TABLES

INTRODUCTORY NETWORK THEORY

Recent Titles in Electrical and Computer
Engineering from PWS Engineering:

Wai-Kai Chen (University of Illinois at Chicago),
Series Editor

INTRODUCTORY NETWORK THEORY
William A. Blackwell and Leonard L. Grigsby

SIGNALS AND SYSTEMS
Alexander D. Poularikas and Samuel Seely

APPLIED ELECTROMAGNETISM
Liang Shen and J. A. Kong

LINEAR NETWORKS AND SYSTEMS
Wai-Kai Chen

FORTRAN 77 FOR ENGINEERS
Garold J. Borse

FORTRAN 77 AND NUMERICAL METHODS FOR ENGINEERS
Garold J. Borse

INTRODUCTORY NETWORK THEORY

William A. Blackwell

Virginia Polytechnic Institute
and State University

Leonard L. Grigsby

Auburn University

PWS Engineering
Boston, Massachusetts

PWS PUBLISHERS

Prindle, Weber & Schmidt • ♣ • Duxbury Press • ♦ • PWS Engineering • ◭
Statler Office Building • 20 Park Plaza • Boston, Massachusetts 02116

Sponsoring Editor: *John E. Block*
Signing Representative: *Jay Bartlett*
Editorial Assistants: *Gabriele Bert and Suzi Shepherd*
Production: *Ex Libris □ Julie Kranhold*
Manuscript Editor: *Linda Thompson*
Design: *John Edeen*
Interior Illustration: *Carl Brown*
Photo Researcher: *Sara B. Hunsaker*
Typesetting: *Jonathan Peck Typographers, Ltd.*
Cover Printing: *John P. Pow Company*
Printing and Binding: *Halliday Lithograph*

PWS Publishers is a division of Wadsworth, Inc.

Library of Congress Cataloging in Publication Data

Blackwell, William A.
  Introductory network theory.

  Includes index.
  1. Electric networks.   I. Grigsby, Leonard L.
II. Title.
TK454.2.B58   1985   621.319′2   84-25843
ISBN 0-534-03771-2

ISBN 0-534-03771-2

Printed in the United States of America

85 86 87 88 89—10 9 8 7 6 5 4 3 2 1

The photomicrograph on the front cover was taken by a process called voltage contrast. A scanning electron microscope is used to probe the surface of a working microprocessor to view the voltages present on the metal lines. The image is enhanced under computer control to make the massive amount of data more readable to the operator.

Photomicrograph courtesy Intel Corporation

Chapter opening photos have been made possible through the courtesy of:

1: Burndy Library. **2:** Edison National Historical Site. **3:** Royal Institution, London. **4:** Burndy Library. **5:** National Museum of American History, #52,202. **6:** National Museum of American History, #66,606. **7:** (*left*) Burndy Library, (*right*) AT&T Bell Labs. **8:** (*left*) MIT Museum, (*right*) General Electric Corporation. **9:** (*left*) National Museum of American History, #51,145, (*right*) Burndy Library. **10:** (*left*) American Museum of American History, Archives Center; (*right*) AT&T Bell Labs. **11:** (*left*) General Electric Corporation, (*right*) RCA. **12:** (*left*) IEEE, (*right*) IEEE. **13:** AT&T Bell Labs. **14:** (*left*) AT&T Bell Labs, (*right*) MIT Museum. **15:** (*left*) The Institute for Advanced Study, (*center*) UPI, (*right*) Intel Corporation.

Preface

The decision to write this book came only after a long and diligent search for a text to be used for the sophomore and junior courses in network theory. We wanted a text with these features:

- A consistent theory with reasonable mathematical preciseness, and with emphasis on the meaning and significance of current and voltage references, topological (interconnection) concepts, and the relationship between a physical network and its mathematical model.

- Sinusoidal steady-state analysis presented on a logical basis, yet treated early enough to be available for electronics and electromagnetic-fields courses taken shortly after the first networks course.

- A thorough treatment of network response for simple networks before the techniques of analysis of larger networks are discussed.

- The treatment of general networks that utilizes systematic procedures amenable to algorithmic formulations for networks including independent sources, dependent sources, and operational amplifiers. Topics to be treated should include linear and nonlinear time-domain algebraic models, state-space linear dynamic models, Laplace-transformed models, frequency-response plots, the concept of resonance, coupled circuit theory, and equivalent networks.

- An introduction to three-phase networks.

- Elementary network graph theory, matrix algebra, and computer techniques presented as tools for network analysis. Matrix algebra, so badly neglected in current undergraduate network texts, is essential if computer techniques are to be fully implemented in networks courses.

- A treatment with specific attention to those network components and techniques needed to support and complement undergraduate electronics courses.

It appeared to us that a book could be developed that would satisfy our requirements better than any of the currently available texts. Our goal has been to develop a presentation practical enough not to offend the practitioner while being consistent enough to satisfy all but the purest networks theorists. Although this is probably too lofty an aspiration, we hope that this book is at least one more step on the way.

Introductory Network Theory is primarily intended to serve in electrical engineering curricula. A physics course in electricity and magnetism is assumed, but not absolutely essential. In Chapters 7 and 8, elementary differential equation theory is desirable but not necessary. The presentation is self-sufficient and includes numerical solution techniques.

In the analysis of large-scale networks, very systematic and well-defined procedures are essential if the analyst is to be successful (in a reasonable number of tries). Throughout this book an emphasis is placed on the student understanding the basis for each step of the modeling procedure. Thus, if an individual has mastered the material, he or she will understand the meaning of plus and minus signs associated with network variables, loop and node orientations, and the classification of a network component as either an energy source or energy sink. These topics, and others of a fundamental nature, are treated very carefully in order to eliminate the all-too-common ambiguities from the modeling process.

Several topics are treated quite differently than in conventional networks texts. A numerical technique based on the Newton-Raphson method is used in Chapter 4 to solve networks containing nonlinear resistors. In Chapter 7, the first-order networks are solved by classical analytic methods and by numerical integration. The main formulation emphasis for second-order networks, treated in Chapter 8, is on state-space modeling, and numerical integration is used to obtain solutions. The analytical solution of second-order network models is deferred until Chapter 12, where the Laplace transform is utilized.

The material included should be more than adequate for six semester hours of coursework. In the belief that network theory is best learned through practice, an extensive set of problems is included. A **Solutions Manual** is available on request from the publisher.

Because of the increasing availability of powerful personal computers, we have emphasized this method of computation. Though the entire course can be taught without the use of digital computation, we feel that its inclusion offers a valuable learning experience for the student. By using a microcomputer the student can work many problems that could not otherwise be solved within his or her time constraints. We have included nine computer programs in Appendix C for solving network problems. These problems are scattered throughout the book and are designated by the symbol ◢.

We have used the BASIC language for the programs in Appendix C for the following reasons:

1.   Nearly every personal computer has BASIC as its primary language, and many students are conversant with it. Modern BASIC is fully adequate for the solution of most of the problems normally associated with undergraduate network analysis.

2.   An interpreter provides more diagnostic tools for debugging.

3.   Run time is not the important item that it is on a central time-share computer.

4.   Our primary interest in using numerical techniques in this course is to make it possible for a student to solve problems that are not practical to do with a hand calculator. The elegance of numerical algorithms and computer programming techniques are of secondary importance.

5.   The basic algorithms used can easily be implemented in any other language to which the student has access.

A User's Guide and an IBM-compatible 5.25-inch floppy disk, with the BASIC programs listed in Appendix C, are available from the publisher. When de facto standards emerge in FORTRAN and Pascal compilers for personal computers, we expect to make programs available in those languages as well.

ACKNOWLEDGMENTS

The writing of a book is a long and arduous task, and we wish to acknowledge the help and support of a number of individuals. In particular we owe many thanks to Professor Daniel B. Hodge, head of Electrical Engineering at Virginia Polytechnic Institute and State University for his support and encouragement. Sandy Crigger, Vicki Trump, and Cheryl West typed and retyped the manuscript over an extended period of time with good humor and dedication. We are much indebted to them for their good work, cheerfulness, and tenacity. We sincerely appreciate the work of our manuscript reviewers John Fagan, University of Oklahoma; Manju Ghalla-Goradia, Cleveland State University; George Lucky, New Mexico State University; and Jacob Castleman, California State Polytechnic Institute at Pomona. Their thoughtful comments and suggestions were most useful to us in completing the manuscript. In addition, we would like to thank David A. Connor, University of Alabama at Birmingham; Thomas M. Scott, Iowa State University; C. W.

Bray, Memphis State University; Robert Mayhan, Ohio State University; William Beasley, Texas A & M University; Sameh A. Mitry, West Virginia University; Shlomo Karni, University of New Mexico; and Donald S. Gage, University of Colorado who also reviewed the manuscript. Last but not least, we express our heartfelt gratitude to our wives, LaRue and Molli. Even though the project lasted much longer than anyone had expected, their enthusiasm never flagged.

William A. Blackwell
Leonard L. Grigsby

To the student

Electrical engineering is an exciting discipline, which requires interest and dedication as well as ability. Traditionally the introductory networks course is the one in which prospective EE students tie their future to this profession, or else seek a more compatible one. As you go through this course, you should think about future options. If the mastering of this material gives you enjoyment and satisfaction, then you have probably found your career. If the lectures, laboratory, and homework bring boredom and drudgery, then engineering is probably not for you.

Electrical network analysis includes most of the mathematical techniques needed for the analysis of all kinds of physical systems. Mastery of these techniques is essential for the understanding of the later electrical engineering courses. If you are ever going to bear down and work hard during your university career, this is a good place to start.

Network theory has one exasperating aspect, which you will soon come to recognize. One simple sign or magnitude error is sufficient to render a long tedious analysis procedure incorrect and useless. This often wastes much valuable time. We try, therefore, to minimize trivial errors by setting up a very systematic and well-defined procedure for analyzing networks. We use these procedures even for small networks when simpler approaches could be used. We want you to learn these general procedures well; they add little, if any, complication to the analysis of simple networks.

Engineering textbooks usually do not contain much of the historical aspect of the discipline. This is regrettable, because the historical perspective gives meaning and interest to the profession. Therefore, we have included pictures and captions for some of the greatest contributors to electrical science. The people included are members of the Centennial Hall of Fame for the Institute of Electrical and Electronics Engineers (IEEE), the professional society for electrical engineering. The IEEE celebrated its centennial anniversary in 1984. Take a bit of time to familiarize yourself with the names and accomplishments of the people who contributed much to make electrical engineering what it is today. This will help you to incorporate technical advances into the more general fabric of history.

This textbook is among the first to emphasize the use of personal computers in the analysis of electric networks. The recent dramatic increase in microcomputer availability has not only made this approach possible but also quite desirable. In Appendix C you will find nine simple BASIC programs that will greatly improve your ability to get numerical answers for network problems. The computer problems fall within the Problems Sections at the end of chapters and are designated by the symbol ◢.

One of the goals of the course is for you to understand the basis for the theory. Therefore, most of the work is analytical. You should know how to integrate a function, invert a matrix, get a Fourier transform for a function, and so forth, but there are times when computational help is needed if a significant problem is to be solved. This is the primary motivation, of course, for using a computer. We suggest, however, that first you use the programs to check the analytical results of simple problems so that you will be familiar with them when you do the more complicated ones.

If the task of typing in the longer programs (and debugging the likely errors) fills you with some dread, perhaps your instructor will be willing to make them available to you on a disk, which is available on request from the publisher.

We hope you enjoy your foray into the intricacies of electrical engineering analysis, and we wish you well.

W.A.B.

L.L.G.

Contents

Power and Energy 55

Resistive Networks 77

Generalized Loop and Nodal Methods for Resistive Networks 167

Resistive 2-Ports 193

10
Three-Phase Networks   389

11
Magnetically Coupled Two-Ports   411

12
The Laplace Transformation   443

13 Fourier Techniques in Network Analysis 485

14 Laplace Transform Analysis of Simple Networks 541

15 Analysis of Larger Networks 587

INTRODUCTORY
NETWORK
THEORY

Giants of the profession
IEEE Centennial Hall of Fame

James Clerk Maxwell (1831–1879)
Physicist and electrical theorist who
developed electromagnetic field theory
and related it to the nature of light; the
author of *Dynamical Theory of the
Electrodynamic Field*; Maxwell also
wrote humorous poetry that often poked
fun at his colleagues.

Reprinted with permission from
"Centennial Hall of Fame,"
IEEE SPECTRUM, April 1984.

Networks and systems

1.1 INTRODUCTION

This book is about electric network theory. To the uninitiated this topic might seem to be an obscure branch of a narrow profession in the broad spectrum of human activities. Not so! Network theory permeates electrical engineering as sand permeates concrete, and the influence of electrical-engineering productivity has become pervasive in every aspect of modern civilization.

Perhaps not all our professional (and nonprofessional) colleagues agree with this viewpoint initially, of course, but given time to reflect, they may come around. No matter—even if you believe that network theory is less than the crown jewel of a fascinating and crucially important profession, it is still a vitally important part of electrical engineering. It encompasses the fundamentals and philosophy of mathematical modeling for a large class of physical systems—not just electric networks. If you never analyze a network outside the classroom, you should still benefit from mastering these topics. Together they define a systematic model-formulation strategy and incorporate mathematical techniques that are widely applicable in analyzing many kinds of physical systems.

1.2 SYSTEMS AND NETWORKS

In this chapter we introduce a number of very fundamental notions that may seem abstract and general. These basic ideas, we hope, are well illustrated with examples. Although some engineering students prefer practical courses to theoretical ones, there is a real need for present and future engineers to be able

1

to reason in abstract or general terms. There is an efficiency of thought thus developed, which makes an extra effort in learning worthwhile.

Everyone is aware of the continuing succession of scientific and engineering feats that have repeatedly staggered the imagination of the world. Consider, for example, the successes of the United States space program. Those activities routinely required the operation of combinations of mechanisms of incredible complexity. As a result, the word *system* took on a significance in the engineering profession that it had never previously attained.

The need for systems engineers first arose in industry when the complexity of devices manufactured for the military services grew to such an extent that often many subcontractors were required to manufacture the parts for one complete mechanism. In a natural development of the terminology, the various parts of such a mechanism were called *components* and the complete device a *system*.

In the manufacture of components for a complex system, there must inevitably be engineering changes from proposed configurations. Very often the change in one component affects the requirements in one or more of the remaining components. The systems engineer came into being primarily to make sure that the design problem was considered from the system viewpoint and that the complete system would still meet its requirements after changes in individual components had been made.

This is roughly the historical development of the term *systems engineer*. From a broader viewpoint, however, every engineer is a systems engineer because no matter how small the device with which he or she is concerned, it may still be regarded as a system made up of subsystems or components. As a broad definition, any entity that may be subdivided into component parts may be considered to be a system. The terms *networks* and *systems* are often used interchangeably.

1.3 PHYSICAL NETWORKS

After the words *system* and *network* became popular in engineering, it became evident that some of the techniques used in the analysis of electric networks were also useful for other collections of component parts, such as transportation networks, traffic networks, economic systems, administrative systems, and biological systems, to name only a few. Thus we need to define the particular kind of network of concern to us in this text. *Physical networks* are those made up of physical objects such as transistors, electron tubes, motors, resistors, electric light bulbs, auto engines, shock absorbers, or springs.

This kind of definition would not be satisfactory to a philosopher because there are many borderline cases where the classification of a network might be questionable. It should be adequate for our purposes, however, since we shall be interested primarily in practical and useful concepts and techniques, rather than in rigorous completeness and generality.

An automobile is a familiar example of a physical system. We may arbitrarily divide an auto into the following components: (1) power system and drive train, (2) body, and (3) suspension system. We can then put everything associated with the car into one of these categories. On the other hand, we may wish to subdivide the power system and drive train into three components: the gasoline power system, the electrical power system, and the drive train. Further, the electrical system could be considered as a set of components including, for example, the alternator, the battery, the distributor, the lights, and the windshield-wiper motors.

1.4 LUMPED NETWORKS

Now that we have a concept of what constitutes a physical network, we need to classify networks on the basis of whether the network has lumped parameters or distributed parameters. We shall use an example to show how the division is made.

Let us consider the automobile battery. If we wish to analyze the operation of an automobile's electric system by considering the battery as one component and concerning ourselves only with the characteristics that can be measured at the terminals, then the battery is a *lumped component*. On the other hand, if we are concerned about the chemical processes taking place at each point inside the battery, then the battery is classified as a *distributed component*. In the latter case, the analysis involves spatial information and is called a *fields*, or *continuum*, problem. A lumped-network analysis involves no spatial data and deals with data that can be measured at terminals external to each component.

In general, distributed networks are much more difficult to analyze than are lumped networks. Fortunately, we shall confine our discussion to the relatively simple problem of the analysis of electric networks that contain only lumped components. In the material to follow, the term *network* can be assumed to imply *lumped network* unless otherwise noted.

1.5 NETWORK ANALYSIS AND SIMULATION

When we analyze a network, as the term is used in this book, we use mathematics to deduce numbers that in some way convey essential information about the condition, or state, of the network. These numbers could indicate a physical condition about voltage, current, power, or any other physical quantity for which measuring instruments are available. Quite often a digital computer or calculator may be used to aid in the process of solving a set of simultaneous equations.

There is a fine line between analysis and simulation when a computer is used. If all the equations of the network model are programmed for solution on a computer, most engineers regard the process as a computer simulation. Sometimes a network is simulated on a computer except for one or two components, which are interfaced to the computer for testing purposes. This is clearly a simulation.

Most often, however, a computer is used to solve a set of equations from which the solution can be written for the network model. In our terminology, this is an analysis. To some extent, this is simply a play on words. However, since you will probably come across the term *simulation* many times in the electrical-engineering literature, we need to relate it to our activities in network analysis.

1.6 OBJECTIVES OF NETWORK ANALYSIS ⎯⎯⎯⎯⎯⎯⎯⎯⎯○

The analysis of a network may be desirable for a number of reasons.

1. Before a component device can be designed, it may be necessary to analyze a network or system to see what is required of the device. The design of an automobile engine, for example, must be based as much as possible on the expected body and transmission system with which it must operate. Thus an analysis of the drive requirements should be completed before the design of the automobile engine is begun.

2. Once the performance requirements for a network are determined and a tentative design based on these requirements is complete, there is always the nagging question, "Will the actual network perform as required?" Of course, it is possible to answer this question by building the network and testing it. This may sometimes be done in the case of relatively simple networks of small components. When networks are built to check performance, they are called *prototype networks*. Often, however, prototype networks are too expensive to build without a lot of confidence that there are no obvious factors that will prevent their successful operation. Thus an analysis of the network based on the preliminary design is usually carried out to establish confidence in its chances for success. Simulation has also proven to be very valuable in these cases.

3. Very often somebody comes up with an idea for changing a component of an operating network to make it more reliable, cheaper to manufacture, or more efficient. Immediately the question arises of how the component change affects the network.

Again, analysis is usually the most economical means of obtaining some data to answer this question.

How do we know when an analysis is acceptable? A very practical criterion, based on our definition of analysis, is that if the numbers that come out of the analysis correlate, within some given tolerance, with numbers representing operational conditions of the network, the analysis is successful. Thus the degree of success of an analysis of a network can never be definitely ascertained until the network itself is operated. By definition, the devices that convert the operating conditions of a network into numbers are called *measuring instruments* or, as we shall more often say, *meters*. At the risk of seeming to emphasize the obvious, we stress that the only means of ascertaining the performance of physical networks in numerical terms is by means of instrumentation, and it is therefore the only way, ultimately, that the success of an analysis can be judged.

1.7 MODELS OF AN ELECTRIC NETWORK ———————————O

In this book we are interested in lumped electric networks. An *electric network* for our purposes is defined as a collection of lumped electric components that are selected and interconnected to produce a desired response.

As we shall use the term, a *mathematical model* of an electric network implies a set of simultaneous equations, the solution to which should correlate with the performance of the network. On the other hand, a physical model is also a network or physical system that performs in the same manner as the network of interest; presumably, it is, for one reason or another, simpler to analyze, or the rules of behavior are better understood by the analyst. Physicists are constantly seeking better physical models of systems of interest to them in the hope of being able to predict as-yet-unknown phenomena. The model of the atom, utilizing the concepts of mechanics, is an example of a constantly improving physical model of great continuing interest to physical scientists.

1.8 THE CONCEPT OF COMPONENTS ———————————O

We defined a physical system as a combination of physical devices and cited an automobile as an example. The mathematical model of such a system is based on two important facets: first, the physical characteristics of the individual components, and second, the manner in which these components are connected together. It is usually possible to subdivide a system into several arrangements of components, as demonstrated by our automobile example. That is, a combination of parts considered to be a component is not, in general, unique.

An interesting example is an electric power utility network. Depending on the requirements of the analysis, a power-generating station may be considered to have furnaces, boilers, steam turbines, electric generators, and electric transformers as components. On the other hand, it might be better for some purposes to consider each complete unit, consisting of the associated furnace, steam generator, steam turbine, and electric generator, as a single component. Still another acceptable, and often useful, viewpoint is to consider the entire power-generating station as one component of the overall network.

Regardless of how the system or network is viewed conceptually, the components chosen are associated with other components of the network by means of some type of connection. We must be able to identify these connections and mathematically describe them if we are to be successful in modeling and analyzing the network. The ability to describe mathematically anything in a physical network implies that a correlation of numbers is to be accomplished. It follows that the points of connection between the components must be available for measurement—at least conceptually. If we are going to talk about these connections, and certainly we must talk about them often, it would be advantageous to adopt a name for them. We choose to call the connection points *terminals*.

1.9   THE CONCEPT OF INTERCONNECTION GEOMETRY

It has been stated that a mathematical model of a network depends on the mathematical models for the components and on the way the components are interconnected to form the network. Now that we have defined the word *terminal*, we can characterize any two-terminal component symbolically with a box and two lines drawn from the box to terminate on dots, as shown in Figure 1.1. In Figure 1.1, the orientations of the terminals *a* and *b* are not significant.

Figure 1.1
Symbolic representations of a two-terminal component.

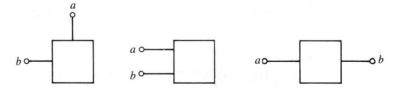

What is important is that two terminals are symbolized, and that there should be an unambiguous correspondence between the terminals and the corresponding connection points of the components so represented. A network made up of two-terminal components is symbolized in Figure 1.2. The various components are designated by boxes named with capital letters, and the interconnection geometry is defined uniquely by the diagram if we make clear the identification of each terminal of each component.

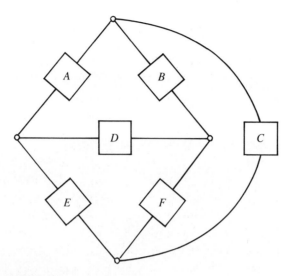

Figure 1.2
Symbolic representation of a network composed of 6 two-terminal components.

1.10 ANALYSIS AND MATHEMATICAL DESIGN

You may find it difficult to understand the basic difference between analysis and mathematical design. We have already discussed the general concept of analysis at some length. We can summarize by saying that analysis is the deduction of network response from the known component characteristics and the interconnection pattern of the components. Mathematical design (sometimes called *synthesis*) is the specification of a network that will realize a certain given response characteristic. More properly, it is the process of finding a set of components with the proper mathematical characteristics, in the proper configuration needed to produce a given mathematical characteristic for a network. Design is usually much more difficult than analysis. Except for some relatively trivial cases, no straightforward technique is known for proceeding on a unique path from specifications to the final design. Often, there are many networks that will achieve a given response. The problem is to pick out the best one for the particular application.

1.11 SUMMARY

Physical networks are made up of physical objects and are therefore of major interest to engineers. The analysis of a physical network is based on a mathematical model of the network. This mathematical model must take into account the characteristics of the network components and their interconnection pattern. If an analysis is to be successful, it must produce numbers characterizing the network response that correspond, within a given tolerance, to numbers obtained from the physical network analyzed with appropriate measuring devices.

Giants of the profession
IEEE Centennial Hall of Fame

Thomas Alva Edison (1847–1931)
He patented 1093 inventions, among
them the phonograph, the incandescent
electric light, and the first commercial
motion pictures; his laboratories served
as a model for modern research
organizations.

Reprinted with permission from
"Centennial Hall of Fame,"
IEEE SPECTRUM, April 1984.

Some basic concepts

2.1 INTRODUCTION

The development of a physical science requires the formulation of a theory that explains all the phenomena observed for the science involved. The science of electricity and magnetism is certainly no exception. Since the ancient Greeks observed the phenomenon of static electricity produced by rubbing amber with a woolen cloth, people have been observing manifestations of electric and magnetic activity and formulating and refining theories to explain their observations better.

Try to place yourself in the situation facing the early experimenters in electricity. You observe things like lightning in a thunderstorm, chaff clinging to glass rods after they have been rubbed with wool, and sparks crackling on a cat's fur after you have stroked it. But you have no theory to explain what you see, and you are not even sure that the phenomena are related. Unlike our abilities to sense some other physical phenomena, we can detect electrical activity only indirectly through light, heat, sound, or force produced. Thus, constructing measuring techniques and a theory for electricity is, perhaps, somewhat more difficult than for the science of mechanics.

Although electrical engineers and technologists are in considerable demand in the world today, the early experimenters found there was no great demand for their electrical expertise and probably carried out their investigations largely as an avocation and to amaze (and shock) their friends. So the development of the science in the early days moved much more slowly than it has since gaining commercial importance.

To understand how our science germinated and developed, let us briefly review a few of the discoveries important to electric network theory and see how they led to the present theory. First we trace the development of the notions of electric charge and electric current. Then we outline a few of the investigations that related electricity and magnetism.

In the middle 1600s a German burgomaster and amateur physicist, Otto Von Guericke, devised a crude electric generator using a spinning sulphur globe, by means of which he could electrify himself and other objects by touching the sphere with his hand. Another century passed before Peter Van Musschenbroek, a professor at Leyden University in Holland, observed that a glass jar filled with water and presumably held by an assistant could be electrified by an electric generator connected to a metal rod placed in the water. Actually, the assistant discovered it first, when he reportedly received a severe shock during the course of the experiment. This discovery relative to storage of electricity led to the development of the *Leyden jar*, in which a glass jar is coated inside and outside with tinfoil. A metal rod through a wooden stopper makes electrical contact with the inner foil accessible from the outside. The electric generator and the Leyden jar made charge, or static, electricity available to experimenters all over the world—including the relatively untutored tinkerers of the English colonies in America.

Medical electronics had its beginnings shortly after the invention of the Leyden jar. Physicians, who had long sought the universal panacea, gleefully joined the pranksters in administering electric-shock treatments to human subjects. This was not a pleasant time for hypochondriacs, who undoubtedly had just cause to mutter "Physician heal thyself."

At this time no one knew the relationship between the electricity of thunderstorms and the frictional type generated and stored by the experimenters. This problem was studied by Benjamin Franklin in America. In 1752 he charged Leyden jars with a kite-carried apparatus and demonstrated not only that Lady Luck was with him, but also that the characteristics of the electricity thus stored were no different than those of the electricity produced by the electrostatic generators then being used. This was a significant event because it raised hope for the possibility of a consistent theory and explanation of electricity.

In addition to his famous kite experiment, Franklin developed the lightning rod to protect buildings from the hazard of lightning in thunderstorms. He also guessed that electricity was a kind of fluid, which flowed from the positive to the negative terminals of a Leyden jar during discharge. Unfortunately, he was wrong in the direction of flow (according to the later electron theory), but his assumption was adopted by other experimenters; it has come down to us as the direction of *conventional current*.

In 1796 Alessandro Volta, inspired by the "twitching frog legs" experiments of another Italian, Luigi Galvani, used the *galvanic effect* associated with two dissimilar metals to produce the first electric battery. This device provided a continuing flow of electric fluid for experimentation, in contrast to the short pulse of the Leyden jar. When more cells were added, stronger effects could be achieved. This ingenious new source of electricity soon became known as the *voltaic pile* and was quickly adopted and used by experimenters across the scientific world. Through evolution, it has come down to us as the modern storage battery. Volta's invention provided experimenters of the day with a practical source of "current electricity"—as contrasted to "charge electricity," which had not been available before for their experiments—and paved the way for investigations into the relationship between electricity and magnetism.

Although the effects of magnetism had been studied by various investigators long before the 19th century, the first discovery of primary interest to us is the discovery by Hans Christian Oersted in 1820 that a compass needle was affected by the presence of an electric current in a nearby conductor. Oersted was a Danish chemist by training. By his own account, the discovery occurred in connection with a lecture/demonstration in which the apparatus had not been previously checked out. Shades of latter-day professors!

Very shortly after Oersted's discovery, a French physicist, André Marie Ampère, extended that work by showing that a solenoidal coil (that is, a coil wound on a cylinder) carrying electric current produces a magnetic effect identical to that of a permanent magnet. The north pole of the solenoid was related to the direction of current flow by the *right-hand rule*—that is, the thumb points north when the fingers point in the direction of current around the solenoid.

Shortly after Ampère's discovery, Johann Schweigger, a German physicist, constructed the first true galvanometer instrument to measure the amount of electric current flowing in a circuit. For the first time, quantitative experimentation in electricity became possible. In 1836 William Sturgeon, an English physicist, made a significantly improved galvanometer by direct application of the results of Ampère's research.

The stage was now set for Michael Faraday, a very prolific English physicist, to devise a set of cleverly contrived experiments that established the principles of electromagnetic induction. These experiments began just prior to 1831, and they went approximately as follows. Faraday set up a solenoidal coil with its terminals connected to a galvanometer and attempted to discover the various ways that a magnet could be used to induce electric current in the coil. He discovered that a permanent magnet inserted into the coil would induce a current, as long as the magnet was moving relative to the coil. When the relative motion stopped, the current stopped. When the direction of the motion was reversed, the current reversed. The same observations were made for a magnet moving in the near vicinity of the coil but not necessarily in the solenoid itself. He also observed that the current was approximately proportional to the number of turns on the coil.

Faraday also prepared a second coil, which was connected through a switch to a voltaic cell, and put this coil in the vicinity of the first coil. For purpose of visualization, we can assume that it is wound on the same cylindrical form as coil 1—but movable relative to it and having no electrical connection to it.

When Faraday closed the switch on coil 2, current was observed in coil 1. As soon as the current in coil 2 became constant, the current in coil 1 became zero. When the polarity of the voltaic cell on coil 2 was reversed, the polarity of the current in coil 1 also reversed. Then, with the current steady in coil 2 and zero in coil 1, Faraday moved coil 2 relative to coil 1. Again, an induced current in coil 1 was observed. Relative motion in the opposite direction produced induced current of the opposite polarity in coil 1. The current indication observed for coil 1, induced by motion of coil 2 relative to coil 1, was the same as if an equivalent permanent magnet had been substituted for coil 2.

Faraday theorized that the induced electric force that produced the current was proportional to the time rate of change of lines of magnetic force that linked coil 1. This view was no doubt influenced by the well-known patterns achieved by scattering iron filings on a surface near a magnet or the plots obtained by using a magnetic compass to determine the direction of magnetic lines of force near a magnet. These lines were visualized by Faraday as forming continuous loops directed through the magnet from south pole to north pole and returning externally from north to south.

After Faraday's researches in electromagnetic induction had been completed, all the necessary concepts were available for the development of electric network theory. The concepts of electric charge, electric current, electric force (electromotive force), and electromagnetic induction had been developed and experimentally justified. Research activity in the science of electricity was at a feverish pitch and the commercial applications were just around the corner.

2.2   BASIC ELECTRIC QUANTITIES

We have presented a brief chronological outline of some of the major discoveries that led to our current physical concepts of electric quantities. Now we turn to the problem of mathematically analyzing electric networks and begin by defining the "basic quantities" and their units as we use them.

What are the basic quantities of electric network theory? Textbook authors do not agree, and good arguments can be made for different points of view. In this book we elect to use electric current and electromotive force (or electric potential) as the basic quantities because, for the most part, they are the quantities that are most convenient to measure and to use in network analyses.

The *electric current* in a device is designated by $i(t)$, a function of time, and is measured in amperes. To be consistent with most other writing on the subject, we use the *conventional current* of Franklin, rather than the oppositely directed flow of electrons. For comparison, 1 ampere of electric current corresponds to 6.24×10^{18} electrons per second flowing past a given point.

The *electromotive force* across a device is designated as $v(t)$, a function of time, and is measured in volts. We also call this quantity *electric potential* or, more often, simply *voltage* because of long, widespread usage of this term. It is convenient to view voltage as a kind of electrical force that causes electrical current to occur, although an equally good argument can be made for the reverse viewpoint.

We now digress a bit to introduce the subject of electric effects in materials. Electric materials can be broadly classified as *conductors* and *non-conductors* (or insulators). Good conductors are those materials in which a large amount of electric current is accompanied by a relatively small amount of voltage. A poor conductor is a material in which a large amount of electric voltage produces a relatively small amount of electric current.

You will undoubtedly jump to the conclusion that a good insulator probably qualifies as a very poor conductor, and a poor insulator probably qualifies as a somewhat better conductor. Since these terms—conductor and insulator—are relative, you are correct.

By definition, the electric voltage across a perfect conductor must be zero and the electric current through a perfect insulator must be zero. Neither, as you might guess, can be obtained in practice, but the former can be approached by cooling a good conductor to near absolute zero, and the latter can be approached in ambient temperatures by good commercial dielectric materials. In network analysis we set these conditions mathematically by applying a short circuit (perfect conductor) and an open circuit (perfect insulator), respectively, in the network.

Two more basic electric quantities will be useful to us in discussing electric network analysis. Some authors call them secondary network variables, and it is convenient for us to view them in that light.

Electric charge, measured in coulombs, is defined as

$$q(t) \doteq \int_{t_0}^{t} i(\tau) \, d\tau + q(t_0) \tag{2.1}$$

If we differentiate both sides of Equation 2.1 with respect to time, we get

$$\frac{d}{dt} q(t) \doteq i(t) \tag{2.2}$$

which indicates that an ampere of electric current is equivalent to a coulomb of electric charge per second flowing past a given point on a conductor. If we are interested only in the electric charge transferred between times t_0 and t, Equation 2.1 becomes

$$q(\tau) \Big|_{t_0}^{t} \doteq \int_{t_0}^{t} i(\tau) \, d\tau \qquad (2.1\text{a})$$

Magnetic flux, measured in webers, is defined as

$$\lambda(t) \doteq \int_{t_0}^{t} v(\tau) \, d\tau + \lambda(t_0) \qquad (2.3)$$

From Equation 2.3 we obtain, by differentiating with respect to time,

$$\frac{d}{dt}\lambda(t) \doteq v(t) \qquad (2.4)$$

which indicates that a volt of electric potential is equivalent to a change of a weber of magnetic flux per second. The magnetic flux established between times t_0 and t can be found from Equation 2.3 as

$$\lambda(\tau) \Big|_{t_0}^{t} \doteq \int_{t_0}^{t} v(\tau) \, d\tau \qquad (2.3\text{a})$$

As you can readily surmise, the definition of the magnetic flux, $\lambda(t)$, exactly parallels that of the electric charge, $q(t)$, to produce a symmetrical arrangement relative to secondary variables used in network analysis.

For the case of voltage associated with a solenoidal coil, the magnetic flux turns out to be the quantity of lines of magnetic force, in webers, that link the coil. For other electrical devices, it is simply a variable, as defined in Equation 2.3.

The physical visualization of flux is usually more difficult than that of charge, but that should not bother you. In network analysis we are primarily interested in the mathematical definition rather than in the physical concept. If we want to measure either $q(t)$ or $\lambda(t)$ in the laboratory, we can use an integrating device, together with a current meter or a voltage meter, respectively.

2.3 THE SI SYSTEM OF UNITS

In order to communicate the results of our network analysis, we must establish a common language. All new terms must be defined precisely and used consistently. We have already defined and discussed some of the basic quantities involved in the analysis of an electric network. We introduce others as they become necessary. Each time a quantity is introduced, we give a unit of measurement of this quantity. Now is an appropriate time to discuss the system of units that we use.

Although the British system of units continues to be popular and in common usage in this country, we use the *International System of Units*, SI, throughout this text. The SI was adopted by the General Conference on Weights and Measures in 1960 and by the National Bureau of Standards in 1964. Eventually, SI should be standard throughout the world. Table 2.1 gives the SI units of measurement for the quantities of interest in the study of network theory. The table also shows the standard abbreviation for each unit. Although this table is not complete, it is sufficient for our purposes.

Table 2.1 The International System of Units (SI)

	Quantity	SI Unit	Abbreviation
Base Units	length mass time current angle	meter kilogram second ampere radian	m kg s A rad
Derived Units with Special Names	frequency force energy power charge voltage capacitance resistance conductance magnetic flux inductance	hertz (1/s) Newton (kg·m/s^2) joule (N·m) watt (J/s) coulomb (A·s) volt (W/A) farad (C/V) ohm (V/A) siemen (A/V) weber (V·s) henry (Wb/A)	Hz N J W C V F Ω S Wb H
Derived Units Without Special Names	area volume linear velocity linear acceleration angular velocity angular acceleration torque	square meter cubic meter meter per second meter per second squared radian per second radian per second squared newton meter	m^2 m^3 m/s m/s^2 rad/s rad/s^2 N·m

The SI system of units has several advantages. One of these is the incorporation of the decimal system to relate larger and smaller units to the basic unit and the use of standard prefixes to signify these powers of ten. Table 2.2 defines these prefixes and gives their standard symbols.

Table 2.2
Prefixes for
Use with Units

Prefix	Symbol	Meaning
exa	E	10^{18}
peta	P	10^{15}
tera	T	10^{12}
giga	G	10^{9}
mega	M	10^{6}
kilo	k	10^{3}
hecto	h	10^{2}
deka	da	10^{1}
deci	d	10^{-1}
centi	c	10^{-2}
milli	m	10^{-3}
micro	μ	10^{-6}
nano	n	10^{-9}
pico	p	10^{-12}
femto	f	10^{-15}
atto	a	10^{-18}

2.4 ORIENTED INSTANTANEOUS METERS ─────────────○

In Chapter 1 we observed that the link between mathematical analysis and physical systems is made by measuring instruments, or instrumentation. The following two quotations indicate that early scientists recognized this fact very fully. In 1883 William Thomson (Lord Kelvin) wrote:

> I often say that when you can measure what you are speaking about and express it in numbers, you know something about it; but when you cannot express it in numbers your knowledge is of a meager and unsatisfactory kind; it may be the beginning of knowledge but you have scarcely in your thoughts advanced to the stage of a science whatever the matter may be.[1]

---

[1]John Bartlett, *Familiar Quotations*, 14th ed. Boston: Little, Brown, 1968.

In a similar vein Henri Poincaré wrote:

The important thing is not to know what force is, but how to measure it. Everything which does not teach us how to measure it is as useless to the mechanician as, for instance, the subjective idea of heat and cold to the student of heat. This subjective idea cannot be translated into numbers, and is therefore useless; a scientist whose skin is an absolutely bad conductor of heat, and who, therefore, has never felt the sensation of heat or cold, would read a thermometer in just the same way as any one else, and would have enough material to construct the whole of the theory of heat.[2]

The type of measuring instrument that we need to correlate with our analysis effort is one that, at least conceptually, has zero time lag in its motion and indicates both positive and negative values. Such a measuring device is called an *instantaneous meter*. It must also have a means of identifying the terminals, since otherwise a positive or negative sign on the number indicated would have no significance. A meter with this terminal identification is said to be *oriented*. Further, we shall idealize our measuring instruments in this text to assume that they do not, when connected to a network, change its performance.

The oriented instantaneous meter that we have defined is conceptual but provides the groundwork for a consistent interpretation of the results of our analysis. We should keep in mind one fundamental point concerning these meters: *A reversal of instrument orientation will always imply a change in sign in the meter reading.*

2.5 CURRENT AND VOLTAGE ——————————————————O

Armed with the concept of an oriented instantaneous meter, we are now ready to discuss the measurement of the basic electric network variables, current and voltage. Our motivation for this discussion is to establish a standard agreement about the meaning of the value of any network variable at any point in time.

There is a large body of physical theory concerning electrical phenomena. We assume that you have obtained the elements from a course in the physics of electricity and magnetism. In the analysis of electric networks the physical theories, while interesting, do not have direct application, since we are primarily interested in calculating numbers that describe the behavior of the network. This is not to say that physical theories are not useful in general. On the contrary, they are extremely useful, particularly in pointing the way toward phenomena not yet observed. In this section we are concerned with measuring the quantities electric current and voltage and describing this measurement so

[2]Henri Poincaré, *Science and Hypothesis* (New York: Dover, 1952).

that another person who knows our conventions can interpret the description without ambiguity.

Although our sight cannot detect it directly, we know that electric current is polarized like the fluid flow for which it was named. Anyone who has tried to start a car with a run-down battery can testify that it does make a difference which way the electric current flows in the battery. If what we call conventional current flows from the positive to negative terminals inside a storage battery, the battery is *charging*. If the current is reversed, the battery is *discharging*.

We measure electric current with an instrument called an *ammeter*. The SI unit for electric current is the ampere. As previously mentioned, we shall think in terms of the conceptually ideal meter—that is, one that reacts in zero time and has a zero-center scale from which the indication is read. If the meter is placed in a network such that it indicates x amperes, the only effect of turning it around (interchanging its terminals) in the same position would be to cause it to read $-x$ amperes. By convention, ammeters are usually oriented with a plus sign or a dot placed near one terminal, as shown in Figure 2.1. Several recognized symbolic representations of such a meter are shown in Figure 2.2.

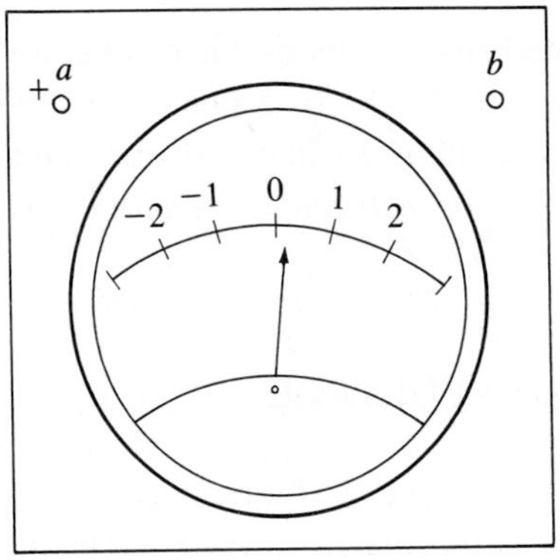

Figure 2.1
A typical zero-center ammeter.

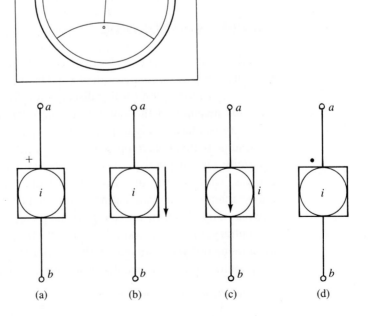

Figure 2.2
Several possible equivalent symbols for oriented ammeters.

(a)   (b)   (c)   (d)

These symbols are equivalent. It is essential that we be able to discriminate between the terminals. However, because of long-standing usage and the intuitive appeal of the arrow, we shall adopt it (Figure 2.2(b)) for symbolic orientation of all instruments associated with the concept of current flow. A positive reading of the ammeter oriented as shown in Figure 2.2(b) corresponds to a flow of conventional electric current in the direction of the arrow. That is, conventional current flows from *a* to *b* through the meter. A negative indication corresponds to a flow in the opposite direction.

In general, the current variables in an electric network vary with time. In order to account for this time variation, we have adopted the symbolism $i(t)$ to stand for our current variable. This variable is often referred to as *instantaneous current*. At times, the time-functional dependence is not shown explicitly, but it is always implied by a lowercase i. Finally, our conceptual meter is capable of following these time variations, and we know the meaning of the positive or negative reading at any particular point in time.

A similar convention is used for the measurement of electric voltage. As for the ammeter, we shall think in terms of a conceptually ideal meter, which reacts in zero time and has a zero-center scale from which the indication is read. Also, the voltmeter must be oriented by some means that discriminates between its terminals. Any one of the methods shown in Figure 2.2 would be adequate. *If i is replaced by v*, the symbols become appropriate symbols for voltmeters. We arbitrarily pick one that is convenient and use the plus (and implied minus) sign, as shown in Figure 2.2(a). The following convention defines the relationship between the physical state of the electric voltage being measured and the numbers used to represent it. A positive indication of the voltmeter signifies that the plus terminal of the voltmeter is at a higher voltage than is the other terminal. A negative reading indicates that the plus terminal is at a lower voltage than the unmarked terminal.

Generally speaking, the voltage variables in an electric network are time-dependent. Therefore, we adopt the symbolism $v(t)$ to represent the voltage variable, often called the *instantaneous voltage*. Our conceptual voltmeter is capable of following instantaneous voltage changes in time, and our sign convention provides a way to interpret the reading without ambiguity.

Finally, there is an essential difference between the conceptual meters that we have just defined. The ammeter measures the current through a component and consequently should be placed end-to-end with the component for which current is to be measured. Thus we say that current is a *through*, or *series*-type, measurement. On the other hand, a voltage measurement is a measurement of the voltage at one point with respect to a second point. Consequently, voltage measurements are made *across*, or *in parallel with*, the component for which the voltage variable is desired. The two-point property of a voltage measurement has led to a symbolism that is often very useful: The voltage at terminal *a* with respect to terminal b is symbolized by v_{ab}, which is read "the voltage at a with respect to b."

The ammeter-voltmeter fundamentals are now illustrated by several examples. In these examples, it is assumed that you have some familiarity with the analysis of very simple networks made up of resistors and batteries.

Example 2.1

Consider the network shown in Figure 2.3. Since the meter connections do not disturb the original network, this network will have a current flow of 6 A in a clockwise direction. Therefore, the meter readings are as follows: $i_1 = 6$ A, $i_2 = -6$ A, $v_1 = 12$ V, and $v_2 = 12$ V.

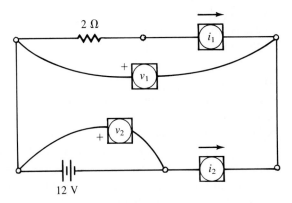

Figure 2,3
A simple network with meters.

Example 2.2

For the network shown in Figure 2.4, the meter readings are as follows: $v_1 = -12$ V, $v_2 = 6$ V, $v_3 = -6$ V, and $v_4 = 6$ V.

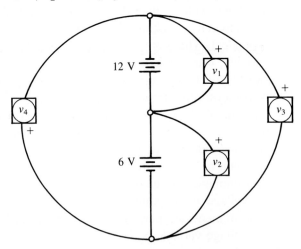

Figure 2.4
A simple network with no current flow.

2.6 MATHEMATICAL MODEL FOR A 1-PORT

A 1-port component (which we shall shorten to 1-port) is by definition a network component with two terminals, two points at which the device is connected to the rest of the network. An alternate way of viewing the 1-port is that there are two points at which measurements may be made to characterize the performance of the device.

An often-used symbol for a 1-port with terminals a and b is shown in Figure 2.5. The 1-port is characterized mathematically by some type of mathematical relationship between the voltage variable and the current variable,

Figure 2.5
Symbolic representation of a general 1-port component.

which represents corresponding voltage and current measurements made at the terminals of the device. The functional relationship may be in analytical form or it may be in the form of an experimental tabulation of data or a graph. We shall refer to this functional relation as the *component terminal characteristic*, whatever the particular form of the relation. The terminal in the name indicates that the measurements are made at the terminals of the component. The words *equation* or *graph* added to the terminology above will indicate the form of the relation. We shall often simply refer to the component terminal characteristic as the *component equation*.

2.7 EFFECT OF INSTRUMENT ORIENTATION

As discussed in Section 2.4, the effect of a reversal of instrument orientation in a network is to change the sign of the indication. Therefore, the component equation for a 1-port may contain a positive or a negative sign. The sign used is arbitrary, in a sense, as indicated by Example 2.3.

Example 2.3

Suppose the 1-port considered is a common electric resistance. If the variables used correlate with the instruments of Figure 2.6(a) and (b) (see next page), the component equation is $v(t) = Ri(t)$. If the variables correlate with the instruments of Figure 2.6(c) and (d), the component equation is $v(t) = -Ri(t)$.

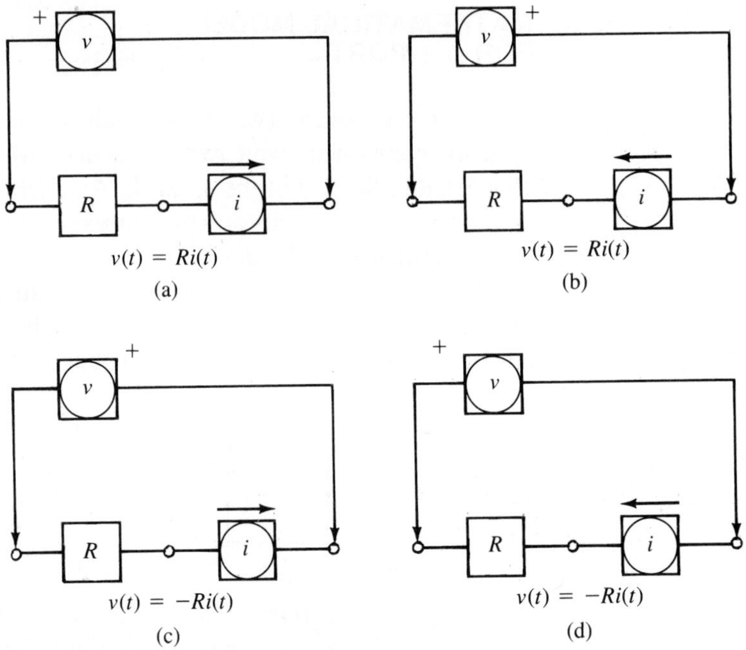

Figure 2.6
Combinations of
instrument orientations
possible for a 1-port.

We have claimed that the sign associated with the component equation is arbitrary. This assertion will now be qualified somewhat. A mathematical model of a 1-port is not complete unless both the component equation and the assumed meter orientations are specified. Either sign may be used if a *corresponding proper combination* of meter orientations is chosen.

2.8 A DIAGRAM TO SPECIFY INSTRUMENT ORIENTATION

As we have noted, all that is required to indicate a meter orientation is some scheme to differentiate between the meter terminals. A line segment with an arrowhead on it is one of the simplest means of accomplishing this job. For example, we might draw the diagram of Figure 2.7(b) to indicate the same information with respect to meter orientation shown in Figure 2.7(a). Furthermore, additional simplification is possible if we standardize our choice of relative polarities of the voltmeter and ammeter. More precisely, if we adopt the convenient convention that the relative polarities of the indicating instruments will always be as shown in Figure 2.7(a), we can use a single, directed line segment called a *measurement diagram* (Figure 2.7(c)) to convey exactly the same information. *This convention is so convenient and useful that we adopt it in the remainder of this text* and designate it as the *standard orienta-*

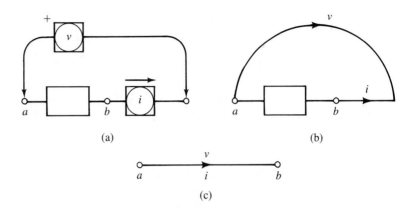

Figure 2.7
Three schemes for indicating meter orientation with respect to a component with terminals *a* and *b*.

tion. Observe that when we use the measurement diagram of Figure 2.7(c) to represent a 1-port component, the oriented line does not symbolize an instrument or instruments. We have already adopted symbols for meters and we shall continue to use them, when convenient, as in Figure 2.7(a).

The line segment with its arrowhead and two accentuated end points carries two pieces of information: (1) the identity of the terminals of the component—that is, the points at which it is connected to other components to form a network—and (2) the polarity of the meters used to measure, at least conceptually, the appropriate current and voltage quantities associated with the component. The information contained in the latter is usually referred to as the *reference directions* for current and voltage.

In other words, the measurement diagram of Figure 2.7(c) indicates that the voltage and current measurement orientations implied by the arrow are as follows:

1. A positive value of v indicates that the voltage of the a terminal is positive with respect to the b terminal. A negative value of v implies that the voltage of the a terminal is negative with respect to the b terminal. Thus all the possible information with regard to the voltage variable associated with the component is known when a magnitude and sign are specified, if this is associated with a measurement diagram. The symbol v_{ab} represents this same measurement—the voltage of a with respect to b.

2. A positive value of i indicates the direction of conventional current flow is from terminal a to terminal b within the component. A negative value of i indicates the converse.

When both a diagram to indicate reference direction and a mathematical relationship between the terminal variables are known, the mathematical model of a 1-port is complete. The following sections will make clear the implications of this statement.

In discussing procedures for modeling networks, it is convenient to work with three types of diagrams to represent the network:

1. A *pictorial-schematic diagram* is one that looks somewhat like the network represented. The symbols on this type of diagram are usually not well standardized. The purpose of this type of diagram is to display information needed to construct schematic or interconnection diagrams, from which a mathematical model of the network can be written directly.

2. An *interconnection diagram* of a network consists of a set of oriented line segments that indicate the pairs of points in the network at which measurements would be made to correspond with chosen network variables and that indicate the polarity of those measurements. An interconnection diagram, therefore, is a set of measurement diagrams. Although the terminology *interconnection diagram* is quite descriptive, this diagram is commonly referred to as a *linear graph*. By and large, we shall use the terminology *linear graph* from this point on. If we do revert to calling this diagram an interconnection diagram, it is to emphasize the nature of the essential information it portrays.

Quite often we shall refer to the line segments of the linear graph as *branches*. On occasion we will refer to the 1-ports as network branches. Although there is a fine distinction, as we have used the terms, it is completely satisfactory for our purposes to use branches and 1-ports synonymously. In Chapter 4 we develop some fundamental concepts associated with the network linear graph, or interconnection diagram. From that point on, the linear graph will play a major role in the formulation of the mathematical equations that describe the behavior of networks.

3. A *schematic diagram* of a network has the same geometry and orientation as a network interconnection diagram. The schematic diagram, however, is also coded to indicate the type of network component on which each measurement is made. The coding is achieved by putting an appropriate symbol on each oriented line segment in the interconnection diagram.

Pictorial-schematic diagrams are not as useful in electric networks as they are in other types of systems, since it is usually possible and customary to draw a schematic directly.

We next develop mathematical models for the common 1-ports of electric networks. These models and the symbols used to depict these components in schematic diagrams are summarized in Tables 2.5 and 2.6 at the end of this chapter.

2.9 RESISTANCE

The most common electric 1-port is the resistor. Every electronic repair shop has bins of them in assorted sizes, since they are the most numerous of the components of familiar electric networks such as radios, audio amplifiers, and television sets. For network-analysis purposes we are not primarily concerned with the size or physical shape of the resistor, but rather with the mathematical model. We can get this by taking the device into a laboratory and simultaneously measuring values of current and voltage.

For the most common type of resistance, laboratory measurements carried out with an experimental setup as shown in Figure 2.8 will yield a curve approximately like that of Figure 2.9.

Figure 2.8
Test system to measure resistor characteristic.
(a) Pictorial-schematic diagram. (b) Schematic diagram of resistor.
(c) Measurement diagram of resistor.

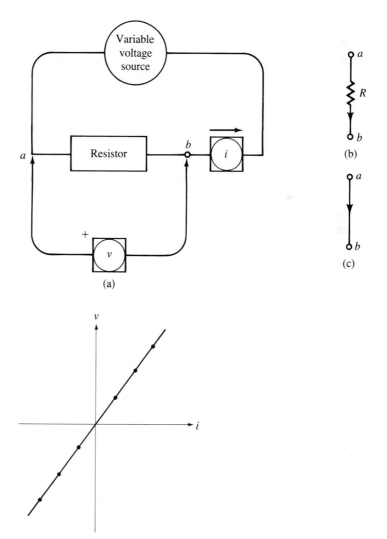

Figure 2.9
Linear-resistor characteristic.

If this plot of v versus i can be approximated by a straight line through the origin, we say the resistor is linear, and the mathematical model is taken to be that of Equation 2.5.

Ohm's Law

> $$v(t) = Ri(t) \quad and \quad a \circ\!\!-\!\!\blacktriangleright\!\!-\!\!\circ b \qquad\qquad (2.5)$$
>
> *where R represents the slope of the curve, is constant, and is called the* resistance *of the 1-port.*

The unit for resistance is the ohm, named after Georg Ohm, a German physicist who studied its properties shortly after the development of the galvanometer.

If the arrowhead on the measurement diagram of Equation 2.5 is reversed, the component equation will remain unchanged. *This is true because a consistent relation (standard orientation) has been maintained between the ammeter and voltmeter orientations.* If the curve in Figure 2.9 is not linear, the resistor is said to be nonlinear, and R is not constant but now depends on i or v. The mathematical model for this type of component will be considered in Section 2.14.

The component equation for the resistor in Equation 2.5 is said to be in *voltage-explicit form.* An alternate, and sometimes useful, form is the *current-explicit form*

$$i(t) = \frac{1}{R} v(t) = Gv(t) \qquad\qquad (2.6)$$

where $G \doteq 1/R$; G is called the *conductance* of the component. The unit for conductance is the siemen.

Not all electric 1-ports can be suitably characterized by an algebraic relationship between the terminal variables. Even some very elementary components require the use of time derivatives of the voltage variables or the current variables in their characteristics. Those electric components for which the characteristic is algebraic are called *resistive components*, or resistors.

2.10 INDUCTANCE

Every conductor of electric current possesses the property of inductance. When a length of wire is formed into a cylindrical coil with many turns, the inductive effect is amplified greatly. As noted earlier, Michael Faraday studied this property and is credited with developing the theory of electromagnetic induction. There is an extensive physical theory to explain this characteristic in terms of more basic models. This phenomenon is usually discussed in the theory of electric and magnetic fields. We shall, however, continue to focus on the component terminal-characteristic equation.

By definition, an electric component that has a terminal characteristic of the form

$$v = L \frac{di}{dt} \quad \text{or} \quad \frac{di}{dt} = \frac{1}{L} v \tag{2.7}$$

where L is a constant, is called an *inductor* and L is called the *inductance* of the component. When v is in volts and i is in amperes, the unit for L is the henry, named after Joseph Henry, an American physicist and first secretary of the Smithsonian Institution, who studied the phenomenon of electromagnetic inductance.

To measure the inductance of a component, a test system of the type illustrated in Figure 2.8 is used. However, we now need to relate voltage to the time derivative of current, and so the current meter should now be replaced by a current-derivative meter. Theoretically, this can be done satisfactorily, but—practically speaking—differentiation is difficult to carry out satisfactorily in the laboratory because of the "noise" always associated with measurement. Fortunately, there is another procedure available if L is constant. Suppose we integrate both sides of Equation 2.7 with respect to time, obtaining

$$\lambda \doteq \int v \, dt = Li \tag{2.8}$$

Integration is simpler to effect satisfactorily in the laboratory than is differentiation. Thus if λ, as defined in Equation 2.8, is plotted versus i, as shown in Figure 2.10, the constant L can be found from the slope of this curve. Figure 2.11 shows a test system for obtaining the data for plotting the curve. By the

Figure 2.10
Characteristic for an inductance.

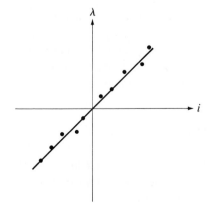

Figure 2.11
(a) Test system for
measuring characteristic
of an electric inductance.
(b) Measurement diagram.
(c) Component schematic
diagram.

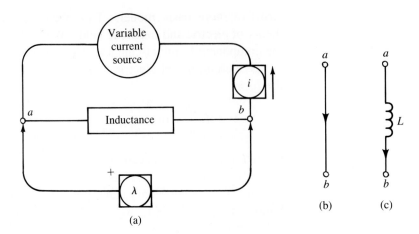

Figure 2.11
(a) Test system for
measuring characteristic
of an electric inductance.
(b) Measurement diagram.
(c) Component schematic
diagram.

use of an oscilloscope, the curve can be displayed directly on a screen if a
repetitive or periodic current source is used.

The alternative form of the component equation for the inductor can be
obtained by rewriting Equation 2.7 as

$$di = \frac{1}{L} v \, dt \tag{2.9}$$

Equation 2.9 can now be solved for current by integrating with respect to time.
Suppose we choose our initial time of integration conveniently as $t = 0$ and our
final time of integration as the arbitrary time t. The limits of integration for the
left-hand side of Equation 2.9 are then seen to be from $i(0)$ to $i(t)$. Thus we
have

$$\int_{i(0)}^{i(t)} di = i(t) - i(0) = \frac{1}{L} \int_{0}^{t} v(\tau) \, d\tau \tag{2.10}$$

or

$$i(t) = \frac{1}{L} \int_{0}^{t} v(\tau) \, d\tau + i(0) = \frac{\lambda(t)}{L} \tag{2.11}$$

If the data are such that the curve of λ versus i can be satisfactorily
approximated by a straight line through the origin, the inductance is *linear*. For
all other cases, it is *nonlinear*.

2.11 CAPACITANCE

The third and last of the *basic electric 1-ports* is the capacitance. If a pair of
good conductors of electric current (that is, conductors of low resistance) are

brought near one another without a conducting link between them, they form a capacitor with a characteristic equation

$$i = C \frac{dv}{dt} \quad \text{or} \quad \frac{dv}{dt} = \frac{1}{C} i \tag{2.12}$$

The familiar tubular capacitor found in some abundance in all kinds of electronic circuitry is made up of two sheets of conducting foil with a sheet of insulating material between them, rolled compactly to minimize the volume required. The C in Equation 2.12 is called the *capacitance*, and its unit is the farad, after Michael Faraday, who also contributed greatly to the knowledge of electric phenomena. For a great majority of electric networks, the capacitors may be assumed constant except for those for which one set of plates can be moved to allow for a deliberate change of capacitance.

A test system for measuring the capacitance of an electric component is shown in Figure 2.12. The system is exactly the same as that for measuring the

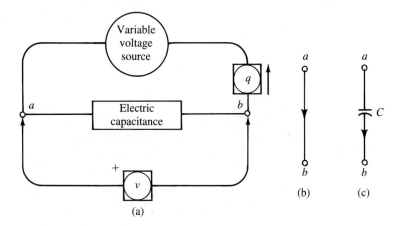

Figure 2.12
(a) Test system for measuring characteristic of an electric capacitance.
(b) Measurement diagram.
(c) Component schematic diagram.

resistance (Figure 2.8), except for a meter to measure the time integral of i rather than an ammeter. This is done because of the considerations discussed in Section 2.10 in connection with the measurement of electric inductance. The integration of both sides of Equation 2.12 yields

$$q \doteq \int i \, dt = Cv \tag{2.13}$$

which is the basis for the measurement technique illustrated in Figure 2.12. The symbol q represents the quantity we have defined as electric charge. If q is plotted versus v, as shown in Figure 2.13, the capacitance C is the slope of the curve when it can be satisfactorily approximated by a straight line through the origin and thus can be considered as a linear device.

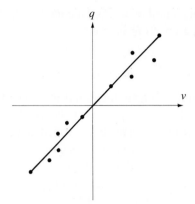

Figure 2.13
Characteristic for an
electric capacitance.

By using integration in a manner exactly the same as for the inductor, we obtain the alternate form of the component equation:

$$v(t) = \frac{1}{C} \int_0^t i(\tau)\, d\tau + v(0) = \frac{q(t)}{C} \qquad (2.14)$$

2.12 ACTIVE COMPONENTS

The three types of components discussed to this point are called *passive* components. A network made up entirely of components of this kind will be inert, or *passive*. If a network is to perform any kind of useful function, it must at least have one source, or *active* component. Some examples of electric network sources are storage batteries, dry-cell batteries, automobile generators, alternators, fuel cells, and solar cells. These examples are typical, but by no means do they exhaust the list. They have in common the ability to "do something"—to create an electric response. Each of the examples cited can be considered to be a two-terminal component, or 1-port. Unlike the R, L, and C components, which are also 1-ports, these are active 1-ports.

The mathematical model for an active 1-port consists of a measurement diagram and a characteristic equation relating the two terminal measurements. We use *standard orientation* and the measurement diagram exactly as discussed in Section 2.8. In this respect the mathematical model is exactly the same as for a passive 1-port. The difference occurs in the form of the component equation.

We choose to classify our active components, or sources, into two groups: either *normal sources* or *ideal sources*. Further, ideal sources are classified as either *independent* or *dependent* sources. The dependent source is covered in detail in Section 2.13. The remaining classifications are best delineated by the following definitions.

Definition 2.1

Independent Current Source

An independent current source is a 1-port component for which the current variable is independent of the voltage variable and is a specified function of time.

Definition 2.2

Independent Voltage Source

An independent voltage source is a 1-port component for which the voltage variable is independent of the current variable and is a specified function of time.

To be completely precise, we should refer to the source in Definition 2.1 as an *ideal independent current source*. However, for the sake of simplicity we shall refer to this source as an *i-source*. In a similar manner we shall refer to the *ideal independent voltage source* as a *v-source*.

The *i*-source and *v*-source are idealized. However, these sources do occur in practice with good approximation over limited operating ranges. Furthermore, it is usually possible to represent a nonideal, or *normal*, source as an interconnection of an ideal source and some passive component. If the component equation is voltage-explicit, the normal source is called a *voltage source*. Likewise, a normal source with a current-explicit component equation is a *current source*. A summary of active components, including the dependent source, is presented in Table 2.6 (at the end of the chapter).

To determine the characteristic curve for an ideal source or a normal source, we could use a test system such as that of Figure 2.14. Note that the

Figure 2.14
(a) Test system for measuring the characteristic of an active 1-port. (b) Corresponding mathematical model.

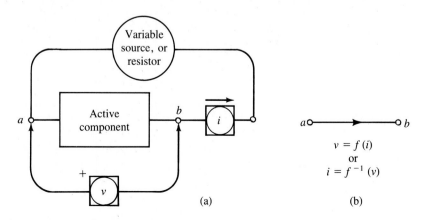

relative instrument orientations are the same as those for the passive 1-ports. In the customary test setups, we would use a passive component, such as a variable resistor, instead of a variable source, as we used in testing passive 1-ports. However, to get the portion of the characteristic in the first quadrant, we must use an active component. This will be made clear when the analysis of simple networks is discussed. Some typical expected characteristics are shown in Figures 2.15, 2.16, and 2.17.

Figure 2.15
Characteristic for a common storage battery.

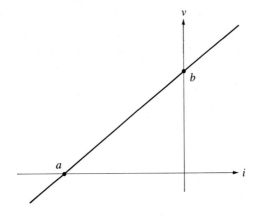

Figure 2.16
Typical characteristic curve for v-source (ideal).

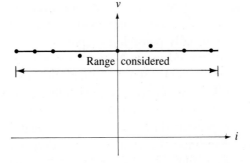

Figure 2.17
Typical characteristic curve for i-source (ideal).

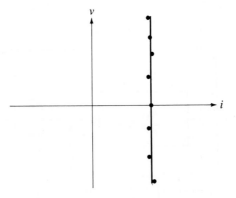

When the characteristic is known to be nearly linear and not ideal, the measurement technique often used is to take data at the points designated by *a* and *b* in Figure 2.15. These points represent the intercepts of the voltage axis and the current axis and thus define a unique straight line. In electric network testing, the terms *open-circuit test* and *short-circuit test* correspond to the voltage-axis and current-axis intercepts, respectively. Open circuit implies zero current and short circuit implies zero voltage at the terminals of the 1-port. These open-circuit and short-circuit tests have interesting interpretations in Sections 4.3, 9.7, and 14.6.

The schematic symbol for an ideal source is a circle, as shown in Figure 2.18. The symbols for *v*-sources and *i*-sources differ only by whether a plus-

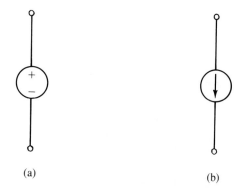

Figure 2.18
Schematic diagrams for ideal sources.
(a) *v*-source. (b) *i*-source.

(a)   (b)

minus sign or an arrow, respectively, is placed inside the circle. The meanings for these reference direction signs are, of course, consistent with those which we established in our earlier discussion of voltage and current measurement. In order to avoid unnecessary complications, the arrow on the corresponding measurement diagram is usually placed to agree with the source orientation. This is not necessary, however, and it should be understood that the arrow or plus-minus sign on the source is actually independent of the reference direction for the measurement diagram. These ideas are best illustrated by example.

Example 2.4

An active component is tested in the laboratory with the experimental setup shown in Figure 2.19. The resulting voltage and current readings are shown in Table 2.3 for various values of the variable resistor. A plot of these values is shown in Figure 2.20. The experimental points are very closely approximated by the straight line shown. Therefore, the active device may be modeled as a normal voltage source having a characteristic equation

$$v = 2i + 10$$

$$(2.15)$$

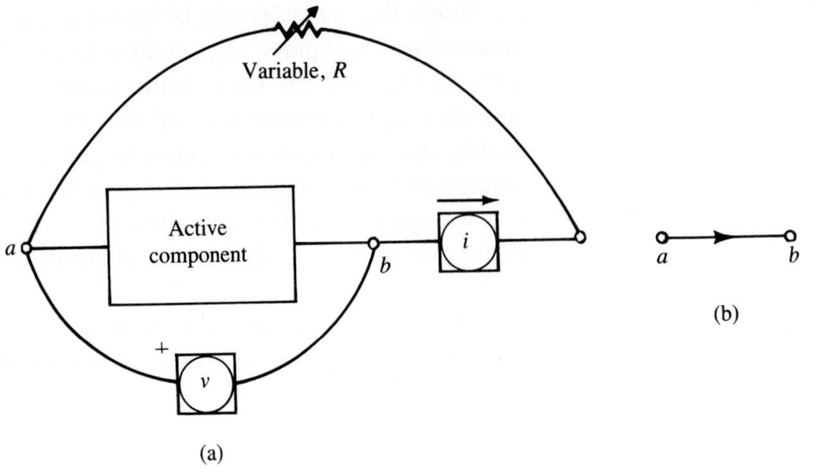

Figure 2.19
(a) Test system for
Example 2.4. (b) Measure-
ment diagram.

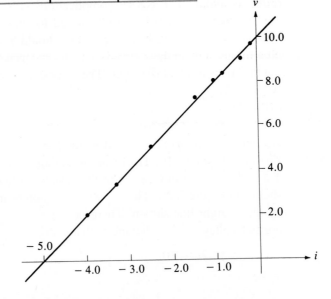

Table 2.3
Experimental Data
for Example 2.4

R (Ohms)	V (Volts)	i (Amps)
50	9.6	−0.19
20	9.1	−0.46
10	8.3	−0.83
8	8.0	−1.0
5	7.2	−1.43
2	5.0	−2.5
1	3.3	−3.3
0.5	2.0	−4.0

Figure 2.20
Experimental data for an
active component.

If we consider v to be the sum of two voltages, v_1 and v_2, then we conclude that the normal source could also be modeled as a 2-Ω resistor and a 10-V v-source connected, as in Figure 2.21. This is only one of many different combinations of 1-ports that might yield the experimental results of Figure 2.20. We explore these possibilities in depth as we build up our ability to analyze larger and more complicated networks.

Figure 2.21
A normal source.

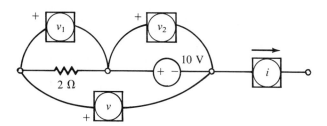

Example 2.5

In order to establish better facility with the meaning of the positive orientations for voltage and current that are established by a measurement diagram, consider Table 2.4. Careful study of this table should also bolster our confidence about the meaning of the model of ideal sources. The table shows several ideal sources, each with an arbitrarily specified measurement diagram and the resulting component equation. Let us examine, in detail, the meaning of some of these examples.

For case A, the measurement diagram gives a positive orientation for the voltage such that any time the voltage across the 1-port is positive, we know that terminal a is positive with respect to b. The specification for the v-source is such that a is always at +50 V with respect to b. Therefore, we have the resulting component equation.

For case C the positive orientation on the measurement diagram agrees with the plus-minus convention on the v-source, thereby leading to the given component equation. We also see that the voltage across the 1-port is given by

$$v_{ab} = 10 \cos 2t \text{ V} \tag{2.16}$$

which implies that a is positive with respect to b when t is such that $\cos 2t$ is positive, and vice-versa when $\cos 2t$ is negative. Nevertheless, the component is completely specified by the designated positive orientation for voltage and the component equation of Equation 2.16.

The measurement diagram for case D indicates that positive current flow is defined as current flow from terminal b to terminal a within the 1-port. Thus current (as defined) is always positive and its value is given by the component equation.

Table 2.4
Some Ideal Source
Examples

Source Type		Source	Measurement Diagram	Component Equation
v-sources	A	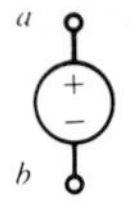 50 V		$v = 50$ V
	B	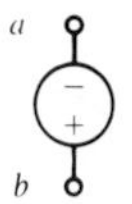 120 V		$v = -120$ V
	C	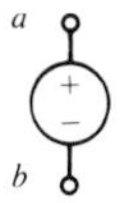 $(10 \cos 2t)$ V		$v = 10 \cos 2t$ V
i-sources	D	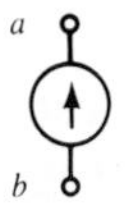 $5e^{-t}$ A		$i = 5e^{-t}$ A
	E	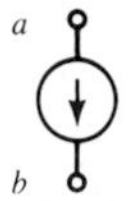 $10 \sin \pi t$ A		$i = -10 \sin \pi t$ A
	F	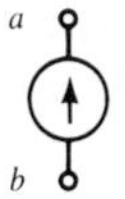 $(10 + 3t)$ A		$i = -(10 + 3t)$ A

This example illustrates several different forms that the specified time-domain functions of ideal sources might take. Two of the more-common source functions, in practical networks, are the *constant source* and the *sinusoidal source*.

The networks used for the analyses of the myriad of electronic devices of today's world contain many constant ideal sources. The description of the constant source is the simplest of our source descriptions and will be encountered many times throughout the book.

In network analysis, the sinusoidal function is often referred to as a *sine wave*.[3] In fact, many of the time-domain functions that we encounter may be called *waveforms*. This is particularly appropriate because these functions can usually be viewed on an oscilloscope in the laboratory.

The general form of a sinusoidal source function is illustrated by

$$v = V_m \cos(\omega t + \theta) \tag{2.17}$$

This type of function occurs often in what follows. Consequently, it is worthwhile spending some time reviewing its characteristics.

We choose, quite arbitrarily, to use the cosine function as the reference function for all sinusoids. With reference to the function of Equation 2.17, we remind you of the following:

1. V_m is the *amplitude* (V).

2. ω is the *radian frequency* (rad/s).

3. θ is the *phase angle* (rad).

4. $(\omega t + \theta)$ is the *argument* of the function (rad).

We recall also that this function repeats every 2π rad of the argument. For this reason, we say that the wave has a *period* of 2π rad. In terms of time, the function repeats every T seconds. Therefore,

$$\omega T = 2\pi$$

from which

$$T = \frac{2\pi}{\omega} \text{ s} \tag{2.18}$$

The repetition rate of the waveform is referred to as the *frequency*, f, and is defined as the number of times that the waveform repeats in 1 s. Thus

$$f = \frac{1}{T} \tag{2.19}$$

and from Equations 2.18 and 2.19, we obtain

$$\omega = \frac{2\pi}{T} = 2\pi f \tag{2.20}$$

The unit for frequency is cycles per second, which is universally designated as hertz (Hz).

---

[3]It is common practice to refer to all sine and cosine functions collectively as sinusoidal functions, or simply as sinusoids. Recall that any sine function can be converted by trigonometric identities to a cosine function, and vice-versa.

The concept of phase angle is illustrated by Figure 2.22.

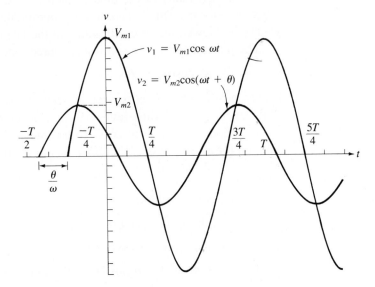

Figure 2.22
Two sinusoidal
waveforms.

From this figure we see that the waveform v_2 passes through its zero points (and its peaks) θ radians before the waveform v_1. Thus we say that θ is the *phase angle* of v_2 with respect to v_1, and for the θ as shown we further say that v_2 *leads* v_1 by θ radians. In a like manner, if θ is negative we say v_2 *lags* v_1. The amount of phase angle lead (or lag) can be converted to time lead (or lag) by calculating θ as a fraction of the period T. That is,

$$t_{\text{lead}} = \frac{\theta}{2\pi} T \text{ s} \tag{2.21}$$

The sinusoidal function is of particular importance for several reasons. You are probably familiar with sinusoidal oscillations or vibrations that occur in physics whenever the damping in a system is negligible. Sinusoidal responses in networks are also of primary interest. In addition, the voltages that exist at the terminals of real sources are often sinusoidal or very nearly so.

The sinusoidal function also possesses a rare property that makes it almost ideal for network analysis. It is one of the very few functions that returns a function of the same form when either integrated or differentiated.

Other source functions will be introduced as needed.

2.13 CONTROLLED SOURCES

In Section 2.12 we introduced the concept of an independent voltage source (*v*-source) and an independent current source (*i*-source). For these sources we have taken as the model the condition that the terminal voltage or the terminal current is a specified function of time, which is independent of any external conditions. That is, an independent voltage source produces a specified voltage at its terminals, regardless of the external network to which this source is connected. Similarly, an independent current source produces a specified current, independent of the network to which it is connected.

In the analysis of networks that contain transistors or other electronic devices, the electronic device is often modeled by a network that contains an ideal source of a completely different nature. These network models often contain voltage sources whose voltages are independent of the current through them but are functions of a voltage or a current at some other location in the network. Similarly, the model may contain current sources whose currents are independent of their terminal voltages but are a function of the current or voltage at some other location in the network. Such sources are called *dependent sources*, or *controlled sources*. Also in common usage is the terminology *dependent generator*. However, we reserve the terminology *generator* for a different concept, which is introduced in Chapter 3. From this point on we shall use the terminology *controlled source*.

Although the functional dependence of the controlled source could theoretically be of a very general nature, it is normally a simple function of the type $x = Ky$, with K constant. This concept and the several possibilities are illustrated in Figure 2.23. Figure 2.23(a) shows a voltage-controlled voltage source (VCVS). In this case μ is a dimensionless proportionality constant, and the source voltage is directly proportional to the voltage at terminal a with respect to terminal b. The other three cases illustrated are a current-controlled voltage source (CCVS), current-controlled current source (CCCS), and voltage-

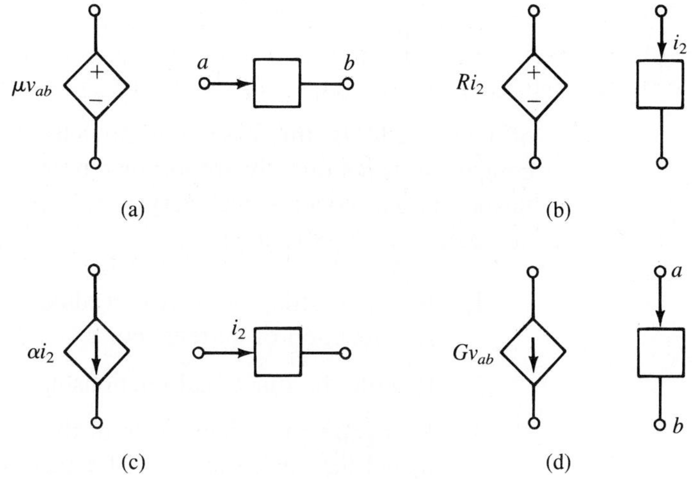

Figure 2.23
Schematic diagrams for controlled sources.
(a) VCVS; (b) CCVS;
(c) CCCS; (d) VCCS.

controlled current source (VCCS), respectively. In these cases the constants of proportionality are R, α, and G, where R has the dimensions of resistance, α is dimensionless, and G has the dimensions of conductance. The mathematical model of a controlled source consists of a measurement diagram and a functional expression for its terminal voltage, or current.

2.14   NONLINEAR 1-PORTS

We have developed mathematical models for a resistor, inductor, and capacitor for the case where these components are linear. Although these models are adequate for a wide range of applications, there are conditions where none of these components may be considered to be linear. We shall now consider the possibility of obtaining mathematical models for these devices when their operation is nonlinear.

Suppose, for example, experimental tests on a resistor yield a characteristic curve, as shown in Figure 2.24, as opposed to the linear characteristic

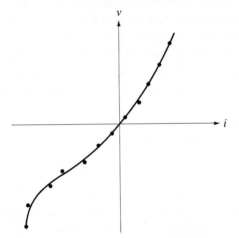

Figure 2.24
Nonlinear resistor
characteristic.

of Figure 2.9. In this case it is obvious that the terminal voltage of this component is not directly proportional to the terminal current and some modification in our model is necessary. One approach to this problem, which may be successful, is as follows:

1. By curve fitting or other procedures, express the terminal voltage as a function of current. For example, $v = f(i)$.

2. Rewrite the functional relationship as $v = f_1(i)i$.

3. Recognize the resemblance of this latter form to Ohm's law and model the device as a resistor that is dependent on the terminal current.

Of course, this technique may fail because it may be impossible to solve for the functional relationship as required by step 2. At any rate, a suitable mathematical model would consist of a measurement diagram and either of the functional expressions above. Note also that a suitable mathematical model would be a measurement diagram and the curve of Figure 2.24 or for that matter a table of values relating terminal voltage to terminal current. All that is required is a component characteristic.

If we had chosen to express the terminal characteristic in current-explicit form, the resulting model would have been a nonlinear conductance that is dependent upon its terminal voltage.

For the case where the inductance characteristic of Figure 2.10 and the capacitance characteristic of Figure 2.13 are nonlinear, a process similar to that for the resistor is appropriate. In the case of inductance, the nonlinear inductance is found to be a function of terminal current. Again, we observe that a suitable mathematical model would be a measurement diagram and an expression for flux, λ, as a nonlinear function of terminal current. Also, as for the resistor, the functional relationship between flux and current does not have to be an analytic expression. In fact, in some cases it may be very difficult or impossible to express this relationship in an analytic form. However, in general the analytic expression is more desirable. In the case of the capacitor, the mathematical model will be a measurement diagram and a functional relationship between charge and terminal voltage. Often the resulting model is a nonlinear capacitance that is dependent upon the terminal voltage.

Example 2.6

Suppose experimental tests on a resistor yield a characteristic curve similar to that of Figure 2.24, and this curve is approximated by the expression $v = 10i^3$. This expression can be rewritten as $v = (10i^2)i$. Therefore, the component is a nonlinear resistor with a resistance $R(i) = 10i^2 \ \Omega$.

Example 2.7

Suppose the characteristic of a nonlinear capacitor is given by $q = v^3$. Since $q = Cv = (v^2)v$, the nonlinear capacitance is $C(v) = v^2$. Now suppose the terminal voltage is $v = e^{-t}$ V; then $q = v^3 = e^{-3t}$ C is the charge on the capacitor. Since

$$q = \int i \, dt$$

$$i = \frac{dq}{dt} = -3e^{-3t}$$

2.15 KIRCHHOFF'S LAWS

Our development of the mathematical models for the electric 1-port components to be used in this text is now complete. At this point we emphasize a vital fact. There is exactly *one* component equation for each 1-port.

As noted in Chapter 1, the mathematical model for a network contains two separate types of information. One necessary ingredient is a mathematical description of each of the components. Since we have defined two variables, voltage and current, and a relationship involving one or both of them for each component, our mathematical model now contains half as many equations as unknowns (or variables). The component equations for a network are dependent on the component characteristics only and, as such, are completely independent of the manner in which the components are interconnected to form a network. The additional equations needed to complete our mathematical model must come from this interconnection information.

Let us now consider the tools for mathematically describing the interconnection of a network. As a preliminary to this discussion, we need several definitions. Since we have standardized on a single arrowhead to indicate both voltage and current orientations, all discussion will be with respect to this arrowhead. This arrowhead may be placed on either the schematic diagram or the interconnection diagram. The arrowhead is usually accompanied by a number coding in order to differentiate between the variables of the different 1-ports of a network (see Figures 2.25 and 2.26).

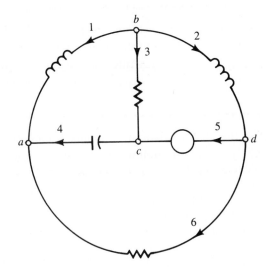

Figure 2.25
An electric network schematic with oriented components.

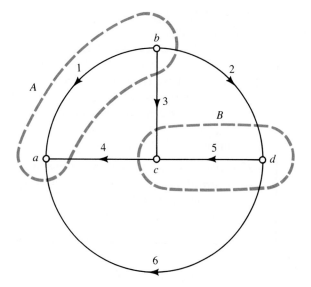

Figure 2.26
A network interconnection
diagram.

Definition 2.3	**Network-Variable Orientation**
	The *orientation for a network variable* is taken to be the direction of the arrowhead. This definition is a natural result of our convention for meter orientations.

Definition 2.4	**Node**
	A *node* in a network is a common point of connection for two or more component terminals.

Definition 2.5	**Loop**
	A *loop* is a closed path traced in a network through network components, which begins and ends at the same node. A closed path that passes through the same node more than once is not considered a loop.

Definition 2.6

> **Oriented Sum**
>
> 1. *Node*. Choose an arbitrary orientation for the node (toward the node or away from the node). The *oriented sum* is the sum of the current variables of all components connected to the node, with each term carrying a plus sign if component orientation agrees with the node orientation and a minus sign if it disagrees.
>
> 2. *Loop*. Choose an arbitrary orientation (direction) around the loop. The *oriented sum* is the sum of the voltage variables for all 1-ports associated with this loop, each with a plus sign if oriented with the loop and a minus sign if oriented opposite to the loop.

It should be clear that a change of loop or node orientation causes a complete sign change in the corresponding oriented sum.

We are now prepared to state one of the more important fundamentals of electric network theory. In 1847 Gustav Kirchhoff, a German physicist, published a paper in which he postulated two principles for electric voltage and current. These two postulates have long since become known as Kirchhoff's laws.

Kirchhoff's Current Law (KCL):

> *In any network, the oriented sum of the instantaneous currents at each node is equal to zero.*

Kirchhoff's Voltage Law (KVL):

> *In any electric network, the oriented sum of the instantaneous voltages around every loop is equal to zero.*

These very fundamental laws are now illustrated with an example.

Example 2.8

Consider the schematic diagram for an electric network shown in Figure 2.25 with arbitrary orientations for the components as shown. This network has a linear graph, as seen in Figure 2.26. If positive orientation is away from the node, the KCL equations are

$$\text{At node } a: \quad -i_1 - i_4 - i_6 = 0 \tag{2.22}$$

$$\text{At node } b: \quad i_1 + i_2 + i_3 = 0 \tag{2.23}$$

$$\text{At node } c: \quad -i_3 + i_4 - i_5 = 0 \tag{2.24}$$

$$\text{At node } d: \quad -i_2 + i_5 + i_6 = 0 \tag{2.25}$$

If clockwise orientation is taken as positive, some KVL equations are

$$\text{Loop } abca: \quad -v_1 + v_3 + v_4 = 0 \tag{2.26}$$

$$\text{Loop } bdcb: \quad v_2 + v_5 - v_3 = 0 \tag{2.27}$$

$$\text{Loop } bdab: \quad v_2 + v_6 - v_1 = 0 \tag{2.28}$$

$$\text{Loop } bdcab: \quad v_2 + v_5 + v_4 - v_1 = 0 \tag{2.29}$$

Several other KVL equations are possible.

All the equations in Example 2.8 could be written from either the schematic diagram or the linear graph. In fact, the nature of the components, as previously mentioned, plays no role in the equations of interconnection and need not be given in this example.

Now suppose we add the KCL equations written for node a and node b (Equations 2.22 and 2.23). The result is

$$i_2 + i_3 - i_4 - i_6 = 0 \tag{2.30}$$

From the rules of linear algebra, we know this is a valid relation that must be satisfied by the network of Figure 2.25. From this it follows that the sum of the instantaneous currents "leaving" the closed surface, enclosed by the dotted line labeled A in Figure 2.26, is equal to zero. Observe that i_1 appears in both Equations 2.22 and 2.23, but with opposite sign. In a similar fashion, by adding Equations 2.24 and 2.25, we get

$$-i_2 - i_3 + i_4 + i_6 = 0 \tag{2.31}$$

as a relation that must be satisfied by the network. This equation would result by setting the sum of the current leaving the closed surface, enclosed by the dotted line B, equal to zero. (In this case, i_5 appears in both equations, but with opposite sign.) It should be apparent that other current equations are possible by the addition of different combinations of the KCL equations.

Expansion of these more generalized concepts for the current equations leads logically to the following:

Definition 2.7

Supernode

A *supernode* of a network is a subnetwork of the network consisting of a set of nodes plus the network 1-ports that have both terminals connected to nodes in the set.

The concept of subnetwork is useful to us in several developments to follow. Any subnetwork of a given network includes in its branches a subset of the complete set of branches of the network.

Kirchhoff's Current Law (Alternate Form)

The oriented sum of the instantaneous currents at any supernode of a network is equal to zero.

Example 2.9

Consider the network linear graph of Figure 2.27. For the supernode labeled A and consisting of nodes a, c, and d (and 1-ports numbered 3 and 7),

$$-i_1 - i_2 + i_4 + i_5 + i_6 - i_8 = 0$$

for a positive orientation away from the supernode. For the supernode labeled B,

$$i_4 + i_5 - i_7 + i_8 = 0$$

Figure 2.27
Linear graph for Example 2.9.

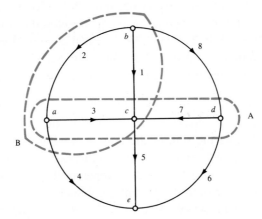

2.16 SUMMARY

In this chapter we considered the concept of instantaneous oriented voltmeters and ammeters and used this concept to develop a convention for interpreting the results of our network analysis. A 1-port electric-network component was defined and the mathematical characteristics (component equations) developed (for a standard orientation of the variables) for those 1-ports of interest in this textbook.

A summary of linear 1-port components is given in Tables 2.5 and 2.6. Some typical examples are given in these tables for component equations and for schematic diagram symbols coded with the component characteristics. Experimental test systems for determining the characteristics of typical 1-ports were introduced and nonlinear components discussed briefly.

We emphasized the importance to mathematical modeling and analysis of electric networks of two disjoint pieces of information—namely, the individual component characteristics and the interconnection information as given by Kirchhoff's voltage and current laws.

Table 2.5 Linear Passive Components

Component	Schematic Symbol	Component Equation Example	Coded Schematic Example
Resistor		$v_1 = 5i_1$ or $i_1 = \frac{1}{5}v_1$	$5\,\Omega$
Inductor		$v_2 = 6\dfrac{di_2}{dt}$ or $i_2 = \dfrac{1}{6}\displaystyle\int_0^t v_2(\tau)\,d\tau + i_2(0)$	$6\,\text{H}$
Capacitor		$v_3 = \dfrac{1}{7}\displaystyle\int_0^t i_3(\tau)\,d\tau + v_3(0)$ or $i_3 = 7\dfrac{dv_3}{dt}$	$7\,\text{F}$

**Table 2.6
Active
Components**

		Source Type	Schematic Symbol	Component Equation Example	Coded Schematic Example
Ideal	Independent	v-source		$v_1 = 10$	10v
		i-source		$i_1 = 5e^{-t}$	$5e^{-t}A$
	Dependent	VCVS		$v_1 = 2v_2$	$2v_2$
		CCVS		$v_1 = 3i_2$	$3i_2$
		VCCS		$i_1 = 4v_2$	$4v_2$
		CCCS		$i_1 = 5i_2$	$5i_2$
	Normal	Voltage		$v_1 = 10i_1 + \cos 4t$	$v_1 = 10i_1 + \cos 4t$
		Current		$i_i = 2v_1 + 5t$	$i_i = 2v_1 + 5t$

PROBLEMS

2.1 Describe an instantaneous meter of some kind that is familiar to you. What does *instantaneous* mean in this context?

2.2 Describe an oriented meter of some kind that is familiar to you. How does the word *oriented* affect the definition?

2.3 An electric battery is often symbolized as shown in Figure 2.28(a), where terminal a is positive with respect to terminal b. State the sign of the indications of the voltmeters connected in the networks shown in (b), (c), (d), and (e) of Figure 2.28.

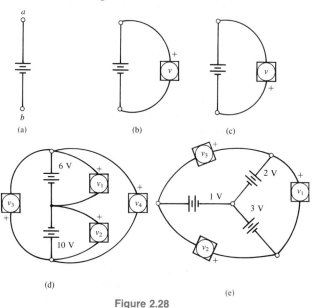

(a)   (b)   (c)

(d)   (e)

Figure 2.28

2.4 In the network of Figure 2.29, what would the magnitude and sign of the ammeter reading be?

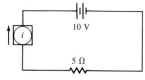

Figure 2.29

2.5 A zero-center ammeter is oriented by an arrow, as shown in Figure 2.30. This meter reads a current, $i = 10 \sin t$ A.

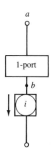

Figure 2.30

(a) State the magnitude and direction of conventional current through the 1-port shown at $t = \pi/2$, $3\pi/4$, and $3\pi/2$ s.

(b) Repeat (a) if the meter reads a current;

$$i = -10 \cos t \text{ A}$$

2.6 A zero-center voltmeter is oriented as shown in Figure 2.31. This meter reads a voltage,

$$v = 5 \cos t \text{ V}$$

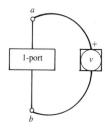

Figure 2.31

(a) State the magnitude and sign of the voltages v_{ab} and v_{ba} at

$$t = \pi/4, 3\pi/4, 3\pi/2, \text{ and } 7\pi/4 \text{ s}$$

(b) Repeat (a) if the meter reads

$$v = 5 - 5 \cos t \text{ V}$$

2.7 Consider the network shown in Figure 2.32. Suppose voltmeter v_4 reads $v_4 = 10 \sin \pi t$ V.

(a) What does voltmeter v_2 read as a function of time?

(b) What does voltmeter v_3 read at $t = \frac{1}{2}$ s?

(c) What does voltmeter v_3 read at $t = \frac{3}{2}$ s?

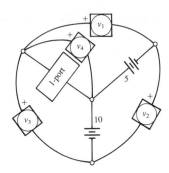

Figure 2.32

(d) What does voltmeter v_1 read at $t = 1$ s?
(e) What does voltmeter v_1 read at $t = \frac{3}{2}$ s?
(f) What is the sum of the voltmeter readings $v_1 + v_2 + v_3$ as a function of time?

2.8 For purposes of plotting voltage versus current for finding a mathematical model for a 1-port, the orientations of Figure 2.6(a) and (b) are equivalent and the orientations of (c) and (d) are equivalent. Explain why this is true.

2.9 (a) Draw a linear graph for the network of Figure 2.3. Orient arrowheads to agree with meter orientations.
   (b) Repeat for Figure 2.4.

2.10 Suppose that for the unknown 1-port of Figure 2.33, measurements in the laboratory indicate that when a voltage source $e = 10 \sin 10t$ V is placed across a component, the current measurement indicates that $i = \cos(10t - 90°)$ A. What is the component and what is its value?

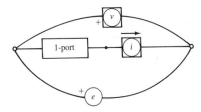

Figure 2.33

2.11 Answer the questions in Problem 2.10 for each of the following functions for i.
   (a) $i = 2 \cos 10t$ A
   (b) $i = -\cos 10t$ A
   (c) $i = \cos(10t + 90°)$ A

Can you be absolutely sure of any of these answers? Why?

2.12 A resistor has a resistance of 10 Ω. Calculate and sketch the current $i(t)$ in this resistor if the voltage across this resistor for $t \geq 0$ is
   (a) $v(t) = 10 \sin 10t$ V   (b) $v(t) = 10t$ V
   (c) $v(t) = 10te^{-t}$ V   (d) $v(t) = 20e^{-2t}$ V

2.13 Repeat Problem 2.12 for a capacitor having a capacitance of 10^{-2} F.

2.14 Repeat Problem 2.12 for an inductor having an inductance of 2 H and $i(0) = 0$.

2.15 The current through a $\frac{1}{2}$-F capacitor is $i(t) = 2t$ A. The voltage at $t = 0$ is -50 V. At what instant $t = t_1$ will the voltage become $v(t_1) = 0$?

2.16 An inductor has an inductance of 1 H. If a constant voltage of 10 V is applied to this inductance for a duration of 10 s, what value would the current have at the end of this period? (The initial current is assumed to be zero.)

2.17 A 5-F capacitor has a measured current wave form as shown in Figure 2.34. Draw the corresponding voltage wave form. Assume the initial voltage is zero.

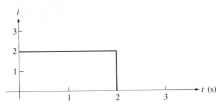

Figure 2.34

2.18 Figure 2.35 shows the voltage measured across a 1-F capacitor. Sketch the current $i(t)$ in this capacitor for $\Delta t = 1$, for $\Delta t = \frac{1}{2}$, and for $\Delta t = \frac{1}{10}$ s. Discuss the limiting case as Δt approaches zero.

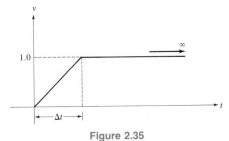

Figure 2.35

2.19 Discuss a situation for an inductor that gives a result analogous to that of Problem 2.18 for the capacitor.

2.20 A 2-H inductor has a voltage given by

$$v(t) = 10e^{-2t} \text{ V for } t \geq 0$$

To what value should the initial current $i(0)$ be adjusted if it is desired that the current $i(t)$ will eventually approach zero as time becomes large?

2.21 In Figure 2.36 the 1-port shown is an independent source. When $R = 2\ \Omega$, voltage measurements indicate v_{ab} is constant with time and $v_{ab} = 10$ V.

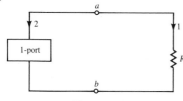

Figure 2.36

(a) Assuming the source is an i-source, give a mathematical model for this source, draw its schematic, and find expected current $i_1(t)$ for $R = 5\ \Omega$ and $R = 10\ \Omega$. What is v_{ab} for each of these cases?

(b) Repeat (a), assuming a v-source.

2.22 The 1-port in Figure 2.36 is some kind of source. When $R = 10\ \Omega$, measurements show $v_1(t) = 50$ V and $i_1(t) = 5$ A. With R changed to $5\ \Omega$, the measurements are $v_1(t) = 50$ V and $i_1(t) = 10$ A. All measurements are constant with time. Describe the source and give its mathematical model. Could the component be identified with either of the above sets of measurements by a single test? Why?

2.23 **(a)** Repeat Problem 2.22 for the following measurements: When $R = 10\ \Omega$, $v_2 = 50$ V and $i_2 = -5$ A; when $R = 40\ \Omega$, $v_2 = 80$ V and $i_2 = -2$ A.

(b) What current i_1 would be read for

$$R = 90\ \Omega?$$

(c) Can the ammeter reading i_2 be caused to read positive by varying the value of R?

2.24 **(a)** Repeat Problem 2.22 for the following measurements: When $R = 0$ (short circuit), $v_2 = 0$, and $i_2 = 1$ A; when $R = \infty$ (open circuit), $v_2 = -50$ V, and $i_2 = 0$.

(b) Is your answer to (a) unique or could it be given in more than one form?

(c) Discuss any practical laboratory precautions that might be necessary for tests of (a).

2.25 For the source-characteristic curve of Figure 2.15, give the component equation if the source is considered: (a) a voltage source, (b) a current source. Answers should be in general terms. Symbolize the current at point a as i_{sc} (short-circuit current) and the voltage at point b as v_{oc} (open-circuit voltage).

2.26 If the capacitance of a nonlinear capacitor is a function of terminal voltage of the form $C = C(v)$, show by use of the basic definition $i = dq/dt$ that the current through the capacitor is given by

$$i(t) = \left[v \frac{d}{dv}\{C(v)\} + C(v)\right] \frac{dv}{dt}$$

with v an arbitrary function of time. Use this expression to verify $i(t)$ for Example 2.7.

2.27 With reference to Problem 2.26, derive a similar expression for inductor voltage for a nonlinear inductor $L = L(i)$. Discuss what happens if $L(i)$ is constant for all i.

2.28 A nonlinear resistor has $R = 20 + i^2\ \Omega$. Sketch the v-i characteristic for this resistor. Find the current if the applied voltage is $v = 48$ V.

2.29 The characteristic curve of a nonlinear resistor is similar to that of Figure 2.24. The curve is adequately described by $v = 100i^2$ in the first quadrant and is symmetric in that if a voltage v gives a current i, then a voltage $-v$ gives a current $-i$. Find an expression for the resistance of this resistor. If the applied voltage is -100 V, calculate i.

2.30 The λ-i characteristic of an inductor is

$$\lambda = 10^{-2}i^2$$

Calculate the voltage across this inductor if $i = 2 \sin 100t$ A.

2.31 The diode is an electrical component with an idealized characteristic, as shown in Figure 2.37.

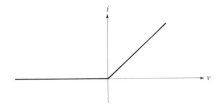

Figure 2.37

(a) If both positive and negative values of v are allowed, is this component linear?
(b) If only positive values of v are allowed, what type component does the diode appear to be?
(c) If only negative values of v are allowed, what type component does the diode appear to be?

2.32 Draw a linear graph for each of the networks of Figure 2.38 and write KCL equations for these diagrams.

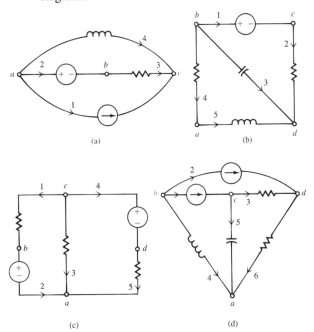

Figure 2.38

2.33 Write five KVL equations and four KCL equations for the linear graph of Figure 2.39. Show that any one of the KCL equations can be obtained from the other three. (This property will be discussed more fully in Chapter 4.)

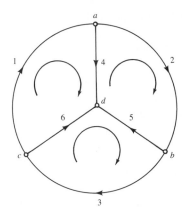

Figure 2.39

2.34 Show that for Figure 2.39 the KVL equation written for elements 1, 2, 3 (clockwise) can be derived by adding the three KVL equations written clockwise, as shown by curved arrows. (This result and these closed paths are discussed more fully in Chapter 4.)

2.35 Write four KCL equations and five KVL equations for Figure 2.40.

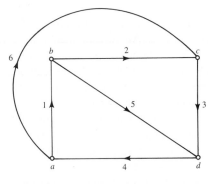

Figure 2.40

2.36 Write three KVL equations for the network of Figure 2.38(d) using double subscript notation (such as v_{ab}).

Giants of the profession
IEEE Centennial Hall of Fame

Michael Faraday (1791–1867)
Chemist and electrical engineer who
invented the generator, discovered
electromagnetic induction, and was the
architect of classical field theory;
through his lectures and writings he was
a great popularizer of science in the
nineteenth century.

Reprinted with permission from
"Centennial Hall of Fame,"
IEEE SPECTRUM, April 1984.

Power and energy

3.1 INTRODUCTION ⎯⎯⎯⎯⎯⎯⎯⎯⎯⎯⎯⎯⎯⎯⎯⎯○

In Chapter 2, we introduced the basic quantities that characterize the performance of a network. We referred to these variables as the *voltage* across a 1-port and the *current* through a 1-port. In Chapter 6 we extend these ideas to include the voltage and current variables at the terminals of a multiterminal, or *multiport*, component. In general, voltages and currents—or their time-integrals or time-derivatives—are the most important variables used in the analysis of networks. *Power* and *energy*, however, are also important variables in network theory. To a large extent their importance stems from the fact that they are much more directly related to the economic side of engineering than are voltage and current.

Electric utility companies charge their customers on the basis of energy used over a given period of time. The energy supplied is very closely related to the amount of fuel required by the company to produce steam and, hence, to the company's fuel cost. The rate at which energy is supplied to a speaker by an audio amplifier is directly related to the volume of sound produced by the speaker. Consequently, we can surmise that the problem of delivering sufficient energy to a load is an extremely important problem indeed.

In this chapter, we formalize the concepts of power and energy as related to 1-port components. In so doing, we are able to classify our components into two distinct groups—those components that can act as sources of energy and those components that cannot function as net energy sources. This leads to their classification as *active* components and *passive* components, respectively.

3.2 POWER AND ENERGY

Although we are primarily concerned in this textbook with the mathematical modeling and analysis of electric networks, it is often quite useful to relate to some basic physics concepts. One such concept is the consideration of conventional current flow as the time rate of flow of positive charge. This leads to the basic relation

$$i(t) = \frac{dq}{dt} \tag{3.1}$$

Electric voltage has been related to the work expended in moving a unit positive charge between the two points for which the voltage is defined. This physical interpretation leads to the relationship

$$v(t) = \frac{dw}{dq} \tag{3.2}$$

where w is the energy in joules.

Suppose we now form the product of the two basic variables, voltage and current. The result, as seen from Equations 3.1 and 3.2, is

$$\begin{aligned} v(t)i(t) &= \frac{dw}{dq} \cdot \frac{dq}{dt} \\ &= \frac{dw}{dt} \end{aligned} \tag{3.3}$$

by the chain rule of differentiation. Thus we have the important result that the product of the voltage and current of a 1-port component is equal to the time rate of transfer of energy to the component. We refer to this new quantity as *power*, or instantaneous power, to emphasize the fact that, in general, it is a function of time.

If the adopted orientation specified in Section 2.8 is maintained consistently for voltage and current, we can assign a very specific meaning to a positive and to a negative value for instantaneous power for any time t. This very fundamental fact of physics can be stated as follows: If at any instant of time, the instantaneous power is positive, the energy flow is into the 1-port. That is, a positive instantaneous power implies that the 1-port is receiving, or absorbing, energy. A negative instantaneous power implies that the 1-port is a source of energy, or is supplying energy. *This very important result of the conventions assumed for the orientations of both current and voltage meters* (standard orientation) *should be noted carefully.*

Let $p(t)$ denote the instantaneous power (in watts) for the 1-port at time t. Then

$$p(t) = v(t)i(t) = \frac{dw}{dt} \tag{3.4}$$

From Equation 3.4, it follows that the energy (in joules) for the 1-port from time t_0 to time t is

$$w(t) - w(t_0) \doteq \Delta w = \int_{t_0}^{t} p(\tau) \, d\tau = \int_{t_0}^{t} v(\tau)i(\tau) \, d\tau \tag{3.5}$$

Since a positive value for instantaneous power indicates that the 1-port is absorbing energy, a positive value for Δw indicates that energy has been absorbed over the interval from t_0 to t. This is equivalent to saying that the component is a *load*, or *energy sink*, over that time period. If Δw is negative over an interval from t_0 to t, energy is transferred from the component over that period and the component is called a *generator*, or *energy source*.

Confusion often arises in the use of the words *passive*, *load*, and *sink* and the words *active*, *source*, and *generator*. The following definitions set forth the conventions adopted in this text.

Definition 3.1

> **Generator**
>
> A component that is supplying energy (an energy source) is designated as a *generator*.

Definition 3.2

> **Load**
>
> A component that is receiving energy (an energy sink) is called a *load*.

Definition 3.3

> **Passive Component**
>
> A component that cannot function as a net energy source when its complete past time history is considered is called a *passive component*.

A component is passive, therefore, if for all t and for all possible conditions of operation,

$$w(t) = \int_{t_0}^{t} p(\tau) \, d\tau \geq 0 \tag{3.6}$$

and $w(t_0) = 0$. All components that are not passive are classified as *active components*, or *sources*.

The word *generator* is used in Definition 3.1, even though it would seem logical to designate an energy source as a source. In the literature of electric network theory, however, including some of the most widely used texts, source is used in the sense that we have used it here—to designate an active 1-port component. The choice of terms in this text is made to conform as nearly as possible to established conventions.

According to our usage in this text, then, a source may be a generator during some time period and a load over some other period. So the terms are not synonymous. As a simple example, an automobile battery is a *load when it is being charged* and a *generator when it is discharging*. It is, however, always an active component, or source. As we shall see, some passive components can be either a load or a generator over certain time periods. The following distinction is important. *Whether a component is active or passive, is an inherent characteristic of the device*. Whether it is a load or generator depends upon the operating conditions during the time interval of interest.

3.3 POWER AND ENERGY FOR A RESISTOR

In Chapter 2, we introduced the concept of linear and nonlinear resistors, where we referred to the positive linear resistor (constant resistance) as a passive component that is dissipative. We now justify this classification.

Since a resistor is a 1-port that is completely characterized by a curve in the v-i plane, it is convenient to consider power and energy with respect to a typical characteristic in this plane. Consider the characteristic shown in Figure 3.1. The instantaneous power associated with this resistor, $p(t) = v(t)i(t)$, is

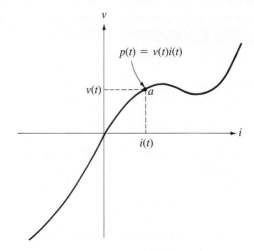

Figure 3.1
Characteristic curve of a resistor.

uniquely determined once an operating point, such as point a in Figure 3.1, is determined. It is obvious that $p(t)$ is positive and the resistor is absorbing energy for any operating point in the first or third quadrants. Likewise, $p(t)$ is negative and the resistor is supplying energy for any operating point in the second or fourth quadrants. From this discussion, we see that $p(t)$ is positive for all possible operating points of a resistor whose characteristic lies completely in the first and third quadrants. Therefore, by Definition 3.3, *any resistor that has a characteristic which lies completely in the first and third quadrants is a passive component.*

Likewise, a resistor that has a characteristic partially or totally in the second and fourth quadrants is an active component. This is true because it is possible to set up operating conditions for this case such that the resistor supplies energy or is a generator for all times of interest. As an immediate consequence of this discussion, we see that the linear resistor, with constant, positive resistance, is a passive component. Finally, a passive resistor can never supply energy to the rest of the network under any operating conditions.

Consider the case of the instantaneous power for a linear resistor,

$$p(t) = v(t)i(t) \tag{3.7}$$

Since $v(t) = Ri(t)$, we have

$$p(t) = R[i(t)]^2 \tag{3.8}$$

or

$$p(t) = \frac{1}{R}[v(t)]^2 \tag{3.9}$$

Equations 3.8 and 3.9 demonstrate that for $R > 0$ and constant, the instantaneous power for the linear resistor is always positive, and this component is passive. That is, it can at no time be a generator. The general expression for energy associated with a 1-port over a time interval from t_0 to t is

$$\Delta w(t) = \int_{t_0}^{t} p(\tau)\, d\tau$$

or

$$\Delta w(t) \doteq w(t)\Big|_{t_0}^{t} = w(t) - w(t_0) = R\int_{t_0}^{t} [i(\tau)]^2\, d\tau$$

$$= \frac{1}{R}\int_{t_0}^{t} [v(\tau)]^2\, d\tau \tag{3.10}$$

The actual form of $\Delta w(t)$ depends on the functional form of $v(t)$ or $i(t)$.

Example 3.1

Let $i(t) = 10$ A for a resistor of 3 Ω and let $w(0) = 0$. Then the instantaneous power is

$$p(t) = 3(10) \cdot (10) = 300 \text{ W}$$

and the energy transferred to the resistor (and dissipated as heat) is

$$w(t) = \int_0^t 300 \, d\tau = 300t \text{ J}$$

Usually $w(0)$ for a resistor has no significance since it is the energy transferred during some time period that is desired. (For example, the heat dissipated in a resistor yesterday is not usually of interest in regard to how it will operate today. An exception, of course, occurs when a neophyte experimenter applies twice-rated voltage to a resistor in the laboratory.) The limits on the integral are thus set to agree with the end points of the interval, and $w(0)$ is set equal to zero or ignored.

Example 3.2

Suppose in Example 3.1 the resistance is -3 Ω. In this case, we have

$$p(t) = -300 \text{ W}$$

and

$$w(t) = -300t \text{ J}$$

Thus we see that the negative resistor is a generator (source of energy) for all time $t > 0$. This is a general result, as readily seen by Equation 3.10 for $R < 0$.

A negative resistance seldom occurs in practice. However, this model of a linear but active resistor is important because some nonlinear resistors have linear characteristics with negative slope over limited operating ranges.

The form of the power and energy expressions for the nonlinear resistor depends on the form of the nonlinearity and does not yield to any general formulation. The nonlinear case is best illustrated by example.

Example 3.3

Consider a nonlinear resistor with $R(i) = 3i^2 \ \Omega$. Then the instantaneous power is

$$p(t) = 3[i(t)]^2 i(t) \cdot i(t)$$
$$= 3[i(t)]^4 \ \text{W}$$

and

$$w(t) = 3 \int_0^t [i(\tau)]^4 \ d\tau \ \text{J}$$

for $w(0) = 0$. We note that $p(t) \geq 0$ and $w(t) \geq 0$ for all t, and their particular form depends on the functional form for $i(t)$.

3.4 POWER AND ENERGY FOR AN INDUCTOR

For an inductor, the component characteristic (given in Chapter 2) is

$$v = \frac{d\lambda}{dt} \tag{3.11}$$

which, for the linear case ($\lambda = Li$, with L constant), reduces to

$$v = L \frac{di}{dt} \tag{3.12}$$

Therefore, the instantaneous power is

$$p(t) = \frac{d\lambda}{dt} \, i(t) \tag{3.13}$$

or

$$p(t) = L \frac{di}{dt} \, i(t) \tag{3.14}$$

where Equation 3.13 is the general relation, linear or nonlinear, and Equation 3.14 is true only for the case where the inductance is linear and constant. In either case, we see that the power can be of either sign, and this component can instantaneously act as either a generator or a load.

From Equation 3.5, we see that the energy for the inductor from time t_0 to time t is

$$\Delta w = \int_{t_0}^t v(\tau) i(\tau) \ d\tau = \int_{t_0}^t \left[\frac{d\lambda}{d\tau} \, i(\tau) \right] d\tau \tag{3.15}$$

Since the inductor characteristic typically gives λ as a function of current i (analytically or graphically), we can often express current as a function of λ in the form

$$i = i(\lambda)$$

From Equation 3.11,

$$v \, d\tau = d\lambda$$

Therefore Equation 3.15 becomes

$$\Delta w = \int_{\lambda(t_0)}^{\lambda(t)} i(\lambda) \, d\lambda \tag{3.16}$$

Therefore, the energy for the inductor over the interval t_0 to t is equal to the area under the current-versus-flux linkage curve. The energy for a typical nonlinear characteristic is shown in Figure 3.2. Note that the figure is shown for λ versus i, since this is the standard form of the inductor characteristic developed in Chapter 2. *Since the integration is with respect to λ, the area representing the energy lies along the vertical axis instead of the horizontal, as usually depicted.*

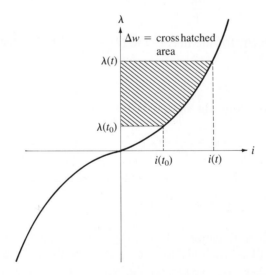

Figure 3.2
Typical λ-i characteristic for an inductor showing energy as an area.

As in the case of the resistor, we can obtain considerable insight into the characteristics of the inductor by consideration of the λ-i curve. We have defined a passive component as a component that cannot function as a net energy source, when its complete time history is considered. More simply, a passive component cannot function as a net energy source over any time interval for which the initial energy is zero.

Consider Equation 3.16 for an inductor whose λ-i characteristic lies totally in the *first and third quadrants*. Starting from a point of zero initial energy ($\lambda(t_0) = 0$), Equation 3.16 gives $\Delta w \geq 0$ for any $t \geq t_0$. This is true since i and $d\lambda$ always carry the same sign in Equation 3.16. Thus we conclude that *an inductor whose λ-i characteristic lies totally in the first and third quadrants is passive*. Likewise, we see that an inductor whose λ-i characteristic lies partially or totally in the second and fourth quadrants is active.

For the linear case, the λ-i characteristic is a straight line through the origin and $\lambda = Li$ with L a constant. In this case, Equation 3.15 becomes

$$\Delta w = L \int_{t_0}^{t} \left[\frac{di}{d\tau} i(\tau) \right] d\tau = L \int_{i(t_0)}^{i(t)} i \, di \tag{3.17}$$

which, after integration and substitution of limits, becomes

$$\Delta w = \frac{L}{2} [i^2(t) - i^2(t_0)] \tag{3.18}$$

Therefore, over the interval from time t_0 to time t, the energy for the linear inductor can be either positive or negative, depending on the relative magnitudes of the currents $i(t)$ and $i(t_0)$. From this we see that this component is capable of functioning either as a generator or as a load over some interval of time.

If we choose $t_0 = -\infty$ and assume that this corresponds to the time of fabrication of the component before it is connected into any network, then $i(-\infty) = 0$. From this, it follows that

$$\Delta w = w(t) = \frac{L}{2} i^2(t) \tag{3.19}$$

which indicates that the net energy flow into a linear inductor over any time period for which the initial energy is zero cannot be negative if the inductance $L \geq 0$. This is true even though the power may be negative at some times within this interval. Therefore, we see that the linear inductor with nonnegative inductance is a passive component. Likewise, a negative inductance is an active component. Negative inductances rarely occur in practice, being confined to some cases of restricted ranges of operation for certain specifically designed electronic networks.

The energy associated with the positive resistor over any time interval is always nonnegative. This follows from the fact that the power is always nonnegative. The energy flow is always into this resistor, and we say that it is *dissipative*, or *lossy*. For these components, the energy transferred to them from other components is retrievable only in the form of heat.

The power for a positive inductor may be either positive or negative. Over a given time interval, the energy associated with the component may be plus or minus. However, starting from an initial zero-energy state, Equation 3.19 indicates that the net energy delivered to the component cannot be negative. Thus, while the positive inductor may serve as either a generator or a load over a given time period, it cannot be a generator over any period that begins with zero energy. In simple terms, this means that positive energy may be regarded as *stored energy* for the positive inductor. No more energy may be delivered (minus energy) than has been transferred in and stored (plus energy) during a prior time period. This discussion leads us to consider the expression

$$w(t) = \frac{L}{2} i^2(t) \tag{3.20}$$

as the energy stored in the inductor as a function of time. Finally, we see from Equation 3.18 that any energy stored in an inductor at time t_0 due to a current flow $i(t_0)$ will be returned to the rest of the network if the current returns to zero.

Since an inductor can store energy and return it to a network in which it is a component, it is called an *energy-storage component*.

Example 3.4

Consider a linear inductor with an inductance of $L > 0$. Suppose the initial current is zero and the current for $t \geq 0$ is given by

$$i(t) = I_M \sin 2\pi t \text{ A}, \qquad I_M \text{ a constant}$$

The voltage across this inductor is

$$v(t) = L \frac{di}{dt} = 2\pi L I_M \cos 2\pi t \text{ V}$$

and the power is

$$p(t) = v(t)i(t) = 2\pi L I_M^2 \cos 2\pi t \sin 2\pi t$$

$$= \pi L I_M^2 \sin 4\pi t \text{ W}$$

Finally, the energy stored in the inductor is

$$w(t) = \int_0^t p(\tau) \, d\tau = \pi L I_M^2 \int_0^t \sin 4\pi\tau \, d\tau$$

$$= \frac{L I_M^2}{4} (1 - \cos 4\pi t) = \frac{L I_M^2}{2} \sin^2 2\pi t \text{ J}$$

Note that the expression for stored energy is the same as that obtained by $\frac{1}{2} L i^2(t)$. From the curves of power and energy versus time (Figure 3.3) or from the expressions for power and energy, we see that the inductor stores energy over the time intervals

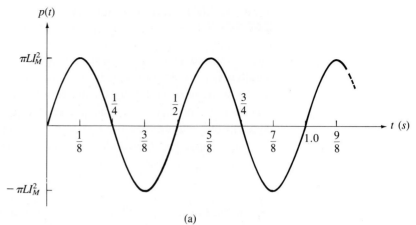

Figure 3.3
Power and energy for
inductor (inductance $= L$ H,
$i = I_M \sin 2\pi t$).
(a) Power curve. (b) Energy
curve.

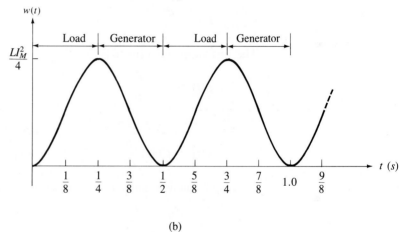

$$0 < t < \tfrac{1}{4}$$

$$\tfrac{1}{2} < t < \tfrac{3}{4}$$

$$\vdots$$

and returns energy over the time intervals

$$\tfrac{1}{4} < t < \tfrac{1}{2}$$

$$\tfrac{3}{4} < t < 1$$

$$\vdots$$

For $L < 0$, the power curve is given by the negative of Figure 3.3(a). The
energy curve is always negative (the negative of Figure 3.3(b)) and the component is active.

3.5 POWER AND ENERGY FOR A CAPACITOR ⎯⎯⎯⎯⎯⎯⎯⎯⎯⎯○

The development of the power and energy relations for a capacitor exactly parallels that for an inductor. In fact, if in the previous section we replace v by i, i by v, λ by q, and L by C, the result is applicable to the capacitor. This procedure is one facet of a concept known as *duality*. In light of this similarity, we shall only summarize the results for the capacitive case.

For a capacitor, the fundamental characteristic is

$$i = \frac{dq}{dt} \tag{3.21}$$

or, for the linear case with $q = Cv$, C constant,

$$i = C\frac{dv}{dt} \tag{3.22}$$

The instantaneous power is

$$p(t) = v(t)\frac{dq}{dt} \tag{3.23}$$

which for the linear case becomes

$$p(t) = Cv(t)\frac{dv}{dt} \tag{3.24}$$

If the q-v characteristic of the capacitor is solved for the voltage in the form

$$v = v(q) \tag{3.25}$$

then the energy relation for the general case is

$$\Delta w = \int_{t_0}^{t} v(\tau)i(\tau)\,d\tau = \int_{q(t_0)}^{q(t)} v(q)\,dq \tag{3.26}$$

and we see that the energy for a capacitor over the interval from t_0 to t is equal to the area under the voltage-versus-charge curve from $q(t_0)$ to $q(t)$. This concept is illustrated by Figure 3.4. As in the case of the inductor in Section 3.4, the integration is along the vertical axis.

For the linear case,

$$\Delta w = \int_{t_0}^{t} v(\tau)i(\tau)\,d\tau = C\int_{t_0}^{t}\left[v(\tau)\frac{dv}{d\tau}\right]d\tau = C\int_{v(t_0)}^{v(t)} v\,dv \tag{3.27}$$

which, after integration and substitution of limits, becomes

$$\Delta w = \frac{C}{2}[v^2(t) - v^2(t_0)] \tag{3.28}$$

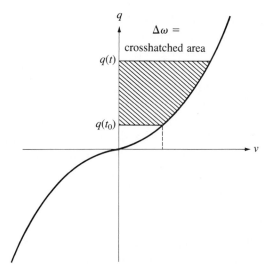

Figure 3.4
Typical *q-v* characteristic for a capacitor showing energy as an area.

In case $w(t_0) = 0$ or, equivalently, $v(t_0) = 0$,

$$w(t) = \frac{C}{2} v^2(t) \tag{3.29}$$

As in the case of the inductor, a capacitor may function as either a load or a generator at any particular time, since $p(t)$ may be either plus or minus at any time. However, as evidenced by Equation 3.29, the net energy flow into a linear capacitor over any time interval for which the initial energy is zero cannot be negative if the capacitance $C > 0$. In contrast, the net energy flow cannot be positive over this same interval if $C < 0$. Therefore, the linear positive capacitor is passive and the linear negative capacitor is active. In general, a capacitor is passive if the *q-v* characteristic curve lies wholly in the first and third quadrants.

Finally, we note that the passive capacitor is storing energy when the power is positive. The energy is stored as a result of an accumulation of charge and a resulting voltage on the plates of the capacitor. Thus we also classify the capacitor as an *energy-storage component*.

3.6 POWER AND ENERGY FOR SOURCES

In this discussion we limit our consideration to the *v*-source and the *i*-source. Because of the nature of the dependent, or controlled, sources (that is, dependence of a terminal variable on one of the terminal variables of another 1-port somewhere in the network), no general development is possible. The power and energy of this source will depend on the form of the variable of dependence and the network to which the source is connected and are best illustrated by examples. We do this in Chapter 4 when we analyze simple networks containing controlled sources. However, controlled sources are active and may be either load or generator. As for the normal source, as previously stated we treat this case as an interconnection of a passive component and an independent source in everything that follows.

The characteristic curves for a v-source and an i-source are given in Chapter 2. These curves are repeated as Figure 3.5. It should be noted that these are, in reality, the characteristic curves for only a particular time t. If the v-source, for example, is time-varying, the horizontal line will shift to a new intercept on the v-axis at some different time. In fact, this line will generally move up and down with time. Of course, if the source is constant with time, the characteristic remains as shown.

The particular form of the power and energy for the v-source and i-source, as well as whether they function as a load or as a generator, depends on the network to which they are connected.

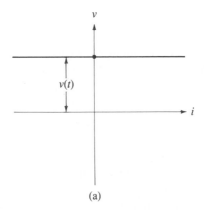

(a)

Figure 3.5
Characteristics for independent sources at time t. (a) v-source. (b) i-source.

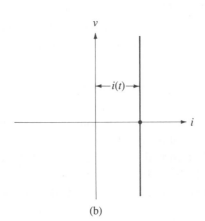

(b)

Example 3.5

Figure 3.6(a) shows a *v*-source and an *i*-source with their terminals connected. Suppose the *v*-source is a constant 10 V and the *i*-source is a constant 5 A. Assume orientations as shown on the linear graph of Figure 3.6(b).

By our conventions,

$$v_1 = 10 \text{ V}$$

$$i_2 = -5 \text{ A}$$

and by application of Kirchhoff's laws,

$$v_2 = v_1 = 10 \text{ V}$$

$$i_1 = -i_2 = 5 \text{ A}$$

Therefore,

$$p_1(t) = v_1 i_1 = 50 \text{ W}$$

$$p_2(t) = v_2 i_2 = -50 \text{ W}$$

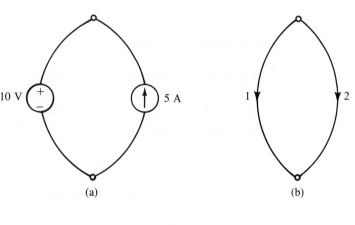

Figure 3.6
A network of two independent sources. (a) The network. (b) The linear graph. (c) An alternate connection of the sources.

(a)

(b)

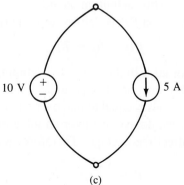

(c)

The v-source is a load and the i-source is a generator for all time. Also,

$$w_1(t) = \int_0^t 50 \, d\tau = 50t \text{ J}$$

$$w_2(t) = -\int_0^t 50 \, d\tau = -50t \text{ J}$$

if both energies are assumed zero at $t = 0$. Therefore, we see that after 1 s has elapsed, the i-source has delivered 50 J of energy to the v-source.

Now suppose that the terminals of the i-source are reversed, as in Figure 3.6(c). Further, suppose the orientations remain the same as before. Then

$$v_1 = v_2 = 10 \text{ V} \quad \text{and} \quad i_2 = -i_1 = 5 \text{ A}$$

$$p_1 = -50 \text{ W} \quad \quad \text{and} \quad p_2 = 50 \text{ W}$$

In this case the v-source supplies energy to the i-source at the rate of 50 J/s (W).

3.7 AVERAGE POWER

In general, the instantaneous power of a 1-port varies with time (although in some simple cases it is constant). It is often convenient to specify the average value of this variation over some specified time interval. Using the standard mathematical definition for the average value of a function, we have

$$P = \frac{1}{t_2 - t_1} \int_{t_1}^{t_2} p(t) \, dt \tag{3.30}$$

where P (in watts) denotes the average value of $p(t)$ over the time interval from time t_1 to time t_2.

This definition is often applied to the case where $p(t)$ is periodic. A function $f(t)$ is defined to be periodic, with a period T, if

$$f(t) = f(t + T)$$

for all t. In this case the averaging interval is usually taken to be one period of the function. For periodic functions the average over any integral number of periods is equal to that over any other integral number of periods. Furthermore, if we do average over an integral number of periods, the initial time does not affect the average. Therefore, we conveniently choose either

$$P = \frac{1}{T} \int_0^T p(t) \, dt \tag{3.31}$$

or $\quad P = \dfrac{1}{T}\displaystyle\int_{-T/2}^{T/2} p(t)\,dt$ (3.32)

for periodic $p(t)$.

This concept of average power is used extensively in network theory—especially in the study of the steady-state operation of networks with sinusoidal sources.

Example 3.6 _____

In Example 3.1, $p(t) = 300$ W. In this case $P = 300$ W also. However, in Example 3.4 we found $p(t)$ to be

$$p(t) = \pi L I_M^2 \sin 4\pi \ \text{W}$$

so

$$P = \frac{\pi L I_M^2}{\tfrac{1}{2}}\int_0^{1/2}\sin 4\pi t\ dt = 0$$

This answer is obviously correct by examination of Figure 3.3.

_____

Question: Will the average power of an inductor always be zero if the current is periodic?

3.8 TELLEGEN'S THEOREM ─────────────────────────────────────○

The principle of conservation of energy is used extensively in classical mechanics as an aid in analysis. This principle also applies to electric networks in a mathematically elegant way. It is not necessary to postulate that an electric network possesses this property. The conservation of power and energy are, in fact, implied by Kirchhoff's laws. The desired result was developed by B. D. H. Tellegen in 1952. In its simplest form, the theorem can be stated as follows.

**Theorem 3.1
Tellegen's
Theorem**

Suppose $i_1, i_2, \ldots, i_n$ and $v_1, v_2, \ldots, v_n$ are the currents and voltages of n 1-port components connected in an arbitrary manner to form a network. Then

$$\sum_{k=1}^{n} v_k i_k = 0$$ (3.33)

In other words, the total power generated by the network is equal to the total power consumed by the network.

3.9 POWER MEASUREMENT

In Chapter 2 we discussed the notion of instantaneous voltage and current meters. These meters are oriented and are uniquely connected to measure the appropriate variables designated by a given measurement diagram for a 1-port component. In this section we introduce the instantaneous power meter, usually called a *wattmeter*.

As in the case of the ammeter (*i*-meter) and voltmeter (*v*-meter), it is convenient to think in terms of a zero-center scale, instantaneous wattmeter (*p*-meter), which can directly read the instantaneous power (with correct sign) for a 1-port component. Since the instantaneous power is defined as

$$p(t) = v(t) \cdot i(t)$$

the wattmeter must sense v and i with proper sign and take the product. This can be done electromechanically, as was the standard for many years, or by using a multiplier circuit along with any means of measuring v and i. In either case the relationship between an oriented wattmeter shown pictorially and the schematic designation is shown in Figure 3.7.

The instantaneous wattmeter is a very convenient construct for analysis purposes and can be built for many applications. For most applications, however, average power is of more importance than instantaneous power. Thus the type of wattmeter that responds to average power over some given time interval is commonly used in industrial applications and laboratories.

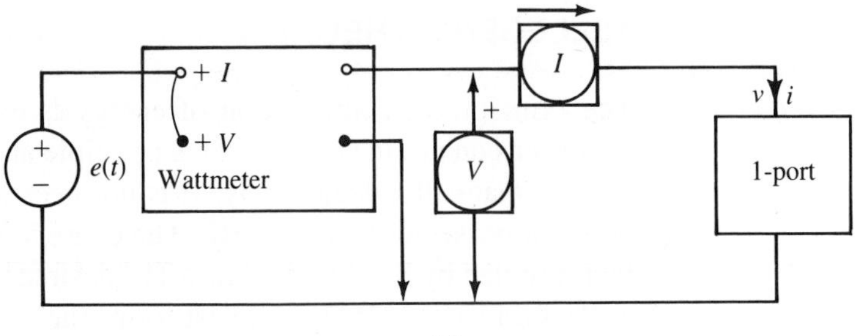

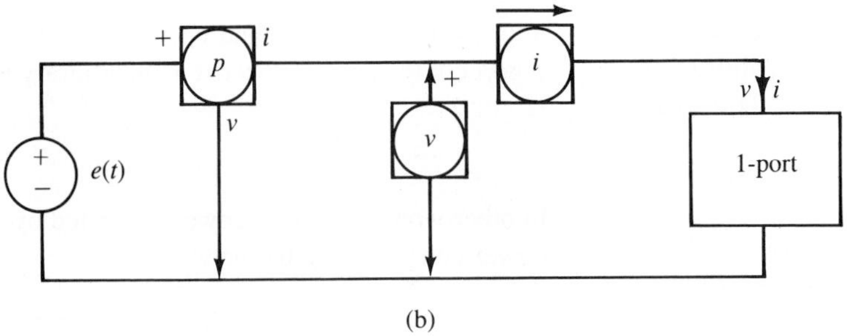

Figure 3.7
Network for measuring the instantaneous v, i, and p quantities for a 1-port. (a) Pictorial diagram and (b) corresponding schematic diagram for the specified orientation of the 1-port component.

(a)

(b)

3.10   SUMMARY

We have defined two additional network variables—power and energy. Although these variables are not usually a direct result of network analysis, their calculation lends further insight into network behavior. Furthermore, in some cases their behavior is of primary concern to the network designer.

Power and energy relations were developed for the majority of the components introduced in Chapter 2. All our components have been classified as either passive or active (an inherent property of the component). However we discovered that all the 1-port components except the resistor may function instantaneously as either an energy supply (generator) or an energy sink (load), depending on the particular operating conditions.

The expressions for the energy stored by linear inductors and capacitors are widely useful in practice. The usefulness of inductors and capacitors in networks is a result of their ability to store and return electrical energy. The resistor, on the other hand, dissipates as heat all energy supplied to it.

PROBLEMS

3.1 A 1-port has a voltage $v = 10 \cos 4\pi t$ V and a current $i = 2 \cos 4\pi t$ A (for all t).
  (a) Calculate the instantaneous power $p(t)$.
  (b) Sketch the curve for $p(t)$ and indicate the intervals of time in which the device is absorbing energy and the intervals in which the device is delivering energy.
  (c) Does the component absorb energy or deliver energy over one period of the given $v(t)$ and $i(t)$?
  (d) Calculate the energy for the 1-port from $t = 0$ to $t = \frac{1}{4}$ s.

3.2 Repeat Problem 3.1, letting

$$i(t) = 2 \cos(4\pi t - \pi/4) \text{ A}$$

3.3 Repeat Problem 3.1, letting

$$i(t) = 2 \cos(4\pi t - 3\pi/2) \text{ A}$$

3.4 A 1-port has a voltage and current $v = \cos 4t$ V and $i = \cos(4t + 45°)$ A. Determine and sketch the instantaneous power for this 1-port. Calculate the energy for the 1-port from $t = 0$ to $t = 5$ s.

3.5 A 1-port has $i = 5$ A and $v = 10 \sin 10t$ V.
  (a) Calculate the instantaneous power and indicate the time intervals for which this component delivers energy.
  (b) Calculate the energy for this component over the interval $t = \pi/20$ to $t = 3\pi/20$ s. Is the component a load or a generator over this interval?

3.6 A constant current flow of 4 A is supplied to a 10-Ω resistor. What is the instantaneous power? How long a time will be required to deliver 900 J of energy to this resistor? Where does this energy go?

3.7 The voltage across a 5-Ω resistor is $v(t) = 100 \cos 5t$ V for $t \geq 0$. Calculate and sketch the time-varying power $p(t)$.

3.8 Calculate the amount of energy that flows into a resistor of 10 Ω, if the resistor has a voltage $10 \cos 2t$ V, for 2π s. Is the starting time important?

3.9 In Example 3.3, a nonlinear resistor is given with $R(i) = 3i^2$. Suppose the current flow through this resistor is $i(t) = 5e^{-t}$ A. Calculate

(a) Instantaneous power.
(b) Energy for the resistor from $t = 0$ to $t = 10$.

3.10 The voltage applied to a 2-Ω resistor is

$$v = 10e^{-t} \text{ V for } t \geq 0$$

Calculate

(a) Instantaneous power.
(b) Energy supplied to this resistor between $t = 0$ and $t = 10$ s.
(c) Energy supplied to this resistor over all positive time—that is, $t = 0$ to $t = \infty$.

3.11 If a constant 100-V source is applied to a 2-H inductor at time $t = 0$ with $i(0) = 0$, calculate the energy for the inductor at $t = 1$ s and at $t = 2$ s. Suppose the source is left connected indefinitely. What happens to the energy?

3.12 The voltage applied to a 3-H inductor is $10 \cos 2t$ V. Assume the initial energy storage at $t = 0$ is zero and calculate

(a) Instantaneous power for $t \geq 0$. Plot and indicate intervals in time when the component stores energy.
(b) Energy stored in the inductor over the interval $t = \pi/8$ to $t = \pi/2$ s.

3.13 A nonlinear inductance is defined by $\lambda = 0.1i^3$. The current flow through this inductor is $i(t) = (1 - e^{-t})$ A. Calculate each of the following:

(a) Instantaneous power $p(t)$.
(b) Energy of the inductor during the time interval $t = 0$ to $t = 10$ s.

3.14 A capacitor has a capacitance of 10^{-3} F. The voltage across this capacitor is given by

$$v(t) = 100(1 - e^{-t}) \text{ V}$$

Assuming that the energy stored at $t = 0$ is zero, calculate the energy stored at $t = 1$ s.

3.15 A 2-F capacitor has $i(t) = 2t$ A and $v = 0$ at $t = 0$.

(a) Find the instantaneous power as a function of time.
(b) During what time interval does the component store energy?
(c) Calculate the change of energy during the interval $t = 1$ s to $t = 2$ s.

3.16 The current through a 1-F capacitor is zero for $t < 0$ and 5 A for $t \geq 0$. Calculate the energy stored in the capacitor at $t = 2$ s and at $t = 2$ h. What is the voltage at $t = 2$ h? Does this problem teach you anything practical? If so, what?

3.17 The current flow through a 0.1-F capacitor is constant at 2 A. Beginning at $t = 0$ with $v(0) = 0$, how long a time will be required to deliver 500 J of energy to the capacitor? What happens to this energy? What is the charge on the capacitor at the time 500 J has been delivered?

3.18 A 12-V battery is modeled as a v-source of 12 V. If this battery is "charged" by a current that is constant at 1 A for 30 min and then reduced linearly to zero over the next 30 min, calculate the energy delivered to this battery over this 1-h time period.

3.19 Calculate the average power for each of the following problems.

(a) Problem 3.6
(b) Problem 3.7
(c) Problem 3.12

3.20 Calculate the average power for Problem 3.10 for the following time intervals.

(a) $t = 0$ to $t = 1$ s.
(b) $t = 1$ to $t = 2$ s.
(c) $t = 0$ to $t = \infty$.

Giants of the profession
IEEE Centennial Hall of Fame

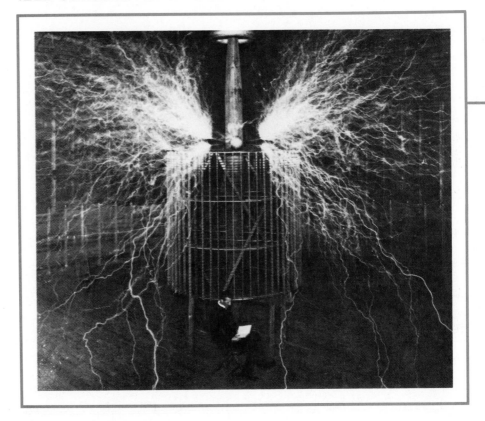

Nikola Tesla (1857–1943)
Electrical engineer who developed the
first alternating-current induction motor;
established a laboratory for studying the
transmission of energy without wires.

Reprinted with permission from
"Centennial Hall of Fame,"
IEEE SPECTRUM, April 1984.

Resistive networks

4.1 INTRODUCTION

In Chapter 2 we studied the properties of basic 1-port network components in detail. Each 1-port in a network is characterized by its terminal relation or its component equation—that is, the relation between its current and voltage. This is a terminal constraint that must be satisfied by the current and voltage at all times regardless of the manner in which the 1-port is connected into the remainder of the network.

In Chapter 2 we also introduced the two Kirchhoff laws for electric networks and observed that these laws do not depend on the nature of the 1-port components that constitute the network. The equations written from Kirchhoff laws are, then, constraints imposed on the network voltages and currents because of the interconnection pattern of the network 1-port components. These relations are often referred to as *interconnection constraints* or *topological constraints*.

Now we begin the study of the fundamental concepts and methods of network analysis—the main theme of this text. Before we actually begin the analysis of particular types of networks, however, we review the status of the mathematical model of our network and introduce a few additional basic concepts.

An electric network may be in one part (connected) or it may be in two or more parts. In this chapter we are concerned only with *one-part* networks and often use *network* synonymously with *connected network*. We use the adjective *connected* when we wish to emphasize an important property of one-part networks.

Consider a connected network made up by some interconnection of 1-port components. Let us denote by b the number of 1-ports, or branches, in this network and by n the number of nodes of the network. The basic question is: How many network equations do we have to write in order to analyze this network? This question can be answered by drawing upon the fundamentals of Chapter 2. First, as previously stated, by analysis of the network we mean the process of deducing or determining the voltage and current for each network 1-port. Thus, in general, there are $2b$ unknowns associated with a network of b 1-port components. It is a fundamental fact of network theory that *any network is completely described by the interconnection constraints (Kirchhoff law equations) and the component terminal constraints (component equations)*. Therefore, we must be able to write a set of $2b$ linearly independent equations from these constraints in order to obtain a unique value for each current and each voltage.[1] We are, in fact, able to develop a procedure for writing such a set of linearly independent equations. Therefore, except for "double-valued" nonlinear components, we have the fortunate circumstance that resistive networks always have a unique solution. This is not to say that the network variables do not vary with time. Rather, the uniqueness of the solution implies that the form of the time variation is specified by the solution and is unique.

How do we obtain these $2b$ linearly independent equations for each network? First, from their very nature, we can obtain b linearly independent equations by simply writing one component equation for each 1-port. Furthermore, these equations are independent of any equations written by Kirchhoff's laws. In Chapter 5 we present a fairly rigorous demonstration that *there are exactly b linearly independent relations specified by Kirchhoff's laws*. However, in this portion of the text, we limit our scope to a statement of this basic fact and some simple techniques for writing a linearly independent set.

We have noted that it is possible by application of Kirchhoff's laws to write many more than b equations. We now define a simple procedure for obtaining one suitable set of linearly independent equations.

Let us begin by stating one of the fundamental facts of network theory: *A connected network with n nodes has $n - 1$ linearly independent KCL equations*. However, the application of KCL at the supernodes of a network having n nodes yields many more than $n - 1$ valid current constraint equations. In Chapter 5 we discuss a very general method for choosing a set of supernodes that yields the proper number of independent equations. However, for our present purposes, the following statement is sufficient: *The KCL equations written at any $n - 1$ nodes of an n-node network are linearly independent*.

---

[1]The reader who is not familiar with the meaning of linear independence of a set of equations should refer to Appendix B.

Furthermore, any additional KCL equations will be dependent and could be derived from the set written for any arbitrarily chosen set of $n - 1$ nodes.

By use of KVL, we can write many valid interconnection constraints on our network voltages. Again, we note that *a connected network with b one-ports and n nodes has $b - n + 1$ linearly independent KVL equations.* Since, in general, there are many more than $b - n + 1$ possible loops in a network, care must be taken to select a set that will yield linearly independent KVL equations.

One possible procedure for selecting a linearly independent set of loops is as follows: Begin with an arbitrary loop and proceed to pick each new loop so that it includes at least one component not contained in any of the previously picked loops. This process assures that at least one new voltage variable appears in each equation and hence guarantees its linear independence. This process may fail to yield the full $b - n + 1$ equations required on a given set of choices but can be made to work by a trial-and-error procedure.

At this point let us consider two systematic methods for selecting a set of $b - n + 1$ independent loops. Although neither method will work for all networks, taken together they are sufficient for our present purposes.

Definition 4.1

Star-tree

Given a network in which at least one node is directly connected to every other node by at least one branch, a set of branches that form this connection is defined as a *star-tree*, and the common node is called the *reference node*.

From this definition we can obtain the following important result: *The unique loops defined by one branch not in the tree and either one or two star-tree elements constitute a particular set of independent loops that are sufficient for writing KVL equations.*

Example 4.1

A star-tree is shown in color in the linear graph in Figure 4.1. For the corresponding five-node, nine-element network, there are

$$b - n + 1 = 9 - 5 + 1 = 5$$

linearly independent KVL equations.

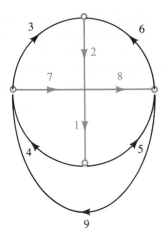

Figure 4.1
A network with a star-tree.

The KVL equations defined by the star-tree are

$$v_3 + v_2 - v_7 = 0$$

$$v_4 + v_7 + v_1 = 0$$

$$v_5 - v_8 + v_1 = 0$$

$$v_6 + v_2 + v_8 = 0$$

$$v_9 + v_7 + v_8 = 0$$

These equations are obviously independent, since a new variable is introduced in each new equation.

We note that a star-tree always contains $n - 1$ elements, since it connects $n - 1$ nodes to the reference node. Therefore, we can always be assured that the elements not in the star-tree ($b - n + 1$ in number) will define a linearly independent set of loops for any network having a star-tree.

Although every network does not contain a star-tree from the outset, a simple stratagem can be used to obtain one if desired. After a reference node has been selected, additional zero-conductance (infinite-resistance) branches can be connected in the network without changing its performance. One of these branches can be placed to connect the reference node to any node not already directly connected to it by a star-tree.

Another widely used scheme for picking a complete set of independent loops is the *mesh method*. To explain this method adequately, we need the concept of a planar network. A *planar network* is a network that can be drawn on the surface of a plane in such a way that no components of the network cross each other. If a planar network is drawn without crossovers, each set of components that define a loop and encircle no other components is called a *mesh. There are $b - n + 1$ meshes for a planar network, and the KVL equations written for these meshes are linearly independent.*

In summary, then, the number of equations necessary in our mathematical model are:

Type of equation	Number of equations	Comments
Component	b	One for each 1-port component
KCL	$n - 1$	Written at all but one node
KVL	$b - n + 1$	Written for all meshes or any independent set of loops

The total number of network equations is

$$b + (n - 1) + (b - n + 1) = 2b$$

which is equal to the number of network unknowns. To analyze a network, we write these equations and solve them for the voltages and currents. The $2b$ equations outlined above are referred to as the *primary mathematical model* (PRIMM) of the network.

Any analysis procedure used must essentially solve these $2b$ equations simultaneously. Because of the nature of the PRIMM and because we do not always need a solution for every variable of the network, we shall devise shortcut methods for solution. In these shortcut methods, we do not always write all the equations of the PRIMM explicitly. However, the complete set of $2b$ equations must always be inherent in our model, and any solution must satisfy the complete PRIMM.

In the remainder of this chapter, we utilize the concepts discussed in this section to analyze some simple but very practical networks. The study of network theory and the analysis of networks is more than the solving for numerical answers of particular network problems. We begin, now, to gain insight into general network behavior by developing some very interesting and useful network properties. This development relies heavily on learning by example.

4.2   ELEMENTARY NETWORK ANALYSIS ⎯⎯⎯⎯⎯⎯⎯○

Some fundamental concepts

In this section we begin the actual analysis of electric networks. We shall, for the present, restrict the discussion to networks consisting entirely of linear resistors and sources. The primary mathematical models for these networks are linear and algebraic. With the aid of examples, we now develop some general analysis procedures that carry over to the study of more general network types.

**Example 4.2
(A simple series
network)**

Consider the network schematic and its linear graph as shown in Figure 4.2. The orientations and the numerical designations for variables have been assigned in a completely arbitrary fashion. Recall that the arrowheads can be shown on the schematic diagram, thereby removing the need for the linear graph. This network has four 1-ports and four nodes. Therefore, the PRIMM contains eight algebraic equations, as follows:

Component equations (CE):

$$v_1 = R_1 i_1$$

$$v_2 = e_2(t)$$

$$v_3 = R_3 i_3$$

$$v_4 = -e_4(t)$$

where $e_2(t)$ and $e_4(t)$ are specified functions of time.

KCL equations (at nodes a, b, and c):

$$i_1 - i_4 = 0$$

$$i_2 - i_1 = 0$$

$$i_3 - i_2 = 0$$

Figure 4.2
A simple series network
schematic diagram.
(a) Network. (b) Linear
graph.

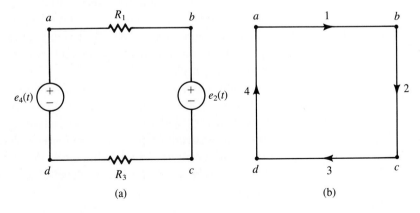

(a)   (b)

KVL equation (for the single mesh):

$$v_1 + v_2 + v_3 + v_4 = 0$$

The solution of the PRIMM can be accomplished in many different ways. We utilize a technique that will later be extended to more general networks. The solution proceeds as follows.

Step 1. From the KCL equations,

$$i_2 = i_1$$

$$i_3 = i_1$$

$$i_4 = i_1$$

From this result we see that each 1-port has the same current through it. This leads naturally to the following definition: *Two 1-port components are said to be in series if they have the same current through them.* Note that the definition specifies the *same* current, not equal current. Thus we see that the four 1-ports in this network are all in series.

Step 2. Use the result of Step 1 to eliminate all currents in the component equations except the current i_1. (We could, of course, just as well have retained i_2, i_3, or i_4.) The result is

$$v_1 = R_1 i_1$$

$$v_2 = e_2(t)$$

$$v_3 = R_3 i_1$$

$$v_4 = -e_4(t)$$

Step 3. Substitute the results of Step 2 into the KVL equation to obtain

$$R_1 i_1 + e_2(t) + R_3 i_1 - e_4(t) = 0$$

and solve as

$$i_1 = \frac{e_4(t) - e_2(t)}{R_1 + R_3}$$

Step 4. Using the answer from Step 3, substitute back to obtain any additional desired voltages or currents. Note that all remaining unknowns can be obtained by simple substitution.

Even though this example is simple to the point of triviality, take careful note of the steps and question, in particular, the motivation for Steps 1, 2, and 3.

**Example 4.3
(A simple parallel
network)**

Figure 4.3 shows a network and linear graph. The PRIMM for this network is as follows.

$$CE: \quad i_1 = 2v_1$$
$$i_2 = 10 \text{ A}$$
$$i_3 = 3v_3$$
$$i_4 = -20e^{-t} \text{ A}$$

$$KVL: \quad v_1 - v_2 = 0$$
$$v_2 - v_3 = 0$$
$$v_3 - v_4 = 0$$

$$KCL: \quad i_1 + i_2 + i_3 + i_4 = 0$$

Figure 4.3
A simple parallel network
schematic diagram.
(a) Network. (b) Linear
graph.

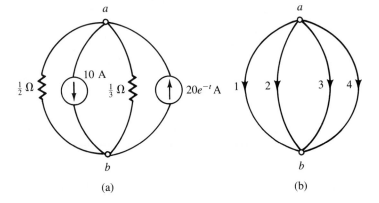

(a)   (b)

Note the similarity between this PRIMM and that for Example 4.2. To aid in the substitution procedure, we have written the component equations explicit in current for this example. We proceed in an analogous fashion to obtain the solution. From the KVL equations we see that all voltages can be written in terms of v_1:

$$v_2 = v_3 = v_4 = v_1$$

Utilizing this result in the CE and substituting them into the KCL, we have

$$2v_1 + 10 + 3v_1 - 20e^{-t} = 0$$

or

$$v_1 = \frac{20e^{-t} - 10}{5} = (4e^{-t} - 2) \text{ V}$$

and

$$v_2 = v_3 = v_4 = (4e^{-t} - 2) \text{ V}$$

Finally,

$$i_1 = 2v_1 = (8e^{-t} - 4) \text{ A}$$
$$i_3 = 3v_3 = (12e^{-t} - 6) \text{ A}$$

and we have the solution for all voltages and currents in the network.

In a manner analogous to the series network we say: *Two 1-port components are in parallel if they have the same voltage across them.*

It is apparent, in retrospect, that much of the detail of these examples could be eliminated, as illustrated by Example 4.4.

Example 4.4

By a straightforward application of KCL, we see that all currents in the network of Figure 4.4 are equal. We emphasize this fact by drawing a single arrow traversing the complete mesh, as shown in Figure 4.5. This current is called a *mesh* or *loop current* and is arbitrarily labeled as i_1. We have also numbered all 1-port variables in order to solve for all network variables.

Figure 4.4
Schematic diagram of a series network.

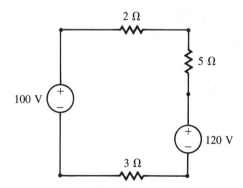

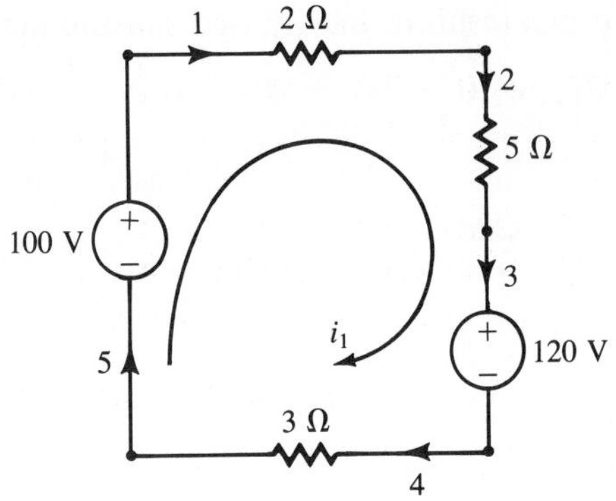

Figure 4.5
Schematic diagram of the network with loop current shown.

Now we can write the single KVL equation in terms of the single unknown i_1 by simply substituting in the individual component equations as we go and utilizing the fact that all currents are equal to i_1. Therefore, we have

$$v_1 + v_2 + v_3 + v_4 + v_5 = 0$$

or

$$2i_1 + 5i_1 + 120 + 3i_1 - 100 = 0$$

which gives

$$i_1 = -2 \text{ A}$$

Immediately

$$i_2 = i_3 = i_4 = i_5 = -2 \text{ A}$$

and

$$v_1 = 2i_1 = -4 \text{ V}$$
$$v_2 = 5i_2 = -10 \text{ V}$$
$$v_4 = 3i_4 = -6 \text{ V}$$

Finally, the instantaneous powers are

$$p_1(t) = v_1 i_1 = (-4)(-2) = 8 \text{ W}$$
$$p_2(t) = v_2 i_2 = (-10)(-2) = 20 \text{ W}$$
$$p_3(t) = v_3 i_3 = (120)(-2) = -240 \text{ W}$$
$$p_4(t) = v_4 i_4 = (-6)(-2) = 12 \text{ W}$$
$$p_5(t) = v_5 i_5 = (-100)(-2) = 200 \text{ W}$$

We see that the 120-V v-source is a generator and supplies energy to the resistors and the 100-V v-source as loads for all time.

Example 4.5

We now apply the shortcut method to the network of Figure 4.3. In this case we can see, by a simple application of KVL, that all 1-port voltages are equal. We could use any one of the voltages as the "key" unknown. In fact, we can use the voltage v_{ab} as the variable.

By writing the single KCL equation, while substituting in the component equations in terms of v_{ab}, we have

$$2v_{ab} + 10 + 3v_{ab} - 20e^{-t} = 0$$

which is, of course, the same as in Example 4.3.

In the above examples we have outlined two definite substitution procedures for use in solving network equations. For series networks the process is

$$\text{KCL} \rightarrow \text{CE} \rightarrow \text{KVL} \qquad \text{(I)}$$

whereas for the parallel case the substitutions are

$$\text{KVL} \rightarrow \text{CE} \rightarrow \text{KCL} \qquad \text{(II)}$$

Even though the substitution may be done implicitly or only in the mind of the analyst, as in the shortcut procedure, one or the other of these substitution processes is followed in all the examples.

If the two substitution procedures worked well only for a network of all series or all parallel components, they would not deserve any special attention. They are, however, of general applicability and worthy of additional consideration at this time.

The substitution process (I) is a technique known as the *loop method*, or *loop-current* formulation, and requires the simultaneous solution of $b - n + 1$ equations for a set of $b - n + 1$ unknown currents (known as loop or mesh currents).

The reasoning behind this formulation and the general outline of the procedure are as follows:

1. Since there are $n - 1$ linearly independent KCL equations, solve these equations for a chosen set of $n - 1$ of the current variables in terms of the remaining $b - n + 1$ current variables.

2. Substitute the results of Step 1 into the component equations to eliminate from the CE the $n - 1$ current variables that were solved for explicitly.

3. Substitute the results of Step 2 into the KVL equations to obtain $b - n + 1$ equations in the remaining $b - n + 1$ currents. It is convenient for this step to have the CE written in *voltage-explicit form*.

The substitution process (II) is a technique known as *nodal analysis*, or *node-voltage formulation*. This process yields a set of $n - 1$ equations expressed in terms of a set of $n - 1$ node voltages. The procedure is completely analogous to that of the loop formulation and need not be outlined any further.

Several points are in order at this time. First, the mesh method requires the simultaneous solution of $b - n + 1$ equations, while the nodal method requires the solution of $n - 1$ simultaneous equations. Therefore, one should compare the number $b - n + 1$ to the number $n - 1$ to decide which formulation is most convenient. Second, a shortcut method is possible by performing the substitutions implicitly or directly on the schematic diagram. This shortcut procedure is particularly easy for the simple networks considered in this chapter.

Finally, several special cases are yet to be considered that require some modification of the general procedures—for example, *i*-sources in a mesh formulation, *v*-sources in a nodal formulation, and controlled sources in either formulation.

Let us now illustrate these procedures with several additional examples.

Mesh and loop analysis

Example 4.6

Consider the network of Figure 4.6. The current and voltage variables have been oriented and numbered in an arbitrary manner, as shown. The PRIMM for this network is

$$\text{CE:} \qquad v_1 = 2i_1$$
$$v_2 = 4i_2$$
$$v_3 = 3i_3$$
$$v_4 = -11 \text{ V}$$
$$v_5 = -17 \text{ V}$$
$$\text{KCL:} \qquad i_1 - i_4 = 0$$
$$i_3 - i_1 - i_2 = 0$$
$$i_2 - i_5 = 0$$
$$\text{KVL:} \quad v_4 + v_1 + v_3 = 0$$
$$v_5 + v_2 + v_3 = 0$$

Even for this fairly simple network, it is apparent that a systematic substitution procedure for solving the ten simultaneous equations is in order. In this case, suppose we solve the KCL equations for i_3, i_4, and i_5 in terms of i_1 and i_2,

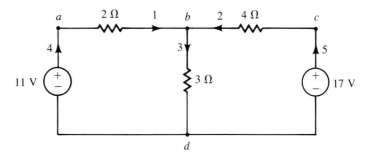

Figure 4.6
A two-mesh network.

substitute these relations into the CE, and substitute the result into the KVL equations. The details are left to the reader, and the final result is

$$5i_1 + 3i_2 = 11 \tag{4.1}$$

$$3i_1 + 7i_2 = 17 \tag{4.2}$$

These equations can now be solved simultaneously for i_1 and i_2, and the result can be substituted back into the KCL equations and the CE to obtain the remainder of the unknowns.

Recall that Equations 4.1 and 4.2 are called mesh equations and can be obtained in a more immediate way directly from the network. Utilizing the KCL equation at node a, we see that a single current flows from d to a to b. Likewise, a single current flows from d to c to b. These two currents are illustrated by single arrows, as shown in Figure 4.7(a). Next, by applying KCL

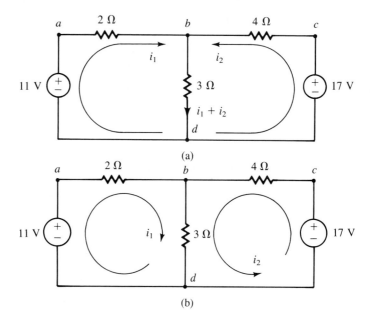

Figure 4.7
(a) Schematic diagram for the short-cut method.
(b) Schematic diagram showing mesh currents.

at node b, we see that the current through the 3-Ω resistor is $i_1 + i_2$ and is so labeled on the diagram of Figure 4.7(a). Now, we can write the two KVL equations for the two meshes directly in terms of i_1 and i_2 if we substitute in the CE as we go. Thus

$$-11 + 2i_1 + 3(i_1 + i_2) = 0 \tag{4.3}$$
$$-17 + 4i_2 + 3(i_1 + i_2) = 0 \tag{4.4}$$

where the loop orientations have been chosen in the direction of the current arrows. If the terms in Equations 4.3 and 4.4 are collected and the constants are transposed, we have

$$5i_1 + 3i_2 = 11 \tag{4.5}$$
$$3i_1 + 7i_2 = 17 \tag{4.6}$$

as expected. With a little thought and some practice, the mesh equations can immediately be written in their final form as in Equations 4.5 and 4.6.

In networks such as in Example 4.6, some people find it helpful to consider the currents i_1 and i_2 as circulating loop or mesh currents that flow throughout their individual meshes, as shown in Figure 4.7(b). The current through the 3-Ω resistor is then correctly given as the sum of the two mesh currents. Of course, this is not strictly correct in that we have no way of detecting two distinct currents through the 3-Ω resistor, but the two currents do, in fact, combine according to KCL at node b to form the current through this resistor. The process is justified because it can aid our thinking patterns and it gives correct mathematical models. The point here, which we hope has been well justified, is that there is one distinct current for each mesh, and all other currents are expressible as linear combinations of these mesh currents.

Example 4.7

The network of Figure 4.8 has two meshes, and the two arbitrary mesh currents have been chosen as shown. Note that mesh current i_1 is equal to the 1-port current i_1. Therefore, no new symbolism is needed for the mesh current. The same is true of i_2. Also note that $i_3 = i_1 - i_2$ as either a superposition of mesh currents or as a result of KCL at node b. The mesh equations written directly in final form are

$$6i_1 - 3i_2 = 3$$
$$-3i_1 + 7i_2 = 4$$

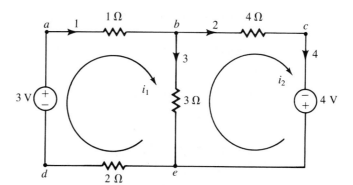

Figure 4.8
Network for Example 4.7.

Keep in mind that these equations are simply the KVL equations for the two meshes, where the branch voltages have been written in terms of the mesh currents.

The two mesh equations have the solution

$$i_1 = i_2 = 1 \text{ A}$$

Therefore,

$$i_3 = i_1 - i_2 = 0$$

Furthermore, we can now solve for any other network variable for which a solution is desired. *It is a fundamental fact of network analysis that the mesh currents are a sufficient set of variables to define all remaining network variables by simple substitution.* Suppose, for example, that we desire the voltage v_{ed}.

$$v_{ed} = 2i_1 = 2 \text{ V}$$

For the voltage v_{be},

$$v_{be} = v_3 = 3i_3 = 0$$

Also note that

$$v_{ae} = v_{ad} + v_{de} = 3 - 2 = 1 \text{ V}$$

or

$$v_{ae} = v_{ab} + v_{be} = i_1 + v_3 = 1 \text{ V}$$

Finally,

$$p_4(t) = v_4 i_4 = v_4 i_2 = -4(1) = -4 \text{ W}$$

Up to this time, we have very carefully avoided the use of any *i*-sources in our considerations of the mesh method. If a network contains *i*-sources and is to be analyzed by the mesh method, some slight modification of the approach is necessary:

1. Write the mesh equations as before, except that each time an *i*-source is encountered in a mesh, a voltage unknown must be introduced for the voltage across this component.

2. Write an additional constraint equation on the mesh currents for each *i*-source in the network. Each of these constraints results from the fact that each *i*-source specifies one current in the network. (This constraint equation sets the *i*-source either equal to a mesh current or to a sum or difference of two mesh currents.)

3. Solve these equations for the mesh currents and proceed as before.

In Step 1 of this procedure, the additional voltage unknown is necessary because, as we recall, a mesh equation is in reality a KVL equation summing the voltages around a loop. Since it is not possible to express the voltage across an *i*-source in terms of the mesh currents—or any other currents for that matter—we have no alternative other than that of introducing an unknown voltage.

At first consideration it appears that the above procedure adds one equation to the set, which must be solved simultaneously for each *i*-source in the network. Technically, this is correct. However, we shall see that "decoupling" of the equations is possible, and the final result is one of simplification. If some currents are known or specified, a simplification in solution should result. This is, in fact, the case, as illustrated by example.

Example 4.8

Figure 4.9 shows the mesh currents of a two-mesh network. Writing the mesh equation for the first mesh, we have

$$v_1 + 4i_1 + 4i_2 = 0$$

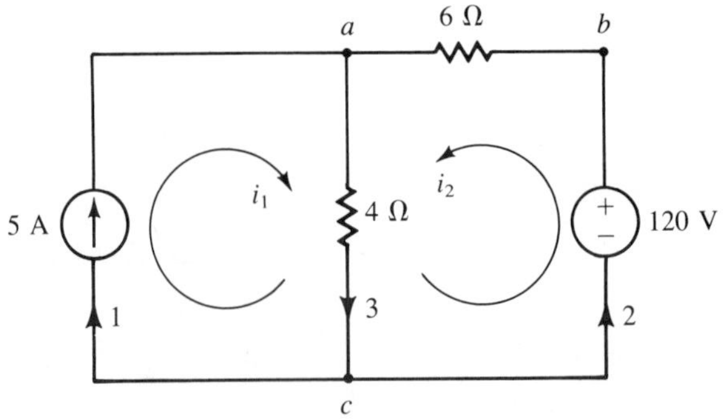

Figure 4.9
A two-mesh network with an *i*-source.

For the second mesh,

$$4i_1 + 10i_2 = 120$$

and the constraint equation is

$$i_1 = 5 \text{ A}$$

We note that the constraint equation can be substituted into the other equations with the result

$$v_1 + 4(5) + 4i_2 = 0$$
$$4(5) + 10i_2 = 120$$

and these two mesh equations are *decoupled*. That is to say, the latter can be solved for i_2 without use of the first equation. Now the first equation can be solved for v_1. Furthermore, it is now possible to solve for any additional network variables that are desired by simple substitution into KCL equations and component equations.

Simple though it is, this last example illustrates some far-reaching implications. Let us consider the subtleties of this example very carefully. Why did the two mesh equations become decoupled and not require simultaneous solution? The answer is that i_1 is known and v_1 did not appear in the equation for the second mesh. This, of course, results because the i-source is in the first mesh but not in the second mesh. Note also that the unknown v_1 appears in no other equations of the PRIMM of this network—not in the CE because 1-port number one is an i-source, and certainly not in the KCL equations—only in the KVL equation for mesh 1. Therefore, the equation for mesh 1 need not—and, in fact, cannot—be used except to solve for the voltage v_1. We call an equation of this type a *dummy equation* and the mesh a *dummy mesh*.

The decoupling described above will occur for any network for which *every i-source is in only one mesh*. Of course, we could not expect this fortunate circumstance to occur for all our problems. Therefore, we ask this question: Is it possible to create the decoupling effect of dummy equations for networks for which one or more i-sources appear in more than one mesh? The answer is yes. Two approaches are fruitful in this regard. First, we might simply redraw the network schematic diagram in an equivalent form and in such a way that each i-source appears in only one mesh. This is possible for many cases but not possible for all networks of interest. Therefore, a second approach of interest is a generalization of the mesh method to a set of loops that are not meshes but for which *each i-source appears in only one loop*. A note of caution: A set of mesh equations is always linearly independent, but $b - n + 1$

loop equations arbitrarily chosen are not guaranteed to be so. Therefore, the analyst must take steps to assure the linear independence of this set of loops. We shall do this in a very formal way later. For now, the procedure of Section 4.1 is sufficient.

Example 4.9

The network of Figure 4.10 has the 5-A i-source common to both meshes. Note that this network can be redrawn in an equivalent form as Figure 4.9 for Example 4.8, and we can use the mesh method. However, suppose we use the loops defined by the arrows shown in Figure 4.11. The two loops shown are certainly linearly independent. You should confirm that this is so. One way is to choose a star-tree that defines the two loops as shown.

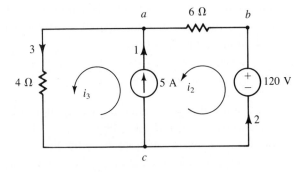

Figure 4.10
A network of Figure 4.9 redrawn in an equivalent form.

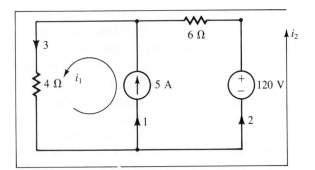

Figure 4.11
Two suitable loops for the network.

The loop and constraint equations for this network are

$$v_1 + 4(i_1 + i_2) = 0$$

$$4i_1 + 10i_2 = 120$$

$$i_1 = 5 \text{ A}$$

where we have used $i_3 = i_1 + i_2$.

In summary, then, the mesh method is a special case of the loop method. Furthermore, the number of simultaneous equations that must be solved simultaneously using this method is $b - n + 1 - N_i$, where N_i is the number of i-sources. There is one dummy loop equation for each i-source that need not be solved or even written unless the voltage across the i-source is needed in the analysis. *Of course, the statements made are contingent on the fact that each i-source appears in one and only one of the loops that have been defined for the network, thereby establishing a set of N_i known loop currents.* Consider the fortunate circumstance where $N_i = b - n + 1$. In this case, either all the loop currents of the network are specified, or all the i-sources are not independent. The case of dependent i-sources can be simply illustrated by two i-sources in series. Note that the dependence here is a different dependence than that of the controlled source. This dependence is imposed by Kirchhoff's current law.

Node-voltage analysis

An n-node network has $n - 1$ linearly independent voltages, and all other voltages in the network are expressible as linear combinations of these voltages. Thus we see that once a suitable set of $n - 1$ voltage variables has been solved for, all other network variables can be found from the PRIMM. The node-voltage method is one technique for formulating a set of $n - 1$ linearly independent equations with $n - 1$ unknown voltages.

The approach that we shall use is as follows, for a network with no v-sources:

1. Choose a suitable set of $n - 1$ node voltages such that all other network voltages can be written as linear combinations of the chosen set.

2. Write equations for the remaining $b - n + 1$ voltages as linear combinations of the chosen set.

3. Write the $n - 1$ independent KCL equations for the network. In these equations, express each current as a function of the chosen unknown voltages by use of the component equations and the relations of Step 2.

The details of this method are illustrated by example.

Example 4.10

It is apparent that any of several sets of two voltage measurements is sufficient to define all the voltages of the network and linear graph shown in Figure 4.12. For example, we might choose v_1 and v_3, or v_3 and v_5, or any other independent

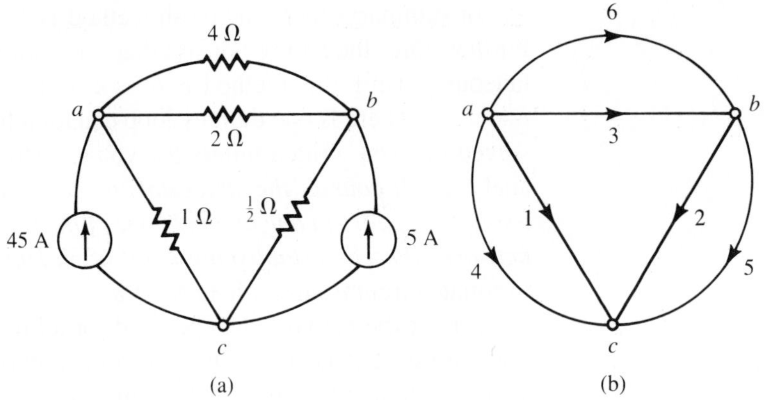

Figure 4.12
Schematic diagram of a
three-node network.
(a) Network. (b) Network
linear graph.

pair. For this example, suppose we choose v_1 and v_2. Following Step 2 of the procedure, we write:

$$v_4 = v_1$$
$$v_5 = v_2$$
$$v_3 = v_1 - v_2 \tag{4.7}$$
$$v_6 = v_1 - v_2$$

Note that we have used the four KVL equations in performing this step.
Next suppose we write KCL equations at nodes a and b. Thus

$$i_1 + i_3 + i_4 + i_6 = 0$$
$$i_2 - i_3 + i_5 - i_6 = 0$$

Now, rewrite these KCL equations in terms of v_1 and v_2 by substituting in the CE and simultaneously eliminating v_3, v_4, v_5, and v_6 by use of Equation 4.7. The result is

$$\frac{v_1}{1} + \frac{v_1 - v_2}{2} - 45 + \frac{v_1 - v_2}{4} = 0 \tag{4.8}$$

$$\frac{v_2}{1/2} - \frac{v_1 - v_2}{2} - 5 - \frac{v_1 - v_2}{4} = 0 \tag{4.9}$$

With practice to gain confidence, we shall be able to write the equations directly in this latter form. Although we never wrote some of the equations explicitly, we have now used all of the equations of the network PRIMM. Further, the substitution process was

$$\text{KVL} \rightarrow \text{CE} \rightarrow \text{KCL}$$

Collecting terms and rewriting Equations 4.8 and 4.9, we have

$$\tfrac{7}{4}v_1 - \tfrac{3}{4}v_2 = 45$$

$$-\tfrac{3}{4}v_1 + \tfrac{11}{4}v_2 = 5$$

for which the solution is

$$v_1 = 30 \text{ V}$$

$$v_2 = 10 \text{ V}$$

and, from Equation 4.7,

$$v_4 = 30 \text{ V}$$

$$v_5 = 10 \text{ V}$$

$$v_3 = v_6 = 20 \text{ V}$$

Now all the network voltages are known and any desired current variables can be found from the individual component equations. For example,

$$i_6 = \tfrac{1}{4}v_6 = \tfrac{1}{4}(20) = 5 \text{ A}$$

In the example just concluded, we note that

$$v_1 = v_{ac}$$

$$v_2 = v_{bc}$$

That is to say, our voltage unknowns were the voltages at nodes a and b, respectively, measured with respect to the common point node c. Thus the name *node voltages*. Although there are many sets of voltages that are suitable as the chosen unknowns, in the procedure we have outlined, these so-called node voltages will always be a linearly independent set. If the node voltages are chosen as unknowns, the second subscript is often omitted and it is understood that all voltages are measured with respect to the remaining *reference* node.

In terms of these node voltages, the procedure can be outlined as follows:

1. Choose one node arbitrarily as the reference node.

2. Define $n - 1$ voltage variables, the unknowns that are to be solved for simultaneously, as the voltages of each of the remaining nodes with respect to the reference node. These unknown voltages, according to personal preference, may be assigned either a numeric subscript or an alphabetic subscript, as outlined above.

3. Proceed, as before, to write the KCL equations in terms of the node voltages.

Finally, note that a node voltage can be used as an unknown, even though this node is not connected directly to the reference node by a single 1-port component. The stratagem of inserting a zero-conductance branch (mentioned in Section 4.1) or its equivalent, a node voltage with an alphabetic subscript to designate a voltage not associated with a 1-port component, may be used.

Example 4.11

Suppose for the simple four-node network of Figure 4.13 we choose node d as the reference and write KCL equations at nodes a, b, and c in terms of the voltages v_a, v_b, and v_c. It is understood that v_a symbolizes v_{ad}, v_b symbolizes v_{bd}, and v_c symbolizes v_{cd}, as previously mentioned. At node a we have

$$\tfrac{1}{2}v_a + \tfrac{1}{4}(v_a - v_b) - 10 = 0$$

where current away from the node is taken as positive and we have, for example, taken the current through the 4-Ω resistor from a to b as

$$\tfrac{1}{4}v_{ab} = \tfrac{1}{4}(v_{ad} - v_{bd}) = \tfrac{1}{4}(v_a - v_b)$$

Likewise, at nodes b and c we have

$$\tfrac{1}{4}(v_b - v_a) + \tfrac{1}{6}(v_b - v_c) = 0$$

and

$$\tfrac{1}{3}v_c + \tfrac{1}{6}(v_c - v_b) + 10 = 0$$

where we have consistently taken current away from the node as the positive reference direction.

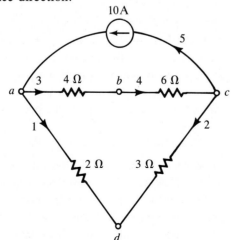

Figure 4.13
Network for Example 4.11.

These equations can be solved for v_a, v_b, and v_c, which—when known—completely specify, by use of KVL, all the voltages of the network. Any current in the network can then, in turn, be found from the individual component equations. Note that $v_b = v_{bd}$ is not the voltage of any 1-port of the network but is measurable, since points b and d are the terminals of 1-port components. Note also that insertion of a zero-conductance branch between nodes b and d (with orientation from b to d) would result in the same equations as if the v of that branch were substituted for v_b. In this way the star-tree approach could be used with this branch and branches 1 and 2 making up the tree.

The approach that has been outlined is perfectly general except for those networks that contain v-sources. We now consider this case.

If a network to be analyzed by the nodal method contains v-sources, the procedure is very similar to that described for loop analysis. In nodal analysis we are summing currents at a node. Therefore, we must introduce an unknown for the current through each v-source. Thus we write our KCL equations at any $n - 1$ nodes of the network and include these current unknowns where required. All other currents are expressed, as previously, in terms of the node voltages. Next, the constraint equations imposed upon the node voltages by the v-sources are written, and the two sets of equations are solved.

The constraint equations can be substituted into the nodal equations, and decoupling will occur for any nodal equation written at a node for which the node voltage is specified as a result of a v-source connected between this node and reference. Two distinct cases are of interest.

Case 1. All v-sources connected at a common node.

Case 2. All v-sources not connected at a common node.

For Case 1, simply choose the node common to all v-sources as the reference. This causes each v-source to specify one node voltage and creates a decoupled, dummy equation at that node, since the current through the v-source appears in that nodal equation and nowhere else in the PRIMM for the network. Thus we see that for a network with N_v v-sources, only $n - 1 - N_v$ of the nodal equations must be solved simultaneously, since N_v of the $n - 1$ independent voltages of the network are specified. The N_v dummy nodal equations are used only if a solution is desired for the currents in the v-sources.

Case 2 is covered in a formal way in Chapter 5. However, the general procedure outlined above can be used to solve problems of this type. To begin, a reference node should be chosen that is common to the maximum number of v-sources. In this case each v-source does not specify one node voltage but a more general constraint on the node voltages. The result is that less decoupling occurs when the constraint equations are substituted into the nodal equations. In any case, however, the number of equations that must be solved simultaneously is less than $n - 1$, since it is always possible to choose a reference such that some of the v-sources specify node voltages.

Example 4.12

Consider again the network of Figure 4.9. The schematic is redrawn in Figure 4.14 for convenience. Suppose we choose node c as the reference node. Then at node a,

$$\tfrac{1}{4}v_a + \tfrac{1}{6}(v_a - v_b) = 5$$

and at node b,

$$i_2 = \tfrac{1}{6}(v_b - v_a)$$

Figure 4.14
Network for Example 4.12.

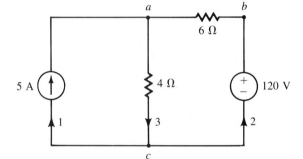

Finally, the constraint equation is

$$v_b = 120 \text{ V}$$

If this constraint equation is substituted into the nodal equations, it is obvious that the two equations are decoupled. The equation at node a can be solved for v_a, and the equation at node b is a dummy equation to use for solving for i_2. You should check the solution against that of Example 4.8.

In order to test our newly developed analytical muscles, let us apply loop-and-nodal analysis methods to some examples of more substance.

Example 4.13

Consider the network schematic diagram and linear graph of Figure 4.15. This network could be redrawn so that each *i*-source appears in only one mesh, thereby creating the desired decoupling of the mesh equations. However, in some networks this is inconvenient or even impossible. For this reason, let us use the more generalized loop method.

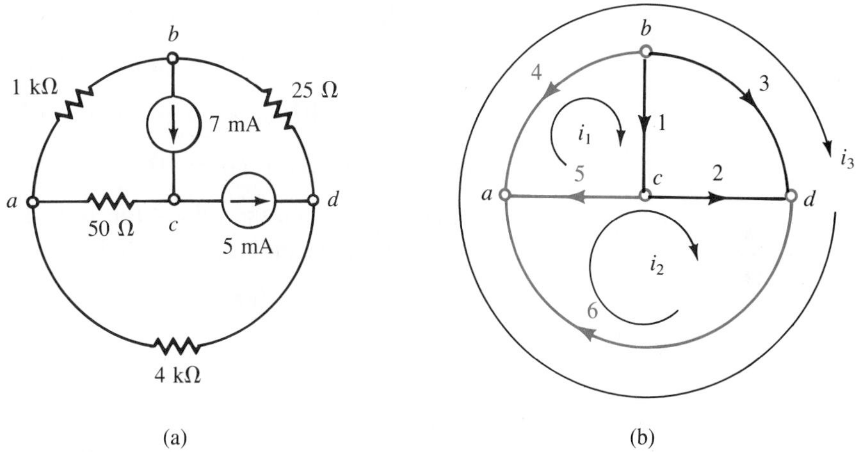

Figure 4.15
Network for Example 4.13.
(a) Schematic diagram.
(b) Linear graph.

(a)   (b)

In order to assure the independence of the loop equations, we shall use a set of loops defined by a star-tree, and at the same time select the star-tree such that each *i*-source appears in only one loop. Such a star-tree is shown in color in Figure 4.14(b). From the definition of the star-tree and the manner in which it creates an independent set of loop equations (Definition 4.1), it is obvious how the star-tree should be chosen in order to create the desired decoupling created by generating a dummy loop equation for each *i*-source. Simply, *choose a set of branches of the graph that does not include the i-sources.*

Question: Can any other star-tree be chosen that will create a set of independent loop equations as convenient as those created by the star-tree shown?

The loops and their associated loop currents, as created by our star-tree, are shown on the linear graph. Note that we have conveniently chosen the loop currents so that they are identical to the non-star-tree branch currents i_1, i_2, and i_3. Because of this we can readily write the star-tree currents in terms of them using the KCL as follows:

$$i_4 = -i_1 - i_3$$
$$i_5 = i_1 - i_2 \qquad\qquad (4.10)$$
$$i_6 = i_2 + i_3$$

Again, we note that this result can be obtained as a superposition of the loop currents flowing in the branches 4, 5, and 6 or by application of KCL at the nodes b, c, and d.

Next, we write the KVL equations for the three loops. In writing these equations, we utilize the CE to write voltages in terms of currents and substitute from Equation 4.10 in order to eliminate i_4, i_5, and i_6 in favor of the selected loop currents i_1, i_2, and i_3. We also introduce an unknown voltage as necessary for each i-source. Thus we have

$$v_1 + 50(i_1 - i_2) - 10^3(-i_1 - i_3) = 0$$
$$v_2 + 4 \times 10^3(i_2 + i_3) - 50(i_1 - i_2) = 0 \qquad (4.11)$$
$$25i_3 + 4 \times 10^3(i_2 + i_3) - 10^3(-i_1 - i_3) = 0$$

By substituting in the known values for i_1 and i_2 (note that the units are mA $= 10^{-3}$ A) and rearranging, we obtain

$$v_1 = -7.1 - 1000i_3 \qquad (4.12)$$
$$v_2 = -19.9 - 4000i_3 \qquad (4.13)$$
$$5025i_3 = -27 \qquad (4.14)$$

The solution for the one unknown loop current is

$$i_3 = -5.373 \times 10^{-3} \text{ A} = -5.373 \text{ mA}$$

At this point, the other currents can be calculated from Equation 4.10 and all voltages can be calculated from the component equations or from the dummy equations (Equation 4.12 and 4.13). The results for the voltages are:

$$v_1 = -1.727 \text{ V} \qquad v_4 = -1.627 \text{ V}$$
$$v_2 = 1.592 \text{ V} \qquad v_5 = 0.10 \text{ V}$$
$$v_3 = -0.1343 \text{ V} \qquad v_6 = -1.492 \text{ V}$$

Example 4.14

Upon examination of the network and linear graph of Figure 4.16, even the most ambitious would probably agree that systematic procedures are indeed in order.

Suppose we select a star-tree consisting of branches 7, 8, 9, and 10. Note that we have not included the i-sources. In order to avoid clutter on the diagram, the loops are not shown. However, the six independent loops as defined by the star-tree are the following sets of elements:

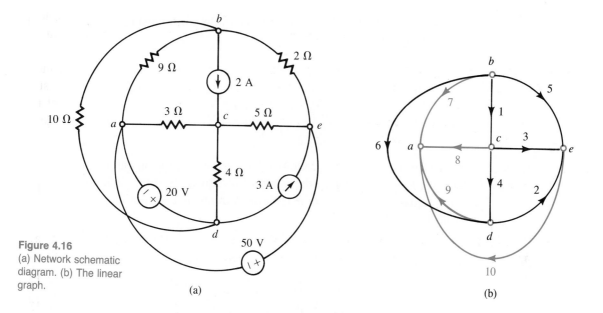

Figure 4.16
(a) Network schematic diagram. (b) The linear graph.

(a)   (b)

Loop number	Network branches included
1	1, 8, 7
2	2, 10, 9
3	3, 10, 8
4	4, 9, 8
5	5, 10, 7
6	6, 9, 7

Note that these loops are, in fact, independent, as promised earlier, since each contains exactly one branch that is not in the star-tree, along with two star-tree branches.

The component equations are

$$i_1 = 2 \text{ A} \qquad\qquad v_6 = 10i_6$$

$$i_2 = 3 \text{ A} \qquad\qquad v_7 = 9i_7$$

$$v_3 = 5i_3 \qquad\qquad v_8 = 3i_8 \qquad\qquad (4.15)$$

$$v_4 = 4i_4 \qquad\qquad v_9 = 20 \text{ V}$$

$$v_5 = 2i_5 \qquad\qquad v_{10} = 50 \text{ V}$$

The independent KCL equations, written in the form most convenient for loop formulation, are

$$i_7 = -i_1 - i_5 - i_6$$
$$i_8 = i_1 - i_3 - i_4$$
$$i_9 = -i_2 + i_4 + i_6$$
$$i_{10} = i_2 + i_3 + i_5$$

(4.16)

We can write the loop equations by writing the KVL equations around each loop while substituting in the component equations from Equation 4.15 and using Equation 4.16 to eliminate those currents that are not loop currents. The result is

$$v_1 + 3(2 - i_3 - i_4) - 9(-2 - i_5 - i_6) = 0$$
$$v_2 + 50 - 20 = 0$$
$$5i_3 + 50 - 3(2 - i_3 - i_4) = 0$$
$$4i_4 + 20 - 3(2 - i_3 - i_4) = 0$$
$$2i_5 + 50 - 9(-2 - i_5 - i_6) = 0$$
$$10i_6 + 20 - 9(-2 - i_5 - i_6) = 0$$

(4.17)

Collecting terms, we obtain

$$v_1 - 3i_3 - 3i_4 + 9i_5 + 9i_6 = -24$$
$$v_2 = -30 \text{ V}$$
$$8i_3 + 3i_4 = -44$$
$$3i_3 + 7i_4 = -14$$
$$11i_5 + 9i_6 = -68$$
$$9i_5 + 19i_6 = -38$$

(4.18)

The first two equations are dummy equations, and the last four are the equations that must be solved simultaneously in order to obtain a network solution by the loop method. If we decide to use nodal analysis on this problem, it is more convenient to write the component equations in current-explicit form. Thus

$$i_1 = 2 \text{ A} \qquad\qquad i_6 = \tfrac{1}{10} v_6$$
$$i_2 = 3 \text{ A} \qquad\qquad i_7 = \tfrac{1}{9} v_7$$
$$i_3 = \tfrac{1}{5} v_3 \qquad\qquad i_8 = \tfrac{1}{3} v_8$$
$$i_4 = \tfrac{1}{4} v_4 \qquad\qquad v_9 = 20 \text{ V}$$
$$i_5 = \tfrac{1}{2} v_5 \qquad\qquad v_{10} = 50 \text{ V}$$

(4.19)

Now if we select v_b, v_c, v_d, and v_e as our node voltage unknowns (node a as the reference), then $v_d = 20$ V and $v_e = 50$ V. Furthermore, an examination of the linear graph indicates that the voltages v_b, v_c, v_d, and v_e are equal to v_7, v_8, v_9, and v_{10}, respectively. Either set can be used as the unknowns. In this example we choose the set with numeric subscripts. Then, in preparation for writing the nodal equations, we express all other voltages in terms of the node voltages by writing the KVL equations from the linear graph. The result is

$$v_1 = v_7 - v_8$$
$$v_2 = v_9 - v_{10} = -30$$
$$v_3 = v_8 - v_{10} = v_8 - 50$$
$$v_4 = v_8 - v_9 = v_8 - 20 \qquad (4.20)$$
$$v_5 = v_7 - v_{10} = v_7 - 50$$
$$v_6 = v_7 - v_9 = v_7 - 20$$

As the final step of the formulation procedure, we write the KCL equations at nodes b, c, d, and e, substituting in the component equations (Equation 4.19) as we go and using Equation 4.20 to eliminate all voltages that are not node voltages. The result is

Node b: $2 + \frac{1}{2}(v_7 - 50) + \frac{1}{10}(v_7 - 20) + \frac{1}{9}v_7 = 0$

Node c: $-2 + \frac{1}{5}(v_8 - 50) + \frac{1}{4}(v_8 - 20) + \frac{1}{3}v_8 = 0$

Node d: $3 - \frac{1}{4}(v_8 - 20) - \frac{1}{10}(v_7 - 20) + i_9 = 0 \qquad (4.21)$

Node e: $-3 - \frac{1}{5}(v_8 - 50) - \frac{1}{2}(v_7 - 50) + i_{10} = 0$

The first two equations are the nodal equations that must be solved simultaneously for the unknown node voltages v_7 and v_8. The last two equations are the dummy equations for the v-sources. Once the first two equations are solved for v_7 and v_8, all other network variables can be obtained by simple algebraic substitution.

Now that we have struggled through both the loop and nodal formulations, let us pause to reflect upon the results. The network solution by the loop method requires the solution of four simultaneous equations, but the solution by nodal methods requires the solution of only two simultaneous equations, and they are uncoupled. We could and should have predicted this in advance, since

$$b - n + 1 - N_i = 10 - 5 + 1 - 2 = 4$$

and

$$n - 1 - N_v = 5 - 1 - 2 = 2$$

For some unknown reason that has confounded professors over the years, beginning students of network analysis almost invariably exhibit a distinct preference for the loop method. This example, however, illustrates quite vividly that we should always look carefully before leaping into the analysis pot.

For networks that contain many components, the analyst may be faced with solving a large number of simultaneous equations, even though a wise choice of nodal versus loop methods has been made. In this case a solution using a digital computer is desirable. BASIC programs for the solution of linear algebraic equations are given in Appendix C for those who want to solve some larger-scale networks.

Controlled sources

To complete our present discussion of the analysis of networks by loop and nodal methods, we now consider the inclusion of controlled sources. The extension is easily made and is summarized as follows:

1. Treat the controlled source as any other ideal source and write the model (loop or node) in the usual fashion.

2. Solve for the variable of dependence (the variable that controls the source) of the source in terms of the model variables (loop currents or node voltages). Substitute this result into the loop or nodal equations and proceed to solve as usual.

We can be sure that we will always be able to perform the solution of Step 2. For example, the loop currents of a network specify all the network currents by KCL. Then, since the voltages can be found from the CE, any network variable can be expressed in terms of the loop currents. The same is true, of course, for the node voltages.

Example 4.15

The mesh equations of the simple network of Figure 4.17 are

$$30i_1 + 20i_2 = 10$$

$$20i_1 + 90i_2 - 5v_{ab} = 0$$

Since

$$5v_{ab} = 5v_3 = 5[20(i_1 + i_2)]$$

$$= 100i_1 + 100i_2$$

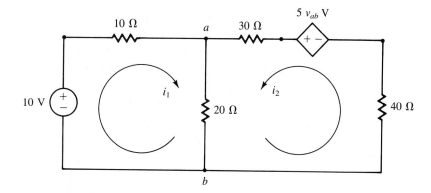

Figure 4.17
A two-mesh network with a dependent voltage source.

the mesh equations become

$$30i_1 + 20i_2 = 10$$

$$-80i_1 - 10i_2 = 0$$

which can be solved for i_1 and i_2. The remainder of the solution proceeds as usual.

4.3 EQUIVALENT NETWORKS— THÉVENIN'S AND NORTON'S THEOREMS

In the previous section we discussed some network-analysis fundamentals and developed the loop and nodal methods for the analysis of resistive networks. In the next several sections, we develop and discuss some additional techniques that are quite useful in network analysis. In much of the following discussion, the explanations are greatly simplified and more efficiently presented by the use of matrix notation. Matrix algebra also proves to be a valuable tool in many of the other analyses that follow. For these reasons, we assume henceforth that the reader is familiar with the fundamentals of matrix algebra. Those in need of review should study Appendix B.

For the most part the techniques of the next several sections are useful because they bring some simplification to the analysis by loop and nodal methods. We begin by discussing equivalent networks.

In general, we consider two networks to be equivalent if they exhibit identical behavior. In this statement, we are typically referring to the external behavior with respect to a set of component terminals. For now we restrict our discussion to two-terminal (1-port) networks.

The 1-port components discussed so far have been tacitly assumed to be simple one-element components. The term 1-*port*, however, can be applied to any subnetwork of one or more components that is connected to the rest of the network at two terminals. Figure 4.18 illustrates one way in which a network can be resolved into three equivalent 1-ports.

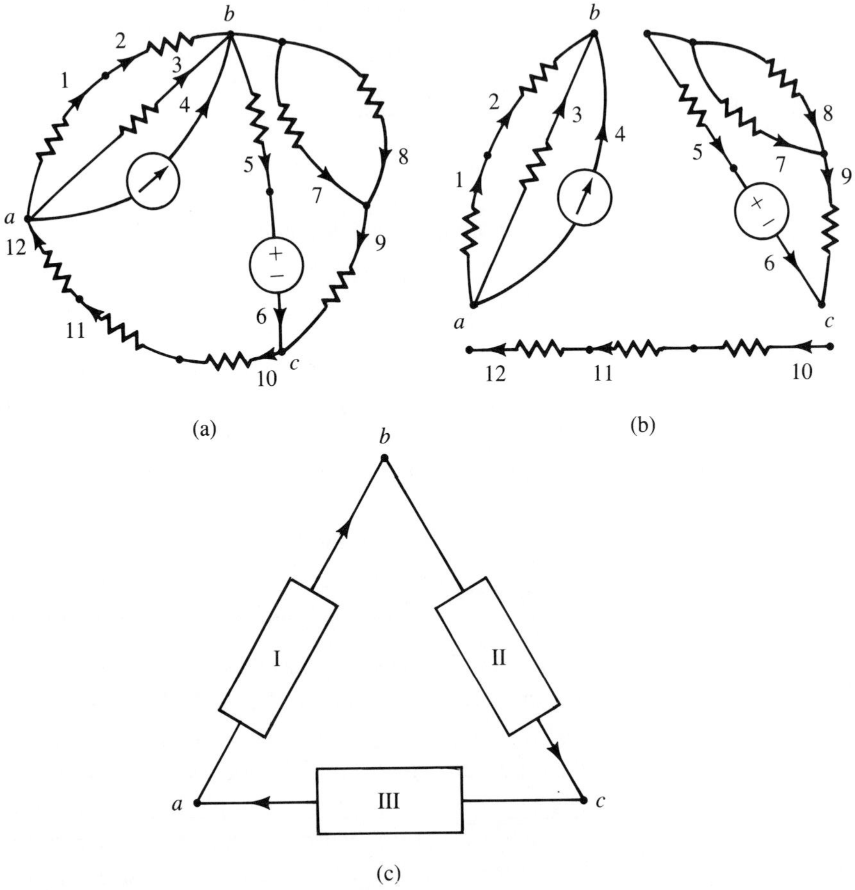

Figure 4.18
Resolution of a network into a set of equivalent 1-ports. (a) Original network. (b) Resolution into three 1-port subnetworks. (c) Schematic diagram of resulting network.

(a)

(b)

(c)

The advantages of using equivalent 1-ports in network analysis stem from the resulting simplification of the mathematical model for the network. The number of simultaneous equations in the model can often be reduced drastically. Each equivalent 1-port requires one measurement diagram and one component equation, just as the simple basic 1-ports do.

Example 4.16

For the network of Figure 4.18(a), the primary mathematical model consists of 24 simultaneous equations because there are 12 elements in the schematic diagram. However, if we can resolve the network into only three equivalent 1-ports, as shown in Figure 4.18(c), the PRIMM will consist of only 6 equations. This reduction of equations is as follows:

Component equations:

Component I:	4 to 1
Component II:	5 to 1
Component III:	3 to 1
Total:	12 to 3

Interconnection equations:

KVL:	$12 - 8 + 1 =$	5 to 1
KCL:	$8 - 1 =$	7 to 2
Total:		12 to 3

Thus we see that the PRIMM for the network of Figure 4.18(c) consists of only 6 simultaneous equations. Furthermore, this network requires the solution of only 1 equation if a loop model is used. To analyze the network of Figure 4.18(c), we need a component equation for each 1-port, as defined in Figure 4.18(b).

Definition 4.2

Equivalent networks

For the purpose of analysis, two 1-port networks are *equivalent* if they have the same component equation.

Note that the "equivalent" component equation is an external characteristic of the 1-port with respect to the two terminals at which measurements are defined. Two equivalent 1-ports are identical in their external behavior in any network, but they may have drastically different internal behavior. The differences are indistinguishable to the rest of the network, however.

Consider a network consisting of resistors, *v*-sources, *i*-sources, and controlled sources, with two terminals emphasized for measurement purposes.[2]

---

[2]Both branches of any controlled source must be included in the subnetwork being modeled by an equivalent component equation.

See Figure 4.19. The internal connections of the individual components may, in general, be completely arbitrary. The network will, of course, have other voltages and currents in general. However, the point here is that we are, at least for the time being, interested only in the voltage at a with respect to b and the current flow into the 1-port at terminal a. More precisely, we are interested in the characteristic that relates these two variables.

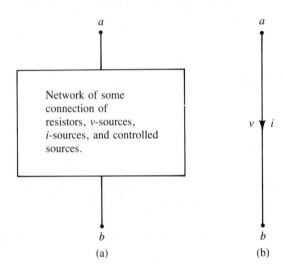

Figure 4.19
One-port equivalent network.

Theorem 4.1

A 1-port network consisting of some connection of resistors and sources will have a component equation that is either of the form

$$v(t) = R_T i(t) + e_T(t) \qquad (4.22)$$

or of the form

$$i(t) = G_N v(t) + i_N(t) \qquad (4.23)$$

where $v(t)$ and $i(t)$ are the terminal variables as illustrated by Figure 4.19(b).

We call Equation 4.22 the *Thévenin-form component equation* and Equation 4.23 the *Norton-form component equation*. The terms in these equations are generally referred to as follows:

R_T: Thévenin-equivalent resistance

$e_T(t)$:   Thévenin-equivalent voltage source

G_N: Norton-equivalent conductance

$i_N(t)$:   Norton-equivalent current source

Most networks will have both forms of equivalent component equations. Either form of the component equation can be solved for the alternate form unless either R_T or G_N is zero. This will, in fact, be the case for v-sources and i-sources, respectively. That is to say, a v-source will only have a Thévenin-form CE and an i-source will only have a Norton-form CE.

The relationships, if they exist, between R_T, G_N, $e(t)$, and $i_N(t)$ are readily obtained by simply solving for the alternate form. We shall derive this equivalence when we discuss equivalent network realizations for our equivalent component equations.

We shall not attempt to prove Theorem 4.1. However, a convincing argument that this result is reasonable is as follows: Suppose we connect a "symbolic" current source $i(t)$ (just an arbitrary function of time, which does not need to be known explicitly) between terminals a and b of the network of Figure 4.19. The result of this connection is shown in Figure 4.20. Unless the

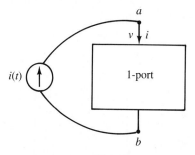

Figure 4.20
Network for finding Thévenin equivalent.

network under consideration is, in fact, an ideal current source (in which case we have probably violated KCL at node a), we can, for any given connection of the allowable components, solve for the voltage at terminal a with respect to terminal b. Furthermore, it is reasonable to expect, on the basis of our experience with networks of this type, that the result of this solution will be in the form of Equation 4.22. That this is the case can be seen by considering the PRIMM of a general network of the type shown in Figure 4.20. This model will be of the general form

$$\mathbf{Ax} = \mathbf{K}_1\,\mathbf{f}(t) + \mathbf{K}_2 i(t)$$

where

$\mathbf{x}$ is a vector of the $2b$ unknown voltages and currents,

$\mathbf{f}(t)$ is a vector of the independent sources,

$i(t)$ is the applied symbolic source, and

$\mathbf{A}$, $\mathbf{K}_1$, and $\mathbf{K}_2$ are the constant coefficient matrices.

If this system of equations has a unique solution,[3] it is given by

$$\mathbf{x} = \mathbf{A}^{-1}\mathbf{K}_1\,\mathbf{f}(t) + \mathbf{A}^{-1}\mathbf{K}_2 i(t)$$

and, since $v(t)$ is included in $\mathbf{x}$, the form of $v(t)$ is determined to be the sum of two terms. The first is some function of time, which is a linear combination of the independent sources, and the second is a constant multiplied times the symbolic source $i(t)$. Symbolically,

$$v(t) = g(t) + ki(t) \qquad (k \text{ constant})$$

which is of the desired form.

In the event that $i(t)$ is completely independent of $v(t)$, we must go to the alternate form for the component equation. In this case, the component equation is given by the specified current function.

An analogous argument can be made for the Norton-form component equation. In this case we apply a symbolic v-source and solve for the resulting current $i(t)$ as a function of the applied symbolic source $v(t)$. This situation is shown in Figure 4.21. This will, of course, not be possible if the given network is such that the voltage $v(t)$ is a given or specified function of time.

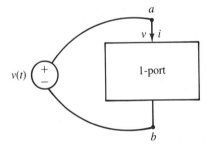

Figure 4.21
Network for finding Norton equivalent.

In addition to providing a convincing argument that we can, in fact, find a component equation in one or both of the forms of Equations 4.22 and 4.23, the above discussion also provides an actual method for finding the equivalent component equation. Simply apply a symbolic source equal to the independent variable in the desired component equation and solve for the dependent variable. The result is the desired component equation.

From our experiences with networks of the type under consideration, we readily see that the equivalent sources $e_T(t)$ and $i_N(t)$ result from the independent sources in the network. That is, if the network contained no independent sources, then $e_T(t)$ and $i_N(t)$ would be zero. Further, the terms R_T and G_N will result from the passive components and the controlled sources. Armed with these ideas, let us examine the equivalent component equations in more detail.

---

[3]The PRIMM may not have a unique solution if the network contains controlled sources. This is discussed more fully in Section 4.6.

Consider the Thévenin form of the component equation:

$$v(t) = R_T i(t) + e_T(t) \tag{4.24}$$

If we set $i(t)$ equal to zero, we have

$$e_T(t) = v(t)\Big|_{i(t) = 0} \tag{4.25}$$

which means that if we make no external connection to the terminals of the 1-port, then the Thévenin equivalent voltage source can be found by calculating the voltage across the "open-circuited" terminals a and b. Note that this voltage will obviously be zero if the network contains no independent sources.

Next, suppose we set all independent sources equal to zero, thereby setting $e_T(t) = 0$. In this case we have

$$R_T = \frac{v(t)}{i(t)}\Big|_{e_T(t) = 0} \tag{4.26}$$

The quantity R_T that results from the calculation of Equation 4.26 is often called the *input resistance,* or *driving-point resistance,* at terminals a–b.

These results constitute a well-known theorem of network theory.

Theorem 4.2 (Thévenin's Theorem)

If the Thévenin-form component equation exists for a 1-port network, it can be found by the following calculations:

1. $e_T(t) = v(t)\Big|_{i(t) = 0 \text{ (terminals } a\text{–}b \text{ open circuited)}}$

2. $R_T = \frac{v(t)}{i(t)}\Big|_{\text{all independent sources} = 0}$

The component equation is then

$$v(t) = R_T i(t) + e_T(t)$$

Thévenin's theorem provides an alternative to the symbolic-source method for finding the Thévenin-form component equation. In order to find this equivalent component equation for a resistive network, we must find the two quantities R_T and $e_T(t)$. In the symbolic-source approach, the complete component equation, and consequently R_T and $e_T(t)$, are found in one operation. If we apply the results of Thévenin's theorem, we use two separate operations or solutions in order to calculate R_T and $e_T(t)$. Although two distinct network analyses are required for this latter approach, this approach is sometimes easier than the single analysis of the symbolic-source approach.

If we are going to calculate R_T by Equation 4.26, we must first determine how we set all the independent sources in the network to zero. The answer lies in the reasoning that zero voltage exists across a short circuit and zero current flows through an open circuit. Therefore, we simply replace all v-sources with short circuits and all i-sources with open circuits. After all independent sources are set to zero, Equation 4.26 indicates that we should apply a symbolic source $i(t)$ and calculate the voltage response, thereby obtaining

$$v(t) = R_T i(t)$$

Actually, we could just as well apply a symbolic voltage source $v(t)$ and calculate the current response as

$$i(t) = Gv(t)$$

In this case the input resistance is given by $R_T = 1/G$. Finally, in some cases, as will be developed shortly, we shall be able to evaluate R_T without applying a symbolic source. In any case, we emphasize again that Equation 4.26 is the basic working definition for the input resistance of a 1-port network.

Now let us turn our attention to the Norton-form 1-port component equation

$$i(t) = G_N v(t) + i_N(t) \tag{4.27}$$

Immediately we see that

$$i_N(t) = i(t)\Big|_{v(t)=0} \tag{4.28}$$

and

$$G_N = \frac{i(t)}{v(t)}\Big|_{i_N(t)=0} \tag{4.29}$$

Since $v(t) = 0$ when terminals a and b are shorted together and since $i_N(t) = 0$ when all independent sources are set to zero, we have the following results.

Theorem 4.3 (Norton's Theorem)

If the Norton-form component equation exists for a 1-port network, it can be found by the following calculations:

$$i_N(t) = i(t)\Big|_{v(t)=0} \quad \text{(terminals } a\text{–}b \text{ shorted)}$$

and

$$G_N = \frac{i(t)}{v(t)}\Big|_{\text{all independent sources}=0}$$

The component equation is then

$$i(t) = G_N v(t) + i_N(t)$$

The quantity G_N is often called the *input*, or *driving-point conductance*, of the network. Comparison of the above results indicates that

$$R_T = \frac{1}{G_N} \qquad (4.30)$$

At times during the analysis of a network, it is helpful to replace several components with a simpler equivalent network. This is an easy matter if either the Thévenin-form or Norton-form component equation is available. For example, the Thévenin-form component equation has the realization shown in Figure 4.22. This is obvious because the terminal voltage $v(t)$ is the sum of two terms—that is,

$$v(t) = v_1(t) + v_2(t)$$

where

$$v_1(t) = R_T i(t)$$

and

$$v_2(t) = e_T(t)$$

and, by a simple application of Kirchhoff's voltage law, we have the desired result.

Figure 4.22
Thévenin equivalent network.

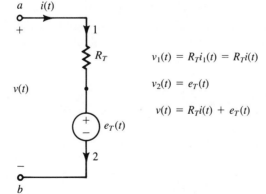

$$v_1(t) = R_T i_1(t) = R_T i(t)$$

$$v_2(t) = e_T(t)$$

$$v(t) = R_T i(t) + e_T(t)$$

Similarly, we recognize that the network of Figure 4.23 is a realization of the Norton-form component equation. The reason for the terminology *Thévenin's equivalent voltage source* and *Norton's equivalent current source* is now clear.

Finally, we emphasize that actual electric networks often contain 1-port subnetworks of the form of Figures 4.22 and 4.23. These 1-port networks are often referred to simply as *sources*. In earlier discussions, we called them *normal sources*.

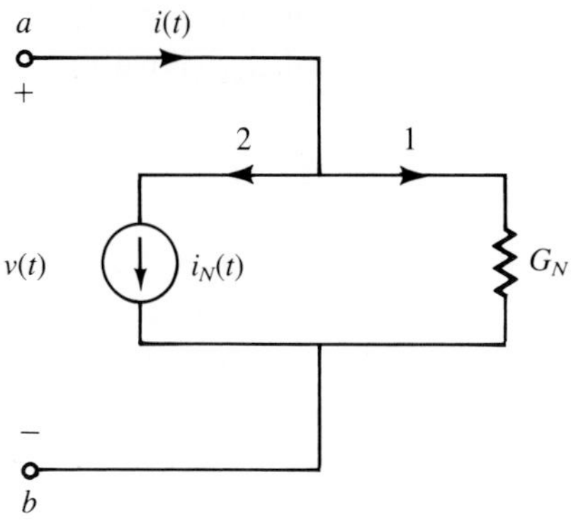

Figure 4.23
Norton equivalent
network.

$v_1 = v_2 = v$

$i_1(t) = G_N v(t)$

$i_2(t) = i_N(t)$

$i(t) = G_N v(t) + i_N(t)$

4.4   SERIES-PARALLEL RESISTORS AND SOURCES

One of the simplest subnetwork configurations for which to derive a 1-port characteristic is a set of series components. Example 4.17 illustrates this concept.

Example 4.17

Let us find the Thévenin-form component equation for the network and the measurement diagram shown in Figure 4.24. If we apply a symbolic current source (Figure 4.25), we can calculate $v(t)$ by a simple application of KVL.

Figure 4.24
A 1-port network.
(a) Network. (b) Measurement
diagram.

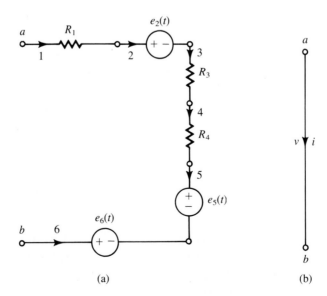

(a)

(b)

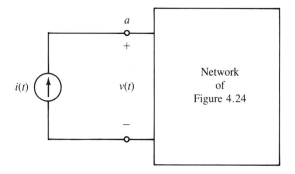

Figure 4.25
Symbolic source applied
to 1-port network.

Immediately, we have

$$v(t) = v_1(t) + v_2(t) + v_3(t) + v_4(t) + v_5(t) - v_6(t)$$
$$= [R_1 + R_3 + R_4]i(t) + e_2(t) + e_5(t) - e_6(t)$$

Therefore,

$$R_T = R_1 + R_3 + R_4$$

and

$$e_T(t) = e_2(t) + e_5(t) - e_6(t)$$

Thus we see that the equivalent resistance of a series connection of resistances is the sum of the individual resistances and that the equivalent voltage source of a series of v-sources is the sum of the individual v-source functions. This result is independent of the order of connection of the components. Furthermore, it is obvious that this result extends to any number of components. In summing the v-source functions, due account must be taken of the source polarity.

Finally, the result of this example is readily obtained by a direct application of Thévenin's theorem.

Example 4.18

The results of Example 4.17 are quite useful for a network of resistances in series. This is illustrated by considering Figure 4.26, a network of n resistors in series. The input, or Thévenin equivalent resistance, is

$$R_T = R_1 + R_2 + \cdots + R_n \tag{4.31}$$

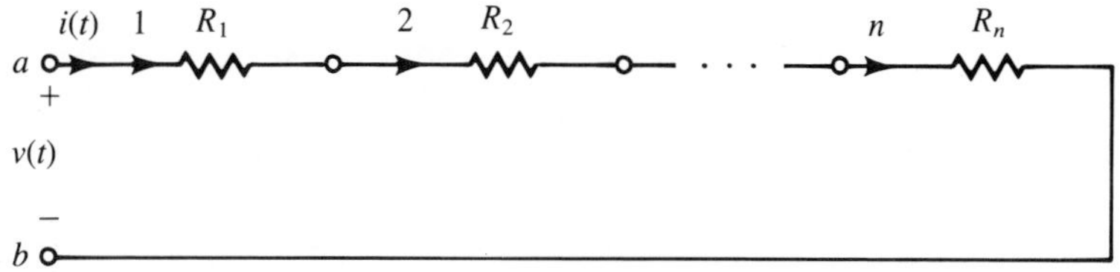

Figure 4.26
A series connection of n
resistors.

The component equation is

$$v(t) = [R_1 + R_2 + \cdots + R_n]i(t)$$

Therefore, the current response to an input voltage $v(t)$ is

$$i(t) = \frac{v(t)}{R_1 + R_2 + \cdots + R_n} = \frac{v(t)}{R_T}$$

and the individual voltages are as summarized in the voltage-divider rule.

Voltage-Divider Rule

$$v_1(t) = R_1 i(t) = \frac{R_1}{R_T} v(t)$$

$$v_2(t) = \frac{R_2}{R_T} v(t)$$

$$\vdots$$

$$v_n(t) = \frac{R_n}{R_T} v(t)$$

The voltage-divider rule is an important result for series-resistive networks.

Example 4.19

The input resistance of the network of Figure 4.27 is

$$R_T = R_1 + R_2 + R_3 = 45 \ \Omega$$

If a v-source is applied so that the terminal voltage is

$$v(t) = (90 \cos 200t) \ V$$

then by the voltage-divider rule,

$$v_1(t) = \frac{R_1}{R_T} v(t) = \frac{10}{45}(90 \cos 200t)$$

$$= (20 \ \cos 200t) \ V$$

Figure 4.27
Network for Example 4.19.

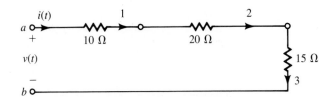

Likewise,

$$v_2(t) = (40 \cos 200t) \text{ V}$$

$$v_3(t) = (30 \cos 200t) \text{ V}$$

Example 4.20

The input resistance of the network of Figure 4.28 is

$$R_T = 50 \text{ } \Omega$$

and the Thévenin equivalent voltage source is

$$e_T(t) = (10 - 10e^{-t}) \text{ V}$$

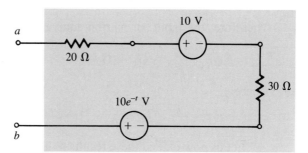

Figure 4.28
Network for Example 4.20.

Both results can be obtained either by the symbolic-source method or by direct application of Thévenin's theorem. The Thévenin equivalent network is shown in Figure 4.29.

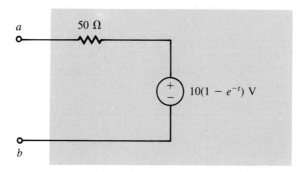

Figure 4.29
Thévenin equivalent network for the 1-port of Figure 4.28.

Let us now turn our attention to the consideration of parallel networks. The network in Figure 4.30 shows n resistors in parallel. A simple analysis indicates that

$$i(t) = i_1 + i_2 + \cdots + i_n$$
$$= G_1 v_1 + G_2 v_2 + \cdots + G_n v_n$$
$$= [G_1 + G_2 + \cdots + G_n]v(t)$$

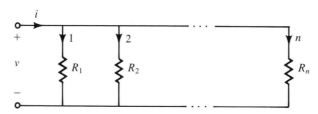

Figure 4.30
Parallel network.

Therefore, the input, or Norton equivalent conductance, is

$$G_N = \frac{1}{R_T} = G_1 + G_2 + \cdots + G_n \qquad (4.32)$$

where

$$G_1 = \frac{1}{R_1}, \ G_2 = \frac{1}{R_2}, \cdots, \ G_n = \frac{1}{R_n}$$

Let us now extend these results to include i-sources by considering another example.

Example 4.21

Suppose we apply a symbolic v-source $v(t)$ to the network of Figure 4.31(b), as shown in Figure 4.31(a). Since the network has only two nodes, the network solution is completely specified by the known source $v(t)$. Writing the one nodal equation (a dummy equation), we obtain the Norton equivalent component equation

$$i(t) = \frac{1}{10}v(t) + \frac{1}{5}v(t) + 10 - 5\cos t$$
$$= 0.3v(t) + 10 - 5\cos t$$

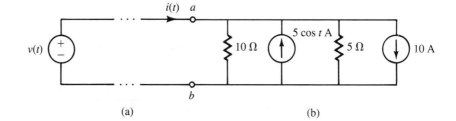

Figure 4.31
(a) Symbolic source.
(b) Network.

(a)   (b)

Therefore,

$$G_N = 0.3 \text{ S}$$

and

$$i_N(t) = (10 - 5 \cos t) \text{ A}$$

The equivalent network is shown in Figure 4.32. This result could also be obtained by a direct application of Norton's theorem. Note that we add the parallel current sources algebraically to obtain the equivalent current source. This is a general result for parallel current sources. The results that we have obtained for series v-sources and parallel i-sources are a direct result of KVL for series elements and KCL for parallel elements.

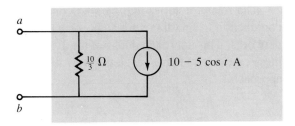

Figure 4.32
Equivalent network.

Some special results concerning two resistances in parallel are useful enough to justify some special attention. From the network of Figure 4.33, we see that

$$G_N = G_1 + G_2$$

$$= \frac{1}{R_1} + \frac{1}{R_2}$$

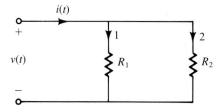

Figure 4.33
Network to develop current divider.

and that

$$R_T = \frac{1}{1/R_1 + 1/R_2} = \frac{R_1 R_2}{R_1 + R_2} \tag{4.33}$$

Thus we see that the equivalent resistance for two resistors in parallel is equal to the *product over the sum of the two resistors,* a result that we shall use repeatedly. Furthermore,

$$i_1(t) = \frac{v(t)}{R_1} = \frac{R_T i(t)}{R_1} = \frac{R_2}{R_1 + R_2} i(t)$$

and

$$i_2(t) = \frac{v(t)}{R_2} = \frac{R_1}{R_1 + R_2} i(t)$$

This latter result is a special case of a more general current-divider rule for n conductances in parallel. In most of our work, we find the special case, in terms of resistances, more useful than the more general rule.

The rules for series and parallel connections of resistances can be used in conjunction to find the equivalent, or input, resistance of many electric 1-port networks. This approach does not always work, and we shall illustrate some of these cases later. However, let us now illustrate the series-parallel combination approach.

Example 4.22

The two resistors in parallel in the network of Figure 4.34 can be replaced by a single resistor by use of Equation 4.33. The new equivalent network is shown in Figure 4.35. Since all resistors are now in series, we see that

$$R_T = 5 + 8 + 2 = 15 \ \Omega$$

Suppose a 60-V v-source is applied to the original network. Using the equivalent network in Figure 4.36, we get

$$i(t) = \frac{60}{15} = 4 \ \text{A}$$

Figure 4.34
Network for Example 4.22.

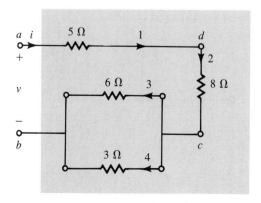

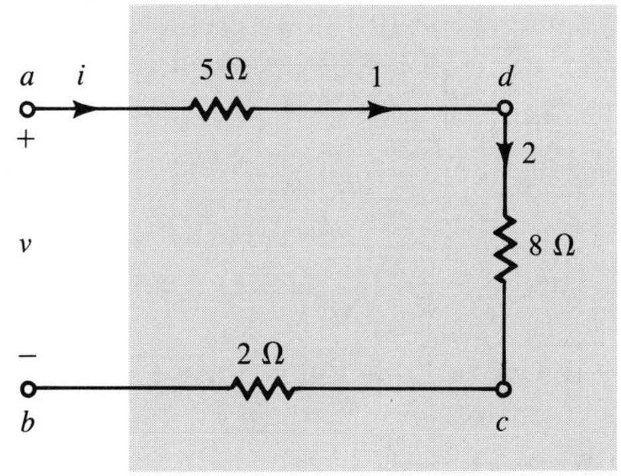

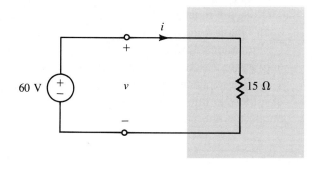

Figure 4.35
Equivalent network.

Figure 4.36
Equivalent network with
source.

From Figure 4.35 we see that

$$i_1 = i_2 = i = 4 \text{ A}$$

$$v_{cb} = 4(2) = 8 \text{ V}$$

and, by the current-divider rule, that

$$i_3 = \frac{3}{3 + 6}(4) = \frac{4}{3} \text{ A}$$

and

$$i_4 = \frac{6}{3 + 6}(4) = \frac{8}{3} \text{ A}$$

4.5 SOURCE TRANSFORMATIONS

If the Thévenin-form component equation of Equation 4.22 is solved for the
current $i(t)$, we have

$$i(t) = \frac{1}{R_T}v(t) - \frac{1}{R_T}e_T(t)$$

and, by comparison to Equation 4.23, we see that

$$G_N = \frac{1}{R_T}$$ (4.34)

and

$$i_N(t) = \frac{-e_T(t)}{R_T}$$ (4.35)

and, by rewriting Equation 4.35, we obtain

$$R_T = -\frac{e_T(t)}{i_N(t)}$$

That is, the input resistance of the network is the negative of the ratio of the open-circuit voltage to the short-circuit current.

Equations 4.34 and 4.35 can be used to transform a Thévenin equivalent network to a Norton equivalent network, or vice versa, as illustrated by Figure 4.37. These equations need not be committed to memory, since direct solution of either Norton-form or Thévenin-form component equations can be used to obtain the alternate forms.

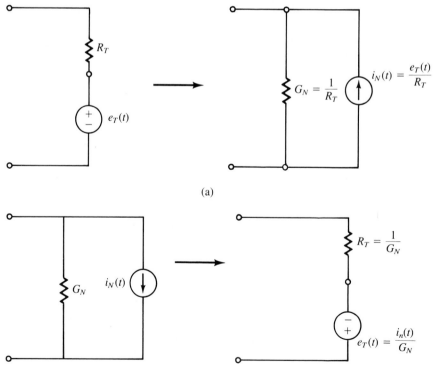

Figure 4.37
(a) Transformation of Thévenin equivalent network to Norton equivalent network.
(b) Transformation of Norton equivalent network to Thévenin equivalent network.

(a)

(b)

Therefore,

$$R_T = 5 + \frac{6(12)}{6 + 12} = 9 \ \Omega$$

Finally, let us perform a direct solution of the Norton-form component equation for this example network. If we apply a symbolic v-source at terminals a–b of Figure 4.38(a) and write nodal equations, we have at node c

$$(\tfrac{1}{5} + \tfrac{1}{12} + \tfrac{1}{6})v_c - (\tfrac{1}{5})v - (\tfrac{1}{6})120 - (\tfrac{1}{12})60 = 0$$

which can be solved for v_c (this is the only nondummy nodal equation):

$$v_c = \tfrac{1}{27}(12v + 1500)$$

The dummy equation at node a yields

$$i = \tfrac{1}{5}(v - v_c)$$

and substituting for v_c gives the desired result (Norton form),

$$i = \frac{v - 100}{9}$$

or the equivalent Thévenin form,

$$v = 9i + 100$$

Example 4.24

Let us now find the Thévenin-form component equation for the network of Figure 4.39(a) for the measurement diagram of Figure 4.39(b). Since it is convenient, we make a source transformation on the dependent source and

Figure 4.39
A network with a controlled source.

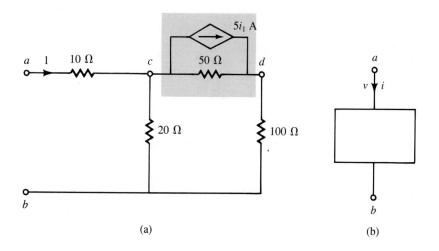

(a)

(b)

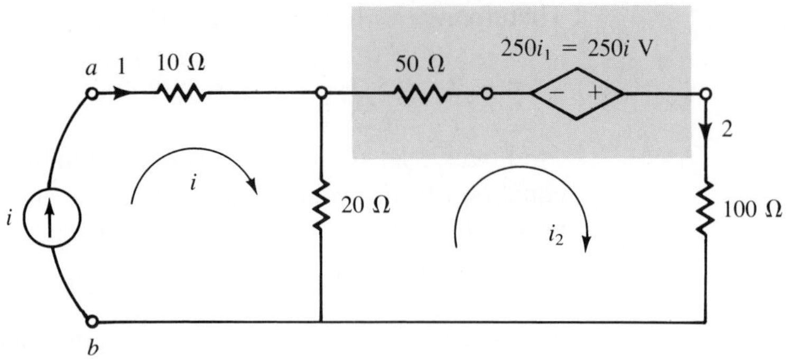

Figure 4.39 (cont'd.)
A network with a
controlled source.

(c)

50-Ω parallel resistor. This is easily done by writing a voltage-explicit (Thévenin-form) component equation for these two components as a 1-port. The resulting equivalent network is shown in Figure 4.39(c). If we apply a symbolic i-source $i(t)$ and write loop equations for Figure 4.39(c), we have

$$-20i(t) + 170i_2(t) - 250i(t) = 0$$

and

$$v(t) = 10i(t) + 20[i(t) - i_2(t)] \qquad \text{(dummy)}$$

Solving the first equation for $i_2(t)$ and substituting into the dummy equation, we obtain

$$v(t) = -\frac{30}{17}i(t)$$

Therefore, we see that this 1-port network is completely equivalent (at its terminals) to a negative resistor, $R = -\frac{30}{17}\,\Omega$.

If we apply Thévenin's theorem directly to this problem, we see immediately that $e_T = v_{ab}$ (o.c.) = 0 and that R_T must be calculated by the symbolic-source method. Thus we would repeat the above calculations or at least do the equivalent.

4.6 LINEARITY AND SUPERPOSITION

With a few exceptions, all the mathematical models that we have used have been linear in nature. This is an appropriate time to present a formal definition for a linear network and discuss some of the characteristics resulting from linearity.

Consider a network consisting of some interconnection of some or all of the following types of components:

1. Linear resistors

2. v-sources

3. i-sources

4. Controlled sources

Such a network is defined to be a linear resistive network. This classification is justified because the PRIMM of a network of this type is a set of linear algebraic equations. The truth of this can be seen because: (1) the KCL and KVL equations are always linear, (2) the component equations for the resistors are linear, (3) the component equations for the v-sources and i-sources are specified functions of time, and (4) the component equations for the controlled sources all specify some current or voltage as being proportional to some other current or voltage in the network (a linear mathematical relation).

If the PRIMM of a network is linear and algebraic, it follows that the loop and nodal models are also a set of linear algebraic equations. In a more general sense, we say that *any network whose primary mathematical model is a set of linear algebraic equations is defined to be a linear resistive network.* The advantages that result from being able to model a network as linear and resistive cannot be overemphasized.

Whether we are considering the complete primary mathematical model, the loop model, or the node-voltage model, the describing equations can be characterized by

$$\mathbf{Ax} = \mathbf{b} \qquad\qquad (4.36)$$

where $\mathbf{x}$ is the vector of unknowns, $\mathbf{A}$ is the matrix of constant coefficients of the equations, and $\mathbf{b}$ is a vector of known constants or functions of time.

Example 4.25

In Example 4.7 the mesh current equations were found to be

$$6i_1 - 3i_2 = 3$$

$$-3i_1 + 7i_2 = 4$$

In matrix form these equations are

$$\begin{bmatrix} 6 & -3 \\ -3 & 7 \end{bmatrix} \begin{bmatrix} i_1 \\ i_2 \end{bmatrix} = \begin{bmatrix} 3 \\ 4 \end{bmatrix}$$

Therefore, we see that in this case

$$A = \begin{bmatrix} 6 & -3 \\ -3 & 7 \end{bmatrix} \qquad x = \begin{bmatrix} i_1 \\ i_2 \end{bmatrix} \qquad b = \begin{bmatrix} 3 \\ 4 \end{bmatrix}$$

Likewise, the node voltage equations in Example 4.10 are

$$\tfrac{7}{4}v_1 - \tfrac{3}{4}v_2 = 45$$

$$-\tfrac{3}{4}v_1 + \tfrac{11}{4}v_2 = 5$$

which can be put in matrix form as

$$\begin{bmatrix} \tfrac{7}{4} & -\tfrac{3}{4} \\ -\tfrac{3}{4} & \tfrac{11}{4} \end{bmatrix} \begin{bmatrix} v_1 \\ v_2 \end{bmatrix} = \begin{bmatrix} 45 \\ 5 \end{bmatrix}$$

and the correlation to Equation 4.36 is readily confirmed. Furthermore, we can deduce that all our loop and nodal equations for linear networks can be placed in the form of Equation 4.36.

Uniqueness of solution

We have taken great pains to develop methods for writing sets of linearly independent equations describing the behavior of resistive networks. While we are writing the equations of one of our mathematical models, the assurance that this model (Equation 4.36) does in fact have a solution would provide us with a large measure of comfort. Furthermore, we should also like to be assured that the solution is unique, so that we need not seek other solutions. Since the model of Equation 4.36 will always contain an equal number of equations as unknowns, these equations will have a unique solution if they are linearly independent and consequently consistent (the inverse of A exists). This is the case for any linear resistive network that contains no controlled sources. If controlled sources are included, the situation is not so clean-cut and pleasing. Since the component equation of a controlled source is dependent upon some other network variable, this component has the potential of destroying the linear independence. We now demonstrate that this may, in fact, happen.

Example 4.26

The loop equations for the network of Figure 4.40 are

$$\begin{bmatrix} 15 & -5 \\ -5 & 25 \end{bmatrix} \begin{bmatrix} i_1 \\ i_2 \end{bmatrix} = \begin{bmatrix} 10 \\ \alpha i_1 \end{bmatrix}$$

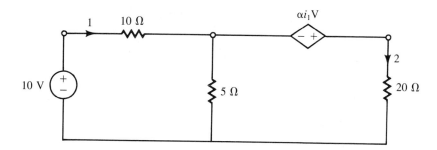

Figure 4.40
A potentially troublesome
network.

or

$$\begin{bmatrix} 15 & -5 \\ (-5 - \alpha) & 25 \end{bmatrix} \begin{bmatrix} i_1 \\ i_2 \end{bmatrix} = \begin{bmatrix} 10 \\ 0 \end{bmatrix}$$

which is of the form $\mathbf{Ax} = \mathbf{b}$.

Let us examine the determinant of $\mathbf{A}$, denoted by $|\mathbf{A}|$:

$$|\mathbf{A}| = 15(25) - 5(5 + \alpha) = 350 - 5\alpha$$

This network does have a unique solution for any value of $\alpha \neq 70$ because $|\mathbf{A}| \neq 0$ except at $\alpha = 70$. However, when $\alpha = 70$ the coefficient matrix $\mathbf{A}$ is singular, its rank is one, and we have a troublesome situation. Since the rank of the augmented matrix $[\mathbf{A}\ \mathbf{b}]$ is two, the system of equations is inconsistent and has no solution for $\alpha = 70$. Finally, we note that if we set the 10-V independent source to zero, the equations are consistent but not linearly independent. In this case, the network has an infinite number of solutions.

It is fortunate that cases such as that illustrated in Example 4.26 are rare and occur only for a precise coincidental combination of the network resistances and the coefficient of the controlled source.

In summary: *Any linear resistive network, with no controlled sources, will always have a unique solution for all voltages and currents. Except in rare cases, the same is true if the network contains controlled sources. However, in this latter case the network equations may have no solution or they may have an infinite number of solutions.*

If the entries in the vector $\mathbf{b}$ are all constant, the solution for all the voltages and currents will be unique and constant. If, however, the entries in $\mathbf{b}$ are functions of time, the solution will yield uniquely specified functions of time. The entries in $\mathbf{b}$ are often referred to as *forcing functions*. Of course, a constant can be considered to be a function of time. From our earlier studies, we also conclude that the entries in $\mathbf{b}$ are linear combinations of the independent sources of the network.

Before leaving this discussion of uniqueness, we mention one other potentially troublesome facet. If a network contains one or more loops made up totally of v-sources, the PRIMM may be inconsistent or may not have a unique solution. The same is true if the network has one or more supernodes whose KCL equations involve only i-sources. These problems are not encountered in this text except for one special case in three-phase networks.

Superposition

Suppose that we have a linear resistive network and a mathematical model for the network in the form of Equation 4.36. As previously discussed this mathematical model might be the PRIMM or it might be a set of loop or nodal equations. The form of the model is repeated for convenience.

$$\mathbf{Ax} = \mathbf{b} \tag{4.37}$$

Now suppose that we apply a set of forcing functions $\mathbf{b}^{(1)}$ and find the solution to be $\mathbf{x}^{(1)}$. This means that

$$\mathbf{Ax}^{(1)} = \mathbf{b}^{(1)} \tag{4.38}$$

and if the solution is unique, we know that we need not search for another $\mathbf{x}$ satisfying Equation 4.37 when $\mathbf{b} = \mathbf{b}^{(1)}$. However, suppose we change the forcing functions so that $\mathbf{b} = \mathbf{b}^{(2)}$ and find a new solution, $\mathbf{x}^{(2)}$. Now

$$\mathbf{Ax}^{(2)} = \mathbf{b}^{(2)} \tag{4.39}$$

We emphasize that $\mathbf{x}^{(1)}$ and $\mathbf{x}^{(2)}$ are the solutions (normally unique) for $\mathbf{b}^{(1)}$ and $\mathbf{b}^{(2)}$.

Suppose now that we add Equations 4.38 and 4.39 to obtain

$$\mathbf{Ax}^{(1)} + \mathbf{Ax}^{(2)} = \mathbf{b}^{(1)} + \mathbf{b}^{(2)}$$

or

$$\mathbf{A}(\mathbf{x}^{(1)} + \mathbf{x}^{(2)}) = \mathbf{b}^{(1)} + \mathbf{b}^{(2)}$$

If we let

$$\mathbf{x}^{(1)} + \mathbf{x}^{(2)} = \mathbf{x}^{(3)}$$

and

$$\mathbf{b}^{(1)} + \mathbf{b}^{(2)} = \mathbf{b}^{(3)}$$

we have

$$\mathbf{Ax}^{(3)} = \mathbf{b}^{(3)} \tag{4.40}$$

Therefore, $\mathbf{x}^{(3)} = \mathbf{x}^{(1)} + \mathbf{x}^{(2)}$ is the solution for our network response to a set of forcing functions $\mathbf{b}^{(3)} = \mathbf{b}^{(1)} + \mathbf{b}^{(2)}$. To help interpret these results, consider the results of two experiments (or mathematical analyses). In the first experiment, we determine the network response due to a set of independent sources (*v*-sources and *i*-sources) that result in the forcing function $\mathbf{b}^{(1)}$. In the second experiment, we determine the response due to a second set of independent sources. The result of adding the two responses will give the correct response for a set of inputs given by the sum of the independent sources from the two individual experiments. Of course, this result is not limited to 2 experiments or analyses. The number of experiments is quite arbitrary. We could calculate or measure the response of any linear resistive network to 13 (or more) different sets of independent sources. If we add the 13 different results for the voltage and current of any network component, the result will be the voltage or current which will result from the application of a set of independent sources equal to the sum of the 13 individual sets of sources. This fundamental result is usually stated in the form of a theorem.

Theorem 4.4 (Superposition Theorem)

Given any linear resistive network containing several sources, the voltage across (or the current through) any network branch can be determined by adding algebraically the individual voltages (or currents) that result from each independent source acting alone, with all other independent sources reduced to zero.

For a network containing five independent sources, Theorem 4.4 indicates that we should run five individual experiments. In each experiment, one and only one independent source is active. All other *v*-sources are replaced by short circuits and all other current sources are replaced by open circuits. Furthermore, each independent source is active in one experiment. Controlled sources are always active.

Many variations are possible in the statement or the application of Theorem 4.4. In the network containing five independent sources, for example, we might run only two experiments. In one experiment we might choose to have two of the sources active and then make the remaining three active in the second experiment.

Example 4.27

Suppose we solve the network of Figure 4.41(a) for the current i_1. With the *i*-source reduced to zero, the network of Figure 4.41(b) results. A loop analysis yields

$$i_1^{(1)} = 4 \text{ A}$$

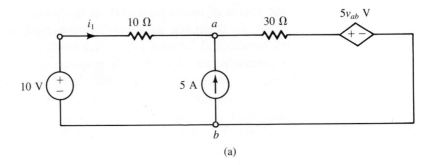

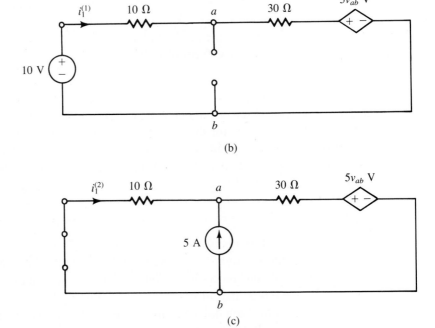

Figure 4.41
Networks for Example
4.27. (a) The original
network. (b) Network with
i-source reduced to zero.
(c) Network with v-source
reduced to zero.

By reducing the v-source to zero and restoring the i-source, we obtain the
network of Figure 4.41(c). A nodal analysis yields

$$v_{ab} = -150 \text{ V}$$

and

$$i_1^{(2)} = 15 \text{ A}$$

Therefore, the result is

$$i_1 = i_1^{(1)} + i_1^{(2)} = 19 \text{ A}$$

You should confirm that this solution is also obtained by loop and nodal
methods.

The results of this example might lead us to ask: Would it not be easier and less time-consuming to analyze this network directly by loop or nodal analysis on the complete network? The answer is yes. In fact, this is generally the case if a network contains one or more controlled sources. Although superposition may never become our favorite analysis technique, we should remember its fundamental importance. It is the failure of superposition that makes the analysis of nonlinear networks so much more difficult.

4.7 POWER, ENERGY, AND MAXIMUM POWER TRANSFER

In Chapter 3 we introduced the fundamental concepts of power and energy. We also developed the power and energy relations for linear resistors and discussed these concepts for ideal sources. These results, when coupled with the analysis methods of this chapter, provide all the necessary tools for power and energy analysis of linear resistive networks. In this section we develop one fundamental and important aspect of power transfer.

The network shown in Figure 4.42 depicts some source network delivering power to a linear, but variable, resistive load. The source network is allowed to be any linear resistive active network—that is, any combination of linear resistors, v-sources, i-sources, and controlled sources. In order to avoid some troublesome but idealized cases, we shall require that both Thévenin and Norton equivalent networks exist for the source network. Now we ask the following very practical question: What is the maximum value of the power that can be delivered to the load and at what value should the load resistance be set in order to attain this maximum?

Figure 4.42
A source delivering power to a load.

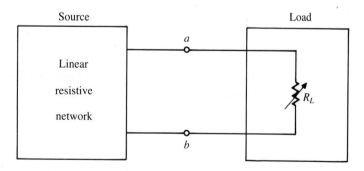

Suppose we replace the source network by a Thévenin equivalent network (Figure 4.43). Then we can readily determine the power delivered to the load as

$$p_L = i^2 R_L = \left(\frac{e_T(t)}{R_T + R_L}\right)^2 R_L \qquad (4.41)$$

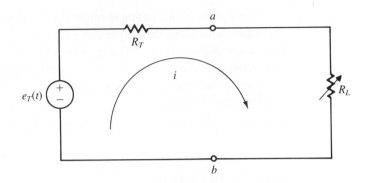

Figure 4.43
Thévenin equivalent
network (for source) and
load.

where the subscript L is used to denote load. At this point we see that this power is not only a function of the load resistance R_L (R_T is constant) but also a function of time if e_T is a function of time. Therefore, this power might be constant (e_T constant), increase indefinitely, vary periodically, or any of many other possibilities for a particular value of the load R_L. Two cases are of particular interest.

Case 1. ($e_T(t)$ constant)   If $e_T(t)$ is constant, p_L is a function only of R_L, and we can maximize this function. If we differentiate Equation 4.41 with respect to R_L and set the result to zero, we obtain

$$\frac{dp_L}{dR_L} = (e_T)^2 \frac{(R_T + R_L)^2 - 2R_L(R_T + R_L)}{(R_T + R_L)^4} = 0$$

or

$$(R_T + R_L)^2 = 2R_L(R_T + R_L)$$

or

$$R_L = R_T \qquad\qquad (4.42)$$

If we substitute this result into Equation 4.41, we obtain the maximum power that can be delivered to the load, namely,

$$p_L(\text{max}) = \frac{e_T^2}{4R_T} \qquad\qquad (4.43)$$

Case 2. ($e_T(t)$ periodic)   Since $e_T(t)$ is periodic, p_L is a periodic function of time for any value of R_L. With p_L periodic, the average power, P_L, is a more useful measure of the power delivered to the load. This power is given by

$$P_L = \frac{1}{T} \int_0^T p_L \, dt = \frac{1}{T} \int_0^T \left(\frac{e_T(t)}{R_T + R_L} \right)^2 R_L \, dt \tag{4.44}$$

where T is the period of $e_T(t)$.

Equation 4.44 can be rewritten to obtain

$$P_L = \left[\frac{1}{T} \int_0^T [e_T(t)]^2 \, dt \right] \frac{R_L}{(R_T + R_L)^2} \tag{4.45}$$

The integral term within the large brackets is a constant since T is a known constant. This constant is simply related to a very important quantity used in the analysis of networks with periodic sources and is discussed more fully in Chapter 9.

Suppose we define the bracketed term as

$$\frac{1}{T} \int_0^T [e_T(t)]^2 \, dt \doteq (E_T)^2 \qquad \text{(a constant)} \tag{4.46}$$

From this definition we see that we can rewrite Equation 4.44 as

$$P_L = (E_T)^2 \frac{R_L}{(R_T + R_L)^2} \tag{4.47}$$

By comparing Equation 4.47 to Equation 4.41 and using the results from Case 1, we can immediately see that the maximum average power which can be delivered to the load is

$$P_L \,(\text{max}) = \frac{E_T{}^2}{4R_T} \tag{4.48}$$

and occurs when

$$R_L = R_T$$

Next we note that the average value of a constant is just the value of the constant and that $E_T = e_T(t)$ if e_T is constant. Therefore, the results of Case 1 also apply to average power and then become identical to Case 2.

Since we have already developed the equivalence between Thévenin's and Norton's equivalent networks, these results could be written in terms of Norton's equivalent. Remember, however, that the equivalent behavior is external; the internal behavior is typically quite different.

The results above constitute the *maximum power transfer theorem* for linear resistive networks. We restate the theorem and then solidify these ideas by working some examples.

**Theorem 4.5
(Maximum Power
Transfer Theorem)**

For a 1-port with the Thévenin-form component equation

$$v(t) = R_T i(t) + e_T(t)$$

the maximum power that can be delivered to a load resistance R_L occurs when the load is adjusted such that

$$R_L = R_T$$

The value of this maximum power transfer is given by

$$p_L \text{ (max)} = P_L \text{ (max)} = \frac{e_T^2}{4R_T}$$

when e_T is constant and is given by

$$P_L \text{ (max)} = \frac{E_T^2}{4R_T}$$

when e_T is time-varying but periodic. In the latter case, E_T^2 is a constant defined by Equation 4.46.

Example 4.28 ───

An electric network, known to be linear and resistive, is enclosed in a black box with two external terminals. Tests in the laboratory determine that this 1-port can be characterized by

$$v = 13.8i + 76$$

Therefore, the maximum power that can be delivered to any resistive load connected across the terminals of this network is

$$p_L \text{ (max)} = \frac{(76)^2}{4(13.8)} = 104.64 \text{ W}$$

and occurs when the load is

$$R_L = 13.8 \ \Omega$$

Example 4.29 ───

The result of replacing the network to the left of the terminals a–b (Figure 4.44) by a Thévenin equivalent network is seen in Figure 4.45. The constant E_T for the Thévenin equivalent voltage source is

$$E_T = \left[\frac{1}{\pi} \int_0^\pi (80 \cos 2t)^2 \, dt \right]^{1/2}$$

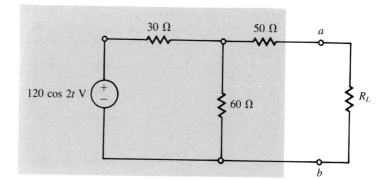

Figure 4.44
Network for Example 4.29.

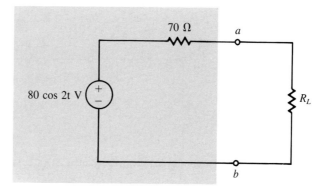

Figure 4.45
Equivalent network for
Example 4.29.

$$= \frac{80}{\sqrt{\pi}} \left[\int_0^{\pi} \cos^2 2t \; dt \right]^{1/2} = \frac{80}{\sqrt{2}} \; V$$

Therefore, the maximum average power that can be delivered to the load is

$$P_L \, (\text{max}) = \frac{(80/\sqrt{2})^2}{4(70)} = 11.43 \; W$$

This maximum will occur when R_L is adjusted to 70 Ω.

Example 4.30 ───

In this example we calculate the maximum power that can be delivered to R_4 by
the network shown in Figure 4.46. We begin by replacing branches 1, 2, and 3
by a Thévenin equivalent and then doing the same for branches 6, 7, and 8.
The result is shown in Figure 4.47. By combining the v-sources and the
resistors, we obtain the network of Figure 4.48. From this network we
calculate

$$p_4 \, (\text{max}) = \frac{(40)^2}{4(23)} = 17.39 \; W$$

and note that this power will be delivered to R_4 when its value is set to 23 Ω.

Figure 4.46
Network for Example 4.30.

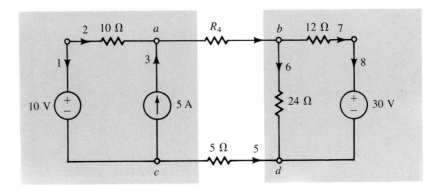

Figure 4.47
Equivalent network.

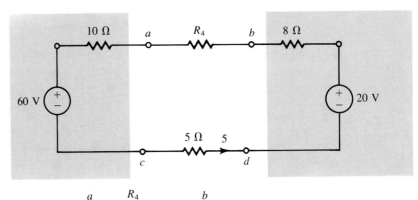

Figure 4.48
Additional equivalent
network.

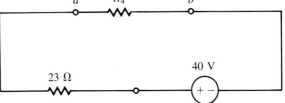

4.8 NONLINEAR NETWORKS

A comprehensive treatment of nonlinear resistive networks is well beyond the scope of this text. However, in keeping with the introductory nature of the treatment to this point, we shall present some straightforward approaches that are sufficient for the analysis of some simple nonlinear resistive networks.

The presence of nonlinear resistors in a network adds a degree of complexity which may, in some cases, be very severe. This added difficulty comes about when we try to solve our model (loop, nodal, or PRIMM). Until now these models have all been a set of linear algebraic equations, but now they become a set of nonlinear algebraic equations. These nonlinear algebraic equations invariably prove to be more difficult to solve for our network variables—severely so in some cases.

Let us now take stock of how we might solve a nonlinear resistive network. In order to introduce the basic concepts, we consider a simple example that illustrates the modeling of a nonlinear network.

Example 4.31

Consider the network shown in Figure 4.49. This network is seen to contain two current-dependent nonlinear resistors.

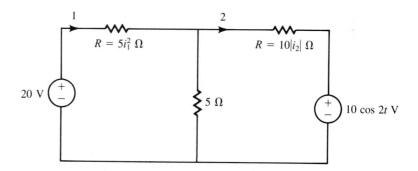

Figure 4.49
A nonlinear resistive
network.

Suppose we consider which of those things we have learned so far that we can still rely upon and what changes we must make if we are going to solve the given network. We have hammered on one especially essential point. Any electric network has two describing characteristics—interconnection equations and component equations. Since the interconnection equations are independent of the types of components, we can still draw a linear graph and write the Kirchhoff law equations. The linear graph is shown in Figure 4.50. The KCL

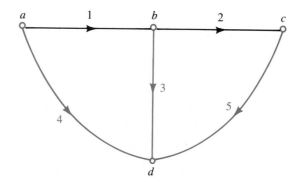

Figure 4.50
Linear graph for the
nonlinear network.

equations at nodes a, b, and c are

$$i_1 + i_4 = 0$$
$$-i_1 + i_2 + i_3 = 0 \tag{4.49}$$
$$-i_2 + i_5 = 0$$

and the KVL equations around the two meshes are

$$v_1 + v_3 - v_4 = 0$$
$$v_2 + v_5 - v_3 = 0 \tag{4.50}$$

Certainly this part of our model (and analysis) is unchanged from that of the linear case. The component equations are

$$v_1 = (5i_1{}^2)(i_1) = 5i_1{}^3$$
$$v_2 = 10|i_2|i_2$$
$$v_3 = 5i_3 \tag{4.51}$$
$$v_4 = 20 \text{ V}$$
$$v_5 = 10 \cos 2t \text{ V}$$

Therefore, just as we should have predicted, the writing of the PRIMM presents no real difficulties. The only difference from the linear case is in the form of the component equations for the nonlinear resistors. The solution of the PRIMM, Equations 4.49, 4.50, and 4.51, is, however, a totally different matter. We can no longer rely on the nice, clean theory of linear algebra.

Now that we have written the PRIMM for this network, it is not difficult to convince ourselves that the majority of the analysis techniques that we have learned can be applied. It is in the solutions of the resulting equations where we run into added difficulties. We could, for example, have written the mesh equations directly. With i_1 and i_2 as mesh currents, we obtain

$$(5i_1{}^2)i_1 + 5(i_1 - i_2) = 20$$
$$10|i_2|i_2 + 5(i_2 - i_1) = -10 \cos 2t$$

or

$$5(i_1 + i_1{}^3) - 5i_2 = 20$$
$$-5i_1 + 5i_2 + 10|i_2|i_2 = -10 \cos 2t \tag{4.52}$$

Obtaining a solution of Equations 4.52 for i_1 and i_2 is not an inviting prospect. We shall not attempt to do so, since our purpose in this example is to illustrate some basic ideas of modeling.

Networks with a Single Nonlinear Resistor

One of the simplest types of nonlinear networks to analyze is one that is linear except for a single nonlinear resistor. Except in some special cases, as previously discussed, we can replace the linear portion of the network by a Thévenin or a Norton equivalent network. Although it is certainly not necessary to do so, we shall assume in what follows that the linear part of the network has been replaced by a Thévenin equivalent. The network can then be represented as shown in Figure 4.51. In this figure R_{NL} denotes the nonlinear resistor. Assume that the component characteristic for this resistor is given in the form of v as some function of i. The functional relationship may be an equation, a graph, or even a table. If needed, the alternate form, i in terms of v, can usually be obtained.

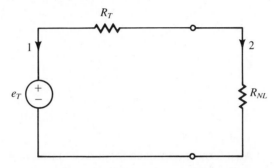

Figure 4.51
General network with single nonlinear R.

Suppose we represent the Thévenin equivalent network by a single 1-port and draw the linear graph shown in Figure 4.52. The loop equation of this network is

$$R_T i_2 + v_2 = e_T \qquad (4.53)$$

where v_2 is a nonlinear function of i_2. There are several fruitful approaches to the solution of this network.

One very popular approach, when e_T is constant, is the graphical solution. From the linear graph we see that

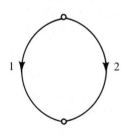

Figure 4.52
Linear graph for Figure 4.51.

$$\text{KCL:} \quad i_1 = -i_2 \qquad (4.54)$$

$$\text{KVL:} \quad v_1 = v_2 \qquad (4.55)$$

The solution now proceeds as follows:

1. Using Equation 4.54, write the component equation for branch 1 in terms of i_2—that is,

$$v_1 = R_T i_1 + e_T$$
$$= -R_T i_2 + e_T$$

2. Plot v_1 as a function of i_2.

3. Plot v_2 as a function of i_2. (This plot may be given.)

4. Equation 4.55 indicates that the solution is the intersection of the two curves plotted in Steps 2 and 3.

A possible graphical solution is shown in Figure 4.53. It is easy to see from this figure that multiple solutions could exist. This happens anytime the nonlinear characteristic is such that it intersects the v_1 characteristic at more than one point.

Figure 4.53
Sketch of graphical
solution.

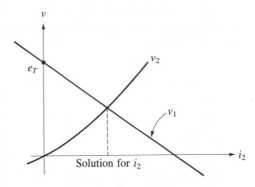

An alternate approach that can be used quite successfully is a "cut-and-try" approach. Suppose the nonlinear relation is some given function or that an equation has been found from the graphical relation so that we know that $v_2 = f_2(i_2)$. Then Equation 4.53 becomes

$$R_T i_2 + f_2(i_2) = e_T \tag{4.56}$$

where f_2 is the specified nonlinear function. Then the procedure is as follows:

1. Estimate the value for i_2.

2. Substitute into Equation 4.56 to see if the equation is satisfied. If it is to within an acceptable tolerance, then the estimate is the solution. If not, a new estimate is created and the process is repeated.

3. Continue until an i_2 is found that satisfies Equation 4.56 to within an acceptable accuracy.

In this process, if the results of one step are used to create an improved estimate for the next step, the technique is referred to as an *iterative method*. Many such standard methods are available and have proven to be a highly successful approach to the solution of nonlinear algebraic equations. One iterative method will be discussed shortly. First we consider two examples and one more approach to solving the network of Figure 4.51.

Example 4.32

Consider the network of Figure 4.54. For this network

$$v_1 = -10i_2 + 20$$
$$v_2 = 8i_2{}^3$$

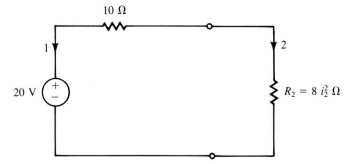

Figure 4.54
Network for Example 4.32.

A very quick and fairly rough graphical solution shows only one intersection and yields an approximate solution $i_2 = 1.05$ A, as seen in Figure 4.55.

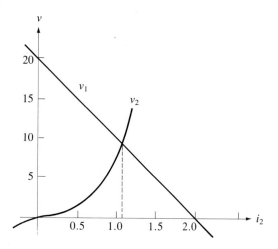

Figure 4.55
Graphical solution for Example 4.32.

The loop equation is

$$10i_2 + 8i_2{}^3 = 20 = e_T$$

and we can refine the solution on i_2, as seen from the given table.

i_2 (Estimate) (A)	e_T (Calculated) = $10i_2 + 8i_2^3$ (V)	Error = $20 - e_T$ (Calculated) (V)
1.05	19.76	0.239
1.06	20.128	−0.128
1.055	19.944	0.056
1.056	19.98	0.02
1.0565	19.999	0.001

Two things are obvious from this table: (1) We can refine the solution to any accuracy we desire, and (2) we can see the direction of necessary change in the estimate of i_2 in order to create an improved estimate from the error calculated in Column 3.

Example 4.33

The network of Figure 4.56 can be reduced to the equivalent network of Figure 4.57. The loop equation for this equivalent network is

$$10i_2 + 5|i_2|i_2 = 10 \tag{4.57}$$

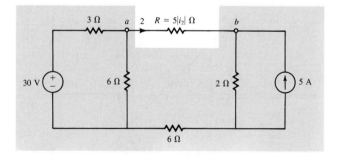

Figure 4.56
Network for Example 4.33.

Either a quick sketch or examination of Equation 4.57 indicates that there is only one solution and that this solution for i_2 must be positive. Therefore, we can rewrite Equation 4.57 as

$$10i_2 + 5i_2^2 = 10 \qquad i_2 > 0$$

The details of the solution are left to you as an exercise but yield $i_2 = 0.732$ A.

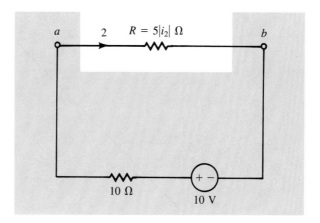

Figure 4.57
Equivalent network.

In some cases, the nonlinear characteristic of the resistor is such that it can be adequately represented by the interconnection of a set of linear characteristics. The techniques that we have discussed so far are sufficient to handle this situation. However, this case is unique enough to merit some special attention and is best illustrated by example.

Example 4.34

The network of Figure 4.58 contains a component known as a *diode*. Suppose the diode has the *v-i* characteristics shown in Figure 4.59. Then it can logically be considered to be a nonlinear resistor. A quick graphical sketch will convince us that the current i_2 must be positive. Examination of the *v-i* characteristic indicates that when i_2 is positive, then $v_2 = 5i_2$, the equation for a 5-Ω linear resistor. Consequently, we can write the loop equation

$$15i_2 + 5i_2 = 50$$

and

$$i_2 = 2.5 \text{ A}$$

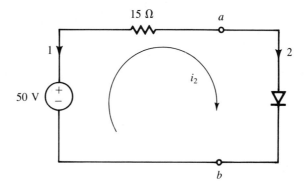

Figure 4.58
A network with a diode.

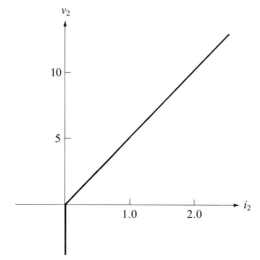

Figure 4.59
The *v-i* characteristic of
the diode.

Therefore

$$v_2 = v_1 = 12.5 \text{ V}$$

and we have the solution using linear techniques.

Next, suppose the polarity of the *v*-source is reversed. In this case we have

$$v_1 = 15i_1 - 50 = -15i_2 - 50$$

and a graphical sketch indicates that the solution occurs at

$$v_2 = -50 \text{ V} \qquad i_2 = 0 = i_1$$

We conclude that when v_2 is positive, the diode behaves like a 5-Ω resistor, and when v_2 is negative, it behaves like an open circuit. In any event the solution is straightforward.

Example 4.35 ───

For this example, suppose that the diode is replaced by a nonlinear resistor with the *v-i* characteristic composed of five linear segments, as shown in Figure 4.60. This characteristic can be described mathematically by

$$
\begin{aligned}
&1. \ v_2 = -50 + 30i_2 &&\text{for} && i_2 \geq 2 \\
&2. \ v_2 = -10 + 10i_2 &&\text{for} && 1 < i_2 < 2 \\
&3. \ v_2 = 0 &&\text{for} && 0 < i_2 \leq 1 \\
&4. \ i_2 = 0 &&\text{for} && -10 \leq v_2 \leq 0 \\
&5. \ v_2 = -10 + 5i_2 &&\text{for} && 0 \leq i_2
\end{aligned}
\qquad (4.58)
$$

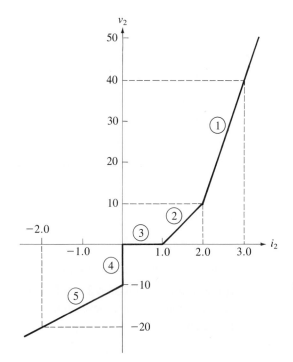

Figure 4.60
Nonlinear resistor characteristic.

The physical interpretations of these expressions should be determined by you. A characteristic of this type is logically referred to as *piecewise-linear*.

   A fruitful approach to the solution for a problem of this type is as follows:

1: Predict which of the linear segments (Equation 4.58) will be intersected by the Thévenin equivalent characteristic for the first 1-port. This can normally be done with excellent accuracy. For example, for the Thévenin equivalent of component 1 of Figure 4.58, we predict with confidence that the intersection occurs on segment 1 of Figure 4.60.

2. Using the linear characteristic for the assumed segment, solve the resulting linear problem. For our example, we have the network of Figure 4.61. (The nonlinear resistor has been replaced by a Thévenin equivalent network having the component equation given by the proper segment from Equation 4.58.) This network is equivalent to the original network as long as i_2 falls in the proper range ($i_2 \geq 2$ in our example). The loop equation for Figure 4.61 is

$$45i_2 = 100$$

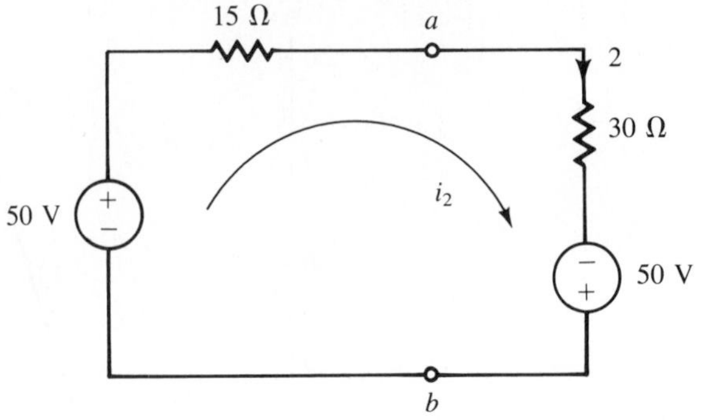

Figure 4.61
Equivalent network.

Therefore,

$$i_2 = 2.222 \text{ A}$$

which is in the assumed range.

3. If the solution from Step 2 yields a current in the assumed range, it is a solution. If not, a new segment is assumed and the process is repeated.

An iterative technique

If a resistive network contains more than one nonlinear resistor, it is usually best to attempt a solution by iterative methods. An iterative technique, generally known as the Newton-Raphson method, has attained a high degree of popularity as a tool to solve nonlinear algebraic equations because of its excellent convergence properties. We now outline this method for two variables. If necessary, you should then be able to extend the approach to larger systems of equations. Consider the following equations:

$$f_1(x_1, x_2) = 0 \tag{4.59}$$

$$f_2(x_1, x_2) = 0 \tag{4.60}$$

Now suppose we assume that $x_1^{(0)}$ and $x_2^{(0)}$ are estimates to the solution of these equations. Further, suppose that $\Delta x_1^{(0)}$ and $\Delta x_2^{(0)}$ are the additions or corrections required to the estimates·so that we do have a solution. This means that

$$f_1(x_1^{(0)} + \Delta x_1^{(0)}, x_2^{(0)} + \Delta x_2^{(0)}) = 0$$

$$f_2(x_1^{(0)} + \Delta x_1^{(0)}, x_2^{(0)} + \Delta x_2^{(0)}) = 0$$

Expanding these two equations in a Taylor series about the initial estimate, we obtain

$$f_1(x_1{}^{(0)}, x_2{}^{(0)}) + \left.\frac{\partial f_1}{\partial x_1}\right]^{(0)} \Delta x_1{}^{(0)} + \left.\frac{\partial f_1}{\partial x_2}\right]^{(0)} \Delta x_2{}^{(0)} + 0_1^2 = 0$$

and

$$f_2(x_1{}^{(0)}, x_2{}^{(0)}) + \left.\frac{\partial f_2}{\partial x_1}\right]^{(0)} \Delta x_1{}^{(0)} + \left.\frac{\partial f_2}{\partial x_2}\right]^{(0)} \Delta x_2{}^{(0)} + 0_2^2 = 0$$

where $]^{(0)}$ denotes that the partial derivatives are evaluated at the initial point $x_1 = x_1{}^{(0)}$ and $x_2 = x_2{}^{(0)}$, and 0_1^2 and 0_2^2 denote terms of second order and higher in $\Delta x_1{}^{(0)}$ and $\Delta x_2{}^{(0)}$.

If we assume that $\Delta x_1{}^{(0)}$ and $\Delta x_2{}^{(0)}$ are small, we can get an approximate solution for the necessary correction factors by neglecting all the higher-order terms. After neglecting 0_1^2 and 0_2^2, we can write the result in matrix form as

$$\begin{bmatrix} \left.\dfrac{\partial f_1}{\partial x_1}\right]^{(0)} & \left.\dfrac{\partial f_1}{\partial x_2}\right]^{(0)} \\[2ex] \left.\dfrac{\partial f_2}{\partial x_1}\right]^{(0)} & \left.\dfrac{\partial f_2}{\partial x_2}\right]^{(0)} \end{bmatrix} \begin{bmatrix} \Delta x_1{}^{(0)} \\[2ex] \Delta x_2{}^{(0)} \end{bmatrix} \approx - \begin{bmatrix} f_1(x_1{}^{(0)}, x_2{}^{(0)}) \\[2ex] f_2(x_1{}^{(0)}, x_2{}^{(0)}) \end{bmatrix} \tag{4.61}$$

which can be symbolized as

$$\mathbf{J}^{(0)} \, \Delta \mathbf{x}^{(0)} \approx -\mathbf{f}(\mathbf{x}^{(0)}) \tag{4.62}$$

where the matrix $\mathbf{J}^{(0)}$ is the 2×2 Jacobian matrix of partial derivatives, evaluated at the initial estimate $x_1 = x_1{}^{(0)}$ and $x_2 = x_2{}^{(0)}$. From Equation 4.61 we calculate the corrections

$$\Delta x^{(0)} \approx [\mathbf{J}^{(0)}]^{-1} [-\mathbf{f}(\mathbf{x}^{(0)})] \tag{4.63}$$

Then the solution is approximated by

$$\mathbf{x}^{(1)} = \mathbf{x}^{(0)} + \Delta \mathbf{x}^{(0)} \tag{4.64}$$

Because of the assumptions that $\Delta x_1{}^{(0)}$ and $\Delta x_2{}^{(0)}$ are small, this approximate solution may or may not be very close to the actual solution. However, it is usually an improvement over the initial guess. Therefore, we need only iterate the equations until Δx becomes small and we obtain a very good approximation to the actual solution. The next iteration is obtained by using $\mathbf{x}^{(1)}$ from Equation 4.64 as the next estimate and calculating a new correction factor.

The results are readily extended to obtain the general recursive relation necessary for the iterative solution. Thus, having an estimate $\mathbf{x}^{(\ell)}$ (the ℓth iterate of **x**), we calculate

$$\Delta \mathbf{x}^{(\ell)} = -[\mathbf{J}^{(\ell)}]^{-1} [\mathbf{f}(\mathbf{x}^{(\ell)})] \tag{4.65}$$

from which we calculate the next estimate (iterate),

$$\Delta \mathbf{x}^{(\ell+1)} = \mathbf{x}^{(\ell)} + \Delta \mathbf{x}^{(\ell)} \tag{4.66}$$

The process is continued until two successive values for both x_1 and x_2 differ by only a specified tolerance. The following is a suitable test for a solution.

Let

$$\Delta \hat{x}_1^{(\ell)} = \left| \frac{\Delta x_1^{(\ell)}}{x_1^{(\ell+1)}} \right| = \left| \frac{x_1^{(\ell+1)} - x_1^{(\ell)}}{x_1^{(\ell+1)}} \right|$$

and

$$\Delta \hat{x}_2^{(\ell)} = \left| \frac{\Delta x_2^{(\ell)}}{x_2^{(\ell+1)}} \right| = \left| \frac{x_2^{(\ell+1)} - x_2^{(\ell)}}{x_2^{(\ell+1)}} \right|$$

Then the process is said to have converged when

$$\max\{\Delta \hat{x}_1^{(\ell)}, \Delta \hat{x}_2^{(\ell)}\} < \epsilon$$

where ϵ is a specified tolerance for the normalized corrections $\Delta \hat{x}_1$ and $\Delta \hat{x}_2$ and max { } denotes the maximum of the two numbers enclosed.

Thus we have converted the solution of the nonlinear equations to the repeated solution of a system of linear equations. It is easy to see that this process may be very time-consuming, especially if the number of equations becomes large. The Jacobian matrix $[\mathbf{J}^{(\ell)}]$ is a matrix of numbers for $\mathbf{x} = \mathbf{x}^{(\ell)}$, but it must be evaluated as such on each iteration of the process. If, for example, we want to solve four equations, $[\mathbf{J}^{(\ell)}]$ is a 4×4 matrix, and at each iteration we must evaluate this coefficient matrix and then solve the four equations

$$[\mathbf{J}^{(\ell)}] \, \Delta \mathbf{x}^{(\ell)} = -\mathbf{f}(\mathbf{x}^{(\ell)})$$

A complex process such as this is best done by a computer program. A program is given in Appendix C for those interested in pursuing this matter.

Example 4.36

Consider the network of Figure 4.62. The resistor R_1 is nonlinear and is described by $R_1 = 10i_1^2$. Likewise, R_2 is nonlinear, as characterized by Figure 4.63. Suppose this v-i characteristic is adequately described by

$$v_2 = 20(1 - e^{-3i_2})$$

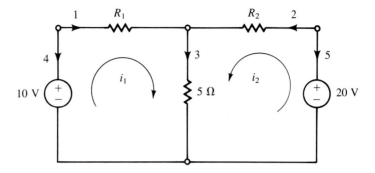

Figure 4.62
Network for Example 4.36.

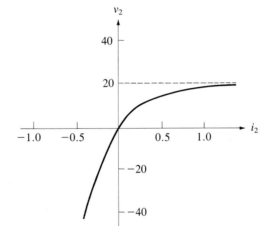

Figure 4.63
Volt-ampere characteristic
of R_2.

Then we can write the loop equations

$$10i_1^2(i_1) + 5(i_1 + i_2) = 10$$

and

$$20(1 - e^{-3i_2}) + 5(i_1 + i_2) = 20$$

which can be rewritten as

$$i_1 + 2i_1^3 + i_2 = 2$$

and

$$i_1 + i_2 + 4(1 - e^{-3i_2}) = 4$$

In terms of our general notation,

$$f_1(x_1, x_2) = x_1 + 2x_1^3 + x_2 - 2 = 0 \qquad (4.67)$$

and

$$f_2(x_1, x_2) = x_1 + x_2 + 4(1 - e^{-3x_2}) - 4 = 0 \qquad (4.68)$$

The Jacobian matrix, as a function of x_1 and x_2, is given by

$$\mathbf{J} = \begin{bmatrix} \dfrac{\partial f_1}{\partial x_1} & \dfrac{\partial f_1}{\partial x_2} \\[2ex] \dfrac{\partial f_2}{\partial x_1} & \dfrac{\partial f_2}{\partial x_2} \end{bmatrix} = \begin{bmatrix} 1 + 6x_1^2 & 1 \\[1ex] 1 & 1 + 12e^{-3x_2} \end{bmatrix} \tag{4.69}$$

Therefore, the iterative relations are

$$\begin{bmatrix} 1 + 6[x_1^{(\ell)}]^2 & 1 \\[1ex] 1 & 1 + 12e^{-3x_2^{(\ell)}} \end{bmatrix} \begin{bmatrix} \Delta x_1^{(\ell)} \\[1ex] \Delta x_2^{(\ell)} \end{bmatrix}$$

$$= - \begin{bmatrix} x_1^{(\ell)} + 2[x_1^{(\ell)}]^3 + x_2^{(\ell)} - 2 \\[1ex] x_1^{(\ell)} + x_2^{(\ell)} + 4(1 - e^{-3x_2^{(\ell)}}) - 4 \end{bmatrix} \tag{4.70}$$

and

$$\begin{bmatrix} x_1^{(\ell+1)} \\[1ex] x_2^{(\ell+1)} \end{bmatrix} = \begin{bmatrix} x_1^{(\ell)} + \Delta x_1^{(\ell)} \\[1ex] x_2^{(\ell)} + \Delta x_2^{(\ell)} \end{bmatrix} \tag{4.71}$$

The selection of an initial estimate to begin the iterative solution is always of some concern. Sometimes it is possible to estimate the order of magnitude and the sign of the unknowns, and this may be all that is necessary. In fact, the algorithm may converge even though a wrong sign is assumed. If the process does not converge, this is usually discovered by noting that the variables grow larger and larger with each iteration and very quickly cause an overflow in the computer.

Suppose in this example that we select

$$x_1^{(0)} = i_1^{(0)} = 1.0 \text{ A} \quad \text{and} \quad x_2^{(0)} = i_2^{(0)} = 1.0 \text{ A}$$

Then a list of the values for fifteen iterations are given in Table 4.1.

Several comments are in order. (1) A built-in convergence test, as earlier defined, will halt the solution after only five iterations with a normalized mismatch less than 1%. (2) The number of iterations required to obtain a solution of acceptable accuracy will depend upon the initial estimate. (3) A different solution might be obtained by starting from a different initial estimate. (4) Any apparent solution given by this method should be checked by sub-stitution into the original equations.

Table 4.1

Iteration number	Maximum mismatch	x_1	x_2
1	25.0230500	0.8630896	−0.0416267
2	1.1916720	0.7961485	0.2171764
3	0.4129152	0.7596403	0.3699234
4	0.0980999	0.7492184	0.4101600
5	0.0052984	0.7486053	0.4123448
6	0.0000145	0.7486036	0.4123507
7	0.0000001	0.7486035	0.4123507
8	0.0000001	0.7486036	0.4123507
9	0.0000001	0.7486035	0.4123507
10	0.0000001	0.7486036	0.4123507
11	0.0000001	0.7486035	0.4123507
12	0.0000001	0.7486036	0.4123507
13	0.0000001	0.7486035	0.4123507
14	0.0000001	0.7486036	0.4123507
15	0.0000001	0.7496035	0.4123507

We close our discussion of nonlinear resistive networks by considering a final example.

Example 4.37

On occasion it is possible to apply the graphical method to networks that contain two nonlinear resistors. To this end, consider the network of Figure 4.64 and the linear graph of Figure 4.65.

The equations needed for the graphical approach are

$$v_1 = 5 + 15e^{0.5i_1} = 5 + 15e^{-0.5i_2}$$

and

$$v_2 = (10 - i_2)i_2$$

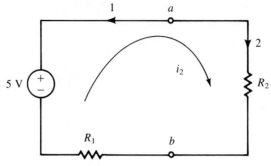

Figure 4.64
Network for Example 4.37.

$$R_1 : \quad v_{R_1} = 15e^{0.5i_1}$$
$$R_2 : \quad v_2 = (10 - i_2)i_2$$

These equations are plotted as Figure 4.66. This graphical approach shows two solutions for i_2 at approximately

$$i_2 = 1.4 \text{ A} \quad \text{and} \quad i_2 = 9.4 \text{ A}$$

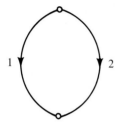

Figure 4.65
Linear graph for Example 4.37.

Figure 4.66
Graphical solution for Example 4.37.

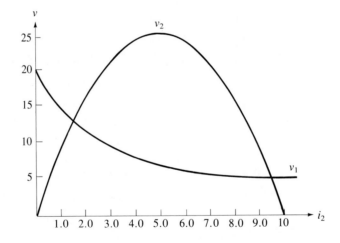

We can also solve this problem using the Newton-Raphson approach. The loop equation is

$$v_2 - v_1 = 0$$

or

$$(10 - i_2)i_2 - 5 - 15e^{-0.5i_2} = 0 = f(i_2)$$

with i_2 playing the role of **x**. The Jacobian matrix is only 1×1 and is

$$\mathbf{J} = \frac{\partial f}{\partial i_2} = 10 - 2i_2 + 7.5e^{-0.5i_2}$$

Therefore,

$$\Delta i_2 = \frac{-f(i_2)}{\partial f / \partial i_2}$$

and the iterative equation becomes

$$i_2^{(\ell+1)} = i_2^{(\ell)} + \Delta i_2^{(\ell)}$$

$$= i_2^{(\ell)} - \frac{(10 - i_2^{(\ell)})i_2^{(\ell)} - 5 - 15e^{-0.5i_2^{(\ell)}}}{10 - 2i_2^{(\ell)} + 7.5e^{-0.5i_2^{(\ell)}}}$$

Although this equation can be iterated by hand, it is best done with a programmable calculator or a computer. The results of such a solution are as follows:

For: $i_2^{(0)} = 1$ A, $i_2 = 1.4377$ A

For: $i_2^{(0)} = 10$ A, $i_2 = 9.4573$ A

which are seen to be refinements of the graphical solutions.

Some final words are in order concerning the iterative method and nonlinear analysis in general:

1. The iterative method is not guaranteed to converge to an answer. If convergence is obtained, the answer that is obtained may not be unique, and others may exist that can only be found by searching from other initial estimates.

2. The nature of the equations describing the nonlinearities, along with the rest of the network, may provide some insight into the nature of the solution(s) and some suitable initial estimates.

3. The solution of nonlinear problems is much more difficult and is not governed by a precise theory, as is the case for linear networks. What works well for one problem may not work at all for another. Generally speaking, the state of the art for these problems consists of a collection of *ad hoc* techniques that have proven valuable in solving some problems. We have discussed some of the better-known approaches.

4.9   SUMMARY

In this chapter we have taken a large step forward in the analysis of electric networks. Limiting our scope to linear resistive networks, we developed two powerful tools: loop and nodal analysis. Equivalent networks, Thévenin's and

Norton's theorems, and source transformations were found to be powerful tools in network simplification and will become trusted friends as we proceed from here to broader horizons of network analysis.

We learned that a unique solution exists for any linear resistive network that does not contain controlled sources. We also discovered that networks with controlled sources have unique solutions except for rare coincidental combinations of numbers.

Power and energy, from Chapter 3, were briefly reviewed for linear resistive networks and an important, practical power transfer theorem was developed.

Finally, we took a side excursion into the analysis of nonlinear resistive networks, where we discovered that the problems were much more complicated. However, we were successful in developing some analysis methods and solving some simple nonlinear networks.

In the next several chapters we return to linear networks and seek to expand our skills to more general rules for loop and nodal analysis and to include energy-storage components in the networks. Many fundamental concepts from this chapter will provide a firm foundation.

PROBLEMS

4.1 Write the $2b$ equations of the PRIMM and solve for the current, voltage, and instantaneous power of each of the 1-ports for the network of Figure 4.67.

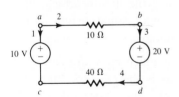

Figure 4.67

4.2 Repeat Problem 4.1 for the network of Figure 4.68.

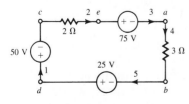

Figure 4.68

4.3 Repeat Problem 4.1 for the network of Figure 4.69.

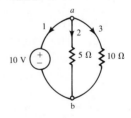

Figure 4.69

4.4 Repeat Problem 4.1 for the network of Figure 4.70.

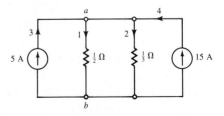

Figure 4.70

4.5 Repeat Problem 4.1 for the network of Figure 4.71.

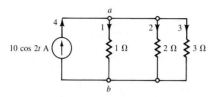

Figure 4.71

4.6 Write PRIMM for the network of Figure 4.72 and solve for i_1, v_2, v_4, v_5, and the power of the source.

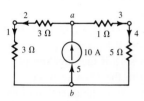

Figure 4.72

4.7 Write PRIMM for the network of Figure 4.73 and solve for i_1, v_2, p_1, and p_2.

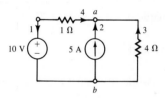

Figure 4.73

4.8 Write PRIMM for the network of Figure 4.74 and solve for all voltages and currents. Also calculate the instantaneous power for each source.

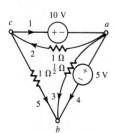

Figure 4.74

4.9 Solve the network of Figure 4.75 for all currents and voltages.

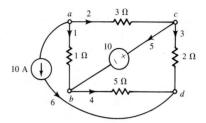

Figure 4.75

4.10 Write mesh equations for the network of Figure 4.69 and solve for i_1, i_2, i_3, and v_1.

4.11 Solve the network of Figure 4.74 for all voltages and currents by the mesh method.

4.12 Solve the network of Figure 4.76 for all currents and voltages by the mesh method.

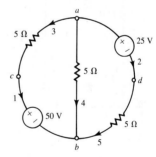

Figure 4.76

4.13 Using the mesh method, solve the network of Figure 4.77 for i_3 and v_{ab}.

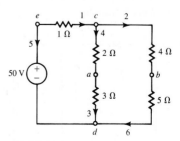

Figure 4.77

4.14 Using the mesh method, calculate the voltage v_{ab} in Figure 4.78.

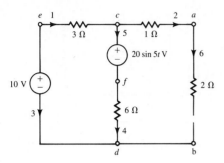

Figure 4.78

4.15 Using the mesh method, solve the network of Figure 4.79 for i_1, i_2, v_{ab}, and the instantaneous power of each branch.

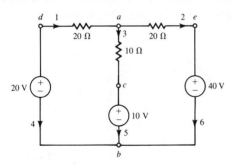

Figure 4.79

4.16 Repeat Problem 4.14 if the v-source, $20 \sin 5t$, is replaced by a 1-Ω resistor.

4.17 Repeat Problem 4.15 if the 20-V v-source is replaced by a short circuit ($R = 0$).

4.18 Solve the network of Figure 4.80 for v_1 and v_2 by the nodal method. Calculate the instantaneous power of each branch.

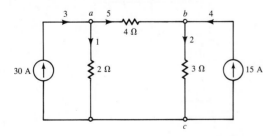

Figure 4.80

4.19 Repeat Problem 4.18 for the network of Figure 4.81.

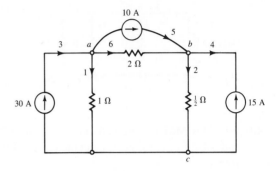

Figure 4.81

4.20 Repeat Problem 4.18 if the direction of current flow is reversed in the 15-A i-source.

4.21 Repeat Problem 4.19 if the direction of the current is reversed in the 10-A i-source.

4.22 Use the mesh method to calculate the currents in the network of Figure 4.70.

4.23 Use the mesh method to solve the network of Figure 4.75.

4.24 Solve the network of Figure 4.73 by loop currents.

4.25 Solve the network of Figure 4.73 by nodal analysis.

4.26 Solve the network of Figure 4.74 by nodal analysis.

4.27 Solve the network of Figure 4.75 by nodal analysis.

4.28 Calculate v_1 and v_2 for the network of Figure 4.82.

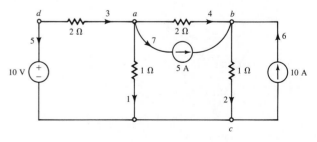

Figure 4.82

4.29 Calculate i_1 and i_2 for the network of Figure 4.83.

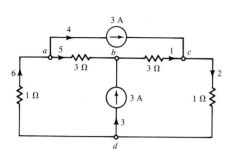

Figure 4.83

4.30 Calculate v_1 and i_3 for the network of Figure 4.84.

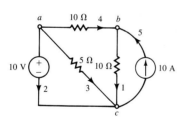

Figure 4.84

4.31 Calculate v_1, i_2, and i_3 for the network of Figure 4.85.

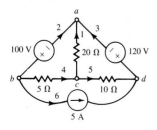

Figure 4.85

4.32 Calculate the voltages v_1 and v_2 for the network of Figure 4.86.

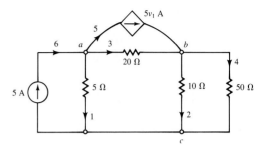

Figure 4.86

4.33 Repeat Problem 4.32 if the 10-Ω resistor is replaced by a 10-V v-source.
4.34 Solve the network of Figure 4.87 for v_2 and i_3.

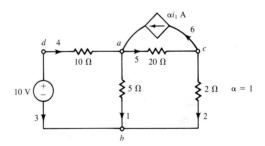

Figure 4.87

4.35 Solve the network of Figure 4.88 for the instantaneous power of the 100-V v-source and the 5-A i-source.

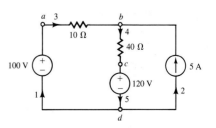

Figure 4.88

4.36 Solve the network of Figure 4.89 for the current and instantaneous power of the 20-Ω resistor and the dependent source.

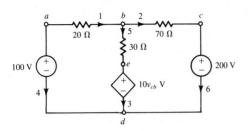

Figure 4.89

4.37 Solve the network of Figure 4.90 for the voltage v_{bd} and the instantaneous power of the 100-V v-source.

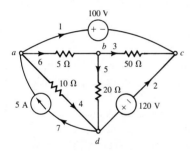

Figure 4.90

4.38 **(a)** Find the equivalent resistance of the network of Figure 4.91 if a and b are considered as the terminals of the equivalent 1-port.
(b) Using the voltage and current-divider concepts, find v_{cb} and i_y if $v_{ab} = 100$ V.

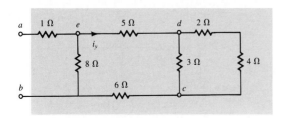

Figure 4.91

4.39 Repeat Problem 4.38 for Figure 4.92.

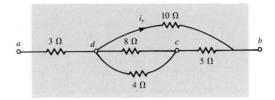

Figure 4.92

4.40 Repeat Problem 4.38 for Figure 4.93.

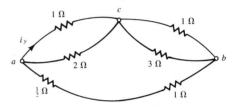

Figure 4.93

4.41 Repeat Problem 4.38 for Figure 4.94.

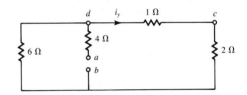

Figure 4.94

4.42 Find the equivalent resistance of the network of Figure 4.95 if a and b are to be the terminals of the equivalent 1-port.

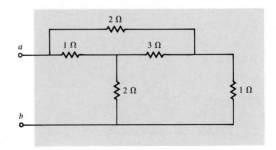

Figure 4.95

4.43 Repeat Problem 4.42 for Figure 4.96.

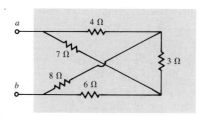

Figure 4.96

4.44 Repeat Problem 4.42 for Figure 4.97.

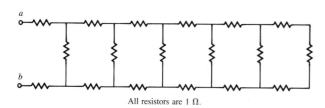

All resistors are 1 Ω.

Figure 4.97

4.45 Repeat Problem 4.42 for Figure 4.98.

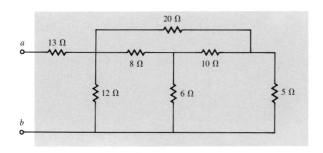

Figure 4.98

4.46 Using nodes a and b as the external terminals, find the Thévenin-form component equation, the Thévenin equivalent network, and the Norton equivalent network for the network of Figure 4.68. (*Hint:* Redraw as Figure 4.99.)

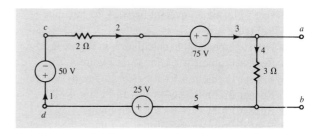

Figure 4.99

4.47 Repeat Problem 4.46 for Figure 4.70.
4.48 Repeat Problem 4.46 for Figure 4.72.
4.49 Repeat Problem 4.46 for Figure 4.74.
4.50 Repeat Problem 4.46 for Figure 4.75.
4.51 Repeat Problem 4.46 for Figure 4.76.
4.52 Repeat Problem 4.46 for Figure 4.77.
4.53 Repeat Problem 4.46 for Figure 4.78.
4.54 Calculate the current i_3 in the network of Figure 4.79 by replacing all the network except the 10-V v-source by a Thévenin equivalent network with nodes b and c as terminals and connecting this equivalent network to the 10-V source.
4.55 Calculate the current i_2 in the network of Figure 4.80 by replacing all the network except the 3-Ω resistor by a Norton equivalent network with nodes b and c as terminals and then connecting this equivalent network to the 3-Ω resistor.
4.56 As in Problem 4.55, use a Norton equivalent to calculate i_2 in Figure 4.81.
4.57 As in Problem 4.55, use a Norton equivalent to calculate i_2 in Figure 4.82.
4.58 As in Problem 4.55, use a Norton equivalent to calculate i_1 in Figure 4.83.
4.59 As in Problem 4.54, use a Thévenin equivalent to calculate i_1 in Figure 4.84.
4.60 Use a Thévenin equivalent network to calculate i_4 in Figure 4.85.
4.61 Use a Thévenin equivalent network to calculate i_2 in Figure 4.86.
4.62 Use a Thévenin equivalent network to calculate i_2 in Figure 4.87.

4.63 Use a Norton equivalent network to calculate i_2 in Figure 4.89.

4.64 Use superposition to calculate i_1 in Figure 4.75.

4.65 Repeat Problem 4.64 for v_4 in Figure 4.76.

4.66 Repeat Problem 4.64 for i_2 in Figure 4.79.

4.67 Repeat Problem 4.64 for v_2 in Figure 4.80.

4.68 Repeat Problem 4.64 for i_1 in Figure 4.82.

4.69 Repeat Problem 4.64 for i_1 in Figure 4.83.

4.70 Repeat Problem 4.64 for i_1 in Figure 4.89.

4.71 A resistor is to be connected between nodes a and b of the network shown in Figure 4.73. What is the maximum power that this resistor can draw from the network and to what value should it be set in order to draw this maximum power?

4.72 Repeat Problem 4.71 for Figure 4.75.

4.73 Repeat Problem 4.71 for Figure 4.76.

4.74 Repeat Problem 4.71 for Figure 4.79.

4.75 Repeat Problem 4.71 for Figure 4.82.

4.76 Repeat Problem 4.71 for Figure 4.86.

4.77 Repeat Problem 4.71 for Figure 4.89.

4.78 In the network of Figure 4.51, $e_T = 40$ V, $R_T = 4\ \Omega$, and R_{NL} is such that $v_2 = i_2 (15 - i_2)$.
Find the current i_2 using the graphical method.

4.79 Repeat Problem 4.78 if $v_2 = 3|i_2|$.

4.80 Repeat Problem 4.78 if $v_2 = 2(e^{0.2i_2} - 1)$.

4.81 In the network of Figure 4.51, the nonlinear resistor has the v-i characteristic of Figure 4.60. Find the current i_2 if
(a) $e_T = 20$ V, $R_T = 10\ \Omega$
(b) $e_T = 20$ V, $R_T = 40\ \Omega$
(c) $e_T = -20$ V, $R_T = 10\ \Omega$

4.82 In the network of Figure 4.51, $e_T = 35$ V, $R_T = 5\ \Omega$, and R_{NL} is characterized by $v_2 = i_2(12.8 - 1.4i_2)$. Use the Newton-Raphson method to find i_2.

4.83 Solve Problem 4.80 by using the Newton-Raphson method.

4.84 Solve the network of Example 4.37 by using the Newton-Raphson method if

$$v_{R_1} = 10e^{i_1}$$

$$v_2 = (8 - 2i_2)i_2$$

4.85 Solve the network of Example 4.36 if

$$R_1 = 5i_1{}^2$$

$$R_2 = 5|i_2|$$

Giants of the profession
IEEE Centennial Hall of Fame

Guglielmo Marconi (1874–1937)
Radio inventor and entrepreneur who
patented wireless telegraphy; made first
transatlantic transmission from England
to Newfoundland, Canada, in 1901; he
shared the Nobel Prize in physics in
1909 with K. F. Braun.

Generalized loop and nodal methods for resistive networks

5.1 INTRODUCTION

In Chapter 4 we discovered two powerful tools for the analysis of electric networks: the loop-current and node-voltage methods. In this chapter we expand these methods to a more generalized approach. Since the methods developed in Chapter 4 can always be made to work for any resistive network, the more generalized approach will not allow us to work with any additional network types. It will, however, provide a very systematic method for always selecting a set of linearly independent equations. Furthermore, these methods will allow us to select a set of convenient minimum-order simultaneous equations to be solved. This latter characteristic can contribute a significant savings in time in the case of large networks.

5.2 SOME LINEAR GRAPH CONCEPTS AND TECHNIQUES

In order to proceed to more generalized loop and nodal analysis methods, we need to develop some additional terminology. We begin by reviewing some familiar terms from earlier chapters in Table 5.1.

**Table 5.1
Definitions**

1. *Linear graph:* A collection of oriented line segments showing the (positive) orientation of the voltage and current variables of each 1-port component in the network and how these components are connected together.

2. *Branch:* The line segments of the linear graph denoting 1-port components. (Occasionally we have also used the term *branch* to refer to the 1-port itself.)

3. *Node:* A point where two or more branches have a common connection.

4. *Path:* A set of branches that may be traversed in order without passing through the same node more than once.

5. *Loop:* A closed path of a linear graph or network.

6. *Planar network (graph):* A network (graph) for which the network diagram can be drawn on the surface of a plane in such a way that no branches cross each other.

7. *Mesh:* A loop of a planar network diagram that encircles no network branches (the network diagram must be drawn without crossovers).

8. *Nonplanar network:* Any network that is not planar.

9. *Star-tree:* The set of branches of a linear graph that connects one node directly to every other node and forms no loops. (Not every linear graph has a star-tree.)

10. *Supernode:* A set of nodes plus all the network branches that have both terminals connected to the nodes in the set.

By review, we recall that a network or linear graph with n nodes and b branches has $n - 1$ linearly independent KCL equations and $b - n + 1$ linearly independent KVL equations. A planar network has $b - n + 1$ meshes, but most networks will have many more than $b - n + 1$ loops and many more than $n - 1$ supernodes. We recall also that with loop analysis we solve a selected set of KVL equations and with nodal analysis we solve a selected set of KCL equations. The thrust of this chapter is to develop systematic methods of selecting which out of these many KVL equations or KCL equations will provide the most appropriate loop or nodal model. The decision is usually based on finding that set which imposes the least computational burden in order to obtain a solution.

At this point we need four additional definitions:

1. *Tree:* A set of branches of a linear graph that connects every node to every other node and contains no loops. (A generalization of the concept of the star-tree. Here there need not be a common, or reference, node, and the manner in which two nodes are connected need not be directly by a single branch.)

2. *Cotree:* The set of branches not in the tree (complement of the tree).

3. *Link:* A branch of the cotree.

4. *Connected graph:* A linear graph that has at least one path (of one or more branches) between any two nodes.

We remark in passing that the term *branch* has sometimes been used to denote only those line segments of the linear graph that belong to the tree. In this text we have consistently referred to all the line segments of the linear graph as branches. Some authors have assigned special names (such as twigs) to the tree branches. However, we shall simply refer to them as tree branches.

Before going on to the main task, we need to discuss connected networks and those that are not connected. According to our definition, we determine that the linear graph of Figure 5.1 is connected or is for a connected network, whereas the one for Figure 5.2 is not. A graph such as the one in Figure 5.2 is referred to as a *two-part graph*.

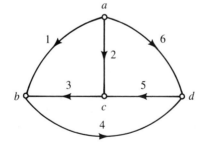

Figure 5.1
Linear graph for a connected network.

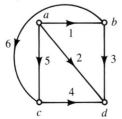
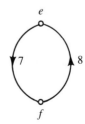

Figure 5.2
Two-part graph.

In order to avoid some unnecessary complications, we shall restrict our discussion to connected networks or, equivalently, to connected graphs. This restriction is justified and leads to no loss in generality because a network of two parts can be connected by a single branch with zero resistance. By KCL no current can flow through this branch. Thus the two nodes that it connects can be coalesced to form a single node, and the resulting one-part network is equivalent to the original two-part one in that the KCL and KVL equations of the two graphs are identical. For our purposes the linear graph of Figure 5.3 is equivalent to the one of Figure 5.2.

Notice that we have distorted or reshaped the second part of the graph in redrawing it as Figure 5.3, illustrating another property of linear graphs, namely, that a linear graph can be distorted, bent, or reshaped and remain topologically identical. This is true because the information portrayed by the graph is unchanged. Finally, we observe that linear graphs of several parts can also be made to be connected by the same stratagem.

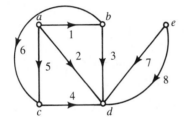

Figure 5.3
Connected equivalent graph.

Although a typical linear graph of interest will have a large number of different trees (How many can you find for Figures 5.1 and 5.3?), each possible set of elements that forms a tree has a property that is vital to us. *Any tree of a connected linear graph contains $n - 1$ branches*. This can be seen by using a construction argument. Given some network, suppose we begin to select a set of branches to use as a tree. The first branch selected will connect two nodes together. Each additional branch selected will add exactly one more node; otherwise it would have to close a loop, which is not allowed. Continuing in this fashion, we see that we need $n - 1$ branches in order to bring all the nodes into the connected set. At this point no more branches can be added without closing a loop. It then follows that *any cotree of a linear graph contains $b - (n - 1) = b - n + 1$ links*. These are interesting results, and it is not coincidental that they agree with the number of linearly independent KCL and KVL equations.

Several results of our linear graph definitions will prove to be fundamental to loop and nodal analysis. We state these as theorems.

Theorem 5.1

> The tree voltages for any tree of a linear graph are sufficient to define all of the voltages of the graph.

To show that this theorem is true, reason as follows: Since a tree of the graph contains no loops, a unique path through the tree exists between any pair of nodes of the graph. Therefore, the voltage between any pair of nodes in the network can be found by KVL as an algebraic sum of tree voltages.

The fact that a unique path through the tree exists between any pair of nodes of the graph leads us to the following fundamental result.

Theorem 5.2

> Each link and the set of tree branches in the path between the two nodes of the link form a unique loop. Furthermore, the set of loops formed by using one link in each loop will be $b - n + 1$ in number and will yield a linearly independent set of KVL equations.

The last part of the theorem follows from the fact that any tree of a graph has $b - n + 1$ associated links and that the loops have been chosen such that each loop contains one distinct link. The loops formed in this manner are defined as the *fundamental loops* of the corresponding tree. This set of loops is suitable for loop analysis, and we shall see that the tree can be chosen in a desirable way.

Example 5.1

The linear graph of a network is shown in Figure 5.4. In this graph, $b = 8$ and $n = 5$. Therefore, the tree has four branches. One possible tree is shown in color as branches 1, 2, 3, and 4. For this tree the KVL equations for the fundamental loops are:

Link 5: $v_5 = -v_2 + v_3 + v_4$

Link 6: $v_6 = v_1 - v_2 + v_3 + v_4$

Link 7: $v_7 = -v_2 + v_3$

Link 8: $v_8 = v_1 - v_2$

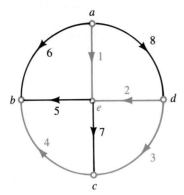

Figure 5.4
Linear graph for Example 5.1.

In matrix form,

$$\begin{bmatrix} v_5 \\ v_6 \\ v_7 \\ v_8 \end{bmatrix} = \begin{bmatrix} 0 & -1 & 1 & 1 \\ 1 & -1 & 1 & 1 \\ 0 & -1 & 1 & 0 \\ 1 & -1 & 0 & 0 \end{bmatrix} \begin{bmatrix} v_1 \\ v_2 \\ v_3 \\ v_4 \end{bmatrix}$$

Other possible trees include branches $(1, 7, 3, 4)$, $(1, 3, 4, 6)$, and $(2, 4, 5, 8)$.

Supernodes

The concept of a supernode was defined in Chapter 2 and KCL was extended to this collection of nodes and branches. In the analysis techniques of Chapter 4, we were not able to take full advantage of the supernode concept. We are now prepared to do so.

Let us formalize the association of the supernode concept with the tree that has been chosen for a linear graph. We introduce the ideas by considering Figure 5.5. This figure shows the six branches that have been chosen as the tree for a seven-node linear graph. The links have temporarily been omitted. If we remove any one branch from this graph, we divide the nodes into two sets. (In some cases one of the sets is only one node.) Suppose we let the set of nodes at the tail of the arrow of the removed element define a supernode. For example, the removal of branch 1 defines a supernode consisting of nodes a, b, and c plus tree branches 2 and 3 and any links that have both ends (terminals) connected to the set of nodes a, b, and c. Any links that have one terminal connected in the set of nodes a, b, and c while the other terminal is connected in the set of nodes d, e, f, and g are cut by the dotted line in the figure and will be included, along with tree branch 1, in the KCL equation for the supernode. If we continue in this fashion, letting each tree branch define one supernode, we obtain $(n - 1) = (7 - 1) = 6$ supernodes. Furthermore, we know that the

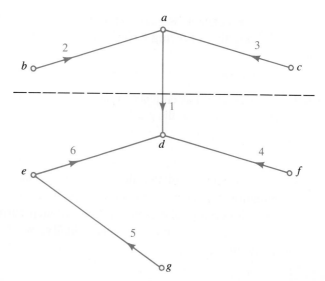

Figure 5.5
A tree of a linear graph.

KCL equations for these supernodes are linearly independent, since each equation contains the current of one unique tree branch. The supernodes formed in this way are defined as *fundamental supernodes* for the corresponding tree. The fundamental supernodes of the graph of Figure 5.5 associated with the tree branches 1, 2, 3, 4, 5, and 6 are shown in Figure 5.6 as the dotted, closed surfaces A, B, C, D, E, and F, respectively. Note that four of the six are simple nodes.

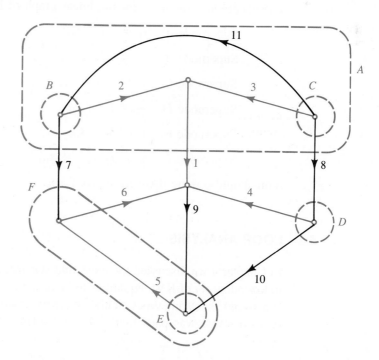

Figure 5.6
Supernodes of the graph.

The concepts we have developed for Figure 5.6 carry over to any network, yielding the following basic results.

Theorem 5.3

> The set of link currents for any tree of a linear graph is sufficient to define all the currents of the graph.

The validity of this theorem follows directly from the fact that the KCL equation for each fundamental supernode involves exactly one unique tree-branch current. Therefore, the tree-branch currents can be found as an algebraic sum of the link currents. Finally, we have the following very useful theorem.

Theorem 5.4

> A unique set of $n - 1$ supernodes is defined by any tree of a connected linear graph.

Example 5.2 ──────────────────────────────────

The supernode equations for the linear graph of Figure 5.6 are:

$$\text{Supernode } A: \quad i_1 = -i_7 - i_8$$
$$\text{Supernode } B: \quad i_2 = -i_7 + i_{11}$$
$$\text{Supernode } C: \quad i_3 = -i_8 - i_{11}$$
$$\text{Supernode } D: \quad i_4 = i_8 - i_{10}$$
$$\text{Supernode } E: \quad i_5 = i_9 + i_{10}$$
$$\text{Supernode } F: \quad i_6 = i_7 + i_9 + i_{10}$$

You should rewrite these in matrix form.

5.3 LOOP ANALYSIS ─────────────────────────────────○

In Chapter 4 we discussed the mesh and star-tree methods of finding a linearly independent set of KVL equations to be used to solve for a set of loop currents. We found that sometimes neither of these approaches yielded a set of loop equations that was particularly desirable. However, we have now overcome these difficulties by introducing a more generalized set of loops. We need only be clever enough to select the tree of the graph in the most expeditious fashion. The resulting fundamental loops are always linearly independent.

Guidelines for the selection of the most appropriate tree are easy to define and use. The primary goal is to create one dummy loop for each *i*-source in the network. This is readily accomplished, as illustrated by Example 5.3.

Example 5.3

In the network of Figure 5.7, the 10-V source in series with the 3-Ω resistor is considered as a single 1-port. The linear graph of the network is shown in Figure 5.8.

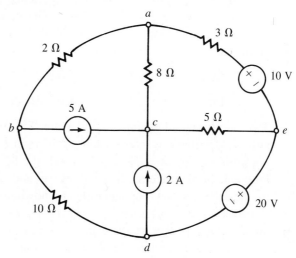

Figure 5.7
Network for Example 5.3.

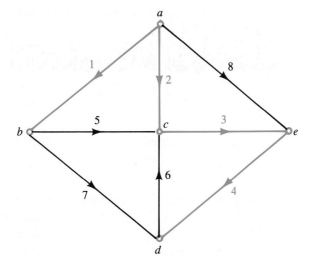

Figure 5.8
Linear graph for Example 5.3.

For this network, the number of i-sources is $N_i = 2$, and the number of v-sources is $N_v = 1$. Since $n = 5$ and $b = 8$, we have

$$n - 1 - N_v = 5 - 1 - 1 = 3$$

and

$$b - n + 1 - N_i = 8 - 5 + 1 - 2 = 2$$

Therefore, a loop analysis will require the solution of only two simultaneous equations, if we can find a suitable set of loop equations. On the other hand, a nodal analysis will require the solution of at least three simultaneous equations. Suppose we decide on the loop approach.

Taking a clue from our earlier experience with the star-tree, we *choose a tree that excludes all i-sources*. One such tree is shown in color in Figure 5.8. The fundamental loops associated with the links consist of the following sets of branches:

Link 5:   5, 2, 1   Link 7:   7, 4, 3, 2, 1

Link 6:   6, 3, 4   Link 8:   8, 3, 2

Two points should be emphasized again. First, we can be sure that these loops will yield a linearly independent set of loop equations because one and only one link appears in each loop. Second, the first two loops will create dummy loop equations, since the link voltages v_5 and v_6 (for the i-sources) will appear in one and only one loop equation and nowhere else in the PRIMM. *These are illustrations of general results that always hold true for a set of fundamental loops for a tree that excludes all i-sources.*

We now formulate the loop equations. The loop currents are the link currents i_5, i_6, i_7, and i_8 (i_5 and i_6 known). The following is a systematic formulation technique, applicable to any network (the substitution order is KCL $\rightarrow$ CE $\rightarrow$ KVL):

Step 1. Using the fundamental supernode equations, write equations expressing the tree branch currents in terms of the link currents.

Step 2. Substitute the results of Step 1 into the component equations, which are written in voltage-explicit form where possible.

Step 3. Using the fundamental loops, write KVL equations. At the same time, substitute the results of Step 2 in order to replace all voltages, except dummy voltages, by expressions in terms of the loop currents. A dummy voltage is introduced for each i-source.

With some practice, it is often possible to go immediately to Step 3 and write the KVL equations directly while substituting from the CE.

For our example we have the following.

Step 1. $i_1 = i_5 + i_7 = 5 + i_7$

$$i_2 = -5 - i_7 - i_8$$
$$i_3 = 2 - i_7 - i_8 \tag{5.1}$$
$$i_4 = 2 - i_7$$

Steps 2 and 3.

$$v_5 = -v_1 + v_2 = -2(5 + i_7) + 8(-5 - i_7 - i_8) \tag{5.2}$$

$$v_6 = -v_3 - v_4 = -5(2 - i_7 - i_8) - 20 \tag{5.3}$$

$$v_7 - v_4 - v_3 - v_2 + v_1 = 10i_7 - 20 - 5(2 - i_7 - i_8)$$
$$- 8(-5 - i_7 - i_8) + 2(5 + i_7) = 0 \tag{5.4}$$

$$v_8 - v_3 - v_2 = 3i_8 + 10 - 5(2 - i_7 - i_8)$$
$$- 8(-5 - i_7 - i_8) = 0 \tag{5.5}$$

The first two equations are dummy equations, while the last two are the loop equations, which must be solved for i_7 and i_8. Rewriting these in a convenient matrix form, we have

$$\begin{bmatrix} v_5 \\ v_6 \end{bmatrix} = \begin{bmatrix} -10 & -8 \\ 5 & 5 \end{bmatrix} \begin{bmatrix} i_7 \\ i_8 \end{bmatrix} + \begin{bmatrix} -50 \\ -30 \end{bmatrix} \tag{5.6}$$

$$\begin{bmatrix} 25 & 13 \\ 13 & 16 \end{bmatrix} \begin{bmatrix} i_7 \\ i_8 \end{bmatrix} = \begin{bmatrix} -20 \\ -40 \end{bmatrix} \tag{5.7}$$

Equation 5.7 can now be solved for i_7 and i_8. Once these currents are known, any other variable can be obtained by algebraic substitution. For example, the tree currents can be found by substituting into Equation 5.1. The voltages v_5 and v_6 can be calculated from the dummy equations (Equation 5.6), and all other voltages can be found from the CE. We have need for Equation 5.6 only if we wish to solve for the dummy voltages, v_5 and v_6.

The technique illustrated by this example has broad application. We need remember only that *the tree should be selected to exclude all i-sources*. With practice the final result in the form of Equation 5.7 can be written directly. However, the substitution technique is systematic and should help to minimize formulation errors.

5.4 NODAL ANALYSIS

In the last section, we found that the concept of a tree of the linear graph could be used to advantage in selecting a set of loops for use in loop analysis. In this approach, we found that we should select a tree such that all i-sources were in the cotree. This approach led to one dummy equation for each i-source and, consequently, to a loop model having the smallest possible number of equations that must be solved simultaneously. The final result was a completely general loop method. In this section we accomplish a similar generalization for the nodal method.

In the loop method, we found no particular constraints upon the placement of v-sources. However, in the generalized nodal approach, we shall end up solving a set of supernode KCL equations for the voltages of the tree branches. Therefore, maximum simplification will occur if we always *select a tree that includes all v-sources*. In this way, N_v of the tree voltages are known and N_v of the supernode equations will be dummy equations. Once an appropriate tree has been selected, a systematic formulation procedure is as follows (the substitution order is KVL → CE → KCL):

Step 1. Using the fundamental loop equations, write equations expressing the link voltages in terms of the voltages of the branches of the tree. (Theorem 5.1 guarantees that this step is always possible.)

Step 2. With the component equations written in current-explicit form everywhere possible (all except v-sources), substitute from Step 1 into these CE.

Step 3. Using the fundamental supernodes, write KCL equations. At the same time, substitute the results of Step 2 in order to replace all currents, except the dummy currents of the v-sources, by expressions in terms of the tree voltages. A current variable (dummy) must be introduced into the model for each v-source.

This method is systematic and perfectly general and always leads to minimum computational effort once nodal methods have been selected. Of course, we should always compare the number of simultaneous equations of this method ($n - 1 - N_v$) to that of the loop method ($b - n + 1 - N_i$).

Example 5.4

The network of Figure 5.9 is one for which the generalized node or supernode approach is quite appropriate. The linear graph, with arbitrary branch numbering and orientation, is shown as Figure 5.10. One appropriate tree, which

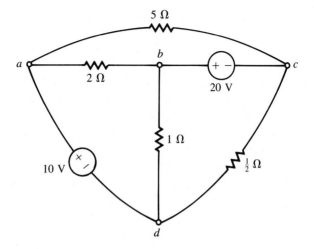

Figure 5.9
Network for Example 5.4.

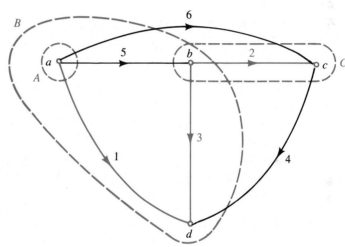

Figure 5.10
Linear graph for
Example 5.4.

includes both v-sources, is shown in color. Following the outlined procedure,
we have the following.

Step 1. $v_4 = -v_2 + v_3 = -20 + v_3$

$v_5 = v_1 - v_3 = 10 - v_3$

$v_6 = v_1 + v_2 - v_3 = 30 - v_3$

Step 2. $i_3 = v_3$

$i_4 = 2v_4 = 2(-20 + v_3)$

$i_5 = \frac{1}{2}v_5 = \frac{1}{2}(10 - v_3)$

$i_6 = \frac{1}{5}v_6 = \frac{1}{5}(30 - v_3)$

Step 3.   Dummy equations (supernodes A and B):

$$i_1 = -i_5 - i_6$$

$$i_2 = i_4 - i_6$$

or

$$i_1 = -\tfrac{1}{2}(10 - v_3) - \tfrac{1}{5}(30 - v_3) = -11 + 0.7v_3 \qquad (5.8)$$

$$i_2 = 2(-20 + v_3) - \tfrac{1}{5}(30 - v_3) = -46 + 2.2v_3 \qquad (5.9)$$

For supernode C:

$$i_3 + i_4 - i_5 - i_6 = 0$$

or

$$v_3 + 2(-20 + v_3) - \tfrac{1}{2}(10 - v_3) - \tfrac{1}{5}(30 - v_3) = 0 \qquad (5.10)$$

Thus we see that the problem reduces to solving one equation (Equation 5.10) for the one unknown tree voltage. This solution yields

$$3.7v_3 = 51$$

$$v_3 = 13.78 \text{ V}$$

Once the solution for v_3 is determined, all other network variables can be determined by algebraic substitution. In particular, the link voltages can be found from the equations of Step 1, and all resistor currents can be calculated from the equations of Step 2. Finally, the dummy currents can be calculated from the dummy equations (Equations 5.8 and 5.9). The results for the currents are: $i_1 = -1.354$ A, $i_2 = -15.68$ A, $i_3 = 13.78$ A, $i_4 = -12.44$ A, $i_5 = -1.89$ A, and $i_6 = 3.244$ A.

In contrast to solving one equation, a loop analysis of this network requires the solution of three simultaneous equations.

Example 5.5

Consider the network of Figure 5.11. A linear graph for this network is shown in Figure 5.12. Note that the 30-V source in series with the 3-Ω resistor has been treated as a single 1-port. The same is true for the 50-V source and 5-Ω resistor. Although dummy nodes could be placed between these sources and their series resistors, there is no essential difference in this approach and absolutely no advantage is gained.

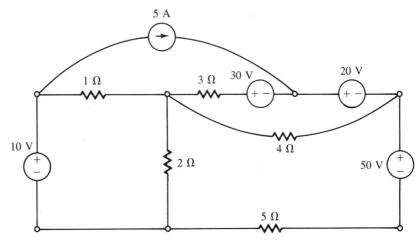

Figure 5.11
Network for Example 5.5.

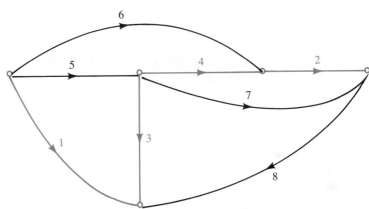

Figure 5.12
Linear graph for
Example 5.5.

For this network, a simple calculation shows that the loop method requires the solution of three simultaneous equations, but the supernode approach leads to only two equations that must be solved simultaneously.

Suppose we shortcut some of the procedure and go directly to the two supernode equations that must be solved for the two unknown tree voltages v_3 and v_4. These equations are

$$i_3 - i_5 - i_6 + i_8 = 0 \tag{5.11}$$

$$i_4 + i_6 + i_7 - i_8 = 0 \tag{5.12}$$

Remember now that the goal of the formulation procedure is to write each of the currents in Equations 5.11 and 5.12 in terms of v_3 and v_4. Thus we obtain

$$\tfrac{1}{2}v_3 - (10 - v_3) - 5 + [-10 + \tfrac{1}{5}(-20 - v_4 + v_3)] = 0 \tag{5.13}$$

$$[-10 + \tfrac{1}{3}v_4] + 5 + \tfrac{1}{4}(v_4 + 20) - [-10 + \tfrac{1}{5}(-20 - v_4 + v_3)] = 0 \tag{5.14}$$

In these equations the bracketed terms correspond to i_8 and i_4. In order to obtain the form shown, it is necessary to write the CE of these 1-ports in current-explicit form. Some analysts prefer to convert these 1-ports to Norton equivalent 1-ports directly on the network before writing the supernode equations. At any rate, by collecting terms we obtain

$$1.7v_3 - 0.2v_4 = 29 \tag{5.15}$$

$$-0.2v_3 + 0.783v_4 = -14 \tag{5.16}$$

You should fill in all the details that have been omitted in obtaining this final result. In fact, it would be advisable to do the complete substitution process in order to see that Equations 5.13 and 5.14 can be written directly after some practice with the substitution process. We wish to emphasize, however, that we can always rely on the complete process. The dummy equations are left as a practice exercise.

5.5 NETWORKS WITH CONTROLLED SOURCES

The extension of our rules for tree selection in order to include networks with controlled sources is relatively straightforward. *Controlled voltage sources should be placed in the tree and controlled current sources should be placed in the cotree.* However, we now have an added dimension. The question is: Is there a preferred location (tree or cotree) for the 1-port whose current or voltage controls the controlled source? The answer to this question is best revealed by example.

Example 5.6

Consider the network of Figure 5.13. A linear graph with a tree that includes the voltage sources and excludes the current sources is shown in Figure 5.14. The current i_x in the 4-Ω resistor controls the current of the controlled source.

Suppose we elect to do loop analysis using the fundamental loops defined by the tree shown. Then, by using the fundamental supernodes, we begin by writing the tree currents in terms of the link currents. We obtain

$$
\begin{aligned}
i_1 &= i_5 - i_6 + i_7 - i_8 \\
i_2 &= i_6 + i_8 \\
i_3 &= -i_5 + i_6 - i_7 \\
i_4 &= i_5 - i_6 - i_8
\end{aligned}
\tag{5.17}
$$

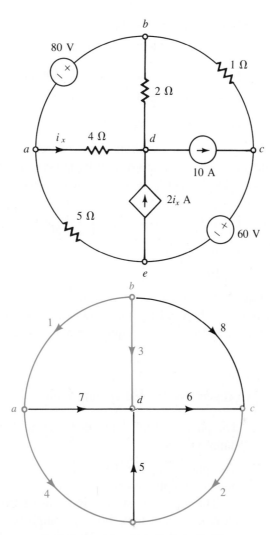

Figure 5.13
Network for Example 5.6.

Figure 5.14
Linear graph for
Example 5.6.

The CE (voltage in terms of current where possible) are

$$v_1 = 80 \text{ V}$$

$$v_2 = 60 \text{ V}$$

$$v_3 = 2i_3$$

$$v_4 = 5i_4$$

$$i_5 = 2i_x = 2i_7$$ (5.18)

$$i_6 = 10 \text{ A}$$

$$v_7 = 4i_7$$

$$v_8 = i_8$$

The KVL equations for the fundamental loops are

$$v_5 - v_3 + v_1 + v_4 = 0 \quad \text{(dummy)}$$

$$v_6 + v_2 - v_4 - v_1 + v_3 = 0 \quad \text{(dummy)}$$

$$v_7 - v_3 + v_1 = 0$$

$$v_8 + v_2 - v_4 - v_1 = 0$$

(5.19)

Using our usual substitution procedure, we substitute Equation 5.17 into Equation 5.18 and the result into Equation 5.19. During this substitution, we replace i_5 by $2i_7$ and i_6 by 10. The result, after simplification, is

$$\begin{bmatrix} v_5 \\ v_6 \end{bmatrix} + \begin{bmatrix} 16 & -5 \\ -16 & 5 \end{bmatrix} \begin{bmatrix} i_7 \\ i_8 \end{bmatrix} + \begin{bmatrix} 10 \\ 50 \end{bmatrix} = \begin{bmatrix} 0 \\ 0 \end{bmatrix}$$

(5.20)

$$\begin{bmatrix} 10 & 0 \\ -10 & 6 \end{bmatrix} \begin{bmatrix} i_7 \\ i_8 \end{bmatrix} = \begin{bmatrix} -60 \\ -30 \end{bmatrix}$$

(5.21)

Equation 5.21 can be solved for i_7 and i_8. Equation 5.20 (the dummy equation) can be used to find v_5 and v_6. Any other variable can be found by algebraic substitution into Equations 5.17 and 5.18.

Two cogent points need amplification:

1. The placing of the controlled current source in the cotree led to a dummy loop.

2. The placing of the 4-Ω resistor in the cotree allowed a simple algebraic replacement of i_x by one of the unknown loop currents, i_7. The replacement of i_x in terms of the model unknowns (loop currents) could have been accomplished if the 4-Ω resistor had been placed in the tree. However, the algebra would have been somewhat more complicated. Also, if the current source were controlled by the voltage v_7 rather than the current i_7, there would be no essential difference in the modeling technique, since $v_7 = 4i_7$. The key point to remember is that we need to solve for the controlling variable in terms of the model unknowns.

Example 5.7

Suppose that we had decided to solve the network of Figure 5.13 by nodal analysis, using the tree of Figure 5.14. We begin by using the fundamental loops to write the link voltages in terms of the three voltages. Thus from Equation 5.19 we obtain

$$v_5 = v_3 - v_1 - v_4$$
$$v_6 = -v_2 + v_4 + v_1 - v_3$$
$$v_7 = v_3 - v_1 \qquad\qquad (5.22)$$
$$v_8 = -v_2 + v_4 + v_1$$

Next we rewrite the CE (current in terms of voltage where possible):

$$v_1 = 80 \text{ V}$$
$$v_2 = 60 \text{ V}$$
$$i_3 = \tfrac{1}{2}v_3$$
$$i_4 = \tfrac{1}{5}v_4$$
$$i_5 = 2i_x = 2i_7 \qquad\qquad (5.23)$$
$$i_6 = 10 \text{ A}$$
$$i_7 = \tfrac{1}{4}v_7$$
$$i_8 = v_8$$

To complete the PRIMM, we rewrite the KCL equations for the fundamental supernodes (Equation 5.17) as

$$i_1 = i_5 - i_6 + i_7 - i_8$$
$$i_2 = i_6 + i_8$$
$$i_3 + i_5 - i_6 + i_7 = 0 \qquad\qquad (5.24)$$
$$i_4 - i_5 + i_6 + i_8 = 0$$

The first two of these equations are the dummy equations and, consequently, are left explicit in i_1 and i_2 for convenience in solving for these two variables. The last two of these equations are the ones that must be solved simultaneously.

The formulation proceeds by substituting Equation 5.22 into Equation 5.23 and this result into Equation 5.24. The result, with the dummy equations excluded, is

$$\tfrac{1}{2}v_3 + 2i_x - 10 + \tfrac{1}{4}(v_3 - 80) = 0$$
$$\tfrac{1}{5}v_4 - 2i_x + 10 + (-60 + v_4 + 80) = 0$$

In order to place these equations in final form, we need to solve for i_x in terms of the model variables v_3 and v_4. We know we can do this because of the fundamental theorems in Section 5.2. Thus

$$i_x = i_7 = \tfrac{1}{4}v_7 = \tfrac{1}{4}(v_3 - 80) = \tfrac{1}{4}v_3 - 20$$

and the final result is

$$1.25v_3 = 70$$

$$-0.5v_3 + 1.2v_4 = -70$$

(5.25)

The formulation is now complete. The remaining details are left as an exercise.

In Example 5.7, the solution for i_x in terms of the unknown tree voltages would have been somewhat more routine if we had selected a tree that included the 4-Ω resistor. We have now gained sufficient insight to state a general guideline for the selection of a tree to be used in loop or nodal analysis. In particular, the following guidelines should be used:

1. The tree should include all v-sources.

2. The tree should exclude all i-sources.

3. The tree should include all controlled voltage sources.

4. The tree should exclude all controlled current sources.

5. If possible, the 1-port that contains the controlling variable of a controlled source should be placed in the cotree if loop analysis is to be used and in the tree if nodal analysis is to be used.

The last guideline is based upon the assumption that the controlling variable is always associated with a resistive 1-port. This is almost always the case in any network of interest. In any case the tree should be selected to provide the simplest possible relationship between the controlling variable and the unknowns in the selected analysis technique. It is often possible to obtain a one-to-one correspondence.

5.6 SUMMARY

In this chapter we outlined systematic methods of network modeling for both loop and nodal analyses. The approach is grounded in properties of the linear graph and allows the selection of an analysis that will minimize the necessary computational burden. Properly applied, the techniques that we have learned to this point are sufficient to solve any resistance network that we may encounter.

PROBLEMS

5.1 Write the KVL and KCL equations for the fundamental loops and the fundamental supernodes of the linear graph of Figure 5.15 if the tree contains branches 1, 2, 3, and 7.

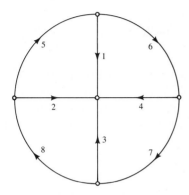

Figure 5.15

5.2 Repeat Problem 5.1 if the tree contains branches 2, 6, 7, and 8.

5.3 Repeat Problem 5.1 if the tree contains branches 2, 4, 5, and 8.

5.4 Write the KVL and KCL equations for the fundamental loops and the fundamental supernodes of the linear graph of Figure 5.16 if the tree contains branches 1, 3, 5, 7, and 11.

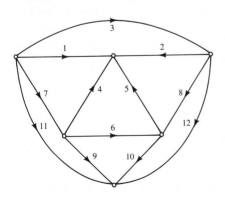

Figure 5.16

5.5 Repeat Problem 5.4 if the tree contains branches 1, 2, 8, 9, and 10.

5.6 Repeat Problem 5.4 if the tree contains branches 1, 9, 10, 11, and 12.

5.7 Repeat Problem 5.4 if the tree contains branches 4, 5, 7, 8, and 12.

5.8 Using a tree consisting of branches 1, 2, 3, and 4, formulate and solve the fundamental loop equations, including the dummy equations, for the network shown in Figure 5.17.

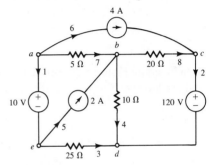

Figure 5.17

5.9 Repeat Problem 5.8 for a tree of branches 1, 2, 7, and 8.

5.10 For the network and linear graph of Figure 5.18, select a suitable tree and use loop analysis to solve for all voltages and currents.

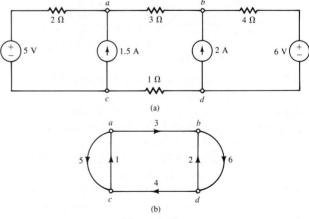

Figure 5.18

5.11 For the network of Figure 5.19, select a suitable tree and use loop analysis to solve for all currents and voltages.

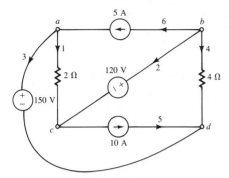

Figure 5.19

5.12 For the network of Figure 5.20, select a suitable tree and use loop analysis to solve for v_5, v_6, i_7, and i_8.

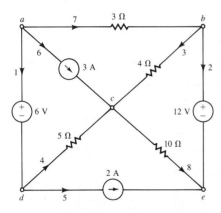

Figure 5.20

5.13 Work out all the details of Example 5.4 and verify the results given.

5.14 Work out all the details of the substitution process for Example 5.5 and verify Equations 5.15 and 5.16. Also, develop the dummy equations for this example. Finally, obtain the solution for all voltages and currents.

5.15 Using a tree consisting of branches 1, 2, 3, and 4, formulate and solve the fundamental supernode equations for i_1, i_2, v_3, and v_4 for the network of Figure 5.17.

5.16 Using a tree consisting of branches 1, 2, 7, and 8, formulate and solve the fundamental supernode equations for all variables in the network of Figure 5.17.

5.17 Select a suitable tree and solve the network of Figure 5.18 by supernode analysis.

5.18 Using a tree consisting of branches 1, 2, and 3, solve the network of Figure 5.19 for v_1, i_2, and i_3 by supernode analysis.

5.19 Select a suitable tree and use supernode techniques to solve the network of Figure 5.20 for i_1, i_2, v_3, and v_4.

5.20 Select a suitable tree and use the loop method to solve the network of Figure 5.21 for all variables. Compare the computational effort of your solution to that which would have been required by nodal analysis.

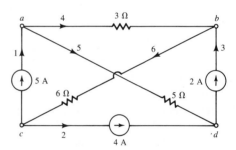

Figure 5.21

5.21 Select a suitable tree and use the supernode method to solve the network of Figure 5.22. Compare the computational effort to that which would have been required by loop methods.

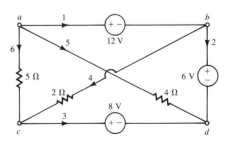

Figure 5.22

5.22 Solve the network of Figure 5.23 for v_5, v_6, and i_2, using the supernode method.

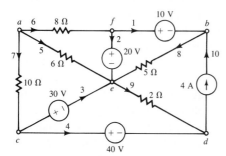

Figure 5.23

5.23 Solve the network of Figure 5.24 for all voltages and currents, using the supernode method.

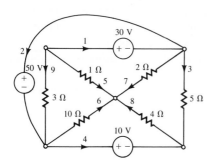

Figure 5.24

5.24 Work out all the details of Examples 5.6 and 5.7 and solve the network of Figure 5.13 for all voltages and currents.

5.25 Select a suitable tree and solve the network of Figure 5.25 by loop analysis.

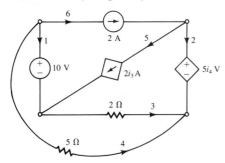

Figure 5.25

5.26 Select a suitable tree and solve the network of Figure 5.26 by loop analysis.

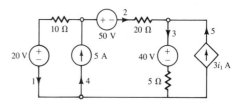

Figure 5.26

5.27 Solve the network of Figure 5.25 by the supernode method.

5.28 Solve the network of Figure 5.27 by the supernode method.

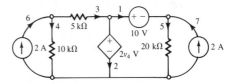

Figure 5.27

5.29 Solve the network of Figure 5.28 for the voltage ratio v_0/v_i (known as *voltage gain*). Also solve for the power gain p_0/p_i, where p_0 is the power in the 10-kΩ resistor and p_i is the output power of the source v_i.

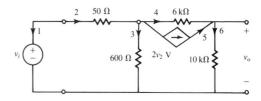

Figure 5.28

5.30 Solve the network of Figure 5.29 for the voltage v_0.

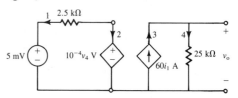

Figure 5.29

Note: For the remainder of the problems in this chapter, it is suggested that the computer program RMATINV, or a similar program, be used to solve the simultaneous equations.

☑ **5.31** Repeat Problem 5.20 using the supernode method.

☑ **5.32** Repeat Problem 5.21 using the loop method.

☑ **5.33** Repeat Problem 5.22 using the loop method.

☑ **5.34** Repeat Problem 5.23 using the loop method.

☑ **5.35** In the network of Figure 5.23, the 20-V source is replaced by a 12-Ω resistor and the 40-V source is replaced by a 3-Ω resistor. Solve the resulting network using the supernode method.

☑ **5.36** Repeat Problem 5.35 using the loop method.

☑ **5.37** In the network of Figure 5.24, the 10-V source is replaced by a 3-Ω resistor. Solve the resulting network using the supernode method.

☑ **5.38** Repeat Problem 5.37 using the loop method.

☑ **5.39** In this chapter we have emphasized two substitution procedures: one that leads to the loop method and one that leads to the supernode method. The primary motivation for emphasizing these approaches is that one or the other of the two methods normally leads to a minimum size set of equations that must be solved simultaneously. However, many other substitution procedures are possible. To illustrate one such procedure solve the network of Figure 5.22 by the following steps:

(a) Choose a suitable tree and write the PRIMM with the KCL equations explicit in tree currents and the KVL equations explicit in link voltages.

(b) Substitute the KCL and KVL equations into the CE thereby eliminating the tree currents and the link voltages from the result.

(c) Write the equations that result from step (b) as a single matrix equation, with tree voltages and link currents as unknowns, and solve the result.

(d) Compare the computational burden of this approach to that of the loop method and of the supernode method.

☑ **5.40** Repeat Problem 5.39 using the network of Figure 5.23.

☑ **5.41** Repeat Problem 5.39 using the network of Figure 5.24.

Giants of the profession
IEEE Centennial Hall of Fame

Heinrich Rudolph Hertz (1857–1894)
Experimental physicist who
demonstrated that electric waves are
essentially the same as those of light,
obeying the same fundamental laws; the
unit of frequency bears his name.

Reprinted with permission from
"Centennial Hall of Fame,"
IEEE SPECTRUM, April 1984.

Resistive 2-ports

6.1 INTRODUCTION

In Chapters 4 and 5 we discussed the analysis of simple networks containing 1-port resistive components and sources. In more general resistive networks, we often want to include 2-port components either for convenience or by necessity. For example, as we shall see, there may be whole subnetworks that can be conveniently represented as resistive 2-ports, in a manner analogous to the 1-port Norton and Thévenin equivalents discussed in Chapter 4. On the other hand, there may be 2-port components such as a transistor, vacuum tube, integrated-circuit amplifier, or electric transformer that cannot be represented satisfactorily by any combination of 1-port components. (This is the primary reason that controlled sources are introduced into network theory.) It is, therefore, essential that we develop a means for characterizing 2-port components so that networks containing both 1-ports and 2-ports can be modeled and analyzed using techniques consistent with those discussed in Chapters 4 and 5.

In this chapter we confine the discussion to 2-port networks that can be represented by 1-port resistances plus independent and/or controlled sources.

Before discussing the details of 2-port resistive models, let us review a few essential facts regarding 1-port component models and their relationships to the primary mathematical model of the network.

Each 1-port component has two variables associated with it—voltage and current. We need one component equation for it relating one or both of the

193

variables. Orientation by the measurement diagram and the standard-orientation convention of the variables are specified. The measurement diagram of the component, together with the measurement diagrams of all the other components in the network, serves to define the linear graph (interconnection diagram) for the network. Finally, the PRIMM for the networks consists of b component equations plus b Kirchhoff law equations in $2b$ unknowns.

Definition 6.1

2-port component

An electric component for which the terminal characteristics can be completely described by two relations involving two voltage variables and two current variables is called a *2-port component*, or simply a *2-port*.

Our definition is consistent with the previously established concept of a 1-port component, since a 1-port is completely described at its terminals by the relationship between one voltage variable and one current variable.

Although 2-port components can have either three or four terminals, in this chapter we confine our discussion to the three-terminal variety. A general block diagram is shown in Figure 6.1(a). The measurement diagram that

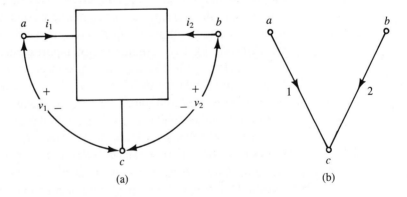

Figure 6.1
Symbols for a 2-port component. (a) General block diagram. (b) Corresponding measurement diagram.

(a)   (b)

accompanies it indicates the location and orientation of the terminal voltage and current variables. Figure 6.2 shows an example of a 2-port component made up of a subnetwork of resistors.

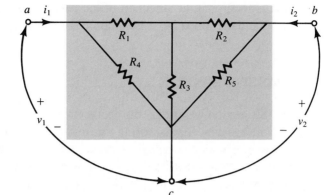

Figure 6.2
Passive resistive 2-port made up of a collection of 1-ports.

Let us examine the problem introduced by including 2-port components in the network. Each 2-port involves four variables—two voltages and two currents. We need to specify variable orientations, still utilizing our standard-orientation convention. Therefore, the measurement diagram to be included in the network linear graph consists of two oriented line segments. We need a component equation for each pair of variables—or the equivalent, each oriented line segment in the measurement diagram. For a 2-port, then, we need two component equations relating four terminal variables. If these requirements are met, we know at least that the PRIMM of a network containing 1-ports and 2-ports will have the required number of component equations (*b*) and Kirchhoff's law equations (*b*) to provide for a unique solution for the 2*b* variables involved.

In the discussion that follows in this chapter, the compact notation of matrix algebra is used because of the much greater efficiency of presentation thus achieved. Every development shown could be carried out in scalar notation, and you are advised to do as much of this kind of translation as is required for understanding until familiarity with matrix methods is achieved.

The instantaneous power associated with a 2-port is defined as

$$p(t) = v_1(t)i_1(t) + v_2(t)i_2(t) \tag{6.1}$$

where the standard orientation of current and voltage references is assumed. (If the relative orientations of v_j and i_j are as shown in Figure 6.1(a) for a 2-port, then we have standard orientation.) As is the case for a 1-port, the sign of $p(t)$ indicates the direction of flow of electrical energy relative to the component. If we have $p(t_1) > 0$, then at $t = t_1$ net flow of electrical energy is into the 2-port. If $p(t_1) < 0$, then at $t = t_1$ net flow of electrical energy is out of the component. Since electrical energy for a component over a time period from t_0 to t can be calculated as

$$w(t) - w(t_0) = \int_{t_0}^{t} p(\tau) \, d\tau \tag{6.2}$$

the amount and the direction of the net energy flow over a given time period can be determined from Equation 6.2 for a known $p(t)$.

6.2   PASSIVE 2-PORTS ⎯⎯⎯⎯⎯⎯⎯⎯⎯⎯⎯⎯⎯⎯⎯⎯◯

In this section we discuss the characterization of 2-port components made up of 1-port resistors. In discussing this topic, it is convenient to think of the 2-port as a box with the actual network inside and only the terminals extending outside. A 2-port of this type is shown in Figure 6.2.

Although there are six different ways that two terminal variables for a 2-port can be written explicitly in terms of the alternate two variables, we shall concern ourselves in this section with only two forms of terminal equations— those with voltages explicit and those with currents explicit. We call the first set the Thevenin-form CE and write them in matrix form as

$$\begin{bmatrix} v_1(t) \\ v_2(t) \end{bmatrix} = \begin{bmatrix} R_{11} & R_{12} \\ R_{21} & R_{22} \end{bmatrix} \begin{bmatrix} i_1(t) \\ i_2(t) \end{bmatrix} \tag{6.3}$$

or

$$\mathbf{v}(t) = \mathbf{R}\mathbf{i}(t) \tag{6.4}$$

where the boldface indicates matrix notation. The motivation for the name will become evident in Section 6.4, where we discuss *active* 2-ports.

For a 2-port network of only 1-port resistors, $\mathbf{R}$ in Equation 6.4 is symmetric and, therefore, $R_{21} = R_{12}$. In determining 2-port CE for such a network either through laboratory measurements or by analytical derivation, this symmetry can serve as a convenient error check. For a resistance network, the R-parameters in Equation 6.3 can be conveniently determined by alternately setting i_1 and i_2 to zero.

For $i_2 = 0$

$$\begin{bmatrix} v_1 \\ v_2 \end{bmatrix} = \begin{bmatrix} R_{11} \\ R_{21} \end{bmatrix} i_1 \tag{6.5}$$

Thus if i_1 is set in the laboratory and v_1 and v_2 are measured, we have the information necessary to determine R_{11} and R_{21}. Likewise, for analytical derivation, if i_1 is assumed (a symbolic source) and v_1 and v_2 are calculated for the network of Figure 6.3 in terms of i_1, then R_{11} and R_{21} can be found. A similar set of statements can be made relative to the situation for $i_1 = 0$, which yields

$$\begin{bmatrix} v_1 \\ v_2 \end{bmatrix} = \begin{bmatrix} R_{12} \\ R_{22} \end{bmatrix} i_2 \tag{6.6}$$

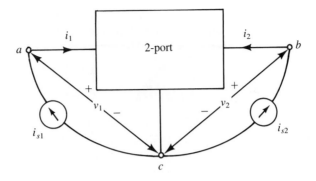

Figure 6.3
Test network for
calculation of Thévenin-
form 2-port component
equations. (Subscript s
denotes symbolic source.)

In summary,

$$R_{11} = \frac{v_1}{i_1}\bigg|_{i_2=0}$$

$$R_{12} = \frac{v_1}{i_2}\bigg|_{i_1=0}$$

$$R_{21} = \frac{v_2}{i_1}\bigg|_{i_2=0}$$

$$R_{22} = \frac{v_2}{i_2}\bigg|_{i_1=0}$$

regardless of how the ratios are obtained. Of course, all four of these parameters can be calculated with one solution of the network shown in Figure
6.3 by applying two symbolic sources and solving for v_1 and v_2 in terms of i_1
and i_2.

Because $i = 0$ corresponds to an open circuit, the parameters in **R** of
Equation 6.4 are often called the *open-circuit* **R**-parameters. An example
illustrates one procedure for deriving the Thévenin-form CE using the
symbolic-source method.

Example 6.1

The resistive 2-port network of Figure 6.4 is to be characterized by Thévenin-
form CE. Symbolic current sources i_{s1} and i_{s2} are connected to form the test
network shown in Figure 6.5. If a star-tree is chosen, as indicated, there are
three loops defined by the network links, of which i_{s1} and i_{s2} are associated
with dummy loops. The KVL equations for these loops are

$$-\begin{bmatrix} v_{s1} \\ v_{s2} \end{bmatrix} = \begin{bmatrix} v_1 \\ v_2 \end{bmatrix} = \begin{bmatrix} 1 & -1 & 0 \\ 0 & -1 & 1 \end{bmatrix} \begin{bmatrix} v_4 \\ v_5 \\ v_6 \end{bmatrix} \tag{6.7}$$

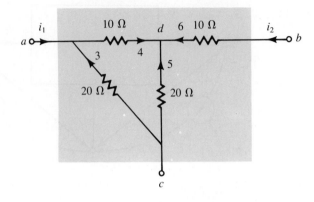

Figure 6.4
Resistive 2-port of
Example 6.1.

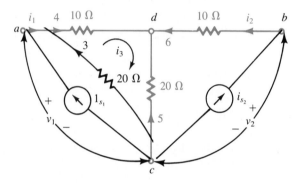

Figure 6.5
Test network for Example
6.1.

The loop-current equation for link 3 is

$$50i_3 + 30i_1 + 20i_2 = 0$$

Therefore,

$$i_3 = -0.6i_1 - 0.4i_2$$

It follows, then, that the star-tree currents are

$$i_4 = i_{s1} + i_3 = 0.4i_1 - 0.4i_2$$

$$i_5 = -i_{s1} - i_{s2} - i_3$$

$$= -0.4i_1 - 0.6i_2$$

$$i_6 = i_{s2} = i_2$$

and

$$\begin{bmatrix} v_4 \\ v_5 \\ v_6 \end{bmatrix} = \begin{bmatrix} 4 & -4 \\ -8 & -12 \\ 0 & 10 \end{bmatrix} \begin{bmatrix} i_1 \\ i_2 \end{bmatrix} \tag{6.8}$$

Substituting Equation 6.8 into Equation 6.7, we have the desired result.

$$\begin{bmatrix} v_1 \\ v_2 \end{bmatrix} = \begin{bmatrix} 1 & -1 & 0 \\ 0 & -1 & 1 \end{bmatrix} \begin{bmatrix} 4 & -4 \\ -8 & -12 \\ 0 & 10 \end{bmatrix} \begin{bmatrix} i_1 \\ i_2 \end{bmatrix}$$

$$\begin{bmatrix} v_1 \\ v_2 \end{bmatrix} = \begin{bmatrix} 12 & 8 \\ 8 & 22 \end{bmatrix} \begin{bmatrix} i_1 \\ i_2 \end{bmatrix} \tag{6.9}$$

You should note that the **R** matrix of Equation 6.9 is indeed symmetric and therefore at least satisfies that requirement. Also, the final substitution in the derivation was made into the dummy loop equations associated with the symbolic current sources. This, as we shall see, is a general pattern for the derivation of CE using symbolic sources. Using Equation 6.9 we can now derive an expression for $p(t)$ for the 2-port. We start with the general 2-port power equation

$$p(t) = v_1(t)i_1(t) + v_2(t)i_2(t)$$

$$= [i_1(t) \quad i_2(t)] \begin{bmatrix} v_1(t) \\ v_2(t) \end{bmatrix} \tag{6.10}$$

Then, by substituting Equation 6.9 for the voltage vector, we get

$$p(t) = [i_1 \quad i_2] \begin{bmatrix} 12 & 8 \\ 8 & 22 \end{bmatrix} \begin{bmatrix} i_1 \\ i_2 \end{bmatrix}$$

$$= 12i_1^2 + 16i_1 i_2 + 22i_2^2 \tag{6.11}$$

It is easy to see that $p(t)$ for this example must always be positive for at least one $i_j \neq 0$. This holds for either $i_1 \neq 0$, $i_2 \neq 0$, or both, regardless of sign. In general $p(t)$ is always positive for a resistive 2-port if either i is nonzero, regardless of the operating condition of the network that contains the 2-port. One way of determining this would be to check that the **R** matrix in Equation 6.9 has the mathematical property of being *positive definite*. (For information on this property, see a text on matrix theory.) Another way to check that $p(t) > 0$ is to assume $i_2 = ki_1$, where $k \neq 0$ (but may be negative), and determine whether a k exists such that $p(t) \leq 0$ in Equation 6.11. (*Hint:* Examine the function for a minimum. If it has one, get an expression for it and show it to be positive.)

A 2-port for which $p(t)$ is always positive (except for $i_1 = i_2 = 0$) is passive by definition.

An equivalent 2-port resistive T network is always easy to construct for CE in Thévenin form if the **R** matrix in Equation 6.4 is symmetric. Figure 6.6 indicates such an equivalent T network in the general form for a passive-resistance 2-port. Figure 6.7 is an equivalent T network for the 2-port of Example 6.1. As far as effects external to the 2-port are concerned, the 2-port of Figure 6.7 is completely equivalent to the 2-port of Figure 6.4.

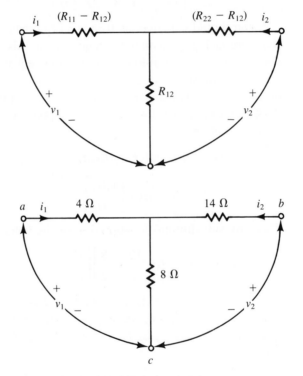

Figure 6.6
Equivalent T network.

Figure 6.7
Equivalent T network for
the 2-port of Example 6.1.

Next we look at the Norton-form CE for a passive-resistance 2-port. The general form for such equations is

$$\begin{bmatrix} i_1(t) \\ i_2(t) \end{bmatrix} = \begin{bmatrix} G_{11} & -G_{12} \\ -G_{21} & G_{22} \end{bmatrix} \begin{bmatrix} v_1(t) \\ v_2(t) \end{bmatrix} \tag{6.12}$$

or

$$\mathbf{i}(t) = \mathbf{G}\mathbf{v}(t) \tag{6.13}$$

For a 2-port network of 1-port resistors only, **G** in Equation 6.13 is symmetric, so $G_{21} = G_{12}$. We could have deduced this from the symmetry of the **R** matrix of Equation 6.3, since $\mathbf{G} = \mathbf{R}^{-1}$ and the inverse of a symmetric matrix is symmetric.

Let us examine Equation 6.12 for a means of conveniently determining the G-parameters in a manner quite analogous to the treatment of R-parameters. If we set $v_2 = 0$ (short-circuit port 2) and apply a voltage to port 1, we have

$$\begin{bmatrix} i_1 \\ i_2 \end{bmatrix} = \begin{bmatrix} G_{11} \\ -G_{21} \end{bmatrix} v_1 \tag{6.14}$$

$$G_{11} = \left. \frac{i_1}{v_1} \right|_{v_2=0}$$

and

$$-G_{21} = \left. \frac{i_2}{v_1} \right|_{v_2=0}$$

In a like manner if we set $v_1 = 0$ (short-circuit port 1), we have

$$\begin{bmatrix} i_1 \\ i_2 \end{bmatrix} = \begin{bmatrix} -G_{12} \\ G_{22} \end{bmatrix} v_2 \tag{6.15}$$

and

$$-G_{12} = \left. \frac{i_1}{v_2} \right|_{v_1=0}$$

$$G_{22} = \left. \frac{i_2}{v_2} \right|_{v_1=0}$$

Since $G_{21} = G_{12}$ for a passive-resistance 2-port, we have a check on the derivation (or measurement) involving this parameter. The G-parameters of Equation 6.12 are often called *short-circuit G-parameters* because of this procedure.

An example will serve to illustrate the derivation of the Norton-form CE by use of symbolic voltage sources. A general test diagram for this derivation is shown in Figure 6.8.

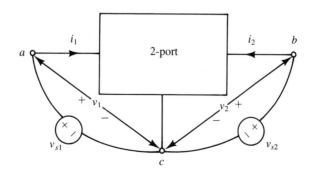

Figure 6.8
Test network for calculation of Norton-form 2-port component equations.

Example 6.2

The resistive 2-port network of Figure 6.4 is to be characterized by Norton-form CE. Symbolic voltage sources v_{s1} and v_{s2} are connected to form the test network shown in Figure 6.9. A star-tree is chosen, for convenience, to include the symbolic voltage sources. The dummy supernode equations for these voltage sources then form the basis for relating i_1 and i_2 to v_1 and v_2. These cutset equations are, in matrix form,

$$-\begin{bmatrix} i_{s1} \\ i_{s2} \end{bmatrix} = \begin{bmatrix} i_1 \\ i_2 \end{bmatrix} = \begin{bmatrix} -1 & 1 & 0 \\ 0 & 0 & 1 \end{bmatrix} \begin{bmatrix} i_3 \\ i_4 \\ i_6 \end{bmatrix} \tag{6.16}$$

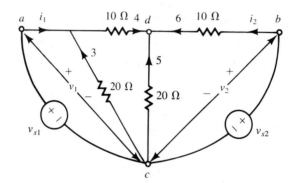

Figure 6.9
Test network for Example 6.2.

The other cutset equation leads to the node-voltage equation

$$(0.1 + 0.1 + 0.05)v_{dc} - 0.1v_{s1} - 0.1v_{s2} = 0$$

$$0.25v_{dc} = 0.1v_1 + 0.1v_2$$

$$v_5 = -0.4v_1 - 0.4v_2$$

Thus

$$v_3 = -v_1$$

$$v_4 = v_1 + v_5 = 0.6v_1 - 0.4v_2$$

$$v_6 = v_2 + v_5 = -0.4v_1 + 0.6v_2$$

and

$$\begin{bmatrix} i_3 \\ i_4 \\ i_6 \end{bmatrix} = \begin{bmatrix} -0.05 & 0 \\ 0.06 & -0.04 \\ -0.04 & 0.06 \end{bmatrix} \begin{bmatrix} v_1 \\ v_2 \end{bmatrix} \tag{6.17}$$

Substituting Equation 6.17 into Equation 6.16 yields the desired result:

$$\begin{bmatrix} i_1 \\ i_2 \end{bmatrix} = \begin{bmatrix} -1 & 1 & 0 \\ 0 & 0 & 1 \end{bmatrix} \begin{bmatrix} -0.05 & 0 \\ 0.06 & -0.04 \\ -0.04 & 0.06 \end{bmatrix} \begin{bmatrix} v_1 \\ v_2 \end{bmatrix}$$

$$\begin{bmatrix} i_1 \\ i_2 \end{bmatrix} = \begin{bmatrix} 0.11 & -0.04 \\ -0.04 & 0.06 \end{bmatrix} \begin{bmatrix} v_1 \\ v_2 \end{bmatrix} \tag{6.18}$$

There are several useful points to note about this derivation:

1. The **G** matrix of Equation 6.18 is symmetric. Thus one condition for correctness is satisfied.

2. The **G** of Equation 6.18 is the inverse of **R** of Equation 6.9. Thus we can find one from the other without a separate derivation.

3. The dummy KCL equations (Equation 6.16) were used for the Norton-form CE derivation to relate the port currents (negative of the symbolic voltage-source currents) to the link currents of the network. In the earlier derivation of the Thévenin-form CE, we used the dummy KVL equations (Equation 6.7) to relate the port voltages (negative of the symbolic current-source voltages) to the star-tree voltages of the network. This is, in fact, a general pattern for such derivations using symbolic sources for the nonexplicit variables (variables on the right-hand side of the equation).

As in the case of the Thévenin-form CE, a simple equivalent circuit can always be constructed for CE in Norton form for a passive resistance 2-port. Figure 6.10 indicates an equivalent π network in the general form for this type of 2-port. The negative signs in the **G** matrix of Equation 6.12 were arbitrarily chosen to make the common branch in the equivalent network G_{12} rather than $-G_{12}$. This agrees with the convention usually adopted by textbook authors.

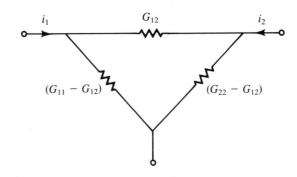

Figure 6.10
Equivalent π network.

Figure 6.11 is an equivalent π network for the 2-port of Example 6.2. As far as effects external to the 2-port are concerned, the network of Figure 6.11 is completely equivalent to both the original 2-port of Figure 6.4 and the equivalent T network of Figure 6.7.

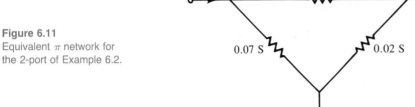

Figure 6.11
Equivalent π network for the 2-port of Example 6.2.

In three-phase power networks, the designations Y and Δ are equivalent to T and π, respectively.

6.3   Y-Δ Transformations

In calculations involving three-phase power networks it is sometimes advantageous to replace a Y-connected 2-port with a Δ-connected 2-port. For this and other reasons, the subject of Y-Δ transformations traditionally has been discussed in network theory textbooks. We include it primarily to illustrate and emphasize the general utility of the equivalent T (Y), and π (Δ) networks discussed in Section 6.2.

Figures 6.12 and 6.13 indicate general forms of the three-phase Y- and Δ-connections for resistive loads. The 2-port CE for the networks are most conveniently written in Thévenin and Norton form, respectively, as follows.

For the equivalent Y network:

$$\begin{bmatrix} v_1(t) \\ v_2(t) \end{bmatrix} = \begin{bmatrix} (R_1 + R_3) & R_3 \\ R_3 & (R_2 + R_3) \end{bmatrix} \begin{bmatrix} i_1(t) \\ i_2(t) \end{bmatrix} \tag{6.19}$$

$$\mathbf{v}(t) = \mathbf{R}\mathbf{i}(t) \tag{6.20}$$

For the equivalent Δ network:

$$\begin{bmatrix} i_1(t) \\ i_2(t) \end{bmatrix} = \begin{bmatrix} (G_a + G_c) & -G_c \\ -G_c & (G_b + G_c) \end{bmatrix} \begin{bmatrix} v_1(t) \\ v_2(t) \end{bmatrix} \tag{6.21}$$

$$\mathbf{i}(t) = \mathbf{G}\mathbf{v}(t) \tag{6.22}$$

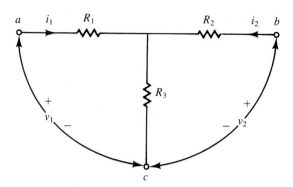

Figure 6.12
Resistive Y (T) network.

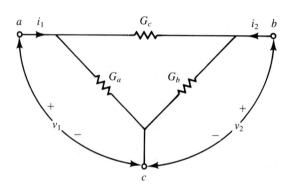

Figure 6.13
Resistive Δ (π) network.

Once we have written the 2-port CE in the forms of Equations 6.19 and 6.21, it is clear that to find the parameters of the Δ network, given the Y network parameters, we simply need to invert $\mathbf{R}$ to find $\mathbf{G}$ in terms of R_1, R_2, and R_3 and then equate terms. The inverse operation yields $\mathbf{R}$ in terms of G_a, G_b, and G_c. You should note, as a convenient memory device, that R_3 and G_c were chosen to be the parameters common to both ports.

To derive the G-parameters in terms of the R-parameters, we note that

$$\mathbf{R}^{-1} = \frac{1}{R_1 R_2 + R_2 R_3 + R_3 R_1} \begin{bmatrix} (R_2 + R_3) & -R_3 \\ -R_3 & (R_1 + R_3) \end{bmatrix} \tag{6.23}$$

Equating terms in Equations 6.23 and 6.21, we have the following results:

$$G_c = \frac{R_3}{R_1 R_2 + R_2 R_3 + R_3 R_1} \tag{6.24}$$

$$G_a = \frac{R_2}{R_1 R_2 + R_2 R_3 + R_3 R_1} \tag{6.25}$$

$$G_b = \frac{R_1}{R_1 R_2 + R_2 R_3 + R_3 R_1} \tag{6.26}$$

To derive the R-parameters in terms of the G-parameters, we use the inverse derivation

$$\mathbf{G}^{-1} = \frac{1}{G_aG_b + G_bG_c + G_cG_a} \begin{bmatrix} (G_b + G_c) & G_c \\ G_c & (G_a + G_c) \end{bmatrix} \tag{6.27}$$

By equating terms in Equations 6.27 and 6.19, we have results that are strikingly similar to those previously derived:

$$R_3 = \frac{G_c}{G_aG_b + G_bG_c + G_cG_a} \tag{6.28}$$

$$R_1 = \frac{G_b}{G_aG_b + G_bG_c + G_cG_a} \tag{6.29}$$

$$R_2 = \frac{G_a}{G_aG_b + G_bG_c + G_cG_a} \tag{6.30}$$

The symmetry of the transformation makes it relatively simple to recall the formulas in Equations 6.24–6.26 and Equations 6.28–6.30 from memory, and many professors urge their students to be able to do so. Given the numerical parameters for either the Y or the Δ network, however, it is probably simpler to write the appropriate parameter matrix and invert it to find the parameters of the other.

Example 6.3

Given the equivalent Y network of Example 6.1 (Figure 6.7), we have the Thévenin-form CE

$$\begin{bmatrix} v_1(t) \\ v_2(t) \end{bmatrix} = \begin{bmatrix} 12 & 8 \\ 8 & 22 \end{bmatrix} \begin{bmatrix} i_1(t) \\ i_2(t) \end{bmatrix} \tag{6.31}$$

If we solve Equation 6.31 for $\mathbf{i}(t)$, the result is

$$\begin{bmatrix} i_1(t) \\ i_2(t) \end{bmatrix} = \frac{1}{200} \begin{bmatrix} 22 & -8 \\ -8 & 12 \end{bmatrix} \begin{bmatrix} v_1(t) \\ v_2(t) \end{bmatrix}$$

$$\begin{bmatrix} i_1(t) \\ i_2(t) \end{bmatrix} = \begin{bmatrix} 0.11 & -0.04 \\ -0.04 & 0.06 \end{bmatrix} \begin{bmatrix} v_1(t) \\ v_2(t) \end{bmatrix} \tag{6.32}$$

To find the equivalent Δ network now, we note that

$$G_c = 0.04 \text{ S} \qquad (R_c = 25 \ \Omega)$$
$$G_a + G_c = 0.11 \text{ S}$$
$$G_a = 0.07 \text{ S} \qquad (R_a = 14.286 \ \Omega)$$
$$G_b + G_c = 0.06 \text{ S}$$
$$G_b = 0.02 \text{ S} \qquad (R_b = 50 \ \Omega)$$

We recognize that the Norton-form CE of Equation 6.32, which was derived by matrix inversion, is identical to Equation 6.18, which was derived from the original 2-port network using symbolic sources. The equivalent Δ network is, therefore, that of Figure 6.11. A similar development will yield the R-parameters for the equivalent Y network when the Δ network is known.

As a further point of interest, we note that the power obtained by summing up the powers associated with all the branches of an equivalent network is identical to that calculated by

$$p(t) = v_1(t)i_1(t) + v_2(t)i_2(t)$$

using the variables of the network ports.

Example 6.4

For the network of Example 6.3 we wish to find $p(t)$ in terms of $i_1(t)$ and $i_2(t)$ using the equivalent Y network.

For

$$
\begin{aligned}
R_1, \quad &p_1(t) = 4i_1^2 \\
R_2, \quad &p_2(t) = 14i_2^2 \\
R_3, \quad &p_3(t) = 8(i_1 + i_2)^2 \\
& = 8i_1^2 + 16i_1i_2 + 8i_2^2
\end{aligned}
$$

The total power is thus

$$p(t) = 12i_1^2 + 16i_1i_2 + 22i_2^2$$

which checks Equation 6.11 of Example 6.2. Equation 6.11 was derived from the definition of 2-port power,

$$p(t) = v_1(t)i_1(t) + v_2(t)i_2(t)$$

and the CE derived for the example network.

6.4   EQUIVALENT *T* AND π NETWORKS FOR ACTIVE 2-PORTS

For 1-port active resistance subnetworks, we observed that if the component equation is written in the form

$$v(t) = R_T i(t) + e_T(t) \tag{6.33}$$

the Thévenin equivalent network is easily obtained by placing a resistance R_T in series with a voltage source $e_T(t)$ and orienting the equivalent network to agree with $e_T(t)$. In like manner the Norton equivalent network for a 1-port with component equation

$$i(t) = G_N v(t) + i_N(t) \qquad (6.34)$$

can be realized by placing a conductance G_N in parallel with a current source $i_N(t)$ and orienting the equivalent 1-port to agree with $i_N(t)$. For these reasons we defined Equations 6.33 and 6.34 as the Thévenin-form and the Norton-form of the component equation, respectively. We have noted that the terms *Thévenin-form* and *Norton-form*, while not as useful, are still valid designations for Equations 6.33 and 6.34, respectively, even though the $e_T(t)$ and the $i_N(t)$ are zero.

For 2-port components the situation is a bit more complicated. Since we have two component equations relating four terminal variables, we have the possibility of solving for six different pairs of variables in terms of the alternate pair rather than the two different explicit variables possible in Equations 6.33 and 6.34.

In this section we continue to confine our discussion to 2-port CE that are solved explicitly in terms of the two voltage variables or in terms of the two current variables. In the first case the component equations in matrix form are written as

$$\begin{bmatrix} v_1(t) \\ v_2(t) \end{bmatrix} = \begin{bmatrix} R_{11} & R_{12} \\ R_{21} & R_{22} \end{bmatrix} \begin{bmatrix} i_1(t) \\ i_2(t) \end{bmatrix} + \begin{bmatrix} e_{T1}(t) \\ e_{T2}(t) \end{bmatrix} \qquad (6.35)$$

By definition, if subscripts 1 and 2 are taken to signify the input and output of the 2-port, respectively, R_{11} is called the *input resistance* and R_{22} is called the *output resistance*. The other resistances, R_{12} and R_{21}, are called *transfer resistances*. This terminology applies only to the open-circuit parameters—that is, the parameters defined by the Thévenin form of the CE.

For a given 2-port network, the Thévenin-form component equations can be calculated by applying two symbolic current sources, as shown in Figure 6.3, and solving for $v_1(t)$ and $v_2(t)$. A similar approach can be used in the laboratory to determine the R values and source-voltage values experimentally. In the latter case a logical procedure for the special case of constants e_{T1} and e_{T2} is to set $i_1(t) = i_2(t) = 0$ (open circuit) first and determine e_{T1} and e_{T2} by measurement. Then i_2 can be set to zero by open-circuiting terminals b and c, and a current source i_1 can be applied between a and c. Then R_{11} and R_{21} could be determined as

$$R_{11} = \left. \frac{v_1 - e_{T1}}{i_1} \right|_{i_2=0}$$

$$R_{21} = \left. \frac{v_2 - e_{T2}}{i_1} \right|_{i_2=0}$$

In a similar way R_{22} and R_{12} can be determined by setting $i_1 = 0$ and applying a current source i_2 between b and c. Then we have

$$R_{12} = \left.\frac{v_1 - e_{T1}}{i_2}\right|_{i_1=0}$$

$$R_{22} = \left.\frac{v_2 - e_{T2}}{i_2}\right|_{i_1=0}$$

In Section 6.2 we noted that the R-parameters for passive resistance networks are often called open-circuit parameters. The same terminology is also used for the R-parameters associated with active resistance 2-ports.

The problem becomes more complicated if e_{T1} and e_{T2} are not constant, but this procedure illustrates a general strategy that can be used to obtain the 2-port component equations.

Just as for the passive case, an equivalent T network is always easy to construct for an active resistance 2-port made up of 1-port components—once the Thévenin-form CE are known. Figure 6.14 illustrates the general form of equivalent networks for this type of 2-port. The placement of the voltage sources is somewhat arbitrary, since the common leg of the T could also be utilized for any voltage source common to the two ports. The T network shown, however, will always work and is as simple as any.

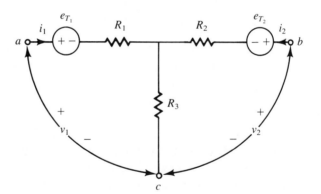

Figure 6.14
Equivalent T (Y) network for an active resistance 2-port.

The determination of Norton-form component equations for a resistive 2-port follows a line of reasoning similar to that for the Thévenin-form equations. In this case the CE have the form

$$\begin{bmatrix} i_1(t) \\ i_2(t) \end{bmatrix} = \begin{bmatrix} G_{11} & -G_{12} \\ -G_{21} & G_{22} \end{bmatrix}\begin{bmatrix} v_1(t) \\ v_2(t) \end{bmatrix} + \begin{bmatrix} i_{N1}(t) \\ i_{N2}(t) \end{bmatrix} \tag{6.36}$$

It follows that the G-parameters in Equation 6.36 can be found by applying two symbolic voltage sources, as shown in Figure 6.8, and solving for $i_1(t)$ and $i_2(t)$.

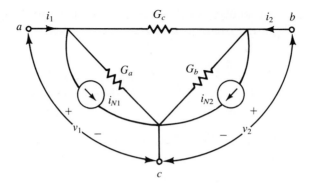

Figure 6.15
Equivalent π (Δ) network
for an active resistance
2-port.

In the laboratory the Norton-form CE can also be determined experimentally (at least theoretically) by short-circuiting both ports simultaneously through ammeters to determine values for i_{N1} and i_{N2}. Then v_1 and v_2 can alternately be set to zero and a voltage source applied to the alternate port. If i_{N1} and i_{N2} are constant, we can then determine the G-parameters by measuring i_1 and i_2 and solving the resulting Equation 6.36.

$$G_{11} = \left.\frac{i_1 - i_{N1}}{v_1}\right|_{v_2=0}$$

$$-G_{21} = \left.\frac{i_2 - i_{N2}}{v_1}\right|_{v_2=0}$$

$$-G_{12} = \left.\frac{i_1 - i_{N1}}{v_2}\right|_{v_1=0}$$

$$G_{22} = \left.\frac{i_2 - i_{N2}}{v_2}\right|_{v_1=0}$$

If i_{N1} and i_{N2} are not constant, the G-parameters for an active 2-port are more difficult to determine in the laboratory.

In the discussion on open-circuit parameters, we defined the terms *input resistance, output resistance,* and *transfer resistance.* Associated with the short-circuit parameters are the analogous terms *input conductance* (G_{11}), *output conductance* (G_{22}), and *transfer conductance* (G_{12} and G_{21}). This terminology is applied only to the parameters defined by the Norton form of the CE.

Example 6.5

Suppose we are given that the CE for an active resistance 2-port are

$$\begin{bmatrix} v_1 \\ v_2 \end{bmatrix} = \begin{bmatrix} 5 & 3 \\ 3 & 4 \end{bmatrix}\begin{bmatrix} i_1 \\ i_2 \end{bmatrix} + \begin{bmatrix} 10 \\ 5 \end{bmatrix} \tag{6.37}$$

An equivalent T network can be drawn from inspection of Equation 6.37, and one is shown in Figure 6.16(a). When Equation 6.37 is solved for the currents, we have

$$\begin{bmatrix} i_1 \\ i_2 \end{bmatrix} = \begin{bmatrix} 0.3636 & -0.2727 \\ -0.2727 & 0.4545 \end{bmatrix} \begin{bmatrix} v_1 \\ v_2 \end{bmatrix} + \begin{bmatrix} -2.272 \\ 0.4545 \end{bmatrix} \tag{6.38}$$

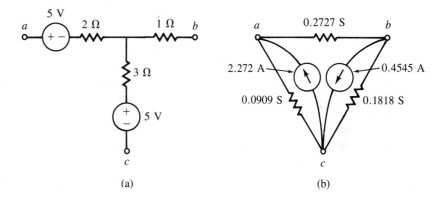

Figure 6.16
Equivalent networks for Example 6.5.

An equivalent π network can be drawn from inspection of Equation 6.38, as shown in Figure 6.16(b). Note that various combinations of sources could be used in both equivalent networks.

Example 6.6

We have an active resistive 2-port for which the CE are given as

$$\begin{bmatrix} i_1 \\ i_2 \end{bmatrix} = \begin{bmatrix} 0.15 & -0.1 \\ -0.1 & 0.14 \end{bmatrix} \begin{bmatrix} v_1 \\ v_2 \end{bmatrix} + \begin{bmatrix} 2 \\ 1 \end{bmatrix} \tag{6.39}$$

An equivalent π network can be drawn from inspection of Equation 6.39 (Figure 6.17(a)). When Equation 6.39 is solved for the voltages, we have

$$\begin{bmatrix} v_1 \\ v_2 \end{bmatrix} = \begin{bmatrix} 12.727 & 9.091 \\ 9.091 & 13.636 \end{bmatrix} \begin{bmatrix} i_1 \\ i_2 \end{bmatrix} - \begin{bmatrix} 34.545 \\ 31.818 \end{bmatrix} \tag{6.40}$$

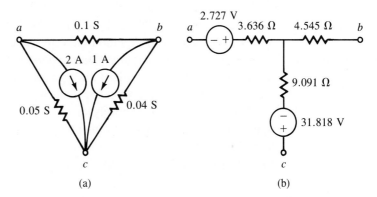

Figure 6.17
Equivalent networks for Example 6.6.

An equivalent T network can be drawn from inspection of Equation 6.40, as shown in Figure 6.17(b). Equations 6.39 and 6.40 could be satisfied by various other source combinations in the equivalent networks.

6.5   EQUIVALENT HYBRID NETWORKS FOR ACTIVE 2-PORTS

In the preceding sections we have discussed 2-ports made up only of 1-port resistances (passive) or 1-port resistances and independent sources. For these cases, it is possible to use either 2-port Thévenin-form or Norton-form CE and to formulate a simple T or π equivalent network. Unfortunately, all electrical 2-ports cannot be satisfactorily represented by CE that are explicit in either the terminal voltages or the currents. Thus we have need for mixed-variable, or hybrid, CE. These, in turn, lead to hybrid equivalent networks.

For example, a transistor used in a stereo amplifier is likely to be modeled at low frequencies with CE of the form

$$\begin{bmatrix} v_1 \\ i_2 \end{bmatrix} = \begin{bmatrix} h_{11} & h_{12} \\ h_{21} & h_{22} \end{bmatrix}\begin{bmatrix} i_1 \\ v_2 \end{bmatrix} \tag{6.41}$$

Figure 6.18 shows the relationship between transistor variables and standard 2-port voltage and current variables.

Figure 6.18
(a) Schematic symbol for a common-emitter NPN transistor with standard 2-port variables.
(b) General 2-port representation for the same transistor. b, c, and e at the terminals designate base, collector, and emitter, respectively.

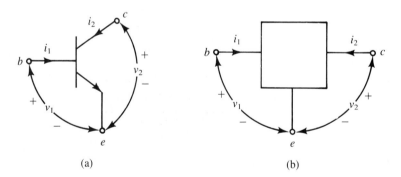

(a)   (b)

The coefficients in Equation 6.41 are called the *hybrid h-parameters*, and for our discussion we assume that the parameters are constant. For CE in this form, an equivalent network of the type illustrated in Figure 6.19 can be drawn directly from the equations using controlled voltage and current sources.

The measurement of purely open-circuit or short-circuit parameters for a transistor is relatively difficult in comparison to laboratory determination of the hybrid h-parameters. This is the primary motivation for using hybrid-form CE for transistor modeling. Unfortunately, an equivalent 2-port network for the

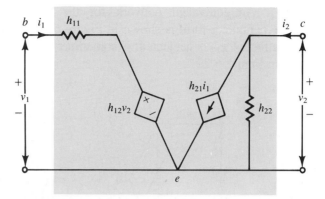

Figure 6.19
Equivalent hybrid
h-parameter 2-port
network.

transistor hybrid *h*-parameter model involves a slight complication in comparison with equivalent networks for the open-circuit and short-circuit parameters. The voltage-controlled voltage source and current-controlled current sources were defined primarily for this application.

As a matter of fact, these two types of controlled sources are simple examples of 2-port components (although we did not treat them as such in Chapter 2) for which the CE are in hybrid form. A demonstration of this is given as a problem.

In many cases h_{12} can be neglected without seriously affecting the validity of the transistor model, and this is often done. For this model the equivalent network becomes that of Figure 6.20.

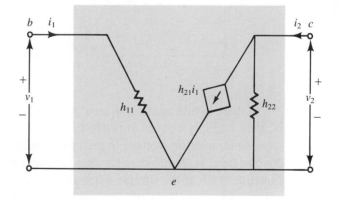

Figure 6.20
Equivalent hybrid
h-parameter 2-port
network.

An alternate means of writing the CE in mixed-variable (or hybrid) form is called the *hybrid g-parameter model*. These equations are the inverse of Equation 6.41 and are written as

$$\begin{bmatrix} i_1 \\ v_2 \end{bmatrix} = \begin{bmatrix} g_{11} & g_{12} \\ g_{21} & g_{22} \end{bmatrix} \begin{bmatrix} v_1 \\ i_2 \end{bmatrix} \tag{6.42}$$

An equivalent network for the general form of the CE in hybrid g-parameter form is shown in Figure 6.21. A simplified model, in which the effect of g_{12} is neglected, is sometimes used. An equivalent network is shown in Figure 6.22.

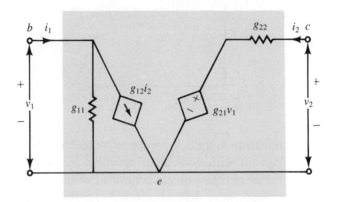

Figure 6.21
Equivalent hybrid
g-parameter 2-port
network.

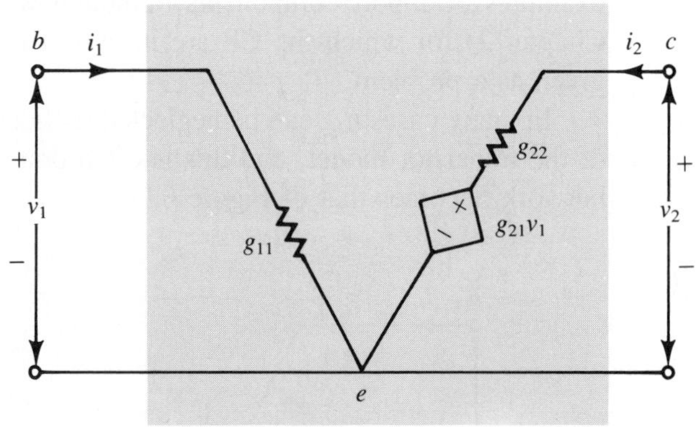

Figure 6.22
Equivalent hybrid
g-parameter 2-port
network.

In these hybrid models, h_{11} and g_{22} have the dimension of resistance. That is, they multiply current to produce voltage. Coefficients g_{11} and h_{22}, on the other hand, multiply voltage to produce current and thus have the dimension of conductance. It should be clear that Equation 6.42 can be found by inverting Equation 6.41, if the inverse exists, and vice versa.

Example 6.7

The hybrid-h CE for a common-emitter transistor have been determined by measurement as

$$\begin{bmatrix} v_1 \\ i_2 \end{bmatrix} = \begin{bmatrix} 800 & 0 \\ 28 & 10^{-5} \end{bmatrix} \begin{bmatrix} i_1 \\ v_2 \end{bmatrix} \tag{6.43}$$

The hybrid h-parameter equivalent 2-port network is shown in Figure 6.23. We can get a hybrid g-parameter model for the transistor by solving Equation 6.43 for i_1 and v_2 to obtain Equation 6.44.

$$\begin{bmatrix} i_1 \\ v_2 \end{bmatrix} = \begin{bmatrix} 1.25 \times 10^{-3} & 0 \\ -3.50 \times 10^3 & 10^5 \end{bmatrix} \begin{bmatrix} v_1 \\ i_2 \end{bmatrix} \tag{6.44}$$

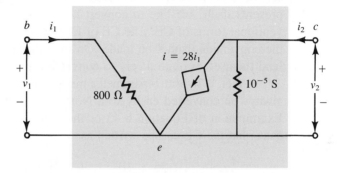

Figure 6.23
Equivalent hybrid
h-parameter network for
the transistor of Example
6.7.

The equivalent network is shown in Figure 6.24.

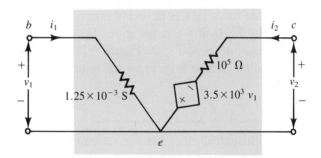

Figure 6.24
Equivalent hybrid
g-parameter network for
the transistor of Example
6.7.

The hybrid g-parameter representation is generally not as useful as the hybrid h-parameter model because it obscures the relationship between i_1 and i_2. In many applications a transistor is viewed as a current-amplifying device, and a model obtained by neglecting the current through the conductance h_{22} is often satisfactory. For this approximation the hybrid h-parameter model is, in general,

$$\begin{bmatrix} v_1 \\ i_2 \end{bmatrix} = \begin{bmatrix} h_{11} & 0 \\ h_{21} & 0 \end{bmatrix} \begin{bmatrix} i_1 \\ v_2 \end{bmatrix} \tag{6.45}$$

For this example, the model is

$$\begin{bmatrix} v_1 \\ i_2 \end{bmatrix} = \begin{bmatrix} 800 \\ 28 \end{bmatrix} i_1 \tag{6.46}$$

The model represented by Equation 6.46 is that of a current-controlled current source. In the next section we shall examine the error caused by this approximation when the transistor is included in a simple network.

In general, we prefer to not use hybrid-form CE in network modeling if a suitable alternative exists. The reason is simple. With hybrid CE involved in the network PRIMM, neither the loop-current nor the node-voltage formulation can be used to obtain a secondary model. Therefore, when the opportunity presents itself, we like to convert hybrid equations to one of the more conventional forms of CE. The CE of Equation 6.46 represent an example where the conversion cannot be made. On the other hand, the CE of Equation 6.43 lend themselves quite nicely to conversion to Norton form.

In fact, a hybrid h-parameter model, in which only h_{12} is neglected, can always be converted easily to a Norton-form model, and this is often done. Examination of Equation 6.43 or the equivalent network (Figure 6.23) indicates that the CE can be written as

$$\begin{bmatrix} i_1 \\ i_2 \end{bmatrix} = \begin{bmatrix} 1.25 \times 10^{-3} & 0 \\ 3.50 \times 10^{-2} & 10^{-5} \end{bmatrix} \begin{bmatrix} v_1 \\ v_2 \end{bmatrix} \tag{6.47}$$

In this form the CE fit nicely into node-voltage formulation, and thus we can avoid the hybrid complication. We could sketch an equivalent network, but there is no need for it. Figure 6.23 is the equivalent network, except for a possible change from input resistance to input conductance.

Example 6.8

To illustrate further the derivation of hybrid-form CE, we next examine the passive resistance network of Example 6.1. You should note that this is not a practical application of hybrid modeling. We are quite content to have CE in the form of Equation 6.9 or 6.18. The calculations presented here, however, are quite generally applicable and should be useful to illustrate the method.

We can begin with CE in either Thévenin or Norton form or with one of the equivalent networks. For this example we choose Equation 6.9 of Example 6.1.

$$\begin{bmatrix} v_1 \\ v_2 \end{bmatrix} = \begin{bmatrix} 12 & 8 \\ 8 & 22 \end{bmatrix} \begin{bmatrix} i_1 \\ i_2 \end{bmatrix} \tag{6.9}$$

Next we rewrite the equation to segregate the variables into v_1, i_2 and i_1, v_2.

$$\begin{bmatrix} 1 & -8 \\ 0 & -22 \end{bmatrix} \begin{bmatrix} v_1 \\ i_2 \end{bmatrix} = \begin{bmatrix} 12 & 0 \\ 8 & -1 \end{bmatrix} \begin{bmatrix} i_1 \\ v_2 \end{bmatrix} \tag{6.48}$$

Solving Equation 6.48, we get the hybrid h-parameter CE.

$$\begin{bmatrix} v_1 \\ i_2 \end{bmatrix} = \frac{1}{22}\begin{bmatrix} 200 & 8 \\ -8 & 1 \end{bmatrix}\begin{bmatrix} i_1 \\ v_2 \end{bmatrix}$$

$$= \begin{bmatrix} 9.09 & 0.364 \\ -0.364 & 4.55 \end{bmatrix} \times 10^{-2}\begin{bmatrix} i_1 \\ v_2 \end{bmatrix} \tag{6.49}$$

Although this 2-port is purely resistive, we need two controlled sources to synthesize an equivalent network. Figure 6.25 indicates the equivalent network that would result from inspection of Equation 6.49.

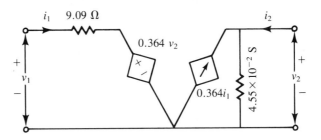

Figure 6.25
Equivalent hybrid h-parameter network for the 2-port of Example 6.8.

The widely different characteristics of the three equivalent networks shown in Figures 6.7, 6.11, and 6.25 should make evident the nonuniqueness of equivalent networks in general. It is useful to note, however, that for purely resistive three-terminal 2-ports, the three-element equivalent T network is unique, as is the three-element equivalent π network. The values of the 1-ports in the equivalent networks are not affected by which port variables are used to define them. Thus the equivalent network is a convenient device to use in transforming 2-port CE from one set of port variables to another.

6.6 THE OP AMP

The age of highly sophisticated techniques for the fabrication of integrated circuits has spawned many new electronic devices. The electronic-network designer now has available a wide array of special-purpose networks of transistors, resistors, capacitors, and so on, which are manufactured on a single chip. Advances in fabrication techniques have resulted in extremely compact, highly reliable, inexpensive devices. One such device is the operational amplifier (op amp).

The name *operational amplifier* was first applied to the electronic amplifiers used in analog computers to perform mathematical operations such as summing, multiplication by a constant, and integration. The modern, solid-state version has become the basic building block in the design of networks for a broad range of applications such as amplification, filtering, signal shaping, signal generation, and switching. Because of its wide application, this device is a key component in the study of electric network analysis.

The network designer is primarily interested in the external, or terminal, characteristics of the integrated-circuit devices available. We shall follow this lead and concentrate our study on the *ideal* model of the op amp and its use as a component in electronic networks. A study of the design and fabrication of the device itself will be left to courses in electronics.

From a terminal standpoint, the symbol of the op amp is seen in Figure 6.26. From this figure we see that this device is in fact a 3-port, having two input terminals, *a* and *b*, and an output terminal, *c*. Thus if the ground, or reference, terminal is common to both the input and the output, terminals *a* and *b* form two input ports and terminal *c* forms an output port.

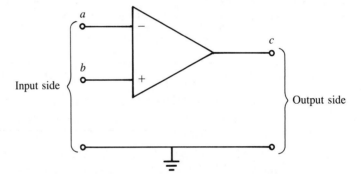

Figure 6.26
Symbol for ideal op amp.

An equivalent network of the ideal op amp, which is suitable for our purposes, is shown in Figure 6.27. As previously stated, we shall not concern ourselves with how the equivalent network comes about, but only with its behavior in electric networks. Of course, the ideal model is not completely attainable. However, the ideal model and the equivalent network are adequate

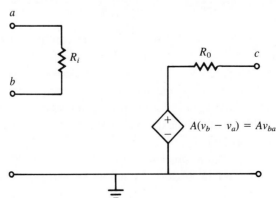

Figure 6.27
Equivalent network for ideal op amp.

for a wide range of applications. The nonideal properties of actual amplifiers will be left to more advanced studies.

The desired characteristics of the ideal model are summarized in Table 6.1.

Table 6.1
Desirable
Characteristics of
Ideal Op Amp

1. The voltage gain, A, is positive and very large (10^6 to 10^8).

2. The input resistance, R_i, is very high (typical values achieved in practice are on the order of 2 MΩ).

3. The ouput resistance, R_o, is relatively small (typical value is on the order of 100 Ω or less).

Example 6.9
(A basic
inverting
network)

One of the most useful op-amp circuits is shown in Figure 6.28. The equivalent network is shown in Figure 6.29 with typical values chosen for R_i and R_o. Let us calculate the output voltage v_o as a function of the input v_i.

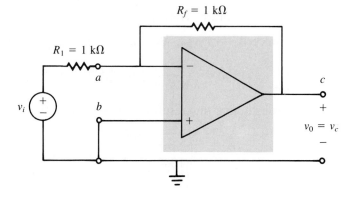

Figure 6.28
Basic inverting network.

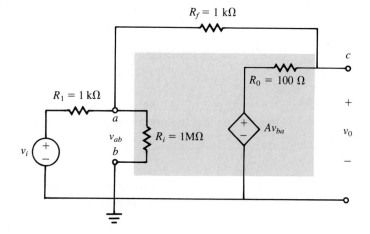

Figure 6.29
Equivalent network.

Utilizing the linear graph of Figure 6.30, the nodal equations at nodes a and c are

$$\frac{v_{ab} - v_i}{1000} + \frac{v_{ab}}{10^6} + \frac{v_{ab} - v_o}{1000} = 0 \tag{6.50}$$

$$\frac{v_o - Av_{ba}}{100} + \frac{v_o - v_{ab}}{1000} = 0 \tag{6.51}$$

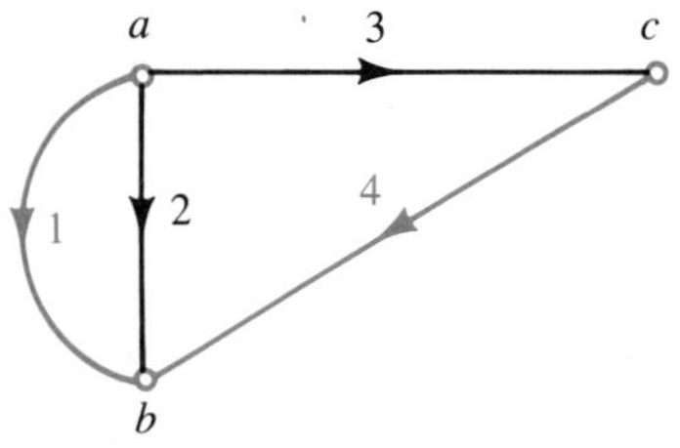

Figure 6.30
Linear graph for the network.

For convenience, we have utilized $v_{cb} = v_o$ in these equations.

Rewriting Equation 6.51 we have

$$10v_o - 10Av_{ba} + v_o - v_{ab} = 0 \tag{6.52}$$

Since $v_{ba} = -v_{ab}$, we can solve for v_{ab} to obtain

$$v_{ab} = \left(\frac{-11}{10A - 1}\right)v_o \tag{6.53}$$

Substituting this result into Equation 6.50 and solving for v_o, we obtain

$$v_o = -\left(\frac{1000}{1000 + \dfrac{2.2 \times 10^4}{10A - 1}}\right)v_i \tag{6.54}$$

$$= -\left(\frac{1}{1 + \dfrac{22}{10A - 1}}\right)v_i$$

Because we have assumed that $A \geq 10^6$, this reduces with good approximation to

$$v_o = -v_i \tag{6.55}$$

Thus we see that the output will always be the negative (inverse) of the input.

Although the use of numbers rather than symbols gives us a more inviting example, it does tend to obscure an important characteristic of this network.

However, the astute reader may have already concluded that the result is dependent only upon the values of the resistors R_1 and R_f. This is, in fact, true.

In retrospect, we can argue from physical reasoning that if

$$R_o \ll R_1 \ll R_i$$

and

$$R_o \ll R_f \ll R_i$$

then the value of R_o can be considered to be negligibly small and replaced by a short circuit. Likewise, the value of R_i is very large and can be approximated by an open circuit. These ideas are exploited in the next example.

Example 6.10

In the network of Figure 6.29, suppose we replace R_i and R_o by open and short circuits, respectively, and represent R_1 and R_f symbolically. The result is the approximate equivalent network shown in Figure 6.31. Nodal analysis readily yields the result that

$$v_o \approx -\left(\frac{R_f}{R_1}\right) v_i \tag{6.56}$$

Verification of the result is given as a problem.

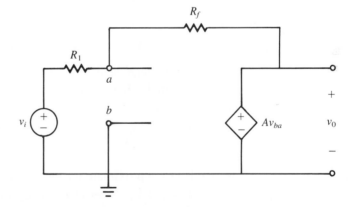

Figure 6.31
Approximate equivalent network.

The terminology *inverting network* arises because of the negative sign in the result shown by Equation 6.56. Further, we note that the gain (R_f/R_1) of the amplifier is independent of the gain, A, as long as A is very high.

If, as in the last example, we make the approximations that R_i is infinite and R_o is zero, we obtain the approximate equivalent network for the op amp shown in Figure 6.32. This approximate equivalent network can be used, with acceptable accuracy, for any application for which the external resistors at the

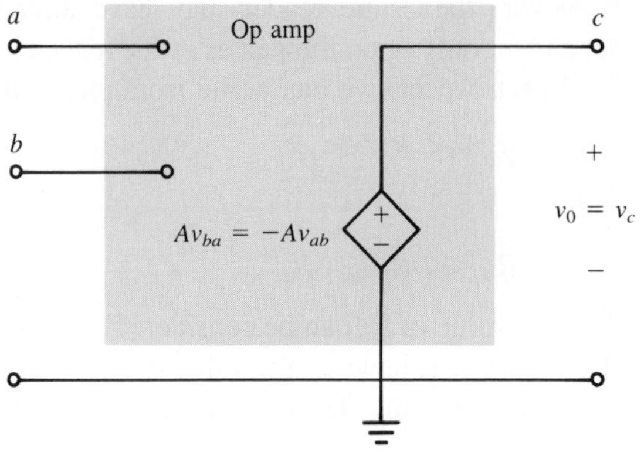

Figure 6.32
Approximate equivalent
network of ideal op amp.

input side do not exceed 100 kΩ and resistors on the output side are large compared to 100 Ω. In what follows, we shall often use the approximate equivalent network. However, we can always utilize the more accurate model of Figure 6.27 when the accuracy of the approximate model is in doubt.

Ues of the approximate model of Figure 6.32 leads us to two additional simplifications:

1. The current flow into the op amp at terminals a and b is assumed to be zero since the input resistance is modeled as infinite.

2. Since

$$v_o = -Av_{ab}$$

the output voltage is independent of what is connected to the output terminals. It is controlled by the dependent source. Furthermore, since

$$v_{ab} = -\frac{1}{A}v_o$$

we are led to approximate v_{ab} by zero since A approaches infinity and v_o is typically constrained to operate between ± 10 V. For example, in Example 6.9 calculation of v_{ab} from Equation 6.53 with $v_o = 10$ V and $A = 10^7$ yields $v_{ab} = -1.1 \times 10^{-6}$ V $= -1.1$ μV.

We now consider an additional example of the application of the op amp.

Example 6.11

Consider the op-amp network of Figure 6.33. Utilizing the approximate op-amp equivalent network, we obtain the network of Figure 6.34 and the linear

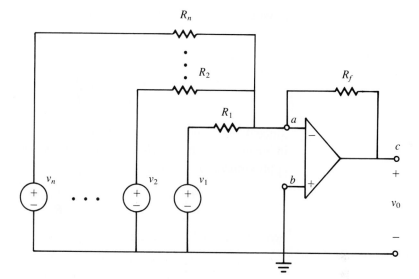

Figure 6.33
Op amp network for
Example 6.11.

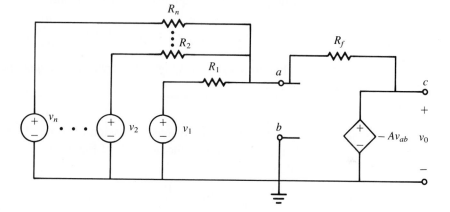

Figure 6.34
Approximate equivalent
network for Example 6.11.

graph of Figure 6.35. Writing the nodal equation at node a, we obtain

$$\frac{v_{ab} - v_1}{R_1} + \frac{v_{ab} - v_2}{R_2} + \cdots$$

$$+ \frac{v_{ab} - v_n}{R_n} + \frac{v_{ab} - (-Av_{ab})}{R_f} = 0 \qquad (6.57)$$

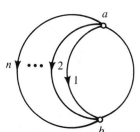

Figure 6.35
Linear graph for Example
6.11.

Single element representing R_f
in series with VCVS

Rewriting this equation, we obtain

$$\left(\frac{1}{R_1} + \frac{1}{R_2} + \cdots + \frac{1}{R_n} + \frac{1+A}{R_f}\right)v_{ab}$$

$$= \frac{v_1}{R_1} + \frac{v_2}{R_2} + \cdots + \frac{v_n}{R_n} \qquad (6.58)$$

Since $A \gg 1$ and we expect that $R_1, R_2, \ldots, R_n$, and R_f are roughly the same in magnitude, the result of solving Equation 6.58 for v_{ab} is very closely approximated by

$$v_{ab} = \frac{R_f}{A}\left(\frac{v_1}{R_1} + \frac{v_1}{R_2} + \cdots + \frac{v_n}{R_n}\right) \qquad (6.59)$$

From Figure 6.34 we write

$$v_o = -Av_{ab}$$

Substituting into Equation 6.59, we obtain

$$v_o = -\left(\frac{R_f}{R_1}v_1 + \frac{R_f}{R_2}v_2 + \cdots + \frac{R_f}{R_n}v_n\right) \qquad (6.60)$$

This network is very aptly referred to as a *summing network*.

We close our current discussion of some of the basic op-amp networks by calling attention to the network of Figure 6.36. Without development we state that

$$v_o = \left(\frac{R_1 + R_f}{R_1}\right)v_i \qquad (6.61)$$

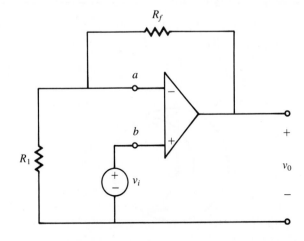

Figure 6.36
Basic noninverting
network.

This network is known as the *basic noninverting network*. For fairly obvious reasons the terminal *a* is universally called the *inverting terminal* and terminal *b* is called the *noninverting terminal*.

In this introduction of the op amp as a network component, you have been asked to accept an idealized model and its equivalent network on faith. We have examined the behavior of this device in several network configurations and have acquired some appreciation for its flexibility as a network component. As we progress in the study of network theory, we shall find many occasions to utilize the equivalent networks of this section. It might be well to place these in our readily accessible memory bank.

When the equivalent network of the op amp was first introduced, we were faced with an imposing 3-port component. As we worked through our study of this device, however, we began to realize that it does not pose a serious problem. Once it is interconnected into a network, it invariably reduces to an interconnection of two or three 1-ports, our old friends, the resistor and the voltage-controlled voltage source.

6.7 ANALYSIS OF NETWORKS CONTAINING 2-PORTS

In the preceding sections of this chapter, we have considered the problem of modeling several of the most common types of 2-port network components. Our emphasis has been on the development of an equivalent network (we hope in the simplest possible form) which, for purpose of analysis, can replace the 2-port in any network situation that does not violate the assumptions on which the model is based.

For any 2-port made up of resistances only, the unnecessary complication of an equivalent network with controlled sources should be avoided. In general, equivalent networks based on open-circuit or short-circuit parameters are preferable to those based on hybrid parameters. In this case, either loop or nodal analysis can be used.

To illustrate the use of equivalent networks, we now consider four examples.

Example 6.12

The Norton-form matrix CE for the 2-port of the network of Figure 6.37 is

$$\begin{bmatrix} i_6 \\ i_7 \end{bmatrix} = \begin{bmatrix} 0.01 & -0.005 \\ -0.005 & 0.02 \end{bmatrix} \begin{bmatrix} v_6 \\ v_7 \end{bmatrix} \tag{6.62}$$

Suppose we want to find v_5 as a function of v_1. We could simply write one node equation at node *b* and substitute all CE into it, finally writing all voltages in terms of v_1 and v_5. No equivalent network for the 2-port is needed. (Note that the port voltages v_6 and v_7 are equal to v_4 and v_5, respectively.)

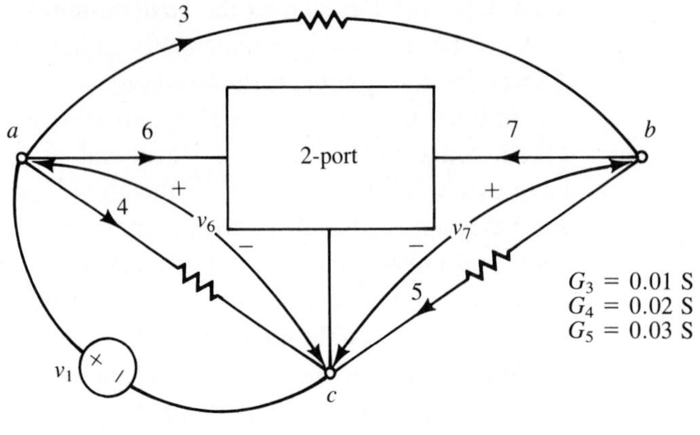

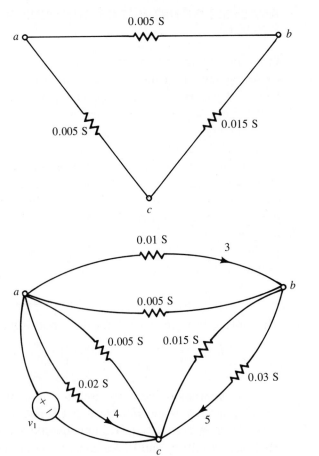

Figure 6.37
Resistive network of
Example 6.12.

$G_3 = 0.01$ S
$G_4 = 0.02$ S
$G_5 = 0.03$ S

We are, however, interested in demonstrating the use of equivalent networks. Therefore, let us replace the 2-port with an equivalent π network, as
shown in Figure 6.38. When this equivalent network is placed into the network
of Figure 6.37, as shown in Figure 6.39, we note that we have three sets of

Figure 6.38
Equivalent π network for
the 2-port of Figure 6.37.

Figure 6.39
Network of Figure 6.37
with the 2-port replaced
by an equivalent
π network.

parallel conductances, which can be combined to form the simplified network of Figure 6.40.

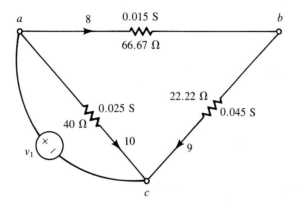

Figure 6.40
Network of Figure 6.39 with parallel conductances combined.

From Figure 6.40 we have several options for finding v_{bc}. For this example, we choose to use the voltage-divider rule and convert the conductances of branches 8 and 9 to equivalent resistances. Now we can write

$$v_{bc} = v_5 = \frac{22.22}{22.22 + 66.67}v_1 \approx 0.25v_1 \tag{6.63}$$

Example 6.13

The network of Figure 6.41 contains a 2-port with the following hybrid h-parameter CE:

$$\begin{bmatrix} v_1 \\ i_2 \end{bmatrix} = \begin{bmatrix} 500 & 10^{-3} \\ 50 & 10^{-5} \end{bmatrix}\begin{bmatrix} i_1 \\ v_2 \end{bmatrix} \tag{6.64}$$

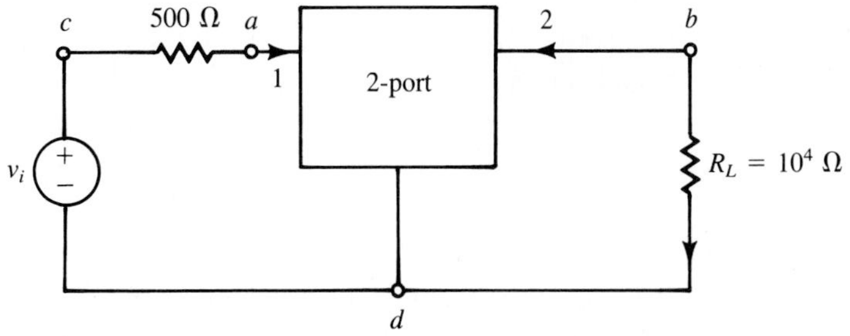

Figure 6.41
Network for Example 6.13.

We desire to find the voltage gain, v_L/v_i, and the power gain, p_L/p_i, of the network using an equivalent network for the 2-port.

The network of Figure 6.42 was obtained by replacing the 2-port of Figure 6.41 with an equivalent hybrid network. At this point we can find a hybrid network model by writing one loop-current equation for the input side and one node equation for the output side.

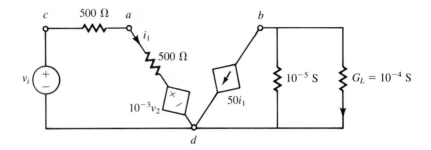

Figure 6.42
Network of Figure 6.41
with 2-port replaced with
an equivalent hybrid
network.

$$v_i = 10^3 i_1 + 10^{-3} v_L$$

$$0 = 50 i_1 + 11 \times 10^{-5} v_L$$

In matrix form this becomes

$$\begin{bmatrix} 10^3 & 10^{-3} \\ 50 & 11 \times 10^{-5} \end{bmatrix} \begin{bmatrix} i_1 \\ v_L \end{bmatrix} = \begin{bmatrix} v_i \\ 0 \end{bmatrix} \qquad (6.65)$$

from which we have

$$\begin{bmatrix} i_1 \\ v_L \end{bmatrix} = \frac{10^2}{6} \begin{bmatrix} 11 \times 10^{-5} \\ -50 \end{bmatrix} v_i = \begin{bmatrix} 1.83 \times 10^{-3} \\ -833 \end{bmatrix} v_i \qquad (6.66)$$

Input power $p_i = 1.83 \times 10^{-3} v_i^2$

Output power $p_L = (833 v_i)^2 \times 10^{-4} = 69.39\ v_i^2$

Power gain $= 37{,}918$

It should be instructive to note what happens to our equivalent network if h_{12} and h_{22} are neglected. From inspection we see that $i_1 = 10^{-3} v_i$ and, therefore, $i_2 = 50 i_1 = 5 \times 10^{-2} v_i$. It follows that $v_L = -5 \times 10^{-2} \times 10^4 v_i = -500 v_i$. In this case the approximation leads to large errors. If the load resistor, R_L, were specified as $10^3\ \Omega$, however, the approximation would be much better. Confirmation of this is left as a problem.

Example 6.14

To illustrate the use of equivalent networks further, we consider the network of Example 6.13 in a slightly different light. Suppose we replace the current-dependent voltage source and the two series resistances on the input side of the network (Figure 6.42) with a Norton equivalent 1-port. Then we have the network of Figure 6.43.

One way to get the Norton equivalent 1-port is to write the Thévenin form of the 1-port equation as

$$v_1 = 10^3 i_1 + 10^{-3} v_2 \qquad (6.67)$$

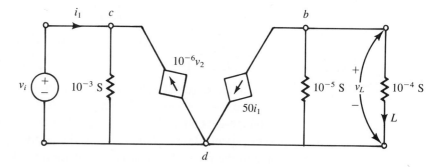

Figure 6.43
2-port network for
Example 6.14.

from which

$$i_1 = 10^{-3}v_1 - 10^{-6}v_2$$

A suitable equivalent 1-port therefore consists of a 1000-Ω resistor in parallel with a current source of magnitude $10^{-6}v_2$ (oriented opposite to i_1). Using the network of Figure 6.43, we can formulate hybrid equations in i_1 and $v_2 = v_L$ by writing node equations at nodes b and c.

One form these equations can take is illustrated in Equations 6.68 and 6.69.

$$i_1 = 10^{-3}v_i - 10^{-6}v_L \tag{6.68}$$

$$50i_1 + 10^{-5}(1 + 10)v_L = 0 \tag{6.69}$$

By substitution of Equation 6.68 into Equation 6.69, we have

$$6 \times 10^{-5}v_L = -5000 \times 10^{-5}v_i$$

from which

$$v_L = -833v_i \tag{6.70}$$

This checks the result of Example 6.13.

Example 6.15

To illustrate a less common use of equivalent networks, we now model the network of Example 6.13 using Norton-form (short-circuit) CE parameters. One means of finding the CE in the short-circuit parameter form is to solve Equation 6.64 for i_1 and i_2. For convenience, we include the 500-Ω series resistance on the input side in the 2-port CE as shown in Equation 6.71:

$$\begin{bmatrix} v_1 \\ i_2 \end{bmatrix} = \begin{bmatrix} 10^3 & 10^{-3} \\ 50 & 10^{-5} \end{bmatrix} \begin{bmatrix} i_1 \\ v_2 \end{bmatrix} \tag{6.71}$$

By factoring Equation 6.71 to get i_1 and i_2 on the left and v_1 and v_2 on the right, we have

$$\begin{bmatrix} 10^3 & 0 \\ -50 & 1 \end{bmatrix} \begin{bmatrix} i_1 \\ i_2 \end{bmatrix} = \begin{bmatrix} 1 & -10^{-3} \\ 0 & 10^{-5} \end{bmatrix} \begin{bmatrix} v_1 \\ v_2 \end{bmatrix} \tag{6.72}$$

The solution of Equation 6.72 yields

$$\begin{bmatrix} i_1 \\ i_2 \end{bmatrix} = \begin{bmatrix} 10^{-3} & -10^{-6} \\ 5 \times 10^{-2} & -4 \times 10^{-5} \end{bmatrix} \begin{bmatrix} v_1 \\ v_2 \end{bmatrix} \tag{6.73}$$

An equivalent hybrid network for a 2-port with Equation 6.73 as CE is shown in Figure 6.44. A new twist to this equivalent network is immediately evident. A voltage-dependent current source must be used on the output side, where we might expect a conductance. This is due to the negative sign on the lower right entry in the parameter matrix of Equation 6.73.

Figure 6.44
Equivalent hybrid network for 2-port of Example 6.14.

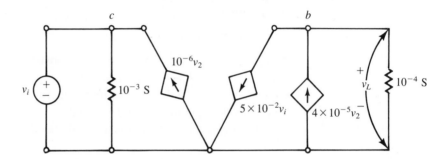

Even though we may have some doubts about the value of the equivalent network because of the three dependent sources, Equation 6.73 is a valid CE for analyzing the network.

To find the relation between $v_L = v_2$ and v_i, we need only write one KCL equation at node b:

$$5 \times 10^{-2}v_i - 4 \times 10^{-5}v_2 + 10^{-4}v_2 = 0 \tag{6.74}$$

Solving Equation 6.74, we find, as in the previous two examples,

$$v_L = -833v_i$$

The KCL equation written at node c could be used to determine the value of i_i in terms of v_i.

6.8   SUMMARY

In this chapter we discussed methods of characterizing 2-port resistive devices and networks. The CE types emphasized are those that utilize open-circuit resistances, short-circuit conductances, and hybrid h-parameters. In each case we have demonstrated how to construct an equivalent network to replace the

2-port for purpose of analysis. Any network containing 2-ports can be analyzed by standard techniques once the 2-ports have been replaced by equivalent networks—if we define standard techniques to include those required to handle controlled sources.

A 2-port equivalent network is merely a schematic diagram of a network that has the same mathematical model as the CE of the 2-port. Thus a given 2-port does not have a unique equivalent network in general. Each form of the CE leads most naturally to a different—but equivalent—network.

Once the logic becomes clear for associating an equivalent network with a particular form of CE, it should not be difficult to recall. In effect, the procedure itself is a sort of self-prompting memory device that is more worthy of concentration than is the memorization of the various equivalent networks.

PROGRAMS

PROBLEMS

6.1 Using the formula for combinations of n things taken m at a time, show that there are six possible different equivalent sets of CE for a 2-port. Why do all six possibilities not exist for some 2-ports? Give two examples of 2-port CE that do not have five equivalent sets.

6.2 How many possible different equivalent sets of CE exist for a 3-port?

6.3 For the 2-port of Figure 6.2, make all resistance values equal to 1 Ω. Find the 2-port CE by the method of Section 6.2 in **(a)** Thévenin form (open-circuit parameters); **(b)** Norton form (short-circuit parameters). Check that $G_N = R_T^{-1}$.

6.4 Explain why open-circuit and short-circuit parameter derivations (Equations 6.5, 6.6, 6.14, 6.15) are equivalent to use of the superposition theorem.

6.5 Find the open-circuit-parameter form and the short-circuit-parameter form of the component equations for the 2-port network of Figure 6.45 for each possible measurement diagram of Figure 6.46. Find an equivalent T network and an equivalent π network that have the same 2-port component equations as those found for the three different measurement diagrams.

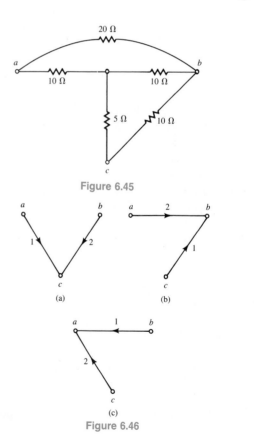

Figure 6.45

(a)

(b)

(c)

Figure 6.46

6.6 Use the symbolic-source method to find the short-circuit-parameter form of the component equations for the 2-port network of Figure 6.47. Use the measurement diagram of Figure 6.46(a). From these results find an equivalent π network. Find $p(t)$ as a function of v_1 and v_2.

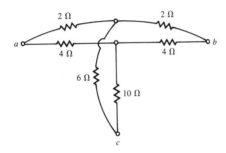

Figure 6.47

6.7 Use the symbolic-source method to find the Thévenin-form component equations (open-circuit parameters) for the network of Figure 6.47. Use the measurement diagram of Figure 6.46(a). Find $p(t)$ as a function of i_1 and i_2.

6.8 Use Y-Δ transformations to find an equivalent π network for the 2-port of Figure 6.2 if all resistors are 1 Ω.

6.9 Use Y-Δ transformations to find an equivalent π network for the 2-port of Figure 6.45.

6.10 Use Y-Δ transformations to find equivalent π and T networks for the 2-port of Figure 6.47.

6.11 The two 2-port networks of Figures 6.45 and 6.47 are interconnected by connecting them at terminals a, b, and c. Find an equivalent π network for this new network. (It is advantageous to represent each 2-port by its equivalent π.)

6.12 Use Y-Δ and series-parallel transformations to find an equivalent T network for the 2-port of Figure 6.48.

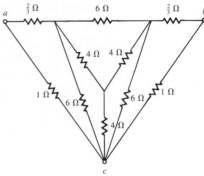

Figure 6.48

6.13 Find the Norton- and Thévenin-form CE for the 2-port network of Figure 6.49 and write them as matrix equations. Also, find $p(t)$ for the 2-port as a function of v_1 and v_2. Under what conditions, for constant v_1 and v_2, is this $p(t) > 0$?

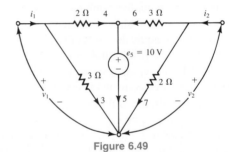

Figure 6.49

6.14 For the resistive 2-port of Example 6.8, find the hybrid h-parameter CE by using the equivalent network of Figure 6.7 and finding the response of v_1 and i_2 to symbolic sources i_1 and v_2.

6.15 Repeat Problem 6.14 using the equivalent network of Figure 6.11.

6.16 For the resistive 2-port of Example 6.8, find the hybrid h-parameter CE directly from the Norton-form CE of Equation 6.32.

6.17 The transistor of Example 6.7 has a load resistor connected so that the equivalent network appears as shown in Figure 6.50. Assume that v_1 is an input sinusoidal voltage of suitable magnitude and frequency for the equivalent network approximation used, and calculate the voltage gain and power gain for the 2-port.

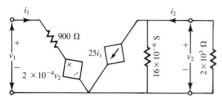

Figure 6.50
Equivalent network for a
low-frequency transistor
amplifier.

6.18 Explain the meaning of "suitable magnitude and frequency for the equivalent network approximation used" as used in Problem 6.17. (You may need a hint from the professor on this.)

6.19 For the transistor network of Figure 6.50, delete the voltage-controlled voltage source and calculate the voltage gain and the power gain. Assume that the network of Figure 6.50 is correct, and find the percent error for voltage gain and power gain caused by this approximation. What does this approximation correspond to, relative to the hybrid h-parameters?

6.20 The network of Figure 6.51 represents the same transistor amplifier shown in Figure 6.50, but with two simplifying approximations. Calculate the voltage gain and power gain of this network and the percent error of each relative to that of the "exact" network of Problem 6.17.

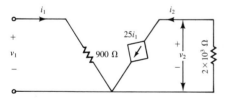

Figure 6.51
Equivalent network of
Figure 6.50 with
approximation
$h_{12} = h_{22} = 0$.

6.21 For the transistor amplifier of Figure 6.52, the hybrid h-parameters are: $h_{11} = 800\ \Omega$, $h_{12} = 0$, $h_{21} = 28$, $h_{22} = 9 \times 10^{-6}$ S, and $R_L = 5000\ \Omega$. Find the voltage gain and power gain of the network.

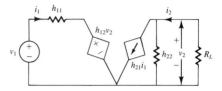

Figure 6.52

6.22 For the network of Figure 6.53, the 2-port hybrid h-parameters are: $h_{11} = 1500\ \Omega$, $h_{12} = 0$, $h_{21} = 40$, and $h_{22} = 5 \times 10^{-6}$ S. The load resistance is $1000\ \Omega$. Find the voltage gain and current gain of the network. How much error in current gain would result from neglecting h_{22}? (Put this in terms of percent change from the gain calculated.)

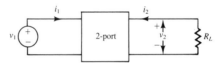

Figure 6.53

6.23 Suppose the output voltage, v_2, for the network of Figure 6.53 is desired for the case when $R_L = \infty$ (open circuit). Explain why the hybrid h-parameter model for the 2-port could not be satisfactory if h_{22} is neglected.

6.24 For the network of Figure 6.52 the hybrid h-parameters are: $h_{11} = 1800\ \Omega$, $h_{12} = 0$, $h_{21} = 32$, $h_{22} = 9 \times 10^{-6}$ S, and $R_L = 2500\ \Omega$. Find the voltage and power gains.

6.25 For the network of Figure 6.53, the 2-port hybrid h-parameters are: $h_{11} = 1000\ \Omega$, $h_{12} = 10^{-4}$, $h_{21} = 30$, $h_{22} = 2 \times 10^{-6}$ S, and $R_L = 2000\ \Omega$. Convert from hybrid h-parameters to Norton-form G-parameters and draw an equivalent network. (*Hint:* Find the currents i_1 and i_2 in terms of v_1 and v_2 to determine the G-parameters.)

6.26 Solve the equivalent network of Problem 6.25 for voltage gain and power gain.

6.27 The CE for the 2-port of Figure 6.53 can be written

$$\begin{bmatrix} i_1 \\ i_2 \end{bmatrix} = \begin{bmatrix} 10^{-3} & 0 \\ 0.04 & 10^{-5} \end{bmatrix} \begin{bmatrix} v_1 \\ v_2 \end{bmatrix}$$

and $R_L = 1000\ \Omega$. Find the voltage gain and the power gain for the network.

6.28 Write the CE for the following 2-ports (assume that the input port is 1 and the output port is 2) in matrix form using appropriate parameter symbols. The symbols used should reflect the form of the equations—that is, open-circuit parameters, R_{ij}; short-circuit parameters, G_{ij}; hybrid h-parameters, h_{ij}; hybrid g-parameters, g_{ij}):
  (a) The voltage-controlled voltage source.
  (b) The voltage-controlled current source.
  (c) The current-controlled voltage source.
  (d) The current-controlled current source.

6.29 Use nodal analysis to verify the voltage gain expression of Equation 6.56.

6.30 For the network of Figure 6.54, find v_0 as a function of v_1 and v_2. Use the approximate equivalent network of Figure 6.32.

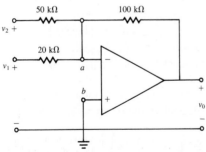

Figure 6.54

6.31 Using one op amp and as many resistors as needed, design a network having the following characteristics:
  (a) $v_0 = -10v_1$
  (b) $v_0 = -v_1 - 2v_2$
  (c) $v_0 = -2v_1 - 0.5v_2 - 3v_3$

6.32 (a) Using the equivalent network of Figure 6.27 for the op amp, develop an equation for the amplifier voltage gain v_0/v_1 for the network of Figure 6.36.

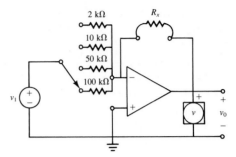

Figure 6.55

  (b) Show that your result reduces to Equation 6.61 as $R_i \to \infty$ and $R_0 \to 0$.
  (c) What is the gain v_0/v_i when $R_f = 0$? (This network is often called a *voltage follower*.)

6.33 The op-amp network of Figure 6.55 has been designed as an ohmmeter to measure the unknown resistance R_x. The ideal voltmeter is to be labeled to read this resistance.
  (a) Develop an expression for R_x in terms of the known voltage source v_1 (a constant) and the voltmeter reading v_0. The switch can be placed in any one of the four positions shown.
  (b) What is the range of resistances that can be read by this meter, and what is the purpose of four switch positions if $|v_0|_{max} = 10$ V and $v_1 = 1$ V?

Note: In Problems 6.34–6.40, use the ideal approximate equivalent network of Figure 6.32 to represent the op amp unless otherwise stated.

6.34 Use the network of Figure 6.56.
  (a) Find the voltage v_0 in terms of v_1 and v_2.
  (b) Simplify the result if $R_3 = R_2$ and $R_4 = R_1$. In this last case, the network is known as a *differential amplifier*.

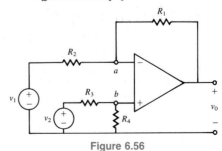

Figure 6.56

6.35 Find a Thévenin equivalent network for the network of Figure 6.54 if $v_2 = 0$ and v_1 is a known function. Treat the output port as the output terminals of the equivalent network.

6.36 Find a Norton equivalent network for the network of Figure 6.57 with respect to the terminals c and d. Use the equivalent network for the op amp with $R_i = 1$ MΩ and $R_0 = 100$ Ω. Assume that v_1 is known. Make reasonable approximations and explain your results.

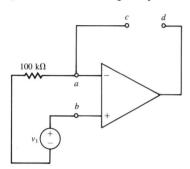

Figure 6.57

6.37 For the network of Figure 6.58, find the current i_L in the load resistor R_L by first replacing the network to the left of terminal pair c-d with a Thevenin equivalent. Then find the load current for each of the following cases.

(a) $R_L = 5$ kΩ.

(b) $R_L = 6$ kΩ in parallel with 3 kΩ.

(c) R_L = value needed for maximum power transfer to the load. Also calculate the power delivered to the load.

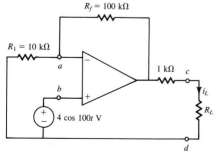

Figure 6.58

6.38 In the network of Figure 6.58, the load resistor is replaced by a voltage source such that $v_{cd} = 25 + 1000i_L$. Calculate the current i_L.

6.39 In the network of Figure 6.58, $R_L = 1$ kΩ. Select design values for the resistors R_f and R_1 so that the load current is $i_L = 4 \cos 100t$ mA.

6.40 In the network of Figure 6.59, find the value of R required to obtain a voltage gain

$$v_0 = -100v_1$$

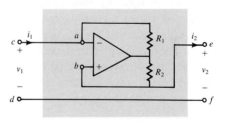

Figure 6.59

6.41 Consider the 2-port network of Figure 6.60.

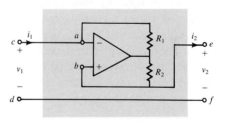

Figure 6.60

(a) For the port variables as shown, find the 2-port component equation in the form

$$\begin{bmatrix} v_1 \\ i_1 \end{bmatrix} \begin{bmatrix} a & b \\ c & d \end{bmatrix} \begin{bmatrix} v_2 \\ i_2 \end{bmatrix}$$

Use the approximate equivalent network and assume $A \to \infty$ to obtain the results. Is it possible to put the results in any of the standard forms discussed in this chapter?

(b) Draw an equivalent network for this case.

(c) The 2-port is loaded at port 2 (terminals e-f) with a resistance R_L. Assuming a given

v_1, find the Thévenin-form component equation for the network as a 1-port at terminals c-d. What is the equivalent network?

6.42 For the 2-port network of Figure 6.61, use the approximate equivalent network for the op amp and find each of the following.

(a) The 2-port CE in Thévenin equivalent form.

(b) The results of part (a) as $A \to \infty$.

(c) The 1-port Thévenin equivalent network at terminals e-f.

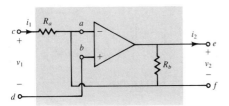

Figure 6.61

6.43 In the network of Figure 6.62, the 2-port component is that of Figure 6.45. Use one of the equivalent networks of Problem 6.5 to solve this network for i_3, i_4, and the total power delivered to the resistive 2-port. Also solve using each of the three different measurement diagrams and the corresponding 2-port CE of Problem 6.5. Finally, solve the network by treating the 2-port as a set of 1-ports.

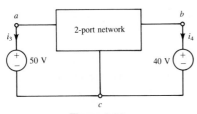

Figure 6.62

6.44 Solve the network of Problem 6.43 for v_3, v_4, and the power delivered to the 2-port network if the sources are changed to $i_3 = -2$ A and $i_4 = -1$ A. Use any (choose a convenient one) of the measurement diagrams and resulting CE of Problem 6.5.

6.45 Write the primary mathematical model for a network consisting of a 2-port and two i-sources as shown in Figure 6.63. Solve for the terminal voltages v_1 and v_2 if the 2-port terminal equations are

$$\begin{bmatrix} v_1 \\ v_2 \end{bmatrix} = \begin{bmatrix} 10 & \sqrt{10} \\ \sqrt{10} & 6 \end{bmatrix} \begin{bmatrix} i_1 \\ i_2 \end{bmatrix}$$

with reference to the measurement diagram of Figure 6.63(b).

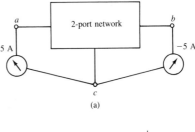

(a)

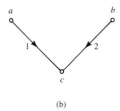

(b)

Figure 6.63

6.46 Given the 2-port component of Problem 6.45 connected to two v-sources shown in Figure 6.64, solve for the terminal currents i_1 and i_2.

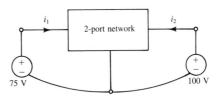

Figure 6.64

6.47 Given the 2-port R-component of Problem 6.45 connected to one v-source and one i-source shown in Figure 6.65, solve for i_1 and v_2 of the 2-port.

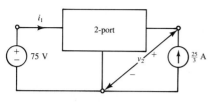

Figure 6.65

6.48 Given the 2-port R-component of Problem 6.45 connected to two i-sources shown in Figure 6.66, find v_1 and v_2 of the 2-port.

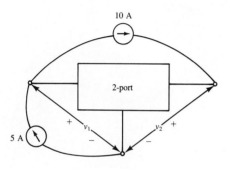

Figure 6.66

6.49 Solve the network of Figure 6.64 if the 2-port is that of Figure 6.47.

6.50 Solve the network of Figure 6.64 if the 2-port is that of Figure 6.48.

6.51 Solve the network of Figure 6.64 if the 2-port is that of Figure 6.49.

6.52 Solve the network of Figure 6.65 if the 2-port is that of Figure 6.47.

6.53 Solve the network of Figure 6.65 if the 2-port is that of Figure 6.48.

6.54 Solve the network of Figure 6.65 if the 2-port is that of Figure 6.49.

6.55 Solve the network of Figure 6.66 if the 2-port is that of Figure 6.47.

6.56 Solve the network of Figure 6.66 if the 2-port is that of Figure 6.48.

6.57 Solve the network of Figure 6.66 if the 2-port is that of Figure 6.49.

6.58 For the network of Example 6.13 (Figure 6.41), assume that $R_L = 10^3$ Ω. Calculate the voltage gain and power gain for each of the following cases.

(a) The network with the 2-port h-parameters as given.

(b) With $h_{12} = h_{22} = 0$.

6.59 Find the 2-port CE for the network of Figure 6.67 in each of the following forms.

(a) Thevenin form.

(b) Norton form.

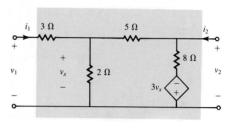

Figure 6.67

6.60 Repeat Problem 6.59 for Figure 6.68.

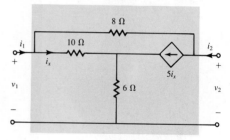

Figure 6.68

6.61 Repeat Problem 6.59 for Figure 6.69.

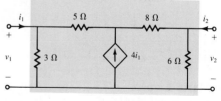

Figure 6.69

6.62 Repeat Problem 6.59 for Figure 6.70.

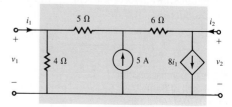

Figure 6.70

Giants of the profession
IEEE Centennial Hall of Fame

André Marie Ampère (1775–1836) Mathematician and physicist; demonstrated the principles of electrodynamics in adjacent current-carrying conductors.

Alexander Graham Bell (1847–1922) Inventor of the telephone and of aids for teaching the deaf; founded the journal *Science*. Shown here with Helen Keller.

Reprinted with permission from "Centennial Hall of Fame," *IEEE SPECTRUM*, April 1984.

First-order networks

7.1 INTRODUCTION

We have developed some detailed analysis techniques for networks that contain only resistors and sources. In all cases the techniques involved the solution of a set of algebraic equations. We begin the analysis, in detail, of networks that contain energy-storage components. In this chapter we now restrict our discussion to those networks that contain only a single energy-storage component. The resulting mathematical models contain derivatives or integrals and we will see that the dynamic, or nonalgebraic, portion of the model can be reduced to a single first-order differential equation. These networks are referred to as *first-order networks*.

7.2 FORMULATING THE EQUATION

Loop or nodal equations can be written for networks made up of sources, resistors, and a single energy-storage component in the same manner that we wrote these equations in Chapters 4 and 5.

Example 7.1

We can write the two mesh equations for the network in Figure 7.1 by simply summing to zero the voltages around the given meshes and expressing each component voltage in terms of the mesh currents. Thus

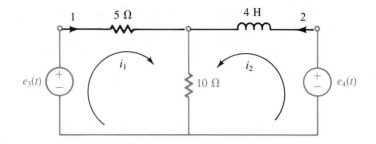

Figure 7.1
A first-order network.

$$-e_3(t) + 5i_1 + 10(i_1 + i_2) = 0$$

$$-e_4(t) + 4\frac{di_2}{dt} + 10(i_1 + i_2) = 0 \tag{7.1}$$

or

$$15i_1 + 10i_2 = e_3(t)$$

$$10i_1 + 10i_2 + 4\frac{di_2}{dt} = e_4(t) \tag{7.2}$$

and we see that, in this case, the mesh equations involve a derivative and are a good deal more difficult to solve than the equations of a two-mesh network with no energy-storage components. One method of solution is to reduce these equations to one algebraic equation and a differential equation in a single variable. Suppose, for example, that Equation 7.1 is solved for i_1 and this result is substituted into Equation 7.2. Then we have, after some algebra,

$$i_1 = \frac{1}{15}\,[e_3(t) - 10i_2] \tag{7.3}$$

and

$$4\frac{di_2}{dt} + \frac{10}{3}i_2 = e_4(t) - \frac{2}{3}\,e_3(t) \tag{7.4}$$

Since $e_3(t)$ and $e_4(t)$ are known functions of time (v-sources), Equation 7.4 is a constant-coefficient, first-order, linear differential equation in the variable $i_2(t)$. You may have already encountered equations of this type in mathematics courses and may be familiar with several techniques for solving them. We shall, however, concentrate on one particular technique for solving this equation.

Once Equation 7.4 is solved for i_2, Equation 7.3 can be used to find i_1. With both mesh currents known, we can find any other network variables as before. That is to say, any other current can be found from KCL and then any component voltage can be found from the CE.

Example 7.2

Suppose the *i*-source of the network in Figure 7.2 is given by $i_3 = J(t)$, a known function of time. Writing the single nodal equation, we have

$$\frac{1}{10} v_1 + \frac{1}{2} \int_0^t v_1(\tau) \, d\tau + i_2(0) + \frac{1}{5} v_1 = J(t)$$

where $i_2(0)$ is a constant—the inductor current at $t = 0$. This equation can be converted to a differential equation simply by differentiating with respect to time. Thus

$$\frac{1}{10} \frac{dv_1}{dt} + \frac{1}{2} v_1 + \frac{1}{5} \frac{dv_1}{dt} = \frac{d}{dt} J(t)$$

or

$$\frac{3}{10} \frac{dv_1}{dt} + \frac{1}{2} v_1 = \frac{d}{dt} J(t) \tag{7.5}$$

Once Equation 7.5 is solved for the node voltage, v_1, we can solve for any other network variable by use of the KVL equations and the CE.

Figure 7.2
Network for Example 7.2.

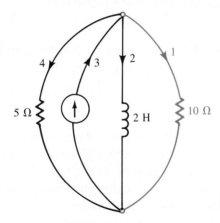

These two examples illustrate how loop and nodal techniques can be extended to networks containing a single energy-storage element. For any network of the type presently under consideration, the approach is essentially the same as that illustrated by these examples:

1. Write the loop or node equations by the usual process, including an integral or derivative term, as appropriate, for the energy-storage component. In this step it is very advantageous to select

the loop currents or node voltages such that one of them corresponds directly to the current or voltage, respectively, of the energy-storage device. (Make the energy-storage component a link for loop analysis or a tree branch for supernode analysis.)

2. By algebraic substitution from the remaining equations, reduce the equation involving the integral or derivative to an equation with only one unknown.

3. If the resulting equation of Step 2 contains an integral, differentiate this equation with respect to time.

4. Solve the first-order differential equation and then proceed as before to obtain the solution for any additional network variables for which a solution is desired.

The major difference injected by the inclusion of the energy-storage component is the necessity of solving a differential equation. Let us now consider this aspect of the problem in more detail.

7.3 SOLUTION OF THE FIRST-ORDER MODEL

Differential equations of the type illustrated by Equations 7.4 and 7.5 can be placed in the following general form:

$$\frac{dx}{dt} = ax + f(t) \tag{7.6}$$

where a is a constant and $f(t)$ is a known function of time. An equation in this form is called a *normal-form differential equation* by mathematicians and a *state equation* by engineers. In the latter case x is called a *state variable*. In either case $f(t)$ is usually called the *forcing function*.

Equation 7.6 is readily solved by the use of the integrating-factor approach. Suppose the entire equation is multiplied by the quantity e^{-at} and rearranged as

$$\frac{dx}{dt}e^{-at} - axe^{-at} = e^{-at}f(t)$$

The left-hand side of this equation is the derivative of a product. Therefore, we have

$$\frac{d}{dt}[xe^{-at}] = e^{-at}f(t) \tag{7.7}$$

which can be integrated with respect to time to obtain a solution for $x(t)$. Suppose we let

$$z(t) = xe^{-at}$$

Then Equation 7.7 can be rewritten as

$$dz = e^{-at}f(t) \, dt$$

Integrating from an arbitrary initial time zero to any later time t gives

$$\int_{z(0)}^{z(t)} dz = \int_0^t e^{-a\tau}f(\tau) \, d\tau$$

where τ has been introduced as a dummy variable of integration. This yields

$$z(t) - z(0) = \int_0^t e^{-a\tau}f(\tau) \, d\tau$$

or

$$x(t)e^{-at} - x(0) = \int_0^t e^{-a\tau}f(\tau) \, d\tau$$

Finally, solving for $x(t)$, we have

$$x(t) = e^{at}x(0) + e^{at} \int_0^t e^{-a\tau}f(\tau) \, d\tau \tag{7.8}$$

where $x(0)$ is the initial value of the state variable at time $t = 0$.

The first term in this solution is often referred to as the *zero-input response* of the network because the $f(t)$ of the given state equation will be some linear combination of the sources of the network. This is true for the two previous examples. If all the sources are set to zero (zero input), then the solution is reduced to

$$x(t) = e^{at}x(0)$$

This portion of the solution is generally called the *homogeneous solution*. This solution is also referred to as the *natural* solution because it results from the nature of the network and is independent of the sources.

In a similar way we see that if $x(0) = 0$, we are left with

$$x(t) = e^{at} \int_0^t e^{-a\tau}f(\tau) \, d\tau$$

which is quite logically referred to as the *zero-state,* or forced, response of the network.

The solution as given in Equation 7.8 is the complete response of the network. Thus the zero-state and zero-input responses are special cases of the complete response. In any case, we have now developed a formal solution for networks described by a first-order model. Once the constant, a, and the functions $f(t)$, are known it is possible to find the state x as a function of time from Equation 7.8.

The zero-input response is a simple exponential response of the form

$$x(t) = e^{at}x(0) \tag{7.9}$$

We shall see later that the constant a is a combination of the values of the network resistances and the capacitance or inductance. *Further, for most cases of interest a is negative.* Therefore, it is convenient to write Equation 7.9 in the form

$$x(t) = e^{-t/T}x(0) \tag{7.10}$$

where

$$T \doteq -\frac{1}{a}$$

and must have the dimensions of time.

The response as given in Equation 7.10 is shown in Figure 7.3 for various values of T. The decaying exponential response for $T > 0$ is of primary interest. The exponential response plays a large role in network analysis and warrants some detailed study.

Consider, for example, the solution for $x(t)$ at a time $t = T$. From Equation 7.10

$$x(T) = e^{-1}x(0) \approx 0.368x(0)$$

Figure 7.3
Typical zero-input responses.

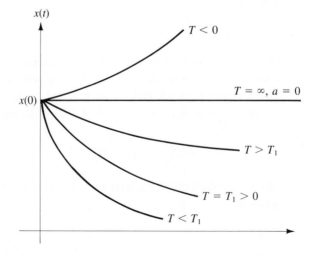

That is, when $t = T$, the zero-state response has decayed to a value that is 36.8% of its original, or initial, value. The quantity T is referred to as the *time constant* of the network. It is obvious that this time constant is a very important parameter in the study of first-order networks. It is also very informative to calculate the approximate value of $x(t)$ for several times that are multiples of the time constant T (Table 7.1). These values are illustrated in Figure 7.4. From Table 7.1 we see, for example, that the response has decayed to a value that is only 0.7% of its initial value in a time equal to five time constants. This means that the zero-input response of a first-order network with a time constant of 1 s will have essentially decayed to zero in 5 s. However, this response will decay to essentially zero in only 5 μs if the time constant is 1 μs. You may find it convenient to memorize the values in Table 7.1. We can, for example, sketch a very good zero-input response curve for a network simply from knowing the time constant and the initial state and recalling the value of the state at $t = 1$, 3, and 5 time constants.

Table 7.1

t	$x(t)$
T	$0.368x(0)$
$2T$	$0.135x(0)$
$3T$	$0.050x(0)$
$5T$	$0.007x(0)$

Figure 7.4
Typical values of zero-input response.

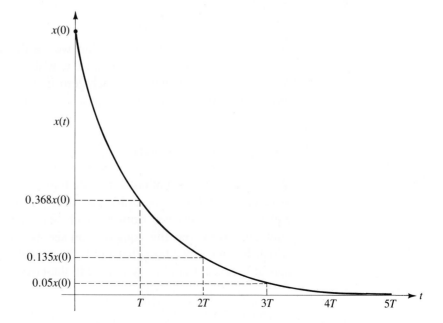

We have made a detailed study of the formal solution to the state equation for the case of zero input. Input signals, which occur often in network analysis, are the sinusoidal input and the nonzero constant input. The general solution for a constant input is simple enough and informative enough to warrant a general development. We do not develop a formal solution for a sinusoidal input. However, this case, as well as any other of interest, can always be handled for particular problems by substituting into the general solution of Equation 7.8.

Now suppose $f(\tau)$ in Equation 7.8 is a constant—let $f(\tau) = K$. Then by straightforward integration (which you should confirm), we get

$$x(t) = e^{at}x(0) - \frac{K}{a}[1 - e^{at}]$$

or, in terms of the time constant,

$$x(t) = e^{-t/T}x(0) + KT[1 - e^{-t/T}]$$

which could be arranged as

$$x(t) = e^{-t/T}[x(0) - KT] + KT \qquad (7.11)$$

If $T > 0$, the first term on the right-hand side of this equation will decay to zero with time, and we see that

$$\lim_{t \to \infty} x(t) = KT$$

for this case. The KT term is often referred to as the *steady-state* response, and the exponential term

$$e^{-t/T}[x(0) - KT]$$

is called the *transient response*. Thus we see that for a network with constant sources ($f(t) = K$), the state variable, x, will eventually become constant, and the derivative dx/dt will approach zero if the time constant is positive. The terminology *steady state* is very descriptive in this case.

7.4 THE STATE EQUATION

We now turn our attention to a straightforward procedure for formulating a state equation for a first-order network. As previously mentioned, a state equation can be derived from a set of loop equations or from a set of nodal equations. However, this equation can also be found in a more direct fashion, which has the advantage that the state variable has more physical intuitive appeal because it is directly related to the energy storage of the network.

Consider a network made up of b 1-ports consisting of resistors, sources, and a single capacitor. The PRIMM of this network consists of $2b$ equations, as follows:

1. $2b - 1$ algebraic equations: KCL equations, KVL equations, source CE, and resistor CE.

2. One equation

$$\frac{dv_c}{dt} = \frac{1}{C} i_c \tag{7.12}$$

where v_c and i_c are capacitor voltage and current, respectively.

The latter equation has the makings of a state equation. In fact, if i_c can be replaced by a linear function of v_c and some function of time, this equation will then be a state equation of the form of Equation 7.6 with $x = v_c$. Since the function of time must arise from the sources, we are faced with a question. Can the $2b - 1$ algebraic equations (which contain i_c in the KCL) be solved for i_c as a function of v_c and the network sources? The answer is yes. Since the $2b - 1$ equations are linearly independent and contain $2b$ unknowns, we know from linear algebra that we can solve this set for any $2b - 1$ variables in terms of the remaining variable. Thus we can solve for i_c in terms of v_c, and this solution will depend on the form of the network sources. Suppose that we have found

$$i_c = kv_c + g(t), \qquad k \text{ constant}$$

By simple substitution we have

$$\frac{dv_c}{dt} = \frac{1}{C}[kv_c + g(t)] = \frac{k}{C}v_c + \frac{1}{C}g(t)$$

which is the desired state equation.

The actual implementation of the solution of i_c as a linear function of v_c and the network sources can be accomplished several ways. One approach, which builds on our resistive-network analysis background, is based on the observation that in solving for i_c in terms of v_c and network sources, v_c is treated as if it were known—as if it were a v-source. Therefore, we can set Equation 7.12 aside for later use and create a new component equation

$$v_c = x(t)$$

the component equation for a symbolic v-source. This equation, combined with the $2b - 1$ algebraic equations, forms the PRIMM of a resistive network made from the original network by replacing the capacitor by a symbolic v-source.

The polarity of this v-source agrees with the arbitrarily chosen orientation for v_c. Any of the analysis techniques we have studied for resistive networks can now be used to solve for i_c, which is now the current through the symbolic v-source.

If the network contains an inductor instead of a capacitor, the approach is quite similar. The equation that will be converted to a state equation is

$$\frac{di_L}{dt} = \frac{1}{L}v_L \qquad (7.13)$$

and now we must solve for v_L in terms of i_L and network sources. This leads us to replace the inductor with a symbolic current source and solve the resulting resistive network for the voltage across this symbolic i-source. Then, by substituting the result into Equation 7.13, we create the desired state equation.

We now apply our newly-developed analytical muscle to some typical first-order networks. If we apply the state-model formulation technique of symbolic sources, the state variable will be *capacitor voltage* if the network contains a capacitor and *inductor current* if the network contains an inductor. These are intuitively satisfying because of their relation to stored energy.

Example 7.3

The network diagram of Figure 7.5 contains a new symbol, which we use to denote a switch. We consider this switch ideal in that when it is open, current flow is interrupted totally; when it is closed, there is zero voltage across the switch. The arrow on the switch indicates the direction of the switch movement, and the time given adjacent to the switch denotes the time at which the switching operation occurs.

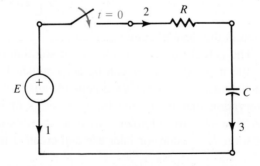

Figure 7.5
A simple RC network with
a constant v-source.

In this network the switch is closed at $t = 0$, at which time the energy stored on the capacitor is $w(0)$. The v-source is constant at E volts. The equation that will be transformed to a state equation is

$$\frac{dv_3}{dt} = \frac{1}{C}i_3 \qquad (7.14)$$

The state variable is the capacitor voltage v_3, and we must solve for i_3 in terms of v_3 and E. Suppose we let

$$v_3 = x(t) \qquad (7.15)$$

a symbolic v-source, and draw the resulting resistive network of Figure 7.6.

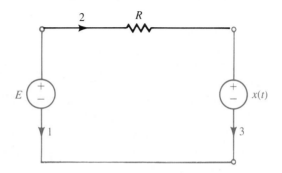

Figure 7.6
A resistive network used for formulating a state equation for the network of Figure 7.5.

This resistive network is readily solved for i_3. Thus

$$i_3 = i_2 = \frac{E - x(t)}{R}$$

and by substituting this result and Equation 7.15 into Equation 7.14, we have

$$\frac{dx}{dt} = -\frac{1}{RC}x + \frac{1}{RC}E \qquad (7.16)$$

Thus, for this network, the time constant is $T = RC$ s. (You should verify from Equation 7.16 that the quantity RC does have the dimension of seconds.) Now the solution to Equation 7.16 is obtained directly from Equation 7.11 as

$$x(t) = e^{-t/RC}[x(0) - E] + E$$

or

$$v_3(t) = e^{-t/RC}[v_3(0) - E] + E \text{ V} \qquad (7.17)$$

where $v_3(0)$ is given by

$$w(0) = \frac{1}{2}Cv_3^2(0) \text{ J}$$

with $w(0)$ known. The response of this network is sketched for $v_3(0) = 0$ in Figure 7.7 (assuming both R and C—and hence T—are positive). The response is seen to be the sum of the transient response and the steady-state response. In this case the capacitor starts in an uncharged, unenergized state and charges exponentially to a steady-state voltage of E volts. After a time of about $5RC$ s, the "transient" has essentially died out; the capacitor is fully energized and has reached steady state.

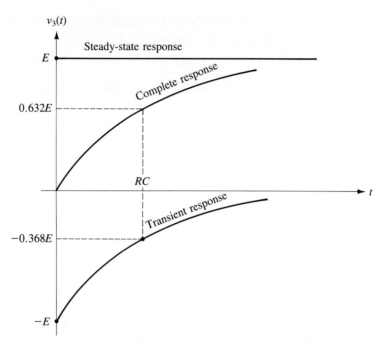

Figure 7.7
Response of the network
of Example 7.3.

Upon the capacitor's reaching steady state, we see that

$$\frac{dv_3}{dt} = 0$$

Therefore, the current in the network, which is

$$i_3 = C\frac{dv_3}{dt} = e^{-t/RC}\left[\frac{E - v_3(0)}{R}\right] \text{ A} \qquad (7.18)$$

will also approach zero in steady state. In steady state the capacitor has become an effective open circuit to current flow. The current is also sketched for $v_3(0) = 0$ in Figure 7.8. Since the state variable is capacitor voltage, we see from this discussion (and the discussion of Equation 7.11) that *a capacitor will tend to become an open circuit in steady state for any first-order network with resistors and constant sources.*

There are several additional cases worth mentioning in passing. Suppose, for example, that $v_3(0) > E$. In this case, the initially charged capacitor temporarily overrides the v-source, the current flow as given by Equation 7.18 is negative and decays to zero, and the capacitor supplies energy to both the v-source and the resistor during the transient. After an elapsed time of about $5RC$ s, the network reaches equilibrium, current stops, and the energy stored on the capacitor is the same as for the case $v_3(0) = 0$.

Finally, consider the case where $v_3(0) = E$. In this case the network starts in equilibrium. The transient response is zero, and no current flows when the switch is closed.

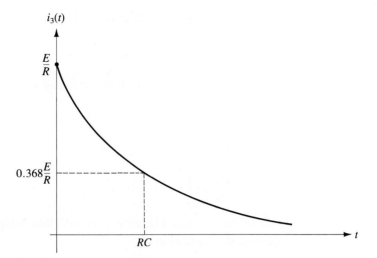

Figure 7.8
Current flow in the
network of Example 7.3.

Example 7.4

In the network of Figure 7.9 the switch has been open but is closed at $t = 0$. In this case we conclude that the current through the inductor at $t = 0$ is $i_3(0) = 0$, since current cannot flow with the switch open. The state variable is $x(t) = i_3$, and the resulting resistive network is seen in Figure 7.10.

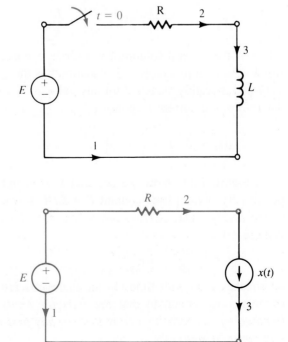

Figure 7.9
Network for Example 7.4.

Figure 7.10
Resistive network
equivalent.

The mesh current in Figure 7.10 is given by the i-source as $x(t)$. Therefore, the voltage v_3 is given by

$$v_3 = E - Rx(t) \tag{7.19}$$

The component equation for the inductor is

$$\frac{di_3}{dt} = \frac{1}{L}v_3$$

or

$$\frac{dx}{dt} = \frac{1}{L}v_3$$

and by substituting Equation 7.19 into this component equation, we have the desired state equation

$$\frac{dx}{dt} = -\frac{R}{L}x + \frac{E}{L}$$

or

$$\frac{di_3}{dt} = -\frac{R}{L}i_3 + \frac{E}{L} \tag{7.20}$$

We see that the time constant of this network is $T = L/R$ s and the complete response is

$$i_3(t) = e^{-Rt/L}\left[i_3(0) - \frac{E}{R}\right] + \frac{E}{R} \tag{7.21}$$

which is the general solution for a series connection of a constant v-source, a resistor, and an inductor. This equation has the same form as that of Equation 7.17 and is readily sketched for any value of $i_3(0)$. In this example, $i_3(0) = 0$. Therefore, the current response is

$$i_3(t) = \frac{E}{R}[1 - e^{-Rt/L}] \tag{7.22}$$

as in Figure 7.11. Now we see that $i_3(t)$ is initially zero and increases exponentially, with a time contant $T = L/R$, toward a final value of E/R A.

In steady state, $i_3(t)$ becomes constant, di_3/dt approaches zero, and the voltage

$$v_3 = L\frac{di_3}{dt} = Ee^{-Rt/L} \tag{7.23}$$

approaches zero with time. In an analogous argument to that given for the capacitor, we conclude that *the inductor tends to become a short circuit (voltage equals zero) at steady state in any first-order network with resistors and constant sources.*

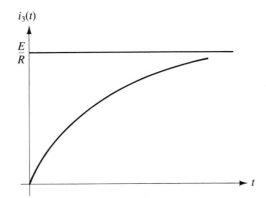

Figure 7.11
Current response for
Example 7.4.

From Equations 7.22 and 7.23 we see that when the switch is first closed, no current flows, the resistor voltage is zero, and the total voltage E appears across the inductor. As time progresses, the current increases, its rate of change decreases, and—consequently—the resistor voltage increases and the inductor voltage decreases. As the network approaches steady state, the inductor is energized fully (as far as possible for this network), current becomes constant to maintain this energy storage, and the full voltage E appears across the resistor. Finally, we note that energy is dissipated in the resistor at a rate

$$p_2(t) = \left(\frac{E}{R}\right)^2 R = \frac{E^2}{R} \quad \text{J/s}$$

at steady state. The source energy rate is

$$p_1(t) = \left(-\frac{E}{R}\right)E = -\frac{E^2}{R} \quad \text{J/s}$$

The negative sign for $p_1(t)$ indicates generated power. We note that the source is supplying energy only to the resistor—the inductor energy is constant and its instantaneous power is zero, all at steady state. This is in contrast to the capacitive network of Example 7.3. In that case the source is supplying no energy at steady state because the current is zero and therefore the resistor is dissipating no energy.

There are two other networks of interest that contain one source, one resistor, and one energy-storage component. These networks are shown in Figure 7.12. The formulation of a state equation and the solution for the network response are straightforward and are left to the problems.

The state-model formulation technique that we have developed is broadly applicable and can be extended to more general networks. In fact, it can be applied directly to a network containing several resistors and several sources but only one energy-storage component. However, we know from the developments in Chapter 4 that it is possible to reduce these networks to an

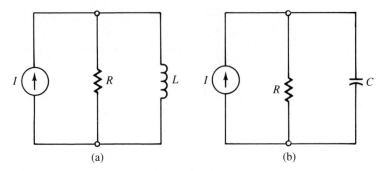

Figure 7.12
Typical first-order
networks with constant
i-sources.

(a)   (b)

equivalent 1-port network containing a source and a resistor, plus the energy-storage component. Therefore, for the time being we restrict ourselves to networks of this type. We do consider, however, some examples of these basic networks with slightly more complex switching arrangements.

Example 7.5

In the network of Figure 7.13, the switch S_1 has been closed and the switch S_2 has been open for a very long time. At $t = 0$, S_1 is opened and S_2 is closed, both in zero time. Let us calculate the voltage $v_1(t)$ for $t \geq 0$.

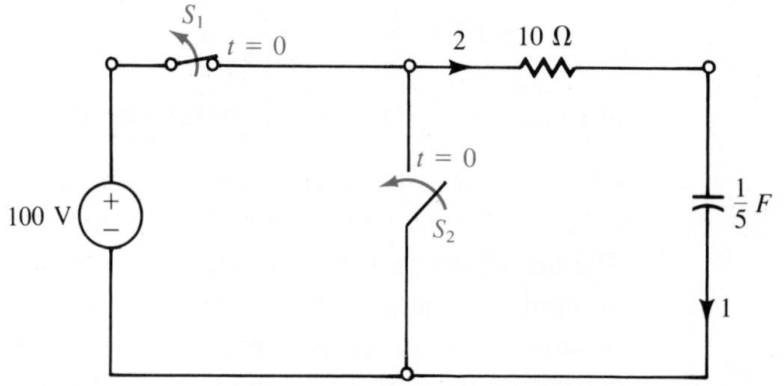

Figure 7.13
Network for Example 7.5.

Just prior to the switching operation, at $t = 0$, the network is in steady state since it has been in this condition for a "very long time." With S_1 closed and S_2 open, the network is a simple series network of the type analyzed in Example 7.3. Therefore, we know the complete response of this network. However, we only need the steady-state solution for $v_1(t)$, since it is the initial condition for the solution for $t \geq 0$. In passing, we note that the time constant of the network response prior to $t = 0$ is $RC = 2$ s. Therefore, the very long time required to attain the steady-state condition is any time greater than about 10 s.

From our analysis of the network of Example 7.3, we immediately conclude that

$$v_1(0^-) = 100 \text{ V}$$

where $t = 0^-$ is taken to be the time instant just before the switching operation begins. Now we ask whether the voltage across the capacitor at the conclusion of the switching is still 100 V. The answer is yes. In fact, *the voltage across a capacitor cannot change in a discontinuous fashion (that is, in zero time) unless the current through the capacitor is infinite*. This is evident from the fact that the capacitor voltage is related to the current by a time integral and consequently cannot change in zero time unless the integrand (current) is infinite in value.

For $t \geq 0$ we again have a simple series network (S_1 open, S_2 closed) of the type of Example 7.3. In this case the initial state is $v_1(0) = 100$ and the network response is for the zero-input case. The time constant of this network is again $T = RC = 2$ s. Therefore, we have

$$v_1(t) = 100e^{-t/2}$$

for $t \geq 0$. The current is

$$i_2 = i_1 = \frac{1}{5}\frac{dv_1}{dt} = -10e^{-t/2}$$

and the resistor voltage is

$$v_2 = 10i_2 = -100e^{-t/2}$$

The capacitor is supplying energy to the resistor until steady state, at which time the resistor has dissipated all the energy stored on the capacitor, and current stops. Technically speaking, this condition is reached only in the limit as t approaches infinity. However, the condition is essentially reached after a time of 10 s (5 time constants). To emphasize this fact we note that

$$w_1(0) = \tfrac{1}{2}\,(\tfrac{1}{5})(100)^2 = 1000 \text{ J}$$

of energy is stored on the capacitor at $t = 0$. But at $t = 10$ s, $v_1(10) = 0.007(100) = 0.7$ and only

$$w_1(10) = \tfrac{1}{2}\,(\tfrac{1}{5})(0.7)^2 = 0.049 \text{ J}$$

of energy is left on the capacitor.

Example 7.6

In the network of Figure 7.14, S_1 has been closed and S_2 has been open for a very long time. (How long is a very long time in this case?) At $t = 0$, S_2 is closed and S_1 is opened, in that order. (What would happen if the reverse sequence of switching were attempted?) Let us solve for $v_1(t)$ and $i_1(t)$ for $t \geq 0$.

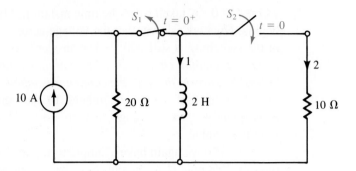

Figure 7.14
Network for Example 7.6.

Prior to $t = 0$ the network is in steady state, the inductor is an effective short circuit, no current flows through the 20-Ω resistor, and $i_1(0^-) = 10$ A. By an argument analogous to that for the capacitor, we conclude that the inductor current cannot change in a discontinuous way unless the voltage across the inductor is infinite. Therefore, for $t \geq 0$ we have the network of Figure 7.15 with $i_1(0) = 10$ A. Note that we do not really care about the value of i_1 at any time in the distant past, whether it had an initial value at the time S_1 was closed, or in what manner it attained steady state. For our purposes these things are not important because they do not affect the value of $i_1(0^-)$.

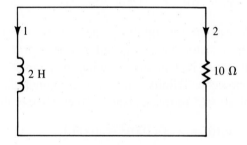

Figure 7.15
Network after switching.

The network of Figure 7.15 is of the form of Example 7.4 and we have only the zero-input response in this case. Therefore, we have

$$i_1(t) = 10e^{-5t}$$

and

$$v_1(t) = 2\frac{di_1}{dt} = -100e^{-5t}$$

for $t \geq 0$. Thus we see that the current response decays exponentially from an initial value of 10 A with a time constant of 0.2 s.

7.5 MORE ON SOURCES—THE STEP AND IMPULSE FUNCTIONS

The use of ideal sources and ideal switches, as in the previous examples, is a satisfactory method of depicting the manner in which networks are suddenly excited by some source. However, it is convenient to have some mathematical source functions to describe such operations, especially if such functions could be represented by a simple symbol on our network diagrams. The step function has been introduced into network analysis with an eye toward this goal.

The *unit step function* is symbolized by $u(t)$ and is shown in Figure 7.16. Mathematically, this function is

$$u(t) = \begin{cases} 1 & t > 0 \\ 0 & t < 0 \end{cases} \qquad (7.24)$$

Figure 7.16
The unit step function.

The value at $t = 0$ is not defined. If this function is multiplied by a constant K, the result is

$$Ku(t) = \begin{cases} K & t > 0 \\ 0 & t < 0 \end{cases} \qquad (7.25)$$

Although the function of Equation 7.25 is simple, it is quite useful in network analysis. For example, the v-source and the switching arrangement in the network of Figure 7.17 can be replaced by the v-source of Figure 7.18, if the switch is moved from position 1 to position 2 at $t = 0$. The result is a network that is equivalent mathematically. It is not necessary to introduce a new symbol. We simply use the v-source symbol and code it with the step-function symbol.

Figure 7.17
Network with v-source and ideal switch.

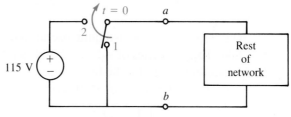

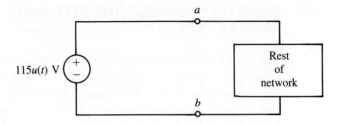

Figure 7.18
Equivalent network using
unit step function.

The unit step function can be used to switch on or off any voltage or current source (or any other variable or function for that matter). For example, the i-source shown in Figure 7.19 produces a current i described by

$$i = \begin{cases} 25 \cos t \text{ A} & t > 0 \\ 0 & t < 0 \end{cases}$$

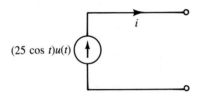

Figure 7.19
An i-source with a unit
step function.

This source function is shown in Figure 7.20.

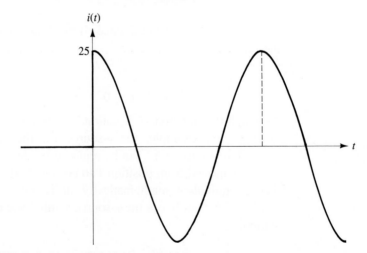

Figure 7.20
The current waveform for
the i-source of Figure
7.19.

The step function is also quite useful in delaying the switching of a source function. The properties of a delayed unit step function follow directly from the basic definition. Thus for the function $u(t - a)$, when the argument $(t - a) > 0$, $u(t - a) = 1$; when $(t - a) < 0$, $u(t - a) = 0$. From this we have

$$u(t - a) = \begin{cases} 1 & t > a \\ 0 & t < a \end{cases} \tag{7.26}$$

The v-source $v = 100u(t - 5)$ V is as shown in Figure 7.21.

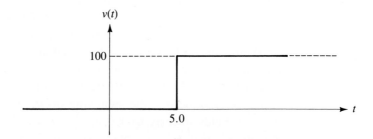

Figure 7.21
The source function
$v = 100u(t - 5)$.

The possibilities for creating ingenious functions are almost limitless. For example, a pulse is shown in Figure 7.22. Another example is seen in Figure 7.23. Other examples—even more creative than these—are left to the imagination.

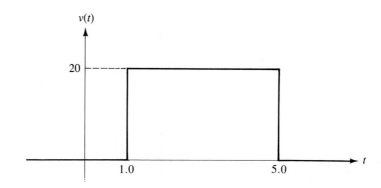

Figure 7.22
The pulse $v =$
$20[u(t - 1) - u(t - 5)]$.

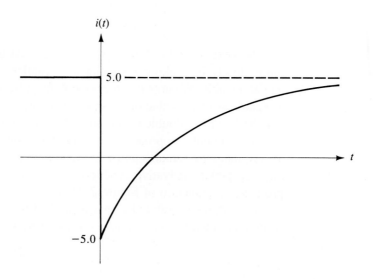

Figure 7.23
The function
$i = 5.0 - 10e^{-at}u(t)$.

Suppose we now consider the differentiation of a step function. Such a differentiation could be necessary, for example, if the voltage across a capacitor contained a step function. Only a little reflection and study of Figure 7.16 is necessary to conclude that the derivative of the unit step function is zero for all $t \neq 0$ (all right so far) but is not defined at $t = 0$. In order to circumvent this difficulty, suppose we consider an approximation to the unit step function as seen in Figure 7.24. In this figure ε is some small positive constant. In other words, we assume that the switching operation begins ε s before $t = 0$; the function builds linearly to 1.0 at $t = \varepsilon$ s and levels off at that point. The derivative is perfectly acceptable (Figure 7.25).

Figure 7.24
An approximation to the unit step function.

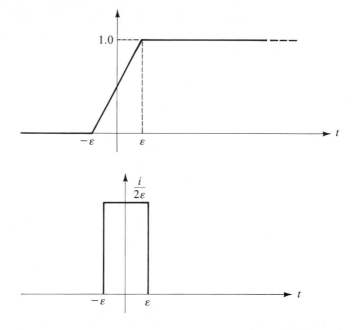

Figure 7.25
The derivative of the function in Figure 7.24.

We next force the function of Figure 7.24 to approximate the unit step more closely by making ε smaller and smaller. This seems perfectly logical and acceptable. We note that the area of the pulse in Figure 7.25 is $2\varepsilon(1/2\varepsilon) = 1$ regardless of the value of ε. As ε is halved, the width of the pulse is halved, but the height is doubled, and so on. In the limit as ε approaches zero, the width of the pulse approaches zero and the height approaches infinity, but the area of the pulse remains unity. We also note that, just as we would expect for any acceptable derivative function, integration of the pulse of Figure 7.25 produces the function of Figure 7.24.

The infinitely high pulse that is created by proceeding to the limit in this fashion is called the *unit impulse function* and is symbolized by $\delta(t)$. Although this impulse is not a function in the strictest mathematical sense, it is a valuable device for network analysis. The formal definition is

$$\delta(t) = \begin{cases} 0 & t \neq 0 \\ \text{undefined} & t = 0 \end{cases} \tag{7.27}$$

but

$$\int_{-\infty}^{\infty} \delta(t) \, dt = 1 \tag{7.28}$$

In addition, we require that

$$\frac{d}{dt} u(t) \doteq \delta(t) \tag{7.29}$$

and

$$\int_{-\infty}^{t} \delta(\tau) \, d\tau \doteq u(t) \tag{7.30}$$

The unit impulse function is also known as the *Dirac delta function*, or simply the *delta function*. This delta function has been introduced at this point solely for the purpose of accounting for the derivative of a function with a jump discontinuity, such as the function $u(t)$.

If you are mathematically inclined, you may be somewhat aghast at the process by which we arrived at this "function." If so, your uneasiness is somewhat justified. However, we ask that you accept this delta function as a formally defined concept with properties defined by Equations 7.27–7.30. We shall see that this formally defined structure will allow us to cope with some unusual problems that would otherwise require a much more complex treatment.

Next consider the derivative of a general step function $Ku(t)$.

$$\frac{d}{dt}[Ku(t)] = K\frac{du(t)}{dt} = K\delta(t) \tag{7.31}$$

and in the reverse direction, we have

$$\int_{-\infty}^{t} K\delta(\tau) \, d\tau = K \int_{-\infty}^{t} \delta(\tau) \, d\tau = Ku(t) \tag{7.32}$$

Consequently, we have the reassurance that the integration of the derivative of a general step function yields the original step function. The corresponding results for a delayed step function are

$$\frac{d}{dt}[Ku(t - a)] \doteq K\delta(t - a) \tag{7.33}$$

and

$$\int_{-\infty}^{t} K\delta(\tau - a)\, d\tau \doteq Ku(t - a) \tag{7.34}$$

where $\delta(t - a)$ is defined by

$$\delta(t - a) = \begin{cases} 0 & t \neq a \\ \text{undefined} & t = a \end{cases} \tag{7.35}$$

$$\int_{-\infty}^{\infty} \delta(t - a)\, dt = 1 \tag{7.36}$$

Thus $\delta(t - a)$ is an impulse function delayed by a s.

We refer to the impulse function $K\delta(t)$ as an impulse function of strength K. We must remember to interpret this *strength as the area of the impulse* (the height is infinite). Thus an impulse of current is represented by a strength (an area) whose dimensions are amp-seconds, or coulombs, and an impulse of voltage is represented by a strength (an area) whose dimensions are volt-seconds, or webers.

The graphical symbol for an impulse function is an arrow with the strength shown in parentheses near the head of the arrow. Figure 7.26 shows the impulse functions $5\delta(t)$ and $-10\delta(t - 4)$.

Figure 7.26
Two-impulse functions.

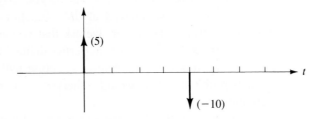

Next consider the integral

$$\int_{a}^{b} f(t)\delta(t - t_1)\, dt$$

with $f(t)$ defined at $t = t_1$ and a and b chosen such that the interval (a, b) includes t_1. Since $\delta(t - t_1) = 0$ except at $t = t_1$, the integrand has a nonzero value only at t_1, and we obtain

$$\int_{a}^{b} f(t)\delta(t - t_1)\, dt = \int_{a}^{b} f(t_1)\delta(t - t_1)\, dt = f(t_1) \tag{7.37}$$

Thus we see that this operation has the effect of picking out the value of the function $f(t)$ at the specific time t_1. This particular property of the impulse function is called the *sampling*, or *sifting*, property.

As a by-product of the development of the sampling property, we also see that

$$f(t) \cdot \delta(t - t_1) = 0 \qquad \text{for } t \neq t_1$$

$$f(t) \cdot \delta(t - t_1) = f(t_1) \cdot \delta(t - t_1) \qquad \text{for } t = t_1$$

Therefore, we see that

$$f(t) \cdot \delta(t - t_1) = f(t_1) \cdot \delta(t - t_1) \qquad \text{for all } t$$

and at $t_1 = 0$,

$$f(t) \cdot \delta(t) = f(0) \cdot \delta(t)$$

Next consider a product function given by

$$g(t) = f(t) \cdot u(t)$$

These two functions are shown in Figure 7.27. The function $g(t)$ can be described mathematically as

$$g(t) = \begin{cases} 0 & \text{for } t < 0 \\ \text{undefined} & \text{for } t = 0 \\ f(t) & \text{for } t > 0 \end{cases}$$

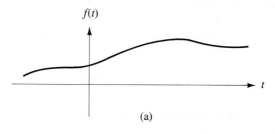

$f(t)$

(a)

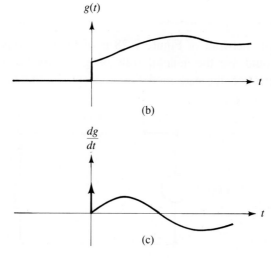

$g(t)$

(b)

$\dfrac{dg}{dt}$

(c)

Figure 7.27
Differentiation of product function.

Further, we note that the jump discontinuity at the origin has a value $f(0)$.
Now consider the derivative

$$h = \frac{d}{dt} g(t) = \frac{d}{dt} [f(t)u(t)]$$

By ordinary rules of derivatives

$$h = \frac{d}{dt} g(t) = \frac{d}{dt} (0) = 0 \qquad \text{for } t < 0$$

$$h = \frac{d}{dt} g(t) = \frac{d}{dt} f(t) \qquad \text{for } t > 0$$

By the rules that we have established for derivatives of jump discontinuities, we see that the derivative at the origin is defined to be an impulse function of strength $f(0)$. Therefore, we can write that

$$h(t) = \frac{d}{dt} [f(t)u(t)] = f(0)\delta(t) + \frac{d}{dt} [f(t)]u(t)$$

where the $u(t)$ restricts the last term to positive time.

Note that we obtain the same results by use of the product rule for differentiation. Thus

$$\frac{d}{dt} [f(t)u(t)] = f(t)\delta(t) + \frac{d}{dt} [f(t)]u(t)$$

$$= f(0)\delta(t) + \frac{d}{dt} [f(t)]u(t)$$

Let us examine some of these points by example.

Example 7.7

The network of Figure 7.28 is of the same type as that of Example 7.4. We could use the general solution given by Equation 7.21. However, we can practice our state-modeling concepts on this network.

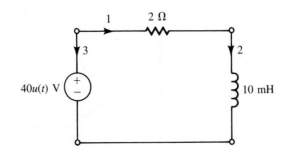

Figure 7.28
RL network with step-function source.

Replacing the inductor by a symbolic current source, we obtain the network of Figure 7.29. From this network

$$v_2(t) = -v_1 + v_3 = -2i_2 + 40u(t)$$

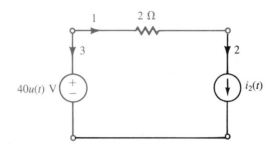

Figure 7.29
Network for developing state model.

Therefore, the state equation is

$$\frac{di_2}{dt} = \frac{1}{10^{-2}}[-2i_2 + 40u(t)]$$

$$= -200i_2 + 4000u(t)$$

By considering the network and the properties of $u(t)$, we conclude that $i_2(0) = 0$. Thus, the state equation becomes

$$\frac{di_2}{dt} = -200i_2 + 4000 \qquad \text{for } t \geq 0$$

$$i_2(0) = 0$$

The solution for any state equation of this form was developed as Equation 7.11. In this case we obtain ($K = 4000$, $T = \frac{1}{200}$)

$$i_2(t) = 20(1 - e^{-200t}) \tag{7.38}$$

Example 7.8 ———————————————————————————————————

Suppose the v-source of Example 7.7 (Figure 7.28), is changed to $v_3 = 40[u(t) - u(t - 1)]$. This can be expressed as

$$v_3 = \begin{cases} 0 & t < 0 \\ 40 & 0 < t < 1 \\ 0 & t > 1 \end{cases}$$

Therefore, during the first second, the source and the solution are the same as that for Example 7.7. So, from Equation 7.38,

$$i_2(t) = 20(1 - e^{-200t}) \qquad \text{for } 0 < t < 1$$

This solution has a time constant of $\frac{1}{200} = 5$ ms. Consequently, $i_2(t)$ will approach a constant value of 20 A very quickly, with respect to the 1-s total period for which this solution is valid. By the end of the 1-s interval, $i_2(t)$ is, for all practical purposes, equal to 20 A. (Note that $e^{-200} = 1.3838965 \times 10^{-87}$.) The buildup of this current is sketched in Figure 7.30(a).

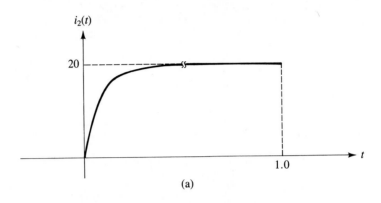

(a)

Figure 7.30
Current response for
Example 7.8. (a) The
buildup of current
(b) Total current.

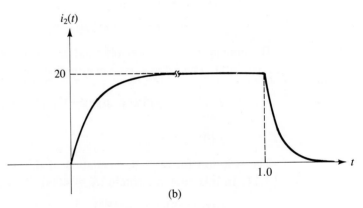

(b)

For $t > 1$ the source goes to zero, and the state model that we need to solve becomes

$$\frac{di_2}{dt} = -200i_2$$

$$i_2(1) = 20 \text{ A}$$

Again, this is our standard-form state equation. In this case we need the unforced solution only. However, there is a new dimension. The initial condition is given at $t = 1$ s rather than $t = 0$. Suppose we simply shift the $t = 0$ axis to the $t = 1$ point by defining a new time variable t' such that

$$t' = t - 1$$

Then, in terms of this new variable, the equations become

$$\frac{di_2}{dt'} = -200i_2$$

$$i_2(0) = 20 \text{ A}$$

and the solution (from Equation 7.11) is

$$i_2(t') = 20e^{-200t'} \qquad \text{for } t' > 0$$

or, in terms of t,

$$i_2(t) = 20e^{-200(t-1)} \qquad t > 1 \text{ s}$$

Now the total solution can be drawn (Figure 7.30(b)).

The impulse function enters into network analysis in at least two basic fashions. One is when the impulse arises as a result of the differentiation of a function with a jump discontinuity. The other occurs when we use source impulse functions as a matter of convenience. We illustrate the first with an example.

Example 7.9

The current in the capacitor in the network of Figure 7.31 is given by

$$i_2(t) = 2\frac{dv_2}{dt} = 2\frac{dv_1}{dt} = 2\frac{d}{dt}[5u(t)] = 10\delta(t) \text{ A}$$

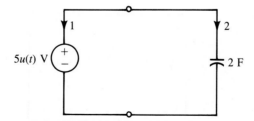

Figure 7.31
Network for Example 7.9.

and the voltage across the capacitor is

$$v_2(t) = \frac{1}{2}\int_{0^-}^{t} i_2(\tau)\, d\tau + v_2(0) = \frac{1}{2}\int_{0^-}^{t} 10\delta(\tau)\, d\tau = 5u(t) \text{ V}$$

The lower limit of 0^- is necessary in order to account for the impulse at $t = 0$. We now have a formal solution. However, an explanation of the physical behavior requires some fancy footwork. Nevertheless, suppose we try. Prior to

$t = 0$, the voltage source is zero, and the capacitor is shorted and consequently has zero voltage and energy. At $t = 0$ the voltage is switched instantaneously from 0 to +5 V. At this point, KVL requires that v_2 also switch instantly to 5 V. Thus the capacitor must go from an uncharged, or deenergized, state to a charged state of 5 V and an energy of $\frac{1}{2}Cv_2^2 = \frac{1}{2}(2)(5)^2 = 25$ J in zero time. Since this charge must be transferred by current flow, this current must be extremely large in order to charge the capacitor in such a short time (0 s). Once the capacitor is charged to 5 V, it remains at this voltage for all $t > 0$.

At this point some professors have been known to remark: If all of this does not disturb you, then you obviously do not understand!

This explanation may be made somewhat more palatable by assuming a model of the network that is less ideal. Suppose the network is known to be more nearly that of Figure 7.32, where a small resistance has been added to account for resistance of the capacitor, the leads, and so on. In this case the state equation is readily determined from Figure 7.33. (Another opportunity to practice state modeling.) The current in the capacitor is

$$i_2 = i_3 = \frac{1}{r}v_3 = \frac{1}{r}[5u(t) - v_2]$$

and the state equation is

$$\frac{dv_2}{dt} = \frac{1}{2}i_2 = \frac{1}{2r}[5u(t) - v_2]$$

or

$$\frac{dv_2}{dt} = -\frac{1}{2r}v_2 + \frac{5}{2r}u(t)$$

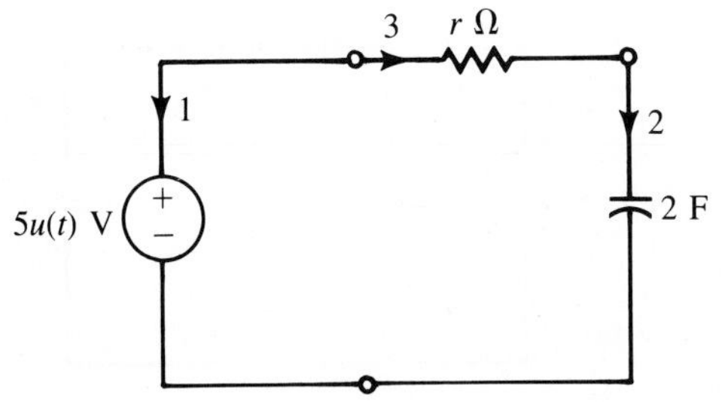

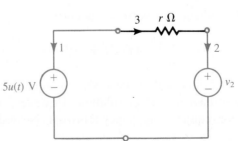

Figure 7.32
A more practical network model.

Figure 7.33
Network used to find state model.

Once again we call on our general solution (Equation 7.11) to obtain

$$v_2(t) = e^{-t/2r}[v_2(0) - 5] + 5$$

and, since $v_2(0) = 0$, we have

$$v_2(t) = 5[1 - e^{-t/2r}]$$

and

$$i_2(t) = 2\frac{dv_2}{dt} = \frac{5}{r}e^{-t/2r}$$

which indicates that the voltage will build up exponentially to 5 V while the current starts at 5/r A and decays exponentially to zero. We note two things. First, the time constant is directly proportional to r; thus the speed of voltage buildup increases as r is made smaller. Second, the initial current flow is inversely proportional to r and also increases as r is decreased. This situation is sketched in Figures 7.34 and 7.35 as r_1 is halved, then halved again, and so on. From these sketches we see that in the limit as r becomes vanishingly small, the current will become an extremely large spike of vanishingly small duration. It is not difficult to imagine this as an approximation to an impulse. We also see from these sketches that the voltage buildup accompanying the current spikes occurs in a time that is approaching zero as the resistance goes to zero.

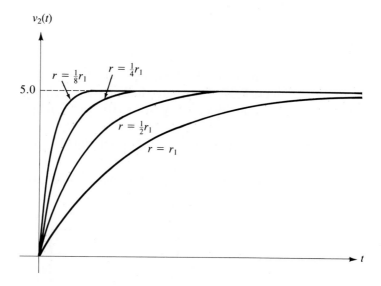

Figure 7.34
Capacitor voltage for
network of Figure 7.32.

This example should not be considered simply as an example of impulsive behavior but as one that illuminates several properties of a simple *RC* network.

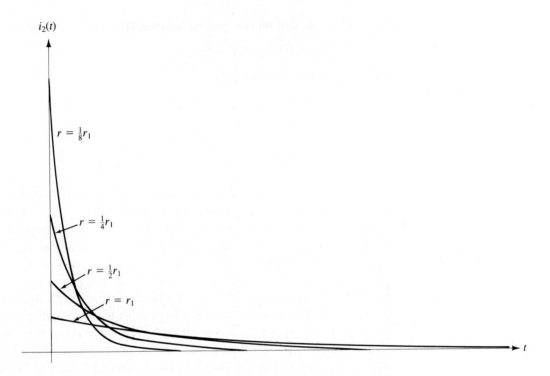

Figure 7.35
Capacitor current for
network of Figure 7.32.

Example 7.10

For the network of Figure 7.36, the voltage of the v-source is sketched in Figure 7.37. This source function, and consequently the voltage v_2, has a jump discontinuity of $+5$ V at $t = 0$. The current in the capacitor is given by

$$i_2(t) = C\,\frac{dv_2}{dt} = 2\,\frac{d}{dt}\,[5e^{-t}u(t)] = 10\delta(t) - 10e^{-t}u(t)$$

Calculation of the capacitor voltage is left as an exercise.

Figure 7.36
Network for Example 7.10.

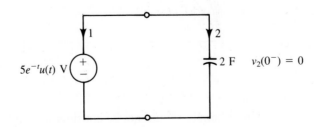

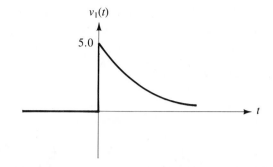

Figure 7.37
The *v*-source for Example 7.10.

The impulse function also enters into network analysis simply because we may decide to use it as a source. The solution of a network to an impulse-function input has long been known as the *impulse response*. Some basic ideas from this impulse response have broad applications in several areas of engineering and applied mathematics. Consequently, we use the first-order network as a vehicle to introduce this subject in a general fashion.

We have seen that any first-order network has a state model of the form

$$\frac{dx}{dt} = ax + f(t) \tag{7.39}$$

Furthermore, in Section 7.3 we derived the solution for this model as

$$x(t) = e^{at}x(0) + e^{at} \int_0^t e^{-a\tau} f(\tau) \, d\tau \tag{7.40}$$

Suppose we choose a forcing function $f(t) = K\delta(t)$; then the solution becomes

$$x(t) = e^{at}x(0) + e^{at}K \tag{7.41}$$

and we see that the forced response is of the exact same form as the natural response. If, as is the usual case for the impulse response, we take the initial state to be zero, then we obtain

$$x(t) = e^{at}K \tag{7.42}$$

which is indistinguishable from the natural response. The impulse function, in fact, imparts an initial energy to the network. Prior to $t = 0$ the network is at rest (no energy storage) and the source is zero. At $t = 0$ the impulse function delivers an infinitely large input to the network over a vanishingly small time interval and consequently delivers energy to the energy-storage element (the L or C element). For any positive time, the source returns to zero and the network is free to deliver the stored energy to the dissipative elements (the resistors) if a path for current flow exists. The result is a natural response—the same as for any initial energy storage.

Consider how this process occurs in the series RL network of Figure 7.38. The state equation is readily seen to be

$$\frac{di}{dt} = \frac{1}{L}v_L = \frac{1}{L}[-Ri + K_1 \, \delta(t)]$$

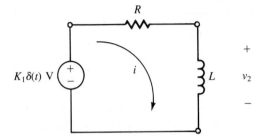

Figure 7.38
Series RL network with impulse input.

The solution as given by Equation 7.42 is

$$i(t) = e^{-Rt/L}\frac{K_1}{L}$$

The constant K_1/L plays the role of an initial current and can be used to establish any desired initial current in the inductance at $t = 0$. Note that the current is of necessity equal to zero before $t = 0$ because the source voltage is zero (a short circuit). Note also that the source reverts to a short circuit for $t > 0$.

Similar responses are readily determined for other specific first-order networks. These are left to the problems.

7.6 A NUMERICAL SOLUTION OF THE STATE EQUATION

Section 7.3 showed that linear first-order networks can be modeled by a linear state equation of the form

$$\dot{x} = ax + f(t) \tag{7.43}$$

We were also successful in developing a solution to this model as a closed-form expression in time, namely,

$$x(t) = e^{at}x(0) + e^{at}\int_0^t e^{-a\tau}f(\tau)\,d\tau \tag{7.44}$$

In the examples considered, the evaluation of the integral term in Equation 7.44 was usually straightforward and fairly simple. We even developed a general form for this integral for the practical case $f(t) = K$. On occasion, however, we may wish to solve networks with a forcing function that is considerably more complicated. This would cause the evaluation of the integral term in Equation 7.44 to be much more of a problem, and we may well wish to use a numerical technique for the evaluation of the integral term. Or, in a more straightforward fashion, we can go directly to a computer solution for Equation 7.43.

If we were concerned only with network models of the form of Equation 7.43, there would be no real justification for introducing numerical approaches. However, in the next chapter we extend modeling and analysis to networks with two energy-storage elements. These networks have differential equation models of second degree and are considerably more complex to solve. A digital computer can perform the laborious portion of the solution, thus allowing the analyst to concentrate on the nature of the finer points of the results.

Finally, the numerical approach that we take can be extended to higher-order networks and to nonlinear networks. It also provides an introduction to the field of numerical solutions of differential equations.

For all these reasons we now discuss one method for solving the state equation with a digital computer. We develop a formula for solving Equation 7.43 by calculating values of the state variable x at specifically defined points in time. The result is a set of tabulated values for $x(t)$ and the corresponding time t. Such a formula is called a *numerical integration algorithm*. The numerical approach yields a table of discrete values for x. In contrast, the analytical approach yields an expression for x as a function of time that holds for all $t \geq 0$.

To develop the algorithm, we rewrite the state equation as

$$\frac{dx}{dt} = ax + f(t) \tag{7.45}$$

and operate on both sides with dt to obtain

$$dx = [ax + f(t)] \, dt$$

Next, we integrate both sides of the equation between the limits of t_k and t_{k+1} and find that

$$\int_{x(t_k)}^{x(t_{k+1})} dx = \int_{t_k}^{t_{k+1}} [ax + f(t)] \, dt = x(t_{k+1}) - x(t_k)$$

Suppose we simplify the notation by using $x(k)$ to denote $x(t_k)$ and $x(k+1)$ to denote $x(t_{k+1})$. In addition, if we symbolize the bracketed term as $g(x, t) = ax + f(t)$, the result is

$$x(k+1) = x(k) + \int_{t_k}^{t_{k+1}} g(x, t) \, dt \tag{7.46}$$

Next, we define a set of discrete points in time, as on the time axis in Figure 7.39. Further suppose that these points are at equally spaced increments of h such that

$$\left. \begin{array}{c} t_k = kh \\ t_{k+1} - t_k = h \end{array} \right\} \quad \text{for } k = 0, 1, 2 \ldots$$

(The equal spacing is not necessary but leads to a convenient result.)

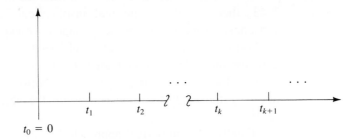

Figure 7.39
The discrete time points
for the numerical
algorithm.

Now we can delineate the problem. Suppose at any time t_k ($k =$ any nonnegative integer), we know:

1. The value of the state $x(k)$.

2. The form of the expression for $g(x, t)$.
   (In our case $g(x, t) = ax + f(t)$,
   with a constant and $f(t)$ a known forcing function.)

The problem: How do we calculate a numerical value for the integral over the interval from t_k to t_{k+1}? Thus the name *numerical integration*.

Many techniques are available for the numerical evaluation of the integral. One of the more popular and powerful approaches is the trapezoidal method. This technique is illustrated by Figure 7.40. Since the value of the definite integral is simply the area under the curve $g(x, t)$, we choose to approximate this area by the area of the trapezoid. Thus

$$\int_{t_k}^{t_{k+1}} g(x, t) \, dt \simeq \frac{1}{2}(t_{k+1} - t_k)\{g[x(k + 1), t_{k+1}]$$

$$+ g[x(k), t_k]\} \tag{7.47}$$

Since $t_{k+1} - t_k = h$ and $g(x, t) = ax + f(t)$, we can write the result for $x(k + 1)$ as

$$x(k + 1) \simeq x(k) + \frac{1}{2}h[ax(k + 1) + f(t_{k+1}) + ax(k) + f(t_k)]$$

and solving for $x(k + 1)$, we have

$$x(k + 1) \simeq \frac{(1 + \frac{1}{2}ha)x(k) + \frac{1}{2}h[f(t_k) + f(t_{k+1})]}{1 - \frac{1}{2}ha} \tag{7.48}$$

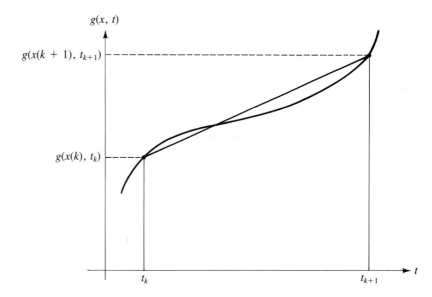

Figure 7.40
Illustration of trapezoidal integration.

and the algorithm is complete. The approximation of Equation 7.48 can be made to be quite accurate by choosing h small.

An outline of how the algorithm can be used to produce the solution for x is appropriate:

Step 1. Identify the given information:
(a) The constant a. (*Note:* This constant is normally negative.)
(b) The initial state $x(0)$.
(c) The forcing function $f(t)$.

Step 2. Choose a solution interval h. (A good beginning value is one-tenth the network time constant.)

Step 3. Evaluate and tabulate the discrete values of the forcing function, $f(0), f(1), f(2), \ldots$, for the number of time points for which a solution is desired. (In actual practice the forcing function may often be entered as a functional expression and the value of the forcing function evaluated as needed in Step 4. However, all that is needed is a set of values at the proper time points.)

Step 4. Beginning at $t = 0$ with $x(0)$, solve Equation 7.48 recursively for $x(1)$, $x(2)$, $x(3)$, $\ldots$, for as many values as desired.

This algorithm is readily implemented on a digital computer or even on a programmable calculator. A BASIC language program, TRAPZ 1, is included in Appendix C.

Example 7.11 _____

In Example 7.7, we found the state model of an RL network to be

$$\frac{di_2}{dt} = -200i_2 + 4000 \tag{7.49}$$

$$i_2(0) = 0$$

and the solution was given as

$$i_2(t) = 20(1 - e^{-200t}), \qquad t \geq 0 \tag{7.50}$$

The state equation of the network (Equation 7.49) is readily solved for the inductor current using the trapezoidal method. Results of the application of Equation 7.48 to this problem are shown in Table 7.2.

Table 7.2
Solution of the
Current for Network
of Example 7.11

Time	$20(1 - e^{-200t})$	Trapezoidal Solution		
		$h = 0.0001$ s	$h = 0.001$ s	$h = 0.005$ s
0.001	3.625384937	3.625494109	3.636363636	
0.002	6.593599079	6.59377784	6.611570248	
0.003	9.023767278	9.023986814	9.045830203	
0.004	11.01342072	11.01366037	11.03749744	
0.005	12.64241118	12.64265644	12.66704336	13.33333333
0.006	13.97611576	13.97635673	14.0003082	
0.007	15.06806072	15.06829089	15.09116126	
0.008	15.96206964	15.962285	15.98367739	
0.009	16.69402224	16.69422060	16.71391787	
0.010	17.29329434	17.29347479	17.31138734	17.77777778
0.011	17.78393683	17.78409935	17.800226	
0.012	18.18564093	18.18578608	18.20018492	
0.013	18.51452844	18.51465718	18.52742402	
0.014	18.78379875	18.78391226	18.7951651	
0.015	19.00425863	19.0043582	19.01422600	19.25925926
0.016	19.18475592	19.18484288	19.19345764	
0.017	19.3325346	19.33261024	19.3401017	
0.018	19.45352555	19.45359113	19.46008321	
0.019	19.55258456	19.55264123	19.55824990	
0.020	19.63368722	19.63373606	19.63856810	19.75308642

0.021	19.70008846	19.70013045	19.70428299	
0.022	19.7544532	19.75448921	19.75804972	
0.023	19.79896329	19.7989941	19.80204068	
0.024	19.83540506	19.83543139	19.83803328	
0.025	19.86524106	19.86526352	19.86748178	19.91769547
0.026	19.88966871	19.88968783	19.89157600	
0.027	19.90966838	19.90968464	19.91128945	
0.028	19.92604273	19.92605653	19.92741864	
0.029	19.9394489	19.9394606	19.94061525	
0.030	19.95042496	19.95043487	19.95141248	19.97256516
0.031	19.95941139	19.95941977	19.96024658	
0.032	19.96676885	19.96677594	19.96747447	
0.033	19.97279264	19.97279862	19.9733882	
0.034	19.97772450	19.97772954	19.97822671	
0.035	19.98176236	19.98176661	19.98218549	19.99085505
0.036	19.98506828	19.98507186	19.98542449	
0.037	19.98777494	19.98777796	19.98807459	
0.038	19.98999097	19.9899935	19.99024284	
0.039	19.9918053	19.99180743	19.99201687	
0.040	19.99329075	19.99329253	19.99346835	19.99695168
0.041	19.99450693	19.99450843	19.99465592	
0.042	19.99550265	19.99550391	19.99562757	
0.043	19.99631788	19.99631894	19.99642256	
0.044	19.99698534	19.99698622	19.997073	
0.045	19.9975318	19.99753254	19.99760518	19.99898389
0.046	19.99797921	19.99797983	19.9980406	
0.047	19.99834552	19.99834603	19.99839686	
0.048	19.99864543	19.99864586	19.99868834	
0.049	19.99889097	19.99889133	19.99892682	
0.050	19.999092	19.9990923	19.99912195	19.99966130

In Table 7.2, an evaluation of the known solution, Equation 7.50, at selected time points is given in the second column. For comparison, the trapezoidal solution is shown for three different solution rates, h, in the last three columns. We note that the numerical solution is extremely accurate for a solution rate of $h = 0.0001$ s. The numerical solution is also quite accurate for $h = 0.001$ and is surprisingly close to the actual solution even when h is taken to be equal to the time constant of 0.005 s. The error for this latter case is a few percent of the actual solution and decreases as the numerical solution proceeds in time. When $h = 0.005$, a limited number of solution points are available.

Example 7.12

Consider the network of Figure 7.41. The state equation is readily determined to be

$$\frac{dv}{dt} = -v + \cos t \qquad t \geq 0 \tag{7.51}$$

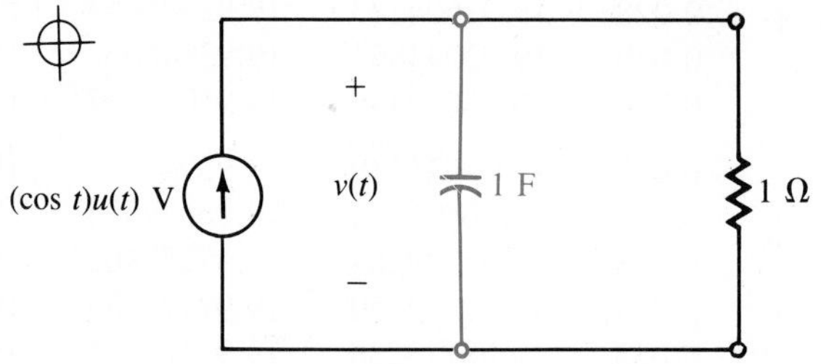

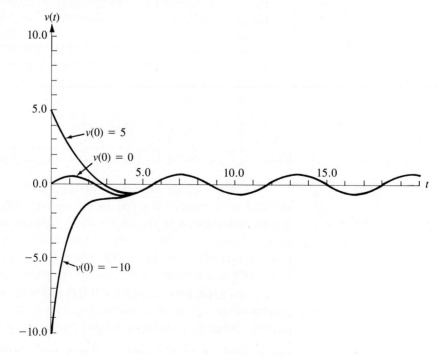

Figure 7.41
Network for Example 7.12.

A computer program is used to solve this equation by the trapezoidal method. The results for three different initial conditions are shown in Figure 7.42. In obtaining this solution, $h = 0.1$ s was chosen. This value is one-tenth of the time constant and the results were within a few tenths of a percent of the actual solution for all time points.

Figure 7.42
Solution of $v(t)$ for Example 7.12.

Example 7.13

As a final example of the numerical method, consider the network of Figure 7.43 with an input *v*-source of the form illustrated in Figure 7.44.

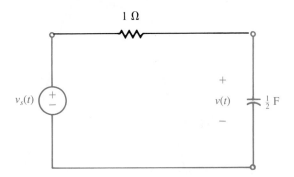

Figure 7.43
Network for Example 7.13.

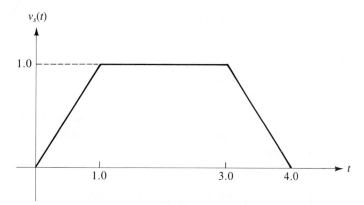

Figure 7.44
Voltage source for
Example 7.13.

In both of the two previous examples, a closed-form time-domain solution can be obtained, without major difficulty, by the solution of the integral in Equation 7.44. However, the state equation for this network is

$$\frac{dv}{dt} = -2v + 2v_s(t) \qquad t \geq 0 \tag{7.52}$$

Therefore, we see that application of Equation 7.44 yields

$$v(t) = e^{-2t}v(0) + e^{-2t} \int_0^t e^{2\tau}[2v_s(\tau)] \, d\tau$$

where $v_s(\tau)$ is not a simply described function of time. Although certainly possible, the evaluation of the integral for all $t \geq 0$ is a somewhat formidable task. Solution by the trapezoidal method, however, is routine. The result, for $v(0) = 0$, is plotted in Figure 7.45. Interpretation of the result is left as an exercise.

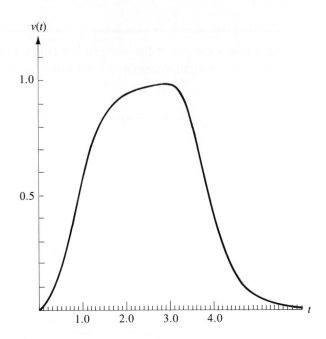

Figure 7.45
Voltage response of
network in Example 7.13.

As a final word on these examples, we note that the forcing function $f(t)$ was provided for the numerical algorithm by a function definition statement in the first two cases but was entered as a table of values for the last example.

7.7 MORE FIRST-ORDER NETWORK ANALYSIS

To conclude this chapter, a few additional examples are presented to help develop a firm understanding of the concepts involved in first-order network analysis. As we stated earlier, the approach that we have taken is applicable to a broad range of networks that contain a single energy-storage element. Thévenin or Norton equivalent networks are often useful in reducing the network to one of the simple forms that we can then handle with confidence. The next example is such a case.

Example 7.14

A fairly general first-order network is shown in Figure 7.46. An application of equivalent network techniques, from Chapter 4, quickly reduces this network to the familiar one of Figure 7.47. (Any remaining uncertainty may be laid to

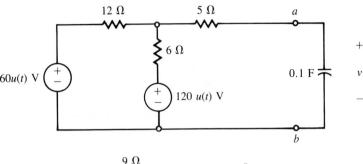

Figure 7.46
Network for Example 7.14.

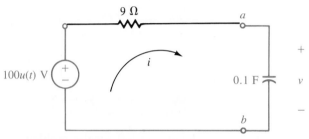

Figure 7.47
Equivalent network for
Figure 7.46.

rest by reviewing Example 4.23.) Therefore, our state-modeling technique
leads to the state equation

$$\frac{dv}{dt} = \frac{1}{C}i = \frac{1}{0.1}\left[\frac{100u(t) - v}{9}\right] = -\frac{1}{0.9}v + \frac{100}{0.9}u(t)$$

which has a now well-known solution,

$$v(t) = e^{-t/0.9}[v(0) - 100] + 100 \text{ V}$$

From the original network we conclude that $v(0) = 0$. (Why is this so?)
Therefore,

$$v(t) = 100(1 - e^{-t/0.09}) \text{ V}, \qquad t \geq 0$$

Now that $v(t)$ is known, other variables in the original network can be determined by fundamental relations and some algebra.

Example 7.15

The network of Figure 7.48 is equivalent to the one of Figure 7.49 (see
Example 4.30). The state equation is given by

$$\frac{di}{dt} = \frac{1}{L}v_L = \frac{1}{2}[40u(t) - 24i] = -12i + 20u(t)$$

and the solution is

$$i(t) = e^{-12t}\left[i(0) - \frac{10}{6}\right] + \frac{10}{6} \text{ A} \qquad t \geq 0$$

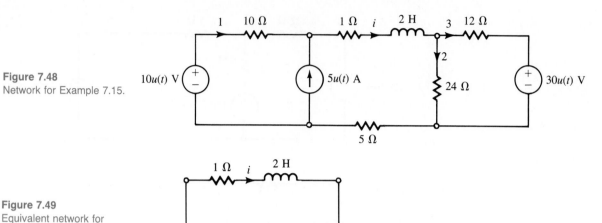

Figure 7.48
Network for Example 7.15.

Figure 7.49
Equivalent network for
Figure 7.48.

Additional details are left for the problems.

Example 7.16

Figure 7.50 shows a first-order network with an op amp. The network to the left of terminal pair c-d is the basic noninverting network. If we use the approximate equivalent network and assume that the voltage at c-d is independent of the load on the op amp (R_2 and C in this case), we conclude that the noninverting network can be replaced by a Thévenin equivalent as seen in

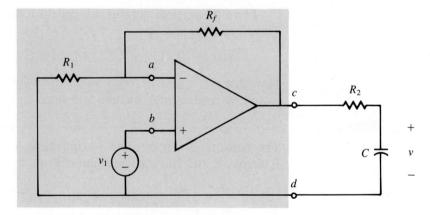

Figure 7.50
Network for Example 7.16.

Figure 7.51. Therefore, the state equation is

$$\frac{dv}{dt} = \frac{1}{C}i = \frac{1}{C}\left(\frac{\dfrac{R_1 + R_f}{R_1}v_1 - v}{R_2}\right)$$

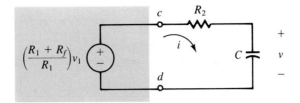

Figure 7.51
An equivalent network for
Figure 7.50.

or

$$\frac{dv}{dt} = -\frac{1}{R_2C}v + \frac{R_1 + R_f}{R_1R_2C}v_1$$

The details of the solution depend upon the form of the v-source v_1 and have already been amply discussed. However, the presence of the op amp caused very little additional complication in the analysis of this first-order network.

Example 7.17

Figure 7.52 shows another first-order network. Again, by using ideal model assumptions for the op amp, we conclude that the voltage at terminal pair c-d is independent of the load (everything to the right of c-d). Since this is a summing network, we conclude that

$$v_{cd} = -\frac{R_f}{R_1}v_1 - \frac{R_f}{R_2}v_2$$

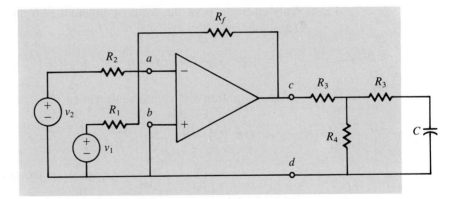

Figure 7.52
Network for Example 7.17.

and the Thévenin equivalent for the complete network to the left of the capacitor is readily determined (Figure 7.53). In this network

$$R_T = R_3 + \frac{R_3R_4}{R_3 + R_4}$$

and

$$e_T = \frac{R_4}{R_3 + R_4}\left(-\frac{R_f}{R_1}v_1 - \frac{R_f}{R_2}v_2\right)$$

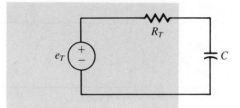

Figure 7.53
An equivalent network for
Figure 7.52.

Once again we have a basic *RC* network of the form that we have now seen
many times.

Example 7.18

The state equation for the network of Figure 7.54 is readily determined to be

$$\frac{dv}{dt} = -\frac{G}{C}v + \frac{I_m}{C}(\cos \omega t)u(t) \tag{7.53}$$

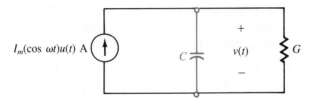

Figure 7.54
Network for Example 7.18.

This equation is in the form of Equation 7.6 and the solution, as given by
Equation 7.8, is

$$v(t) = e^{-Gt/C}v(0) + e^{-Gt/C}\int_0^t e^{G\tau/C}\left(\frac{I_m}{C}\cos \omega\tau\right) d\tau \tag{7.54}$$

After integration and some manipulation, the result is

$$v(t) = \left[v(0) - \frac{I_m G}{G^2 + (\omega C)^2}\right]e^{-Gt/C}$$

$$+ \frac{I_m}{G^2 + (\omega C)^2}(G \cos \omega t + \omega C \sin \omega t) \tag{7.55}$$

for all $t \geq 0$.

   This is a rather formidable result and you might well inquire about the
relative merits of this approach as compared to the numerical approaches of the
previous section. Certainly it is a rather simple matter to numerically integrate
Equation 7.53 and plot a curve of the voltage response of this network if a
computer is available. This was done for some specific network constants in
Example 7.12. However, our motivation here is to lay a foundation for understanding the response of networks with sinusoidal sources. The steady-state
response of such networks is of particular importance in the study of network
analysis.

Examine Equation 7.55 in some detail. In a manner similar to earlier examples, we conclude that the first term in the response is a transient term and will decay toward zero with a time constant equal to C/G s.

The rest of the response merits some special attention. We call the second term in the response the *steady-state response*, (a name that we justify shortly) and symbolize it as v_{ss}. Then

$$v_{ss} = \frac{I_m}{G^2 + (\omega C)^2}(G \cos \omega t + \omega C \sin \omega t) \qquad (7.56)$$

By use of trigonometric identities, we can rewrite this result as

$$v_{ss} = \frac{I_m}{\sqrt{G^2 + (\omega C)^2}} \cos(\omega t - \theta) \qquad (7.57)$$

where

$$\theta = \tan^{-1}\frac{\omega C}{G}$$

In earlier examples we saw that the steady-state response of first-order networks with constant inputs was also constant and easily calculated. In a similar fashion, we see that the steady-state response of this RC network to a sinusoidal input is also sinusoidal.

Now that we have been through this solution one time, we can always write the steady-state solution for a parallel RC network by inspection. We know that the response will be sinusoidal and has two particular characteristics:

1.   The amplitude of the response is equal to the amplitude of the source divided by the factor $\sqrt{G^2 + (\omega C)^2}$.
2.   The response lags the input by an angle $\theta = \tan^{-1}(\omega C/G)$.

In this example we used a cosine function as the input. However, the results (1 and 2) would have been the same for any sinusoidal function. You should give some thought to the several steps in this example if the source is $I_m\cos(\omega t + \alpha)$, where α is an arbitrary angle.

The results in this example are illustrative of steady-state solutions for networks with sinusoidal sources and are extended to general linear networks in Chapter 9.

Finally, if we let $I_m = 1$, $\omega = 1$, $G = 1$, and $C = 1$, the network becomes that of Example 7.12 and the numerically determined curves of Figure 7.42 clearly indicate a sinusoidal steady-state response with the correct characteristics. Also note that the steady-state response is essentially attained in 5 s (5 time constants), independent of the value of the initial condition.

7.8 SUMMARY

In this chapter we dealt with the problem of modeling and analysis of networks that contain a single energy-storage element. We discussed extension of the loop and nodal methods to these networks and developed a systematic procedure for obtaining the state model for a general first-order network.

We found that the solution for the network variables was somewhat more complicated than for the earlier resistive network cases because of the necessity to solve a differential equation. However, we did obtain a general form for the solution of any first-order state equation and found that the solutions of most first-order networks are relatively routine.

Anticipating that higher-order differential equation models were lurking somewhere in the unexplored territory ahead, we turned to the digital computer and to numerical solutions for help with the detailed calculations. As we broaden our network horizons, we will see that the computer is, indeed, a powerful ally. We will also develop other mathematical skills to help us cope with an increasing network complexity.

PROBLEMS

7.1 In the network of Figure 7.55, the switch is closed at $t = 0$ with zero energy storage in the inductor.
(a) Solve for the current $i_1(t)$.
(b) Calculate the energy stored in the inductor at $t = \frac{1}{4}$ s, $t = \frac{3}{4}$ s, and $t \to \infty$.

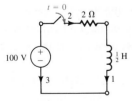

Figure 7.55

7.2 In the network of Figure 7.56, the switch closes at $t = 0$ with $v_3(0) = 200$ V. Calculate $i_2(t)$, $v_3(t)$, and the energy stored on the capacitor, all for $t \geq 0$.

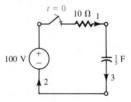

Figure 7.56

7.3 In the network of Figure 7.57, the switch is opened at $t = 0$ (previously closed for a very long time). Calculate $v_1(t)$ for $t \geq 0$.

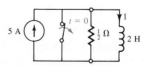

Figure 7.57

7.4 In the network of Figure 7.58, the switch is opened at $t = 0$ after having been closed for a very long time. Calculate the energy stored on the capacitor for $t \geq 0$.

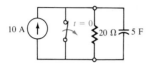

Figure 7.58

7.5 Develop a state equation and an expression for the complete response for the networks of Figure 7.12. Answers will be in terms of $I, R, L,$ and C and should include arbitrary initial values for the state variables.

7.6 In the network of Example 7.3, $R = 2\ \Omega$, $C = \frac{1}{8}$ F and $E = 50$ V. Sketch on one time axis, approximately to scale, the response $v_3(t)$ for each of the following cases.
(a) $v_3(0) = 100$ V   (b) $v_3(0) = 50$ V
(c) $v_3(0) = -100$ V   (d) $v_3(0) = -50$ V

7.7 In the network of Example 7.3, $C = \frac{1}{10}$ F, $E = 50$ V and $v_3(0) = 0$. Sketch on one time axis, approximately to scale, the response $v_3(t)$ for each of the following.
(a) $R = 1\ \Omega$ (b) $R = 2\ \Omega$
(c) $R = 5\ \Omega$ (d) $R = 10\ \Omega$

7.8 In the network of Example 7.4, $R = 10\ \Omega$, $L = 10$ mH, and $E = 120$ V. Sketch on one time axis, approximately to scale, the response $i_3(t)$ for each of the following cases. Also sketch a similar set of curves for $v_3(t)$.
(a) $i_3(0) = 24$ A   (b) $i_3(0) = 12$ A
(c) $i_3(0) = -24$ A   (d) $i_3(0) = -12$ A

7.9 In the network of Example 7.4, $L = 10$ mH, $E = 120$ V and $i_3(0) = 0$. Sketch on one time axis, approximately to scale, the response $i_3(t)$ for each of the following.
(a) $R = 1\ \Omega$ (b) $R = 2\ \Omega$
(c) $R = 10\ \Omega$ (d) $R = 100\ \Omega$

7.10 In the network of Figure 7.59, the switch S_1 has been closed and switch S_2 open for a very long time. At $t = 0$, S_2 is closed and S_1 is then opened, all in zero time. Calculate $i_1(t)$ for $t \geq 0$. Sketch this current response.

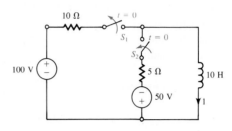

Figure 7.59

7.11 In the network of Figure 7.60, the switch S_1 has been closed and S_2 open for a very long time. At $t = 0$, S_2 is closed and then S_1 is opened. Calculate $v_1(t)$ for $t \geq 0$. Calculate $p_2(t)$ for $t \geq 0$. Discuss the energy transfer of this network.

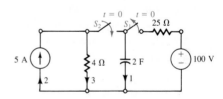

Figure 7.60

7.12 The switch in the network of Figure 7.61 has been open for a long time but closes at $t = 0$. Calculate $i(t)$ for $t \geq 0$.

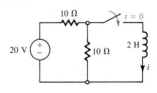

Figure 7.61

7.13 Solve the network of Figure 7.62 for i_1, i_2, and v_3 by the following methods:
(a) Use loop analysis.
(b) Replace the inductor by a symbolic source; then formulate and solve a state equation for the resulting two-loop resistive network.
(c) Replace all the network external to the 2-H inductor by a 1-port Thévenin equivalent; then formulate and solve a state equation for the resulting network.

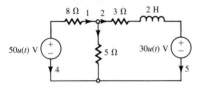

Figure 7.62

7.14 Solve the network of Figure 7.63 for v_1, v_2, and v_3 by the following methods.
(a) Use nodal analysis.
(b) Replace the capacitor by a symbolic source; then formulate and solve a state equation for the resistive network.
(c) Replace all the network external to the capacitor by a 1-port Thevenin equivalent; then formulate and solve a state equation for the resulting network.

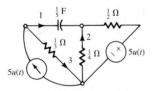

Figure 7.63

7.15 In the network of Figure 7.64, the switch has been open for a very long time and is closed at $t = 0$. Formulate a state model and solve for $i_1(t)$ and $i_2(t)$ for $t \geq 0$.

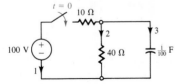

Figure 7.64

7.16 In the network of Figure 7.65, the switch is closed at $t = 0$ with $v_1(0) = 20$ V. Formulate a state model and solve for $i_3(t)$ for $t \geq 0$.

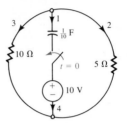

Figure 7.65

7.17 Solve the network of Figure 7.66 for $v_1(t)$ and the currents in the resistors.

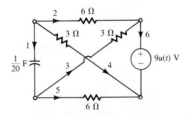

Figure 7.66

7.18 Solve the networks of Figure 7.67 for $v(t)$.

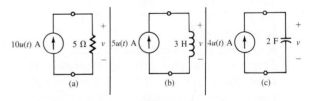

Figure 7.67

7.19 Solve the networks of Figure 7.68 for $i(t)$.

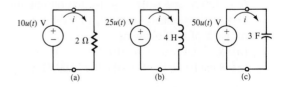

Figure 7.68

7.20 Solve the network of Figure 7.69 for $v_3(t)$ and $i_2(t)$.

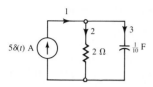

Figure 7.69

7.21 Solve the network of Figure 7.70 for $i_3(t)$.

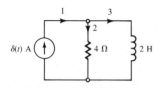

Figure 7.70

7.22 Solve the network of Figure 7.71 for $i(t)$.

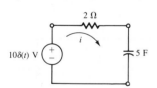

Figure 7.71

In Problems 7.23–7.32, use a trapezoidal integration program such as TRAPZ1 and other algebraic routines as necessary to solve for the variables listed.

7.23 Solve the network of Figure 7.60 for v_1, i_3, and p_2.

7.24 Solve the network of Figure 7.62 for i_2 and v_3.

7.25 Solve the network of Figure 7.63 for v_1 and i_2.

7.26 Solve the network of Figure 7.66 for v_1, i_2, and p_6.

7.27 Solve the network of Figure 7.62 for i_2 if the sources are changed to $v_4 = 50e^{-2t}u(t)$ and $v_5 = 30(\cos 10t)u(t)$.

7.28 Solve the network of Figure 7.66 for v_1 if the source is changed to $v_6 = 9[u(t) - u(t - 0.01)]$.

7.29 Solve the network of Figure 7.66 for v_1 and p_6 if the source is changed to $v_6 = 10t[u(t) - u(t - 1)]$.

7.30 Verify the state equation and the solution given in Example 7.15 and solve for i_1, i_2, and v_3. (It is necessary to find $i(0)$ from the given network.)

7.31 Formulate a state equation for the network of Figure 7.72 and solve for $v_1(t)$, $i_2(t)$, and $p_6(t)$.

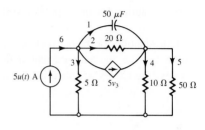

Figure 7.72

7.32 Solve the network of Figure 7.73 for v_{out}.

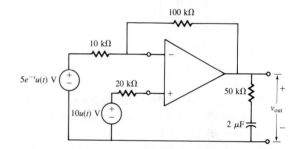

Figure 7.73

7.33 Find the state equation for the network of Figure 7.74. Solve for the capacitor voltage and the voltage across the 1-Ω resistor as functions of time.

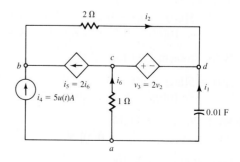

Figure 7.74

7.34 Use the trapezoidal integration routine TRAPZ1 to find the solution numerically for the network of Problem 7.33. *Hint:* Use an integration time increment of one-tenth the time constant to begin and halve, if necessary, to get $v_1(0.18)$ within 1% of the analytical solution. Print out the capacitor voltage and $v(t)$ versus time, with the analytical solution for the capacitor voltage as a check.

7.35 Find the state equation for the network of Figure 7.75. Solve for the inductor current and the voltage across the CCCS as functions of time.

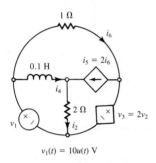

Figure 7.75

7.36 Solve the state equation of Problem 7.35 numerically, by use of the trapezoidal integration routine TRAPZ1. Print out values of the numerical solution for $i_4(t)$ and $v_5(t)$ versus time, along with the analytical solution for $i_4(t)$ as a check.

7.37 Work Problem 7.33 for
$i_4(t) = 5[u(t) - u(t - 0.2)]$ A.

7.38 Work Problem 7.34 for
$i_4(t) = 5[u(t) - u(t - 0.2)]$ A.

7.39 Work Problem 7.33 for
$$i_4(t) = 5[u(t) - u(t - 0.2)]$$
$$- 10[u(t - 0.2) - u(t - 0.3)] \text{ A}$$

7.40 Work Problem 7.34 for
$$i_4(t) = 5[u(t) - u(t - 0.2)]$$
$$- 10[u(t - 0.2) - u(t - 0.3)] \text{ A}$$

7.41 Work Problem 7.35 for
$v_1(t) = 10[u(t) - u(t - 0.5)]$ V.

7.42 Work Problem 7.36 for
$v_1(t) = 10[u(t) - u(t - 0.5)]$ V.

7.43 Work Problem 7.35 for
$$v_1(t) = 20[u(t) - u(t - 0.25)]$$
$$- 10[u(t - 0.25) - u(t - 0.75)] \text{ V}$$

7.44 Work Problem 7.36 for
$$v_1(t) = 20[u(t) - u(t - 0.25)]$$
$$- 10[u(t - 0.25) - u(t - 0.75)] \text{ V}$$

7.45 Formulate the state equation for the network of Figure 7.76 using the inductor current as the state variable. The voltage source is specified by
$$v_1(t) = 10[u(t) - u(t - t_1)]$$
$$- 10[u(t - t_1) - u(t - t_2)] \text{ V}$$
where $t_1 = 0.1$ s and $t_2 = 0.2$ s. Solve the state equation for all time intervals of interest, and write the solution for $i_1(t)$ and $v_5(t)$.

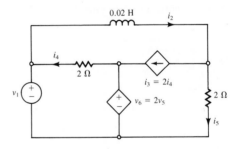

Figure 7.76

7.46 Use the trapezoidal integration TRAPZ1 routine to solve the network of Problem 7.45 numerically. Print out the variables of interest versus time, with the analytical solution for the inductor current as a check. Carry the solution out to five time constants plus t_2.

7.47 Work Problem 7.46 for $t_1 = 0.1$ and $t_2 = 0.15$ s.

7.48 Work Problem 7.46 for $t_1 = 0.05$ and $t_2 = 0.15$ s.

7.49 Work Problem 7.46 for $t_1 = 0.025$ and $t_2 = 0.075$ s.

7.50 Work Problem 7.46 for $t_1 = 0.05$ and $t_2 = 0.3$ s.

Giants of the profession
IEEE Centennial Hall of Fame

Oliver Heaviside (1850–1925)
Controversial mathematician and
discoverer of the Heaviside layer in the
upper atmosphere that reflects radio
waves back to earth; devised the theory
of loading coils for telephone lines;
advanced nonconformist mathematical
techniques for circuit analysis.

Charles Proteus Steinmetz (1865–1923)
Colorful GE mathematician and
engineer who elucidated the theory of
hysteresis and played a major role in the
introduction of complex quantities into
the analysis of alternating current.

Reprinted with permission from
"Centennial Hall of Fame,"
IEEE SPECTRUM, April 1984.

Second-order networks

8.1 INTRODUCTION

In Chapter 7 we studied first-order networks in detail. In this chapter we move on to electric networks of second order—that is, networks whose PRIMM includes a second-order differential equation portion. The emphasis is upon techniques for the formulation of a second-order state model. However, we will extend the loop and supernode approaches to formulate an equivalent model.

The solution of a second-order network is normally a much more laborious task than that for the first-order networks encountered to this point. Numerical integration of the state equations can be a considerable blessing. Analytical approaches to the solution by means of the Laplace transform are also developed in detail in Chapter 12.

It is often possible to replace an interconnected network of inductances (or capacitances) by a single equivalent inductance (capacitance). Some basics of this approach are presented preliminary to the main thrust of this chapter.

8.2 EQUIVALENT INDUCTANCE AND CAPACITANCE

Consider first the case of several inductances in series as seen in Figure 8.1(a). We seek to find a single inductance L_{eq}, as shown in Figure 8.1(b), which is

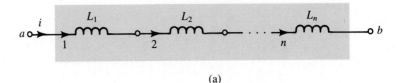

(a)

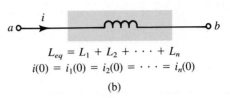

$$L_{eq} = L_1 + L_2 + \cdots + L_n$$
$$i(0) = i_1(0) = i_2(0) = \cdots = i_n(0)$$

(b)

Figure 8.1
(a) Several inductances in series. (b) An equivalent inductance for the series connection.

mathematically equivalent with respect to the terminals a and b. We immediately recognize that for the series connection

$$v_{ab} = L_1 \frac{di_1}{dt} + L_2 \frac{di_2}{dt} + \cdots + L_n \frac{di_n}{dt}$$

and since

$$i_1 = i_2 = \cdots = i_n = i$$

we have

$$v_{ab} = (L_1 + L_2 + \cdots + L_n) \frac{di}{dt} \tag{8.1}$$

For L_{eq} we write

$$v_{ab} = L_{eq} \frac{di}{dt} \tag{8.2}$$

and the two networks are equivalent if

$$L_{eq} = L_1 + L_2 + \cdots + L_n \tag{8.3}$$

and

$$i(0) = i_1(0) = i_2(0) = \cdots = i_n(0) \tag{8.4}$$

Next, suppose several inductances are connected in parallel, as in Figure 8.2(a). Again, we seek an equivalent inductance L_{eq}. In this case we have

$$i = i_1 + i_2 + \cdots + i_n$$

$$= \frac{1}{L_1} \int_0^t v_{ab} \, d\tau + i_1(0) + \frac{1}{L_2} \int_0^t v_{ab} \, d\tau + i_2(0) + \cdots$$

$$+ \frac{1}{L_n} \int_0^t v_{ab} \, d\tau + i_n(0)$$

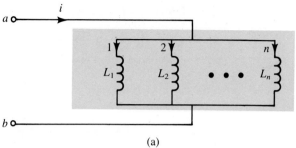

Figure 8.2
(a) Inductances in parallel.
(b) An equivalent
inductance.

(a)

$$L_{eq} = \cfrac{1}{\cfrac{1}{L_1} + \cfrac{1}{L_2} + \cdots + \cfrac{1}{L_n}}$$

$$i(0) = i_1(0) + i_2(0) + \cdots + i_n(0)$$

(b)

or

$$i = \left(\frac{1}{L_1} + \frac{1}{L_2} + \cdots + \frac{1}{L_n}\right) \int_0^t v_{ab}\, d\tau + i_1(0)$$

$$+ \cdots + i_n(0) \qquad (8.5)$$

and for L_{eq}

$$i = \frac{1}{L_{eq}} \int_0^t v_{ab}\, d\tau + i(0) \qquad (8.6)$$

Thus the two networks are equivalent if

$$\frac{1}{L_{eq}} = \frac{1}{L_1} + \frac{1}{L_2} + \cdots + \frac{1}{L_n}$$

or

$$L_{eq} = \cfrac{1}{\cfrac{1}{L_1} + \cfrac{1}{L_2} + \cdots + \cfrac{1}{L_n}} \qquad (8.7)$$

and

$$i(0) = i_1(0) + i_2(0) + \cdots + i_n(0) \qquad (8.8)$$

Analogous situations for series and parallel capacitors are shown in Figures
8.3 and 8.4. By a development similar to that for the inductances, it is easy to
show two properties.

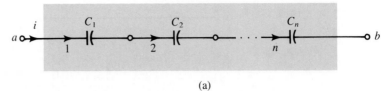

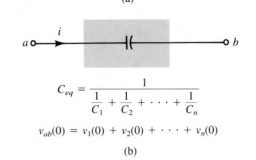

(a)

Figure 8.4
(a) Capacitances in parallel. (b) An equivalent capacitance.

$$C_{eq} = \frac{1}{\dfrac{1}{C_1} + \dfrac{1}{C_2} + \cdots + \dfrac{1}{C_n}}$$

$$v_{ab}(0) = v_1(0) + v_2(0) + \cdots + v_n(0)$$

(b)

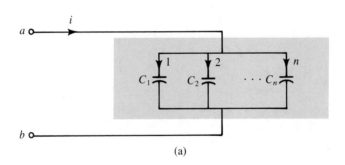

(a)

Figure 8.3
(a) Several capacitances in series. (b) An equivalent capacitance.

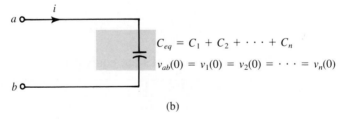

$$C_{eq} = C_1 + C_2 + \cdots + C_n$$

$$v_{ab}(0) = v_1(0) = v_2(0) = \cdots = v_n(0)$$

(b)

For n capacitors in series:

$$C_{eq} = \frac{1}{\dfrac{1}{C_1} + \dfrac{1}{C_2} + \cdots + \dfrac{1}{C_n}} \tag{8.9}$$

and

$$v_{ab}(0) = v_1(0) + v_2(0) + \cdots + v_n(0) \tag{8.10}$$

For n capacitors in parallel:

$$C_{eq} = C_1 + C_2 + \cdots + C_n \tag{8.11}$$

and

$$v_{ab}(0) = v_1(0) = v_2(0) = \cdots = v_n(0) \tag{8.12}$$

These relations for series and parallel inductances and capacitances are reminiscent of the techniques that we learned for finding equivalent resistances in Chapter 4. Many of the ideas learned there are applicable here. However, there are some subtle differences, which we discuss as we proceed. It is also possible to develop equivalent inductances and capacitances for other purely inductive and purely capacitive networks that do not involve combinations of series and parallel connections. However, the series/parallel relations are sufficient for our present needs and are now illustrated by several examples.

Example 8.1 _____

In Figure 8.5, we seek an equivalent inductance L_{eq} for the three inductances shown in part (a) of the figure. Using the relations that we developed earlier, we have

$$L_{eq} = L_1 + \frac{L_2 L_3}{L_2 + L_3} = L_1 + L_{23}(eq)$$

where $L_{23}(eq)$ = equivalent inductances of L_2 in parallel with L_3, and we have

$$i(0) = i_1(0)$$

Figure 8.5
A network of inductances
and an equivalent.

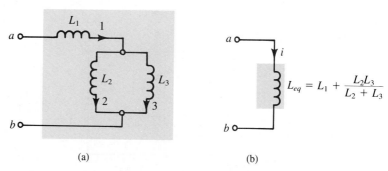

(a)   (b)

We also note that the conditions at $t = 0$ are constrained by

$$i_1(0) = i_2(0) + i_3(0)$$

Next, we note the following voltage- and current-divider relations:

$$v_2 = v_3 = \frac{L_{23}(eq)}{L_{23}(eq) + L_1} v_{ab} \tag{8.13}$$

$$v_1 = \frac{L_1}{L_{23}(eq) + L_1} v_{ab} \tag{8.14}$$

$$i_2(t) - i_2(0) = \frac{L_3}{L_2 + L_3}[i_1(t) - i_1(0)] \qquad (8.15)$$

and

$$i_3(t) - i_3(0) = \frac{L_2}{L_2 + L_3}[i_1(t) - i_1(0)] \qquad (8.16)$$

You should derive these relations to understand them in detail.

Example 8.2

Figure 8.6 shows an example of the successive steps in the reduction of a network of capacitances to a single equivalent capacitance. We also note that the initial condition is given by

$$v_{ab}(0) = v_4(0)$$

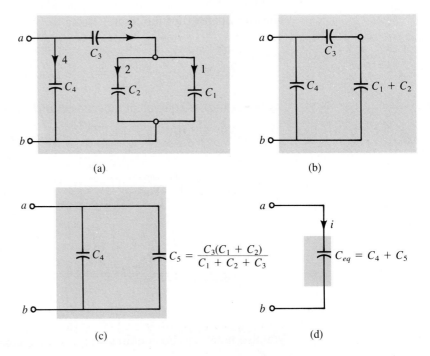

Figure 8.6
Reduction of a network of capacitances to an equivalent.

Example 8.3

A simple capacitive network is shown in Figure 8.7 and an equivalent network is shown in Figure 8.8. This latter network is a standard form of first-order network of Chapter 7 (even though the original network contained two energy-storage elements). We have little difficulty calculating $v_{bd}(t)$ for the network of Figure 8.8. (True?) Once this voltage is known, we see that

$$i_2(t) = i_3(t) = i_4(t) = \frac{3}{4}\frac{d}{dt}v_{bd}$$

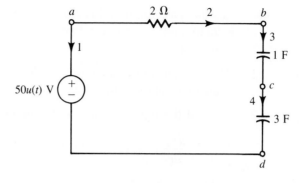

Figure 8.7
A simple network with two
capacitors.

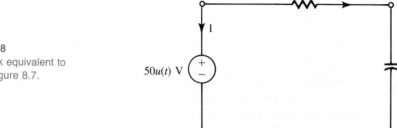

Figure 8.8
A network equivalent to
that of Figure 8.7.

The voltage-divider rule for this case gives

$$v_3(t) - v_3(0) = \frac{C_4}{C_3 + C_4}[v_{bd}(t) - v_{bd}(0)] = \frac{3}{4}[v_{bd} - v_{bd}(0)] \quad (8.17)$$

and

$$v_4(t) - v_4(0) = \frac{C_3}{C_3 + C_4}[v_{bd}(t) - v_{bd}(0)] = \frac{1}{4}[v_{bd} - v_{bd}(0)] \quad (8.18)$$

8.3   MODELING OF SECOND-ORDER NETWORKS

We now turn our attention to the problem of finding a suitable mathematical model for second-order networks. Although some attention will be given to loop and supernode techniques, the major emphasis in this chapter is on state modeling and solutions for state models.

Consider a network made up of *b* 1-ports consisting of resistors, sources, and two energy-storage elements. Further suppose that the network contains no loops that contain capacitors only or only capacitors and *v*-sources. Finally, suppose the network contains no supernodes such that all leads or electrical connections that pass through this closed surface are either inductor terminals or only inductor and *i*-source terminals. The PRIMM of this network consists of $2b$ equations as follows:

1. $2b - 2$ algebraic equations: KCL equations, KVL equations, source CE and resistor CE.

2. 2 CE of the type (for energy-storage elements)

$$\frac{dx_1}{dt} = k_1 y_1 \tag{8.19}$$

and

$$\frac{dx_2}{dt} = k_2 y_2 \tag{8.20}$$

where x_1 and y_1 are complementary variables for an energy-storage element. That is, if x_1 is a capacitor voltage, then y_1 is a capacitor current; if x_1 is an inductor current, then y_1 is an inductor voltage. Likewise, x_2 and y_2 are complementary. This simply means that these latter two equations are the differential-equation form of the CE for the two energy-storage components.

Equations 8.19 and 8.20 will become two simultaneous differential equations in two unknowns if it is possible to substitute for y_1 and y_2 in terms of x_1, x_2, and known functions of time (sources). By a line of reasoning similar to that for the first-order case, we recognize that we can solve the $2b - 2$ algebraic equations for y_1 and y_2 as linear functions of x_1 and x_2 plus some function of time. When these relations are substituted into Equations 8.19 and 8.20, the result will be of the form

$$\frac{dx_1}{dt} = a_{11}x_1 + a_{12}x_2 + f_1(t) \tag{8.21}$$

$$\frac{dx_2}{dt} = a_{21}x_1 + a_{22}x_2 + f_2(t) \tag{8.22}$$

where a_{11}, a_{12}, a_{21}, and a_{22} are constant and $f_1(t)$ and $f_2(t)$ are known functions of time.

The two coupled, ordinary, linear, constant-coefficient differential equations above are called *state equations*. Since two dynamic or differential equations are required for the description of this network, we refer to Equations 8.21 and 8.22 as a *second-order state model* and the network as a *second-order network*. Later we show that Equations 8.21 and 8.22 are equivalent to a single second-order differential equation—further justifying this terminology.

The procedure for formulating the state equations for a second-order network is summarized as follows:

1. Write the CE for the energy-storage elements in the form of Equations 8.19 and 8.20. (These equations are the basis for the state equations.)

2. Solve the remaining $2b - 2$ algebraic equations of the PRIMM for the complementary variables of the energy storage elements.

3. Substitute the results of Step 2 into the equations of Step 1.

In Step 2 the state variables are treated as if they were known. Just as for the first-order case, this leads us to replace the capacitors with symbolic v-sources and the inductors with symbolic i-sources. Then we perform Step 2 by solving the resulting resistive network. This is true because, in the procedure we have outlined, the capacitor voltages and inductor currents are state variables. This resistive-network, symbolic-source method is very convenient for performing the algebra of Step 2 but certainly is not necessary. Any approach for solving the $2b - 2$ equations for the appropriate variables is suitable.

There are other possible choices of state variables. Furthermore, there are other mathematical models equivalent to the state model. The state model is, however, ideally suited for our present purposes.

Example 8.4

Consider the series RLC network shown in Figure 8.9. Proceeding with Step 1 of the outlined procedure, we have

$$\frac{dv_3}{dt} = \frac{1}{C}i_3$$

and

$$\frac{di_4}{dt} = \frac{1}{L}v_4$$

Figure 8.9
A second-order network.

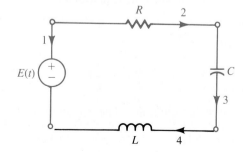

To convert these two equations to state equations, we must solve for i_3 and v_4 in terms of v_3, i_4, and the source $E(t)$ (Step 2). This second step is very conveniently done by treating v_3 and i_4 as known symbolic sources—namely,

$$v_3(t) = x_1(t)$$

and

$$i_4(t) = x_2(t)$$

This leads to the resistive network shown in Figure 8.10. Furthermore, we have

$$\frac{dx_1}{dt} = \frac{1}{C}i_3 \tag{8.23}$$

and

$$\frac{dx_2}{dt} = \frac{1}{L}v_4 \tag{8.24}$$

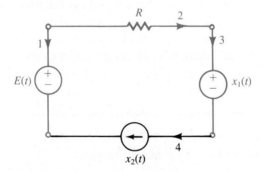

Figure 8.10
Resistive network for
formulating a state model.

The network of Figure 8.10 can be solved by inspection, since the loop current is given by the source $x_2(t)$. Therefore, we have immediately

$$i_3(t) = i_2(t) = x_2(t)$$
$$v_4(t) = -v_3 - v_2 + v_1 = -x_1(t) - Rx_2(t) + E(t)$$

Substituting this result into Equations 8.23 and 8.24, we have

$$\frac{dx_1}{dt} = \frac{1}{C}x_2$$

$$\frac{dx_2}{dt} = -\frac{1}{L}x_1 - \frac{R}{L}x_2 + \frac{1}{L}E(t)$$

the desired state equations. These equations could also be written

$$\frac{dv_3}{dt} = \frac{1}{C}i_4 \tag{8.25}$$

$$\frac{di_4}{dt} = -\frac{1}{L}v_3 - \frac{R}{L}i_4 + \frac{1}{L}E(t) \tag{8.26}$$

or in matrix form as

$$\begin{bmatrix} \dfrac{dv_3}{dt} \\ \dfrac{di_4}{dt} \end{bmatrix} \doteq \frac{d}{dt}\begin{bmatrix} v_3 \\ i_4 \end{bmatrix} = \begin{bmatrix} 0 & \dfrac{1}{C} \\ -\dfrac{1}{L} & -\dfrac{R}{L} \end{bmatrix}\begin{bmatrix} v_3 \\ i_4 \end{bmatrix} + \begin{bmatrix} 0 \\ \dfrac{1}{L} \end{bmatrix}E(t)$$

Example 8.5

An alternate mathematical model can be written for the network of Figure 8.9 in a very simple manner using the loop method. Considering i_4 as the loop current, we have

$$L\frac{di_4}{dt} + Ri_4 + \frac{1}{C}\int_0^t i_4(\tau)\, d\tau + v_3(0) = E(t)$$

as the loop equation. The integral term can be eliminated by differentiation, yielding

$$L\frac{d^2i_4}{dt^2} + R\frac{di_4}{dt} + \frac{1}{C}i_4 = \frac{dE(t)}{dt} \tag{8.27}$$

Equation 8.27 is equivalent to Equations 8.25 and 8.26. In fact, Equation 8.27 can be obtained from Equation 8.26 by differentiating Equation 8.26 and substituting Equation 8.25 into the result of this differentiation. *Thus we can see that the two state equations are equivalent to a single second-order differential equation.* This is a general result that is best illustrated by considering a standard linear second-order differential equation

$$\frac{d^2y}{dt^2} + a_1\frac{dy}{dt} + a_0 y = f(t) \tag{8.28}$$

where a_1 and a_0 are constant coefficients.

This equation might arise, for example, from the loop or node model of a network with two energy-storage components. This equation is readily converted to an equivalent state model by the following change of variables: Let

$$x_1 = y \tag{8.29}$$

and

$$x_2 = \dot{x}_1 = \dot{y} \tag{8.30}$$

Then, by differentiation of Equation 8.30,

$$\dot{x}_2 = \ddot{y} = -a_1\dot{y} - a_0 y + f(t)$$

or

$$\dot{x}_2 = -a_1 x_2 - a_0 x_1 + f(t)$$

Thus we have the two state equations

$$\dot{x}_1 = x_2 \tag{8.31}$$

$$\dot{x}_2 = -a_0 x_1 - a_1 x_2 + f(t) \tag{8.32}$$

In Example 8.5 we wrote a loop model for a single-loop, second-order network. This loop-modeling technique extends directly to any second-order network with any number of loops. For that matter it also extends to higher-order networks. As before, the procedure is simple:

1. Choose an independent set of loop currents and their associated loops.

2. Write KVL equations around these loops, expressing each component voltage in terms of the loop currents.

The only new aspects of this loop model are the integral or derivative terms due to the energy-storage elements.

In the case of supernode methods, the procedure is summarized as follows:

1. Choose a tree and an associated set of supernodes.

2. Write KCL equations at these supernodes, expressing each component current in terms of the tree voltages.

The result of modeling by either the loop or nodal procedure will, in general, be a set of simultaneous integrodifferential equations.

We now have the basic rules necessary to obtain loop, supernode, and/or state models for second-order networks. All that remains is to obtain the confidence, through practice, that we can apply these techniques to any second-order network that we encounter.

Example 8.6

Consider the network of Figure 8.11. Following the procedures outlined for obtaining a state model, we first write the CE for the energy-storage components:

$$\frac{dv_1}{dt} = 4i_1 \tag{8.33}$$

and

$$\frac{di_3}{dt} = 8v_3 \tag{8.34}$$

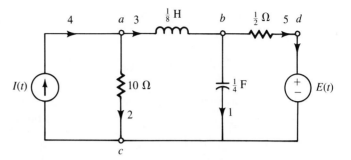

Figure 8.11
Network for Example 8.6.

These two equations will eventually become the state equations for this network. Our next task is clear. We must solve for i_1 and v_3 in terms of v_1, i_3, and the two source functions. This is very conveniently accomplished by utilizing the resistive network in Figure 8.12. In this latter network we have replaced the inductance by a symbolic current source x_2 (we could just as well have called this source i_3) and the capacitance by a symbolic voltage source x_1.

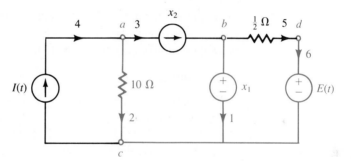

Figure 8.12
Resistive network used to formulate state model.

Solution of the network of Figure 8.12 for v_3 and i_1 is routine, and this solution will obviously be in terms of the two sources and the two state variables (x_1 and x_2 or, equivalently, v_1 and i_3). The network has only one unknown loop current if loop methods are chosen. Likewise, a single node voltage can be used. Thus at node a we write

$$\frac{1}{10}v_2 = I(t) - x_2 \quad \rightarrow \quad v_2 = 10[I(t) - x_2] \tag{8.35}$$

Then

$$v_3 = v_2 - x_1 = 10I(t) - 10x_2 - x_1 \tag{8.36}$$

and

$$i_1 = x_2 - 2v_5 = x_2 - 2x_1 + 2E(t) \tag{8.37}$$

When these results are substituted into Equations 8.33 and 8.34, we obtain the two state equations (also noting $v_1 = x_1$ and $i_3 = x_2$)

$$\frac{dx_1}{dt} = -8x_1 + 4x_2 + 8E(t)$$

$$\frac{dx_2}{dt} = -8x_1 - 80x_2 + 80I(t)$$

You may prefer voltage and current to the formal x (state-variable) symbolism. Rewriting the equations in this form and putting in matrix notation, we obtain

$$\frac{d}{dt}\begin{bmatrix} v_1 \\ i_3 \end{bmatrix} = \begin{bmatrix} -8 & 4 \\ -8 & -80 \end{bmatrix}\begin{bmatrix} v_1 \\ i_3 \end{bmatrix} + \begin{bmatrix} 8 & 0 \\ 0 & 80 \end{bmatrix}\begin{bmatrix} E(t) \\ I(t) \end{bmatrix} \qquad (8.38)$$

We conclude this example by noting that if (and its no small *if*) we could solve Equation 8.38 for $v_1(t)$ and $i_3(t)$, then all other network variables could be found by algebraic substitution into Equations 8.35–8.37 and other KCL, KVL, and CE.

Example 8.7

In this example we formulate nodal equations for the network of Figure 8.11. Using our usual approach, we select node c as the reference, giving v_1, v_2, and v_6 as the node voltages (see Figure 8.13). Then at nodes a and b, we have

$$b: \quad \frac{1}{4}\frac{dv_1}{dt} + 2(v_1 - E(t)) + 8\int_0^t (v_1 - v_2)\, d\tau - i_3(0) = 0 \qquad (8.39)$$

$$a: \quad 8\int_0^t (v_2 - v_1)\, d\tau + i_3(0) + 0.1v_2 - I(t) = 0 \qquad (8.40)$$

The dummy equation at node d is

$$i_6 = i_5 = 2[v_1 - E(t)] \qquad (8.41)$$

In order to complete the solution of this network by this approach, we must:

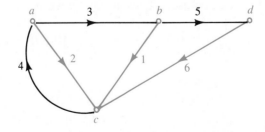

Figure 8.13
Linear graph for network of Figure 8.11.

1. Solve the integrodifferential equations of Equations 8.39 and 8.40. Once this is done, all node voltages are known!

2. Solve Equation 8.41 for the dummy varable i_6 if needed.

3. Use Kirchhoff's laws and CE to find all other network variables, as desired, from the node voltages.

If a loop approach is taken with i_3, i_4, and i_5 as the loop currents (see Figure 8.13), then we have for the loops defined by links 3 and 5:

$$\frac{1}{8}\frac{di_3}{dt} + 10(i_3 - I(t)) + 4\int_0^t (i_3 - i_5)\, d\tau + v_1(0) = 0$$

and

$$\frac{1}{2}i_5 + 4\int_0^t (i_5 - i_3) - v_1(0) + E(t) = 0$$

For the dummy loop we have

$$v_4 = -v_2 = -10[I(t) - i_3]$$

Again we are faced with the necessity of solving a pair of imposing integrodifferential equations. Once the loop currents are found, the rest of the solution proceeds, as always, by algebraic substitution.

Example 8.8

As a final illustration of different but equivalent mathematical models, we convert the state model of Equation 8.38 to a single second-order differential equation. For convenience, we rewrite Equation 8.38 as

$$\frac{dv_1}{dt} = -8v_1 + 4i_3 + 8E(t) \tag{8.42}$$

$$\frac{di_3}{dt} = -8v_1 - 80i_3 + 80I(t) \tag{8.43}$$

Differentiate Equation 8.42 and substitute Equation 8.43 into the result to obtain

$$\frac{d^2v_1}{dt^2} = -8\frac{dv_1}{dt} + 4(-8v_1 - 80i_3 + 80I(t)) + 8\frac{d}{dt}[E(t)]$$

Next substitute for i_3 from Equation 8.42 and collect terms:

$$\frac{d^2v_1}{dt^2} + 88\frac{dv_1}{dt} + 672v_1 = 640E(t) + 320I(t) + 8\frac{d}{dt}[E(t)] \tag{8.44}$$

Now, since $E(t)$ and $I(t)$ are known functions of time, this last result is in exactly the same form as the second-order differential equation of Equation 8.28. Note that this example illustrates the general procedure for deriving an equivalent second-order differential equation from a second-order state model.

8.4   SOLUTION OF THE SECOND-ORDER NETWORK ⎯⎯⎯⎯⎯⎯⎯⎯⎯⎯⎯⎯⎯○

In the examples of the last section, we saw the emergence of some fundamental ideas relative to the mathematical models for second-order networks. This is an appropriate time to generalize and summarize these results. For any linear second-order network, the following conditions hold:

1. Loop or supernode methods lead to a set of equations, which must be solved simultaneously for the unknown loop currents or the unknown tree voltages. This set of equations has the following properties:

    (a)   Constant coefficient integrodifferential.

    (b)   Mathematical order of two.

    (c)   Number of equations equals:

$$b - n + 1 - N_i \qquad \text{for loop method}$$

$$n - 1 - N_v \qquad \text{for supernode method}$$

    (where all symbols are as previously defined).

2. State-model approaches lead to a set of simultaneous equations with the following properties:

    (a)   Constant-coefficient, first-order differential.

    (b)   Mathematical order of two.

We cannot delay the inevitable any longer; if we aspire to be network analysts, we must face the task of solving these equations. The crux of the matter is that we have a simple choice—the solution of one or more integrodifferential equations or the solution of two first-order differential equations. In the broadest sense, the two jobs are equivalent because the integrodifferential equations can be always reduced, by algebraic manipulation, to a second-order differential equation. As we have shown, this second-order equation can then be converted to a second-order state model.

As network analysts, we have access to two general approaches to solve the second-order model. One is an analytical, closed-form mathematical approach to the solution. The second approach is either by simulation by a physical network model or by numerical techniques with a computer.

Analytical approaches to the solution of differential equations are usually based on classical differential equation theory or on the Laplace transform. You may already have encountered the classical approach in mathematics courses. In any event, we will leave this presentation to the mathematicians.

When faced with the task of solving a second-order (or higher) differential equation model, the typical up-to-date electrical engineer will likely turn to the

Laplace transform or, more probably, to the support of a computer. If the Laplace transform is to be used for the solution, it makes little difference whether a state model is used or whether the loop or supernode approach is chosen. In other words, the choice between the state model versus the integrodifferential equation model is not a major concern. However, just as in the past, the choice between the loop and supernode methods may be critical for a network with several loops and/or several nodes.

A numerical approach to the solution of the dynamic model of a network normally requires a state model. For this reason, and since it does not matter in the Laplace approach, we tend to emphasize the state-model approach from this point on.

The analysis of networks by Laplace transform methods is treated in detail in Chapters 12, 14, and 15. We now turn our attention to the major thrust of this section—the development of a numerical algorithm for the solution of a second-order state model.

For any linear second-order network, the state equations can be placed in the following general form:

$$\frac{dx_1}{dt} = a_{11}x_1 + a_{12}x_2 + f_1(t) \tag{8.45}$$

$$\frac{dx_2}{dt} = a_{21}x_1 + a_{22}x_2 + f_2(t) \tag{8.46}$$

In matrix form, these equations are

$$\begin{bmatrix} \dfrac{dx_1}{dt} \\ \dfrac{dx_2}{dt} \end{bmatrix} = \frac{d}{dt}\begin{bmatrix} x_1 \\ x_2 \end{bmatrix} = \begin{bmatrix} a_{11} & a_{12} \\ a_{21} & a_{22} \end{bmatrix}\begin{bmatrix} x_1 \\ x_2 \end{bmatrix} + \begin{bmatrix} f_1(t) \\ f_2(t) \end{bmatrix} \tag{8.47}$$

which can be symbolized as

$$\frac{d}{dt}\mathbf{x} = \mathbf{A}\mathbf{x} + \mathbf{f}(t) \tag{8.48}$$

Following a procedure exactly analogous to that of Section 7.6 for the first-order case, we rewrite Equation 8.48 as

$$d\mathbf{x} = [\mathbf{A}\mathbf{x} + \mathbf{f}(t)]\,dt$$

Next we integrate this equation from t_k to t_{k+1} to obtain

$$\mathbf{x}(k+1) = \mathbf{x}(k) + \int_{t_k}^{t_{k+1}} [\mathbf{A}\mathbf{x} + \mathbf{f}(t)]\,dt$$

As in the first-order case, we take a trapezoidal approximation to the integral to obtain

$$\mathbf{x}(k + 1) = \mathbf{x}(k) + \tfrac{1}{2}h[\mathbf{Ax}(k + 1) + \mathbf{f}(t_{k+1})$$
$$+ \mathbf{Ax}(k) + \mathbf{f}(t_k)] \qquad (8.49)$$

where

$$h = t_{k+1} - t_k$$

$$\mathbf{x}(k + 1) = \mathbf{x}(t_{k+1})$$

$$\mathbf{x}(k) = \mathbf{x}(t_k)$$

Equation 8.49 is then rewritten as

$$[\mathbf{U} - \tfrac{1}{2}h\mathbf{A}]\mathbf{x}(k + 1) = [\mathbf{U} + \tfrac{1}{2}h\mathbf{A}]\mathbf{x}(k) + \tfrac{1}{2}h[\mathbf{f}(t_{k+1}) + \mathbf{f}(t_k)] \quad (8.50)$$

Since $\mathbf{A}$ is constant, the matrices $[\mathbf{U} - \tfrac{1}{2}h\mathbf{A}]$ and $[\mathbf{U} + \tfrac{1}{2}h\mathbf{A}]$ are constant for any selected solution rate h. Suppose we symbolize these as

$$[\mathbf{U} - \tfrac{1}{2}h\mathbf{A}] = \mathbf{B} = \begin{bmatrix} b_{11} & b_{12} \\ b_{21} & b_{22} \end{bmatrix} \qquad (8.51)$$

and

$$[\mathbf{U} + \tfrac{1}{2}h\mathbf{A}] = \mathbf{D} = \begin{bmatrix} d_{11} & d_{12} \\ d_{21} & d_{22} \end{bmatrix} \qquad (8.52)$$

Further, let

$$\begin{bmatrix} b_{11} & b_{12} \\ b_{21} & b_{22} \end{bmatrix}^{-1} = \frac{1}{b_{11}b_{22} - b_{12}b_{21}} \begin{bmatrix} b_{22} & -b_{12} \\ -b_{21} & b_{11} \end{bmatrix}$$

$$= \begin{bmatrix} c_{11} & c_{12} \\ c_{21} & c_{22} \end{bmatrix} = \mathbf{C} \qquad (8.53)$$

Then the solution for $x(k + 1)$ can be written as

$$\mathbf{x}(k + 1) = \mathbf{C}\{\mathbf{Dx}(k) + \tfrac{1}{2}h[\mathbf{f}(t_{k+1}) + \mathbf{f}(t_k)]\} \qquad (8.54)$$

which is a perfectly acceptable form for the result. However, it may be instructive to write this matrix equation as two separate equations. To this end, we simplify the equation further by the following notation:

$$\mathbf{CD} = \mathbf{K} = \begin{bmatrix} k_{11} & k_{12} \\ k_{21} & k_{22} \end{bmatrix}$$

Then Equation 8.54 can be rewritten as two scalar equations:

$$x_1(k + 1) = k_{11}x_1(k) + k_{12}x_2(k) + \tfrac{1}{2}h\{c_{11}[f_1(t_{k+1}) + f_1(t_k)]$$
$$+ c_{12}[f_2(t_{k+1}) + f_2(t_k)]\} \qquad (8.55)$$

$$x_2(k + 1) = k_{21}x_1(k) + k_{22}x_2(k) + \tfrac{1}{2}h\{c_{21}[f_1(t_{k+1}) + f_1(t_k)]$$
$$+ c_{22}[f_2(t_{k+1}) + f_2(t_k)]\} \qquad (8.56)$$

Either Equation 8.54 or the scalar version of Equations 8.55 and 8.56 is readily implemented in a digital computer program. If subroutines are available to perform the necessary matrix operations, Equation 8.54 or maybe Equation 8.50 might be preferred. An implementation of Equations 8.55 and 8.56 that requires no external matrix subroutines is shown in Appendix C as TRAPZ2.

In order to use the algorithm of Equations 8.55 and 8.56, the following outline is suggested:

I.   Required information to start solution:
   A.   Coefficient matrix **A**.
   B.   Forcing function vector $\mathbf{f}(t)$.
   C.   Initial state $\mathbf{x}(0)$ at $t_0 = 0$.

II.   Necessary preliminary activities. Select a solution interval h and calculate:
   A.   **B** and **D** from Equations 8.51 and 8.52.
   B.   **C** from Equation 8.53.
   C.   **K** = **CD**.

III.   Solution for x_1 and x_2:
Starting with $x_1(0)$ and $x_2(0)$, solve Equations 8.55 and 8.56 for x_1 and x_2 at successive values of time by solving these equations recursively for $k = 1, 2, 3, \ldots$. A method of evaluating $f_1(t)$ and $f_2(t)$ at t_k and t_{k+1} is required.

Example 8.9

A simple series *RLC* network was considered in Example 8.4. The state model was found to be

$$\frac{d}{dt}\begin{bmatrix} v_3 \\ i_4 \end{bmatrix} = \begin{bmatrix} 0 & \dfrac{1}{C} \\ -\dfrac{1}{L} & -\dfrac{R}{L} \end{bmatrix}\begin{bmatrix} v_3 \\ i_4 \end{bmatrix} + \begin{bmatrix} 0 \\ \dfrac{1}{L} \end{bmatrix} E(t)$$

Suppose $L = 2$ H, $C = \frac{1}{8}$ F, and $E(t) = 10u(t)$ V. Numerical solutions for $v_3(t)$ and $i_4(t)$ for seven different values of R are given in Figures 8.14 and 8.15. These curves show that the response of both state variables becomes more damped as the resistance is increased. They also show that, as time proceeds, the capacitor is approaching an open circuit with a voltage of 10 V and the inductor is approaching a short circuit.

A set of solution curves such as these are readily obtained for any second-order network by use of a computer program based on the algorithm of Equations 8.55 and 8.56.

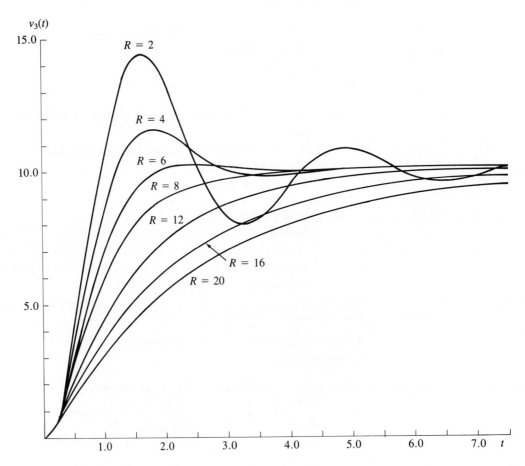

Figure 8.14
Capacitor voltage
response for Example 8.9.

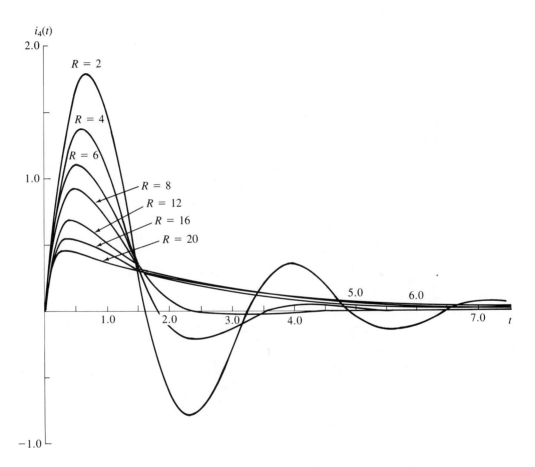

Figure 8.15
Inductor current response
for Example 8.9.

Example 8.10

Replacing the capacitor in the network of Figure 8.16 with a symbolic v-source and the inductor by a symbolic i-source, we obtain the resistive network of Figure 8.17. This network is appropriate for the formulation of the state model.

The CE of the energy-storage components are

$$\frac{dv_1}{dt} = 100i_1 \tag{8.57}$$

$$\frac{di_2}{dt} = 10v_2 \tag{8.58}$$

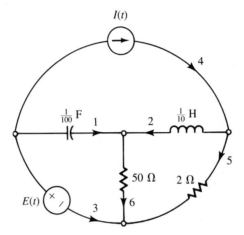

Figure 8.16
Network for Example 8.10.

We convert these two equations to state equations by solving the network of Figure 8.17 for i_1 and v_2 in terms of v_1, i_2, and the two sources $E(t)$ and $I(t)$.

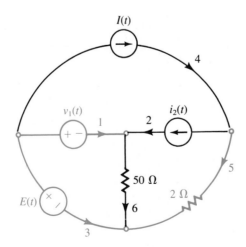

Figure 8.17
Network for formulating state model.

Branches 1, 3, and 5 are appropriate choices as a tree for this purpose. Either a loop or supernode formulation requires the solution of only a single nondummy equation. In either case, we readily obtain the state model as

$$\frac{d}{dt}\begin{bmatrix} v_1 \\ i_2 \end{bmatrix} = \begin{bmatrix} -2 & -100 \\ 10 & -20 \end{bmatrix}\begin{bmatrix} v_1 \\ i_2 \end{bmatrix} + \begin{bmatrix} 2E(t) \\ 20I(t) - 10E(t) \end{bmatrix} \tag{8.59}$$

Again, a solution can easily be obtained by numerical integration. The results are shown in Figures 8.18 and 8.19 for $E(t) = 10u(t)$ V and $I(t) = e^{-5t}u(t)$ A. We note that as time proceeds, $I(t)$ approaches zero, the capacitor approaches an open circuit, the inductor approaches a short circuit, and the state variables approach expected, constant values.

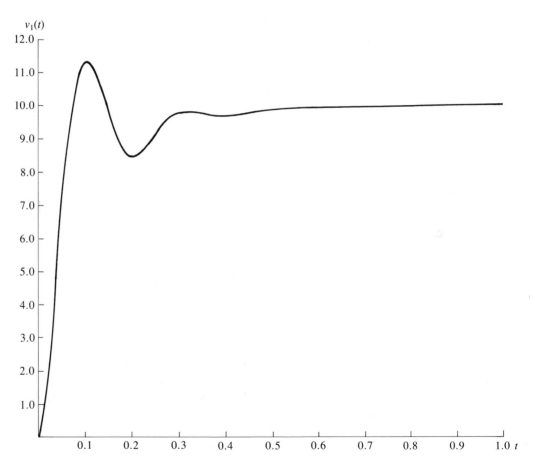

Figure 8.18
Capacitor voltage for
Example 8.10.

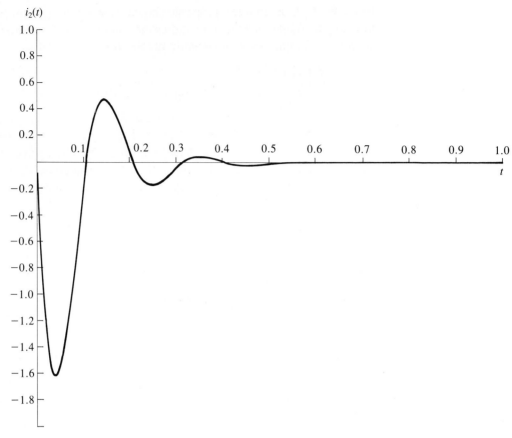

Figure 8.19
Inductor current for
Example 8.10.

8.5   HIGHER-ORDER NETWORKS ─────────────────────────────○

The state-modeling and the numerical-solution techniques that have been discussed can be extended readily to networks of higher order. The approach is
exactly the same—only the dynamic order of the mathematical model changes.
This further complicates the process of obtaining an analytical solution and
makes the numerical approach even more attractive.

Example 8.11 ──

A fourth-order network is shown in Figure 8.20. The resistive network of
Figure 8.21 is appropriate for the formulation of the state equations. Only one

tree can be chosen that includes all v-sources; it is shown by the colored elements. This is a fortunate circumstance because all tree voltages are specified v-sources and any other variable can be found by simple algebra.

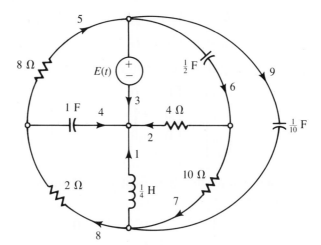

Figure 8.20
Network for Example 8.11.

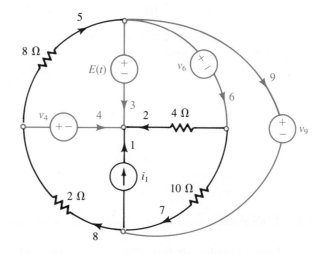

Figure 8.21
Network for formulating state model.

The matrix form of the CE for the energy-storage elements is

$$\frac{d}{dt}\begin{bmatrix} i_1 \\ v_4 \\ v_6 \\ v_9 \end{bmatrix} = \begin{bmatrix} 4 & 0 & 0 & 0 \\ 0 & 1 & 0 & 0 \\ 0 & 0 & 2 & 0 \\ 0 & 0 & 0 & 10 \end{bmatrix}\begin{bmatrix} v_1 \\ i_4 \\ i_6 \\ i_9 \end{bmatrix} \qquad (8.60)$$

Since all tree voltages are known, we easily obtain

$$v_1 = -v_9 + E(t)$$

$$i_4 = i_8 - i_5 = \tfrac{1}{2}[E(t) - v_9 - v_4] - \tfrac{1}{8}[v_4 - E(t)]$$

$$i_6 = i_2 + i_7 = \tfrac{1}{4}[E(t) - v_6] + \tfrac{1}{10}(v_9 - v_6)$$

$$i_9 = i_1 + i_8 - i_7 = i_1 + \tfrac{1}{2}[E(t) - v_4 - v_9] - \tfrac{1}{10}(v_9 - v_6)$$

Collecting these results in matrix form, we have

$$\begin{bmatrix} v_1 \\ i_4 \\ i_6 \\ i_9 \end{bmatrix} = \begin{bmatrix} 0 & 0 & 0 & -1 \\ 0 & -\frac{5}{8} & 0 & -\frac{1}{2} \\ 0 & 0 & -\frac{7}{20} & \frac{1}{10} \\ 1 & -\frac{1}{2} & \frac{1}{10} & -\frac{6}{10} \end{bmatrix} \begin{bmatrix} i_1 \\ v_4 \\ v_6 \\ v_9 \end{bmatrix} + \begin{bmatrix} 1 \\ \frac{5}{8} \\ \frac{1}{4} \\ \frac{1}{2} \end{bmatrix} E(t) \tag{8.61}$$

Substituting this last result into Equation 8.60, we obtain the desired state model:

$$\frac{d}{dt}\begin{bmatrix} i_1 \\ v_4 \\ v_6 \\ v_9 \end{bmatrix} = \begin{bmatrix} 0 & 0 & 0 & -4 \\ 0 & -\frac{5}{8} & 0 & -\frac{1}{2} \\ 0 & 0 & -\frac{7}{10} & \frac{2}{10} \\ 10 & -5 & 1 & -6 \end{bmatrix} \begin{bmatrix} i_1 \\ v_4 \\ v_6 \\ v_9 \end{bmatrix} + \begin{bmatrix} 4 \\ \frac{5}{8} \\ \frac{1}{2} \\ 5 \end{bmatrix} E(t) \tag{8.62}$$

Although we will not do so, the algorithm of Equation 8.50 can be used to solve this state model. It is necessary only to dimension the matrices and vectors to account for the fourth-order system.

8.6   SUMMARY

In this chapter we formulated loop, supernode, and state models for second-order networks or networks with two energy-storage components. We also noted that several energy-storage components can, in some cases, be reduced to a single equivalent component, and we derived formulas for this reduction. The solution of second-order networks was restricted, for the present, to a numerical integration approach. Finally, we extended the state-model formulation and numerical-solution procedures to higher-order networks.

Problems

8.1 Find the equivalent capacitance of the network of Figure 8.22.

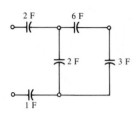

Figure 8.22

8.2 Find the equivalent capacitance of the network of Figure 8.23.

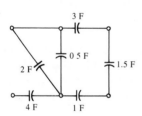

Figure 8.23

8.3 Find the equivalent inductance of the network of Figure 8.24.

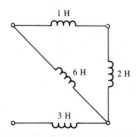

Figure 8.24

8.4 Find the equivalent inductance of the network of Figure 8.25.

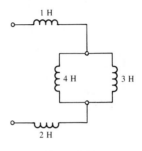

Figure 8.25

8.5 Find the equivalent capacitance of the network of Figure 8.26.

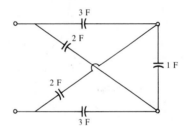

Figure 8.26

In Problems 8.6–8.10, formulate state equations for the networks specified. Put state variables in numerical order.

8.6 The network of Figure 8.27.

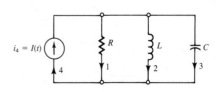

Figure 8.27

8.7 The network of Figure 8.28.

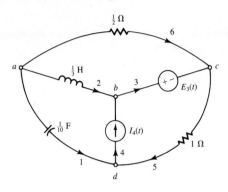

Figure 8.28

8.8 The network of Figure 8.29.

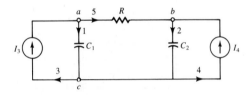

Figure 8.29

8.9 The network of Figure 8.30.

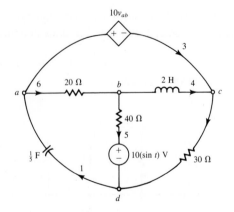

Figure 8.30

8.10 The network of Figure 8.31.

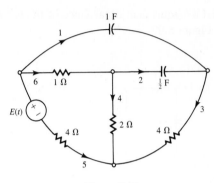

Figure 8.31

8.11 Formulate the node voltage equations for the network of Figure 8.28. Use node c as reference.

8.12 Formulate the node voltage equations for the network of Figure 8.29. Use node c as reference.

8.13 Formulate the node voltage equations for the network of Figure 8.30. Use node d as reference.

8.14 Formulate the mesh equations for the network of Figure 8.31.

8.15 Formulate the mesh equations for the network of Figure 8.32.

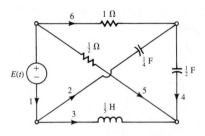

Figure 8.32

8.16 Choose an appropriate tree and formulate a loop model for the network of Figure 8.28.

8.17 Solve the state model of Problem 8.6 numerically for several values of R if

$$L = 1 \text{ H}, C = 1 \text{ F, and } I(t) = 5u(t) \text{ A}$$

8.18 Solve the state model of Problem 8.7 numerically if $E_3(t) = 100u(t)$ V and $I_4(t) = 5u(t)$ A.

8.19 Solve the state model of Problem 8.9 numerically for zero initial conditions.

8.20 Solve the state model of Problem 8.10 numerically if $E(t) = 100u(t)$ V.

8.21 Formulate a state model for the network of Figure 8.32.

8.22 Formulate a state model for the network of Figure 8.33.

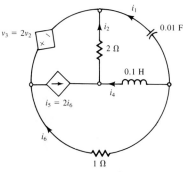

Figure 8.34

8.24 Solve Problem 8.23 for $v_1(0) = 0$ and $i_4(0) = 5$ A.

8.25 Formulate state equations using capacitor voltage and inductor current as variables for the network of Figure 8.35. Solve numerically for $v_1(t) = 10u(t)$ V and $v_3(0) = i_4(0) = 0$.

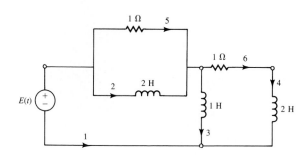

Figure 8.33

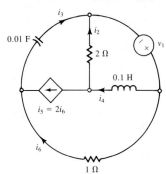

Figure 8.35

For the following problems use the second-order trapezoidal integration program TRAPZ2. The initial time increment for numerical integration chosen should be about one-tenth the shortest time constant involved. After the first successful run, halve the time increment to check how much change occurs. When an analytical solution is not available, judgment may be required to determine when a numerical solution is acceptable.

Each solution should be run for t equal to five time constants (based on the longest time constant) after the last change in the network source.

8.23 Formulate state equations in capacitor voltage and inductor current for the network of Figure 8.34. Solve numerically for $v_1(0) = 10$ V and $i_4(0) = 0$.

8.26 Solve Problem 8.25 for

$$v_1(t) = 10[u(t) - u(t - 0.05)] \text{ V}.$$

8.27 Solve Problem 8.25 if $v_3(0) = 10$ V.

8.28 Solve Problem 8.25 for

$$v_1(t) = 10[u(t) - u(t - 0.1)]$$
$$- 20[u(t - 0.1) - u(t - 0.15)] \text{ V}.$$

8.29 Investigate the behavior of the network of Figure 8.35 if the orientation of $i_5(t)$ is reversed and all other relations remain the same. (The CE for branch 5 is unchanged.) Use the conditions of Problem 8.25 first and then try the source of Problem 8.26.

Giants of the profession
IEEE Centennial Hall of Fame

Georg Simon Ohm (1789–1854)
Mathematician and experimenter whose
analysis established the relationship
between voltage, current, and resistance;
the unit of resistance bears his name.

Joseph Henry (1797–1878)
Physicist who, independently of Michael
Faraday, discovered electromagnetic
induction, the self-inductance of an
electrical field, and the oscillatory
nature of electrical discharges such as
lightning.

Steady-state solutions

9.1 INTRODUCTION

The PRIMM of a linear time-invariant network is, in general, a set of linear algebraic equations and first-order linear differential equations. The solution of such a model consists of a complementary (transient) component and a particular (steady-state) component.

The steady-state solution is by definition that part of the solution due to the sources of the network and which has the same time-functional form as those sources. This definition may have some shortcomings from a theoretical standpoint, owing to a number of rather transitory sources utilized in the analysis of electric networks. Even so, it will be adequate for our purposes.

Steady-state solutions are often very important in engineering calculations. For example, the transient operation of an electric motor driving a refrigerator compressor may only last for 1% to 5% of the operating time of the compressor. The user is probably far more interested in its energy consumption during steady-state operation than in its transient performance, unless transient performance significantly affects equipment life.

In Chapter 13 we use the Laplace transform to derive the sinusoidal steady-state solution. At that point, you will (we fervently hope) understand the basis for the procedure for phasor modeling given without formal justification in Section 9.3. Meanwhile, we can find steady-state solutions for networks with sinusoidal sources by means of a rather simple, straightforward procedure without understanding precisely how or why it works.

9.2   STEADY-STATE SOLUTION FOR CONSTANT SOURCES

The concept of steady-state response for networks with constant sources was introduced in Section 7.4 in connection with solutions for first-order networks. We learned that to calculate the steady-state solution in a network containing a capacitor, we need only replace the capacitor with an *open circuit* and solve the resulting resistive network. For a network containing an inductor, we replace the inductor with a *short circuit* and solve the resulting resistive network. In this section we expand these concepts to a general *RLC* network.

The derivation of a procedure to find the steady-state solution for a network with constant sources is based on the PRIMM of the network. If only constant sources are present, then steady-state operation is defined as that condition when none of the variables are changing—or, equivalently, all the variables are constant.

For every inductance in the network, therefore, at steady state

$$v_L = L\frac{di}{dt} = 0 \tag{9.1}$$

In a similar fashion, for every capacitor in the network

$$i_C = C\frac{dv}{dt} = 0 \tag{9.2}$$

A bit of reflection will quickly lead one to the realization that the inductor of Equation 9.1 is equivalent to a short circuit, and the capacitor of Equation 9.2 is equivalent to an open circuit—under the condition of steady-state response to constant sources. Thus to analyze a given network for steady-state response with constant sources, we need only replace capacitors by open circuits and inductors by short circuits. In effect, inductor branches may be simply shrunk to a node, and capacitor branches may be deleted from the network diagram to formulate the constant-source steady-state network model.

Example 9.1

The schematic diagram of Figure 9.1(a) reduces to the diagram of Figure 9.1(b) for the purpose of steady-state calculations. We note first that the loop-current equation for i_7 is a trivial one, in that $i_7 = 0$. The other steady-state loop equations are

$$(R_1 + R_2)i_1 + R_2 i_3 + e_4 = 0 \tag{9.3}$$

$$v_3 + R_2 i_3 + R_2 i_1 = 0 \qquad \text{(Dummy loop)} \tag{9.4}$$

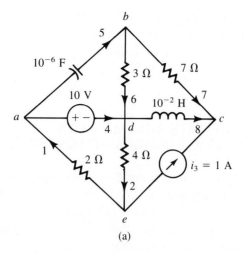

(a)

Figure 9.1
(a) Schematic diagram of a network with constant sources. (b) Equivalent steady-state network.

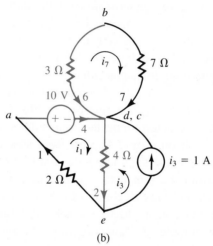

(b)

When the parameter values are inserted, Equation 9.3 becomes

$$6i_1 + 4 + 10 = 0$$

from which $i_1 = -\frac{7}{3}$ A.

Now we can use the dummy-loop equation to find

$$v_3 = \frac{16}{3} \text{ V}$$

As this example illustrates, it is usually considerably simpler to get steady-state solutions for constant sources by using a steady-state equivalent network model rather than the original network model. This follows because the number of equations in the PRIMM is reduced by *twice* the number of energy-storage branches in the network.

9.3   STEADY-STATE SOLUTION FOR SINUSOIDAL SOURCES—PHASORS

Now let us consider the very important case of steady-state solutions for networks with sinusoidally time-varying sources. Networks of this type are commonly designated as ac (alternating-current) networks. In the remainder of this chapter, we assume that all sources, both voltage and current, are sinusoidal and of the same constant frequency.

When we use the term *sinusoidal function* we mean either a sine or cosine function of time in general. To simplify the discussion in this chapter, however, we *always use cosine* source functions. This does not limit us in any way, since any sinusoidal function can be expressed as a cosine function with the proper phase-angle displacement.

We do not have the theoretical background at this point to develop the method of phasors in a rigorous fashion. Therefore, we present a detailed procedure for determining the sinusoidal steady-state solution for a network, and justify it only by extension from special-case examples. The procedure presented is universally known as the *phasor technique*. Its value stems principally from the fact that a phasor network PRIMM is algebraic (although complex), and thus algebraic techniques may be used for solution.

The concept of phasor variables is largely based on the relationship between a complex exponential function and real sinusoidal functions often called *Euler's formula*:

$$e^{j\theta} = \cos\theta + j\sin\theta$$

We use j instead of i (as most mathematicians do) to represent $\sqrt{-1}$ because i is used for electric current in all modern electrical engineering texts.

The use of the phasor technique in network analysis requires a knowledge of complex algebra. For a review of the subject, see Appendix A.

From Euler's formula for a time-varying angle,

$$e^{j\omega t} = \cos\omega t + j\sin\omega t \tag{9.5}$$

it is clear that there is an equivalence relationship between the complex time-varying exponential and the real sinusoidal functions $\sin\omega t$ and $\cos\omega t$.

To understand the basis for the phasor method, consider the series *RLC* network of Figure 9.2. Using the methods discussed in Chapter 8, we can write a second-order state model for the network with general parameters as follows:

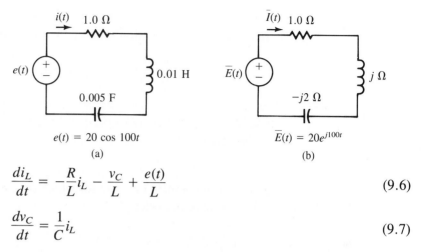

Figure 9.2
(a) A series *RLC* network
with a sinusoidal *v*-source.
(b) An equivalent network
for sinusoidal steady-state
analysis.

$$\frac{di_L}{dt} = -\frac{R}{L}i_L - \frac{v_C}{L} + \frac{e(t)}{L} \tag{9.6}$$

$$\frac{dv_C}{dt} = \frac{1}{C}i_L \tag{9.7}$$

We find an equivalent second-order differential equation by solving Equation 9.7 for i_L and substituting into Equation 9.6. Thus

$$i_L = C\frac{dv_C}{dt}$$

and

$$\frac{d}{dt}i_L = C\frac{d^2v_C}{dt^2}$$

substituted in Equation 9.6 yields

$$\frac{d^2v_C}{dt^2} + \frac{R}{L}\frac{dv_C}{dt} + \frac{v_C}{LC} = \frac{e(t)}{LC} \tag{9.8}$$

We now assume $e(t) = E_m\cos(\omega t + \theta)$. Note that any sinusoidal function can be written in the cosine form if the proper phase angle θ is used.

Our next step is designed to reduce the work associated with finding the steady-state solution for Equation 9.8 with a sinusoidal forcing function. Suppose we use a forcing function

$$\bar{E}(t) = E_m e^{j(\omega t + \theta)} = E_m e^{j\theta} e^{j\omega t} \tag{9.9}$$

The function $\bar{E}(t)$ is called a *time-varying phasor*.

By Euler's formula we note that

$$\bar{E}(t) = E_m[\cos(\omega t + \theta) + j\sin(\omega t + \theta)]$$

and thus that $e(t)$ equals the real part of $\bar{E}(t)$. Solving a linear differential equation for the particular solution with an exponential forcing function is quite simple. The standard procedure is to assume a solution of the form

$$\bar{A}e^{j\omega t} = Ae^{j\alpha}e^{j\omega t}$$

where $\bar{A}$ is a complex number with magnitude A and phase angle α.

We now form a differential equation based on Equation 9.8 but having the exponential forcing function (phasor function) indicated as Equation 9.9.

$$\frac{d^2\bar{V}_C(t)}{dt^2} + \frac{R}{L}\frac{d\bar{V}_C(t)}{dt} + \frac{1}{LC}\bar{V}_C(t) = \frac{1}{LC}E_m e^{j\theta}e^{j\omega t} \qquad (9.10)$$

The symbol $\bar{V}_C(t)$ represents a phasor voltage and is related to $v_C(t)$ as $\bar{E}(t)$ is related to $e(t)$. That is, $v_C(t)$ is equal to the real part of the phasor $\bar{V}_C(t)$.

Now we assume

$$\bar{V}_C(t) = \bar{V}_C e^{j\omega t} \qquad (9.11)$$

where $\bar{V}_C$ is a complex constant for which the magnitude is V_{Cm} and the phase angle is α. It follows that

$$\frac{d}{dt}\bar{V}_C(t) = j\omega(\bar{V}_C e^{j\omega t}) \qquad (9.12)$$

and

$$\frac{d^2}{dt^2}\bar{V}_C(t) = (j\omega)^2(\bar{V}_C e^{j\omega t}) \qquad (9.13)$$

When Equations 9.11–9.13 are substituted into Equation 9.10, we have

$$[(j\omega)^2 + \frac{R}{L}(j\omega) + \frac{1}{LC}]\bar{V}_C e^{j\omega t} = \frac{1}{LC}E_m e^{j\theta}e^{j\omega t} \qquad (9.14)$$

Note that the effect of substituting the assumed solution into Equation 9.10 is to replace the derivative operator by $j\omega$.

Equation 9.14 can be conveniently rewritten as

$$[(j\omega L)(j\omega C) + R(j\omega C) + 1](V_{Cm}e^{j\alpha})e^{j\omega t} = E_m e^{j\theta}e^{j\omega t} \qquad (9.15)$$

to associate $j\omega$ with L and with C. This association is quite important in what we do in this chapter.

To illustrate the simplification that results from using an exponential forcing function to represent a sinusoidal function, we use the parameters of Figure 9.2 ($R = 1\ \Omega$, $L = 0.01$ H, $C = 0.005$ F) to get the following differential equation.

$$\frac{d^2}{dt^2}v_C(t) + 100\frac{d}{dt}v_C(t) + (2 \times 10^4)v_C(t)$$

$$= (2 \times 10^4)(20\cos 100t) \qquad (9.16)$$

which corresponds to Equation 9.8.

The corresponding differential equation with a phasor forcing function is

$$\frac{d^2}{dt^2}\bar{V}_C(t) + 100\frac{d}{dt}\bar{V}_C(t) + (2 \times 10^4)\bar{V}_C(t) = (4 \times 10^5)e^{j100t} \quad (9.17)$$

Next we substitute the assumed solution

$$\bar{V}_C(t) = \bar{V}_C e^{j100t} \text{ V} \tag{9.18}$$

into Equation 9.17. The result is

$$[(j100)^2 + 100(j100) + 2 \times 10^4]\bar{V}_C e^{j100t}$$
$$= (4 \times 10^5)e^{j100t} \tag{9.19}$$

We can divide both sides by e^{j100t} since its magnitude is unity for all t. Solving Equation 9.19 we have

$$\bar{V}_C = \frac{4 \times 10^5}{10^4(1 + j)} \tag{9.20}$$

If the numerator and denominator of Equation 9.20 are multiplied by the conjugate of $(1 + j)$, we get

$$\bar{V}_C = 40 \frac{(1 - j)}{(1 + j)(1 - j)} = \frac{40(1 - j)}{1^2 + 1^2}$$
$$= 20\sqrt{2}e^{-j45°} \text{ V} \tag{9.21}$$

Thus

$$\bar{V}_C(t) = 20\sqrt{2}e^{j(100t - 45°)} \text{ V}$$

and

$$v_C(t) = 20\sqrt{2}\cos(100t - 45°) \text{ V} \tag{9.22}$$

which is the steady-state solution to Equation 9.16.

To review the essential parts of the procedure, we replaced $e(t) = 20\cos 100t$ by an exponential function, called a *time-varying phasor*,

$$\bar{E}(t) = 20e^{j100t} \text{ V} \tag{9.23}$$

and assumed a solution of the form

$$\bar{V}_C(t) = \bar{V}_C e^{j100t} \text{ V} \tag{9.24}$$

Then we substituted Equation 9.24 into the transformed differential equation (Equation 9.17), which produced a complex algebraic equation (Equation 9.19). We should note that this substitution is equivalent to substituting $j100$ ($j\omega$ in general) for the derivative operator in Equation 9.17. This substitution produced the complex algebraic equation (Equation 9.19).

The same kind of procedure could have been used with the state equations (Equations 9.6 and 9.7) to produce the same result. Justification of this is left to the problems.

We note in passing that since we have a solution for $v_C(t)$, the solution for $i_L(t)$ can be found either from Equation 9.7,

$$i_L(t) = 0.005 \frac{dv_C}{dt}$$

by differentiating $v_C(t)$, or by using the solution for the phasor voltage $\overline{V}_C(t)$. In the first case we have

$$i_L(t) = 0.005 \frac{d}{dt} [20\sqrt{2} \cos(100t - 45°)]$$

$$= -10\sqrt{2} \sin(100t - 45°) \text{ A}$$

$$= 10\sqrt{2} \cos(100t + 45°) \text{ A}$$

Using the second approach, we transform Equation 9.7 (by substituting $j100$ for d/dt) into

$$\overline{I}_L(t) = 0.005(j100)\overline{V}_C(t)$$

$$= j0.5[20\sqrt{2}e^{-j45°}e^{j100t}]$$

$$= 10\sqrt{2}e^{j90°}e^{-j45°}e^{j100t}$$

$$= 10\sqrt{2}e^{j(100t+45°)} \text{ A} \tag{9.25}$$

Thus by both methods the steady-state value of $i_L(t)$ is

$$i_L(t) = 10\sqrt{2} \cos(100t + 45°) \text{ A}$$

Although we used a series *RLC* network to illustrate the basis for finding the sinusoidal steady-state solution by the phasor technique, the method clearly applies to any second-order network. Given any pair of linear network state equations with a sinusoidal forcing function, we could use exactly the same technique to arrive at a steady-state solution. In fact, the method applies to a linear network of any order that is excited with a sinusoidal source or sources.

We next outline the operational aspects of the phasor technique. To obtain a phasor model for a linear electric network with sinusoidal sources, use the following procedure:

1. Replace every sinusoidal source with an equivalent cosine function of the form $A \cos(\omega t + \theta)$.

2. Represent each cosine function by an exponential function (a time-varying phasor).

$$A \cos(\omega t + \theta) \rightarrow Ae^{j(\omega t + \theta)} = Ae^{j\theta}e^{j\omega t} \tag{9.26}$$

   Note that the cosine function is the real part of the exponential function in Equation 9.26.

3. We can either work with the exponential function of Equation 9.26 or we can take one further simplifying step. Most authors use the *constant phasor* source representation $Ae^{j\theta} \doteq A\underline{/\theta}$; we also use this option. The multiplier $e^{j\omega t}$ can always be associated with the solution as a step toward writing it back in the time domain.

4. Replace every inductance, L, in the network by an *impedance*, $j\omega L$. In the phasor model, inductor voltage is related to inductor current by $\bar{V} = j\omega L \bar{I}$, where the bar denotes *phasor* variable.

5. Replace every capacitance, C, in the network by an *impedance*, $1/j\omega C$. In the phasor model, capacitor current is related to capacitor voltage by $\bar{I} = j\omega C \bar{V}$.

6. Resistance models in the network are unchanged, except that the variables are phasors.

7. The Kirchhoff law equations are unchanged for the phasor model, except that the voltage and current variables are phasor quantities.

8. The phasor network PRIMM is a set of linear, complex algebraic equations with phasor variables, which can be solved using loop-current, node-voltage, or other formulation techniques.

9. Once the phasor network model is solved, the variables found are of the form $B\underline{/\alpha} \doteq B e^{j\alpha}$. This solution contains magnitude and relative phase information. This may be adequate for a given analysis. If time-domain solutions are required, Steps 10 and 11 complete the procedure.

10. For each constant phasor $B e^{j\alpha}$ of the solution, the equivalent time-varying phasor is

$$B e^{j\alpha} e^{j\omega t} \equiv B e^{j(\omega t + \alpha)} \tag{9.27}$$

11. The sinusoidal function corrresponding to the time-varying phasor of Equation 9.27 is $B \cos(\omega t + \alpha)$. Note that this is the *real* part of $B e^{j(\omega t + \alpha)}$.

We now use the phasor technique to analyze the same network we used earlier to justify the method.

Example 9.2

The electric network of Figure 9.2(a) includes a sinusoidal voltage source

$$e(t) = 20 \cos 100t \text{ V} \tag{9.28}$$

To solve the network for sinusoidal steady state, we first convert the v-source to a time-varying phasor

$$\bar{E}(t) = 20 e^{j100t} \text{ V} \tag{9.29}$$

Suppose we assume that the current in each of the passive network elements is oriented consistent with $i(t)$. Using KVL, we can write

$$e(t) = v_R(t) + v_L(t) + v_C(t) \tag{9.30}$$

for which the corresponding phasor equation is

$$20e^{j100t} = \bar{V}_R(t) + \bar{V}_L(t) + \bar{V}_C(t) \qquad (9.31)$$

Since

$$\bar{V}_R(t) = \bar{I}(t)$$
$$\bar{V}_L(t) = j\bar{I}(t)$$
$$\bar{V}_C(t) = -j2\bar{I}(t)$$

we can write

$$20e^{j100t} = (1 + j - j2)\bar{I}(t) \qquad (9.32)$$

Thus

$$\bar{I}(t) = \frac{20e^{j100t}}{(1 - j)} = 10(1 + j)e^{j100t}$$

$$= 10\sqrt{2}e^{j45°}e^{j100t} = 10\sqrt{2}e^{j(100t + 45°)} \text{ A} \qquad (9.33)$$

The real time-domain solution for $i(t)$ is found by taking the real part of $\bar{I}(t)$.

$$i(t) = 10\sqrt{2}\cos(100t + 45°) \text{ A} \qquad (9.34)$$

The phasor voltages associated with the passive elements can be found from the phasor form of the CE. Thus

$$\bar{V}_R(t) = \bar{I}(t) = 10\sqrt{2}e^{j(100t + 45°)} \text{ V}$$
$$\bar{V}_L(t) = j\bar{I}(t) = 10\sqrt{2}e^{j90°}e^{j(100t + 45°)}$$
$$= 10\sqrt{2}e^{j(100t + 135°)} \text{ V}$$
$$\bar{V}_C(t) = -j2\bar{I}(t) = 20\sqrt{2}e^{-j90°}e^{j(100t + 45°)}$$
$$= 20\sqrt{2}e^{j(100t - 45°)} \text{ V}$$

From the t-varying phasor voltages, we can write the sinusoidal t-functions as follows:

$$v_R(t) = 10\sqrt{2}\cos(100t + 45°) \text{ V}$$
$$v_L(t) = 10\sqrt{2}\cos(100t + 135°) \text{ V}$$
$$v_C(t) = 20\sqrt{2}\cos(100t - 45°) \text{ V}$$

Example 9.3

The electric network of Figure 9.3(a) includes a sinusoidal current source,

$$i(t) = 10 \sin 50t = 10 \cos(50t - 90°) \text{ A} \qquad (9.35)$$

Figure 9.3
(a) A parallel RLC network with a sinusoidal i-source.
(b) An equivalent network for sinusoidal steady-state analysis.

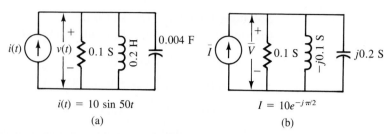

$i(t) = 10 \sin 50t$
(a)

$I = 10e^{-j\pi/2}$
(b)

The corresponding time-varying phasor current is

$$\bar{I}(t) = 10e^{j(50t-90°)} = 10e^{-j90°}e^{j50t} \text{ A} \tag{9.36}$$

In this example we use the constant-phasor form of the current source to solve for the sinusoidal steady-state voltage across the parallel RLC network.

$$\bar{I} = 10e^{-j90°} \text{ A} \tag{9.37}$$

Let us assume that the current orientation in each passive element is down. Then we can write the phasor KCL equation

$$10e^{-j90°} = \bar{I}_R + \bar{I}_L + \bar{I}_C \tag{9.38}$$

Each phasor current can be written in terms of the common voltage $\bar{V}$. (Note that the values on the equivalent network shown as Figure 9.3(b) correspond to siemens, not ohms.)

$$\bar{I}_R = 0.1\bar{V}$$
$$\bar{I}_L = -j0.1\bar{V}$$
$$\bar{I}_C = j0.2\bar{V}$$

Therefore, we can write

$$10e^{-j90°} = (0.1 - j0.1 + j0.2)\bar{V}$$

or

$$-j10 = 0.1(1 + j)\bar{V} \tag{9.39}$$

Solving for $\bar{V}$ from Equation 9.39, we get

$$\bar{V} = \frac{-j10}{0.1(1 + j)} = \frac{-j100(1 - j)}{2}$$
$$= 50(-1 - j) = 50\sqrt{2}e^{-j135°} \text{ V} \tag{9.40}$$

The corresponding time-varying phasor voltage is

$$\bar{V}(t) = \bar{V}e^{j50t} = 50\sqrt{2}e^{j(50t-135°)} \text{ V} \tag{9.41}$$

and the real t-function is

$$v(t) = 50\sqrt{2}\cos(50t - 135°) \text{ V} \tag{9.42}$$

Solutions for $i_R(t)$, $i_L(t)$, and $i_C(t)$ can be found by using the phasor CE and transforming in a similar fashion. Details are left to you, but the results are

$$i_R(t) = 5\sqrt{2}\ \cos(50t - 135°) \text{ A}$$

$$i_L(t) = 5\sqrt{2}\ \cos(50t + 135°) \text{ A}$$

$$i_C(t) = 10\sqrt{2}\ \cos(50t - 45°) \text{ A}$$

For these solutions, the characteristics of the sinusoidal functions are

Radian frequency: 50 rad/s

Period: $\dfrac{\pi}{25}$ s

Frequency: $\dfrac{25}{\pi}$ Hz

9.4   PHASOR QUANTITIES

As we have seen, phasor variables can be used to represent sinusoidal variables in the steady-state analysis of electric networks. The phasor technique enables us to find solutions for linear networks by solving sets of complex linear algebraic equations.

There are several types of phasors in general use. To use the phasor method effectively we need a symbolism that distinguishes phasor quantities from time-domain quantities. Given a t-domain function

$$v(t) = V_m \cos(\omega t + \alpha)$$

any of the following phasor representations may be used:

$$\bar{V}(t) = V_m e^{j\alpha} e^{j\omega t} \qquad \text{(Time-varying phasor)} \qquad (9.43)$$

$$\bar{V} = V_m e^{j\alpha} \qquad \text{(Constant phasor)} \qquad (9.44)$$

$$\bar{V}_r = \frac{1}{\sqrt{2}} V_m e^{j\alpha} \qquad \text{(Root-mean-square phasor)} \qquad (9.45)$$

For convenience in writing and printing, engineers often write

$$e^{j\alpha} = 1\underline{/\alpha}$$

They also shorten the term *root-mean-square* phasor to *rms* phasor.

The rms phasor is mentioned for primarily one reason. In sinusoidal steady-state analyses, the calculation of average power is often of great interest. As we shall see in the next section, the calculation of *average power* for sinusoidal voltage and current is made very similar to that for constant variables by the use of *rms phasors*. Consequently, the electric power industry specifies alternating voltage and current magnitudes in rms quantities—almost without exception. Except for this widespread usage, the rms phasor offers no particular advantage in analysis. In this book the time-varying phasor of Equation 9.43 or the constant-phasor of Equation 9.44 may be assumed unless the rms phasor is specifically designated.

The bars over the capital letters in $\bar{V}(t)$, $\bar{V}$, and $\bar{V}_r$ are used to indicate that the quantities are phasors. The constant phasor is very important. All calculations can be carried out with this form for single-frequency sources because $e^{j\omega t}$ may be factored out of the source vector function. That is, if a network PRIMM has a source vector of the form

$$\begin{bmatrix} \bar{V}_1(t) \\ \bar{V}_2(t) \\ \bar{I}_3(t) \\ \bar{I}_4(t) \end{bmatrix} = \begin{bmatrix} (V_{1m}e^{j\alpha_1})e^{j\omega t} \\ (V_{2m}e^{j\alpha_2})e^{j\omega t} \\ (I_{3m}e^{j\alpha_3})e^{j\omega t} \\ (I_{4m}e^{j\alpha_4})e^{j\omega t} \end{bmatrix}$$

then it can be written

$$\begin{bmatrix} \bar{V}_1(t) \\ \bar{V}_2(t) \\ \bar{I}_3(t) \\ \bar{I}_4(t) \end{bmatrix} = \begin{bmatrix} V_{1m}e^{j\alpha_1} \\ V_{2m}e^{j\alpha_2} \\ I_{3m}e^{j\alpha_3} \\ I_{4m}e^{j\alpha_4} \end{bmatrix} e^{j\omega t} = \begin{bmatrix} V_{1m}\underline{/\alpha_1} \\ V_{2m}\underline{/\alpha_2} \\ I_{3m}\underline{/\alpha_3} \\ I_{4m}\underline{/\alpha_4} \end{bmatrix} e^{j\omega t}$$

In vector notation, this is

$$\bar{\mathbf{X}}(t) = \bar{\mathbf{X}}e^{j\omega t} \tag{9.46}$$

where $\bar{\mathbf{X}}$ is a vector of constant phasors. It should be clear that a phasor PRIMM source vector of the form $\bar{\mathbf{X}}e^{j\omega t}$ produces phasor voltage and current solutions of the same form. That is, every phasor variable of the network has the form of a constant phasor multiplied by $e^{j\omega t}$. Since this is always true, the constant phasor source vector $\bar{\mathbf{X}}$ may be used to derive the same information about the network. Very often only *magnitudes* and relative phase angles are desired in a network analysis. If the *t*-domain solution is desired, however, it can be obtained from the constant-phasor solution by first converting it to the time-variable phasor solution and then taking the real part of it. The examples of Section 9.3 illustrate this procedure.

The phasor $\bar{A} = a_1 + ja_2 = |\bar{A}|e^{j\theta}$ can be represented by a diagram in the complex plane showing the magnitude and phase angle. This type of graphical depiction is called a *phasor diagram* and is often quite useful in allowing phase relationships between various network variables to be more easily visualized—particularly in three-phase networks. An example is shown in Figure 9.4.

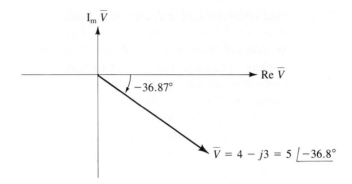

Figure 9.4
Phasor diagram for
$\bar{V} = 5\underline{/-36.87°}$.

$\bar{V} = 4 - j3 = 5\underline{/-36.8°}$

If drawn to scale, phasor diagrams can be used to find the sum or difference of two phasors graphically, but this is a relatively minor application. An example of the use of a phasor diagram to sum two phasors graphically is shown in Figure 9.5.

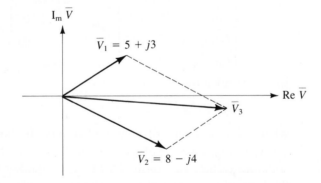

Figure 9.5
Phasor diagram for finding
$\bar{V}_3 = \bar{V}_1 + \bar{V}_2$ graphically.

The whole theory of phasor applications could be developed quite nicely without phasor diagrams, but much would be lost in ease of visualization of relative phase angles between a set of several sinusoidal variables. This will be appreciated more fully when we get to the subject of resonance in this chapter and to three-phase networks in Chapter 10.

Phasor diagrams are normally drawn for constant phasors but apply as well to the time-varying phasor $\bar{V}(t) = \bar{V}e^{j\omega t}$ at some fixed time. The choice of $t = 0$ is convenient for this purpose, since then the phasor diagrams for the time-varying and constant phasors are the same.

9.5 COMPLEX POWER

The basic definition of power, as given in Chapter 3, is $p(t) = v(t)i(t)$. For the case of a 1-port component operating at sinusoidal steady state, let

$$v(t) = V_m \cos \omega t$$

$$i(t) = I_m \cos(\omega t + \theta)$$

Then the instantaneous (time-varying) power is

$$p(t) = V_m I_m (\cos^2 \omega t \cos \theta - \cos \omega t \sin \omega t \sin \theta)$$

$$= \tfrac{1}{2} V_m I_m [(1 + \cos 2\omega t)\cos \theta - \sin 2\omega t \sin \theta]$$

$$= \tfrac{1}{2} V_m I_m [\cos \theta + \cos(2\omega t + \theta)] \tag{9.47}$$

When dealing with sinusoidal (time-varying) steady-state quantities in network analysis, it is often more convenient to consider *average power* than instantaneous power. The average power of a component is directly related to the energy associated with it over a given time period. This energy may be transmitted or received, depending upon the particular network and component.

The average power over an interval T is defined as

$$P = \frac{1}{T} \int_{t_0}^{t_0+T} p(t) \, dt \tag{9.48}$$

For sinusoidal steady-state operation, then, the average power over any interval that is a multiple of the period

$$T = \frac{1}{f} = \frac{2\pi}{\omega}$$

of the source, or sources, is

$$P = \tfrac{1}{2} V_m I_m \cos \theta \tag{9.49}$$

This result is obtained by substituting Equation 9.47 into Equation 9.48. Integration limits of 0 and $2\pi/\omega$ may be used for convenience, since the result does not depend upon t_0. By convention, the term *average power,* when associated with a sinusoidal steady-state solution, always implies the average power over one complete period.

The passive 1-port network components have the following instantaneous power relations, obtained by putting appropriate values of θ into Equation 9.47:

$$\text{Resistance } (\theta = 0): \quad p(t) = \frac{1}{2} V_m I_m (1 + 2 \cos 2\omega t)$$

$$\text{Inductance } \left(\theta = -\frac{\pi}{2}\right): \quad p(t) = \frac{1}{2} V_m I_m \sin 2\omega t$$

$$\text{Capacitance } \left(\theta = \frac{\pi}{2}\right): \quad p(t) = -\frac{1}{2} V_m I_m \sin 2\omega t$$

Of these three power equations, it is obvious that only the first has a nonzero average over a complete period. At this point we can see a motivation for the definition of root-mean-square phasors as having $1/\sqrt{2}$ times the magnitude of the equivalent cosine functions. In terms of *rms* magnitudes, the average value of $p(t)$ (for a resistance) is

$$P = \left(\frac{V_m}{\sqrt{2}}\right)\left(\frac{I_m}{\sqrt{2}}\right) = V_r I_r = R I_r^2 = \frac{V_r^2}{R}$$

This is directly analogous to the expression for power for a resistor with constant voltage and current.

The general expression for average power for sinusoidal steady state in terms of rms quantities is obtained from Equation 9.49:

$$P = \tfrac{1}{2} V_m I_m \cos \theta = V_r I_r \cos \theta$$

The factor $\cos \theta$ is quite appropriately called the *power factor* because it multiplies the apparent power, $V_r I_r$, as judged from the analogous constant steady-state case. Electric utility companies prefer power factors near unity because of the following considerations:

1. Average power is proportional to $I_r \cos \theta$ because the line voltage is approximately constant.

2. Transmission-line heating-power loss is proportional to $I_r^2 R$. At a given power supplied, I_r depends upon $\cos \theta$. That is,

$$I_r = \frac{P}{V_r \cos \theta}$$

3. The only way to reduce transmission-line power loss effectively is to increase the power factor ($\cos \theta$) or to reduce R (use larger-diameter wires in the line). It can easily be seen that the latter alternative would be unpopular because of increased costs.

To gauge the amount of increased current required due to the power factor, electric-power engineers have adopted the concept of *complex power:*

$$\overline{S} \doteq V_r(I_r \cos \theta - jI_r \sin \theta) = P + jQ \tag{9.50}$$

where $|\overline{S}|$ is defined as the apparent power, P is the average power, and Q is defined to be the reactive power for a 1-port component for which the terminal phasor variables are

$$\bar{V} = \sqrt{2}\, V_r\, \underline{/\alpha} \tag{9.51}$$

$$\bar{I} = \sqrt{2}\, I_r\, \underline{/\alpha + \theta} \tag{9.52}$$

The units of these quantities are as follows:

$$\text{Apparent power, } |\bar{S}|:\quad \text{volt-amperes (VA)}$$
$$\text{Power, } P:\quad \text{watts (W)}$$
$$\text{Reactive power, } Q:\quad \text{volt-amperes reactive (VAR)}$$

It is evident that—except for the sign—Q is equal to the coefficient of the term

$$(\tfrac{1}{2}V_m I_m \sin \theta)\sin 2\omega t$$

which is part of the equation just before Equation 9.47. The sign is an arbitrary choice that associates

$$Q > 0 \quad \text{with} \quad \theta < 0 \qquad \text{(Current-lagging voltage)}$$
$$Q < 0 \quad \text{with} \quad \theta > 0 \qquad \text{(Current-leading voltage)}$$

This convention probably resulted from the fact that electric-power-system engineers ordinarily deal with inductive loads, for which $\theta < 0$, and they prefer to deal primarily with *positive* reactive volt-amperes. A typical example is an air-conditioner load that requires a complex power of

$$\bar{S} = 4000 + j3000 = 5000\underline{/36.9} \text{ VA}$$

Complex power is very conveniently calculated from the phasor voltage and current variables. Suppose the phasor variables are of the form of Equations 9.51 and 9.52. Then

$$\bar{V}_r \bar{I}_r^* = (V_r\underline{/\alpha})(I_r\underline{/-\alpha - \theta} = V_r I_r\underline{/-\theta}$$
$$= V_r I_r(\cos \theta - j \sin \theta)$$

In this expression, $\bar{I}^*$ denotes the conjugate of $\bar{I}$, and the voltage and current are rms phasors. The resulting expression is identical to the definition of complex power, as shown in Equation 9.50. If $\bar{V}_r$ and $\bar{I}_r$ are in rectangular form, such as

$$\bar{V}_r = V_1 + jV_2$$
$$\bar{I}_r = I_1 + jI_2$$

then the product

$$\bar{V}_r \bar{I}_r^* = (V_1 + jV_2)(I_1 - jI_2)$$

produces the complex power in its rectangular form,

$$\bar{S} = P + jQ = (V_1 I_1 + V_2 I_2) + j(V_2 I_1 - V_1 I_2) \tag{9.53}$$

For a given 1-port component, the power factor is defined to be $\cos \theta$, where θ is the angle of the current with respect to the voltage. Since $P = V_r I_r \cos \theta$, the power factor can be found from

$$p.f. = \cos \theta = \frac{P}{|\overline{S}|}$$

For the air-conditioner load mentioned earlier, $\overline{S} = 4000 + j3000$ VA, it is convenient for the power company to regard its responsibility as that of supplying 4000 W (4 kW) and 3000 reactive volt-amperes (3 kVAR). The power requirement is, in general, not under the control of the company. Further, since its time integral, energy, is the usual basis for charges against the customer, a large steady-load power requirement is usually considered desirable.

On the other hand, Q represents required system capacity, which produces no revenue. The power company would like to reduce it to zero if economically feasible. In theory, the reduction of Q can be accomplished quite easily. If the load complex power is

$$\overline{S}_1 = P_1 + jQ_1$$

then another load can be placed in parallel with a complex power of

$$\overline{S}_2 = 0 - jQ_1$$

The total complex power of the combined loads is then

$$\overline{S} = P_1 + j0$$

If the load reactive volt-amperes are positive ($Q > 0$), then a capacitor is the type of 1-port to use for power-factor compensation. The capacitors, often included with electric motors for home air conditioners, are examples of this type of compensation.

Electric-power utilities in the United States operate at a frequency of 60 Hz and at approximately constant peak voltage (even though customers often claim that they do not). Therefore, the size of a capacitor required to correct the power factor is essentially determined by the reactive volt-amperes required at the voltage involved.

For a capacitor, the complex power can be expressed in terms of rms voltage as follows:

$$\overline{S} = jQ_C = \overline{V}_r \overline{I}_r^*$$
$$= \overline{V}_r (j\omega C \overline{V}_r)^*$$
$$= -j\omega C |V_r|^2 \text{ VA} \tag{9.54}$$

Suppose a capacitor is to be put in parallel with an inductive load with complex power

$$\overline{S} = 3000 + j4000 = 5000\underline{/53.1°} \text{ VA}$$

at an rms voltage of magnitude 100 V and 60-Hz frequency. The uncorrected load power factor is 0.6, and we wish to correct it to 1.0 with a properly sized capacitor.

The volt-amperes reactive for the capacitor should be

$$\overline{S}_C = -j4000 \text{ VA}$$

Thus from Equation 9.54, we have

$$10^4 \omega C = 4000$$

$$C = \frac{4}{2\pi(60)10} = 1.06 \times 10^{-3} \text{ F}$$

$$= 1060 \text{ } \mu\text{F}$$

Since the magnitude of the current required is

$$|\overline{I}_C| = \frac{4000}{100} = 40 \text{ A}$$

the capacitor would have to be sturdy enough to operate at 40 A for long periods of time without overheating. A standard-size capacitor of perhaps 1000 μF and rated at 115 V and 5 kVA would probably be chosen.

Power capacitors cost money, and the higher the voltage and kVA ratings, the more they cost. Perhaps we would be satisfied with a power factor of 0.9 in order to spend less for the capacitor. In that case, the corrected complex power would have a phase angle of 25.84° and would be

$$\overline{S} = 3000 + j1453 \text{ VA}$$

instead of

$$\overline{S} = 3000 + j0 \text{ VA}$$

as was the case for unity power factor. Thus our capacitor VA rating at 100 V rms would be

$$4000 - 1453 = 2547 \text{ VAR}$$

and the capacitance would be

$$C = \frac{2547}{(100)^2 2\pi(60)} = 6.756 \times 10^{-4} \text{ F}$$

$$= 675.6 \text{ } \mu\text{F}$$

9.6   PHASOR IMPEDANCE AND ADMITTANCE ⊸⊸⊸⊸⊸⊸⊸⊸⊸⊸⊸○

In Section 9.3 we learned the mechanics of converting a t-domain model of an electric network to a phasor model for the sole purpose of calculating the sinusoidal steady-state solution. As one step in the process, we defined a t-varying phasor that corresponds to a sinusoidal variable. For a linear network with constant parameters, sinusoidal sources produce sinusoidal responses in all branches. Therefore, phasor variables can be utilized throughout the network.

As we have seen, the use of phasors greatly simplifies steady-state solutions by transforming a set of t-domain differential equations (or integrodifferential equations) into a set of complex algebraic equations. The component equations in the phasor model are algebraic relations between phasor voltages and currents.

A word of explanation is now in order. We have used the term *phasor model* several times without comment on its meaning. We certainly do not mean that the model is a phasor. In their basic form, phasors are time-varying complex variables, which have equivalence relationships to time-varying sinusoidal functions. It is convenient, however, to designate the network equations that relate the phasor voltages and currents as the *phasor model*. We also use the terms *phasor impedance* and *phasor admittance*, respectively, to denote the algebraic relationship between phasor voltage and current, $\bar{Z} = \bar{V}/\bar{I}$ and $\bar{Y} = \bar{I}/\bar{V}$, for a component.

The reader should note this carefully. The terms *phasor, phasor variable, phasor voltage*, and *phasor current* always indicate complex variables that have a one-to-one relationship to real time-varying sinusoids. As a modifying adjective in any other context, *phasor* simply indicates that the noun modified is associated with the network model that involves phasor variables.

To see how this comes about, let us examine the t-domain relationship between the voltage and current for an inductance and convert it to a phasor relationship. For an inductor,

$$v(t) = L \frac{d}{dt} i(t) \tag{9.55}$$

Since by assumption $i(t)$ is a sinusoidal function, Equation 9.55 may be converted to a phasor relationship by changing the variables to t-varying phasors,

$$\bar{V}(t) = L \frac{d}{dt} \bar{I}(t) \tag{9.56}$$

By setting $\bar{I}(t) = I_m e^{j\theta} e^{j\omega t}$ in Equation 9.56, we find

$$\bar{V}(t) = j\omega L(I_m e^{j\theta} e^{j\omega t})$$

$$= j\omega L \bar{I}(t) \tag{9.57}$$

Thus the complex factor $j\omega L$ multiplied times the t-varying phasor current for the inductor is equal to the phasor voltage. It should be clear that this relationship also holds for the constant phasors. That is,

$$\bar{V} = j\omega L \bar{I} \doteq \bar{Z}_L \bar{I} \tag{9.58}$$

for the inductor. By analogy to the term *resistance*, for which $V = RI$, we use the term *impedance* for the factor $(\bar{Z}_L)$ that multiplies current to produce voltage. For an inductor, $\bar{Z}_L \doteq j\omega L$ is the phasor-model impedance at the radian frequency ω. This impedance is also called the *ω-domain impedance* and written $\bar{Z}(j\omega)$.

By a similar derivation, we find that for a capacitor

$$\bar{I}(t) = j\omega C \bar{V}(t) = \bar{Y}_C \bar{V}(t) \tag{9.59}$$

and

$$\bar{I} = j\omega C \bar{V} = \bar{Y}_C \bar{V} \tag{9.60}$$

In this case we call $\bar{Y}_C \doteq j\omega C$ the *phasor-model admittance,* by analogy to *conductance* for a resistive component. We also designate it by the name *ω-domain admittance* and symbolize it by $\bar{Y}_C(j\omega)$.

For a resistance the phasor CE has the same form,

$$\bar{V}(t) = R\bar{I}(t) = \bar{Z}_R \bar{I}(t)$$

or

$$\bar{I}(t) = G\bar{V}(t) = \bar{Y}_R \bar{V}(t)$$

as it has in the t-domain model. Therefore, the ω-domain impedance of a resistor is R and the ω-domain admittance is $G \doteq 1/R$.

Of course the inductance also has an ω-domain admittance, and the capacitance has an ω-domain impedance, as illustrated by the following equations:

$$L: \quad \bar{I} = \frac{1}{j\omega L}\bar{V} = \frac{-j}{\omega L}\bar{V} = \bar{Y}_L \bar{V} \tag{9.61}$$

$$C: \quad \bar{V} = \frac{1}{j\omega C}\bar{I} = \frac{-j}{\omega C}\bar{I} = \bar{Z}_C \bar{I} \tag{9.62}$$

As is the case with resistive networks, the impedance of a 1-port made up of a set of 1-ports in series is equal to the sum of the impedances:

$$\bar{Z}_t = \bar{Z}_1 + \bar{Z}_2 + \cdots + \bar{Z}_n$$

In like manner, the admittance of a 1-port made up of n 1-ports in parallel is equal to the sum of the admittances:

$$\bar{Y}_t = \bar{Y}_1 + \bar{Y}_2 + \cdots + \bar{Y}_n$$

The equivalent ω-domain impedance (or admittance) for a passive 1-port of any complexity always reduces to a complex number at a given frequency. Therefore, it is possible to synthesize an equivalent 1-port network at that frequency, using a series (or parallel) combination of components. If the impedance (or admittance) is expressed in rectangular form, the relationship between the $\bar{Z}(j\omega)$ (or $\bar{Y}(j\omega)$) and the equivalent phasor-model 1-port is the simplest.

Example 9.4

Suppose that we wish to synthesize equivalent 1-ports for the following phasor models at $\omega = 10$ rad/s and 100 rad/s, respectively: (a) $\bar{Z}(j10) = 1 + j5\ \Omega$; (b) $\bar{Y}(j100) = 0.1 + j0.01$ S.

Solution: (a) For a series combination of $R = 1\ \Omega$ and $L = 5/10 = 0.5$ H, $\bar{Z}(j10) = 1 + j5\ \Omega$. (b) For a parallel combination of $R = 10\ \Omega$ and $C = 0.01/100 = 10^{-4}$ F, $\bar{Y}(j100) = 0.1 + j10^{-2}$ S.

This example is certainly not exhaustive with respect to the various ways in which the admittance and impedance could be realized. For example, if a parallel combination of components is desired, then the admittance corresponding to $\bar{Z}(j10) = 1 + j5\ \Omega$ could be found in rectangular form. Then the parallel combination needed can be found by inspecting the resulting admittance $\bar{Y}(j10) = \frac{1}{26} - j\frac{5}{26}$ S.

In order to simplify the notation and terminology associated with phasor models, it is convenient to designate the imaginary part of an impedance as the *reactance* and denote it by the symbol X. Thus any 1-port impedance can be designated as

$$\bar{Z} \doteq R + jX$$

where the sign of X depends on the components and topology of the 1-port. For example, the impedance of an inductor can be written as

$$\bar{Z}_L = j\omega L = jX_L$$

where X_L is called the *inductive reactance*. In like manner, the impedance of a capacitor can be shown as

$$\bar{Z}_C = \frac{1}{j\omega C} = j\left(-\frac{1}{\omega C}\right) = jX_C$$

where X_C is called the *capacitive reactance*. It should be clear that $|\bar{Z}|$, R, and X must all have the same units (ohms) since they represent the ratio of phasor voltage magnitude to current magnitude.

Having defined the concept of reactance, we are now challenged by a need for a similar name for the imaginary part of complex admittance. It is customary to write admittance in the form

$$Y = G + jB$$

The admittance of an inductor is

$$\bar{Y}_L = \frac{1}{j\omega L} = j\left(-\frac{1}{\omega L}\right) = jB_L$$

where B_L is called the *inductive susceptance*. For a capacitor the admittance is

$$\bar{Y}_C = j\omega C = jB_C$$

where B_C is called the *capacitive susceptance*. For a combination of R and L in parallel, we have

$$\bar{Y} = G + \frac{1}{j\omega L} = G + jB_L$$

which is analogous to the parallel resistance rule in resistive networks. Susceptance, like admittance, is measured in siemens.

9.7 THÉVENIN AND NORTON PHASOR EQUIVALENTS ⎯⎯⎯⎯⎯⎯⎯⎯⎯⎯⎯⎯⎯◯

The phasor-model equivalent 1-port CE for a subnetwork can be derived by a direct extension of the techniques presented in Chapter 4. If we desire the Thévenin phasor model ($\bar{V}$-explicit), then a symbolic phasor i-source ($\bar{I}_s$) is used to excite the 1-port. The phasor voltage for the 1-port is then found as a function of $\bar{I}_s$. Recall that the 1-port phasor voltage is the negative of the voltage of the symbolic current source.

Example 9.5 ⎯⎯⎯⎯⎯⎯⎯⎯⎯⎯⎯⎯⎯⎯⎯⎯⎯⎯⎯⎯⎯⎯⎯⎯⎯⎯⎯⎯

Suppose we desire the phasor impedance for the 1-port network shown in Figure 9.6. First we apply a symbolic phasor i-source, as shown in Figure 9.7. The loop equations for this test network are

$$\left(R + j\omega L + \frac{1}{j\omega C}\right)\bar{I}_1 - \frac{1}{j\omega C}\bar{I}_s = 0 \tag{9.63}$$

$$\bar{V}_s - \frac{1}{j\omega C}\bar{I}_1 + \frac{1}{j\omega C}\bar{I}_s = 0 \qquad \text{(Dummy)} \tag{9.64}$$

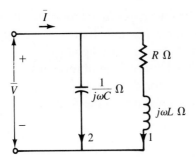

Figure 9.6
One-port passive network.

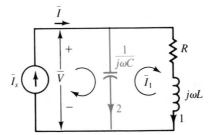

Figure 9.7
Test network to compute
phasor impedance.

The solution for Equation 9.63 is

$$\bar{I}_1 = \frac{\bar{I}_s}{j\omega C\left[R + j\left(\omega L - \dfrac{1}{\omega C}\right)\right]} = \frac{\bar{I}_s}{j\omega C[R + j(X_L + X_C)]}$$

From the dummy-loop equation, we have

$$\bar{V} = -\bar{V}_s = \frac{(1/j\omega C)(R + j\omega L)}{R + j\omega L + 1/j\omega C}\,\bar{I} \tag{9.65}$$

The impedance of Equation 9.65 is of the form

$$Z(j\omega) = \frac{\bar{Z}_1\bar{Z}_2}{\bar{Z}_1 + \bar{Z}_2}$$

which is an algorithm for finding the equivalent impedance for two impedances
in parallel. The result, of course, can be found more readily by this algorithm
than by carrying out the derivation.

The general procedure for finding the ω-domain admittance of a 1-port
subnetwork is analogous to that of Example 9.5, except that a symbolic phasor
v-source is used. Then the relation $\bar{I} = -\bar{I}_s$ is used to get the phasor component
equation

$$\bar{I} = \bar{Y}(j\omega)\bar{V} + \bar{J}$$

Example 9.6

For the 1-port network of Figure 9.6, the use of a phasor v-source such that $\bar{V}_s = \bar{V}_1$ allows the formulation of a phasor node model that contains only one dummy equation. For a tree consisting of the v-source

$$\bar{I} = -\bar{I}_s = \bar{I}_C + \bar{I}_L$$

$$= \frac{R + j\omega L + 1/j\omega C}{(1/j\omega C)(R + j\omega L)} \bar{V} = \bar{Y}(j\omega)\bar{V}$$

This result checks the calculation of $\bar{Z}(j\omega)$ of Example 9.5.

The discussion of this section applies not only to passive networks, but also to active phasor equivalent 1-ports and 2-ports. If there are internal sources, the component equations can be written in either the Thévenin or the Norton form. The concept of symbolic sources is very useful in these derivations.

Example 9.7

Equivalent Thévenin and Norton networks are to be found for the 1-port phasor network of Figure 9.8(a). We elect to apply a symbolic i-source and solve for the phasor voltage to obtain the Thévenin-form CE.

The loop equations are

$$(10 - j5)\bar{I}_1 + j5\bar{I}_s = -100\underline{/0°} \tag{9.66}$$

$$\bar{V}_s + j5\bar{I}_s - (-j5)\bar{I}_1 = 0 \quad \text{(Dummy)} \tag{9.67}$$

From Equation 9.66 we have

$$\bar{I}_1 = \frac{-100 - j5\bar{I}_s}{10 - j5} = (-8 - j4) + \frac{1}{5}(1 - j2)\bar{I}_s$$

The dummy-loop equation then yields

$$\bar{V} = -\bar{V}_s = j5I_1 + j5I_s$$

$$= (20 - j40) + (2 + j6)\bar{I}_s$$

Since $\bar{I} = \bar{I}_s$, we have

$$\bar{V} = (2 + j6)\bar{I} + 20(1 - j2) \tag{9.68}$$

The Norton-form component equation is found by solving Equation 9.68 for $\bar{I}$.

$$\bar{I} = \frac{1}{20}(1 - j3)\bar{V} + (5 + j5)$$

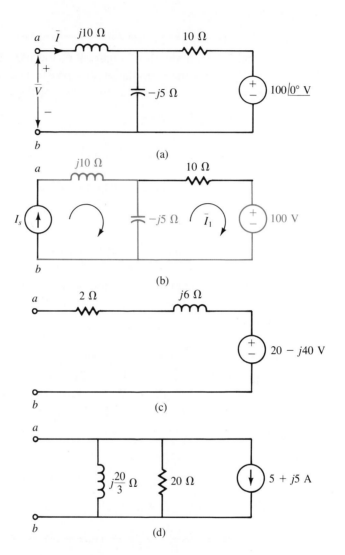

Figure 9.8
(a) 1-port phasor network.
(b) Test network to
determine Thévenin-form
CE. (c) Thévenin
equivalent network.
(d) Norton equivalent
network.

The corresponding Thévenin and Norton equivalent 1-port networks are shown in Figure 9.8(c) and (d).

Example 9.8

We wish to find the Thévenin and Norton equivalent 2-port networks for the phasor network of Figure 9.9(a). The network is the same as that for Example 9.7 except that a 10-Ω resistor is placed across terminals a and b.

The Norton-form component equations are simplest to solve for in this case. A pair of symbolic phasor v-sources can be connected to correspond to $\overline{V}_1$ and $\overline{V}_2$. Since this forms a star-tree of v-sources, no simultaneous equations

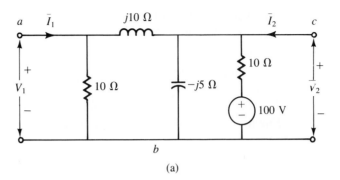

(a)

Figure 9.9
(a) 2-port active phasor network. (b) Norton equivalent 2-port network. (c) Thévenin equivalent 2-port network.

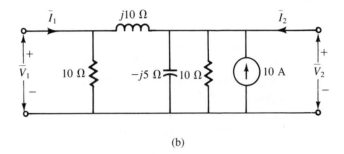

(b)

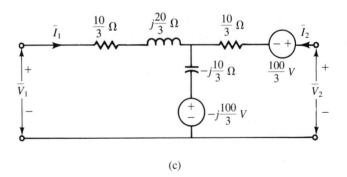

(c)

need be solved. In fact, if the 1-port Thévenin network, consisting of a 10-Ω resistance in series with a 100-V source, is converted into its Norton 1-port equivalent, we have the Norton equivalent 2-port network of Figure 9.9(b).

From this network we can write the following Norton-form CE by inspection:

$$\begin{bmatrix} \bar{I}_1 \\ \bar{I}_2 \end{bmatrix} = \frac{1}{10} \begin{bmatrix} (1-j) & j \\ j & (1+j) \end{bmatrix} \begin{bmatrix} \bar{V}_1 \\ \bar{V}_2 \end{bmatrix} - \begin{bmatrix} 0 \\ 10 \end{bmatrix} \tag{9.69}$$

The matrix equation in Equation 9.69 can be solved for the phasor voltages to yield the Thévenin form of the component equations:

$$\begin{bmatrix} \bar{V}_1 \\ \bar{V}_2 \end{bmatrix} = \frac{10}{3} \begin{bmatrix} (1 + j) & -j \\ -j & (1 - j) \end{bmatrix} \begin{bmatrix} \bar{I}_1 \\ \bar{I}_2 \end{bmatrix} + \frac{100}{3} \begin{bmatrix} -j \\ 1 - j \end{bmatrix} \tag{9.70}$$

The corresponding Thévenin equivalent 2-port network can be drawn from Equation 9.70 and is shown in Figure 9.9(c).

9.8 SINUSOIDAL STEADY-STATE ANALYSIS

In the earlier sections of this chapter we have become familiar with various specific applications and characteristics of phasors in steady-state ac network analysis. Now we review these topics and summarize the results as we consider the problem of analyzing a general ac network for steady-state operation using a phasor model.

Let us first examine the transformation of the basic network model—the PRIMM. We recall that the PRIMM consists of three sets of equations: (1) the KCL, (2) the KVL, and (3) the CE.

The first two sets are linear algebraic equations with constant (unity magnitude) coefficients. It follows that the transformation of these equations from the t-domain to the ω-domain *does not change the form of the equations at all*. The only change is the substitution of phasor variables for t-domain variables.

In general, the CE are made up of linear algebraic equations with constant coefficients (such as resistors, controlled sources, and Thévenin equivalent 1-ports) and linear differential and/or integral equations with constant coefficients.

The transformation of the algebraic CE, of course, presents no problem. The phasor form of the equations is exactly the same as the t-domain form except for the phasor variables.

As we have seen, for those CE that involve derivatives, the transformation is more complex—but still quite simple. On the basis that at sinusoidal steady state every voltage and current variable is a sinusoid, we have the following relations for an inductor and a capacitor:

$$v_L(t) = L \frac{d}{dt} i_L(t) = L \frac{d}{dt} I_m \cos(\omega t + \alpha)$$

$$= -\omega L I_m \sin(\omega t + \alpha)$$

$$= \omega L I_m \cos(\omega t + \alpha + 90°) \tag{9.71}$$

$$i_C(t) = C\frac{d}{dt}v(t) = C\frac{d}{dt}V_m\cos(\omega t + \beta)$$

$$= -\omega CV_m\sin(\omega t + \beta)$$

$$= \omega CV_m\cos(\omega t + \beta + 90°) \tag{9.72}$$

The phasor equivalents for Equations 9.71 and 9.72 are, respectively,

$$\bar{V}_L(t) = \bar{V}_Le^{j\omega t} = \omega LI_me^{j90°}e^{j(\omega t + \alpha)}$$

$$= j\omega L\bar{I}_L(t)$$

$$= j\omega L\bar{I}_Le^{j\omega t} \tag{9.73}$$

$$\bar{I}_C(t) = \bar{I}_Ce^{j\omega t} = \omega CV_me^{j90°}e^{j(\omega t + \beta)}$$

$$= j\omega C\bar{V}_C(t)$$

$$= j\omega C\bar{V}_Ce^{j\omega t} \tag{9.74}$$

From Equations 9.73 and 9.74, we can write the constant-phasor forms of the CE as

$$\bar{V}_L = j\omega L\bar{I}_L \tag{9.75}$$

$$\bar{I}_C = j\omega C\bar{V}_C \tag{9.76}$$

If the CE for the inductor and capacitor are written in the integral forms

$$i_L(t) = \frac{1}{L}\int v(t)\,dt$$

$$v_C(t) = \frac{1}{C}\int i(t)\,dt$$

a similar derivation yields the inverse forms of Equations 9.75 and 9.76. In this derivation, however, we must remember to discard integration constants because they are not part of the sinusoidal steady-state solution.

From this discussion we see that, in effect, the phasor transformation of a time-domain PRIMM converts a set of real linear algebraic, differential, and/or integral equations into a set of linear algebraic equations with complex coefficients.

There are no changes in the rules for picking a suitable set of loops or supernodes for the KVL and KCL. There are also no changes in the rules for formulating the loop equations and the supernode equations. The phasor transformation thus makes the analysis of an ac network very analogous to the analysis of a resistance network. All mathematical operations in both are algebraic and linear. In the phasor model of an ac network, impedance and admittance, respectively, correspond to the resistance and conductance of the resistive network. We even carry over the units, ohms and siemens, from the resistance-network terminology to ac networks.

To illustrate phasor techniques applied to fairly general types of ac networks, we present two examples. In Example 9.9, we formulate the phasor PRIMM and carry out the formulation of node equations by substitution. In Example 9.10, we write loop equations from inspection of the network.

Example 9.9

The electric network of Figure 9.10 includes two sinusoidal sources, as shown beside the t-domain network. The corresponding time-varying phasor sources are shown with the ω-domain network. A star-tree of branches 1, 2, and 3 is chosen to include the v-source.

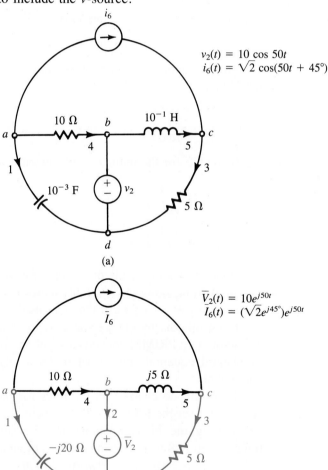

$$v_2(t) = 10 \cos 50t$$
$$i_6(t) = \sqrt{2} \cos(50t + 45°)$$

Figure 9.10
Network for Example 9.9.
(a) A t-domain ac network.
(b) The equivalent phasor-model network.

(a)

$$\overline{V}_2(t) = 10e^{j50t}$$
$$\overline{I}_6(t) = (\sqrt{2}e^{j45°})e^{j50t}$$

The phasor KVL equations for the network are

$$\bar{V}_4 = \bar{V}_1 - \bar{V}_2 \qquad (9.77)$$

$$\bar{V}_5 = \bar{V}_2 - \bar{V}_3 \qquad (9.78)$$

$$\bar{V}_6 = \bar{V}_1 - \bar{V}_3 \qquad \text{(Dummy)} \qquad (9.79)$$

The phasor CE, in the proper form for formulating node-voltage equations, are

$$\bar{I}_1 = j0.05\bar{V}_1 \qquad (9.80)$$

$$\bar{I}_3 = 0.2\bar{V}_3 \qquad (9.81)$$

$$\bar{I}_4 = 0.1\bar{V}_4 \qquad (9.82)$$

$$\bar{I}_5 = -j0.2\bar{V}_5 \qquad (9.83)$$

The phasor KCL are

$$\bar{I}_1 + \bar{I}_4 + \bar{I}_6 = 0 \qquad (9.84)$$

$$\bar{I}_3 - \bar{I}_5 - \bar{I}_6 = 0 \qquad (9.85)$$

$$\bar{I}_2 - \bar{I}_4 + \bar{I}_5 = 0 \qquad \text{(Dummy)} \qquad (9.86)$$

To formulate node-voltage equations, we first eliminate the link voltages from Equations 9.80–9.83 by use of the KVL. The results are

$$\bar{I}_1 = j0.05\bar{V}_1 \qquad (9.87)$$

$$\bar{I}_3 = 0.2\bar{V}_3 \qquad (9.88)$$

$$\bar{I}_4 = 0.1(\bar{V}_1 - \bar{V}_2) \qquad (9.89)$$

$$\bar{I}_5 = -j0.2(\bar{V}_2 - \bar{V}_3) \qquad (9.90)$$

We substitute the resulting equations into the KCL to obtain the following:

$$(0.1 + j0.05)\bar{V}_1 = -\bar{I}_6 + 0.1\bar{V}_2 \qquad (9.91)$$

$$(0.2 - j0.2)\bar{V}_3 = \bar{I}_6 - j0.2\bar{V}_2 \qquad (9.92)$$

Note that because the only branch between nodes a and c is an i-source, Equations 9.91 and 9.92 are uncoupled and may be solved separately. The solutions are

$$\bar{V}_1 = 4(-1 - j2) = 8.94\underline{/243.4°} \text{ V}$$

$$\bar{V}_3 = 5 + j0 = 5\underline{/0°} \text{ V}$$

From these tree voltages, we can find the link voltages from the KVL.

$$\bar{V}_4 = \bar{V}_1 - \bar{V}_2 = -14 - j8 = 16.12\underline{/209.7°}\ \text{V}$$

$$\bar{V}_5 = \bar{V}_2 - \bar{V}_3 = 10 - 5 = 5\underline{/0°}\ \text{V}$$

$$\bar{V}_6 = \bar{V}_1 - \bar{V}_3 = -9 - j8 = 12.04\underline{/-138.4°}\ \text{V}$$

With all voltages known, we can now write the branch phasor currents.

$$\bar{I}_1 = j0.05\bar{V}_1 = 0.4 - j0.2 = 0.447\underline{/-26.6°}\ \text{A}$$

$$\bar{I}_3 = 0.2\bar{V}_3 = 1 + j0 = 1\underline{/0°}\ \text{A}$$

$$\bar{I}_4 = 0.1\bar{V}_4 = -1.4 - j0.8 = 1.612\underline{/209.7°}\ \text{A}$$

$$\bar{I}_5 = -j0.2\bar{V}_5 = 0 - j = 1\underline{/-90°}\ \text{A}$$

$$\bar{I}_2 = \bar{I}_4 - \bar{I}_5 = -1.4 + j0.2 = 1.414\underline{/171.9°}\ \text{A}$$

Note that $\bar{V}_6$ and $\bar{I}_2$ are the variables associated with the i-source and v-source, respectively, and are found from the dummy KVL and KCL equations.

Now that we have finished the phasor calculations, we can check the validity of our solutions for node voltages by checking whether the KCL equations (other than the dummy equation) are satisfied. The rectangular form of the phasor is most convenient for this check. Details are left to you. *Question:* Why could we not use the KVL equations for the check?

Finally, we write the real-time functions that correspond to the phasor currents.

$$i_1(t) = 0.447\cos(50t - 26.6°)\ \text{A}$$

$$i_3(t) = \cos 50t\ \text{A}$$

$$i_4(t) = 1.612\cos(50t - 150.3°)\ \text{A}$$

$$i_5(t) = \cos(50t - 90°)\ \text{A}$$

$$i_2(t) = 1.414\cos(50t + 171.9°)\ \text{A}$$

Example 9.10

The electric network of Figure 9.11(a) includes two sinusoidal sources,

$$i_3(t) = \sqrt{2}\sin\left(1000t + \frac{\pi}{4}\right)\ \text{A} \tag{9.93}$$

and

$$v_4(t) = 4\cos(1000t + \pi)\ \text{V} \tag{9.94}$$

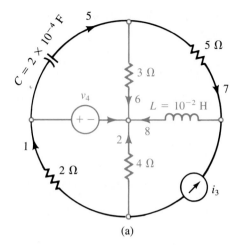

(a)

Figure 9.11
(a) Network of Example
9.10 for a time-domain
analysis. (b) Phasor
equivalent network.

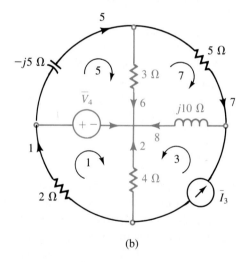

(b)

The CE for the capacitor and the inductor are, respectively,

$$i_5(t) = 2 \times 10^{-4} \frac{d}{dt} v_5(t)$$

and

$$v_8(t) = 10^{-2} \frac{d}{dt} i_8(t)$$

To solve the network for sinusoidal steady state, we first convert $i_3(t)$ to a cosine function,

$$i_3(t) = \sqrt{2} \cos\left(1000t - \frac{\pi}{4}\right) \text{ A} \tag{9.95}$$

The time-varying phasors corresponding to $i_3(t)$ and $v_4(t)$ are then

$$\bar{I}_3(t) = \sqrt{2}e^{-j\pi/4}e^{j1000t} \text{ A} \tag{9.96}$$

$$\bar{V}_4(t) = 4e^{j\pi}e^{j1000t} \text{ V} \tag{9.97}$$

The constant-phasor equivalents for $\bar{I}_3(t)$ and $\bar{V}_4(t)$ are

$$\bar{I}_3 = \sqrt{2}e^{-j\pi/4} \equiv \sqrt{2} \underline{/-\pi/4} = 1 - j1 \text{ A}$$

$$\bar{V}_4 = 4e^{j\pi} = 4\underline{/\pi} = -4 + j0 \text{ V}$$

The phasor CE for the network can be written in the form of phasor voltages explicit in terms of phasor currents as follows:

$$\bar{V}_1 = 2\bar{I}_1$$
$$\bar{V}_2 = 4\bar{I}_2$$
$$\bar{V}_5 = -j5\bar{I}_5$$
$$\bar{V}_6 = 3\bar{I}_6$$
$$\bar{V}_7 = 5\bar{I}_7$$
$$\bar{V}_8 = j10\bar{I}_8$$

It is clear that all inverse relationships also exist, so we are free to formulate a phasor model using either loop-current or node-voltage variables. A star-tree of branches 2, 4, 6, and 8 is suitable for either formulation and is chosen.

A quick check indicates that there are three equations to be solved simultaneously with either method. We elect to use the loop-current method with the loops defined by the tree chosen and indicated on Figure 9.11(b).

The phasor loop model in matrix form is symbolized as

$$\bar{\mathbf{Z}}_\ell \bar{\mathbf{I}}_\ell = \bar{\mathbf{f}}$$

This is written as Equation 9.98 for the network.

$$\begin{bmatrix} 6 & 0 & 0 \\ 0 & 3-j5 & -3 \\ 0 & -3 & 8+j10 \end{bmatrix} \begin{bmatrix} \bar{I}_1 \\ \bar{I}_5 \\ \bar{I}_7 \end{bmatrix} + \begin{bmatrix} 4\bar{I}_3 + \bar{V}_4 \\ -\bar{V}_4 \\ j10\bar{I}_3 \end{bmatrix} = 0 \tag{9.98}$$

Next we calculate the determinant of the coefficient matrix $\bar{\mathbf{Z}}_\ell$.

$$\Delta = 6[(3 - j5)(8 + j10) - 9]$$
$$= 6[(74 - 9) + j(30 - 40)] = 6(65 - j10)$$
$$= 6 \times 65.8\underline{/-8.75°} = 390 - j60$$

The inverse matrix is

$$\bar{\mathbf{Z}}_\ell^{-1} = \frac{1}{\Delta} \begin{bmatrix} (65 - j10) & 0 & 0 \\ 0 & 6(8 + j10) & 18 \\ 0 & 18 & 6(3 - j5) \end{bmatrix} \qquad (9.99)$$

where the determinant $\Delta = 390 - j60$. Therefore, $\bar{\mathbf{I}}_\ell = \bar{\mathbf{Z}}_\ell^{-1}\,\bar{\mathbf{f}}$ is

$$\begin{bmatrix} \bar{I}_1 \\ \bar{I}_5 \\ \bar{I}_7 \end{bmatrix} = \begin{bmatrix} 0.1667 & 0 & 0 \\ 0 & (0.097 + j0.169) & (0.045 + j0.007) \\ 0 & (0.045 + j0.007) & (0.057 - j0.068) \end{bmatrix}$$

$$\begin{bmatrix} +j4.0 \\ -4 \\ -10-j10 \end{bmatrix} \qquad (9.100)$$

from which

$$\begin{bmatrix} \bar{I}_1 \\ \bar{I}_5 \\ \bar{I}_7 \end{bmatrix} = \begin{bmatrix} +j0.667 \\ -0.770 - j1.195 \\ -1.429 + j0.088 \end{bmatrix} = \begin{bmatrix} 0.667\ \underline{/+90°} \\ 1.42\underline{/-122.78°} \\ 1.432\underline{/176.5°} \end{bmatrix} \qquad (9.101)$$

For our example, the time-varying phasor current solutions are

$$\bar{I}_1(t) = 0.667e^{j90°}e^{j1000t} = 0.667e^{j(1000t + 90°)} \text{ A}$$
$$\bar{I}_5(t) = 1.42e^{-j122.8°}e^{j1000t} = 1.42e^{j(1000t - 122.8°)} \text{ A}$$
$$\bar{I}_7(t) = 1.432e^{j176.5°}e^{j1000t} = 1.432e^{j(1000t + 176.5°)} \text{ A}$$

Thus the actual time-varying currents are

$$i_1(t) = 0.667 \cos(1000t + 90°) \text{ A}$$
$$i_5(t) = 1.42 \cos(1000t - 122.8°) \text{ A}$$
$$i_7(t) = 1.432 \cos(1000t + 176.5°) \text{ A}$$

When the sinusoidal steady-state solution for a network is obtained by the algebraic technique described in this section, the principal work involved is that of solving a set of simultaneous linear algebraic equations with complex coefficients. The BASIC computer program, CMATINV in Appendix C, can be very useful for inverting complex matrices of order 3 and above. The network model must be transformed from a time-domain model to a phasor model (sometimes called an ω-domain model), but this transformation affects only the energy-storage components and the sinusoidal sources. Both are easily carried out. The magnitudes and the phase angles in the phasor model are exactly the same as those of the t-domain model. Therefore, the inverse transformation—from ω-domain to t-domain—is equally simple.

As a final pair of examples, we use the networks of Figures 9.2 and 9.3 to demonstrate that the old workhorse rules of resistive networks—the voltage-divider rule and the current-divider rule—are valid in phasor calculations.

Example 9.11

For the series network of Figure 9.2(b), we found that

$$\bar{I} = \frac{\bar{E}}{(R + j\omega L + 1/j\omega C)} = \frac{\bar{E}}{\bar{Z}} = 10\sqrt{2}\underline{/45°} \text{ A}$$

Since $\bar{I}$ is common to all three components, the component voltages can be written

$$\bar{V}_R = R\bar{I} = \frac{R}{\bar{Z}}\bar{E}$$

$$\bar{V}_L = j\omega L\bar{I} = \frac{jX_L}{\bar{Z}}\bar{E}$$

$$\bar{V}_C = \frac{1}{j\omega C}\bar{I} = \frac{jX_C}{\bar{Z}}\bar{E}$$

By inserting $\omega = 100$ rad/s, $R = 1\ \Omega$, $L = 0.01$ H, $C = 0.005$ F, and $\bar{E} = 20\underline{/0°}$, we get

$$\bar{V}_R = 10\sqrt{2}\underline{/45°} \text{ V}$$

$$\bar{V}_L = 10\sqrt{2}\underline{/135°} \text{ V}$$

$$\bar{V}_C = 20\sqrt{2}\underline{/-45°} \text{ V}$$

If we want to know the voltage across the RL combination ($\bar{V}_{RL} = \bar{V}_R + \bar{V}_L$), we can use the voltage-divider rule as follows:

$$\bar{V}_{RL} = \frac{R + j\omega L}{\bar{Z}}\, \bar{E} = \frac{1 + j}{1 - j}\, 20\underline{/0^\circ}$$

$$= \frac{j2}{2}\,(20 + j0) = j20 = 20\underline{/90^\circ}\ \text{V}$$

Example 9.12

For a parallel network of Figure 9.3(b), we found the solution

$$\bar{V} = \frac{\bar{I}}{G + j(B_C + B_L)} = \frac{\bar{I}}{\bar{Y}} = 50\sqrt{2}\underline{/-135^\circ}\ \text{V}$$

Since $\bar{V}$ is common to all components, the component currents can be written

$$\bar{I}_R = G\bar{V} = \frac{G}{\bar{Y}}\,\bar{I}$$

$$\bar{I}_L = \frac{1}{j\omega L}\,\bar{V} = \frac{jB_L}{\bar{Y}}\,\bar{I}$$

$$\bar{I}_C = j\omega C\bar{V} = \frac{jB_C}{\bar{Y}}\,\bar{I}$$

By inserting $\omega = 50$ rad/s, $G = 0.1$ S, $L = 0.2$ H, $C = 0.004$ F, and $\bar{I} = 10\underline{/-90^\circ}$, we get

$$\bar{I}_R = 5\sqrt{2}\underline{/-135^\circ}\ \text{A}$$
$$\bar{I}_L = 5\sqrt{2}\underline{/135^\circ}\ \text{A}$$
$$\bar{I}_C = 10\sqrt{2}\underline{/-45^\circ}\ \text{A}$$

It should be clear from the last two examples that the voltage-divider and current-divider rules carry over from resistive networks with only minor modifications.

9.9 TRANSFER FUNCTIONS, FREQUENCY RESPONSE, AND RESONANCE

To this point in the steady-state analysis of networks with sinusoidal sources, we have been concerned with the calculation of the response of a network to a source or a set of sources that are operating at a single fixed frequency. In this

section, we broaden our viewpoint and study the changes in the behavior of
networks as the frequency is varied over a wide range. This type of study is
known as a *frequency-response* analysis and is an important concept in many
electrical-engineering disciplines.

The ability of a network to select or respond vigorously to signals of some
frequencies while filtering or not responding to signals of other frequencies is a
characteristic of primary importance in communications. The frequency-
response characteristic of a network or electrical system is one that is readily
determined in the laboratory, and much can be learned about the system from
the results of such an experiment. For these reasons (and others that will
become apparent as we proceed), the ability to calculate or determine the
frequency response of a network is a valuable asset to an electrical engineer.

Transfer function

The idea of a *transfer function* is a useful concept that arises often in the study
of networks and more general systems. In order to introduce the basic concept,
suppose we consider a fairly general network. Let the network be made up of
an interconnection of some or all of our linear elements—resistors, inductors,
capacitors, controlled sources, and op amps. However, the network is excited
by a single independent source—an *i*-source or a *v*-source. Further suppose
that this source is sinusoidal and the frequency is variable. In general terms,
this source is

$$f(t) = F_m \cos(\omega t + \alpha) \tag{9.102}$$

where $f(t)$ stands for either a voltage or a current source. The corresponding
phasor representation is

$$\bar{F}(t) = (F_m \underline{/\alpha})e^{j\omega t} \tag{9.103}$$

with the constant phasor

$$\bar{F} \doteq F_m \underline{/\alpha} \tag{9.104}$$

Notice that the frequency dependence of the source is submerged by use of the
constant phasor but is apparent from the time-varying phasor of Equation
9.103.

Now suppose we calculate the steady-state solution for either a current or a
voltage at some location in the network. Certainly this is straightforward for a
particular frequency. Suppose, however, that we wish to calculate this response for many frequencies. One approach would be to solve the network for
each different value of frequency and tabulate the response as a function of
frequency. A more sophisticated and practical approach, however, is to solve
for the response as a function of frequency directly.

Let the response be symbolized by $x(t)$. Then for networks as described above, it is always possible to find the constant-phasor representation of the steady-state solution in the following form:

$$\bar{X}(j\omega) = \bar{T}(j\omega)\bar{F} \qquad (9.105)$$

where $\bar{T}(j\omega)$ is a complex-valued function of frequency that is developed from the network. This function is called a *transfer function* relating the response or output, X, to the input, F. More precisely, it is

$$\bar{T}(j\omega) \doteq \frac{\bar{X}(j\omega)}{\bar{F}} \qquad (9.106)$$

Thus $\bar{T}(j\omega)$ is defined as the ratio of the phasor output to the phasor input described as a function of frequency. In this development, the dependence of the output upon frequency is emphasized by the notation $\bar{X}(j\omega)$.

Example 9.13

Consider the 1-port network of Figure 9.12. Three transfer functions of interest are

$$\bar{T}_1(j\omega) = \frac{\bar{V}(j\omega)}{\bar{I}} = R + j\omega L$$

$$\bar{T}_2(j\omega) = \frac{\bar{V}_R(j\omega)}{\bar{V}} = \frac{R}{R + j\omega L}$$

$$\bar{T}_3(j\omega) = \frac{\bar{V}_L(j\omega)}{\bar{V}} = \frac{j\omega L}{R + j\omega L}$$

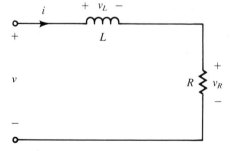

Figure 9.12
Network for Example 9.13.

Note that the first is simply the 1-port impedance and the other two result from the voltage-divider rule.

Example 9.14

The network of Figure 9.13 has several possible transfer functions. (How many can you name?) One is

$$\frac{\bar{V}_2(j\omega)}{\bar{V}} = \frac{\dfrac{4(1/j0.1\omega)}{4 + 1/j0.1\omega}}{1 + \dfrac{4(1/j0.1\omega)}{4 + 1/j0.1\omega}} = \frac{\dfrac{4}{j0.1\omega}}{4 + \dfrac{5}{j0.1\omega}} = \frac{4}{5 + j0.4\omega}$$

$$= \frac{4}{\sqrt{25 + 0.16\omega^2}} \underline{/-\tan^{-1}0.08\omega}$$

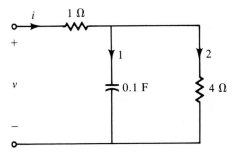

Figure 9.13
Network for Example 9.14.

The last example illustrates a general property of transfer functions. A typical transfer function has both a magnitude and an angle, which are functions of frequency. Also recall that a transfer function is restricted to a single input.

Frequency response

As stated earlier, a frequency-response analysis is a study of the behavior of a network as a function of source frequency. In order to examine the interrelationship of transfer functions and frequency response further, let us reconsider the basic result of Equation 9.105. Rewriting, we have

$$\bar{X}(j\omega) = \bar{T}(j\omega)\bar{F}$$

Written out in polar form,

$$X_m(\omega)\underline{/\theta(\omega)} = \left[T(\omega)\underline{/\beta(\omega)}\right]\left[F_m\underline{/\alpha}\right] \tag{9.107}$$

where

$$T(\omega) = \text{magnitude of transfer function}$$

$$\beta(\omega) = \text{angle of transfer function}$$

$$X_m(\omega) = \text{peak value of sinusoidal response}$$

$$\theta(\omega) = \text{phase angle of sinusoidal response}$$

all of which are functions of the source frequency ω.
From Equation 9.107 we see that

$$X_m(\omega) = T(\omega)F_m \tag{9.108}$$

and

$$\theta(\omega) = \alpha + \beta(\omega) \tag{9.109}$$

Therefore, the amplitude of the sinusoidal steady-state response is equal to the amplitude of the source function multiplied by the magnitude of the transfer function. Furthermore, the phase angle of the response relative to the source function is exactly the angle on the complex quantity representing the transfer function.

Frequency-response data are normally presented as plots of the magnitude $X_m(\omega)$ and the phase $\theta(\omega)$ versus the frequency ω. Alternatively, because of the results of Equations 9.108 and 9.109, the results may be presented as plots of the transfer function magnitude and angle versus frequency. Since the amplitude and phase of the source are usually assumed to be constant in undergraduate textbooks, the same information is displayed in either case.

An examination of the magnitude plot of the transfer function immediately reveals the manner in which a signal of a particular frequency is amplified or attenuated by the network. Likewise, the angle plot reveals the phase shift that will be imparted to an output variable relative to the input source at a particular frequency.

Example 9.15

In Example 9.14, we found the transfer function $\bar{T}(j\omega) = \bar{V}_2(j\omega)/\bar{V}$ to be defined by

$$T(\omega) = \frac{4}{\sqrt{25 + 0.16\omega^2}} \quad \text{and} \quad \beta(\omega) = -\tan^{-1}0.08\omega$$

By calculating a few points, we can sketch the magnitude and angle plots (Figure 9.14). The BASIC computer program FREQRES in Appendix C can be very useful for this calculation.

A physical interpretation of the plots is possible. For example, as ω approaches zero, the impedance of the capacitor is approaching infinity—an open circuit. In this case, the network behaves like a pure resistive network and the transfer function reduces to that of a voltage divider for the 4-Ω resistor in

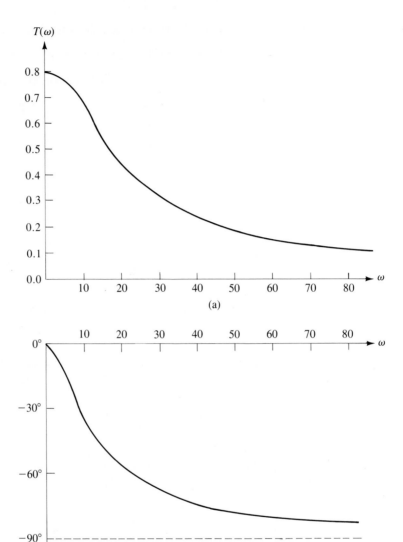

Figure 9.14
Frequency response
for Example 9.15.
(a) Magnitude. (b) Angle.

series with the 1-Ω resistor. The interpretation of the network behavior as ω approaches infinity is equally informative and is left as an exercise.

In the sketching or plotting of magnitude and angle plots, a base 10 logarithm scale is often used for the frequency axis. This has the effect of spreading out that portion of the plot of primary interest and also allowing for a wider range of frequencies in the plot. This idea is best illustrated by example.

Example 9.16 ————————————————————————————————

If a tree is chosen as shown in the network of Figure 9.15, a nodal equation can be used to find the transfer function $\bar{T}(j\omega) = \bar{V}_0(j\omega)/\bar{I}$. The result is

$$\bar{T}(j\omega) = \frac{j0.2\omega}{10 + j\omega}$$

Figure 9.15
Network for Example 9.16.

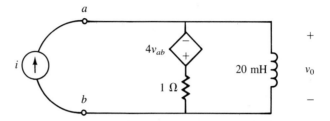

Therefore,

$$T(\omega) = \frac{0.2\omega}{\sqrt{100 + \omega^2}}$$

and

$$\beta(\omega) = 90 - \tan^{-1}0.1\omega$$

A sketch of these magnitude and angle functions is shown in Figure 9.16. On these sketches the frequency is shown on a logarithmic scale. Note that all frequency points shown are powers of ten. Of course, intermediate points could be shown if desired.

Figure 9.16
Frequency response for network of Figure 9.15.
(a) Magnitude.

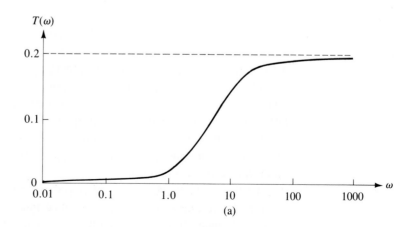

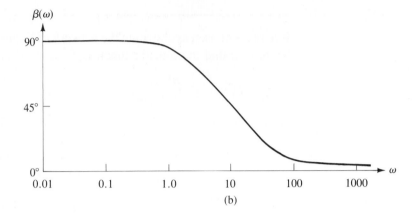

Figure 9.16 (cont'd.)
(b) Angle.

Additional frequency-response characteristics will arise as we study the subject of resonance.

Resonance

The concept of resonance is an important characteristic of electric networks. It is this phenomenon that permits frequency discrimination in communication networks.

Definition 9.1

Resonance
A 1-port network containing at least one inductor and one capacitor is defined to be *resonant* if the impedance of the network is purely real.

From the definition we see that a network displaying the resonance property appears the same as a pure resistance or is operating at unity power factor. This is true even though it contains energy-storage components!

The condition of resonance is a property that depends upon frequency as well as the size and interconnection of the network elements. Resonance can be attained by tuning or varying the frequency. However, it can also be obtained by varying the value of a network component. The latter approach requires that the network component be variable or at least that it be designed specifically to attain the resonant condition.

An electric network (or any other system) normally displays a more peaked or dramatic response at or near resonance than at other frequencies removed from resonance. It is not difficult to see why this property of a frequency response is crucial in the study of networks, as well as of other engineering disciplines. The selectivity aspects of resonance can be used to enhance the performance of communications devices. Knowledge of the resonant frequency or frequencies of a mechanical system, as well as of the frequencies that are present in the mechanical vibrations to which the system will be subjected, is an essential part of a successful design. Would you like to take off in an airplane with an extreme peak in the frequency-response characteristics of the wings at frequencies near 2 rad/s if you thought there was a significant chance that these frequencies might be excited by vibrations from the runway just before liftoff?

In the remainder of this section, we study some basic resonant electric networks. The series *RLC* network of Figure 9.17 can be adjusted to operate at resonance at a particular frequency. In this case we refer to the condition as *series resonance*. For this network the phasor-domain loop equation is

$$\left(R + j\omega L + \frac{1}{j\omega C}\right)\bar{I} = \bar{V}$$

from which

$$\bar{I} = \frac{\bar{V}}{R + j(\omega L - 1/\omega C)} \tag{9.110}$$

or

$$\bar{T}(j\omega) = \bar{Y}(j\omega) = \frac{\bar{I}(j\omega)}{\bar{V}} = \frac{1}{R + j(\omega L - 1/\omega C)} \tag{9.111}$$

and we see that resonance (unity power factor) occurs when

$$\omega L = \frac{1}{\omega C} \tag{9.112}$$

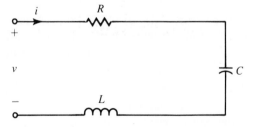

Figure 9.17
Series *RLC* network.

This is the general condition; it can be achieved by adjusting any one of the three variables in Equation 9.112 if the other two are fixed. Thus for fixed *L* and *C*, the resonant frequency is

$$\omega_0 \doteq \frac{1}{\sqrt{LC}} \tag{9.113}$$

Note that at this frequency, the transfer function is

$$T_0(j\omega) = \frac{1}{R}$$

and the current is

$$\bar{I}_0(j\omega) = \frac{\overline{V}}{R} \tag{9.114}$$

The current is maximum and is in phase with the voltage.

If it is desired that a network be frequency-selective and that the currrent be maximized at a given frequency ω_0, then a series *RLC* network tuned to ω_0 can be used. The peaking effect of such a network is illustrated in Figure 9.18.

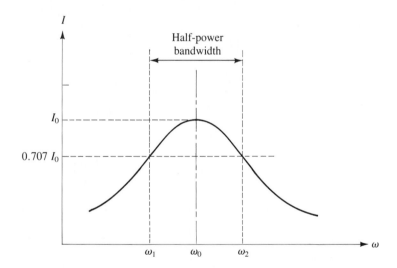

At resonance, I is inversely proportional to R, so it is evident that the magnitude of I_0 can be controlled by varying the value of R. Of course, there are practical limitations in reducing the R-coefficient to arbitrarily small values.

The power dissipated in an R-load is proportional to I^2. When discussing resonant series networks, we say that the *half-power frequencies* are those at which the current magnitude is $0.707I_0$, as shown in Figure 9.18.

At the half-power frequencies ω_1 and ω_2,

$$|Z(j\omega)| = \sqrt{2}R = \left| R + j\left(\omega L - \frac{1}{\omega C} \right) \right| \tag{9.115}$$

Therefore, it follows that

$$\frac{1}{\omega_1 C} - \omega_1 L = R \tag{9.116}$$

$$\omega_2 L - \frac{1}{\omega_2 C} = R \qquad (9.117)$$

Equations 9.116 and 9.117 make evident the fact that reduction of R for given L and C causes a corresponding reduction in $\omega_2 - \omega_1$. This frequency band is defined as the *half-power bandwidth*. As R becomes very small, it can be seen that

$$\omega_1 \to \frac{1}{\sqrt{LC}} \doteq \omega_0$$

$$\omega_2 \to \frac{1}{\sqrt{LC}} \doteq \omega_0$$

The series *RLC* network thus becomes more selective as R is reduced.

Another basic form of resonance is displayed by the parallel *RLC* network of Figure 9.19. This type of resonance is aptly referred to as *parallel resonance*. For this network, the phasor nodal equation is

$$\left(G + j\omega C + \frac{1}{j\omega L} \right) \bar{V} = \bar{I} \qquad (9.118)$$

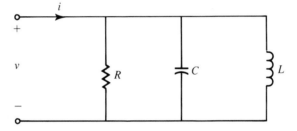

Figure 9.19
A parallel *RLC* network.

Solving for the parallel-network voltage, we have

$$\bar{V} = \frac{\bar{I}}{G + j[\omega C - 1/(\omega L)]} \qquad (9.119)$$

As for the series *RLC* network, resonance occurs for

$$\omega C = \frac{1}{\omega L}$$

which corresponds to

$$\omega^2 = \frac{1}{LC} \doteq \omega_0{}^2 \qquad (9.120)$$

At $\omega = \omega_0$,

$$\bar{V} = \frac{\bar{I}}{G} \doteq \bar{V}_0 \qquad (9.121)$$

For $\omega > \omega_0$, $\omega C > 1/\omega L$ and $\bar{I}$ leads $\bar{V}$. For $\omega < \omega_0$, $\omega C < 1/\omega L$ and $\bar{V}$ leads $\bar{I}$.

Half-power bandwidth is defined for the parallel network as indicated in Figure 9.20. Increasing the value of the parallel R (decreasing G) results in an increase in the magnitude of $\bar{V}_0$ and a decrease in the bandwidth.

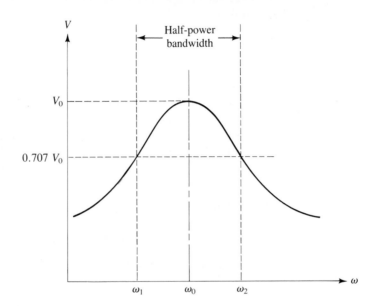

Figure 9.20
Frequency response of a parallel *RLC* network.

A much more practical form of parallel *RLC* network is that of Figure 9.21. Parallel tuned circuits of electronic equipment take this form, since a coil of wire (inductor) inherently has resistance associated with it.

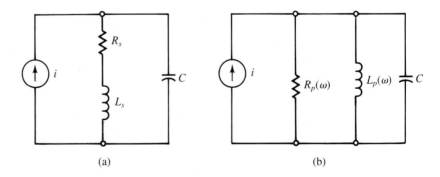

Figure 9.21
A parallel *RLC* network equivalent to a practical inductor in parallel with a *C*-component.

The effect on the sinusoidal steady-state solution of varying R_s in the network of Figure 9.21 can be deduced from the results for parallel *RLC* networks. To do this, we replace the series RL network by an equivalent parallel RL network. If we let subscripts s and p denote series and parallel, respectively, then for the RL branch of Figure 9.21, we obtain a parallel equivalent consisting of

$$R_p = \frac{R_s^2 + \omega^2 L_s^2}{R_s} \tag{9.122}$$

$$\omega L_p = \frac{R_s^2 + \omega^2 L_s^2}{\omega L_s} \tag{9.123}$$

Thus to make R_p large—with corresponding increase in V_0 and decrease in bandwidth—we must decrease R_s. It should also be observed that as $R_s \to 0$, $L_p \to L_s$. Note also that equivalent R_p and L_p are functions of ω. Finally, we emphasize that the condition for resonance is

$$\omega L_p = \frac{1}{\omega C}$$

which should be solved for ω_0! The derivation makes an interesting exercise.

Example 9.17

An active RC network as seen in Figure 9.22 can exhibit a peaking effect in much the same fashion as a resonant RLC network. Using the ideal model for

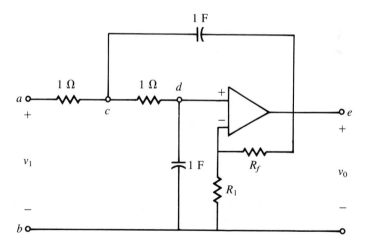

Figure 9.22
Network for Example 9.17.

the op amp, we can redraw the network in phasor form as shown in Figure 9.23. Selecting node b as the reference node, we see that nodal analysis leads to four node-voltage equations. However, the equation at node a is a dummy equation. Further we note that

$$\bar{V}_0 = k\bar{V}_3$$

Figure 9.23
Phasor equivalent network.

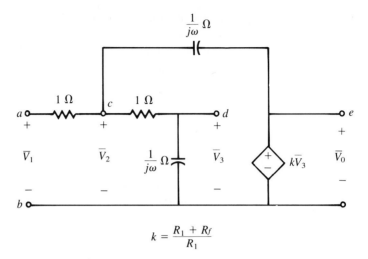

$$k = \frac{R_1 + R_f}{R_1}$$

By utilizing this result and writing the nodal equations at nodes c and d, we obtain

$$\begin{bmatrix} 2 + j\omega & -1 - kj\omega \\ -1 & 1 + j\omega \end{bmatrix} \begin{bmatrix} \bar{V}_2 \\ \bar{V}_3 \end{bmatrix} = \begin{bmatrix} \bar{V}_1 \\ 0 \end{bmatrix}$$

From these equations we find the transfer function to be

$$T(j\omega) = \frac{\bar{V}_0}{\bar{V}_1}(j\omega) = \frac{k}{1 + (3 - k)j\omega + (j\omega)^2}$$

The magnitude and angle plots of this function are shown in Figures 9.24 and 9.25 for three different values of k. Figure 9.24 shows that this network attenuates signals of high frequencies but passes or amplifies signals at low frequencies. For this reason this network is commonly referred to as a *low-pass filter* network.

A computer is quite useful in calculating frequency-response characteristics of this type and is a real time-saver for transfer functions involving higher-degree polynomials in $j\omega$.

9.10   MAXIMUM POWER TRANSFER AT STEADY STATE

In many electric network applications—particularly in communication circuits —it is desirable to achieve a maximum transfer of power from a normal source to a load impedance. As a common example, an electric guitar and amplifier may be regarded as a 1-port normal source when in operation. For a guitar enthusiast, an optimum situation exists when maximum audio power is emanating from the speaker. This situation occurs when maximum electric power

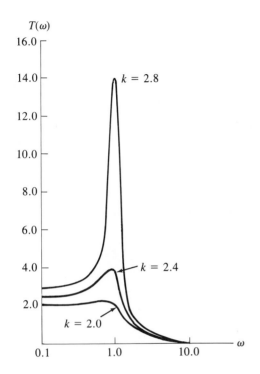

Figure 9.24
Magnitude plot for
Example 9.17.

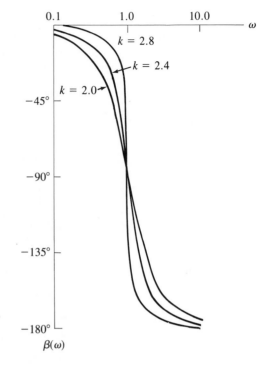

Figure 9.25
Angle plot for Example
9.17.

Figure 9.26
Schematic diagram of a
Thévenin 1-port and load
impedance.

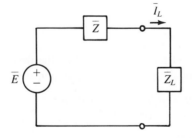

is being transferred from the amplifier to the speaker. The problem is, then, to match the speaker to achieve maximum power transfer, given a particular guitar-amplifier.

A normal source, as we have seen, may be represented at its terminals by either a Thévenin or a Norton equivalent 1-port. Our development will utilize the phasor Thévenin 1-port, with the Norton 1-port being left to the problems.

The network of Figure 9.26 contains a load impedance $\bar{Z} = R_L + jX_L$ connected across the terminals of a Thévenin equivalent 1-port. Let us suppose that we are able to vary R_L and X_L independently for the first investigation.

Theorem 9.1

Given an active phasor 1-port with Thévenin impedance $\bar{Z} = R + jX$ connected to a passive load impedance $\bar{Z}_L = R_L + jX_L$. Maximum power is absorbed by the load when $R_L = R$ and $X_L = -X$.

Proof: The average-load power is

$$P_L = \frac{I_L{}^2 R_L}{2}$$

where I_L is the peak value of the sinusoidal current. But since

$$I_L{}^2 = \left| \frac{\bar{E}}{R + R_L + j(X + X_L)} \right|^2 = \frac{E^2}{(R + R_L)^2 + (X + X_L)^2}$$

it follows that

$$P_L = \frac{E^2}{2} \left[\frac{R_L}{(R + R_L)^2 + (X + X_L)^2} \right]$$

We first maximize P_L with respect to X_L:

$$\frac{\partial P_L}{\partial X_L} = -\frac{E^2}{2} \frac{2(X + X_L)R_L}{[(R + R_L)^2 + (X + X_L)^2]^2}$$

When $\partial P_L / \partial X_L$ is set equal to zero, we obtain

$$X + X_L = 0$$

for the nontrivial case where $E \neq 0$ and $R_L \neq 0$.

If we now set $X_L = -X$, we obtain

$$P_L = \frac{E^2}{2} \frac{R_L}{(R + R_L)^2}$$

for the average-load power. Now we find the maximum of P_L with R_L as a variable. Differentiating the power expression with respect to R_L, we have

$$\frac{\partial P_L}{\partial R_L} = \frac{E^2}{2} \frac{(R + R_L)^2 - 2(R + R_L)R_L}{(R + R_L)^4} = 0$$

from which $R^2 - R_L{}^2 = 0$.

Theorem 9.1 is useful from a theoretical standpoint, but it has limited practical value because R_L and X_L can rarely be controlled independently. A more practical situation is one in which the magnitude Z_L can be varied, with the ratio of X_L to R_L remaining constant. We examine this case next.

Theorem 9.2

Given an active phasor 1-port with Thévenin impedance $\bar{Z} = R + jX$ connected to a passive load impedance, $\bar{Z}_L = Z_L \underline{/\theta}$. If Z_L is variable and θ fixed, then maximum average-load power occurs with $|\bar{Z}_L| = |\bar{Z}|$.

Proof:

$$P_L = \frac{I_L{}^2 R_L}{2}$$

$$= \frac{E^2}{2} \frac{Z_L \cos \theta}{(R + Z_L \cos \theta)^2 + (X + Z_L \sin \theta)^2}$$

Differentiating P_L with respect to Z_L and equating to zero, we obtain

$$(R + Z_L \cos \theta)^2 \cos \theta + (X + Z_L \sin \theta)^2 \cos \theta$$
$$- 2Z_L \cos^2\theta (R + Z_L \cos \theta) - 2Z_L \cos \theta \sin \theta (X + Z_L \sin \theta) = 0$$

which simplifies to

$$R^2 - Z_L{}^2(\cos^2 \theta + \sin^2 \theta) + X^2 = 0$$

or

$$Z_L{}^2 = R^2 + X^2$$

Thus if only the magnitude of the load impedance can be varied for matching purposes, maximum power is transmitted to the load when $|\bar{Z}_L| = |\bar{Z}|$. In Chapter 11 the use of electric transformers as impedance-magnitude-matching devices is discussed.

Although the derivations have been made in terms of phasor models, the results apply as well to active resistive 1-ports with resistive load. This is true in the resistive case regardless of the *t*-function form of the Thévenin *v*-source (or the Norton *i*-source). Demonstration of this is left to the problems.

9.11 SCALING OF IMPEDANCE FUNCTIONS

In most of our examples and problems, the numbers for the network components have been chosen for ease in computation. Values of 1 Ω, 2 H, and $\frac{1}{2}$ F are nice for analysis purposes but are not generally useful in practical electric networks.

For example, in a microwave network we might be dealing with frequencies in the gigahertz range (10^9 Hz), so that a resonant parallel circuit would have an LC product of approximately 10^{-19}. If L is in the 10^{-6} H range, then C would be approximately 10^{-13} F. These are not nice numbers to work with, so we could shrug our shoulders and justify using academic numbers by noting that the mastering of network theory does not depend on using practical numbers. Fortunately, however, we do not need to take such an ivory-tower stance to justify working with simple numbers.

By the use of scaling, we can convert practical numbers into convenient numbers. To juggle the size of practical inductors and capacitors to convenient size for analysis, we have two scaling options—impedance-magnitude scaling and frequency scaling.

To see how impedance-magnitude scaling works, let us consider a series *RLC* 1-port for which the impedance is

$$\bar{Z}(j\omega) = j\omega L + R + \frac{1}{j\omega C} \tag{9.124}$$

The impedance magnitude can be scaled up or down by a factor K_m to produce an impedance

$$\bar{Z}'(j\omega) = K_m\bar{Z}(j\omega) = K_m\left(j\omega L + R + \frac{1}{j\omega C}\right) \tag{9.125}$$

or

$$Z'(j\omega) = j\omega L' + R' + \frac{1}{j\omega C'} \tag{9.126}$$

where the prime denotes the scaled quantities (impedance and network component values of the scaled impedance).

Equating like terms in Equations 9.125 and 9.126, we have the following relations between the original component values and the scaled values:

$$L' = K_m L$$

$$R' = K_m R$$

$$C' = \frac{C}{K_m}$$

It should be clear that we do not gain any flexibility by considering admittance scaling also. Everything that can be done by magnitude scaling to juggle relative values of *L* and *C* can be done with either impedance-magnitude or admittance-magnitude scaling. We have chosen to discuss the scaling of impedance magnitude.

Example 9.18 _____

The series *RLC* network of Figure 9.27 has a resonant radian frequency of 10^5 rad/s. We scale the impedance magnitude by a factor of 10^{-2} to bring both the capacitance and the inductance to 10^{-5}. The resistance in the scaled network is then 1 Ω.

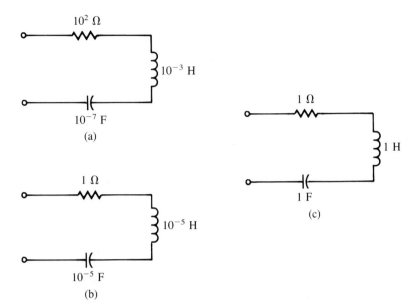

Figure 9.27
(a) Unscaled series network. (b) Impedance magnitude-scaled network ($K_m = 10^{-2}$). (c) Network with both impedance magnitude scaling ($K_m = 10^{-2}$) and frequency scaling ($K_f = 10^{-5}$).

With this scaling, we have not produced particularly good numbers for L and C, but we have brought them into the same range. Now we can use frequency scaling to try to improve the situation further.

In frequency scaling we change the value of frequency at which a particular impedance (magnitude and phase) occurs. Let the scaled frequency be ω' and let

$$\omega' = K_f \omega \qquad (9.127)$$

If we again take a general series impedance

$$\bar{Z}(j\omega) = j\omega L + R + \frac{1}{j\omega C}$$

and substitute

$$\omega = \frac{\omega'}{K_f}$$

we have

$$\bar{Z}'(j\omega') = j\omega'\left(\frac{L}{K_f}\right) + R + \frac{1}{j\omega'\left(\dfrac{C}{K_f}\right)} \qquad (9.128)$$

Thus if the scaled impedance is symbolized by

$$\bar{Z}'(j\omega') = j\omega'L' + R' + \frac{1}{j\omega'C'} \tag{9.129}$$

the scaled values of the network elements are

$$L' = \frac{L}{K_f}$$

$$R' = R$$

$$C' = \frac{C}{K_f}$$

Since K_f operates on L and C in the same manner, we can use frequency scaling to bring inductor and capacitor values that are in the same range into a more convenient range.

Example 9.19

For the network of Example 9.18, we can bring the scaled values of L and C to unity by using $K_f = 10^{-5}$. The scaled resonant frequency will also be unity.

$$\omega_0' = 10^{-5}\omega_0 = 1 \text{ rad/s}$$

The resistance R is unaffected by frequency scaling. The twice-scaled network is shown in Figure 9.27(c).

Scaling is usually applied only to passive network functions. Frequency scaling does not affect any CE that does not involve ω. Thus resistances and dependent sources are not affected. Magnitude scaling affects only those dependent sources in which the CE involves both current and voltage. Thus the CCCS and VCVS are not affected (since the coefficient in each case is dimensionless). For the CCVS where $v_j = Ai_k$, the scaled coefficient is $A' = K_m A$ (A has the unit of resistance). For the VCCS where $i_j = Bv_k$, the scaled coefficient is $B' = B/K_m$ (B has the unit of conductance).

Although we took a series RLC network to justify the scaled relationships for the various components, the results obtained are quite general. For the more complicated network, the choice of K_m and K_f to produce convenient numbers might not be so obvious as in our example. Once K_m and K_f are chosen, however, the scaled relationships follow from our results. If the results are not to our liking, we can always choose new scale factors and try again.

9.12 SUMMARY

In this chapter we discussed the analysis of networks in steady-state operation for sources of constant magnitude and for sinusoidal sources.

For constant sources, steady-state operation occurs when the time derivatives of all network voltages and currents are zero. The t-domain model for a network in such an operation thus becomes a set of algebraic equations, and the number of equations in the network PRIMM is reduced by twice the number of inductors *plus* capacitors in the network.

The phasor technique is very useful for steady-state analysis of networks that contain constant-frequency sources with constant maximum amplitudes. A phasor is characterized by the fact that its magnitude and phase angle correspond, respectively, to the magnitude and the phase angle of the sinusoidal function that it represents.

If only a steady-state analysis of a network is desired, it is convenient to begin directly with a network phasor model (also called the ω-domain model). This is done by replacing each source by its phasor equivalent and each L and C by its complex impedance or admittance. The problem of analysis is then reduced to one involving simultaneous complex linear algebraic equations.

The concept of complex power is useful in defining the operating condition of an electric-power system. The components of complex power—real average power and reactive volt-amperes—are readily calculated from the appropriate phasor voltages and currents. The power factor is defined as the ratio of real average power to apparent power (volt-amperes) and thus is a convenient quantity for partially characterizing a network in sinusoidal operation.

The property of resonance is often utilized in communication networks to discriminate between information transmitted at different frequencies. The sharpness of selectivity of a particular network is commonly defined by the specification of its half-power bandwidth.

PROBLEMS

9.1 Find the steady-state solutions to the following differential equations by the method of Section 9.2—that is, by setting the t-derivative terms equal to zero. The t-derivative operator is symbolized by p.

(a) $px + 10x = 50u(t)$

(b) $p^2x + 3px + 2x = 50u(t)$

(c) $p^3x + 6p^2x + 5px + 2x = 10u(t)$

(d) $p\begin{bmatrix} x_1 \\ x_2 \end{bmatrix} = \begin{bmatrix} -2 & 1 \\ 1 & -2 \end{bmatrix}\begin{bmatrix} x_1 \\ x_2 \end{bmatrix} + \begin{bmatrix} -10 \\ 5 \end{bmatrix}u(t)$

(e) $p\begin{bmatrix} x_1 \\ x_2 \end{bmatrix} = \begin{bmatrix} -1.5 & 1 \\ 2 & -2 \end{bmatrix}\begin{bmatrix} x_1 \\ x_2 \end{bmatrix} + \begin{bmatrix} 20 \\ -10 \end{bmatrix}u(t)$

(f) $p\begin{bmatrix} x_1 \\ x_2 \end{bmatrix} = \begin{bmatrix} -4 & 3.5 \\ 7 & -7.5 \end{bmatrix}\begin{bmatrix} x_1 \\ x_2 \end{bmatrix} + \begin{bmatrix} k_1 \\ k_2 \end{bmatrix}u(t)$

9.2 The network of Figure 9.28 was used in Example 8.10 to demonstrate numerical solution techniques for second-order systems. For $i_4(t) = u(t)$ A and $e_3(t) = 10u(t)$ V, find the steady-state solution for all currents by the method of Section 9.2.

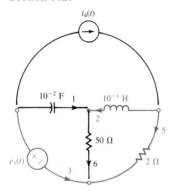

Figure 9.28

9.3 For the network of Figure 9.28, as in Example 8.10, $i_4(t) = e^{-5t}u(t)$ A and $e_3(t) = 10u(t)$ V. If steady state is defined as the solution as $t \to \infty$, find the steady-state value of all voltages by the method of Section 9.2.

9.4 Find the steady-state solutions to the following differential equations by the method of Section 9.3.

(a) $px + 10x = 10 \cos 5t$

(b) $p^2x + 3px + 2x = 10 \cos(t + 30°)$

(c) $p^3x + 6p^2x + 5px + 2x = 20 \sin t$

(d) $p \begin{bmatrix} x_1 \\ x_2 \end{bmatrix} = \begin{bmatrix} -2 & 1 \\ 1 & -2 \end{bmatrix} \begin{bmatrix} x_1 \\ x_2 \end{bmatrix} + \begin{bmatrix} 10 \cos t \\ -5 \sin t \end{bmatrix}$

(e) $p \begin{bmatrix} x_1 \\ x_2 \end{bmatrix} = \begin{bmatrix} -1.5 & 1 \\ 2 & -2 \end{bmatrix} \begin{bmatrix} x_1 \\ x_2 \end{bmatrix}$
$+ \begin{bmatrix} 5 \cos(2t + 45°) \\ 10 \cos 2t \end{bmatrix}$

(f) $p \begin{bmatrix} x_1 \\ x_2 \end{bmatrix} = \begin{bmatrix} -4 & 3.5 \\ 7 & -7.5 \end{bmatrix} \begin{bmatrix} x_1 \\ x_2 \end{bmatrix} + \begin{bmatrix} \cos 5t \\ -\sin 5t \end{bmatrix}$

9.5 Find the steady-state solutions for the following equations. Write the solutions in rectangular form (the form $\cos(\omega t + \theta) + j \sin(\omega t + \theta)$).

(a) $p^2x + 3px + 2x = 10e^{j10t}$

(b) $p^3x + 6p^2x + 5px + 2x = 20e^{j(2t + 60°)}$

9.6 The network of Figure 9.29 is excited by the following two sources:

$$v_2 = 100 \cos 100t \text{ V} \qquad i_6 = 5 \sin 100t \text{ A}$$

Use the phasor technique to solve for the steady-state values of all network currents and for $v_6(t)$. Write the answers in cosine form. Use branches 2, 4, and 5 as a tree.

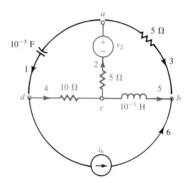

Figure 9.29

9.7 The network of Figure 9.28 is excited by the following two sources:

$$v_3 = 10 \cos 40t \text{ V} \qquad i_4 = -2 \sin 40t \text{ A}$$

Use the phasor technique to solve for the steady-state values of all network currents. Write in cosine form. Use branches 2, 3, and 5 as a tree.

9.8 The network of Figure 9.28 is excited by the following two sources:

$$v_3 = -10 \sin 25t \text{ V} \qquad i_4 = 2 \cos 25t \text{ A}$$

Use the phasor technique to solve for the steady-state values of all network voltages. Write in cosine form. Use branches 2, 3, and 5 as a tree.

9.9 For the network of Figure 9.29 and source functions

$$v_2 = 10 \cos 50t \text{ V}$$

$$i_6 = \sqrt{2} \cos(50t + 45°) \text{ A}$$

draw the phasor network model and, using a tree of branches 2, 4, and 5, formulate the phasor loop equations and solve for the phasor loop currents. Write the constant-phasor solution for all currents and all voltages of the network.

9.10 Repeat Problem 9.9 for source functions

$$v_2 = 50 \cos(100t - 120°) \text{ V}$$

$$i_6 = 5 \cos 100t \text{ A}$$

9.11 Repeat Problem 9.6 for source functions

$$v_2 = 20 \cos 200t \text{ V}$$

$$i_6 = 2 \sin(200t + 60°) \text{ A}$$

9.12 For the network of Figure 9.30 and the source functions

$$v_1 = \cos 10^4 t \text{ V}$$

$$v_2 = \cos(10^4 t + 90°) \text{ V}$$

$$i_4 = 2 \sin(10^4 t - 90°) \text{ A}$$

$$i_3 = -\cos 10^4 t \text{ A}$$

use a tree of branches 1, 2, 5, and 7 to formulate phasor loop equations. Solve the loop equations and find all network currents in cosine form.

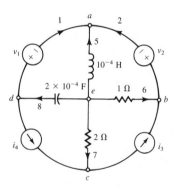

Figure 9.30

9.13 Solve the network of Problem 9.12 by formulating phasor node equations with node a as reference. (A zero-current element may be inserted in the linear graph between nodes a and c for the purpose of writing the node voltage equations.) Find every network voltage in cosine form. Find the t-variable phasor form for each network current.

9.14 Find the phasor impedance, Z, and admittance, Y, in rectangular form of the 1-port networks of Figure 9.31 at the radian frequencies given.

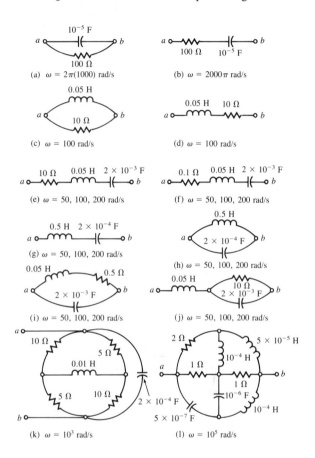

Figure 9.31

9.15 Find the phasor Thévenin and Norton equivalent 1-port models for the networks of Figure 9.32:

(a) with respect to terminals a and b for networks (a) through (d)

(b) network of (e) with respect to terminals b and d

(c) network of (e) with respect to terminals a and c

(d) network of (e) with respect to terminals c and d

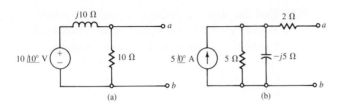

(a)

(b)

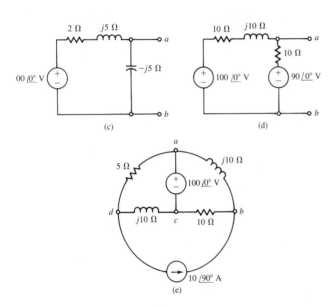

(c)

(d)

(e)

Figure 9.32

9.16 Calculate the complex power in rectangular form for a 1-port component having the following quantities associated with it.
(a) $\bar{I} = 10 + j10$ A, $\bar{V} = 100e^{j\,130°}$ V
(b) $i(t) = 2 \cos 377t$ A,
$v(t) = 150 \sin(377t + 30°)$ V
(c) $|\bar{V}| = 220$ V, $|\bar{I}| = 25$ A,
p.f. (power factor) $= 0.8$ ($\bar{I}$ lags $\bar{V}$)
(d) $\bar{V} = 250e^{j\,45°}$ V, $\bar{Z} = 10 - j5$ Ω
(e) $\bar{I} = 10$ A, $\bar{Z} = 10 - j5$ Ω
(f) $|\bar{V}|\cdot|\bar{I}| = 5000$ VA, $\bar{Y} = 8 - j6$ S

9.17 Given the following information about quantities associated with a 1-port network, find the indicated unknowns.
(a) $\bar{S} = 1000 + j200$ VA, $\bar{V} = 100$ V.
p.f. $=$?, $\bar{I} = $?
(b) $|\bar{S}| = 10,000$ VA, $\bar{V}_r = 115(1 + j)$ V,
p.f. $= 0.8$. $\bar{I}_r = $? (V and I rms)

(c) $|\bar{S}| = \sqrt{P^2 + Q^2} = 1500$ VA,
$P = 1000$ W, $Q = $?, p.f. $= $?
(d) $P = 5000$ W, $|\bar{V}_r| = 200$ V, $|\bar{I}_r| = 40$ A
($\bar{I}$ lags $\bar{V}$), $Q = $?, p.f. $= $?

9.18 Solve the network of Figure 9.33 and find the complex power associated with each branch. Demonstrate that the sum of the complex powers vanishes when every branch of the network is included.

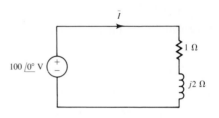

Figure 9.33

9.19 Solve Problem 9.18, except use the networks of Figure 9.34.

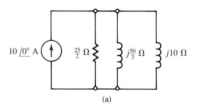

(a)

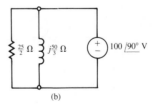

(b)

Figure 9.34

9.20 Find the complex power associated with each of the components of the two networks of Figure 9.35. Note for each source whether it is a load or generator with respect to average power. Also note whether it is supplying inductive or capacitive vars.

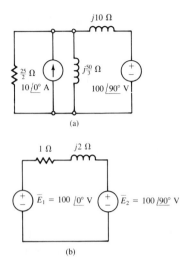

(a)

(b)

Figure 9.35

9.21 Determine the size of each capacitor needed at $f = 60$ Hz to obtain unity power factor for the networks of Figure 9.36.

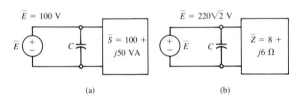

(a)

(b)

Figure 9.36

9.22 Find the frequency f for which each of the 1-ports of Figure 9.37 are resonant. Also find the half-power frequencies.

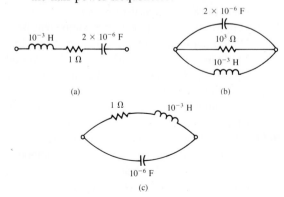

(a)

(b)

(c)

Figure 9.37

9.23 Find the half-power frequencies for each of the 1-port networks of Figure 9.37 for (a) $R = 100$ Ω and (b) $R = 10$ Ω. Tabulate the half-power bandwidth for each network for the values of resistance used in Problem 9.22 and in this problem.

9.24 Find the steady-state voltage on each capacitor of Figure 9.38 if $e(t) = 100u(t)$ V.

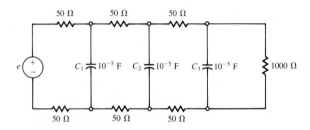

Figure 9.38

9.25 Write the 2-port Thévenin-form phasor model for the network of Figure 9.39 for every 2-port diagram shown. Sketch an equivalent phasor π network for a given ω.

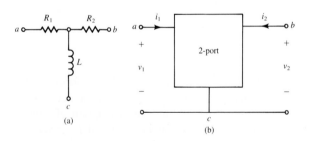

(a)

(b)

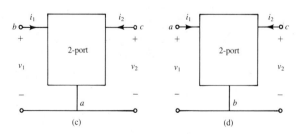

(c)

(d)

Figure 9.39

9.26 Write the 2-port Thévenin-form phasor model for the network of Figure 9.40 for every 2-port diagram of Figure 9.39. Sketch an equivalent phasor π network for a given ω.

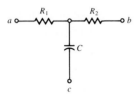

Figure 9.40

9.27 Write the 2-port Norton-form phasor model for the network of Figure 9.41 for every 2-port diagram of Figure 9.39. Sketch an equivalent phasor T network for a given ω.

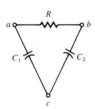

Figure 9.41

9.28 Find the Thévenin and the Norton forms of the 2-port component equations for the network of Figure 9.42 for the 2-port diagram of Figure 9.39(b). Sketch equivalent π and T networks.

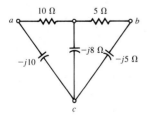

Figure 9.42

9.29 Solve Problem 9.28 for the network of Figure 9.43.

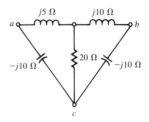

Figure 9.43

9.30 The following phasors represent sinusoidal t-functions. Write the functions in the form $A \cos(\omega t + \theta)$.
   (a) $\bar{V}(t) = 100e^{j100t}$
   (b) $\bar{I}(t) = [(1 + j2)/10e^{j56\cdot9°}]e^{j50t}$
   (c) $\bar{V}(t) = e^{j60°}e^{j10t} - 2e^{-j30}e^{j10t}$
   (d) $\bar{I}(t) = 10e^{j(2t+45°)} + (3 + j4)e^{j2t}$

9.31 Combine each of the following sets of functions into one cosine function by the use of phasors.
   (a) $f_1(t) = 2\cos(at + 60°) + \cos at$
   (b) $f_2(t) = 5\cos 2t + 3\sin 2t$
   (c) $f_3(t) = 10\sin(377t + 30°)$
        $+ 5\cos(377t - 60°)$
   (d) $f_4(t) = \cos 10t + \cos(10t + 120°) +$
        $\cos(10t + 240°)$

9.32 Find the value of resistive load that would dissipate maximum average power when connected to each of the active 1-ports of Problem 9.15 (Figure 9.32). Find the maximum possible value of the average load power.

9.33 Suppose that an active 1-port component has a Norton admittance of $\bar{Y} = G + jB$. Let a load admittance $\bar{Y}_L = G_L + jB_L$ be variable, in both G_L and B_L (B_L may be of either sign). Find the condition such that maximum average power is transmitted to the load. (*Hint:* The argument parallels the proof of Theorem 9.1.)

9.34 Carry out the derivation paralleling the proof of Theorem 9.2 for an active 1-port component with a Norton admittance $\bar{Y} = G + jB$ and a load admittance of $\bar{Y}_L = Y_L \underline{/\theta}$.

9.35 If an active 1-port component has a Thévenin-form component equation $v(t) = Ri + e(t)$, then maximum power is transmitted to a resistive load R_L when $R_L = R$, regardless of the form of $e(t)$. Use a derivation similar to those for Theorems 9.1 and 9.2 to prove this statement.

9.36 For the network of Figure 9.44, assume that the operational amplifier is ideal (see Section 6.6) and the input voltage is

$$e(t) = E \cos \omega t \text{ V}$$

Find the output voltage $v_0(t)$ at steady state as a function of ω, using phasor analysis.

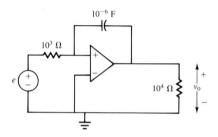

Figure 9.44

9.37 Work Problem 9.36 with a capacitor of 10^{-5} F.
9.38 Work Problem 9.36 with a capacitor of 10^{-7} F.
9.39 For the network of Figure 9.45, assume that the operational amplifier is ideal and the input voltage is

$$e(t) = 5 \cos 10^3 t \text{ V}$$

Find the output voltage $v_0(t)$ at steady state using phasor analysis.

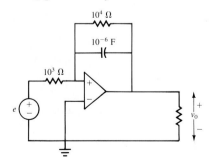

Figure 9.45

9.40 Repeat Problem 9.39 with $\omega = 10^4$ rad/s.
9.41 Repeat Problem 9.39 with $\omega = 10^2$ rad/s.
9.42 For the network of Figure 9.46, assume that the voltage source is

$$e = E \cos \omega t \text{ V}$$

Use phasor analysis to find $\bar{V}_2$ in terms of E and ω.

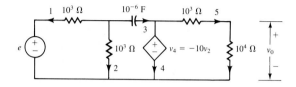

Figure 9.46

9.43 In Problem 9.42 let $E = 10$ V and $\omega = 10^3$ rad/s. Find $v_0(t)$.
9.44 In Problem 9.42 let $E = 10$ V and $\omega = 10^2$ rad/s. Find $v_0(t)$.
9.45 For the network of Figure 9.47, assume that the voltage source is

$$e = 5 \cos 10^3 t \text{ V}$$

Use phasor analysis to find $v_0(t)$.

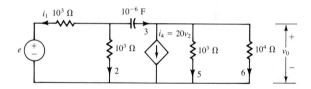

Figure 9.47

9.46 In Problem 9.45 let $\omega = 10^2$ rad/s and find $v_0(t)$.
9.47 In Problem 9.45 let $\omega = 10^4$ rad/s and find $v_0(t)$.
9.48 Use impedance magnitude and frequency scaling to get equivalent networks for Figure 9.37 in which each inductor and capacitor has a magnitude of unity (H and F).
9.49 Use impedance magnitude and frequency scaling on the network of Figure 9.31(k) to derive an equivalent network in which the in-

ductor and capacitor have magnitudes of 1 H and 1 F, respectively.

9.50 Use impedance magnitude and frequency scaling on the network of Figure 9.31(l) to derive an equivalent network in which the 10^{-4}-H inductor and the 10^{-6}-F capacitor have magnitudes of 2 H and 2 F, respectively.

The computer program FREQRES can be used to advantage for Problems 9.51–9.66, 9.68, and 9.69.

9.51 For the network of Figure 9.48, calculate and plot the magnitude and angle of the transfer function $\bar{T}(j\omega) = \bar{Y}(j\omega) = \bar{I}/\bar{V}_1$ for values of the resistor of 0.2, 0.5, and 1 Ω. Show all three curves for the magnitude on a single plot and all three curves for the angle on another plot.

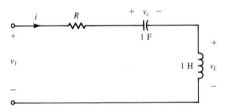

Figure 9.48

9.52 Repeat Problem 9.51 if $L = 0.01$ H.
9.53 Repeat Problem 9.51 if $L = 1.0$ mH and $C = 0.1$ F.
9.54 Repeat Problem 9.51 except use the transfer function $\bar{V}_L/\bar{V}_1$.
9.55 Repeat Problem 9.51 except use the transfer function $\bar{V}_C/\bar{V}_1$.
9.56 For the network of Figure 9.49, calculate and plot the magnitude and angle of the transfer function $\bar{T}(j\omega) = \bar{Z}(j\omega) = \bar{V}/\bar{I}$ for values of the resistor of 1, 2, and 5 Ω. Show all three curves for the magnitude on a single plot and all three curves for the angle on another plot.

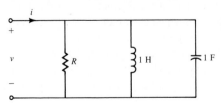

Figure 9.49

9.57 Repeat Problem 9.56 if $C = 0.1$ F.
9.58 Repeat Problem 9.56 if $C = 0.01$ F and $L = 10$ mH.

In Problems 9.59–9.66, calculate and plot the frequency-response characteristics of the specified transfer functions.

9.59 $\bar{T}(j\omega) = \bar{V}_1/\bar{I}$ for Figure 9.50.
9.60 $\bar{T}(j\omega) = \bar{V}_1/\bar{I}$ for Figure 9.50 except $R_L = 5$ Ω.
9.61 $\bar{T}(j\omega) = \bar{V}_0/\bar{V}_1$ for Figure 9.50.

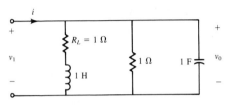

Figure 9.50

9.62 $\bar{T}(j\omega) = \bar{V}_1/\bar{I}$ for Figure 9.51.
9.63 $\bar{T}(j\omega) = \bar{V}_0/\bar{V}_1$ for Figure 9.51.

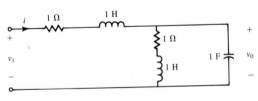

Figure 9.51

9.64 $\bar{T}(j\omega) = \bar{V}_0/\bar{V}_1$ for Figure 9.52.

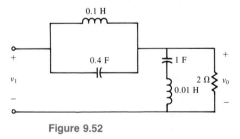

Figure 9.52

9.65 $\bar{T}(j\omega) = \bar{V}_0/\bar{V}_1$ for Figure 9.53. Use $R_2 = R_3 = 1$ Ω, $C_1 = 4.3$ F, $C_2 = 0.36$ F, and plot curves for three different values of the op-amp circuit gain $k \doteq (R_1 + R_f)/R_1$. Use $k = 1$, 5, and 10.

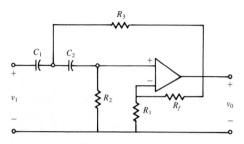

Figure 9.53

9.66 $T(j\omega) = \bar{V}_0/\bar{V}_1$ for Figure 9.54. Use $C_1 = C_2 = 1$ F, $R_3 = R_4 = 2\ \Omega$, $R_2 = 1\ \Omega$, and plot curves when $k \doteq (R_1 + R_f)/R_1$ is given by $k = 1$, 3, and 5.

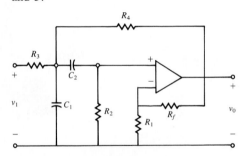

Figure 9.54

9.67 For the network of Figure 9.53, develop an expression for the transfer function $\bar{V}_0/\bar{V}_1$. Your answer should be expressed in terms of G_1, G_2, G_3, C_1, C_2, and k where $k \doteq (R_1 + R_f)/R_1$.

9.68 Repeat Problem 9.67 for the network of Figure 9.54. Answer should be in terms of G_1, G_2, G_3, G_4, C_1, C_2, and k. Let $G_1 = G_2 = G_3 = G_4 = 1$ S, $C_1 = C_2 = 1$ F. Calculate and plot enough transfer function characteristics to examine the behavior of this network as k is varied where $k > 0$. Discuss the potential applications of a network of this type.

9.69 For the network of Figure 9.54, let $G_1 = G_2 = G_3 = G_4 = 1$ S. Investigate the frequency response of this network as C_1 and C_2 are varied but held equal. For each value of capacitance, use several appropriate values of $k \doteq (R_1 + R_f)/R_1$.

For Problems 9.70–9.80, use CMATINV or a similar complex matrix inversion program to find the solutions to the problems as indicated.

9.70 Problem 9.6.   **9.74** Problem 9.10.
9.71 Problem 9.7.   **9.75** Problem 9.11.
9.72 Problem 9.8.   **9.76** Problem 9.12.
9.73 Problem 9.9.   **9.77** Problem 9.13.
9.78 The network of Figure 9.55.

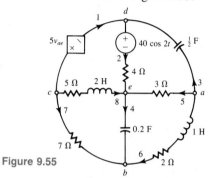

Figure 9.55

9.79 The network of Figure 9.56.

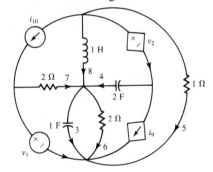

Figure 9.56 $v_2 = 2v_7$ $i_9 = 2i_6$
$v_1 = 5 \sin 4t$ V $i_{10} = 10 \cos 4t$ A

9.80 The network of Figure 9.57.

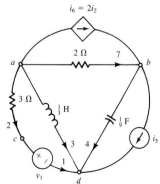

Figure 9.57 $v_1 = 9 \cos 10t$ V
$i_5 = 2 \sin 10t$ A

Giants of the profession
IEEE Centennial Hall of Fame

Edwin H. Armstrong (1890–1954)
His four major inventions included the super-heterodyne receiver and frequency modulation in radio communications. Here, on the beach, Armstrong tunes in the first "portable" radio, a gift to his bride, 1923.

Lee de Forest (1873–1961)
Colorful and controversial inventor of the triode-amplifier vacuum tube; he was also an aficionado of poetry, painting, and music. The photo shows de Forest with the three-element vacuum tube used to amplify speech, 1946.

Reprinted with permission from
"Centennial Hall of Fame,"
IEEE SPECTRUM, April 1984.

10

Three-phase networks

10.1 INTRODUCTION

The term *three-phase network* is applied to any electric network for which the sources are three balanced sinusoidal time functions. The meaning of *balanced* will become clear in the next section. Three-phase networks are very important to the electric-power industry because essentially all electric energy is generated with three-phase alternators and transmitted by three-phase transmission lines.

One of the primary advantages of three-phase power stems from the fact that the power taken by a balanced three-phase load is constant—not pulsating, as is the case for a single-phase load. For this and other reasons, a balanced load is very desirable on a three-phase system.

A three-phase alternating-current (ac) motor provides a balanced load to the power system, and thus most ac motors above 1 or 2 hp operate on three-phase power. Although a significant amount of the loads of an electric-power company may be single-phase, a strong attempt is made to distribute these loads to form a balanced three-phase load at the generating station.

General network-modeling techniques are certainly applicable to three-phase networks. These techniques would be required to obtain a complete analysis of network operation. In general, however, the operation of a three-phase network at steady state is of great interest to electric-power engineers. Fortunately, there are many special techniques and shortcuts available for balanced three-phase networks operating at steady state. Thus a special treatment of three-phase network analysis by phasor techniques is desirable.

Throughout this chapter we are concerned with sinusoidal steady-state analysis only. Therefore phasor (ω-domain) models are used consistently. Also, in keeping with the usual practice of electric-power engineers, *rms voltages and currents are used throughout*.

To be complete from a theoretical standpoint, this chapter should probably treat three-phase voltage *and* current sources. In practice, however, essentially all three-phase power systems operate at approximately constant-voltage conditions, so only three-phase voltage sources are considered. The extension to current sources, if needed, is a simple one. We therefore believe that the extra space required for their treatment is not justified in this book.

10.2 BALANCED THREE-PHASE SOURCES AND LOADS

Balanced loads and voltage sources for three-phase electric networks invariably occur in the *delta* (Δ) or *wye* (Y) configurations or a combination of the two.[1] Figure 10.1 illustrates these configurations.

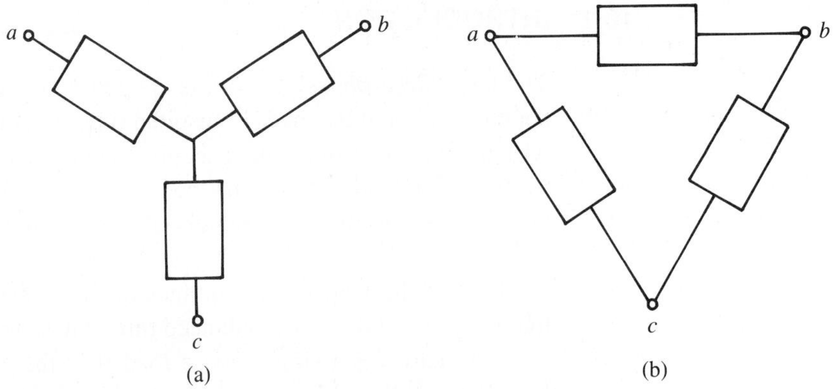

Figure 10.1
One-port components connected for three-phase operation. (a) $Y(T)$ connection. (b) $\Delta(\pi)$ connection.

A three-phase load is said to be *balanced* if the ω-domain impedance of each of the three single-phase loads is the same.

A set of three-phase sinusoidal voltage sources is said to be balanced if the maximum value of each of the voltages is the same and if the phase angles of two of the voltages are 120° and $-120°$ relative to the third. As an example, the following set of three sinusoidal functions is a balanced set by this definition:

$$X_1 = A\cos(\omega t + 45°)$$
$$X_2 = A\cos(\omega t + 165°)$$
$$X_3 = A\cos(\omega t + 285°)$$

(10.1)

[1]Electric-power engineers have used the names *delta* and *wye*, respectively, for the configurations that electronics and networks engineers call π and T. Since we are discussing a power subject here, we use the appropriate power terminology.

The direction of rotation of a three-phase electric motor depends upon the order in which the applied balanced voltages become maximum. This order is called the *phase sequence* of the balanced set. For the example shown in Equation 10.1, the sequence is 321. Equivalent statements of the phase sequence are 132 and 213. It is, however, customary to refer to the two possible orders as 123 and 321.

We restrict the type of system considered in this chapter to the simple configuration illustrated in Figure 10.2. In general, the source may be connected Δ or Y. Likewise the load may be connected in either manner. If *both* source and load are Y-connected, the transmission line connecting them may consist of four wires—one of which ties together the center (or neutral) junctions of the Y's. Otherwise the transmission line is always a three-wire line.

Figure 10.2
Simple power system.

In many practical problems the transmission-line impedance may be neglected in comparison with the load impedance. A simpler model results when such an approximation can be made. We consider the case of zero impedance in the transmission line as well as the nonzero impedance case for the various load configurations.

In specifying operating voltages and currents of an electric-power system, the rms currents in the lines and the rms voltages measured between lines are usually used. With Y-loads and Y-sources, the line currents correspond to the load and source currents. The line-to-line voltages do not correspond to the load voltages but are related in a simple manner.

Consider the Y-configuration of Figure 10.3. Double-subscript notation is convenient to describe the relationship between the line-to-line voltages (here-

Figure 10.3
Set of Y-connected
v-sources.

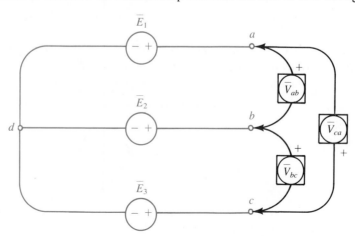

after abbreviated to *line voltages*). The notation $\bar{V}_{ab}$ denotes the rms phasor voltage of a with respect to b. Using this notation, let us assume that the phasor representation of the Y voltages is

$$\bar{E}_1 = \bar{V}_{ad} = E\underline{/\theta}$$

$$\bar{E}_2 = \bar{V}_{bd} = E\underline{/\theta - 120°} = (-0.5 - j0.866)E\underline{/\theta} \qquad (10.2)$$

$$\bar{E}_3 = \bar{V}_{cd} = E\underline{/\theta - 240°} = (-0.5 + j0.866)E\underline{/\theta}$$

We would like to find the line voltages $\bar{V}_{ab}$, $\bar{V}_{bc}$, and $\bar{V}_{ca}$. For convenience, we connect a set of meters on the system of Figure 10.3 to measure these line voltages. For the system thus formed, the Y-voltages constitute a star-tree of voltages.

Thus using the resulting loops, we can write

$$\bar{V}_{ab} + \bar{V}_{bd} + \bar{V}_{da} = 0$$

or

$$\bar{V}_{ab} = \bar{V}_{ad} + \bar{V}_{db}$$

$$\bar{V}_{ab} = E\underline{/\theta} - E\underline{/\theta - 120°} = (1.5 + j0.866)E\underline{/\theta} = \sqrt{3}E\underline{/\theta + 30°}$$

Similarly,

$$\bar{V}_{bc} = \bar{V}_{bd} + \bar{V}_{dc} = \sqrt{3}E\underline{/\theta - 90°}$$

$$\bar{V}_{ca} = \bar{V}_{cd} + \bar{V}_{da} = \sqrt{3}E\underline{/\theta + 150°}$$

These relations may be visualized most quickly from the phasor diagram of Figure 10.4.

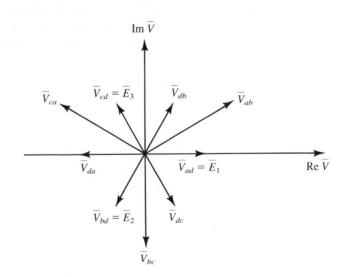

Figure 10.4
Phasor diagram for the phasor voltages of Equation 10.2 for $\theta = 0$.

10.3 FOUR-WIRE Y NETWORK

Consider the network of Figure 10.5. The phasor three-phase source consists of

$$\bar{V}_1 = E\underline{/0°}$$
$$\bar{V}_2 = E\underline{/-120°}$$
$$\bar{V}_3 = E\underline{/120°}$$

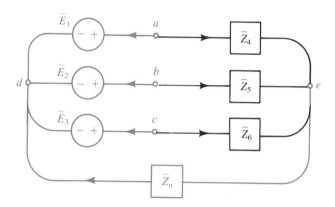

Figure 10.5
Four-wire YY-connected
three-phase network.
(Formulation star-tree
indicated by colored
lines.)

If the transmission-line impedance is nonzero, it is considered as part of the load in the following discussion.

The impedance of the neutral line (between nodes d and e) is designated as $\bar{Z}_n$. If a formulation tree is chosen consisting of the three sources and the neutral line, we may use either three loop equations or one node equation to analyze the system. For our immediate purpose the node equation is most useful. If node d is taken as the reference and one equation is written at node e, we obtain

$$(\bar{Y}_n + \bar{Y}_4 + \bar{Y}_5 + \bar{Y}_6)\bar{V}_n = \bar{Y}_4\bar{E}_1 + \bar{Y}_5\bar{E}_2 + \bar{Y}_6\bar{E}_3 \qquad (10.3)$$

where $\bar{Y} \equiv 1/\bar{Z}$.

For the balanced case, $\bar{Y}_4 = \bar{Y}_5 = \bar{Y}_6 = \bar{Y}$ and $\bar{E}_1 + \bar{E}_2 + \bar{E}_3 = 0$. Thus for the balanced three-phase network, Equation 10.3 becomes

$$(\bar{Y}_n + 3\bar{Y})\bar{V}_n = \bar{Y}(\bar{E}_1 + \bar{E}_2 + \bar{E}_3) = 0 \qquad (10.4)$$

Equation 10.4 makes evident the fact that the voltage across the neutral line of the balanced four-wire system depicted in Figure 10.5 is always zero despite the magnitude of $\bar{Z}_n$. Thus there is no current in the neutral line of a balanced four-wire system.

The currents in the loads of Figure 10.5 can be found as functions of the sources to which the loads are connected. By expressing the load voltages in terms of the tree voltages in the CE, we obtain

$$\bar{I}_4 = \frac{\bar{V}_1}{Z} = \frac{E\underline{/0°}}{Z\underline{/\alpha}} = \frac{E}{Z}\underline{/-\alpha}$$

$$\bar{I}_5 = \frac{\bar{V}_2}{Z} = \frac{E\underline{/-120°}}{Z\underline{/\alpha}} = \frac{E}{Z}\underline{/-120° - \alpha}$$

$$\bar{I}_6 = \frac{\bar{V}_3}{Z} = \frac{E\underline{/120°}}{Z\underline{/\alpha}} = \frac{E}{Z}\underline{/120° - \alpha}$$

Therefore, the currents are also balanced and have the same relative phases as do their corresponding sources. This development is for a general balanced three-phase system without specification of the impedance of the neutral line. For this case it is clear that only one current need be calculated. If the phase sequence of the voltages is known, the proper phase angle can be assigned to two currents once the remaining one is known.

Even if the network is unbalanced, one node-voltage equation (Equation 10.3) is still sufficient. In general, of course, the neutral current is not zero.

The complex power transmitted to the three-phase load can be found from

$$\bar{S} = P + jQ = \bar{V}_4\bar{I}_4^* + \bar{V}_5\bar{I}_5^* + \bar{V}_6\bar{I}_6^* \tag{10.5}$$

which for the balanced case reduces to

$$\bar{S} = 3\bar{V}_4\bar{I}_4^* = -3\bar{E}_1\bar{I}_1^* \tag{10.6}$$

Equation 10.6 follows from Equation 10.5 because the phase angle of each phasor load current, relative to the corresponding phasor voltage, is the same. Equation 10.5 is a general expression for power for a three-phase load if the voltages and currents are associated with the individual 1-port (single-phase) loads.

The magnitude of each line voltage is $\sqrt{3}V_4$. Thus the three-phase power expression, Equation 10.6, can be written in terms of the line-voltage magnitude as

$$\bar{S} = 3V_4I_4\underline{/\alpha} = \sqrt{3}V_LI_L\underline{/\alpha} \tag{10.7}$$

where V_L and I_L are line-voltage and line-current rms magnitudes, respectively, and α is the load-impedance angle. The power factor of the load is

$$\text{p.f.} = \cos \alpha$$

10.4   THREE-WIRE Y NETWORK

In this section we consider the system discussed in the previous section but with the neutral connection removed. For the balanced case we found that no current was present in the neutral. From this we can conclude that no change in the operation would result if the neutral line were removed.

One node equation is sufficient to model the three-wire network of Figure 10.6. By using the artifice of replacing the neutral with an element of $\bar{Y}_n = 0$, we may regard the three-wire network as a four-wire network. (This is also equivalent to assuming an ideal current source with $\bar{I} = 0$.)

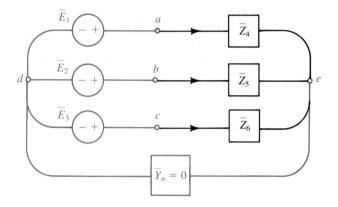

Figure 10.6
Three-wire YY-connected three-phase network. Zero-admittance neutral inserted for convenience.

Using the star-tree indicated, we obtain a node equation which is the same as Equation 10.3 with $\bar{Y}_n = 0$:

$$(\bar{Y}_4 + \bar{Y}_5 + \bar{Y}_6)\bar{V}_n = \bar{Y}_4\bar{E}_1 + \bar{Y}_5\bar{E}_2 + \bar{Y}_6\bar{E}_3 \qquad (10.8)$$

so that under balanced conditions, $\bar{V}_n = 0$ and

$$\bar{V}_4 = \bar{E}_1 \qquad \bar{V}_5 = \bar{E}_2 \qquad \bar{V}_6 = \bar{E}_3$$

This confirms our previous conclusion that the operation of the three-wire and four-wire YY networks are identical under balanced conditions.

If the loads are not identical, then

$$\bar{V}_{ed} = \bar{V}_n = \frac{\bar{Y}_4\bar{E}_1 + \bar{Y}_5\bar{E}_2 + \bar{Y}_6\bar{E}_3}{\bar{Y}_4 + \bar{Y}_5 + \bar{Y}_6}$$

$$\bar{V}_4 = \bar{E}_1 - \bar{V}_n$$

$$\bar{V}_5 = \bar{E}_2 - \bar{V}_n$$

$$\bar{V}_6 = \bar{E}_3 - \bar{V}_n$$

The complex power for the unbalanced three-wire YY network can be found by

$$\bar{S} = \bar{V}_4 \bar{I}_4^* + \bar{V}_5 \bar{I}_5^* + \bar{V}_6 \bar{I}_6^*$$

where

$$\bar{I}_4 = \frac{\bar{V}_4}{\bar{Z}_4} = \frac{\bar{E}_1 - \bar{V}_n}{\bar{Z}_4}$$

$$\bar{I}_5 = \frac{\bar{V}_5}{\bar{Z}_5} = \frac{\bar{E}_2 - \bar{V}_n}{\bar{Z}_5}$$

$$\bar{I}_6 = \frac{\bar{V}_6}{\bar{Z}_6} = \frac{\bar{E}_3 - \bar{V}_n}{\bar{Z}_6}$$

For the balanced case,

$$\bar{I}_4 = \frac{\bar{E}_1}{\bar{Z}_4}$$

$$\bar{I}_5 = \frac{\bar{E}_2}{\bar{Z}_5}$$

$$\bar{I}_6 = \frac{\bar{E}_3}{\bar{Z}_6}$$

and

$$\bar{S} = 3EI_L \underline{/\alpha}$$

where α is the phase angle of the balanced load impedance. In terms of line-to-line voltage V_L, this can be written

$$\bar{S} = \sqrt{3} V_L I_L \underline{/\alpha}$$

The power factor of the load is given by

$$\text{p.f.} = \cos \alpha$$

10.5   YΔ NETWORK

In this section we investigate the operation of a system composed of a set of Y-connected voltage sources and a Δ-connected load. The analysis is particularly simple if the transmission-line impedances are considered zero. Figure 10.7 shows the schematic diagram for such a system.

Since the ideal voltage sources form a complete star-tree, we note that

$$\bar{V}_4 = \bar{E}_2 - \bar{E}_3$$

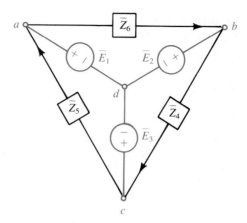

Figure 10.7
YΔ network with zero
transmission-line
impedance.

and thus that

$$\bar{I}_4 = \frac{\bar{E}_2 - \bar{E}_3}{\bar{Z}_4}$$

If we use the phasor voltages of Equation 10.2,

$$\bar{E}_1 = E\underline{/\theta}$$

$$\bar{E}_2 = E\underline{/\theta - 120°}$$

$$\bar{E}_3 = E\underline{/\theta - 240°}$$

and the phasor diagram of Figure 10.4, we find that the currents are

$$\bar{I}_4 = \frac{\sqrt{3}E}{\bar{Z}_4}\underline{/\theta - 90°}$$

$$\bar{I}_5 = \frac{\sqrt{3}E}{\bar{Z}_5}\underline{/\theta + 150°}$$

$$\bar{I}_6 = \frac{\sqrt{3}E}{\bar{Z}_6}\underline{/\theta + 30°}$$

If the load is balanced, $\bar{Z}_4 = \bar{Z}_5 = \bar{Z}_6$, and clearly the currents are balanced. The solution is simple even for unbalanced loads.

The complex power associated with the Δ-load is the sum of the three complex powers

$$\bar{S} = \bar{V}_4\bar{I}_4^* + \bar{V}_5\bar{I}_5^* + \bar{V}_6\bar{I}_6^*$$

For balanced conditions this simplifies to

$$\bar{S} = 3\bar{V}_4\bar{I}_4^* = 3V_4I_4\underline{/\alpha} \tag{10.9}$$

It is possible to express the three-phase power in terms of line voltages and line currents for this case as well as for the Y-load already discussed. From the schematic diagram of Figure 10.7, we note that the line currents are the currents of the voltage sources: .

$$\bar{I}_1 = \bar{I}_{ad} = \bar{I}_5 - \bar{I}_6 = \bar{I}_{ca} + \bar{I}_{ba}$$

$$\bar{I}_2 = \bar{I}_{bd} = \bar{I}_{ab} + \bar{I}_{cb}$$

$$\bar{I}_3 = \bar{I}_{cd} = \bar{I}_{bc} + \bar{I}_{ac}$$

If we assume that the phasor currents in the Δ are

$$\bar{I}_{ca} = I_5 = I\underline{/0° + \theta}$$

$$\bar{I}_{ab} = I_6 = I\underline{/-120° + \theta} \qquad (10.10a)$$

$$\bar{I}_{bc} = I_4 = I\underline{/120° + \theta}$$

then

$$\bar{I}_{ad} = I_1 = \sqrt{3}I\underline{/30° + \theta}$$

$$\bar{I}_{bd} = I_2 = \sqrt{3}I\underline{/-90° + \theta} \qquad (10.10b)$$

$$\bar{I}_{cd} = I_3 = \sqrt{3}I\underline{/150° + \theta}$$

Figure 10.8 is a phasor diagram indicating the relative magnitudes and phase angles of the Δ-load currents and the line currents.

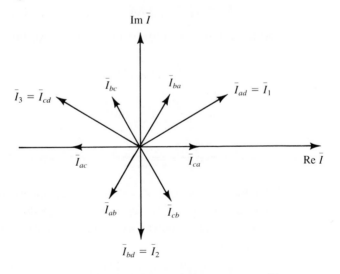

Figure 10.8
Phasor diagram for Equation 10.10 with $\theta = 0$.

The magnitude of each of the line currents is $\sqrt{3}$ times the magnitude of the balanced Δ-load currents. Thus the three-phase power expression, Equation 10.9, can be written

$$\bar{S} = P + jQ = \sqrt{3}V_L I_L \underline{/\alpha} = \sqrt{3}V_L I_L(\cos\alpha + j\sin\alpha)$$

where V_L and I_L are line-voltage and line-current rms magnitudes, respectively, and α is the load-impedance angle. The power factor of the load is

$$\text{p.f.} = \cos \alpha$$

10.6 ΔΔ NETWORK

Suppose the three-phase source of Figure 10.7 was Δ-connected instead of Y-connected as we assumed in Section 10.5. It is clear that no change in the line and Δ-load currents would occur if the line voltages were unchanged.

If a set of balanced v-sources is assumed connected in Δ, there is a problem of determining currents in the three-phase source thus formed. This problem arises because no tree exists in the system I-diagram that contains all v-sources. Thus every supernode equation that involves one v-source current must involve two. If each source is regarded as a Thévenin equivalent 1-port with arbitrarily small (but equal) impedance, the currents can be shown to be balanced for a balanced three-phase load.

No such problem arises when the open-Δ (or V) source connection is used. The open-Δ connection is, as the name implies, a Δ with one 1-port missing. Figure 10.9 illustrates a three-phase open-Δ source connected to a Δ-load. Since the two single-phase sources can be included in a tree of the system, the source currents can be found. If zero impedance is assumed in the transmission lines ($Z_a = Z_b = Z_c = 0$), the sources make up a complete tree and no simultaneous solution of equations is necessary.

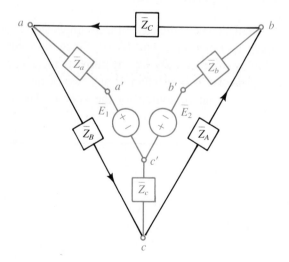

Figure 10.9

Three-phase network with an open-Δ-connected source.

The currents in the loads are then found as

$$\bar{I}_A = \frac{\bar{E}_2}{\bar{Z}_A}$$

$$\bar{I}_B = \frac{\bar{E}_1}{\bar{Z}_B}$$

$$\bar{I}_C = \frac{-(\bar{E}_1 + \bar{E}_2)}{\bar{Z}_C}$$

If the transmission-line impedances are present and not balanced, three loop or three node equations are needed to model the network. If the line impedances and the load impedances are balanced, then a load Δ-to-Y (π-to-T) transformation will allow the line currents to be solved for on a single-phase basis.

In any event the complex power $\bar{S}$ can be found by

$$\bar{S} = P + jQ = \bar{V}_A \bar{I}_A^* + \bar{V}_B \bar{I}_B^* + \bar{V}_C \bar{I}_C^*$$

which becomes, for balanced impedances,

$$\bar{S} = \sqrt{3} V_L I_L \underline{/\alpha}$$

where V_L is the rms voltage magnitude measured between lines at the load, I_L is the rms line-current magnitude, and α is the angle of the 1-port load impedances. As in previous cases, the power factor of the load is

$$\text{p.f.} = \cos \alpha$$

10.7 ΔY NETWORK

We now consider the case of a Δ-connected set of v-sources and a Y-connected load, as shown in Figure 10.10. Since the v-sources form a loop, it is impossible to solve directly for the currents in them.

An open Δ consisting of any two of the sources would provide an equivalent three-phase source for the system. The currents in the sources for this

Figure 10.10
Three-phase network with Δ-connected sources and Y-connected loads.

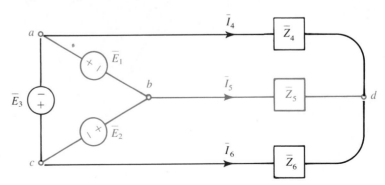

kind of connection could be determined. The line currents and voltages would be, of course, the same as for the complete Δ-source. The treatment that follows is applicable to either open-Δ or Δ-connected sources.

Suppose that a formulation star-tree is chosen to include $\bar{E}_1$, $\bar{E}_2$, and $\bar{Z}_5$. One node equation is sufficient to model the network even with unbalanced load impedances. This equation is

$$(\bar{Y}_4 + \bar{Y}_5 + \bar{Y}_6)\bar{V}_{db} = \bar{Y}_4\bar{E}_1 - \bar{Y}_6\bar{E}_2 \tag{10.11}$$

From the solution of Equation 10.11, we obtain the load voltages and currents:

$$\bar{V}_5 = \bar{Z}_5\bar{I}_5 = \bar{V}_{bd}$$

$$= \frac{\bar{Y}_6\bar{E}_2 - \bar{Y}_4\bar{E}_1}{\bar{Y}_4 + \bar{Y}_5 + \bar{Y}_6}$$

$$\bar{V}_4 = \bar{V}_5 + \bar{E}_1 = \bar{Z}_4\bar{I}_4$$

$$\bar{V}_6 = \bar{V}_5 - \bar{E}_2 = \bar{Z}_6\bar{I}_6$$

For the balanced-load case in which

$$\bar{Y}_4 = \bar{Y}_5 = \bar{Y}_6 = \bar{Y}$$

Equation 10.11 simplifies to

$$3\bar{Y}\bar{V}_{db} = \bar{Y}(\bar{E}_1 - \bar{E}_2)$$

or

$$\bar{V}_{bd} = \tfrac{1}{3}(\bar{E}_2 - \bar{E}_1) \tag{10.12}$$

Let us assume that the phasor v-sources are

$$\bar{E}_1 = E\underline{/0°}$$

$$\bar{E}_2 = E\underline{/-120°} \tag{10.13}$$

$$\bar{E}_3 = E\underline{/120°}$$

Then, as shown on the phasor diagram of Figure 10.11,

$$V_5 = \frac{E}{3}(1\underline{/-120°} - 1\underline{/0°})$$

$$= \frac{E}{\sqrt{3}}\underline{/-150°}$$

$$\bar{V}_4 = \frac{E}{\sqrt{3}}\underline{/-30°}$$

$$\bar{V}_6 = \frac{E}{\sqrt{3}}\underline{/90°} \tag{10.14}$$

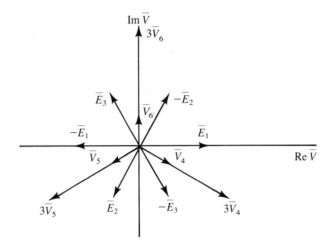

Figure 10.11
Phasor diagram illustrating relationships between the phasor v-sources and the load voltages for a balanced ΔY network.

From the above we see that for the balanced-load case, we could determine $\bar{V}_4$ by a phasor-diagram approach and solve for

$$\bar{I}_4 = \frac{\bar{V}_4}{\bar{Z}_4}$$

The other two line currents have the same magnitude as $\bar{I}_4$ and a phase-angle relationship of $\pm 120°$ depending on the phase sequence of the three-phase source. For our assumed sources

$$\bar{I}_5 = |\bar{I}_4|\underline{/\theta_4 - 120°} = \bar{I}_4(1\underline{/-120°})$$
$$\bar{I}_6 = \bar{I}_4(1\underline{/120°})$$

The complex power taken by the three-phase load is

$$\bar{S} = \bar{V}_4\bar{I}_4^* + \bar{V}_5\bar{I}_5^* + \bar{V}_6\bar{I}_6^* \qquad (10.15)$$

in general, where $\bar{V}$ and $\bar{I}$ are in rms volts and amperes, respectively. If the load is balanced, Equation 10.15 becomes

$$\bar{S} = 3\bar{V}_4\bar{I}_4^* = \sqrt{3}V_LI_L\underline{/\alpha}$$

as for the other balanced three-phase connections.

10.8   THREE-PHASE POWER MEASUREMENTS ———————————————————O

In the discussion of three-phase electric-power networks operating at sinusoidal steady state, we have observed that the complex power associated with a three-phase component is the sum of the powers associated with each phase. In instantaneous power terms,

$$p(t) = p_a(t) + p_b(t) + p_c(t)$$
$$= v_a i_a + v_b i_b + v_c i_c$$

From this general expression we can deduce a method for measuring three-phase power. One wattmeter can be connected to each single-phase load (Figure 10.12) if such measurements are accessible.

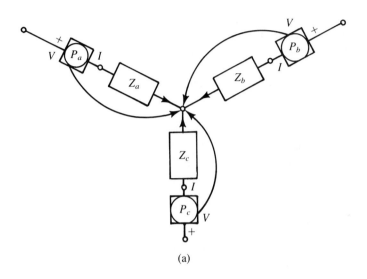

(a)

Figure 10.12
Two types of passive three-phase load connections with appropriately connected wattmeters to measure the single-phase powers.
(a) Wye connection.
(b) Delta connection.

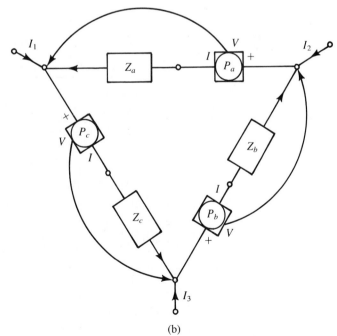

(b)

If only the total power of a three-terminal, three-phase component is desired, some economy of instrumentation is possible. From the developments in Chapter 6 we know that any three-terminal electric component can be externally characterized as a 2-port with a two-element star-tree measurement diagram. Using the port voltage and current variables, we can write the power as

$$p(t) = v_1 i_1 + v_2 i_2$$

Figure 10.13 schematically illustrates the wattmeter connections needed to measure the power for a three-phase, 2-port component—either active or passive.

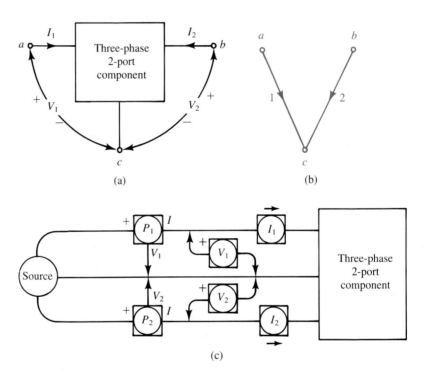

Figure 10.13
Three-phase power measurement by the two-wattmeter method.
(a) Three-phase 2-port component.
(b) Corresponding measurement diagram.
(c) Instrumentation system to measure voltages, currents, and powers for the measurement diagram used.

To confirm that the power expression derived from considering the three-phase load as a general 2-port component is correct, we consider the Y-connected network of Figure 10.12(a). The power for the three single-phase loads can be summed to yield

$$p(t) = v_a i_a + v_b i_b + v_c i_c$$

But

$$i_c = -i_a - i_b$$

and, therefore,

$$p(t) = v_a i_a + v_b i_b - v_c i_a - v_c i_b$$
$$= (v_a - v_c)i_a + (v_b - v_c)i_b$$
$$= v_1 i_1 + v_2 i_2$$
$$= p_1(t) + p_2(t)$$

It is left to the problems to show that the same type of result holds for the Δ-connected load of Figure 10.12(b).

Our development of the two-wattmeter method for measuring power for a three-terminal, 2-port component has not, of course, been restricted to three-phase components. The subject is appropriately treated here, though, since its application is largely in three-phase power systems. Although the development is in terms of instantaneous powers, the results can be extended directly to the measurement of average power by the use of averaging meters.

10.9 SUMMARY

In this chapter we found that three-phase networks can be modeled by the same procedures that apply to networks in general. Because of the balanced sinusoidal sources, however, much simpler phasor models are possible if the load impedances are also balanced. For the sinusoidal steady-state solution of a balanced three-phase network model, simultaneous equations are never required. That is, a single solution for one load current or voltage is sufficient to define all other variables of the network. We find that this property leads to the use of single-phase equivalent schematic diagrams to represent three-phase balanced networks.

In general, when we obtain such a simplification it is necessary to transform the load connection (Y or Δ) to match the source connection, or vice versa. When this is done, the load voltage is defined by the source voltage directly, and a simple phasor calculation defines the load current. If the sources are i-sources, the calculation is analogous.

In Chapter 6 we showed that for balanced loads the transformation from Y to Δ or vice versa is

$$3\bar{Z}_Y = \bar{Z}_\Delta$$

Use of this relation to match the load connection to the source connection results in an equivalent load-current calculation of the form

$$\bar{I}_1 = \frac{\bar{V}_1}{\bar{Z}} = \frac{\bar{E}_1}{\bar{Z}}$$

where the subscript simply indicates that the equivalent load impedance is associated with the number 1 source. The actual load currents, if an impedance transformation has been required, can be found from the equivalent load currents.

For every balanced three-phase source-load combination, we also found that the three-phase complex power expression is

$$\bar{S} = P + jQ = \sqrt{3}V_L I_L \underline{/\alpha} = \sqrt{3}V_L I_L(\cos \alpha + j \sin \alpha)$$

where α is the angle associated with the load impedance, V_L the rms line-to-line voltage magnitude, and I_L the rms line-current magnitude.

This common expression for complex power for all balanced three-phase networks is a result of the fact that (1) for balanced Y-loads, line-to-line voltage magnitude is $\sqrt{3}$ times the individual load-voltage magnitude, and (2) for balanced Δ-loads, line-current magnitude is $\sqrt{3}$ times the individual load-current magnitude.

PROBLEMS

For Problems 10.1–10.16 assume as given, unless specifically stated otherwise, the following balanced three-phase phasor v-sources:

$$\bar{E}_1 = 100\underline{/0°} \text{ V rms}$$
$$\bar{E}_2 = 100\underline{/-120°} \text{ V rms}$$
$$\bar{E}_3 = 100\underline{/-240°} \text{ V rms}$$

10.1 Write the balanced phasor voltages given above as real t-variable functions.

10.2 Write the given balanced phasor voltages in rms rectangular form.

10.3 Given that three v-sources $\bar{E}_1$, $\bar{E}_2$, and $\bar{E}_3$ are connected Y as shown in Figure 10.14, write the line-to-line voltages indicated in polar form.

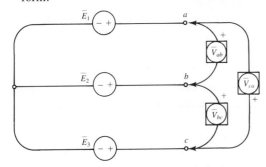

Figure 10.14

10.4 Suppose that in Figure 10.14, the line-to-line voltages are known to be in phasor form,

$$\bar{V}_{ab} = 150\underline{/0°} \text{ V} \qquad \bar{V}_{bc} = 150\underline{/-120°} \text{ V}$$
$$\bar{V}_{ca} = 150\underline{/-240°} \text{ V}$$

Find the phasor voltages $\bar{E}_1$, $\bar{E}_2$, and $\bar{E}_3$.

10.5 In the network of Figure 10.15, $\bar{Y}_4 = \bar{Y}_5 = \bar{Y}_6 = 0.4 + j0.3$ S and $\bar{Y}_n = 1.0$ S. Find $\bar{I}_4$, $\bar{I}_5$, $\bar{I}_6$, and $\bar{I}_n$ and the three-phase average power for the load.

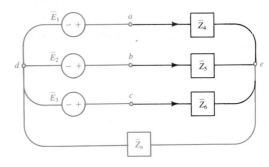

Figure 10.15

10.6 In the network of Figure 10.15, $\bar{Y}_4 = \bar{Y}_5 = \bar{Y}_6 = 0.866 - j0.5$ S and $\bar{Y}_n = 1.0$ S. Find $\bar{I}_4$, $\bar{I}_5$, $\bar{I}_6$, $\bar{I}_n$, and the three-phase average power for the load.

10.7 In the network of Figure 10.15, $\bar{Y}_4 = \bar{Y}_5 = 1.0 + j0, \bar{Y}_6 = 0.6 - j0.8$, and $Y_n = 1.0\,\text{S}$. Find $\bar{I}_4, \bar{I}_5, \bar{I}_6, \bar{I}_n, \bar{V}_4, \bar{V}_5, \bar{V}_6$, and $\bar{V}_n$.

10.8 Solve Problem 10.7 for the case of $\bar{Z}_n = 0$.

10.9 Solve Problem 10.7 for the case of $\bar{Y}_n = 0$ (Figure 10.16).

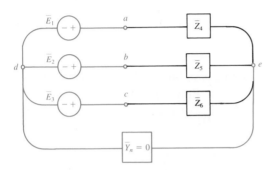

Figure 10.16

10.10 Solve Problem 10.6 for the case of $\bar{Y}_n = 0$ (Figure 10.16).

10.11 In the network of Figure 10.17, $\bar{Y}_4 = \bar{Y}_5 = \bar{Y}_6 = 0.8 - j0.6\,\text{S}$. Find $\bar{I}_4, \bar{I}_5, \bar{I}_6, \bar{I}_1, \bar{I}_2, \bar{I}_3$, and the three-phase power of the load.

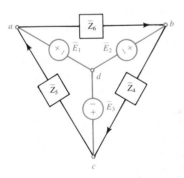

Figure 10.17

10.12 In the network of Figure 10.17, $\bar{Y}_4 = 0.8 - j0.6, \bar{Y}_5 = 1.0 + j0$, and $\bar{Y}_6 = 0.3 - j0.4\,\text{S}$. Find $\bar{I}_4, \bar{I}_5, \bar{I}_6, \bar{I}_1, \bar{I}_2, \bar{I}_3$, and the total average three-phase load power.

10.13 In the network of Figure 10.18, the load impedances are balanced, $\bar{Z}_A = \bar{Z}_B = \bar{Z}_C = 8 + j6\,\Omega$. The line impedances are also bal-

anced, $\bar{Z}_a = \bar{Z}_b = \bar{Z}_c = 1.0 + j0\,\Omega$. Find the load currents $\bar{I}_A, \bar{I}_B$, and $\bar{I}_C$ and the currents in the open-Δ source, $\bar{I}_1$ and $\bar{I}_2$.

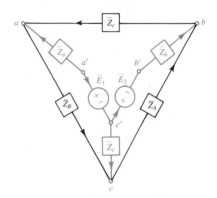

Figure 10.18

10.14 In the network of Figure 10.19, $\bar{Z}_a = \bar{Z}_b = \bar{Z}_c = 4 + j3\,\Omega$. Find $\bar{I}_a, \bar{I}_b, \bar{I}_c, \bar{I}_1, \bar{I}_2, \bar{I}_3$, and the average three-phase load power.

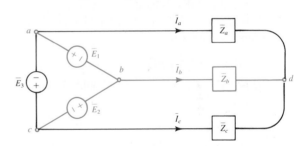

Figure 10.19

10.15 In the network of Figure 10.19, $\bar{Z}_a = 5 + j0, \bar{Z}_b = 4 + j3, \bar{Z}_c = 3 + j4\,\Omega$. Find $\bar{I}_a, \bar{I}_b, \bar{I}_c$, and the average three-phase load power.

10.16 Given the network of Figure 10.16, suppose that the Δ-load of Figure 10.18 is also connected in addition to the Y-load. Both three-phase loads are balanced:

Δ-load: $\bar{Z}_A = \bar{Z}_B = \bar{Z}_C = 0.866 + j0.5\,\Omega$

Y-load: $\bar{Y}_4 = \bar{Y}_5 = \bar{Y}_6 = 0.4 - j0.3\,\text{S}$

Find the source currents $\bar{I}_1, \bar{I}_2$, and $\bar{I}_3$ and the total source power (three-phase). Compare this with the sum of the power calculated for the two balanced three-phase loads.

10.17 Derive Equation 10.4, including all details.

10.18 For the *YY* three-wire connection with a balanced three-phase source, derive the condition on load impedances such that neutral voltage $\bar{V}_n = 0$.

10.19 For the Δ-connected 2-port shown in Figure 10.12, prove that the instantaneous power expression

$$p_0(t) = v_1 i_1 + v_2 i_2$$

is equivalent to

$$p_0(t) = v_a i_a + v_b i_b + v_c i_c$$

10.20 Assume a balanced set of voltages in the network shown in Figure 10.20

$$\bar{V}_1 = 10\underline{/0°} \text{ V}$$
$$\bar{V}_2 = 10\underline{/-120°} \text{ V}$$
$$\bar{V}_3 = 10\underline{/-240°} \text{ V}$$

where the magnitudes are rms. Find the expression for three-phase $p(t)$ by expressing each load phasor $\bar{V}$ and $\bar{I}$ as a real sinusoidal *t*-function and using

$$p(t) = p_1(t) + p_2(t) + p_3(t)$$

(*Hint:* The three-phase $p(t)$ should be constant.)

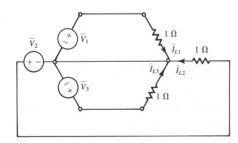

Figure 10.20

10.21 In a balanced three-phase system, as shown in Figure 10.21, the effective power factor of the load can be corrected to a more desirable value (closer to unity) by connecting a three-phase capacitor bank in parallel with the inductive load, as shown. The capacitor bank can be connected in either a Δ- or a Y-connection.

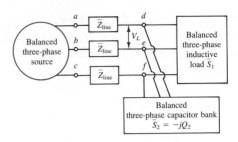

Figure 10.21

Suppose the three-phase inductive load is $\bar{S}_1 = P_1 + jQ_1$ with

$$|\bar{S}_1| = 10 \text{ kVA}$$

$$\text{p.f.} = \frac{P_1}{|\bar{S}_1|} = 0.8$$

and the line voltage at the load is held constant at $V_L = 440$ V.

(a) Find the complex power rating $\bar{S}_2$ of the three-phase capacitor bank that will cause the total load (the inductive load and the capacitor bank in parallel) to operate at a power factor of 0.9. Note that the total complex three-phase power, $\bar{S}_0$, at *d-e-f* is given by $\bar{S}_0 = \bar{S}_1 + \bar{S}_2$.

(b) Find the value of each capacitor in the bank if they are connected Δ ($f = 60$ Hz).

(c) Repeat part (b) for a Y-connection.

(d) Discuss the differences in the two connections.

(e) If $\bar{Z}_{\text{line}} = 4 + j16$ Ω, calculate the line voltage and the complex power output required at the source with and without the capacitor compensation. Explain why the compensated system is more desirable.

10.22 Using the network of Problem 10.6,

(a) Calculate the capacitance of each leg of a Y-connected bank that will, when connected in parallel with the load, cause the three-phase source to operate at unity power factor. The frequency is 60 Hz.

(b) Repeat part (a) if the capacitors are connected Δ.

(c) Compare the results of the two connections.

10.23 Repeat Problem 10.22 for the network of Problem 10.11.

10.24 For the network of Figure 10.21, $\overline{S}_1 = 10 + j8$ KVA, $V_L = 500$ V, and $\overline{Z}_{line} = 0$.

(a) Calculate the capacitance of a Y-connected capacitor bank that will cause the source to operate at unity power factor.

(b) Repeat part (a) if $\overline{Z}_{line} = 8 + j10$ Ω.

Giants of the profession
IEEE Centennial Hall of Fame

Ernst F. W. Alexanderson (1878–1975)
His career spanned 50 years with
General Electric; 350 patents including
the high-frequency radio alternator; he
was the first chief engineer for RCA.
Shown here with thyratron power
circuits, 1938.

Vladimir Zworykin (1889–1982)
Early television pioneer of the
Westinghouse Electric Corp. and RCA;
inventor of the iconoscope and
kinescope. Shown here with the
iconoscope that he developed as the all-
electronic "eye" of the TV camera,
1940.

Reprinted with permission from
"Centennial Hall of Fame,"
IEEE SPECTRUM, April 1984.

11

Magnetically coupled two-ports

11.1 INTRODUCTION

A *magnetically coupled* 2-*port* (or inductive 2-port) is an electric component consisting of a pair of coils, or inductors, which are located in such physical proximity that the operating conditions of one affects the other. Unlike the three-terminal 2-ports discussed earlier, the inductive 2-port is a two-terminal-pair device (except for special situations where one pair of terminals is connected). The measurement diagram, therefore, consists in general of a pair of directed line segments without a common node.

This class of electrical devices is discussed in textbooks under various headings, including coupled circuits, mutual inductance, and electric transformers, and is of great importance because of its wide use both in electric power systems and in communications networks.

In our modern society, no one is likely to be long out of the immediate vicinity of several such devices. Every radio and television receiver has many coupled inductors, and electric-power transformers hang so thickly in most urban areas that they are a constant source of annoyance to esthetically minded citizens.

In this chapter we deal with two forms of mathematical models for the magnetically coupled 2-port. The general model is discussed first, and then the concept of an ideal transformer is introduced. In the attempt to obtain a satisfactory model for any network, there is a need for searching out the simplest forms of component equations that are adequate for the purpose. This need motivates our examination of two radically different mathematical models for inductively coupled 2-port components.

11.2 *t*-DOMAIN MODEL

Suppose that two inductors are located close enough to each other that some of the magnetic flux, ϕ, set up by one inductor links the other one. Let ϕ_1 be the flux of coil 1 and ϕ_2 be the flux of coil 2. By Faraday's law,

$$v_1 = \pm n_1 \frac{d\phi_1}{dt}$$

$$v_2 = \pm n_2 \frac{d\phi_2}{dt} \tag{11.1}$$

where the number of turns of coils 1 and 2 are n_1 and n_2, respectively. We assume the total flux to be made up of two components,

$$\phi_1 = \phi_{11} \pm \phi_{12}$$

$$\phi_2 = \pm \phi_{21} + \phi_{22} \tag{11.2}$$

where ϕ_{jk} is the magnetic flux in webers set up by a current in coil k and linking coil j. Thus the flux ϕ_1 that links coil 1 is the sum of the flux set up by coil 1 (ϕ_{11}) and the flux set up by coil 2 (ϕ_{12}).

It is convenient to assume a reference relationship between the ϕ_k reference and that for v_k and i_k, as shown in Figure 11.1, such that the signs in Equation 11.1 are positive. This convention is followed in the remainder of our discussion.

Figure 11.1
Right-hand reference convention for electric and magnetic references.

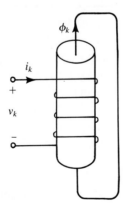

The right-hand rule can be used as a convenient memory device to recall the relative orientations of current and flux. If the fingers of the right hand curl around a coil in the direction of the current, the thumb points in the direction of the resulting magnetic flux.

For the case of two inductors in close proximity such that they have mutual flux linkages, we can obtain a relationship between the terminal voltages and the magnetic fluxes by substituting Equation 11.2 into Equation 11.1:

$$v_1 = n_1 \dot{\phi}_{11} \pm n_1 \dot{\phi}_{12}$$
$$v_2 = \pm n_2 \dot{\phi}_{21} + n_2 \dot{\phi}_{22} \tag{11.3}$$

where the dot signifies derivative with respect to time.

In Equation 11.3 two of the coefficients have an ambiguous sign. We take n_1 and n_2 as always positive and affix the plus or minus sign depending on whether the reference direction for ϕ_1 and ϕ_2 is the same or opposite, respectively, in the common flux path linking the coils. Figure 11.2 illustrates two physical situations that result in different signs. The two windings are placed on a magnetic core exactly the same way in both situations, but because of a difference in choice of reference for the variables associated with coil 2, the signs are different. For the inductors of Figure 11.2(a), the sign on the coupling terms is positive, and for (b) it is negative.

Figure 11.2
Winding diagrams for a pair of coupled inductors.
(a) Mutual flux reinforcing.
(b) Mutual flux opposing.

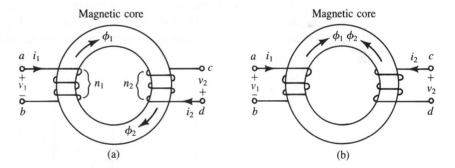

For the purpose of component modeling, it is convenient to express the magnetic flux ϕ_{jk} in terms of its associated current i_k. To do this we write

$$\frac{d\phi}{dt} = \frac{d\phi}{di} \frac{di}{dt}$$

For convenience we define

$$n_j \left| \frac{d\phi_{jk}}{di_k} \right| = \begin{cases} L_k & \text{if } j = k \\ M_{jk} & \text{if } j \neq k \end{cases}$$

The term L_k is called the *self-inductance* of the kth inductor and the term M_{jk} is called the *mutual inductance* of inductors j and k. Since n_j is positive, L and M are always positive.

Using this symbolism, we can now write Equation 11.3 (with positive mutual terms) in matrix form as

$$\begin{bmatrix} v_1 \\ v_2 \end{bmatrix} = \begin{bmatrix} L_1 & M_{12} \\ M_{21} & L_2 \end{bmatrix} \frac{d}{dt} \begin{bmatrix} i_1 \\ i_2 \end{bmatrix} \qquad (11.4)$$

Equation 11.4 is ideal in the sense that the resistance of the coils is neglected. Experimental evidence indicates that $M_{12} = M_{21}$ for an inductive 2-port. Therefore, we drop the subscripts, as is common in electric-network texts, and simply write M for each of the mutual-inductance coefficient terms. Now that our conventions are established, we write the component equations for the 2-port of Figure 11.2(a) as

$$\begin{bmatrix} v_1 \\ v_2 \end{bmatrix} = \begin{bmatrix} L_1 & M \\ M & L_2 \end{bmatrix} \frac{d}{dt} \begin{bmatrix} i_1 \\ i_2 \end{bmatrix} \qquad (11.5)$$

For the 2-port of Figure 11.2(b), we have as component equations

$$\begin{bmatrix} v_1 \\ v_2 \end{bmatrix} = \begin{bmatrix} L_1 & -M \\ -M & L_2 \end{bmatrix} \frac{d}{dt} \begin{bmatrix} i_1 \\ i_2 \end{bmatrix} \qquad (11.6)$$

The corresponding measurement diagrams for Equations 11.5 and 11.6 are shown in Figure 11.3(a) and (b), respectively. Equations 11.5 and 11.6 are designated as component equations for the *mutual-inductance model* of the two coupled inductors.

Figure 11.3
Measurement diagrams to correspond to the 2-ports of Figure 11.2.

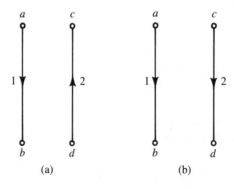

(a)   (b)

In drawing a schematic diagram of a network that includes a pair of coupled inductors, it is usually not convenient to draw a winding diagram to show how the inductors are situated physically with respect to each other. The dot convention serves to provide the equivalent information in a more convenient manner. Figure 11.4 indicates schematic diagrams for the 2-port of Figure 11.2 using the dot convention for orienting the terminals.

The dots (plus signs on the devices) can be located by the following procedure: One terminal of the primary coil (coil 1) is arbitrarily picked as the dotted terminal. The reference for i_1 is taken into the dotted terminal. The reference direction for i_2 is determined such that the fluxes set up by positive i_1 and i_2 are in the same direction in that part of the magnetic path that links the coils. The terminal on the secondary coil (coil 2), which the i_2 reference enters, is made the dotted terminal.

There are other equally good procedures for affixing and interpreting the dots, but this one is as simple as any and is completely adequate. Note that the placement of the dots on a schematic diagram for an inductive 2-port is independent of the choice of references for v and i.

Using a schematic diagram of the type illustrated in Figure 11.4, we determine if the sign on M in the component equations is positive or negative, respectively, by whether the i references are oriented in the same or opposing ways with respect to their dotted terminals. On the schematic diagram of Figure 11.4(a), both references are into the dotted terminals. Therefore the sign on M is plus. If they had both been out of the dotted terminals, the results would have been the same. The relative orientations of the references and the dotted terminals of Figure 11.4(b) are opposite, and therefore the sign on M is negative.

Figure 11.4
Schematic diagram of the mutual inductance model of an inductive 2-port. (a) Positive mutual coupling. (b) Negative mutual coupling.

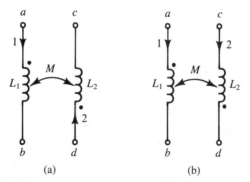

(a)   (b)

If $L_1 L_2 - M^2 \neq 0$, we can write (from Equation 11.5)

$$\frac{d}{dt}\begin{bmatrix} i_1 \\ i_2 \end{bmatrix} = \frac{1}{L_1 L_2 - M^2}\begin{bmatrix} L_2 & -M \\ -M & L_1 \end{bmatrix}\begin{bmatrix} v_1 \\ v_2 \end{bmatrix} \tag{11.7}$$

This form of the component equations is suitable for formulating state models of networks containing the inductive 2-port. The state-model formulation procedure of Chapter 8 applies to the case of inductive 2-ports as well as to the 1-ports discussed in that chapter.

Example 11.1

To illustrate the procedure for formulating state equations for networks containing inductive 2-ports, we carry out a formulation for the network of Figure 11.5. First we write the component equations for the energy-storage components:

$$i_1 = C_1 \frac{dv_1}{dt}$$

$$\begin{bmatrix} v_2 \\ v_3 \end{bmatrix} = \begin{bmatrix} L_2 & -M_{23} \\ -M_{23} & L_3 \end{bmatrix} \begin{bmatrix} \dfrac{di_2}{dt} \\ \dfrac{di_3}{dt} \end{bmatrix} \tag{11.8}$$

Figure 11.5
(a) Schematic diagram of a network containing an inductive 2-port.
(b) Equivalent network for formulating a state model. The state variables are represented by ideal sources.

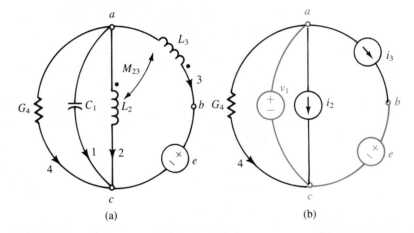

The sign on M_{23} is negative in Equation 11.8 since the relative placement of the polarity dots and the current references indicate negative mutual coupling. The state variables of the network are v_1, i_2, and i_3. The schematic diagram of Figure 11.5(b) is convenient to use for the process of eliminating nonstate variables from the equations. The variables to be eliminated in favor of state variables and source variables are i_1, v_2, and v_3.

To simplify the final form of the state equations, let $L_2 = 0.010$ H and $L_3 = M_{23} = 0.005$ H. We can write the component equations of the energy-storage components in derivative-explicit vector form as

$$\frac{d}{dt} \begin{bmatrix} v_1 \\ i_2 \\ i_3 \end{bmatrix} = \begin{bmatrix} \dfrac{1}{C_1} & 0 & 0 \\ 0 & 200 & 200 \\ 0 & 200 & 400 \end{bmatrix} \begin{bmatrix} i_1 \\ v_2 \\ v_3 \end{bmatrix} \tag{11.9}$$

Inspection of Figure 11.5(b) reveals that

$$
\begin{bmatrix} i_1 \\ v_2 \\ v_3 \end{bmatrix} = \begin{bmatrix} -G_4 & -1 & -1 \\ 1 & 0 & 0 \\ 1 & 0 & 0 \end{bmatrix} \begin{bmatrix} v_1 \\ i_2 \\ i_3 \end{bmatrix} + \begin{bmatrix} 0 \\ 0 \\ -1 \end{bmatrix} e
\tag{11.10}
$$

By substituting Equation 11.10 into Equation 11.9, we obtain the vector state equation of the network:

$$
\frac{d}{dt}\begin{bmatrix} v_1 \\ i_2 \\ i_3 \end{bmatrix} = \begin{bmatrix} -\dfrac{G_4}{C_1} & \dfrac{-1}{C_1} & \dfrac{-1}{C_1} \\ 400 & 0 & 0 \\ 600 & 0 & 0 \end{bmatrix} \begin{bmatrix} v_1 \\ i_2 \\ i_3 \end{bmatrix} + \begin{bmatrix} 0 \\ -200 \\ -400 \end{bmatrix} e
$$

If there are no capacitors present in the network, differential loop equations can be formulated by the substitution method, because all CE can be written with the *v*-variable explicit. To write loop equations direct from the schematic diagram of a network in which both ports of an inductive 2-port are in the same formulation loop is, in general, difficult compared to formulation for 1-ports only. If the inductive 2-ports can be included in the formulation cotree together with the *i*-sources, however, the loop equations can be written about as simply as for a network of 1-ports.

By choosing a formulation tree such that the inductive 2-ports are excluded, we ensure that no loop contains both ports. Thus the mutual inductance terms are added—with proper signs—to the off-diagonal coupling terms, but the main diagonal terms are the same as they would be if *M* were zero.

Example 11.2

We formulate loop differential equations in matrix form for the network of Figure 11.6. The letter *p* is used to symbolize the time-derivative operator:

$$
\begin{bmatrix} R_3 + R_4 + pL_1 & R_3 + R_4 - pM \\ R_3 + R_4 - pM & R_3 + R_4 + R_5 + pL_2 \end{bmatrix}\begin{bmatrix} i_1 \\ i_2 \end{bmatrix} + \begin{bmatrix} R_4 i_6 + e_7 \\ (R_4 + R_5)i_6 \end{bmatrix} = 0
$$
$$
v_6 + R_4 i_1 + (R_4 + R_5)i_2 + (R_4 + R_5)i_6 = 0 \quad \text{(Dummy)}
\tag{11.11}
$$

The terms on the main diagonal of the coefficient matrix of Equation 11.11 are exactly what they would have been with no mutual coupling present. If the loops had been chosen so that one passed through both L_1 and L_2, then the entry in the coefficient matrix corresponding to that loop would contain the effects of mutual coupling and the off-diagonal terms would contain both mutual inductance and self-inductance. Although it is possible to state a procedure that will allow us to write the loop equations directly for such a

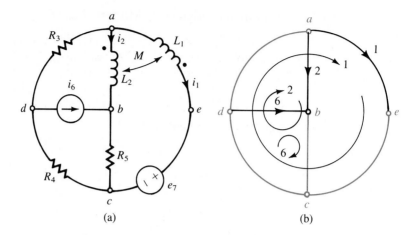

Figure 11.6
(a) Schematic diagram of a network containing an inductive 2-port.
(b) Corresponding linear graph showing formulation tree and loops used for Example 11.2.

(a)   (b)

situation, it is just complicated enough that we elect to omit it in favor of other more important subjects. In any event, the substitution procedure can always be used.

11.3 ω-DOMAIN MODEL

The steady-state analysis of networks with sinusoidal source functions was treated at some length in Chapter 9. The phasor model, which so greatly simplifies such an analysis, is directly applicable to networks containing inductive 2-ports.

Given a t-domain component model, the corresponding phasor model can be obtained by replacing d/dt by $j\omega$ and deleting the initial conditions. Thus Equation 11.5 transforms into the phasor model

$$\begin{bmatrix} \bar{V}_1 \\ \bar{V}_2 \end{bmatrix} = j\omega \begin{bmatrix} L_1 & M \\ M & L_2 \end{bmatrix} \begin{bmatrix} \bar{I}_1 \\ \bar{I}_2 \end{bmatrix} \tag{11.12}$$

or, symbolically, $\bar{\mathbf{V}} = j\omega\mathbf{L}\bar{\mathbf{I}}$.

If $L_1 L_2 - M^2 \neq 0$, Equation 11.12 can be solved for currents, yielding

$$\begin{bmatrix} \bar{I}_1 \\ \bar{I}_2 \end{bmatrix} = \frac{1}{j\omega(L_1 L_2 - M^2)} \begin{bmatrix} L_2 & -M \\ -M & L_1 \end{bmatrix} \begin{bmatrix} \bar{V}_1 \\ \bar{V}_2 \end{bmatrix} \tag{11.13}$$

Equation 11.13 can be symbolized as

$$\bar{\mathbf{I}} = \frac{1}{j\omega}\mathbf{L}^{-1}\bar{\mathbf{V}}$$

The phasors $\bar{\mathbf{I}}$ and $\bar{\mathbf{V}}$ can be either time-varying or constant, so long as consistency is maintained in relating them.

Example 11.3

The network of Figure 11.6 is used to illustrate the formulation and solution of a phasor model of a network containing an inductive 2-port. Constant maximum-value phasors are used:

$$\bar{I}_6 = -3 + j3 = 4.24\underline{/135°} \text{ A}$$

$$\bar{E}_7 = -j6 = 6\underline{/-90°} \text{ V}$$

$$L_1 = M = 0.005 \text{ H}$$

$$L_2 = 0.010 \text{ H}$$

$$\omega = 400 \text{ rad/s}$$

$$R_3 = R_4 = 1 \text{ }\Omega$$

$$R_5 = 2 \text{ }\Omega$$

The schematic diagram for the phasor network is shown as Figure 11.7. The phasor loop equations corresponding to Equation 11.11 are

$$\begin{bmatrix} 2 + j2 & 2 - j2 \\ 2 - j2 & 4 + j4 \end{bmatrix} \begin{bmatrix} \bar{I}_1 \\ \bar{I}_2 \end{bmatrix} + \begin{bmatrix} -j6 - 3 + j3 \\ 3(-3 + j3) \end{bmatrix} = 0$$

Figure 11.7
(a) Schematic diagram of the phasor network corresponding to Figure 11.6. (b) Corresponding linear graph showing formulation tree.

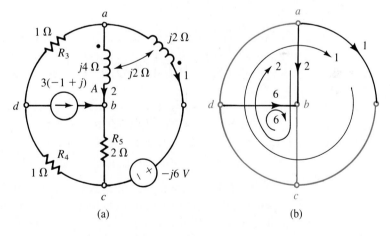

(a)   (b)

Solving for the phasor currents, we have

$$\begin{bmatrix} \bar{I}_1 \\ \bar{I}_2 \end{bmatrix} = \frac{1}{24} \begin{bmatrix} 4 - j4 & 2 + j2 \\ 2 + j2 & 2 - j2 \end{bmatrix} \begin{bmatrix} 3 + j3 \\ 9 - j9 \end{bmatrix}$$

$$= \frac{1}{24} \begin{bmatrix} 60 \\ -j24 \end{bmatrix} = \begin{bmatrix} 2.5 \\ -j \end{bmatrix} = \begin{bmatrix} 2.5\underline{/0°} \\ 1\underline{/-90°} \end{bmatrix}$$

The dummy-loop equation is

$$\bar{V}_6 + 3(-3 + j3) + 3\bar{I}_2 + \bar{I}_1 = 0$$

from which

$$\overline{V}_6 = (9 - j9) - 2.5 - 3(-j)$$
$$= 6.5 - j6 = 8.86\underline{/-42.8°} \text{ V}$$

Example 11.4

The phasor loop model for the network of Figure 11.8 is

$$\begin{bmatrix} \overline{Z}_1 + j\omega L_1 & j\omega M \\ j\omega M & j\omega L_2 + \overline{Z}_2 \end{bmatrix} \begin{bmatrix} \overline{I}_1 \\ \overline{I}_2 \end{bmatrix} = \begin{bmatrix} \overline{E} \\ 0 \end{bmatrix}$$

Figure 11.8
Schematic diagram of a
network in which an
impedance $\overline{Z}_2$ is
connected to an active
1-port by an inductive
2-port.

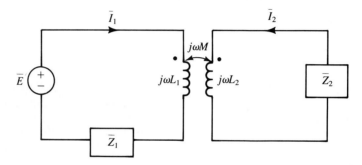

The solution is

$$\begin{bmatrix} \overline{I}_1 \\ \overline{I}_2 \end{bmatrix} = \frac{1}{(\overline{Z}_1 + j\omega L_1)(\overline{Z}_2 + j\omega L_2) + \omega^2 M^2} \begin{bmatrix} \overline{Z}_2 + j\omega L_2 \\ -j\omega M \end{bmatrix} \overline{E}$$

$$\overline{I}_1 = \frac{\overline{Z}_2 + j\omega L_2}{(\overline{Z}_1 + j\omega L_1)(\overline{Z}_2 + j\omega L_2) + \omega^2 M^2} \overline{E} \qquad (11.14)$$

$$\overline{I}_2 = \frac{-j\omega M}{(\overline{Z}_1 + j\omega L_1)(\overline{Z}_2 + j\omega L_2) + \omega^2 M^2} \overline{E} \qquad (11.15)$$

In this example, the variables in the right-hand loop are completely dependent upon the mutual inductance M, since there is no connection between
that circuit and the active one. Equation 11.15 indicates this.

Inductive 2-ports are most often used where sinusoidal steady-state conditions are very important considerations. For this reason, the phasor model is
widely used in discussing the characteristics and properties of these 2-ports. In
the remainder of this chapter, therefore, we restrict ourselves to phasor modeling in discussing inductive 2-ports.

11.4 COEFFICIENT OF COUPLING ⎯⎯⎯⎯⎯⎯⎯⎯⎯⎯⎯⎯○

Although the characterization of an inductive 2-port by its self-inductances and mutual inductances is adequate for many purposes, there are often more convenient ways of modeling when the coupling is close. Close coupling, by definition, occurs when nearly all flux generated by one coil links the other.

The general concept of *degree of coupling* is illustrated quite well by considering the equivalent impedance of a 1-port made up by connecting the two ports of an inductive 2-port in series and in parallel.

First we consider the series connections. The connection in (a) of Figure 11.9 is called *series aiding* and the connection in (b) is called *series opposing*.

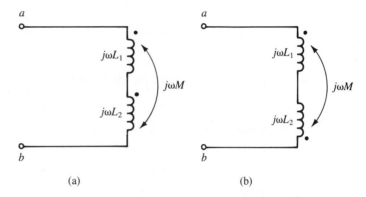

Figure 11.9
Inductive 1-ports
consisting of series-
connected inductive
2-ports.

(a)   (b)

If we put a symbolic phasor *i*-source on each circuit, we obtain these equations.

$$\textit{Series aiding:} \quad \overline{V} = j\omega(L_1 + L_2 + 2M)\overline{I} = j\omega L_e \overline{I}$$
$$\textit{Series opposing:} \quad \overline{V} = j\omega(L_1 + L_2 - 2M)\overline{I} = j\omega L_e \overline{I}$$

(11.16)

where L_e signifies equivalent inductance.

In a similar way, for the parallel connections of Figure 11.10, we derive the following relations.

$$\textit{Parallel aiding:} \quad \overline{V} = \frac{j\omega(L_1 L_2 - M^2)}{L_1 + L_2 - 2M}\overline{I} = j\omega L_e \overline{I}$$
$$\textit{Parallel opposing:} \quad \overline{V} = \frac{j\omega(L_1 L_2 - M^2)}{L_1 + L_2 + 2M}\overline{I} = j\omega L_e \overline{I}$$

(11.17)

The equivalent 1-port inductance L_e can never be negative for the various connections. If it could, such an inductor could deliver energy from an initially unenergized state, since

$$w = \frac{1}{2}L_e i^2$$

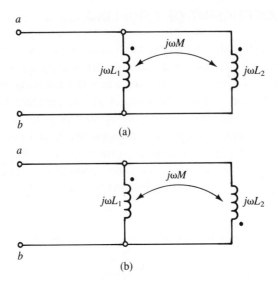

Figure 11.10
Inductive 1-ports
consisting of parallel-
connected inductive
2-ports.

would then be negative for all i. Therefore, we conclude that

$$L_1 + L_2 - 2M \geq 0 \qquad (11.18)$$

from Equation 11.16. Assuming $L_1 + L_2 > 2M$, we conclude from Equation 11.17 that

$$L_1 L_2 - M^2 \geq 0 \qquad (11.19)$$

on the basis of $L_e \geq 0$.

Equations 11.18 and 11.19 put upper bounds on M in terms of L_1 and L_2. If M satisfies the inequality

$$0 \leq M \leq \sqrt{L_1 L_2}$$

it will also satisfy Equation 11.18. The proof of this is left to the problems.

We have now established a theoretical upper limit on M as

$$M = \sqrt{L_1 L_2}$$

This value corresponds to *perfect coupling*. A pair of coils of equal self-inductance and with perfect coupling, connected series opposing, has zero equivalent inductance, as shown by Equation 11.16. For this case, we cannot invert the phasor component equations to obtain current explicitly as shown by Equation 11.13.

We define the coefficient of coupling k to be the ratio of M to the maximum value it can have:

$$k \doteq \frac{M}{\sqrt{L_1 L_2}}$$

The coefficient of coupling ranges from zero at no mutual coupling to unity for perfect coupling. It enables us to compare on a normalized scale the mutual-coupling characteristics of 2-port inductors of widely varying sizes. As a broad rule of thumb, low values of k are associated with high-frequency communication networks, while high values are associated with low-frequency applications—power and audio systems.

The mutual-inductance models of the inductive 2-port that we have examined, utilizing self-inductances and mutual inductances, are generally most convenient for low values of k. When k is near unity, the inductive 2-port, often called an *electric transformer* for this case, can be modeled more conveniently for many applications by the use of the concept of unity coupling.

11.5 UNITY COUPLING

When, for convenience in modeling, the coefficient of coupling is assumed to be unity for an inductive 2-port, the normal phasor component equations (Equation 11.13) become

$$\begin{bmatrix} \bar{V}_1 \\ \bar{V}_2 \end{bmatrix} = j\omega \begin{bmatrix} L_1 & \sqrt{L_1 L_2} \\ \sqrt{L_1 L_2} & L_2 \end{bmatrix} \begin{bmatrix} \bar{I}_1 \\ \bar{I}_2 \end{bmatrix} \tag{11.20}$$

which can be written

$$\begin{bmatrix} \bar{V}_1 \\ \bar{V}_2 \end{bmatrix} = j\omega \begin{bmatrix} L_1 & L_1 \sqrt{\dfrac{L_2}{L_1}} \\ L_1 \sqrt{\dfrac{L_2}{L_1}} & L_1 \dfrac{L_2}{L_1} \end{bmatrix} \begin{bmatrix} \bar{I}_1 \\ \bar{I}_2 \end{bmatrix} \tag{11.21}$$

Let $\sqrt{L_2/L_1}$ be symbolized by N. The inductance of a coil is approximately proportional to the number of turns squared. For near-unity coupling, therefore,

$$N^2 = \frac{L_2}{L_1} \approx \frac{n_2{}^2}{n_1{}^2}$$

where n_1 and n_2 are the number of turns on coil 1 and coil 2, respectively. Thus N is approximately the ratio of the turns of coil 2 to those of coil 1.

Using the symbolism for the turns ratio, the component equations become

$$\begin{bmatrix} \bar{V}_1 \\ \bar{V}_2 \end{bmatrix} = j\omega L_1 \begin{bmatrix} 1 & N \\ N & N^2 \end{bmatrix} \begin{bmatrix} \bar{I}_2 \\ \bar{I}_1 \end{bmatrix} \tag{11.22}$$

Equation 11.22 cannot be solved for $\bar{I}_1$ and $\bar{I}_2$ any more than can Equation 11.20, but we can solve for $\bar{V}_2$ and $\bar{I}_1$. For the case where $\bar{V}_1$ is known and the network to be solved is like that of Figure 11.8, this form of component equation is more convenient:

$$
\begin{bmatrix} \overline{V}_2 \\ \overline{I}_1 \end{bmatrix} = \frac{1}{j\omega L_1} \begin{bmatrix} j\omega N L_1 & 0 \\ 1 & -j\omega N L_1 \end{bmatrix} \begin{bmatrix} \overline{V}_1 \\ \overline{I}_2 \end{bmatrix}
$$

$$
= \begin{bmatrix} N & 0 \\ \dfrac{1}{j\omega L_1} & -N \end{bmatrix} \begin{bmatrix} \overline{V}_1 \\ \overline{I}_2 \end{bmatrix} \tag{11.23}
$$

From inspection of Equation 11.23, we see that if $\overline{V}_1$ is given, $\overline{V}_2 = N\overline{V}_1$ is known. If $\overline{I}_2$ can be determined by a simple calculation such as

$$
\overline{I}_2 = \frac{-\overline{V}_2}{\overline{Z}}
$$

as would be the case in Example 11.4, then $\overline{I}_1$ can be found as

$$
\overline{I}_1 = \frac{1}{j\omega L_1}\overline{V}_1 - N\overline{I}_2 = \frac{1}{j\omega L_1}\overline{V}_1 + \frac{N\overline{V}_2}{\overline{Z}}
$$

$$
= \left(\frac{1}{j\omega L_1} + \frac{N^2}{\overline{Z}} \right)\overline{V}_1 \tag{11.24}
$$

For problems of this type, no simultaneous equations need be solved. In any event, the simple relationship between $\overline{V}_1$ and $\overline{V}_2$ allows one variable to be eliminated from the primary model of a network. Figure 11.11 shows a schematic diagram that corresponds to component equations in the form of Equation 11.23.

Figure 11.11
(a) Schematic diagram for an inductive 2-port with unity coupling using an ideal-transformer symbol. (b) Corresponding measurement diagram. For the ideal transformer, $\overline{I}_1'' = -N\overline{I}_2$, $\overline{V}_2 = N\overline{V}_1$.

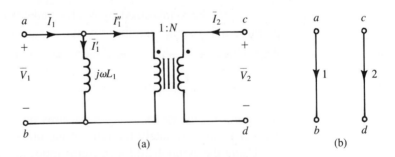

The schematic diagram consists of an ideal transformer with an impedance $j\omega L_1$ connected across the terminals of coil 1. The ideal transformer is symbolized as a pair of coils with three parallel lines drawn between them. The turns ratio is indicated as $1{:}N$ and polarity dots are located appropriately. With the current-reference arrows alike with respect to the dots, the component equations of the ideal transformer in Figure 11.11 are

$$\bar{V}_2 = N\bar{V}_1$$

$$\bar{I}_1'' = -N\bar{I}_2$$

The schematic diagram of Figure 11.11 shows

$$\bar{V}_2 = N\bar{V}_1$$

$$\bar{I}_1 = \bar{I}_1' + \bar{I}_1'' = \frac{1}{j\omega L_1}\bar{V}_1 - N\bar{I}_2$$

since

$$\bar{I}_1' = \frac{1}{j\omega L_1}\bar{V}_1$$

$$\bar{I}_1'' = -N\bar{I}_2$$

Thus the schematic diagram of the 2-port corresponds to Equation 11.23. Since these component equations are explicit neither in voltage nor in current, the standard procedures for formulating either loop equations or supernode equations do not apply. This does not cause difficulty in simple networks such as the one discussed earlier in this section. Where this type of approximation is made in more complex networks, however, a slight modification in the formulation procedure allows loop or supernode equations to be formulated. This is illustrated in Section 11.6.

11.6 IDEAL TRANSFORMER

In many practical cases an inductive 2-port with near-unity coupling can be adequately modeled as an *ideal transformer*. This model is identically that of the unity-coupled case with the further approximation that, in Figure 11.11, $\bar{I}_1''$ is so much larger than $\bar{I}_1'$ that $\bar{I}_1'$ may be neglected. This is often the case if $j\omega L_1$ is large enough and $\bar{I}_2 \neq 0$. The component equations and schematic diagram for the ideal transformer were introduced in the discussion of unity coupling.

For many networks containing electric-power transformers, the ideal-transformer model is adequate and greatly simplifies the model for the complete network.

There are several characteristics of the ideal transformer that might serve to justify the name *ideal*, but probably the input-power relationship is most apt. The total complex power associated with a 2-port can be written

$$\bar{S} = \bar{V}_1\bar{I}_1^* + \bar{V}_2\bar{I}_2^* \tag{11.25}$$

Since

$$V_2 = N\bar{V}_1$$

$$I_2 = -\frac{1}{N}\bar{I}_1$$

we note that

$$\bar{S} = 0$$

The transformer is thus ideal in the sense that there is zero net complex power transmitted to the device. That is, all complex power transmitted into the ideal transformer at one port is transmitted out at the other port. To illustrate the solutions of network models including ideal transformers, we now present examples typical of those already used for the other forms of inductive 2-port models.

Example 11.5

The first network considered is that of Figure 11.12(a). This is the same network used for Example 11.3 except that the pair of coupled inductors is replaced with an ideal transformer with $N = \sqrt{L_2/L_1} = \sqrt{2}$. We deliberately make each ideal-transformer current a loop current to effect a simplification in the loop model, as demonstrated later. If it were not possible to do this, then a different model would have to be used because a supernode equation that relates both currents of an ideal transformer and i-sources may be inconsistent with the ideal-transformer component equation that relates the currents. Furthermore, no loop should consist only of v-sources and the two ideal-transformer elements. If so, that loop equation may not be consistent with the ideal-transformer component equation that relates to voltages.

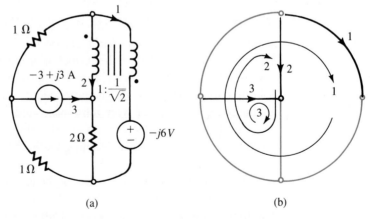

Figure 11.12
(a) Schematic diagram and (b) Linear graph of the network of Figure 11.6 with an ideal transformer replacing the inductive 2-port.

(a)   (b)

In this case, both criteria are satisfied. We now write the loop-current equations for the network *leaving the ideal-transformer voltages in the equations:*

$$\text{Loop 1:} \quad 2\bar{I}_1 + 2\bar{I}_2 + 1(-3 + j3) - j6 + \bar{V}_1 = 0$$

$$\text{Loop 2:} \quad 2\bar{I}_1 + 4\bar{I}_2 + 3(-3 + j3) + \bar{V}_2 = 0 \tag{11.26}$$

$$\text{Loop 3:} \quad \bar{V}_3 + 3(-3 + j3) + \bar{I}_1 + 3\bar{I}_2 = 0 \qquad \text{(Dummy)}$$

In writing these equations, we have used all the component equations except for those of the ideal tranformer. For the reference arrows chosen and the polarity dots shown,

$$\bar{V}_2 = -\sqrt{2}\bar{V}_1$$
$$\bar{I}_1 = \sqrt{2}\bar{I}_2$$

We now use these component equations to eliminate $\bar{V}_2$ and $\bar{I}_1$ from Equation 11.26 to obtain the loop equations

$$\begin{bmatrix} (2\sqrt{2} + 2) & 1 \\ (2\sqrt{2} + 4) & -\sqrt{2} \end{bmatrix} \begin{bmatrix} \bar{I}_2 \\ \bar{V}_1 \end{bmatrix} = \begin{bmatrix} 3 + j3 \\ 9 - j9 \end{bmatrix} \tag{11.27}$$

$$\bar{V}_3 = -(3 + \sqrt{2})\bar{I}_2 + 9 - j9 \qquad \text{(Dummy)}$$

The model to be solved includes two simultaneous equations in $\bar{I}_2$ and $\bar{V}_1$. The only simplification in this model as compared to the one obtained in Example 11.3 is that this one involves only real numbers in its coefficient matrix. Whether this transformer model is adequate or not depends on how accurate the ideal-transformer component equations are in the PRIMM of the particular network.

In general, the use of an ideal-transformer model in a network that requires a model of simultaneous equations is not justifiable on the basis of reducing the work involved in an analysis. The next example, however, demonstrates a case where the amount of work is definitely reduced.

Example 11.6

The network of Example 11.4 is used, with an ideal transformer replacing the general inductive 2-port model (Figure 11.13). The loop equations are

$$-\bar{E} + \bar{V}_1 + \bar{Z}_1\bar{I}_1 = 0$$
$$\bar{Z}_2\bar{I}_2 + \bar{V}_2 = 0 \tag{11.28}$$

Figure 11.13
A network in which an impedance $\bar{Z}_2$ is connected to an active 1-port by an ideal transformer.

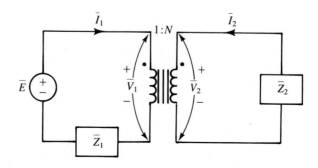

When we substitute the ideal-transformer component equations

$$\bar{V}_1 = \frac{1}{N}\bar{V}_2$$

$$\bar{I}_2 = -\frac{1}{N}\bar{I}_1$$

into Equation 11.28, we obtain

$$\bar{E} = \frac{1}{N}\bar{V}_2 + \bar{Z}_1\bar{I}_1$$

$$\bar{V}_2 = \frac{\bar{Z}_2}{N}\bar{I}_1 \tag{11.29}$$

By substitution, Equation 11.29 can be transformed into

$$\bar{E} = \left(\bar{Z}_1 + \frac{\bar{Z}_2}{N^2}\right)\bar{I}_1$$

$$\bar{V}_2 = \frac{\bar{Z}_2}{N}\bar{I}_1 \tag{11.30}$$

which requires the solution of only one equation. Equation 11.30 is analogous to Equation 11.14,

$$\bar{E} = \left[(\bar{Z}_1 + j\omega L_1) + \frac{\omega^2 M^2}{Z_2 + j\omega L_2}\right]\bar{I}_1$$

for the general inductive 2-port. The advantage of this model, with regard to simplicity, is quite apparent. The use of an ideal-transformer model results in this kind of simplification, however, only when there are no loops in the network that include both inductors of the coupled pair. By contrast, we see that the use of an ideal transformer in Example 11.5 produced no obvious simplification in the network model.

11.7   REFLECTED IMPEDANCE

The analysis of a network of the type shown in Figure 11.14(a) often requires only that the effect of the load impedance on the current on the primary side of the 2-port (coil 1) be known. For this kind of calculation, the concept of reflected impedance is useful.

We now examine this concept from the standpoint of the following models: (1) a general inductive 2-port, (2) a unity-coupled inductive 2-port, and (3) an ideal transformer.

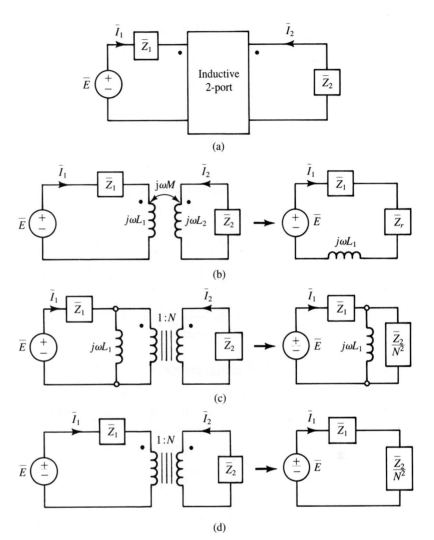

Figure 11.14
(a) Network containing an inductive 2-port with a load impedance across the secondary. Equivalent networks containing equivalent 1-port loads based on the reflected impedance concept. (b) Mutual-inductance 2-port model. (c) Unity-coupling 2-port model. (d) Ideal-transformer 2-port model.

General inductive 2-port

In Example 11.4 we derived a relation between $\bar{E}$ and $\bar{I}_1$ for the *general inductive 2-port* network as

$$\bar{E} = \left[(\bar{Z}_1 + j\omega L_1) + \frac{\omega^2 M^2}{\bar{Z}_2 + j\omega L_2} \right] \bar{I}_1 \qquad (11.31)$$

If the secondary circuit (coil 2) were open and $\bar{I}_2 = 0$ or if $M = 0$, the impedance of the primary circuit would be $\bar{Z}_1 + j\omega L_1$. Therefore, the *effect in the primary* of the mutual coupling and the load impedance $\bar{Z}_2$ can be considered as an additional impedance,

$$\bar{Z}_r = \frac{\omega^2 M^2}{\bar{Z}_2 + j\omega L_2} \tag{11.32}$$

put in series with the primary impedance. This impedance, $\bar{Z}_r$, is called the *reflected impedance*. The equivalent network with respect to the primary side is shown in Figure 11.14(b).

Unity-coupled inductive 2-port

For the network of Figure 11.14(a) with the inductive 2-port modeled as a unity-coupled transformer (Figure 11.14(c)), we can derive the relationship between $\bar{E}$ and $\bar{I}_1$ to be

$$\bar{E} = \left[\bar{Z}_1 + \frac{1}{(N^2/\bar{Z}_2) + (1/j\omega L_1)} \right] \bar{I}_1 \tag{11.33}$$

The equivalent network with respect to the primary side is shown on the right side of Figure 11.14(c).

Ideal transformer

The *ideal-transformer model* inserted into the network of Figure 11.14(a) results in a schematic diagram like that of the unity-coupled coils, except that the parallel impedance $j\omega L_1$ is deleted. The schematic diagram of the entire network and the equivalent network with respect to the primary are shown in Figure 11.14(d).

For this ideal-transformer model, the relationship between $\bar{E}$ and $\bar{I}_1$ is

$$\bar{E} = \left(\bar{Z}_1 + \frac{\bar{Z}_2}{N^2} \right) \bar{I}_1 \tag{11.34}$$

One of the great advantages of using an ideal-transformer model, when it is adequate, can be seen in Equation 11.34. An impedance $\bar{Z}_2$ across the secondary side of the transformer looks like an impedance $\bar{Z}_2/N^2$ from the primary side. That is, the equivalent 1-port component equation of an ideal transformer and an impedance $\bar{Z}_2$ is, as indicated in Figure 11.14(d),

$$\bar{V}_1 = \frac{\bar{Z}_2}{N^2} \bar{I}_1 \tag{11.35}$$

where N is the turns ratio of the secondary to the primary and may, of course, be either greater or less than unity. The terms *primary* and *secondary* are simply convenient expressions to denote to which side the source and the load impedance, respectively, are connected.

In Chapter 9 we discussed conditions for matching a load to an active 1-port so that maximum power is transmitted to the load. Given a Thévenin equivalent for the active 1-port,

$$\bar{V}_1 = \bar{E} + \bar{Z}_1 \bar{I}_1$$

and a load impedance $\bar{Z}$ with fixed phase and variable magnitude, we found that the condition for maximum power is

$$|\bar{Z}| = |\bar{Z}_1|$$

Equation 11.35 indicates that with an ideal transformer, we can alter the apparent magnitude of an impedance by a factor $1/N^2$. Thus a transformer with near-unity coupling may be used to match an impedance to an active 1-port provided the transformer's primary self-impedance is large enough, compared to the impedance being matched, that it may be assumed infinite. Impedance-matching transformers are customarily specified on the basis of the turns ratio and impedance level.

Example 11.7

The network of Figure 11.15(a) represents a phonograph pickup (source), an audio amplifier for which the component equations over some frequency range are assumed to be

$$\bar{I}_1 = 0 \qquad \text{(Infinite input impedance)}$$

$$\bar{V}_2 = 2.4 \times 10^5 \bar{V}_1 + 3200 \bar{I}_2$$

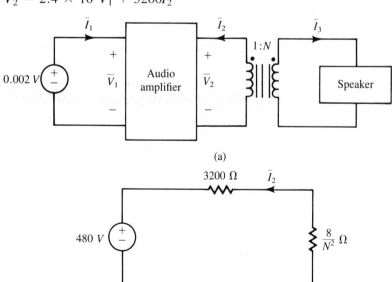

Figure 11.15
Simple audio system utilizing an ideal transformer for impedance matching for maximum power transfer.

and a speaker of impedance $\bar{Z} = 8 + j0\ \Omega$. The problem is to pick a matching transformer (assumed to be ideal) to maximize the power transmitted to the speaker.

The network of Figure 11.15(b) shows the Thévenin equivalent network for the active 1-port consisting of the pickup and amplifier connected to the 1-port equivalent for the transformer and speaker. For maximum power transfer, the equivalent load impedance must equal the Thévenin impedance of the active 1-port. Therefore,

$$N^2 = \frac{8}{3200} = \frac{1}{400}$$

and

$$N = \frac{1}{20}$$

In this example we have used resistance instead of the more general impedance, but the procedure is identical except for the fact that impedance magnitudes are matched for maximum power transfer.

11.8   IRON-CORE TRANSFORMER

For many applications, the *iron-core electric-power transformer* can be satisfactorily represented by the unity-coupled or ideal-transformer model. Power companies are vitally interested in two aspects of transformer operation, however, for which these models are completely inadequate.

Most important, perhaps, is the performance of the transformer with a short circuit on its secondary. Using our simplified unity-coupled model, a short-circuited secondary reflects zero impedance into the primary, and thus the current for a constant input voltage is unlimited. Actually the resistances of the two windings plus a net reactive effect due to nonperfect coupling result in a predictable current under secondary short circuit.

Second, with the secondary unloaded, there is a net flow of power into the transformer owing to hysteresis characteristics of the iron core, in addition to the loss due to the resistance of the windings. Where this effect is significant, an adequate equivalent network model must account for this power loss with an appropriately placed resistor.

An equivalent network that recognizes the effect of winding resistance and imperfect coupling is shown in Figure 11.16(a). Here we have assumed that the

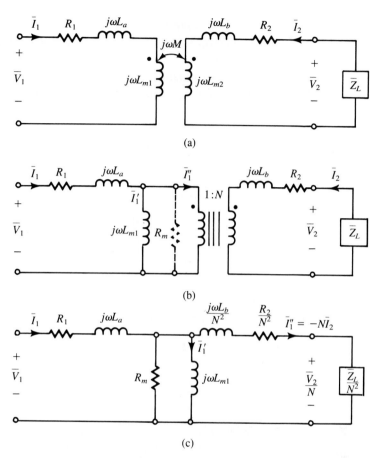

Figure 11.16
(a) Equivalent network of an actual transformer and load using a unity-coupled 2-port. (b) Unity-coupled 2-port replaced by its equivalent network. (c) Equivalent 1-port replacing ideal transformer and load.

primary and secondary inductances can be represented as a sum of two inductances:

$$L_1 = L_{m1} + L_a$$
$$L_2 = L_{m2} + L_b$$

where $M^2 = L_{m1}L_{m2}$ and L_a and L_b are called *leakage inductances* of the primary and secondary, respectively. In other words, we have chosen L_{m1} and L_{m2} such that we can consider these two inductances to have unity coupling. The actual transformer equivalent circuit then consists of a unity-coupled transformer plus series impedances to account for winding resistances and leakage flux.

In Figure 11.16(b) we have replaced the unity-coupled transformer with the equivalent network developed in Section 11.5 involving an ideal transformer and an inductive impedance connected across the primary. In addition, dotted lines show a resistance in parallel with $j\omega L_{m1}$ that can be used, if desired, to account for transformer losses with zero load current.

The 1-port equivalent network utilizing reflected impedances is shown in Figure 11.16(c). If $\bar{V}_2$ and $\bar{I}_2$ are desired from this diagram, they may be found as indicated.

The determination of the various impedances from test measurements can be understood from the approximate equivalent networks of Figure 11.17.

Figure 11.17
Approximate equivalent networks for an actual transformer with secondary (a) open and (b) shorted.

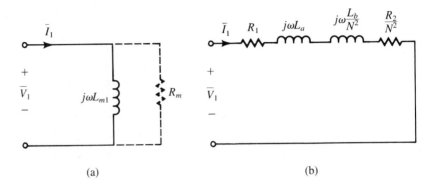

(a)   (b)

For a practical transformer,

$$R_1 \approx \frac{R_2}{N^2}$$

$$L_a \approx \frac{L_b}{N^2}$$

(11.36)

The resistance relation can be justified on the basis of the comparative length and cross section of the winding conductors. The inductance relation is based on turns ratio only. Furthermore, R_m and ωL_{m1} are both orders of magnitude larger than R_1 and ωL_a, respectively. Using these approximate relations, we can now justify the determination of the various parameters by the open-circuit and short-circuit secondary tests.

With the secondary open-circuited and a voltage $\bar{V}_1$ applied,

$$\bar{I}_1 \approx \left(\frac{1}{R_m} + \frac{1}{j\omega L_{m1}} \right) \bar{V}_1$$

(11.37)

as indicated in Figure 11.17(a). The resistor R_m is chosen to account for the power input at this operating condition. By measuring V_2, we can determine the turns ratio approximately as

$$N \approx \left| \frac{\bar{V}_2}{\bar{V}_1} \right|$$

With the secondary short-circuited and a voltage $\bar{V}_1$ applied,

$$\bar{V}_1 \approx \left[R_1 + \frac{R_2}{N^2} + j\omega \left(L_a + \frac{L_b}{N^2} \right) \right] \bar{I}_1$$

(11.38)

as shown in Figure 11.17(b). Using the approximate relations indicated in Equation 11.36, we can determine the values of R_1, R_2, L_a, and L_b from Equation 11.38 when the magnitudes and relative phase angle of $\bar{V}_1$ and $\bar{I}_1$ are known. This determination is usually made with an ac rms voltmeter, an rms ammeter, and a wattmeter (average power meter).

11.9   SUMMARY

An inductive 2-port can be modeled using mutual inductances or an ideal transformer. For 2-ports with coupling coefficients well below unity, the mutual-inductance model is usually used. Those 2-ports with coupling coefficients near unity are often called electric transformers.

Polarity dots on an inductive 2-port indicate relative coil-winding polarities so that, given the primary and secondary v- and i-orientations, the proper signs may be used in the component equations without a detailed knowledge of how the windings are put on. Polarity dot positions are determined by the winding polarity—not by the v- and i-orientations!

If an inductive 2-port is not perfectly coupled, the t-domain component equations can be solved for the time derivatives of the currents. With this form of the component equations, the state model of a network containing inductive 2-ports can be formulated by the methods of Chapter 8. The formulation problem is no more complex than with noncoupled inductances.

Standard loop and supernode models can be formulated by the substitution procedure for networks containing inductive 2-ports, using either t-domain or ω-domain mutual-inductance models. If the 2-ports can be included in the formulation cotree, loop equations can be written from inspection with only a slight extension from the 1-port formulation procedure.

Coupling coefficients are useful in specifying coupling characteristics of inductive 2-ports on a normalized scale. The concept of an ideal transformer is useful (as a part of an equivalent model, at least) when the coupling coefficient is near unity.

An ideal transformer has zero input admittance with open-circuited secondary and zero input impedance with short-circuited secondary. The total complex power associated with it vanishes under all conditions of operation. The component equations, for i-reference arrows alike with respect to the polarity dots, are $\bar{V}_2 = N\bar{V}_1$ and $\bar{I}_1 = -N\bar{I}_2$. Although these component equations are simple, they do not necessarily simplify the complete network model if both windings of the transformer are in a single connected network.

The unity-coupled transformer model utilizes an ideal transformer but is a bit more realistic than the ideal-transformer model in that its input admittance with open-circuited secondary is $1/j\omega L_1$. This is achieved in the schematic diagram by connecting an impedance, $j\omega L_1$, across the primary terminals of the ideal-transformer model.

For many practical networks containing inductive 2-ports, there are no electric connections between the primary and secondary windings. For this type of system, the equivalent 1-port representation of an inductive 2-port with its secondary load impedance is often very useful. Which 2-port model of the inductor is used depends on the specific network. If the ideal-transformer model is adequate, it is by far the simplest, since a secondary impedance $\bar{Z}$ reflects into the primary as $\bar{Z}/N^2$.

An actual iron-core transformer can be modeled by a combination of ideal transformer, resistances, and 1-port inductors. All parameters for the transformer equivalent circuit, including N, can be determined to a fair approximation by open-circuit and short-circuit tests.

PROBLEMS

11.1 Assume for the inductive 3-port of Figure 11.18 that ϕ links all three coils completely. Suppose that $\phi = 10 \sin 400t$ Wb. Assume that the numbers of turns on the coils are n_1, n_2, and n_3 and write $v_1(t)$, $v_2(t)$, and $v_3(t)$, paying particular attention to the sign of each expression.

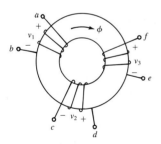

Figure 11.18

11.2 Suppose for Problem 11.1 that all of ϕ links coil 1, 0.8ϕ links coil 2, and 0.5ϕ links coil 3. Write the corresponding expressions for $v_1(t)$, $v_2(t)$, and $v_3(t)$.

11.3 Given for the configuration of Figure 11.18 that

$$\phi = \begin{cases} 0 & 0 \leq t < T \\ -50(t - T) & T < t \leq T + 2 \\ -100 & T + 2 < t \end{cases}$$

and that ϕ links all coils completely. Write expressions for $v_1(t)$, $v_2(t)$, and $v_3(t)$ for $t > 0$

and sketch the functions versus time if $n_1 = 10$, $n_2 = 20$, and $n_3 = 5$.

11.4 Suppose for the configuration of Figure 11.18 that all the magnetic flux ϕ links all three coils. Suppose, further, that an alternating voltage $v_1(t) = 100 \cos 50t$ V is applied to coil 1. Write expressions for $\phi(t)$ and for v_{ce} if terminals d and f are connected together. Use $n_1 = 10$, $n_2 = 20$, and $n_3 = 5$ as the numbers of turns per coil.

11.5 For the configuration of Figure 11.19, write the Faraday law equations (Equation 11.3) choosing the correct sign. Reference directions for ϕ_1 and ϕ_2 should be taken to agree with reference directions of i_1 and i_2, respectively.

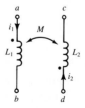

Figure 11.19

11.6 Change the reference directions for v_2 and i_2 in Figure 11.19 and repeat Problem 11.5.

11.7 Change the reference directions for v_1, v_2, i_1, and i_2 in Figure 11.19 and repeat Problem 11.5.

11.8 Consider only coils 1 and 2 of Figure 11.18 and put magnetic polarity dots on an appropriate pair of terminals.

11.9 Repeat Problem 11.8 for coils 1 and 3.

11.10 Put magnetic polarity dots on the coil terminals of Figure 11.20.

11.11 Use magnetic polarity markings of dot, triangle, and square to mark relative magnetic polarities of coil pairs 1–2, 1–3, and 2–3 of Figure 11.18. Each coil will thus have two different polarity marks on it.

11.12 Write the terminal characteristic equations for the 2-port of Figure 11.20 in the t-domain if $L_1 = 4$ H, $L_2 = 9$ H, and $M = 5$ H.

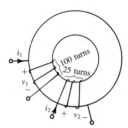

Figure 11.20

11.13 Suppose that the two coils of Figure 11.20 are connected in series to form a 1-port. What values of inductance are possible? Use $L_1 = 4$ H, $L_2 = 9$ H, and $M = 5$ H.

11.14 Solve Problem 11.13, except connect the two coils in parallel instead of in series.

11.15 Calculate the inductance formed by the series-connected inductors of Figure 11.21.

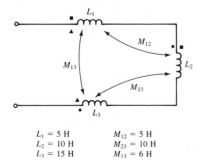

$L_1 = 5$ H $M_{12} = 5$ H
$L_2 = 10$ H $M_{23} = 10$ H
$L_3 = 15$ H $M_{13} = 6$ H

Figure 11.21

11.16 Assume that coil 2 is reversed in the series connection of Figure 11.21. Find the total inductance of the 1-port formed by the three series inductors.

11.17 Formulate the state equations for the network of Figure 11.22 for $M = 1$ H. Find the steady-state solution by converting to a phasor model.

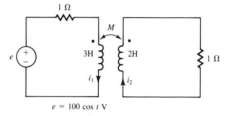

$e = 100 \cos t$ V

Figure 11.22

11.18 Formulate the state equations for the network of Figure 11.23 for $M = 1$ H. Find the steady-state solution by converting to a phasor model.

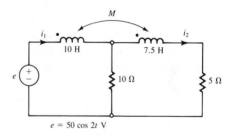

$e = 50 \cos 2t$ V

Figure 11.23

11.19 Formulate the state equations for the network of Figure 11.24 with $M = 0.04$ H.

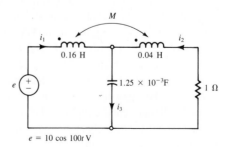

$e = 10 \cos 100t$ V

Figure 11.24

11.20 Formulate the state equations for the network of Figure 11.25 with $M = 0.04$ H.

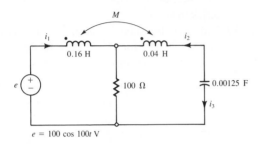

$e = 100 \cos 100t$ V

Figure 11.25

11.21 Change the position of the polarity dot on L_3 of Figure 11.5 to the opposite (a) end of the coil and formulate state equations for the network.

11.22 Formulate state equations for the network of Figure 11.6 assuming that $R_3 = R_4 = R_5 = 1\,\Omega$, $L_1 = L_2 = 2$ H, and $M = 1$ H.

11.23 Formulate and solve the phasor loop model of the network of Figure 11.22 with $M = 1$ H. Compare with the steady-state solution to Problem 11.17. Use the loop currents shown.

11.24 Formulate and solve the phasor loop model of the network of Figure 11.23 with $M = 1$ H. Use the loop currents indicated.

11.25 Formulate and solve the phasor loop model of the network of Figure 11.24 using $\bar{I}_1$ and $\bar{I}_2$ as the phasor loop currents. Let $k = 0.5$.

11.26 Formulate and solve the phasor loop model of the network of Figure 11.25 using $\bar{I}_1$ and $\bar{I}_2$ as the phasor loop currents. Let $k = 0.6$.

11.27 Assume that the inductors of Figure 11.22 are unity-coupled ($k = 1$). Draw a schematic diagram using an equivalent 2-port utilizing unity coupling. Formulate a phasor model for this schematic diagram using the method described in Section 11.5, and solve for $\bar{I}_1$ and $\bar{I}_2$.

11.28 Assume that the inductors of Figure 11.24 are unity-coupled ($k = 1$). Draw a schematic diagram for the network using an equivalent 2-port utilizing unity coupling. Formulate a phasor model for the schematic diagram using the method described in Section 11.5, and solve for $\bar{I}_1$ and $\bar{I}_2$.

11.29 Repeat Problem 11.27 for the network of Figure 11.25. The coils are perfectly coupled.

11.30 Formulate a phasor model for the network of Figure 11.22 (with $k = 1$) using an equivalent 2-port network with unity coupling to represent the coupled coils. Solve for $\bar{I}_1$ by using the concept of reflected impedance to obtain the effect of the second loop on the first.

11.31 Formulate a phasor model for the network of Figure 11.22 using an ideal transformer approximation to the unity-coupled 2-port. Solve for $\bar{I}_1$, and compare the solution to the solution for Problem 11.30.

11.32 The inductive 2-port of Figure 11.26 is modeled as an ideal transformer. Solve the phasor network for $\bar{I}_1$ and $\bar{I}_2$ by (a) writing two loop equations, (b) using the concept of reflected impedance and finding the equivalent 1-port impedance, Z_0, connected across the source at terminals ab, and (c) finding the Thevenin equivalent 1-port for the network to the left of terminals cd.

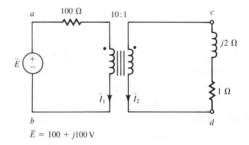

$\bar{E} = 100 + j100$ V

Figure 11.26

11.33 The inductive 2-port of Figure 11.27 is modeled as an ideal transformer. Solve the phasor

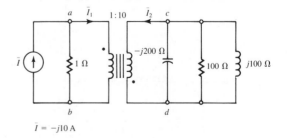

$\bar{I} = -j10$ A

Figure 11.27

network for $\bar{V}_{ab}$ and $\bar{V}_{cd}$ by (a) writing super-node equations, (b) finding the admittance of the 1-port network connected to the source at ab, and (c) finding the Norton equivalent 1-port for the network to the left of terminals cd.

11.34 Find the impedance of the 1-port of Figure 11.28 at terminals ab. This inductive 2-port connection is known as an *autotransformer*.

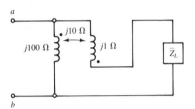

Figure 11.28

11.35 Find the impedance of the equivalent 1-port for the network of Figure 11.29 if $N = \frac{1}{5}$.

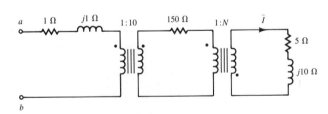

Figure 11.29

11.36 Choose N in the network of Figure 11.29 such that power transmitted to the impedance $5 + j10$ is maximum for a source with terminal equation

$$\bar{V}_{ab} = 10 + (5 + j5)\bar{I}_{ab}$$

connected to terminals ab. For this value of N, solve for $\bar{I}$.

11.37 Find the impedance of the 1-port network of Figure 11.30.

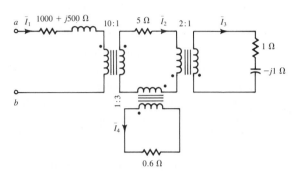

Figure 11.30

11.38 Find every phasor current indicated on the network of Figure 11.30 for an ideal source connected to terminals ab such that $\bar{V}_{ab} = 2000$ V.

11.39 The inductive 2-port of Figure 11.31 is modeled as an ideal transformer. Choose N such that maximum power is transferred to the secondary. For this N, solve for both $\bar{I}_1$ and $\bar{I}_2$.

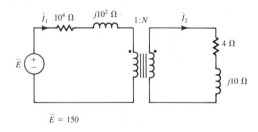

Figure 11.31

11.40 A pair of coupled coils have the following parameters: $L_1 = 100$ H, $L_2 = 1$ H, and $M = 9$ H. Here $R_1 = 5\ \Omega$ and $R_2 = 0.04\ \Omega$. Draw a transformer-type equivalent network with all parameters referred to the primary (number 1) side of the transformer. (Iron losses are neglected.)

11.41 A 10-kVA 60-Hz, 2300/230-V distribution transformer, tested both with the low-voltage side (secondary) open-circuited and with the secondary short-circuited, yields the following data:

Open-circuit data	Short-circuit data
$|\bar{V}_1| = 2300$ V	$|\bar{V}_1| = 120$ V
$|\bar{I}_1| = 0.2$ A	$|\bar{I}_1| = 150$ A
p.f. $= 0.6$ lag	p.f. $= 0.5$ lag

Assume that the winding resistances are equal and the leakage reactances are equal, *when referred to the same winding of the transformer*. Draw an equivalent network for the transformer referred to the high-voltage winding. Indicate the values of all impedances (or admittances).

11.42 Derive Equation 11.17 for both parallel-aiding and parallel-opposing connections.

11.43 Explain why, if an ideal-transformer model is to be used as part of a network model, there must exist (a) a cotree that contains the coupled coils and all *i*-sources and (b) a tree that contains the coupled coils and all *v*-sources.

11.44 Derive Equation 11.33.

11.45 Justify that $R_1 \approx R_2/N^2$ for a well-designed two-winding transformer. *Hint:* Start with the assumption that the design is for full-load conditions, and that no copper is to be wasted.

11.46 Give an approximate range of values of $|\bar{Z}_L|$ such that the ideal transformer model would be adequate to represent the inductive 2-port of Figure 11.22. Assume that $M \approx \sqrt{6}$, and justify your conclusion.

11.47 Develop an argument to justify neglecting R_m and $j\omega L_{m_1}$ in the short-circuit test network of Figure 11.17(b).

Giants of the profession
IEEE Centennial Hall of Fame

Michael Pupin (1858–1935)
Professor of electrical engineering at
Columbia University for more than 40
years; an early experimenter with
X-rays; his autobiography, *From
Immigrant to Inventor*, won a Pulitzer
Prize.

Harry Nyquist (1889–1976)
Pioneer in communications systems
whose signal-transmission studies laid
the groundwork for modern information
theory; holder of 138 patents; he
invented the vestigial sideband
transmission system.

Reprinted with permission from
"Centennial Hall of Fame,"
IEEE SPECTRUM, April 1984.

The Laplace transformation

12.1 INTRODUCTION

In Chapters 7 and 8 we formulated mathematical models in the t-domain for some simple networks with energy-storage elements. The solution for a first-order state model was developed in detail and the second-order model was discussed briefly. Further, we noted that for more complex networks the state model could, in general, be of higher order, thereby requiring the solution of a system of simultaneous linear differential equations. It is for this reason that we now introduce the Laplace transform, by means of which we are able to transform systems of ordinary linear differential equations with constant coefficients into algebraic equations that are also linear in the transformed variables.

12.2 DEFINITION OF THE LAPLACE TRANSFORM

There have been many techniques used to introduce the Laplace transform to engineering students which avoid the direct statement of the integral definition. It is doubtful, however, that any eventual advantage can thus be gained. All the important properties of the transform stem directly from this definition. We, therefore, begin our discussion of the subject in the manner traditional to mathematics.

Definition 12.1

Given a function $f(t)$, its Laplace transform, $\mathcal{L}\{f(t)\}$, is

$$\mathcal{L}\{f(t)\} = \int_0^\infty f(t)e^{-st}\,dt$$

if the integral exists.

The notation $F(s) \doteq \mathcal{L}\{f(t)\}$ is often used to symbolize a transformed function. When a time function (or t-function) is Laplace-transformed, it is said to be transformed from the t-domain to the s-domain. This results from the fact, of course, that a transformed function is a function of the variable s.

Example 12.1

Let $f(t) = u(t)$, the unit step function, where

$$u(t) = \begin{cases} 1 & t > 0 \\ 0 & t < 0 \end{cases}$$

Then, if s is real and positive,

$$F(s) = \int_0^\infty u(t)e^{-st}\,dt = \int_0^\infty e^{-st}\,dt = \left[\frac{e^{-st}}{-s}\right]_0^\infty = \frac{1}{s}$$

Example 12.2

Let $f(t) = u(t - 1)$; then

$$F(s) = \int_0^\infty u(t-1)e^{-st}\,dt = \int_1^\infty e^{-st}\,dt = -\left[\frac{e^{-st}}{s}\right]_1^\infty = \frac{e^{-s}}{s}$$

12.3   TRANSFORMS OF ELEMENTARY FUNCTIONS

There are a number of functions that occur repeatedly in the analysis of electric networks. You should become familiar with them as quickly as possible. In this section we shall derive some of these transforms to illustrate the procedure. We are also interested in recording the transform pairs together for use later.

Theorem 12.1

$$\mathcal{L}\{Ke^{at}\} = \frac{K}{s-a}$$

Proof:

$$\mathcal{L}\{Ke^{at}\} = K \int_0^\infty e^{at} e^{-st} \, dt$$

$$= K \int_0^\infty e^{-(s-a)t} \, dt$$

$$= -\frac{K}{s-a}\left[e^{-(s-a)t} \right]_0^\infty$$

$$= \frac{K}{s-a} \qquad \text{(If } s \text{ is real and } s > a)$$

Theorem 12.1 is very useful in the development of Laplace transforms of more complex functions that can be expressed in terms of exponential functions. By taking the special case of $a = 0$, we have the Laplace transform of the unit step function.

Example 12.3

$$\mathcal{L}\{K\,u(t)\} = \mathcal{L}\{Ke^0\} = \frac{K}{s}$$

The constant a in Theorem 12.1 may be complex; thus we have the next result.

Example 12.4

$$\mathcal{L}\{Ke^{(a+j\omega)t}\} = \frac{K}{s-(\alpha+j\omega)}$$

From Theorem 12.1 we shall now find the transforms for two of the most important functions in network analysis.

Theorem 12.2

$$\mathcal{L}\{\cos \omega t\} = \frac{s}{s^2 + \omega^2}$$

Proof:

$$\mathcal{L}\{\cos \omega t\} = \mathcal{L}\left\{\frac{e^{j\omega t} + e^{-j\omega t}}{2}\right\}$$

$$= \frac{1}{2}\left(\frac{1}{s - j\omega} + \frac{1}{s + j\omega}\right)$$

$$= \frac{s}{s^2 + \omega^2}$$

Theorem 12.3

$$\mathcal{L}\{\sin \omega t\} = \frac{\omega}{s^2 + \omega^2}$$

The proof is left as an exercise.

The following theorem is often called the *substitution theorem* and the *s-domain shifting theorem*.

Theorem 12.4

Let $\mathcal{L}\{f(t)\} = F(s)$; then

$$\mathcal{L}\{e^{-at}f(t)\} = F(s + a)$$

Proof:

$$\mathcal{L}\{e^{-at}f(t)\} = \int_0^\infty f(t)e^{-(s+a)t}\, dt$$

If $\lambda \doteq s + a$, then in our symbolism

$$\int_0^\infty f(t)e^{-\lambda t}\, dt \equiv F(\lambda) = F(s + a)$$

This is a very useful theorem, as illustrated in the following example.

Example 12.5

$$\mathcal{L}\{e^{-at}\cos \omega t\} = \frac{s + a}{(s + a)^2 + \omega^2}$$

Theorem 12.5

$$\mathcal{L}\{t^n\} = \frac{n!}{s^{n+1}} \qquad n \geq 0$$

Proof: The theorem holds for $n = 0$. By induction the theorem is true if, holding for n, we can demonstrate that it holds for $n + 1$:

$$\mathcal{L}\{t^{n+1}\} = \int_0^{\infty} t^{n+1} e^{-st} \, dt$$

We now integrate by parts using

$$\int u \, dv = uv - \int v \, du$$

where

$$u = t^{n+1} \qquad\qquad dv = e^{-st} \, dt$$

$$du = (n + 1)t^n \, dt \qquad v = -\frac{1}{s}e^{-st}$$

Thus

$$\mathcal{L}\{t^{n+1}\} = -\frac{t^{n+1}e^{-st}}{s}\bigg|_0^{\infty} + \frac{n + 1}{s} \int_0^{\infty} t^n e^{-st} \, dt$$

The first term is zero at the limits. The integral is exactly $\mathcal{L}\{t^n\}$, which we have demonstrated to hold for $n = 0$. Thus

$$\mathcal{L}\{t^{n+1}\} = \frac{n + 1}{s} \mathcal{L}\{t^n\} = \frac{(n + 1)!}{s^{n+2}}$$

and the theorem is proved.

The proof of Theorem 12.5 was carried out in some detail for two reasons: first, to illustrate the use of the induction method of proof, which you would do well to master if you have not already; and, second, to bring to mind, because of its great usefulness in the material to be discussed shortly, the method of integration by parts.

The impulse function $\delta(t)$, while not a true function in the mathematical sense, is very useful in engineering analysis. Although it is zero everywhere except at $t = 0$, it is assigned the formal property

$$\int_{-\varepsilon}^{\varepsilon} \delta(t) \, dt = 1 \tag{12.1}$$

where ε is any real number greater than zero. For the integral to be nonzero, we must integrate across the origin. Thus when we take the Laplace transform of an impulse function, we must interpret the lower limit as 0^- (arbitrarily close to zero but negative).

Theorem 12.6

$$\mathcal{L}\{\delta(t)\} = 1$$

Proof:

$$\mathcal{L}\{\delta(t)\} = \int_{0^-}^{\infty} \delta(t)e^{-st} \, dt = e^0 = 1$$

by the sampling property of the impulse function.

Example 12.6 ───────────────────────────────

$$\mathcal{L}\{5\delta(t-1)\} = \int_{0^-}^{\infty} 5\delta(t-1)e^{-st} \, dt = 5e^{-s} \tag{12.2}$$

To show this result, we set $\tau = t - 1$ and Equation 12.2 becomes

$$\int_{-1}^{\infty} 5\delta(\tau)e^{-s(\tau+1)} \, d\tau = 5e^{-s} \tag{12.3}$$

Example 12.7 ───────────────────────────────

$$\mathcal{L}\{t^2\delta(t-2)\} = \int_{0^-}^{\infty} t^2\delta(t-2)e^{-st} \, dt = 4e^{-2s} \tag{12.4}$$

The result in Equation 12.4 follows from the property $\delta(t) \cdot f(t) = \delta(t)f(0)$. In this example $t^2 e^{-st}\delta(t-2) \equiv 4e^{-2s}\delta(t-2)$.

Example 12.8 ───────────────────────────────

$$\mathcal{L}\{(t-2)^2 \, \delta(t)\} = \int_{0^-}^{\infty} (t-2)^2 \, \delta(t)e^{-st} \, dt = (-2)^2 = 4 \tag{12.5}$$

12.4 TRANSFORMS OF DERIVATIVES ───────────────○

In this section we arrive at the property of the Laplace transform that largely accounts for its usefulness in network analysis—the transformation of differential equations into algebraic equations.

Theorem 12.7

Let $\mathcal{L}\{f(t)\} = F(s)$ and $(d/dt)f(t)$ be defined; then

$$\mathcal{L}\left\{\frac{d}{dt}f(t)\right\} = sF(s) - f(0) \tag{12.6}$$

Proof: For convenience let $f'(t) \doteq (d/dt)f(t)$:

$$\mathcal{L}\{f'(t)\} = \int_0^\infty f'(t)e^{-st}\, dt$$

Integrate by parts, letting $u = e^{-st}$ and $dv = f'(t)dt$:

$$du = -se^{-st}\, dt \qquad v = f(t)$$

Then

$$\mathcal{L}\{f'(t)\} = e^{-st}f(t)\Big|_0^\infty + s\int_0^\infty f(t)e^{-st}\, dt$$

$$= 0 - f(0) + sF(s)$$

If the function $f(t)$ has a jump discontinuity at the origin, we find ourselves on the horns of a dilemma. Theorem 12.7 is based on the existence of the derivative $f'(t)$, but in this case the assumption does not hold over a t-interval that includes $t = 0$. On the other hand, we must use 0^- as the lower limit of the Laplace transform integral to be consistent if we want to include impulse functions in network theory. Therefore, with some reluctance we again turn to formal methods and define

$$\mathcal{L}\{f'(t)\} = sF(s) - f(0^-)$$

and recognize that if $f(t) = g(t)u(t)$, where $g(t)$ is continuous at the origin, then $f'(t)$ must contain an impulse function of strength equal to the magnitude of the discontinuity.

Example 12.9

Let $f(t) = 10u(t)$. For this function, $f(0^-) = 0$. By Theorem 12.7,

$$\mathcal{L}\{f'(t)\} = s\left(\frac{10}{s}\right) - 0 = 10$$

$$\mathcal{L}^{-1}\{10\} = 10\delta(t) = f'(t)$$

Thus $f'(t)$ is an impulse of strength 10 at $t = 0$ and 0 for $t > 0$.

Example 12.10

Let $g(t) = (10 \cos 2t)u(t)$.

$$\mathcal{L}\{g'(t)\} = s\left(\frac{10s}{s^2 + 2^2}\right) - 0 = \frac{10s^2}{s^2 + 2^2} = 10\left(1 - \frac{4}{s^2 + 4}\right)$$

$$10\mathcal{L}^{-1}\left\{1 - \frac{4}{s^2 + 4}\right\} = 10\delta(t) - 20 \sin 2t = g'(t) \qquad (12.7)$$

For this example, had we chosen to use 0^+ for the lower limit in Theorem 12.7, the only change in the statement would be to change from $g(0^-)$ to $g(0^+)$. In this example $g(0^+) = 10$; therefore,

$$\mathcal{L}\{g'(t)\} = s\left(\frac{10s}{s^2 + 4}\right) - 10 = -\frac{40}{s^2 + 4}$$

$$\mathcal{L}^{-1}\left\{-\frac{40}{s^2 + 4}\right\} = -20 \sin 2t = g'(t) \qquad (12.8)$$

Both Equations 12.7 and 12.8 are valid solutions for $g'(t)$. The solution shown as Equation 12.8, however, is valid only for $t > 0$.

In case you are becoming demoralized at this point by the quandary of which lower limit on the Laplace transform integral is preferable, 0^- or 0^+, we can offer some comfort. For nearly all network models, excepting some pathological ones dreamed up by professors to trip students, the initial conditions are the same at 0^+ and 0^-. Thus for most practical networks, we need not be concerned about the theoretical niceties of the initial conditions. To be consistent, however, and to make our theory applicable to impulse-function sources and responses, we use the 0^- lower limit on the Laplace transform integral for the remainder of this book.

Theorem 12.7 may be used successively to obtain the Laplace transform of higher-order time derivatives.

Theorem 12.8

$$\mathcal{L}\left\{\frac{d^2}{dt^2}f(t)\right\} = s^2F(s) - sf(0^-) - f'(0^-)$$

Proof: By Theorem 12.7,

$$\mathcal{L}\{f''(t)\} = s\mathcal{L}\{f'(t)\} - f'(0^-)$$

But $\mathcal{L}\{f'(t)\} = sF(s) - f(0^-)$, and thus the theorem follows.

Theorem 12.8 opens the disquieting possibility of Laplace transforms of second (and higher) derivatives of functions with jump discontinuities. It is true that we can handle these types of singularity functions *formally*, as the following example illustrates.

Example 12.11

Given the function

$$h(t) = 5[u(t) - u(t - 2)]$$

then

$$\mathcal{L}\{h'(t)\} = 5s\left[\frac{1}{s} - \frac{e^{-2s}}{s}\right] = 5 - 5e^{-2s}$$

since $h(0^-) = 0$.

Thus the *t*-domain solution is

$$h'(t) = 5\delta(t) - 5\delta(t - 2)$$

Furthermore,

$$\mathcal{L}\{h''(t)\} = 5s - 5se^{-2s}$$

since $h'(0^-) = 0$. The inverse transform is

$$h''(t) = 5\delta'(t) - 5\delta'(t - 2)$$

and so on.

By means of the theorems developed up to this point, an ordinary linear differential equation in the *t*-domain may be transformed into an algebraic linear equation in the *s* (or Laplace-transform) variable.

Example 12.12 ———————————————————————————————————————

Given the differential equation

$$\frac{d^2}{dt^2} x(t) + 5\frac{d}{dt} x(t) + 2x(t) = 50 \cos 10t$$

the Laplace-transformed equation is

$$s^2 X(s) - sx(0^-) - x'(0^-) + s5X(s) - 5x(0^-) + 2X(s) = \frac{50s}{s^2 + 10^2}$$

or

$$(s^2 + 5s + 2)X(s) = \frac{50s}{s^2 + 10^2} + (s + 5)x(0^-) + x'(0^-)$$

from which

$$X(s) = \frac{1}{s^2 + 5s + 2}\left[\frac{50s}{s^2 + 100} + (s + 5)x(0^-) + x'(0^-)\right]$$

12.5   TRANSFORMS OF INTEGRALS ————————————————————————O

We have stressed formulation techniques that lead to secondary models containing sets of simultaneous first-order differential equations. The importance of the state model to us stems mainly from its usefulness for numerical solution by digital computers, but it has great mathematical importance in rigorous investigations into the theory of differential equations.

Mathematical models are often formulated, however, using integral component characteristics such as

$$i = \frac{1}{L}\int_0^t v\, dt + i(0)$$

$$v = \frac{1}{C}\int_0^t i\, dt + v(0)$$

to obtain secondary models. When time-derivative and time-integral component characteristics are used in the same model, we say that the model contains integrodifferential equations. It is customary to differentiate integrodifferential equations to obtain a set of differential equations when classical solution techniques are used. By use of the Laplace transform technique, however, the integrodifferential equations may be transformed directly.

Theorem 12.9

Let $F(s)$ be the Laplace transform of $f(t)$; then

$$\mathcal{L}\left\{\int_0^t f(\tau)\, d\tau\right\} = \frac{F(s)}{s}$$

Proof:

$$\mathcal{L}\left\{\int_0^t f(\tau)\, d\tau\right\} = \int_{0^-}^\infty e^{-st}\left[\int_0^t f(\tau)\, d\tau\right] dt$$

Integrate by parts. Let

$$u = \int_0^t f(\tau)\, d\tau \qquad du = f(t)\, dt$$

$$dv = e^{-st}\, dt \qquad v = -\frac{1}{s}e^{-st}$$

Then

$$\mathcal{L}\left\{\int_0^t f(\tau)\, d\tau\right\} = -\frac{1}{s}e^{-st}\int_0^t f(\tau)\, d\tau\Big|_{0^-}^\infty + \frac{1}{s}\int_0^\infty f(t)e^{-st}\, dt$$

$$= -[0-0] + \frac{F(s)}{s}$$

Example 12.13

Let $f(t) = \displaystyle\int_0^t \cos \omega\tau\, d\tau$. Find $\mathcal{L}\{f(t)\}$.

By Theorem 12.9,

$$F(s) = \frac{1}{s}\,\mathcal{L}\{\cos \omega t\}$$

$$= \frac{1}{s}\left\{\frac{s}{s^2 + \omega^2}\right\}$$

$$= \frac{1}{s^2 + \omega^2}$$

As a check we integrate and then take the Laplace transform.

$$\mathcal{L}\{f(t)\} = \mathcal{L}\left\{\frac{1}{\omega}\sin \omega t\right\} = \frac{1}{\omega}\frac{\omega}{s^2 + \omega^2} = \frac{1}{s^2 + \omega^2}$$

Example 12.14

Find the Laplace transform of $\frac{1}{3} t^3 = \int_0^t \tau^2 \, d\tau$:

$$\mathscr{L}\left\{\int_0^t \tau^2 \, d\tau\right\} = \frac{1}{s} \mathscr{L}\{t^2\} = \frac{1}{s} \mathscr{L}\left(\int_0^t 2\tau \, d\tau\right) = \frac{1}{s^2} \mathscr{L}\{2t\} = \frac{1}{s^2}\left(\frac{2}{s^2}\right)$$

As the examples demonstrate, Theorem 12.9 can be used effectively as a memory device to recall the Laplace transform of functions for which we know the transform of the derivative. Table 12.1 lists a number of transform pairs for elementary and often-used t functions.

**Table 12.1
Transform pairs for
some elementary
t-functions**

	t-function	Laplace transform
1	$\delta(t)$	1
2	$u(t)$	$\dfrac{1}{s}$
3	t^n	$\dfrac{n!}{s^{n+1}}$
4	e^{-at}	$\dfrac{1}{s+a}$
5	$\cos \omega t$	$\dfrac{s}{s^2+\omega^2}$
6	$\sin \omega t$	$\dfrac{\omega}{s^2+\omega^2}$
7	$e^{-at}f(t)$	$F(s+a)$
8	$\dfrac{d}{dt}f(t)$	$sF(s) - f(0^-)$
9	$\displaystyle\int_0^t f(\tau)\,d\tau$	$\dfrac{F(s)}{s}$
10	$e^{-at}\cos \omega t$	$\dfrac{s+a}{(s+a)^2+\omega^2}$
11	$e^{-at}\sin \omega t$	$\dfrac{\omega}{(s+a)^2+\omega^2}$

12.6 SHIFTING THEOREMS

In network modeling we occasionally have need for a simple means of shifting source functions. By using sums and differences of shifted functions, for example, we can synthesize more complex functions. Since the Laplace transform is a linear operation, the transforms of such complex functions are easy to write as linear combinations of the Laplace-transformed constituent functions.

Theorem 12.10

Given $F(s)$ as the Laplace transform of $f(t)$, then if $a > 0$,

$$\mathcal{L}\{f(t - a)u(t - a)\} = e^{-as}F(s)$$

Proof:

$$\mathcal{L}\{f(t - a)u(t - a)\} = \int_{0^-}^{\infty} f(t - a)u(t - a)e^{-st}\,dt$$

Let $\lambda = t - a$. Then $t = \lambda + a$, and the lower limit becomes $\lambda = -a$. Now

$$\mathcal{L}\{f(t - a)u(t - a)\} = \int_{-a}^{\infty} f(\lambda)u(\lambda)e^{-s(\lambda + a)}\,d\lambda$$

$$= e^{-as}\int_{0^-}^{\infty} f(\lambda)e^{-s\lambda}\,d\lambda \qquad (12.9)$$

since the integrand is zero for $\lambda < 0$. The integral of Equation 12.9 is $F(s)$, so the theorem is proved.

Theorem 12.11

Given $F(s)$ as the Laplace transform of $f(t)$, then if $a > 0$,

$$\mathcal{L}\{f(t)u(t - a)\} = e^{-as}\mathcal{L}\{f(t + a)u(t)\}$$

Proof:

$$\int_{0^-}^{\infty} f(t)u(t - a)e^{-st}\,dt = \int_{a}^{\infty} f(t)e^{-st}\,dt$$

Let $\lambda = t - a$; then $t = a$ transforms to $\lambda = 0$.

$$\int_{a}^{\infty} f(t)e^{-st}\,dt = \int_{0}^{\infty} f(\lambda + a)e^{-s(\lambda + a)}\,d\lambda = e^{-as}\int_{0}^{\infty} f(\lambda + a)e^{-s\lambda}\,d\lambda$$

The right-hand expression is equal to the right-hand expression in the theorem except for the variable of integration.

Example 12.15

As an example of the use of the first shifting theorem, consider the Laplace transform of $g'(t)$, where

$$g(t) = \left[10 \cos 2\left(t - \frac{\pi}{4}\right)\right]u\left(t - \frac{\pi}{4}\right)$$

By Theorems 12.10 and 12.7, we have

$$\mathcal{L}\{g'(t)\} = e^{-(\pi/4)s}s\left[\frac{20}{s^2 + 4}\right]$$

since $\cos 2(t - \pi/4) = \sin(2t)$ and $\sin(0^-) = 0$.

Now we look at an example of the second shifting theorem.

Example 12.16

Given

$$f(t) = (10 \cos 2t)u\left(t - \frac{\pi}{2}\right)$$

$$\mathcal{L}\{f(t)\} = e^{-(\pi/2)s}\mathcal{L}\left\{10 \cos\left(2t + \frac{\pi}{2}\right)\right\}$$

$$= e^{-(\pi/2)s}\left(\frac{-20}{s^2 + 4}\right)$$

since $\cos(2t + \pi/2) = -\sin 2t$.

Finally, we have an example that results in the transform of an impulse function.

Example 12.17

Given

$$h(t) = 10 \cos 2tu(t - \pi)$$

$$H(s) = 10e^{-\pi s}\mathcal{L}\{[\cos 2(t + \pi)]u(t)\}$$

$$= 10e^{-\pi s}\mathcal{L}\{[\cos 2t]u(t)\}$$

$$= 10e^{-\pi s}\frac{s}{s^2 + 4}$$

$\mathcal{L}\{h'(t)\} = sH(s)$ since $h(0^-) = 0$. Therefore,

$$\mathcal{L}\{h'(t)\} = 10e^{-\pi s} \frac{s^2}{s^2 + 4}$$

$$= 10e^{-\pi s}\left(1 - \frac{4}{s^2 + 4}\right)$$

Thus the inverse transform is

$$h'(t) = 10\{\delta(t - \pi) - 2\sin 2(t - \pi)u(t - \pi)\}$$
$$= 10\delta(t - \pi) - 20(\sin 2t)u(t - \pi)$$

12.7 TRANSFORMATION OF AN INTEGRODIFFERENTIAL EQUATION ⊸

We have now developed enough properties of the Laplace transform to transform simple t-domain linear differential equations and integrodifferential equations with constant coefficients into linear algebraic s-domain equations.

Example 12.18

Given the integrodifferential equation

$$\frac{d}{dt}x + 3x + 2\int_0^t x\, d\tau = 5u(t)$$

Transforming the entire equation term by term, we have

$$sX(s) - x(0^-) + 3X(s) + 2\frac{X(s)}{s} = \frac{5}{s}$$

The solution, in the s-domain, of this linear algebraic equation in the variable $X(s)$ is

$$X(s) = \frac{5 + sx(0^-)}{s^2 + 3s + 2}$$

In most instances, an analysis of a network by any technique finally requires that a t-domain solution be obtained. Thus the s-domain solution which we have obtained in Example 12.18 may be useless unless we have a simple technique for deducing the t-domain solution from it.

The time-domain function corresponding to an s-domain function can be found from the inverse Laplace transform

$$f(t) = \frac{1}{2\pi j} \int_{c-j\infty}^{c+j\infty} F(s)e^{st} \, ds \qquad (12.10)$$

where $F(s) \doteq \mathcal{L}\{f(t)\}$ and c is a real number that depends on $F(s)$. Evaluation of the integral in Equation 12.10 requires an understanding of complex variable theory. Fortunately, we are able to use a simpler technique to find the inverse transform for network models. Whatever procedure is used (provided that it is valid), we are assured that the inverse transform is unique. That is, there is a one-to-one correspondence between a function in the t-domain and its Laplace transform.

One means for finding the inverse transform is based on the stratagem of breaking the s-domain solution, $X(s)$, into a sum of functions of simpler form such that we can recognize the t-domain form of the transform pair. The mechanism for doing this, *when the s-domain solution is a ratio of polynomials (rational function)*, is the partial-fraction expansion. Fortunately for us, a wide class of important problems in network analysis yields s-domain solutions that are in the form of ratios of polynomials. For these networks, the technique to be discussed is applicable.

12.8 PARTIAL-FRACTION EXPANSION— SIMPLE POLES

From algebra it is a well-known fact that a polynomial of degree n has n factors or zeros. For the simple case of $n = 2$, these factors can be found by means of the quadratic formula or by completing the square. For $n \geq 3$ the problem is more complex. In this text no attention will be devoted to the problem of factoring a polynomial, although the use of the partial-fraction expansion depends upon the ability to find the factors of the denominator polynomial in the s-domain solution. Fortunately, the task of factoring polynomials of large degree is amenable to computer solution. See POLYROOT, Appendix C.

Let us begin the discussion of partial-fraction expansion by considering a Laplace-transformed function of the form

$$A(s) = \frac{K(s - s_3)}{s(s - s_1)(s - s_2)} \qquad (12.11)$$

where s_1, s_2, and s_3 are constants, no two of which are equal. Now $A(s)$ can be written as a sum of rational functions of the form

$$A(s) = \frac{A_0}{s} + \frac{A_1}{s - s_1} + \frac{A_2}{s - s_2} \qquad (12.12)$$

where there is one term in the summation for each denominator factor and A_1, A_2, and A_3 are constants. We have specifically excluded in this discussion the case of repeated factors in the *denominator* of $A(s)$.

Before discussing the determination of the A's, let us consider for a moment the reason the partial-fraction form is useful. If we know that $A(s)$ is a Laplace-transformed function, then we can write the *t*-domain solution $a(t)$ by inspection of Equation 12.12, since

$$\mathcal{L}\{f_1(t) + f_2(t) + f_3(t)\} = F_1(s) + F_2(s) + F_3(s)$$

Thus for Equation 12.12,

$$a(t) = A_0 + A_1 e^{s_1 t} + A_2 e^{s_2 t} \qquad \text{for } t \geq 0$$

To find the values of the A's, there is a choice of at least two procedures. One is to multiply both sides of the equation

$$A(s) = \frac{K(s - s_3)}{s(s - s_1)(s - s_2)} = \frac{A_0}{s} + \frac{A_1}{s - s_1} + \frac{A_2}{s - s_2} \qquad (12.13)$$

by $s(s - s_1)(s - s_2)$; multiply the right side out and equate coefficients of terms of like degree. A set of simultaneous equations in the A's results. A simpler scheme, which involves no simultaneous solution, is as follows. To find A_i, multiply both sides of Equation 12.13 by $s - s_i (s_0 \equiv 0)$ and take the limit of both sides as $s \to s_i$. The limit of every term of the form

$$\lim_{s \to s_i} (s - s_i) \frac{A_k}{s - s_k} = 0 \qquad \text{for } i \neq k$$

Thus

$$A_i = \lim_{s \to s_i} (s - s_i) A(s)$$

for the case of no repeated denominator factors.

Example 12.19 _____

We expand

$$A(s) = \frac{10(s + 1)}{s(s + 2)(s + 5)}$$

in a partial-fraction expansion:

$$A(s) = \frac{A_0}{s} + \frac{A_1}{s + 2} + \frac{A_2}{s + 5}$$

$$A_0 = \lim_{s \to 0} sA(s) = \lim_{s \to 0} \frac{10(s + 1)}{(s + 2)(s + 5)} = 1$$

$$A_1 = \lim_{s \to -2} (s + 2)A(s) = \lim_{s \to -2} \frac{10(s + 1)}{s(s + 5)} = \frac{5}{3}$$

$$A_2 = \lim_{s \to -5} (s + 5)A(s) = \lim_{s \to -5} \frac{10(s + 1)}{s(s + 2)} = -\frac{8}{3}$$

If $A(s)$ is a ratio of polynomials in s, those values of s for which $|A(s)|$ vanishes are called *zeros* of $A(s)$, and those values of s for which $|A(s)|$ is unbounded are called *poles* of $A(s)$. For the $A(s)$ of Example 12.19, the poles are $s = 0, -2, -5$. The one zero is $s = -1$.

The partial-fraction expansion applies to functions with complex poles as well as those with real poles only. If the coefficients of a polynomial are real (as is the case with lumped-system models) the complex zeros will occur in complex-conjugate pairs. That is, if one zero is $s = -1 + j$, another is $s = -1 - j$ for a polynomial with real coefficients.

The partial-fraction expansion can be used only for ratios of polynomials for which the degree of the numerator polynomial is less than that of the denominator. For cases where the degree of the numerator is equal to or greater than the degree of the denominator, division must be used to get an expression suitable for partial-fraction expansion.

12.9 PARTIAL-FRACTION EXPANSION— MULTIPLE POLES

Let us suppose that a Laplace-transformed solution $Z(s)$ for a system model is a ratio of polynomials and that $Z(s)$ has two second-order poles (repeated denominator factors) as illustrated by

$$Z(s) = \frac{K(s - s_1)}{s^2(s - s_2)^2(s - s_4)} \tag{12.14}$$

If the denominator of such a function has a factor of the type $(s - s_i)^n$, we say that the function has a pole of order n at $s = s_i$. The partial-fraction expansion of $Z(s)$ is of the form

$$Z(s) = \frac{A_1}{s} + \frac{A_2}{s^2} + \frac{B_1}{s - s_2} + \frac{B_2}{(s - s_2)^2} + \frac{C_1}{s - s_4} \tag{12.15}$$

The evaluation of C_1 follows the same procedure defined in Section 12.8. Multiply both sides of Equation 12.15 by $(s - s_4)$ and take the limit as $s \to s_4$. This yields

$$C_1 = \lim_{s \to s_4} (s - s_4)Z(s) = \frac{K(s_4 - s_1)}{s_4^2(s_4 - s_2)^2} \tag{12.16}$$

To find A_2, we multiply both sides of Equation 12.16 by s^2 and let $s \to 0$:

$$A_2 = \lim_{s \to 0} s^2 Z(s) = \frac{Ks_1}{s_2{}^2 s_4} \tag{12.17}$$

Similarly,

$$B_2 = \lim_{s \to s_2} (s - s_2)^2 Z(s) = \frac{K(s_2 - s_1)}{s_2{}^2 (s_2 - s_4)} \tag{12.18}$$

The same kind of procedure will fail when we attempt to find A_1 and B_1. To illustrate this fact, we multiply both sides of Equation 12.15 by s and take the limit as $s \to 0$. The result is

$$\lim_{s \to 0} Z(s) = A_1 + \lim_{s \to 0} \frac{A_2}{s}$$

The right-hand limit does not exist, so an alternative method must be sought.

Suppose that we again multiply both sides of Equation 12.15 by s^2 and differentiate with respect to s. If the limit is now taken as $s \to 0$,

$$\lim_{s \to 0} \frac{d}{ds} s^2 \left(\frac{A_2}{s^2} + \frac{B_1}{s - s_2} + \frac{B_2}{(s - s_2)^2} + \frac{C_1}{s - s_4} \right) = 0 \tag{12.19}$$

Thus

$$A_1 = \lim_{s \to 0} \frac{d}{ds} A_1 s = \lim_{s \to 0} \frac{d}{ds} s^2 Z(s) \tag{12.20}$$

This same approach yields

$$B_1 = \lim_{s \to s_2} \frac{d}{ds} (s - s_2)^2 Z(s) \tag{12.21}$$

If $Z(s)$ is a ratio of polynomials and has a pole of order n, then the part of the partial-fraction expansion due to that pole would have the form

$$\frac{A_1}{s - s_i} + \frac{A_2}{(s - s_i)^2} + \frac{A_3}{(s - s_i)^3} + \cdots + \frac{A_n}{(s - s_i)^n} \tag{12.22}$$

Thus the partial-fraction expansion can be written

$$Z(s) = \frac{A_1}{s - s_i} + \frac{A_2}{(s - s_i)^2} + \cdots + \frac{A_n}{(s - s_i)^n} + F(s) \tag{12.23}$$

where $F(s)$ is that part of the expansion due to all other poles of $Z(s)$. To evaluate the A coefficients, both sides of Equation 12.23 are multiplied by $(s - s_i)^n$ to produce

$$(s - s_i)^n Z(s) = (s - s_i)^{n-1} A_1 + (s - s_i)^{n-2} A_2 + \cdots$$
$$+ (s - s_i) A_{n-1} + A_n + (s - s_i)^n F(s) \tag{12.24}$$

From Equation 12.24,

$$A_n = \lim_{s \to s_i} (s - s_i)^n Z(s)$$

If both sides are differentiated with respect to s, the following expression is obtained:

$$\frac{d}{ds}[(s - s_i)^n Z(s)] = (n - 1)(s - s_i)^{n-2} A_1 + (n - 2)(s - s_i)^{n-3} A_2 + \cdots + A_{n-1}$$

$$+ (s - s_i)^{n-1}\left[(n - 1)F(s) + (s - s_i)\frac{d}{ds}F(s)\right] \qquad (12.25)$$

By taking the limit as $s \to s_i$, we obtain

$$A_{n-1} = \lim_{s \to s_i} \frac{d}{ds}[(s - s_i)^n Z(s)] \qquad (12.26)$$

Another differentiation with respect to s allows us to evaluate A_{n-2} as

$$A_{n-2} = \frac{1}{2!} \lim_{s \to s_i} \frac{d^2}{ds^2}[(s - s_i)^n Z(s)] \qquad (12.27)$$

This procedure can be repeated until after $n - 1$ differentiations we have

$$(n - 1)!A_1 = \lim_{s \to s_i} \frac{d^{(n-1)}}{ds^{(n-1)}}[(s - s_i)^n Z(s)] \qquad (12.28)$$

Example 12.20

We consider the partial-fraction expansion of

$$Z(s) = \frac{10(s + 1)}{s^2(s + 2)^2(s + 3)}$$

$Z(s)$ has a simple pole at $s = -3$ and second-order poles at $s = 0$ and $s = -2$. Thus the partial-fraction expansion of $Z(s)$ is of the form

$$Z(s) = \frac{A_1}{s} + \frac{A_2}{s^2} + \frac{B_1}{s + 2} + \frac{B_2}{(s + 2)^2} + \frac{C_1}{s + 3}$$

$$C_1 = \lim_{s \to -3} (s + 3)Z(s) = \frac{10(-2)}{(-3)^2(-1)^2} = -\frac{20}{9}$$

$$A_2 = \lim_{s \to 0} \frac{10(s + 1)}{(s + 2)^2(s + 3)} = \frac{5}{6}$$

$$B_2 = \lim_{s \to -2} \frac{10(s + 1)}{s^2(s + 3)} = -\frac{5}{2}$$

The procedure for finding A_1 is now examined in more detail. For convenience in differentiating, we multiply out the denominator of $s^2Z(s)$:

$$A_1 = \lim_{s \to 0} \frac{d}{ds} \left[\frac{10(s + 1)}{s^3 + 7s^2 + 16s + 12} \right]$$

$$= 10 \lim_{s \to 0} \left[\frac{s^3 + 7s^2 + 16s + 12 - (s + 1)(3s^2 + 14s + 16)}{(s^3 + 7s^2 + 16s + 12)^2} \right]$$

$$= 10 \left(\frac{12 - 16}{12^2} \right) = \frac{-40}{144} = \frac{-5}{18}$$

By a similar procedure, we find

$$B_1 = 10 \lim_{s \to -2} \left[\frac{s^3 + 3s^2 - (s + 1)(3s^2 + 6s)}{(s^3 + 3s^2)^2} \right]$$

$$= \frac{5}{2}$$

Thus

$$Z(s) = \frac{5}{18} \left[-\frac{1}{s} + \frac{3}{s^2} + \frac{9}{s + 2} - \frac{9}{(s + 2)^2} - \frac{8}{s + 3} \right]$$

In those *special cases for which there is only one second-order pole* the differentiation procedure may be avoided by the following approach. Suppose the partial-fraction expansion of a function $Z(s)$ is of the form

$$Z(s) = \frac{A_1}{s - s_1} + \frac{A_2}{(s - s_1)^2} + F(s) \tag{12.29}$$

where $F(s)$ includes all terms not associated with the second-order pole s_1. The coefficients of $F(s)$ are easily obtained, since they are associated with simple poles. With those coefficients known, we can obtain A_1 by multiplying Equation 12.29 by s and letting $s \to \infty$:

$$\lim_{s \to \infty} sZ(s) = A_1 + \sum \text{coefficients of } F(s) \tag{12.30}$$

If, as is often the case, the degree of the numerator of $Z(s)$ is at least two less than the degree of the denominator, then

$$\lim_{s \to \infty} sZ(s) = 0$$

which simplifies the procedure still more. From the discussion of this procedure it should be clear that it will work for the case of more than one second-order pole provided all except one of the coefficients of the fractions of first degree are known.

Example 12.21

Suppose that for the function

$$Z(s) = \frac{10(s + 1)}{s^2(s + 2)^2(s + 3)}$$

of Example 12.20 we know

$$A_1 = -\frac{5}{18} \quad \text{and} \quad C_1 = -\frac{20}{9}$$

Then, using our shortcut procedure, we obtain

$$B_1 = \lim_{s \to \infty} sZ(s) - \left(-\frac{5}{18} - \frac{20}{9}\right)$$

$$= \lim_{s \to \infty} \frac{10(s + 1)}{s(s + 2)^2(s + 3)} + \frac{45}{18}$$

$$= \frac{5}{2}$$

12.10 TIME-DOMAIN SOLUTIONS FROM s-DOMAIN SOLUTIONS

The use of the partial-fraction expansion to obtain the t-domain solution is justified on the basis that the Laplace transform is linear, that is, by the definition

$$\mathcal{L}\{f_1(t) + f_2(t) + f_3(t)\} = \int_0^\infty [f_1(t) + f_2(t) + f_3(t)]e^{-st}\, dt$$

$$= \int_0^\infty f_1(t)e^{-st}\, dt + \int_0^\infty f_2(t)e^{-st}\, dt$$

$$+ \int_0^\infty f_3(t)e^{-st}\, dt$$

$$= \mathcal{L}\{f_1(t)\} + \mathcal{L}\{f_2(t)\} + \mathcal{L}\{f_3(t)\}$$

Therefore, if we can express the Laplace-transformed function as a sum of s-domain functions, each of which is a Laplace transform, we can evaluate the inverse transform term by term. For linear electric networks the s-domain solutions characteristically have the form of a ratio of polynomials. For this s-domain form of solution, the t-domain solution can always be found by the partial-fraction expansion, provided the s-domain source functions are ratios of polynomials and the poles of the s-domain solution can be found. Each term in the partial-fraction expansion is of the type

$$\frac{A_n}{(s - s_i)^n}$$

Transform pairs 7 and 3 of Table 12.1 indicate that

$$\mathcal{L}^{-1}\left\{\frac{A_n}{(s - s_i)^n}\right\} = e^{s_i t}\,\mathcal{L}^{-1}\left\{\frac{A_n}{s^n}\right\} = e^{s_i t}\,\frac{(t^{n-1})}{(n - 1)!} \qquad (12.31)$$

For the special case $n = 1$, the general result of Equation 12.31 reduces to

$$\mathcal{L}^{-1}\left\{\frac{A_1}{s - s_i}\right\} = A_1 e^{s_i t}$$

Example 12.22 ──

The t-domain solution for the s-domain function of Example 12.20,

$$Z(s) = \frac{10(s + 1)}{s^2(s + 2)^2(s + 3)}$$

$$= \frac{5}{18}\left[-\frac{1}{s} + \frac{3}{s_2} + \frac{9}{s + 2} - \frac{9}{(s + 2)^2} - \frac{8}{s + 3}\right]$$

is

$$z(t) = \frac{5}{18}(-1 + 3t + 9e^{-2t} - 9te^{-2t} - 8e^{-3t}) \qquad \text{for } t > 0$$

──

The time function

$$e^{-at}(k_1 \cos \omega t + k_2 \sin \omega t) \qquad (12.32)$$

occurs so often in physical-system analysis that it warrants some special comment. Solutions of the form Equation 12.32 occur when the s-domain solution has complex poles. When these occur, the part of the partial-fraction expansion due to these poles can be written

$$\frac{\bar{A}}{s - \bar{s}_1} + \frac{\bar{A}^*}{s - \bar{s}_1^*} = \frac{A_1 + jA_2}{s + a - j\omega} + \frac{A_1 - jA_2}{s + a + j\omega} \qquad (12.33)$$

where the overbar denotes a complex number and the asterisk indicates the complex conjugate.

The s-domain functions of Equation 12.33 can be transformed to the t-domain directly and combined to obtain the real function required in the

t-domain. Because of its frequency of occurrence, however, it may be advantageous to combine the two terms of Equation 12.33 in the s-domain to obtain

$$\frac{2[A_1(s + a) - A_2\omega]}{(s + a)^2 + \omega^2} \tag{12.34}$$

The inverse transform for Equation 12.34 is, by transform pairs 10 and 11 of Table 12.1,

$$2e^{-at}(A_1 \cos \omega t - A_2 \sin \omega t) \tag{12.35}$$

Example 12.23 ───

Given the s-domain function

$$Z(s) = \frac{s + 6}{s^2 + 4s + 85}$$

Instead of using the partial-fraction expansion, we complete the square in the denominator and arrange terms to obtain the form of Equation 12.34:

$$Z(s) = \frac{(s + 2) + 4}{(s + 2)^2 + 81}$$

$$\mathcal{L}^{-1}\{Z(s)\} = e^{-2t}(\cos 9t + \frac{4}{9} \sin 9t)$$

───

One further comment is in order. It is evident that with some experience, the solution (Equation 12.35) could be written directly from the partial-fraction expansion, Equation 12.33. In general, however, tables are used in practical application, and any special effort to commit any except for the most elementary transforms to memory is not worthwhile. It is usually more rewarding to concentrate on the more fundamental aspects of inversion by partial-fraction expansion.

From Examples 12.22 and 12.23, we observe several relationships between the s-domain and t-domain solutions that prove to be useful in network analysis and design. Each term of a partial-fraction expansion can always be put in the form

$$F_i(s) = \frac{A}{(s - p)^n} \qquad n = 1, 2, 3, \ldots \tag{12.36}$$

where A and the pole p may be real or complex. The corresponding t-domain solution is

$$f_i(t) = Ae^{pt} \frac{t^{n-1}}{(n - 1)!} \equiv Be^{pt}t^{n-1}$$

If we let p be complex,

$$p = \sigma + j\omega$$

then we can say that for $n = 1$,

$$f_i(t) = Ae^{\sigma t}e^{j\omega t} = Ae^{\sigma t}(\cos \omega t + j \sin \omega t)$$

$$\lim_{t \to \infty} |f_i(t)| = \begin{cases} 0 & \sigma < 0 \\ |A| & \sigma = 0 \\ \infty & \sigma > 0 \end{cases} \tag{12.37}$$

For $n \geq 2$,

$$f_i(t) = \frac{A}{(n-1)!} t^{n-1}e^{\sigma t}e^{j\omega t} = Bt^{n-1}e^{\sigma t}(\cos \omega t + j \sin \omega t)$$

and

$$\lim_{t \to \infty} |f_i(t)| = \begin{cases} 0 & \sigma < 0 \\ \infty & \sigma \geq 0 \end{cases} \tag{12.38}$$

If the pole p is real, Equations 12.37 and 12.38 still hold, of course, since $|e^{j\omega t}| = 1$ for any finite value of ω.

The function $f_i(t)$ is said to be *absolutely stable* if its magnitude tends to zero as t becomes large. It is said to be *unstable* if its magnitude is unbounded as t approaches ∞ and *conditionally stable* if its magnitude remains bounded.

Using these definitions, we see that for a t-domain solution corresponding to an s-domain term of the form of Equation 12.36, the solution is *absolutely stable* for the real part of p negative ($\sigma < 0$) and *unstable* for the real part of p positive ($\sigma > 0$).

Example 12.24

For the rational function $Z(s)$ of Example 12.23, the poles are $p_1 = -2 + j9$ and $p_2 = -2 - j9$. Since the real parts of both poles are negative, $z(t)$ is absolutely stable. We can confirm this by examining the behavior of $|z(t)|$ as $t \to \infty$. If the denominator of $Z(s)$ were $(s - 2)^2 + 81$, then $p_1 = 2 + j9$ and $p_2 = 2 - j9$ and the solution would be unstable.

12.11 SOLUTION OF SIMULTANEOUS DIFFERENTIAL EQUATIONS

The Laplace transform of a linear ordinary differential equation with constant coefficients is a linear algebraic equation with s-domain variables and coefficients that are polynomials in s. Linear algebra may be used to obtain the s-domain solution for a set of transformed simultaneous equations of this type. The t-domain solution can then be obtained by the methods of the previous sections.

The following example demonstrates the procedure for solving two simultaneous differential equations. There is a direct extension to any number of simultaneous equations.

Example 12.25

Consider the two equations

$$\frac{d}{dt} x_1(t) + x_1(t) + x_2(t) = u(t) \qquad x_1(0^-) = 0$$

$$\frac{d}{dt} x_2(t) + 3x_2(t) + 2x_1(t) = 0 \qquad x_2(0^-) = 2$$

(12.39)

The Laplace-transformed equations are

$$(s + 1)X_1(s) + X_2(s) = \frac{1}{s}$$

$$2X_1(s) + (s + 3)X_2(s) = 2$$

By Cramer's rule the solution is

$$X_1(s) = \frac{-s + 3}{s(s^2 + 4s + 1)}$$

$$X_2(s) = \frac{2(s^2 + s - 1)}{s(s^2 + 4s + 1)}$$

(12.40)

and by use of the partial-fraction expansion, we have the s-domain solution in a convenient form for inversion.

$$X_1(s) = \frac{k_1}{s} + \frac{k_2}{s + 3.732} + \frac{k_3}{s + 0.268}$$

$$X_2(s) = \frac{k_4}{s} + \frac{k_5}{s + 3.732} + \frac{k_6}{s + 0.268}$$

(12.41)

For $t > 0$, the corresponding t-domain solution in vector form is

$$\begin{bmatrix} x_1(t) \\ x_2(t) \end{bmatrix} = \begin{bmatrix} k_1 \\ k_4 \end{bmatrix} + \begin{bmatrix} k_2 \\ k_5 \end{bmatrix} e^{-3.732t} + \begin{bmatrix} k_3 \\ k_6 \end{bmatrix} e^{-0.268t}$$

(12.42)

The calculation of the constants is left to the problems. In Equation 12.42, the constant vector is the steady-state solution of Equation 12.39 for the constant forcing function u. The other two vectors make up the transient solution. In Section 9.2 we discussed a technique for finding the steady-state solution for

constant forcing functions by setting the *t*-derivatives equal to zero and ignoring initial conditions.

We now turn to an example of the use of the Laplace transform in finding
the steady-state solution to simultaneous differential equations with sinusoidal
forcing functions.

Example 12.26

Suppose we are given the differential equations of Example 12.25 except that
the constant source is replaced by a sinusoidal forcing function. In matrix
state-model form, we have

$$\begin{bmatrix} \dfrac{d}{dt}x_1(t) \\ \dfrac{d}{dt}x_2(t) \end{bmatrix} = \begin{bmatrix} -1 & -1 \\ -2 & -3 \end{bmatrix}\begin{bmatrix} x_1(t) \\ x_2(t) \end{bmatrix} + \begin{bmatrix} 5\cos 10t \\ 0 \end{bmatrix} \tag{12.43}$$

$$x_1(0) = 0, x_2(0^-) = 2$$

After taking the Laplace transform, Equation 12.43 becomes

$$\begin{bmatrix} sX_1(s) \\ sX_2(s) \end{bmatrix} - \begin{bmatrix} 0 \\ 2 \end{bmatrix} = \begin{bmatrix} -1 & -1 \\ -2 & -3 \end{bmatrix}\begin{bmatrix} X_1(s) \\ X_2(s) \end{bmatrix} + \begin{bmatrix} \dfrac{5s}{s^2 + 100} \\ 0 \end{bmatrix} \tag{12.44}$$

Separating the knowns and unknowns in Equation 12.44 yields

$$\begin{bmatrix} (s+1) & 1 \\ 2 & (s+3) \end{bmatrix}\begin{bmatrix} X_1(s) \\ X_2(s) \end{bmatrix} = \begin{bmatrix} \dfrac{5s}{s^2+100} \\ 2 \end{bmatrix} \tag{12.45}$$

The solution by Cramer's rule is

$$\begin{bmatrix} X_1(s) \\ X_2(s) \end{bmatrix} = \dfrac{1}{\Delta(s)}\begin{bmatrix} (s+3) & -1 \\ -2 & (s+1) \end{bmatrix}\begin{bmatrix} \dfrac{5s}{s^2+100} \\ 2 \end{bmatrix} \tag{12.46}$$

where $\Delta(s) = s^2 + 4s + 1$.

After multiplying out Equation 12.46 and factoring $s^2 + 100$, we have

$$\begin{bmatrix} X_1(s) \\ X_2(s) \end{bmatrix} = \begin{bmatrix} \dfrac{5s(s+3)}{\Delta(s)(s+j10)(s-j10)} \\ \dfrac{-10s}{\Delta(s)(s+j10)(s-j10)} \end{bmatrix} + \dfrac{2}{\Delta(s)}\begin{bmatrix} -1 \\ s+1 \end{bmatrix} \tag{12.47}$$

It should be clear that the right-hand vector of Equation 12.47 is due to the initial condition and thus is part of the transient solution. Therefore, we concentrate on the left-hand solution vector, which contains the steady state. If we neglect the initial condition, Equation 12.47 yields for X_1

$$X_1(s) = \frac{5s(s + 3)}{(s^2 + 4s + 1)(s + j10)(s - j10)}$$

$$= \frac{k_1}{s - j10} + \frac{k_2}{s + j10} + \frac{k_3}{s + 3.732} + \frac{k_4}{s + 0.268} \qquad (12.48)$$

It should be clear that k_3 and k_4 are associated with the transient solution, so our objective is to find k_1 and k_2. Let the subscript s denote steady-state solution. Then

$$X_{1s}(s) = \frac{k_1}{s - j10} + \frac{k_2}{s + j10} \qquad (12.49)$$

From Equation 12.48 we find

$$k_1 = \lim_{s \to j10} \frac{5s(s + 3)}{(s^2 + 4s + 1)(s + j10)} = \frac{j50(3 + j10)}{(-99 + j40)(j20)}$$

$$= \frac{5}{2} \frac{(3 + j10)}{(-99 + j40)} = 0.02259 - j0.2434 \qquad (12.50)$$

and

$$k_2 = \lim_{s \to -j10} \frac{5s(s + 3)}{(s^2 + 4s + 1)(s - j10)} = \frac{-j50(3 - j10)}{(-99 - j40)(-j20)}$$

$$= \frac{5}{2} \frac{(3 - j10)}{(-99 - j40)} = 0.02259 + j0.2434$$

$$= k_1^* \qquad (12.51)$$

We note that k_2 is the conjugate of k_1. This is not a coincidence but is a general result for partial-fraction coefficients for denominator terms of the form $(s^2 + \omega^2) = (s - j\omega)(s + j\omega)$. Thus the calculation for k_2 can serve as a check on the accuracy of the calculation of k_1. The generality of this result can be recognized by noting that every factor in the calculation of k_2 is the complex conjugate of that for k_1 when $j\omega$ is substituted for s.

We now put the s-domain steady-state solution for x_1 in a form convenient for inversion, using Equation 12.34.

$$X_{1s}(s) = \frac{0.02259 - j0.2434}{s - j10} + \frac{0.02259 + j0.2434}{s + j10}$$

$$= \frac{0.04518s}{s^2 + 100} + \frac{0.4868(10)}{s^2 + 100} \qquad (12.52)$$

The corresponding t-domain function is

$$X_{1s}(t) = 0.04518 \cos 10t + 0.4868 \sin 10t$$

$$= 0.04518 \cos 10t + 0.4868 \cos(10t - 90°)$$

$$= 0.4889 \cos(10t - 84.7°) \tag{12.53}$$

To find the steady-state solution for x_2, we use the same procedure; this yields

$$X_2(s) = \frac{-10s}{(s^2 + 4s + 1)(s^2 + 100)} \tag{12.54}$$

$$= \frac{k_5}{s - j10} + \frac{k_6}{s + j10} + \frac{k_7}{s + 3.732} + \frac{k_8}{s + 0.268}$$

from Equation 12.47 when the initial condition is ignored. The steady-state part of Equation 12.54 is

$$X_{2s}(s) = \frac{k_5}{s - j10} + \frac{k_6}{s + j10} \tag{12.55}$$

where

$$k_5 = \lim_{s \to j10} \frac{-10s}{(s^2 + 4s + 1)(s + j10)} = 0.0434 + j0.0175$$

and

$$k_6 = k_5^* = 0.0434 - j0.0175$$

Thus

$$X_{2s}(s) = \frac{0.0868s}{(s^2 + 100)} - \frac{0.035(10)}{(s^2 + 100)} \tag{12.56}$$

from which the t-domain solution is

$$X_{2s}(t) = 0.0868 \cos 10t - 0.035 \sin 10t$$

$$= 0.0936 \cos(10t + 22°) \tag{12.57}$$

12.12   SINUSOIDAL STEADY-STATE SOLUTIONS

As we saw in Example 12.26, the sinusoidal steady-state solution for one or more differential equations may be calculated by finding the partial-fraction terms in the s-domain solutions that correspond to the source function or functions. We now apply this solution technique to justify the phasor-model approach introduced in Section 9.3.

The term *transfer function* was introduced in Section 9.9 as the ratio of an output to an input variable in the ω-domain. In electric network theory, these variables are normally either $\bar{I}(j\omega)$ or $\bar{V}(j\omega)$ and the transfer function is a ratio of polynomials in the variable $j\omega$. The concept of transfer function applies equally well to Laplace-transformed (s-domain) network models (also with initial conditions ignored).

For a network with one input voltage, $v_i(t)$, and one output voltage, $v_o(t)$, the s-domain transfer relationship can be written as

$$V_o(s) = G(s)V_i(s) \tag{12.58}$$

The transfer function $G(s)$ will be a *rational function*—that is, a ratio of polynomials with real coefficients. This is our reason for discussing the partial-fraction expansion of such functions.

In Example 12.26, the s-domain solution shown as Equation 12.47 illustrates how the concept of transfer function can be applied to the Laplace transform of a pair of differential equations with a forcing function. If $x_1(t)$ is taken as the output variable and $(5 \cos 10t)$ is the input function, then—for initial conditions set to zero—the transfer relationship is

$$X_1(s) = \left[\frac{(s + 3)}{(s^2 + 4s + 1)}\right]\left[\frac{5s}{s^2 + 100^2}\right] \tag{12.59}$$

where the transfer function

$$G_1(s) = \frac{(s + 3)}{s^2 + 4s + 1} \tag{12.60}$$

is a ratio of polynomials with real coefficients.

For the relationship between the variable $X_2(s)$ and the forcing function (input), we have

$$X_2(s) = \left(\frac{-2}{s^2 + 4s + 1}\right)\left(\frac{5s}{s^2 + 100}\right) \tag{12.61}$$

where the transfer function is

$$G_2(s) = \frac{-2}{s^2 + 4s + 1} \tag{12.62}$$

In defining both transfer functions, we have ignored initial conditions—or the equivalent, set them to zero. In fact, the very definition of transfer function implies that response due to initial conditions is not included. Otherwise we could not get a simple linear relationship between s-domain input and output variables. Therefore, the procedure used in this special case can be extended to the general case.

To begin our justification of the phasor method, we assume a transfer function relationship

$$X(s) = G(s)F(s)$$

between a network input $F(s)$ and an output $X(s)$. The transfer function $G(s)$ is a ratio of polynomials with real coefficients.

$$G(s) = \frac{N(s)}{D(s)}$$

Next we assume that

$$f(t) = F_m \cos \omega t$$

so that

$$F(s) = \frac{sF_m}{s^2 + \omega^2}$$

For this case,

$$X(s) = \frac{N(s)}{D(s)} \cdot \frac{sF_m}{s^2 + \omega^2} = \frac{\bar{A}}{s - j\omega} + \frac{\bar{A}^*}{s + j\omega} + \text{other terms} \quad (12.63)$$

where the other terms are due to the zeros of $D(s)$ and do not contribute to the steady-state solution. (If $D(s)$ has a factor $(s^2 + \omega^2)$, a problem in defining steady state arises, but we assume that this is not the case.) The t-domain steady-state solution for Equation 12.63 is

$$x_{ss}(t) = \bar{A}e^{j\omega t} + \bar{A}^*e^{-j\omega t} \quad (12.64)$$

where

$$\bar{A} = \lim_{s \to j\omega} \frac{N(s)}{D(s)} \cdot \frac{sF_m}{(s + j\omega)}$$

$$= \frac{N(j\omega)}{2D(j\omega)} F_m = \frac{G(j\omega)}{2} F_m \quad (12.65)$$

It follows that

$$\bar{A}^* = \frac{G(-j\omega)}{2} F_m \quad (12.66)$$

Now we represent the transfer function

$$G(j\omega) = \frac{N(j\omega)}{D(j\omega)} = |G(j\omega)| e^{j\theta(j\omega)} = G_1(j\omega) + jG_2(j\omega)$$

where $G_1(j\omega)$ and $G_2(j\omega)$ are real functions and $\theta = \tan^{-1}[G_2(j\omega)/G_1(j\omega)]$.

Since $G(s)$ is a rational function, $G(-j\omega) = G^*(j\omega) = |G(j\omega)|e^{-j\theta(j\omega)}$. Therefore, the solution of Equation 12.64 can be written as

$$x_{ss}(t) = \frac{F_m}{2}[G(j\omega)e^{j\omega t} + G(-j\omega)e^{-j\omega t}]$$

$$= \frac{F_m|G(j\omega)|}{2}(e^{j\omega t}e^{j\theta(j\omega)} + e^{-j\omega t}e^{-j\theta(j\omega)}) \qquad (12.67)$$

By use of Euler's relationship, Equation 12.67 can be written in the form

$$x_{ss}(t) = F_m|G(j\omega)| \cos[\omega t + \theta(j\omega)] \qquad (12.68)$$

In deriving Equation 12.68, we went through a set of steps remarkably similar to those discussed in our introduction to phasors in Chapter 9. To clarify the relationship, we now solve the same problem by a slightly different approach.

Suppose we consider a source function

$$f_1(t) = F_m e^{j\omega t}$$

instead of

$$f(t) = F_m \cos \omega t$$

Clearly, $f_1(t)$ is a complex function for which the angle is ωt. By Euler's relation,

$$f_1(t) = F_m(\cos \omega t + j \sin \omega t)$$

so it seems reasonable that if we find the steady-state solution for

$$X_1(s) = G(s)F_1(s) \qquad (12.69)$$

the real part of the solution should correspond to Equation 12.67 and the imaginary part should correspond to a function $F_m \sin \omega t$. In this case, what seems reasonable is correct and can be deduced by superposition.

Let us now derive the steady-state solution to Equation 12.69. First we have

$$X_1(s) = G(s)\frac{F_m}{s - j\omega} = \frac{\bar{B}}{s - j\omega} + \text{other terms}$$

from which

$$X_{1ss}(s) = \frac{\bar{B}}{s - j\omega}$$

By the partial-fraction expansion,

$$\bar{B} = \lim_{s \to j\omega} F_m G(s) = F_m G(j\omega)$$

$$= F_m |G(j\omega)| e^{j\theta(j\omega)} \qquad (12.70)$$

and the *t*-domain steady-state solution is

$$\bar{X}_{1ss}(t) = F_m \left| G(j\omega) \right| e^{j[\omega t + \theta(j\omega)]} \tag{12.71}$$

Using Euler's relation, we can write Equation 12.71 in the form

$$\bar{X}_{1ss}(t) = F_m \left| G(j\omega) \right| \{\cos[\omega t + \theta(j\omega)] + j \sin[\omega t + \theta(j\omega)]\} \tag{12.72}$$

which shows that the solution of Equation 12.68 is just the real part of the solution of Equation 12.72.

We can summarize these results as follows:

1. The steady-state response at any branch of a network due to a single sinusoidal source is also sinusoidal in form.

2. The amplitude of the response is the product of the source amplitude and the magnitude of the transfer function $G(j\omega)$.

3. The phase angle of the response is the sum of the source phase angle and the angle of $G(j\omega)$.

Equation 12.71 is the time-variable phasor solution that corresponds to Equation 12.68. The complex constant $\bar{B}$ of Equation 12.70 is the corresponding constant phasor. We carried out the solution by means of Laplace transform techniques, but the result is exactly the same as if we had used the phasor procedures of Chapter 9.

Now we demonstrate an application of the phasor technique to the steady-state solution for simultaneous linear differential equations with a sinusoidal forcing function.

Example 12.27

Let us consider the phasor solution to the differential equations of Example 12.26. The *s*-domain transfer function for $\bar{X}_1(s)$ is

$$G_1(s) = \frac{s + 3}{s^2 + 4s + 1}$$

and the forcing function is $5 \cos 10t$. Thus the time-varying phasor solution is

$$\bar{X}_1(t) = G_1(j10)5e^{j10t}$$

$$= \frac{5(3 + j10)}{-99 + j40} e^{j10t}$$

$$= (0.04517 - j0.4868)e^{j10t}$$

$$= 0.4889 \, e^{j(10t - 84.7°)} \tag{12.73}$$

Now we note that both the magnitudes and the phase angles of $\bar{X}_1(t)$ (Equation 12.73) and $X_{1s}(t)$ (Equation 12.53) are the same.

For $X_2(s)$ the transfer function is

$$G_2(s) = \frac{-2}{s^2 + 4s + 1}$$

Since the forcing function is the same, the time-varying phasor solution is

$$\bar{X}_2(t) = [G_2(j10)]5e^{j10t}$$

$$= \frac{-10}{-99 + j40}\, e^{j10t}$$

$$= (0.0868 + j0.0351)e^{j10t}$$

$$= 0.0936e^{j(10t + 22°)} \tag{12.74}$$

which checks in magnitude and phase the solution shown as Equation 12.56.

The approach taken in this section, using the Laplace transform to find the sinusoidal steady-state solution, can be generalized to other types of periodic forcing functions. The transfer function relationship

$$X(s) = G(s)F(s)$$

is written in a partial-fraction expansion. Then those terms in the expansion that correspond to the poles of $F(s)$ make up the s-domain steady-state solution. The inverse transform yields the t-domain steady-state solution.

12.13   CONVOLUTION

Quite often the s-domain solution of a network model may be obtained in the form

$$X(s) = G(s)F(s)$$

where $G(s)$ is a ratio of polynomials and $F(s)$ is the Laplace transform of a source. If the inverse transform for the transform function $g(t) = \mathcal{L}^{-1}\{G(s)\}$ is known, then the t-domain solution $x(t) = \mathcal{L}^{-1}\{X(s)\}$ can be found from the convolution integral. In this case,

$$x(t) = \mathcal{L}^{-1}\{G(s)F(s)\} = \int_0^t g(u)f(t - u)\, du \tag{12.75}$$

The relationship can be proved as follows: Let

$$x(t) = \int_0^t g(u)f(t - u) \, du$$

where u is a variable of integration (not related to the unit step function). Then

$$X(s) = \int_C^\infty \left[\int_0^t g(u)f(t - u) \, du \right] e^{-st} \, dt \tag{12.76}$$

Now $f(t - u) = 0$ for $t - u < 0$, which corresponds to $u > t$. Therefore, $x(t)$ can be written

$$x(t) = \int_0^\infty g(u)f(t - u) \, du$$

and

$$X(s) = \int_0^\infty \left[\int_0^\infty g(u)f(t - u) \, du \right] e^{-st} \, dt \tag{12.77}$$

Now we change the order of integration and note that, since $f(t - u) = 0$ for $t < u$, the double integral can be written

$$X(s) = \int_0^\infty g(u) \left[\int_u^\infty f(t - u)e^{-st} \, dt \right] du \tag{12.78}$$

We now use the substitution $\lambda = t - u$ to get the inside integral into a convenient form. The change of variable yields $t = u + \lambda$ and $dt = d\lambda$. At the upper limit, $t = \infty \to \lambda = \infty$, and at the lower limit $t = u \to \lambda = 0$. Thus

$$X(s) = \int_0^\infty g(u) \left[\int_0^\infty f(\lambda) \, e^{-s\lambda} \, d\lambda \right] e^{-su} \, du$$

$$= \left[\int_0^\infty g(u)e^{-su} \, du \right] \left[\int_0^\infty f(\lambda)e^{-s\lambda} \, d\lambda \right]$$

$$= G(s) \cdot F(s) \tag{12.79}$$

If the change of variable $\lambda = t - u$ is made in Equation 12.75, we produce

$$x(t) = \int_0^t g(t - \lambda)f(\lambda) \, d\lambda \equiv \int_0^t g(u)f(t - u) \, du \tag{12.80}$$

(How do you justify the fact that the limits are the same?)

Suppose we symbolize the convolution of $g(t)$ and $f(t)$ as

$$g(t) * f(t) \doteq \int_0^t g(u)f(t - u) \, dt \tag{12.81}$$

From Equation 12.80, it should be clear that

$$g(t) * f(t) = f(t) * g(t)$$

Example 12.28

For the simple RC network of Figure 12.1, the state equation is

$$\frac{dv_c}{dt} = -2v_c + 2e(t) \qquad (12.82)$$

Figure 12.1
Network for Example
12.28.

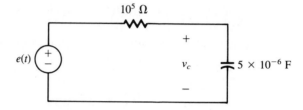

If we assume that the initial capacitor voltage is zero, the Laplace-transformed equation becomes

$$(s + 2)V_c(s) = 2E(s) \qquad (12.83)$$

and

$$V_c(s) = \left(\frac{2}{s + 2}\right)E(s) \qquad (12.84)$$

Suppose we designate

$$G(s) = \frac{2}{s + 2}$$

Then $g(t) = 2e^{-2t}$. Using the convolution integral, we can calculate the response of the network to various voltage excitation functions.

First we assume a very simple source function $e(t) = 50e^{-t}$. The response of the network capacitor voltage can be found from

$$v_c(t) = \mathscr{L}^{-1}\left\{\left(\frac{2}{s + 2}\right)\left(\frac{50}{s + 1}\right)\right\} \qquad (12.85)$$

Using the convolution integral, we find the solution as follows:

$$v_c(t) = 100 \int_0^t e^{-2u}e^{-(t-u)}\,du$$

$$= 100e^{-t}\int_0^t e^{-2u}\,e^u\,du$$

$$= -100e^{-t}e^{-u}\Big|_0^t = -100(e^{-2t} - e^{-t})$$

$$= 100(e^{-t} - e^{-2t}) \qquad (12.86)$$

This solution can be checked by using Equation 12.85.

Example 12.29

As a second example we assume that $e(t) = 50[u(t) - u(t - 10)]$. The Laplace-transform solution is

$$v_c(t) = \mathscr{L}^{-1}\left\{\left(\frac{2}{s + 2}\right)\frac{50}{s}(1 - e^{-10s})\right\} \tag{12.87}$$

Using the convolution integral, we obtain the following solution:

$$v_c(t) = 100\int_0^t e^{-2(t-x)}[u(x) - u(x - 10)]\,dx$$

$$= 100e^{-2t}\int_0^t e^{2x}\,dx$$

$$= 100e^{-2t}\left(\frac{e^{2x}}{2}\right)\Big|_0^t$$

$$= 50e^{-2t}(e^{2t} - 1)$$

$$= 50(1 - e^{-2t}) \qquad 0 < t < 10 \tag{12.88}$$

For $t > 10$, the convolution integral becomes

$$v_c(t) = 100e^{-2t}\int_0^{10} e^{2x}\,dx$$

$$= 100e^{-2t}\left(\frac{e^{2x}}{2}\right)\Big|_0^{10}$$

$$= 50e^{-2t}(e^{20} - 1)$$

$$\cong 50e^{-2(t-10)} \qquad t > 10 \tag{12.89}$$

The solution represented by Equations 12.88 and 12.89 can be found by taking the Laplace transform inverse shown as Equation 12.87. The result is usually written as

$$v_c(t) = 50[(1 - e^{-2t})u(t) - (1 - e^{-2(t-10)})u(t - 10)] \tag{12.90}$$

Confirmation of the equivalence of the two solutions is left as an exercise.

12.14 SUMMARY

Ordinary linear equations with constant coefficients can be changed into linear algebraic equations by use of the Laplace transform. We say in network analysis—where t is the independent variable—that this transformation carries the mathematical model from the t-domain to the s-domain.

Linear algebra may be used to obtain the s-domain solution for the transformed model. In many cases, enough information is available directly from the s-domain solution so that the inverse transform need not be taken. These cases are not discussed here, but they arise in connection with electronic-network and feedback-control system design, as well as in other applications.

To obtain the t-domain solution from the equivalent s-domain solution, the method of partial-fraction expansion is widely used. The method applies to all s-domain solutions that are ratios of polynomials in s. In linear network analysis, the s-domain solutions are always ratios of polynomials if the Laplace transform of each source is a ratio of polynomials.

REFERENCES

1. Churchill, R. V., J. W. Brown, and R. F. Verhey, *Complex Variables and Applications,* 3rd ed. New York: McGraw-Hill, 1974.
2. Karni, S., *Intermediate Network Analysis.* Boston: Allyn and Bacon, 1971, Appendix B.
3. LePage, W., *Complex Variables and the Laplace Transform for Engineers.* New York: McGraw-Hill, 1961.
4. McGillem, C. D., and G. R. Cooper, *Continuous and Discrete Signal and System Analysis.* New York: Holt, Rinehart & Winston, 1974, Chapter 6.
5. Scott, R. E., *Linear Circuits.* Reading, Mass.: Addison-Wesley, 1960, Chapters 20–22.
6. Van Valkenburg, M. E., *Network Analysis.* Englewood Cliffs, N.J.: Prentice-Hall, 1974, Chapter 7.
7. Ziemer, R. E., W. H. Tranter, and D. R. Fannin, *Signals and Systems: Continuous and Discrete.* New York: Macmillan, 1983, Chapter 4.

PROBLEMS

12.1 Find the Laplace transform of the following functions by use of the integral definition: (a) t^2, (b) te^{at}, (c) $\sinh at$, (d) $tu(t - T)$, (e) $e^{at} \cos bt$, (f) $t \cos bt$, (g) $\cos(bt + \theta)$.

12.2 Use Theorem 12.1 to derive the Laplace transform of (a) $\cos(bt + \theta)$, (b) $\sinh at$, (c) $\cosh(bt + a)$, (d) $\sin at$.

12.3 Use Theorem 12.4 and Table 12.1 to find the Laplace transform of the following functions: (a) $e^{at} \sin(bt + \theta)$, (b) $e^{at}t^n$, (c) $e^{at} \cosh bt$.

12.4 Use Theorem 12.8 to show that

$$\frac{d^3}{dt^3}f(t) = s^3F(s) - s^2f(0^-) - sf'(0^-) - f''(0^-)$$

12.5 Laplace-transform the differential equation

$$2\frac{d^2}{dt^2}x(t) + 3\frac{d}{dt}x(t) + x(t) = \cos 10t$$

$$x(0^-) = 0 \qquad x'(0^-) = 10$$

and solve the resulting equation for $X(s)$.

12.6 Laplace-transform the equation
$$(d^3/dt^3)x + 5(d^2/dt^2)x + 6(d/dt)x = e^{-t}$$
with all zero initial conditions on x.

12.7 Laplace-transform the following state equations and solve for $V_1(s)$ and $V_2(s)$.

$$\frac{dv_1}{dt} = -2v_1 + v_2 + f_1(t)$$

$$\frac{dv_2}{dt} = v_1 - 2v_2 + f_2(t)$$

$$v_1(0^-) = 0 \qquad f_1(t) = e^{-t}$$
$$v_2(0^-) = 0 \qquad f_2(t) = 2\cos 5t$$

12.8 Repeat Problem 12.7 with the forcing functions set equal to zero and
$$v_1(0^-) = 10 \qquad v_2(0^-) = -5$$

12.9 Repeat Problem 12.7 with the forcing functions as shown but with the initial conditions of Problem 12.8.

12.10 Repeat Problem 12.7 for $f_1(t) = f_2(t) = u(t)$.

12.11 Use Theorem 9.9 to find the Laplace transform of

(a) $t^4 = \int_0^t 4\tau^3 \, d\tau$

(b) $(\cos \omega t - 1) = -\int_0^t (\sin \omega\tau)\omega \, d\tau$

12.12 Laplace-transform the following state equations and solve for $X_1(s)$ and $X_2(s)$.

$$\frac{dx_1}{dt} = -4x_1 + \frac{7}{2}x_2 + f_1(t)$$

$$\frac{dx_2}{dt} = 7x_1 - \frac{15}{2}x_2 + f_2(t)$$

$$x_1(0^-) = 50 \qquad f_1(t) = 0$$
$$x_2(0^-) = 0 \qquad f_2(t) = 0$$

12.13 Repeat Problem 12.12 for $f_1(t) = 10\cos 2t$, $x_1(0^-) = x_2(0^-) = f_2(t) = 0$.

12.14 Repeat Problem 12.12 for $f_1(t) = f_2(t) = x_1(0^-) = 0, x_2(0^-) = 100$.

12.15 Find the partial-fraction expansion of the following s-functions, and write the corresponding t-functions.

(a) $A(s) = \dfrac{10(s + 1)}{(s + 2)(s + 5)}$

(b) $A(s) = \dfrac{5}{s(s + 1)(s + 10)}$

(c) $A(s) = \dfrac{(s + 5)(s + 2)}{s(s + 1)(s + 3)(s + 4)}$

(d) $A(s) = \dfrac{s^2 + 1}{s^3 + 4s^2 + 3s}$

(e) $A(s) = \dfrac{s + 1}{(s + 1)^2 + 4}$

(f) $A(s) = \dfrac{K}{s^2 + 2s + 5}$

12.16 Use the shortcut method to evaluate the partial-fraction expansion for each.

(a) $G(s) = \dfrac{10(s + 1)}{(s + 2)^2(s + 5)}$

(b) $G(s) = \dfrac{10(s + 1)}{(s + 2)(s + 5)^2}$

(c) $G(s) = \dfrac{5}{s^2(s + 1)(s + 10)}$

(d) $G(s) = \dfrac{(s + 5)(s + 2)}{s(s + 1)(s + 3)(s + 4)^2}$

12.17 Find the partial-fraction expansion of the following s-functions, and write the corresponding t-functions.

(a) $F(s) = \dfrac{10(s + 1)}{(s + 2)^2(s + 5)^2}$

(b) $F(s) = \dfrac{10(s + 1)}{(s + 5)(s + 2)^2}$

(c) $F(s) = \dfrac{10}{s^2(s + 1)^2(s + 10)}$

12.18 Find the t-domain solution corresponding to the s-domain solution of Problem 12.5.

12.19 Find the t-domain solution corresponding to the s-domain solution of Problem 12.6.

12.20 Find the t-domain solution for Problem 12.7.

12.21 Find the t-domain solution for Problem 12.8.

12.22 Find the t-domain solution for Problem 12.9.

12.23 Find the t-domain solution for the equations of Problem 12.12 by use of the partial-fraction expansion of the solutions for $X_1(s)$ and $X_2(s)$.

12.24 Solve the following integrodifferential equations, using the Laplace transform $[x(0^-) = 0]$.

(a) $\quad 2\dfrac{d}{dt}x + 4x + \displaystyle\int_0^t x\,d\tau + 10 = 0$

(b) $\quad \dfrac{d}{dt}x + 2x + 5\displaystyle\int_0^t x\,d\tau - 5 = \cos 10t$

12.25 Find the t-domain solution for Problem 12.13.

12.26 Find the t-domain solution for Problem 12.14.

12.27 Use the partial-fraction expansion technique to find the constants k_i in the solution to Example 12.25.

12.28 Find the solution to the following pair of differential equations by use of the Laplace transform:

$$(p^2 + 4p + 1)v_1(t) + 2pv_2(t) = 0$$

$$2pv_1(t) + pv_2(t) = u(t)$$

$$v_1'(0^-) = 0$$

$$v_1(0^-) = 0$$

$$v_2(0^-) = 0$$

where p is the t-derivative operator.

12.29 Find the solution to the differential equations of Problem 12.28 except that the initial conditions are changed to $v_1'(0^-) = -2$, $v_2(0^-) = 1$, $v_1(0^-) = 0$.

12.30 Given a transfer function

$$G(s) = \frac{10(s + 1)}{(s + 2)(s + 3)}$$

that relates an output voltage $V_2(s)$ to an input voltage $V_1(s)$. If $v_1(t) = 100u(t)$, find the steady-state value of $v_2(t)$ by the method of Section 9.2.

12.31 Find the constants A_1 and A_2 of Equation 12.35 for solution of Example 12.23.

12.32 For

$$G(s) = \frac{s + 1}{s^2 + 2s + 1}$$

show that $G(-j\omega)$ is the conjugate of $G(j\omega)$.

12.33 Apply the reasoning (relative to steady-state calculations) of Section 12.12 to the case of a forcing step function $Ku(t)$, and justify the procedure of Section 9.2.

12.34 Use the phasor technique to find the steady-state solution for the differential equation

$$(p^3 + 2p^2 + 3p + 1)X(t) = 10\cos(t + 45°)$$

where $p \doteq d/dt$.

12.35 Find the steady-state solution for the differential equation of Problem 12.5 by the method of phasors.

Giants of the profession
IEEE Centennial Hall of Fame

John Bardeen (1908–   )
Coinventor, with Walter H.
Brattain, of the point-contact
transistor; shared the Nobel
Prize in Physics in 1956 for
the transistor with Brattain
and William Shockley and
won another Nobel Prize for
the theory of superconductors
in 1973.

William B. Shockley (1910–   )
Physicist who invented the
junction transistor and who shared
the 1956 Nobel Prize in Physics
with John Bardeen and Walter H.
Brattain.

Walter H. Brattain (1902–   )
Coinventor, with John Bardeen, of
the point-contact transistor; shared
the Nobel Prize in Physics in
1956, with Bardeen and William
Shockley.

Fourier techniques in network analysis

13.1 INTRODUCTION

As we saw in Chapter 12, the Laplace transform is very useful for obtaining the general solution for the mathematical model of a linear network. A broad class of source functions can be included, and initial conditions are accounted for in a very systematic way. This is our most potent analytical tool for finding complete solutions to systems of linear differential equations.

In many network analyses, however, a complete solution may not be needed. We have seen how phasors simplify sinusoidal steady-state computations. In this chapter we explore additional ways of using sinusoidal functions to help in the analysis of networks.

In any dynamic linear network a sinusoidal source function produces a set of sinusoidal responses. If, on the other hand, a nonsinusoidal periodic source function is introduced, the responses may be different in waveform at different points in the network. In general, the responses will not have the same waveform as the source. In fact, as we know, even with sinusoidal sources the response will be radically different as the source frequency is changed.

The Fourier series enables us to represent a periodic time function with a sum of sinusoidal functions plus a constant. By using the principle of superposition, we can then consider each term individually in computing the network response. If we are interested only in steady-state response, the phasor technique may be used to find a Fourier series for each response desired. Thus the waveform of the steady-state responses can be obtained.

The Fourier transform is an integral transform akin to the Laplace transform but not as widely applicable. It follows as a natural development from the Fourier series and allows us to represent nonperiodic functions of the pulse type as a continuous function of frequency. It can be used in network analysis for some fairly specialized applications, but it is much more useful in the theory of communications systems. It is introduced here primarily because of its importance in that area.

13.2 ORTHOGONAL FUNCTIONS ⎯⎯⎯⎯⎯⎯⎯⎯⎯⎯⎯⎯⎯○

Before beginning the discussion of the Fourier series, it is helpful to discuss a more general concept—orthogonality of functions.

Definition 13.1

> Two functions $f_1(t)$ and $f_2(t)$ are said to be *orthogonal* over some time interval t_1 to t_2 if
>
> $$\int_{t_1}^{t_2} f_1(t)f_2(t)\, dt = 0$$
>
> If $f_1(t) = f_2(t)$, the integral cannot be zero unless $t_1 = t_2$ or $f_1(t) = 0$. Therefore, a nonzero function cannot be orthogonal to itself over any nonzero interval.

In analysis it is often convenient to represent a function as a sum of simpler functions. This is illustrated by the following equation:

$$g(t) = a_1 g_1(t) + a_2 g_2(t) + a_3 g_3(t) \tag{13.1}$$

where the a_i coefficients are assumed to be constant and the g_i functions are assumed known. If the g_i functions are orthogonal over the interval t_1 to t_2, then

$$\int_{t_1}^{t_2} g_i(t)g_j(t)\, dt = 0 \qquad \text{for } i \ne j$$

This property suggests a means for evaluating the constants a_1, a_2, and a_3. If we multiply both sides of Equation 13.1 by $g_1(t)$ and integrate with respect to t from t_1 to t_2, we obtain

$$\int_{t_1}^{t_2} g(t)g_1(t)\, dt = a_1 \int_{t_1}^{t_2} g_1^2(t)\, dt$$

since $g_1(t)$ is orthogonal to $g_2(t)$ and $g_3(t)$ over the interval of integration. Thus we have that

$$a_1 = \frac{\displaystyle\int_{t_1}^{t_2} g(t)g_1(t)\, dt}{\displaystyle\int_{t_1}^{t_2} g_1{}^2(t)\, dt}$$

In Section 13.3 we examine a particular set of orthogonal functions.

13.3 FOURIER SERIES

The Fourier series is important to the study of electrical engineering for several reasons. Voltage and current variables with nonsinusoidal but periodically recurring waveforms are common in network analyses. By use of the Fourier series technique, we can represent a network source function of this type as a summation of sine and cosine terms. Then, using the principle of super-position, find the steady-state solution for the network by the phasor method. There are also many occasions where the response of a 2-port network to a periodic source function can be estimated by using the network ω-domain transfer function and the Fourier series for the source. Finally, an understanding of the Fourier series provides a very good basis for the mastery of the Fourier transform and numerical methods for approximating it.

As defined earlier, a function $f(t)$ is periodic with period T if $f(t) = f(t + T)$. Consider a periodic network source function. The following theorem enables us to represent it as a sum of sinusoidal functions.

Theorem 13.1

Let $f(t)$ be periodic with period T and let $f(t)$ be continuous except for a finite number of discontinuities. Then $f(t)$ can be represented by an infinite series,

$$f(t) = \frac{a_0}{2} + a_1 \cos \omega_0 t + a_2 \cos 2\omega_0 t + \cdots + a_n \cos n\omega_0 t + \cdots$$
$$+ b_1 \sin \omega_0 t + b_2 \sin 2\omega_0 t + \cdots + b_n \sin n\omega_0 t + \cdots \quad (13.2)$$

where $\omega_0 \doteq 2\pi/T$ is called the *fundamental radian frequency* of the series. The series defined by Equation 13.2 is known as a *Fourier series*.

The Fourier series converges to the function except at points of discontinuity, where it converges to $\frac{1}{2}[f(t^-) + f(t^+)]$, the average value of the function on each side of the discontinuity.

We now show that the functions on the right side of Equation 13.2 are orthogonal over any time period $T = 2\pi/\omega_0$. For simplicity we shall work with

$$g(x) = \frac{a_0}{2} + a_1 \cos x + a_2 \cos 2x + \cdots + a_n \cos nx + \cdots$$

$$+ b_1 \sin x + b_2 \sin 2x + \cdots + b_n \sin nx + \cdots$$

$$= \frac{a_0}{2} + \sum_{n=1}^{\infty} a_n \cos nx + \sum_{n=1}^{\infty} b_n \sin nx \qquad (13.3)$$

where $x \doteq \omega_0 t$. This series is made up of functions which are orthogonal over period 2π since $\omega_0 T = 2\pi$. To define $g(x)$ for a periodic function of time $f(t)$, we determine the period in time units and make this correspond to 2π radians. The series represented by Equation 13.3 is just as general as is Equation 13.2 and has the advantage that the period of orthogonality is always 2π rather than the true time period T. The coefficients in Equations 13.2 and 13.3 are, of course, identically the same. The actual fundamental frequency ω_0 can always be found by

$$\omega_0 = \frac{2\pi}{T} \ \text{rad}/\text{s} \qquad (13.4)$$

if T is in seconds.

If we are given a function $g(x)$ to be represented in a Fourier series as indicated by Equation 13.3, our problem is to evaluate the coefficients for enough terms to satisfactorily represent the function. It can be shown that the effect of neglecting a term ($a_n \cos nx$ or $b_n \sin nx$) becomes less significant as n becomes larger. In the typical case a series of three or four terms is often adequate. As illustrated in Section 13.2, we use the orthogonality property of the functions of Equation 13.3 to evaluate the coefficients.

The following set of definite integrals is useful to us in the coefficient evaluation:

$$\int_0^{2\pi} \cos nx \cos mx \ dx = \begin{cases} 0 & \text{if } m \neq n \\ \pi & \text{if } m = n \end{cases} \qquad (13.5)$$

$$\int_0^{2\pi} \sin nx \sin mx \ dx = \begin{cases} 0 & \text{if } m \neq n \\ \pi & \text{if } m = n \end{cases} \qquad (13.6)$$

$$\int_0^{2\pi} \sin nx \cos mx \ dx = 0 \qquad \text{for all } m \text{ and } n \qquad (13.7)$$

$$\int_0^{2\pi} \sin mx \ dx = \int_0^{2\pi} \cos mx \ dx = 0 \qquad (13.8)$$

In these integrals m and n are assumed to be positive integers.

To evaluate a_0 in Equation 13.3, we need merely integrate both sides fom 0 to 2π (or from x_1 to $x_1 + 2\pi$). It is clear from Equation 13.8 that all integrals involving sinusoidal terms on the right side vanish and that

$$\int_0^{2\pi} g(x)\ dx = \int_0^{2\pi} \frac{a_0}{2}\ dx = \pi a_0$$

or

$$a_0 = \frac{1}{\pi} \int_0^{2\pi} g(x)\ dx \qquad\qquad (13.9)$$

From this we see that a_0 is twice the average value of $g(x)$ over the interval.

To find a_n we multiply both sides of Equation 13.3 by cos nx and integrate with respect to x from 0 to 2π. The only nonzero integral on the right side of the equation is

$$a_n \int_0^{2\pi} \cos^2 nx\ dx = \pi a_n$$

This can be confirmed by checking all right-side integrals against Equations 13.5–13.7. Thus

$$a_n = \frac{1}{\pi} \int_0^{2\pi} g(x)\cos nx\ dx \qquad\qquad (13.10)$$

Multiplying through Equation 13.3 by sin nx and integrating with respect to x from 0 to 2π, we obtain

$$b_n = \frac{1}{\pi} \int_0^{2\pi} g(x)\sin nx\ dx \qquad\qquad (13.11)$$

If $g(x)\cos nx$ and $g(x)\sin nx$ are integrable analytically, the general coefficients may be obtained as functions of n. If not, then any appropriate numerical integration procedure (such as NUMINT in Appendix C) may be used to evaluate the coefficients individually.

The coefficients may be evaluated in a completely different manner if desired. It is necessary to estimate the number of terms needed, however, in advance of the calculation. Suppose that five terms were judged sufficient—the constant and two each of the sine and cosine terms. We generate five equations which are linear in the unknown coefficients by inserting in the five-term series five different values of x between 0 and 2π. For each value of x we know $g(x)$ and the functions cos x, cos $2x$, sin x, and sin $2x$. Therefore, we can write, in matrix form,

$$
\begin{bmatrix}
g(x_1) \\
g(x_2) \\
g(x_3) \\
g(x_4) \\
g(x_5)
\end{bmatrix}
=
\begin{bmatrix}
1 & \cos x_1 & \cos 2x_1 & \sin x_1 & \sin 2x_1 \\
1 & \cos x_2 & \cos 2x_2 & \sin x_2 & \sin 2x_2 \\
1 & \cos x_3 & \cos 2x_3 & \sin x_3 & \sin 2x_3 \\
1 & \cos x_4 & \cos 2x_4 & \sin x_4 & \sin 2x_4 \\
1 & \cos x_5 & \cos 2x_5 & \sin x_5 & \sin 2x_5
\end{bmatrix}
\begin{bmatrix}
\dfrac{a_0}{2} \\
a_1 \\
a_2 \\
b_1 \\
b_2
\end{bmatrix}
$$

If the sample values of x_i have been picked wisely, the inverse of the matrix will exist and the coefficients can be found. The series thus defined will fit the data points. There is a big disadvantage here, though. If we decide that five terms are not enough and we want to add two more, we must go through the complete process again, because in the usual case all the coefficients will change. This is not necessary when using Equations 13.9–13.11 to evaluate coefficients, since the calculations are independent of each other.

The Fourier series representation of a function can be written as either a sine or a cosine series, if desired, by combining the sine and cosine terms of like frequencies. For example, the nth harmonic terms

$$
a_n \cos nx + b_n \sin nx \tag{13.12}
$$

can be combined to form a single term,

$$
C_n \cos(nx + \phi_n) \tag{13.13}
$$

where $C_n = \sqrt{a_n^2 + b_n^2}$ and $\phi_n = -\tan^{-1}(b_n/a_n)$.

Probably the simplest way to remember the form of Equation 13.13 from Equation 13.12 is to use phasors to obtain the sum. The phasor representation of Equation 13.12 is $(a_n - jb_n)e^{jnx}$:

$$
(a_n - jb_n)e^{jnx} = \left(\sqrt{a_n^2 + b_n^2}\right)e^{j\phi_n}e^{jnx} \tag{13.14}
$$

The real part of Equation 13.14 equals Equation 13.13.

Example 13.1 _____

Consider the periodic function of Figure 13.1. The function is defined as

$$
f(x) =
\begin{cases}
2 & 0 < x < \pi \\
-1 & \pi < x < 2\pi
\end{cases}
$$

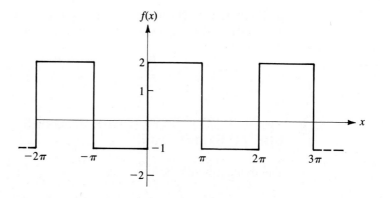

Figure 13.1
Periodic function.

The coefficients are found as follows:

$$a_0 = \frac{1}{\pi}\left[\int_0^{\pi} 2\,dx + \int_{\pi}^{2\pi}(-1)\,dx\right] = 2 - 1 = 1$$

$$a_1 = \frac{1}{\pi}\left(\int_0^{\pi} 2\cos\,dx - \int_{\pi}^{2\pi}\cos x\,dx\right) = 0$$

$$a_n = \frac{1}{\pi}\left(\int_0^{\pi} 2\cos nx\,dx - \int_{\pi}^{2\pi}\cos nx\,dx\right) = 0$$

$$b_1 = \frac{1}{\pi}\left(\int_0^{\pi} 2\sin x\,dx - \int_{\pi}^{2\pi}\sin x\,dx\right)$$

$$= \frac{1}{\pi}\left[\left(-2\cos x\right)_0^{\pi} - \left(-\cos x\right)_{\pi}^{2\pi}\right]$$

$$= \frac{1}{\pi}(2 + 2 + 1 + 1) = \frac{6}{\pi}$$

$$b_n = \frac{1}{\pi}\left(\int_0^{\pi} 2\sin nx\,dx - \int_{\pi}^{2\pi}\sin nx\,dx\right)$$

$$= \frac{1}{\pi}\left[\left(-\frac{2}{n}\cos nx\right)_0^{\pi} + \left(\frac{1}{n}\cos nx\right)_{\pi}^{2\pi}\right]$$

$$= \begin{cases} 0 & \text{for } n \text{ even} \\ \dfrac{6}{n\pi} & \text{for } n \text{ odd} \end{cases}$$

The series for $f(x)$ is

$$f(x) = \frac{1}{2} + \frac{6}{\pi}\sin x + \frac{6}{3\pi}\sin 3x + \frac{6}{5\pi}\sin 5x + \cdots$$

If this function $f(x)$ had been set up to represent a function of t with period $T = 0.01$ s, then $\omega_0 = 2\pi/T = 200\pi$, and the t-function series would be

$$f(\omega_0 t) = \frac{1}{2} + \frac{6}{\pi} \sin 200\pi t + \frac{6}{3\pi} \sin 600\pi t + \cdots$$

13.4 SIMPLIFICATION OF FOURIER SERIES DUE TO SYMMETRIES

The evaluation of the integrals

$$\int_0^{2\pi} g(x)\cos nx \, dx \quad \text{and} \quad \int_0^{2\pi} g(x)\sin nx \, dx$$

may be simplified considerably if the function possesses certain symmetrical characteristics. The first types of symmetries commonly encountered are those displayed by *even functions* and *odd functions*.

Definition 13.2

A function $f(t)$ is said to be *even* if $f(t) = f(-t)$. Observing from the point $t = 0$, an even function appears the same viewed in the direction of increasing t or decreasing t.

The cosine function is one important example of an even function. Another example is a function that is constant for all t.

Definition 13.3

A function $f(t)$ is said to be *odd* if $f(t) = -f(-t)$. (The sine function is an odd function.)

As a result of Definitions 13.2 and 13.3, for any function $f(t)$ we can define corresponding even and odd functions as follows:

$$f_e(t) = \frac{f(t) + f(-t)}{2} \tag{13.15}$$

$$f_o(t) = \frac{f(t) - f(-t)}{2} \tag{13.16}$$

By summing these equations, we get

$$f(t) = f_e(t) + f_o(t) \tag{13.17}$$

Thus we conclude that every function can be written as the sum of an even function and an odd function. We also note that the difference of Equations 13.15 and 13.16 yields

$$f(-t) = f_e(t) - f_o(t) \tag{13.18}$$

From Equations 13.15 and 13.16, we note that $f(t)$ cannot be both even and odd unless $f(t) \equiv 0$.

A sum of even functions is even and a sum of odd functions is odd, as the next theorems show.

Theorem 13.2

Let $g(t) = f_0(t) \pm f_2(t)$, where $f_0(t)$ and $f_2(t)$ are even. Then $g(t)$ is even.

Proof (for sum): Since $f_0(t) = f_0(-t)$ and $f_2(t) = f_2(-t)$,

$$g(t) = f_0(-t) + f_2(-t) = g(-t)$$

and therefore $g(t)$ is even.

The difference of two even functions is even by the same line of reasoning. It follows from this property that a Fourier cosine series

$$f(x) = a_0 + \sum_{n=1}^{\infty} a_n \cos nx \tag{13.19}$$

is even.

Theorem 13.3

Let $g(t) = f_1(t) \pm f_3(t)$, where $f_1(t)$ and $f_3(t)$ are odd. Then $g(t)$ is odd.

Proof (for sum): Since $f_1(t) = -f_1(-t)$ and $f_3(t) = -f_3(-t)$,

$$g(t) = -f_1(-t) - f_3(-t)$$
$$= -[f_1(-t) + f_3(-t)] = -g(-t)$$

Thus a Fourier sine series

$$g(x) = \sum_{n=1}^{\infty} b_n \sin nx \tag{13.20}$$

is an odd function.

The properties of Theorems 13.2 and 13.3, along with multiplication and division, are summarized in Table 13.1.

Table 13.1
Combinations of even and odd functions

	Even*	Odd *
1	$f_2 \pm f_4$	$f_1 \pm f_3$
2	$f_2 \cdot f_4$	$f_1 \cdot f_2$
3	$f_1 \cdot f_3$	$\dfrac{1}{f_1},\ f_1 \neq 0$
4	$\dfrac{1}{f_2},\ f_2 \neq 0$	

*A function f_k is even (or odd) if its subscript is even (or odd).

There are two more properties of odd and even functions that are of great value in evaluating Fourier series coefficients:

1. If $f(t)$ is even, then

$$\int_{-a}^{a} f(t)\ dt = 2 \int_{0}^{a} f(t)\ dt \tag{13.21}$$

2. If $f(t)$ is odd, then

$$\int_{-a}^{a} f(t)\ dt = 0 \tag{13.22}$$

The limit a in Equations 13.21 and 13.22 can be arbitrarily large or small. In particular, the properties hold as a approaches ∞.

We have seen that the only function that is both even and odd is the zero function, $f(x) \equiv 0$ for all x. It can be shown that the sum or difference of an even function and an odd function is neither even nor odd unless one function is zero.

It follows, therefore, that if a function is even it can be represented by a Fourier cosine series (Equation 13.19) and if a function is odd it can be represented by a Fourier sine series (Equation 13.20). *Thus if a function can be classified as even or odd, one set of the coefficients is known to be zero.* Often a function that does not have even or odd symmetry may be made to possess one of them by a proper translation of either the $f(x)$-axis or the x-axis.

For example, if the function of Figure 13.1 were shifted down $\frac{1}{2}$ unit to reduce the average value to zero, it would be an odd function. Except for a_0, the coefficients for the series would be unchanged.

If the function of Figure 13.1 were shifted to the left $\pi/2$ radians, the result—$f_1(x)$—would be an even function,

$$f_1(x) = \begin{cases} 2 & 0 < x < \frac{\pi}{2},\ -\frac{\pi}{2} < x < 0 \\ -1 & \frac{\pi}{2} < x < \pi,\ -\pi < x < -\frac{\pi}{2} \end{cases}$$

The Fourier series for the periodic function $f_1(x)$ is

$$f_1(x) = \frac{1}{2} + \frac{6}{\pi}\cos x - \frac{6}{3\pi}\cos 3x + \cdots$$

We summarize this discussion of even and odd symmetry by stating the results in the form of two theorems.

Theorem 13.4

If $f(x)$ is periodic and even, then $f(x) = \dfrac{a_0}{2} + \displaystyle\sum_{n=1}^{\infty} a_n \cos nx$.

Theorem 13.5

If $f(x)$ is periodic and odd, then $f(x) = \displaystyle\sum_{n=1}^{\infty} b_n \sin nx$.

Another form of symmetry that is often useful in evaluating the Fourier series coefficients for a function is called *half-wave symmetry*.

Definition 13.4

A function is said to have *half-wave symmetry* if $f(x) = -f(x + \pi)$.

If a function has half-wave symmetry, it is only necessary to integrate over an interval of π radians (half a period) rather than over 2π radians.

Theorem 13.6

Let $f(x)$ have half-wave symmetry. Then the Fourier series coefficients for $f(x)$ are given by

$$a_n = \begin{cases} 0 & \text{for } n \text{ even (including } n = 0) \\ \dfrac{2}{\pi}\displaystyle\int_0^\pi f(x)\cos nx \, dx & \text{for } n \text{ odd} \end{cases}$$

$$b_n = \begin{cases} 0 & \text{for } n \text{ even} \\ \dfrac{2}{\pi}\displaystyle\int_0^\pi f(x)\sin nx \, dx & \text{for } n \text{ odd} \end{cases}$$

Proof: We shall develop a proof for a_n and leave b_n as an exercise.

$$a_0 = 0$$

$$a_n = \frac{1}{\pi}\int_0^{2\pi} f(x)\cos nx \, dx \qquad n > 0$$

$$= \frac{1}{\pi}\left[\int_0^\pi f(x)\cos nx \, dx + \int_\pi^{2\pi} f(x)\cos nx \, dx\right] \qquad (13.23)$$

Since $f(x)$ has half-wave symmetry,

$$\int_\pi^{2\pi} f(x)\cos nx \, dx = -\int_\pi^{2\pi} f(x + \pi)\cos nx \, dx$$

If we let $\lambda = x + \pi$, we find that

$$-\int_\pi^{2\pi} f(x + \pi)\cos nx \, dx = -\int_0^\pi f(\lambda)\cos n\lambda \cos n\pi \, d\lambda \qquad (13.24)$$

Equation 13.24 yields

$$\int_0^\pi f(x)\cos nx \, dx \qquad \text{if } n \text{ is odd} \qquad (13.25)$$

$$-\int_0^\pi f(x)\cos nx \, dx \qquad \text{if } n \text{ is even} \qquad (13.26)$$

Putting Equations 13.25 and 13.26 back into Equation 13.23 for

$$\int_\pi^{2\pi} f(x)\cos nx \, dx$$

we obtain the result for a_n in Theorem 13.6. A similar approach will yield the result for b_n.

Example 13.2

The function $g(x)$ of Figure 13.2 has half-wave symmetry. The coefficients of the Fourier series for $g(x)$ are

$$a_0 = 0$$

$$a_n = \frac{2}{\pi} \left[\int_0^{\pi/2} 2 \cos nx \, dx + \int_{\pi/2}^{\pi} (-1) \cos nx \, dx \right]$$

$$= \frac{2}{\pi} \left[\left(\frac{2}{n} \sin nx \right)_0^{\pi/2} - \left(\frac{1}{n} \sin nx \right)_{\pi/2}^{\pi} \right] \quad \text{for } n \text{ odd}$$

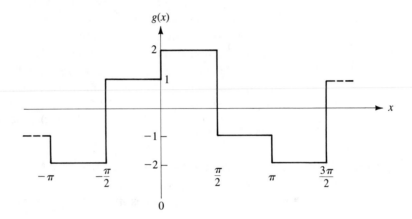

Figure 13.2
Perodic function with half-wave symmetry.

Therefore,

$$a_n = \begin{cases} 0 & \text{for } n \text{ even} \\ \dfrac{6}{n\pi} \sin \dfrac{n\pi}{2} & \text{for } n \text{ odd} \end{cases}$$

$$b_n = \frac{2}{\pi} \left(\int_0^{\pi/2} 2 \sin nx \, dx - \int_{\pi/2}^{\pi} \sin nx \, dx \right)$$

$$= \frac{2}{\pi} \left[\left(-\frac{2}{n} \cos nx \right)_0^{\pi/2} + \left(\frac{1}{n} \cos nx \right)_{\pi/2}^{\pi} \right] \quad \text{for } n \text{ odd}$$

and

$$b_n = \begin{cases} 0 & \text{for } n \text{ even} \\ \dfrac{2}{n\pi} & \text{for } n \text{ odd} \end{cases}$$

The series representation of $g(x)$ is

$$g(x) = \frac{6}{\pi} \cos x - \frac{6}{3\pi} \cos 3x + \frac{6}{5\pi} \cos 5x - \cdots$$

$$+ \frac{2}{\pi} \sin x + \frac{2}{3\pi} \sin 3x + \frac{2}{5\pi} \sin 5x + \cdots$$

$$= \frac{2}{\pi} \left[\sqrt{10} \cos(x - 18.4°) - \frac{\sqrt{10}}{3} \cos(3x + 18.4°) + \cdots \right]$$

If a function $f(x)$ has half-wave symmetry and is also either even or odd, $f(x)$ is said to possess *quarter-wave symmetry*. Such a function satisfies the hypothesis of Theorem 13.6, and thus the Fourier series that represents it has only odd harmonic terms. Furthermore, $f(x)$ satisfies the hypothesis of either Theorem 13.4 or Theorem 13.5, and therefore the Fourier series that represents it contains only cosine terms or sine terms, depending upon whether it is even or odd, respectively.

Theorem 13.7

Let a function $f(x)$ possess quarter-wave symmetry.

(1) If $f(x)$ is an even function,

$$b_n = 0 \qquad \text{for all } n$$

$$a_n = \begin{cases} 0 & \text{for } n \text{ even} \\ \dfrac{4}{\pi} \displaystyle\int_0^{\pi/2} f(x)\cos nx \, dx & \text{for } n \text{ odd} \end{cases}$$

(2) If $f(x)$ is an odd function,

$$b_n = \begin{cases} 0 & \text{for } n \text{ even} \\ \dfrac{4}{\pi} \displaystyle\int_0^{\pi/2} f(x)\sin nx \, dx & \text{for } n \text{ odd} \end{cases}$$

$$a_n = 0 \qquad \text{for all } n$$

Proof: We prove the theorem for (1) and leave (2) as an exercise. Since the function has half-wave symmetry, we know by Theorem 13.6 that $b_n = a_n = 0$ for n even and that

$$a_n = \frac{2}{\pi} \int_{-\pi/2}^{\pi/2} f(x)\cos nx \, dx$$

where the limits are taken for convenience as shown instead of from 0 to π. Therefore,

$$a_n = \frac{2}{\pi}\left[\int_{-\pi/2}^{0} f(x)\cos nx \ dx + \int_{0}^{\pi/2} f(x)\cos nx \ dx\right]$$

Since we have assumed the function even, $f(x) = f(-x)$. Therefore, $b_n = 0$ and the first integral is

$$\int_{-\pi/2}^{0} f(x)\cos nx \ dx = -\int_{-\pi/2}^{0} f(-x)\cos(-nx)(-dx)$$

$$= \int_{0}^{-\pi/2} f(-x)\cos(-nx)(-dx)$$

$$= \int_{0}^{\pi/2} f(x)\cos nx \ dx$$

and the result for a_n follows. A similar argument can be made for (2).

Example 13.3 ──────────────────────────────────────

The function $f(x)$ shown in Figure 13.3 has half-wave symmetry and is odd.

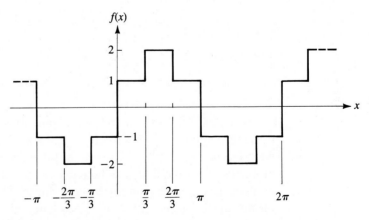

Figure 13.3
Periodic function with odd and half-wave symmetry.

Therefore, its Fourier series consists of odd harmonic sine terms only. The coefficients are as follows:

$$a_n = 0 \qquad\qquad n = 0, 1, 2, \ldots$$

$$b_n = 0 \qquad\qquad n \text{ even}$$

$$b_n = \frac{4}{\pi}\int_{0}^{\pi/2} f(x)\sin nx \ dx \qquad n \text{ odd}$$

$$= \frac{4}{\pi}\left(\int_{0}^{\pi/3} \sin nx \ dx + \int_{\pi/3}^{\pi/2} 2 \sin nx \ dx\right)$$

$$= \frac{4}{\pi n} \left[\left(-\cos nx \right)_{0}^{\pi/3} + \left(-2 \cos nx \right)_{\pi/3}^{\pi/2} \right]$$

$$= \frac{4}{\pi n} \left(1 + \cos n\frac{\pi}{3} \right)$$

$$b_1 = \frac{4}{\pi}(1 + \cos 60°) = \frac{6}{\pi}$$

$$b_3 = \frac{4}{3\pi}(1 + \cos 180°) = 0$$

$$b_5 = \frac{4}{5\pi}(1 + \cos 300°) = \frac{6}{5\pi}$$

$$b_7 = \frac{4}{7\pi}(1 + \cos 60°) = \frac{6}{7\pi}$$

$$b_9 = \frac{4}{9\pi}(1 + \cos 180°) = 0$$

The Fourier series for the function is

$$f(x) = \frac{6}{\pi} \left(\sin x + \frac{1}{5} \sin 5x + \frac{1}{7} \sin 7x + \cdots \right)$$

Now that we have derived the expressions for the coefficients a_n and b_n using the simpler expressions $\sin nx$ and $\cos nx$ and presented some examples, we translate the results to a more useful form for most electrical engineering problems. Sinusoidal source function specifications are likely to be given in terms of time rather than in terms of angle. Therefore, to translate from our results of Equations 13.9–13.11 to integrals involving time, we use the relations

$$x \rightarrow 2\pi f_0 t = \omega_0 t \text{ rad}$$

$$dx \rightarrow 2\pi f_0 dt = \omega_0 dt \text{ rad}$$

$$x = 2\pi \text{ rad} \rightarrow t = T \text{ s}$$

where

$$f_0 = \frac{1}{T} \text{ Hz}$$

Therefore, by direct substitution we have

$$a_n = \frac{2}{T} \int_0^T g(t)(\cos 2\pi n f_0 t)\, dt \qquad\qquad (13.27)$$

$$b_n = \frac{2}{T} \int_0^T g(t)(\sin 2\pi n) f_0 t\, dt \qquad\qquad (13.28)$$

We now look at another example to demonstrate the use of axis shifts to take advantage of a symmetry that may not be present in the original function. Sometimes a simple shift up or down on the function axis will create half-wave symmetry, $f(t) = -f(t + T/2)$. Thus a new function $f_1(t)$ is formed for which the average value $a_0/2$ is zero. A similar shift could create even or odd symmetry and halve the number of coefficient calculations.

Example 13.4 ──

The function $f(x)$ of Figure 13.1 has no symmetry as it stands. Suppose we define a new function

$$f_1(x) = f(x) - \frac{a_0}{2} = f(x) - \frac{1}{2}$$

We note that $f_1(x)$ is odd and has half-wave symmetry. Thus without calculation we know that for $f_1(x)$, $a_n = 0$ for all n and $b_n = 0$ for n even. Our task is reduced to finding

$$b_n = \frac{4}{\pi} \int_0^{\pi/2} f_1(x) \sin nx\, dx = \frac{6}{n\pi} \qquad \text{for } n = 1, 3, 5 \ldots$$

We can write the Fourier series for $f(x) = f_1(x) + \frac{1}{2}$ as

$$f(x) = \frac{1}{2} + \frac{6}{\pi}\left[\sin x + \frac{1}{3} \sin 3x + \frac{1}{5} \sin 5x + \cdots \right]$$

which checks the results of Example 13.1.

If we should prefer even symmetry, the angle axis could be shifted by defining a new function

$$f_2(x) = f_1\left(x - \frac{\pi}{2} \right)$$

This places the new origin at $x = \pi/2$ of the old system. With even and half-wave symmetry we know that $a_0 = 0$, $b_n = 0$ for all n, and $a_n = 0$ for n even. Our job is to find the a_n for odd harmonics. This time we use the time-function form.

Let $T = 10^{-3}$ s, so that $f_0 = 10^3$ Hz. Then we need to evaluate

$$a_n = \frac{8}{T} \int_0^{T/4} f(t)\cos(2\pi n \times 10^3 t)\, dt$$

$$= \frac{8 \times 1.5 \times 10^3}{2\pi n \times 10^3} \sin(2\pi n \times 10^3 t)\Big|_0^{2.5 \times 10^{-4}}$$

$$= \frac{6}{n\pi} \sin n\frac{\pi}{2}$$

Therefore,

$$a_n = \begin{cases} \dfrac{6}{n\pi} & n = 1, 5, 9, \ldots \\[2ex] -\dfrac{6}{n\pi} & n = 3, 7, 11, \ldots \end{cases}$$

which can be written as

$$a_{(2n-1)} = \frac{6}{n\pi}(-1)^{(n+1)} \qquad \text{for } n = 1, 2, 3, \ldots$$

The Fourier series for $f_2(t)$ is

$$f_2(t) = \frac{6}{\pi}\left(\cos 2\pi \times 10^3 t - \frac{1}{3} \cos 6\pi \times 10^3 t + \frac{1}{5} \cos 10\pi \times 10^3 t \right.$$
$$\left. - \frac{1}{7} \cos 14\pi \times 10^3 t + \cdots \right)$$

From this solution the Fourier series for $f_1(t)$ and $f(t)$ can be written using

$$f_1\left(t - \frac{T}{4}\right) = f_2(t)$$

or

$$f_1(t) = f_2\left(t + \frac{T}{4}\right)$$

and

$$f(t) = \frac{1}{2} + f_1(t)$$

13.5 STEADY-STATE ANALYSIS FOR PERIODIC SOURCES

Thus far we have discussed only the mechanics of finding a Fourier series to represent a periodic function. In this section we discuss an important application. Suppose we have a network or system that contains a periodic source and for which we desire the steady-state solution. We proceed as follows:

1. Represent the source function with a Fourier cosine series, including as many harmonics as necessary for the accuracy desired.

2. Regard the source as a set of series or parallel single-frequency sources depending upon whether it is a *v*-source or *i*-source, respectively.

3. Use the superposition principle to find that part of the total solution due to each sinusoidal source function. The phasor technique is generally employed for this calculation. If there are *n* terms in the Fourier series representing the source function, there will be *n* separate networks to solve.

4. Write the Fourier series for the desired variables by combining the phasor solutions.

It should be clear that the general Fourier series for the source function can be used. Since we have adopted a convention of letting a phasor represent a cosine function, however, it is most convenient to use a cosine series. If the source function is even or can be made even by a translation of axis, no b_n coefficients need be calculated. If not, then C_n and ϕ_n coefficients must be found as indicated in Equation 13.13 and we have

$$f(x) = a_0 + \sum_{n=1}^{\infty} C_n \cos(nx + \phi_n) \tag{13.28}$$

as the Fourier series for the source function where $x = \omega_0 t$.

Example 13.5

Suppose we have the series *RL* circuit of Figure 13.4. A square-wave voltage of period $T = 2\pi \times 10^{-3}$ s and magnitude $\pi/4$ is applied. If $t = 0$ is chosen such that $v(t)$ is even, as shown in Figure 13.5, we know from Example 13.1 that the Fourier series can be written

$$v(t) = \cos 1000t - \frac{1}{3} \cos 3000t + \frac{1}{5} \cos 5000t + \cdots \text{ V}$$

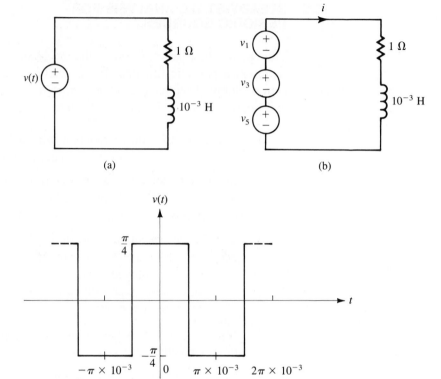

Figure 13.4
(a) An *RL* series network with a square-wave voltage applied. (b) A circuit equivalent to (a) with the approximation that three terms of the Fourier series for *v(t)* are adequate.

Figure 13.5
Square-wave *v*-function with even symmetry and zero average value.

Let us assume that three terms of the Fourier series will approximate $v(t)$ adequately. We can find the steady-state solution to the network of Figure 13.5(b) by obtaining the phasor solution for the network for each of the v-sources and then adding the individual solutions:

$$\bar{I}_1 = \frac{1\underline{/0°}}{1 + j1000 \times 10^{-3}} = \frac{1}{\sqrt{2}}\underline{/-45°}$$

$$\bar{I}_3 = \frac{-\frac{1}{3}\underline{/0°}}{1 + j3} = \frac{-1}{3\sqrt{10}}\underline{/-71.6°} = \frac{1}{3\sqrt{10}}\underline{/108.4°}$$

$$\bar{I}_5 = \frac{\frac{1}{5}\underline{/0°}}{1 + j5} = \frac{1}{5\sqrt{26}}\underline{/-78.7°}$$

The first three terms of the Fourier series for the current are then

$$i(t) = \frac{1}{\sqrt{2}}\cos(1000t - 45°) - \frac{1}{3\sqrt{10}}\cos(3000t - 71.6°)$$

$$+ \frac{1}{5\sqrt{26}}\cos(5000t - 78.7°)\ \text{A}$$

In effect, the series *RL* network has acted as a low-pass filter for the current. We note that the magnitudes of the third and fifth harmonics are reduced by factors of $1/\sqrt{10}$ and $1/\sqrt{26}$, respectively, relative to the corresponding voltage harmonics, while the magnitude of the first harmonic is reduced by only $1/\sqrt{2}$.

13.6 POWER CONSIDERATIONS FOR A PERIODIC FUNCTION

In Example 13.5 we used three terms of a Fourier cosine series to represent a square-wave voltage source. We might well be concerned with how satisfactory our approximation was and thus how close our analysis would check a set of experimental measurements. In this section we develop one measure of the *goodness of fit* for a Fourier series which contains a finite number of terms.

The question of how many terms should be included in a Fourier series is a pertinent one. Truncation of a series always introduces errors, but practical considerations in network analysis require that only a finite number of terms be used. The question is where to truncate.

Consider the graphs of Figure 13.6 for the even square-wave function of Example 13.5. Fourier series plots for two, three, four, and eight terms are shown.

Looking at Figure 13.6(a) and (b), we see that the addition of the fifth harmonic helps considerably to improve the general conformance of the series to the square-wave function. The addition of the seventh harmonic in (c) shows a further improvement. Figure 13.6(d) shows the partial sum including the fifteenth harmonic, and now the approximation is very good indeed.

We note, however, that a marked oscillation occurs near the discontinuity. This phenomenon is called the *Gibbs effect*, and it will continue to be present no matter how many harmonics we include in the Fourier series. The effect is present in any Fourier series representation of a discontinuous function. Each term in a Fourier series is a continuous function. Sums of continuous functions are continuous. Thus a series of continuous functions can never perfectly represent a discontinuous function (in all respects) at a point of discontinuity. This is a drawback of the Fourier series that makes it unsatisfactory for some applications.

In Figure 13.6 it is clear that the addition of another term improves the approximation, but how do we put a quantitative value on the goodness of the fit? No one measure is universally satisfactory, but one based on power considerations is widely used.

Figure 13.6

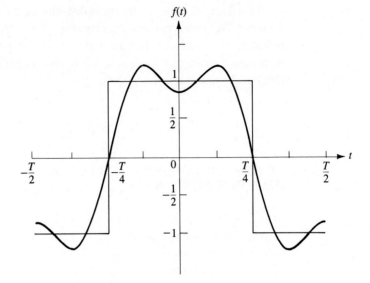

(a) Plot of $f(t) = (4/\pi)(\cos \omega_0 t - \frac{1}{3} \cos 3\omega_0 t)$

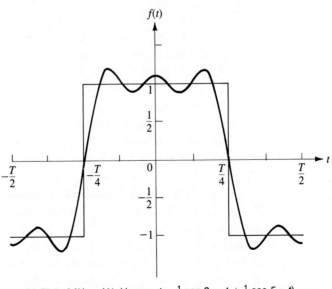

(b) Plot of $f(t) = (4/\pi)(\cos \omega_0 t - \frac{1}{3} \cos 3 \omega_0 t + \frac{1}{5} \cos 5\omega_0 t)$

In communications theory the instantaneous power, $p(t)$, of a function $x(t)$ is widely taken to be $x^2(t)$. To fit this convention to network analysis, let us consider the power associated with a 1-Ω resistor.

$$p(t) = v^2(t) = i^2(t)$$

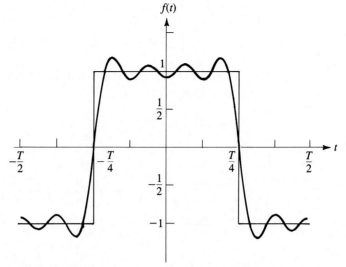

(c) Plot of $f(t) = (4/\pi)(\cos \omega_0 t - \frac{1}{3} \cos \omega_0 t + \frac{1}{5} \cos 5\omega_0 t - \frac{1}{7} \cos 7\omega_0 t)$

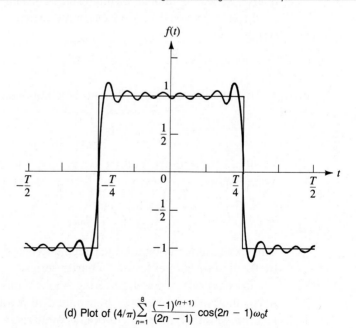

(d) Plot of $(4/\pi)\sum_{n=1}^{8} \dfrac{(-1)^{(n+1)}}{(2n-1)} \cos(2n-1)\omega_0 t$

We elect to use $v(t)$ for the development that follows. Suppose $v(t)$ is periodic with period T and represented by a Fourier series

$$v(t) = \frac{a_0}{2} + \sum_{n=1}^{\infty} (a_n \cos n\omega_0 t + b_n \sin n\omega_0 t)$$

The average power associated with $v(t)$ (applied to a 1-Ω resistor) is

$$P = \frac{1}{T} \int_{t_1}^{t_1+T} p(t) \, dt = \frac{1}{T} \int_{t_1}^{t_1+T} v^2(t) \, dt \tag{13.29}$$

Because of the orthogonality property, all terms vanish when integrated over a complete period except the following:

$$P = \frac{1}{T} \left[\int_0^T \left(\frac{a_0}{2} \right)^2 dt + \int_0^T \sum_{n=1}^{\infty} a_n^2 \cos^2 n\omega_0 t \, dt + \int_0^T \sum_{n=1}^{\infty} b_n^2 \sin^2 n\omega_0 t \, dt \right] \tag{13.30}$$

These integrals are the ones that we encountered when evaluating the Fourier series coefficients in Section 13.3. Thus we can write the result as

$$P = \frac{a_0^2}{4} + \frac{1}{2} \sum_{n=1}^{\infty} (a_n^2 + b_n^2) \tag{13.31}$$

Equation 13.31 is an expression of average power for $v(t)$ in terms of its Fourier series coefficients. This result is usually called *Parseval's theorem*.

From Equation 13.31 we can write the rms value of the periodic function $v(t)$ as

$$V_r = \sqrt{\frac{a_0^2}{4} + \frac{1}{2} \sum_{n=1}^{\infty} (a_n^2 + b_n^2)} \tag{13.32}$$

If the voltage function has no dc component, this becomes

$$V_r = \sqrt{\frac{1}{2} \sum_{n=1}^{\infty} (a_n^2 + b_n^2)} \tag{13.33}$$

If we truncate the Fourier series for a function at the Mth harmonic, the average power over a complete period for the series can be written as

$$P' = \frac{a_0^2}{4} + \frac{1}{2} \sum_{n=1}^{M} (a_n^2 + b_n^2) \tag{13.34}$$

This expression can be used to judge how good an approximation is provided by the first M harmonics of a Fourier series.

In many electrical-engineering applications, particularly in communications, the amount of power transmitted to a load by a signal (voltage) is of paramount importance. Therefore, a comparison of the power associated with a periodic function to that associated with its truncated Fourier series representation is useful in assessing whether the representation is adequate.

Let us discuss one measure. Suppose the average power of a periodic function $v(t)$ is P and the average power of its truncated Fourier series representation is P'. It is reasonable to define an average *power error* (APE) as

$$\text{APE} = P - P' \tag{13.35}$$

and a ratio of power error to power

$$\text{APER} = \frac{P - P'}{P} = \frac{\text{APE}}{P}$$

as the *power error ratio*. The power error ratio becomes smaller as more terms are added to the truncated Fourier series representation because P' approaches P as a limit, and all terms in Equation 13.34 are positive. The expression we have called average power error is closely related to an error measure called *integral-square error*, much used by communications and control specialists.

Example 13.6

In this example we apply the average power error ratio to test the closeness of our three-term Fourier series approximation to the square-wave voltage source of Example 13.5. The average power of the square-wave voltage source is

$$P = \frac{1}{T} \int_{-T/2}^{T/2} p(t)\, dt = \frac{1}{T} \int_{-T/2}^{T/2} v^2\, dt$$

$$P = \frac{1}{T} \int_{-T/2}^{T/2} \left(\frac{\pi}{4}\right)^2 dt = \left(\frac{\pi}{4}\right)^2 = 0.61685 \text{ W}$$

The average power for the three-term truncated Fourier series fundamental and harmonics is as follows:

$$P_1 = \frac{(1)^2}{2} = 0.5000 \text{ W}$$

$$P_3 = \frac{1}{2}\left(\frac{1}{3}\right)^2 = 0.0556 \text{ W}$$

$$P_5 = \frac{1}{2}\left(\frac{1}{5}\right)^2 = 0.0200 \text{ W}$$

$$P' = P_1 + P_3 + P_5 = 0.5756 \text{ W}$$

Thus the average power error ratio is

$$\text{APER} = \frac{0.61685 - 0.5756}{0.61685} = 0.0669 \qquad (6.69\%)$$

By adding additional terms to the series, we can reduce the error ratio. Adding the seventh harmonic reduces the error ratio to 5.03%, and it drops to 4.03% when the ninth harmonic is added. With this information in hand, an analyst might be able to make a decision on truncation for a particular application.

An ideal filter in electrical-network theory is a 2-port that passes a sinusoidal voltage (or current) through without attenuation or phase shift for a given range of frequency. Outside that range the output is zero. The Fourier series is a useful mechanism to investigate the effects of such a filter on a periodic voltage (or current), as we now demonstrate.

Example 13.7

Suppose the square-wave voltage of Example 13.5 is applied to a 1-Ω resistor through a 2-port filter that passes all frequencies up to and including the ninth harmonic, $f_9 = 9000/2\pi$ Hz (see Figures 13.7 and 13.8). Our problem is to determine the average power error ratio, where P' is the power dissipated in the resistor and P is the average power available (for a 1-Ω resistor) at the source.

Figure 13.7
Graph of an ideal filter amplitude characteristic.

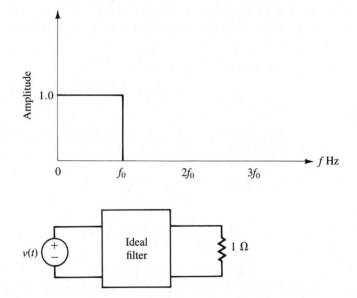

Figure 13.8
Network of Example 13.7.

From our calculations in Example 13.6, we know that the average power error ratio corresponding to the truncated Fourier series that includes the ninth harmonic is 0.0403. This is a measure of the effect of the filter on the periodic square wave.

To conclude the discussion on power considerations for periodic functions, we note two very important properties of the Fourier series. Assuming that we have made the decision to represent a periodic function with a Fourier series, we have these assurances:

1. The coefficients found by the formulas of Equations 13.9–13.11 provide the best fit possible (for a given number of harmonics) in minimizing the average power error.

2. Each harmonic term added to a truncated series representation reduces the average power error.

13.7 EXPONENTIAL FOURIER SERIES

The Fourier series

$$f(x) = \frac{a_0}{2} + \sum_{n=1}^{\infty} a_n \cos nx + \sum_{n=1}^{\infty} b_n \sin nx \tag{13.36}$$

can be written in an alternative manner known as the exponential Fourier series. The exponential series has an elegant mathematical form and is useful in many theoretical developments.

To develop the exponential series, note that Equation 13.36 can be written

$$f(x) = \frac{a_0}{2} + \sum_{n=1}^{\infty} a_n \frac{e^{jnx} + e^{-jnx}}{2} - j\sum_{n=1}^{\infty} b_n \frac{e^{jnx} - e^{-jnx}}{2}$$

$$= \frac{a_0}{2} + \sum_{n=1}^{\infty} \frac{(a_n - jb_n)e^{jnx}}{2} + \sum_{n=1}^{\infty} \frac{(a_n + jb_n)e^{-jnx}}{2} \tag{13.37}$$

Suppose we let $\bar{c}_n = (a_n - jb_n)/2$. Then $\bar{c}_n^* = (a_n + jb_n)/2$ and we may write Equation 13.37 as

$$f(x) = \frac{a_0}{2} + \sum_{n=1}^{\infty} \bar{c}_n e^{jnx} + \sum_{n=1}^{\infty} \bar{c}_n^* e^{-jnx} \tag{13.38}$$

If we define $\bar{c}_{-n}$ to be $\bar{c}_n^*$ and $\bar{c}_0$ to be $a_0/2$, Equation 13.38 becomes

$$f(x) = \sum_{n=-\infty}^{-1} \bar{c}_n e^{jnx} + \bar{c}_0 + \sum_{n=1}^{\infty} \bar{c}_n e^{jnx}$$

$$= \sum_{n=-\infty}^{\infty} \bar{c}_n e^{jnx} \tag{13.39}$$

Equation 13.39 is the exponential Fourier series of the function $f(x)$. We defined $\bar{c}_n$ by

$$\bar{c}_n = \frac{a_n - jb_n}{2} \tag{13.40}$$

Therefore, we may evaluate the coefficients of Equation 13.39 by first evaluating a_n and b_n. Since $\bar{c}_{-n} = \bar{c}_n^*$, it is only necessary to evaluate $\bar{C}_n$ for $n = 0$,

1, 2, . . . , N, where N is the highest harmonic desired. For practical applications the calculation of $\bar{c}_n$ by Equation 13.40 may be the most direct and simple procedure. For theoretical purposes, however, it is often desirable to use an alternative approach. If we put in the integral definitions for a_n and b_n in Equation 13.40, we have

$$\bar{c}_n = \frac{1}{2\pi} \int_0^{2\pi} f(x)(\cos nx - j \sin nx)\, dx$$

$$= \frac{1}{2\pi} \int_0^{2\pi} f(x) e^{-jnx}\, dx \qquad (13.41)$$

We note that $\bar{c}_0$ as given by Equation 13.41 agrees with the definition of $a_0/2$. From the definition of $\bar{c}_n$ it follows that if $f(x)$ is an even function, $\bar{c}_0 = a_0/2$ and $\bar{c}_n = \bar{c}_{-n} = a_n/2$, $n = 1, 2, 3, \ldots$. If $f(x)$ is an odd function, $\bar{c}_0 = 0$ and $\bar{c}_n = -\bar{c}_{-n} = -jb_n/2$, $n = 1, 2, 3, \ldots$. Table 13.2 summarizes the relations between $\bar{c}_n$, a_n, and b_n for even, odd, and half-wave symmetry.

Example 13.8 ───

The coefficients of the Fourier series representing the function $g(x)$ of Example 13.2 are

$$a_n = \frac{6}{n\pi} \sin \frac{n\pi}{2} \qquad \text{for } n \text{ odd}$$

$$b_n = \frac{2}{n\pi} \qquad \text{for } n \text{ odd}$$

$$a_n = b_n = 0 \qquad \text{for } n \text{ even}$$

The coefficients for the exponential Fourier series are, therefore,

$$\bar{c}_n = \begin{cases} \dfrac{3 \sin \dfrac{n\pi}{2} - j}{n\pi} & \text{for } n \text{ odd} \\[4mm] 0 & \text{for } n \text{ even} \end{cases}$$

$$\bar{c}_{-n} = \begin{cases} \dfrac{3 \sin \dfrac{n\pi}{2} + j}{n\pi} & \text{for } n \text{ odd} \\[4mm] 0 & \text{for } n \text{ even} \end{cases}$$

**Table 13.2
Fourier series
coefficient
relationships**

$$f(t) = \frac{a_0}{2} + \sum_{n=1}^{\infty} a_n \cos n\omega_0 t + \sum_{n=1}^{\infty} b_n \sin n\omega_0 t$$

$$= \sum_{n=-\infty}^{\infty} \bar{c}_n e^{jn\omega_0 t}$$

$$c_0 = \frac{a_0}{2} = \frac{1}{T} \int_{-T/2}^{T/2} f(t)\, dt \qquad \bar{c}_n = \frac{a_n - jb_n}{2}$$

$$\bar{c}_{-n} = \bar{c}_n^* = \frac{a_n + jb_n}{2}$$

$f(t)$ (periodic)	General	Half-wave symmetry $f(t) = -f\left(t + \dfrac{T}{2}\right)$
General	$\bar{c}_n = \dfrac{1}{T} \displaystyle\int_{-T/2}^{T/2} f(t)e^{-jn\omega_0 t}\, dt$ $a_n = \bar{c}_n + \bar{c}_{-n} \qquad n \neq 0$ $b_n = j(\bar{c}_n - \bar{c}_{-n})$	$\bar{c}_n = \dfrac{2}{T} \displaystyle\int_{0}^{T/2} f(t)e^{-jn\omega_0 t}\, dt \; n \text{ odd}$ $\bar{c}_n = 0 \qquad\qquad\qquad n \text{ even}$ $a_n = \bar{c}_n + \bar{c}_{-n}$ $b_n = j(\bar{c}_n - \bar{c}_{-n})$
Even $f(t) = f(-t)$	$\bar{c}_n = \dfrac{2}{T} \displaystyle\int_{0}^{T/2} f(t)\cos n\omega_0 t\, dt$ $a_n = 2\bar{c}_n$ $b_n = 0$	$\bar{c}_n = \dfrac{4}{T} \displaystyle\int_{0}^{T/4} f(t)\cos n\omega_0 t\, dt$ $a_n = \begin{cases} 2\bar{c}_n & n \text{ odd} \\ 0 & n \text{ even} \end{cases}$ $b_n = 0$
Odd $f(t) = -f(-t)$	$\bar{c}_n = -j\dfrac{2}{T} \displaystyle\int_{0}^{T/2} f(t)\sin n\omega_0 t\, dt$ $\bar{c}_0 = 0$ $a_n = 0$ $b_n = j2\bar{c}_n$	$\bar{c}_n = -j\dfrac{4}{T} \displaystyle\int_{0}^{T/4} f(t)\cos n\omega_0 t\, dt$ $\bar{c}_0 = 0$ $a_n = 0$ $b_n = \begin{cases} j2\bar{c}_n & n \text{ odd} \\ 0 & n \text{ even} \end{cases}$

A few terms of the exponential Fourier series are

$$g(x) = \frac{\sqrt{10}}{\pi}(\cdots + \frac{1}{5}e^{-j(5x-18.4°)} - \frac{1}{3}e^{-j(3x+18.4°)}$$

$$+ e^{-j(x-18.4°)} + e^{j(x-18.4°)}$$

$$- \frac{1}{3}e^{j(3x+18.4°)} + \frac{1}{5}e^{j(5x-18.4°)} + \cdots)$$

We now find the coefficients for the exponential and the trigonometric Fourier series of a sawtooth function by using Equation 13.41 and Table 13.2.

Example 13.9

Given the sawtooth waveform of Figure 13.9, we wish to find the Fourier series coefficients. The function is odd; therefore, $c_0 = 0$ and

$$\bar{c}_n = \frac{2A}{T^2} \int_{-T/2}^{T/2} t e^{-jn\omega_0 t} \, dt = -j\frac{4A}{T^2} \int_0^{T/2} t \sin n\omega_0 t \, dt$$

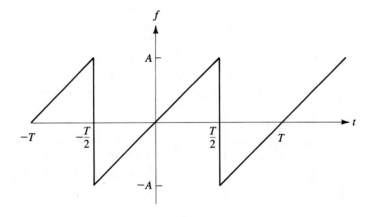

Figure 13.9
The sawtooth function of Example 13.9.

Integrating by parts, we have, for $n \neq 0$

$$\bar{c}_n = \frac{-j4A}{T^2}\left\{\frac{-t}{n\omega_0}\cos n\omega_0 t \Big|_0^{T/2} + \frac{1}{n\omega_0}\int_0^{T/2}\cos n\omega_0 t \, dt\right\}$$

$$= \frac{-j4A}{T^2}\left\{-\frac{T}{2n\omega_0}\cos n\omega_0\frac{T}{2} + \frac{1}{n^2\omega_0^2}\sin n\omega_0 t \Big|_0^{T/2}\right\}$$

$$= \frac{j2A}{n\omega_0 T}\cos n\omega_0\frac{T}{2}$$

since $\sin n\omega_0 t$ is zero for $t = 0$ and $t = n(T/2)$. Thus

$$\bar{c}_n = \begin{cases} \dfrac{jA}{\pi n} & n \neq 0 \text{ and even} \\[3mm] -\dfrac{jA}{\pi n} & n \text{ odd} \end{cases}$$

and

$$b_n = j2c_n = \begin{cases} -\dfrac{2A}{\pi n} & n \text{ even} \\[3mm] \dfrac{2A}{\pi n} & n \text{ odd} \end{cases}$$

$$a_n = 0$$

The exponential series can thus be written as

$$f(t) = j\frac{A}{\pi} \sum_{n=-\infty}^{1} \frac{(-1)^n}{n} e^{jn\omega_0 t} + j\frac{A}{\pi} \sum_{n=1}^{\infty} \frac{(-1)^n}{n} e^{jn\omega_0 t}$$

A few terms of the series may help to visualize the symmetry:

$$f(t) = j\frac{A}{\pi} \left[\left(\cdots \frac{1}{3} e^{-j3\omega_0 t} - \frac{1}{2} e^{-j2\omega_0 t} + e^{-j\omega_0 t} \right) + \left(-e^{j\omega_0 t} + \frac{1}{2} e^{j2\omega_0 t} \right. \right.$$
$$\left. \left. - \frac{1}{3} e^{j3\omega_0 t} + \cdots \right) \right]$$

Note that the coefficients of terms for $n < 0$ are conjugates of terms for $n > 0$, and thus the pairs may be combined to form sine functions. Using the coefficients b_n, we can write the trigonometric series as

$$f(t) = \frac{2A}{\pi} \sum_{n=1}^{\infty} \frac{(-1)^{n+1}}{n} \sin n\omega_0 t$$

$$= \frac{2A}{\pi} \left[\sin \omega_0 t - \frac{1}{2} \sin 2\omega_0 t + \frac{1}{3} \sin 3\omega_0 t + \cdots \right]$$

The Fourier series for some common periodic functions useful in electrical engineering are shown in Table 13.3.

We have seen how frequency techniques (Fourier series) can be quite useful in the analysis of systems containing periodic sources. Frequency-response characteristics of a system in the form of a transfer function are generally not difficult to obtain experimentally. With this information, the output waveform of a system corresponding to a periodic source function can

Table 13.3 Fourier series for some simple periodic functions

Waveform	Trigonometric series	Exponential series coefficients	
	$\dfrac{4A}{\pi}\displaystyle\sum_{n=1}^{\infty}\dfrac{1}{(2n-1)}\sin(2n-1)\omega_0 t$	$\dfrac{-j2A}{\pi n}$	$n = \pm1,\ \pm3,\ \pm5,\ \ldots$
		0	n even
	$\dfrac{4A}{\pi}\displaystyle\sum_{n=1}^{\infty}\dfrac{(-1)^{n+1}}{(2n-1)}\cos(2n-1)\omega_0 t$	$\dfrac{2A}{|n|\,\pi}$	$n = \pm1,\ \pm5,\ \pm9,\ \ldots$
		$\dfrac{-2A}{|n|\,\pi}$	$n = \pm3,\ \pm7,\ \pm11,\ \ldots$
		0	n even
	$\dfrac{8A}{\pi^2}\displaystyle\sum_{n=1}^{\infty}\dfrac{1}{(2n-1)^2}\cos(2n-1)\omega_0 t$	$\dfrac{4A}{\pi^2 n^2}$	n odd
		0	n even
	$\dfrac{2A}{\pi}\displaystyle\sum_{n=1}^{\infty}\dfrac{(-1)^{(n+1)}}{n}\sin n\omega_0 t$	$-j\,\dfrac{A(-1)^{(|n|+1)}}{\pi n}$	$n = \pm1,\ \pm2,\ \pm3,\ \ldots$
		0	$n = 0$
Full-wave rectified cosine wave	$\dfrac{2A}{\pi}\left[1 - 2\displaystyle\sum_{n=1}^{\infty}\dfrac{(-1)^n}{(4n^2-1)}\cos 2n\omega_0 t\right]$	$\dfrac{2A}{\pi}$	$n = 0$
		$\dfrac{2A}{\pi(n^2-1)}$	$n = \pm2,\ \pm6,\ \pm10,\ \ldots$
		$\dfrac{-2A}{\pi(n^2-1)}$	$n = \pm4,\ \pm8,\ \pm12,\ \ldots$
Half-wave rectified cosine wave	$\dfrac{A}{\pi}\left[1 + \dfrac{\pi}{2}\cos\omega_0 t \right.$ $\left. - 2\displaystyle\sum_{n=1}^{\infty}\dfrac{(-1)^n}{(4n^2-1)}\cos 2n\omega_0 t\right]$	$\dfrac{A}{\pi}\quad n = 0,\qquad \dfrac{A}{4}\quad n = \pm1$	
		$\dfrac{A}{\pi(n^2-1)}$	$n = \pm2,\ \pm6,\ \pm10,\ \ldots$
		$-\dfrac{A}{\pi(n^2-1)}$	$n = \pm4,\ \pm8,\ \pm12,\ \ldots$

be predicted in the form of a Fourier series. That is, if we know the relationship in phase and magnitude between the i-variable or v-variable chosen as output and a sinusoidal function corresponding to a source at each frequency of interest, we can calculate the steady-state magnitude and phase of each harmonic of a Fourier series for the output if we know the Fourier series of the source.

This turns out to be a useful procedure both for actual calculations and for its conceptual value. For a given source function, for example, using frequency concepts we can estimate the frequency-response characteristics required of a 2-port network such that the periodic output conforms within limits to the shape of the periodic input. In the case of an electric-power-supply filter, we might want frequency-response characteristics to reduce the fundamental and all harmonics of the output to negligible values in comparison to the constant, or dc, value.

13.8 FOURIER TRANSFORM

In transmitting information over communication networks, we generally would like the output to resemble the input closely, where the closeness of the resemblance must be defined somehow. Very often the signals (source functions) sent via communication networks are pulses of nonrepetitive nature. Thus a Fourier series cannot represent the signal. For such signals a Fourier integral (or Fourier transform) may exist. If so, ω-domain techniques— including phasor models—can be used to characterize the response of a linear network to such a signal.

We found in Section 13.7 that for a periodic function $f(t)$, we could write an exponential Fourier series as

$$f(t) = \sum_{n=-\infty}^{\infty} \bar{c}_n e^{jn\omega_0 t} = \frac{1}{2\pi} \sum_{n=-\infty}^{\infty} \omega_0(\bar{c}_n T)e^{jn\omega_0 t} \qquad (13.42)$$

where

$$\bar{c}_n = \frac{1}{T} \int_{-T/2}^{T/2} f(t)e^{-jn\omega_0 t}\, dt \qquad (13.43)$$

$$\omega_0 = \frac{2\pi}{T}$$

We now develop the Fourier transform as a limiting case of the exponential Fourier series. For convenience, we write Equations 13.42 and 13.43 as follows:

$$f(t) = \frac{1}{2\pi} \sum_{n=-\infty}^{\infty} \omega_0(\bar{c}_n T)e^{jn\omega_0 t} = \frac{1}{2\pi} \sum_{n=-\infty}^{\infty} \omega_0 \bar{a}_n(\omega_0)e^{jn\omega_0 t} \qquad (13.44)$$

where

$$\bar{a}_n(\omega_0) \doteq \bar{c}_n(\omega_0) \cdot T$$

and

$$\bar{a}_n(\omega_0) = \int_{-T/2}^{T/2} f(t)e^{-jn\omega_0 t}\, dt \tag{13.45}$$

Now consider Equations 13.44 and 13.45 as $\omega_0 \to 0$ ($T \to \infty$). We define

$$\omega \doteq n\omega_0$$

$$\Delta\omega \doteq \omega_0$$

$$\bar{F}(j\omega) \doteq \bar{a}_n(\omega_0)$$

In the limit as $T \to \infty$, we have

$$f(t) = \frac{1}{2\pi} \lim_{\Delta\omega \to 0} \sum_{n=-\infty}^{\infty} \bar{F}(j\omega)e^{j\omega t}\, \Delta\omega$$

$$= \frac{1}{2\pi} \int_{-\infty}^{\infty} \bar{F}(j\omega)e^{j\omega t}\, d\omega \tag{13.46}$$

$$\bar{F}(j\omega) = \lim_{T \to \infty} \int_{-T/2}^{T/2} f(t)e^{-j\omega t}\, dt$$

$$= \int_{-\infty}^{\infty} f(t)e^{-j\omega t}\, dt \tag{13.47}$$

We now define this relation to be the Fourier transform of $f(t)$ as

$$\mathscr{F}\{f(t)\} \equiv \bar{F}(j\omega) \doteq \int_{-\infty}^{\infty} f(t)e^{-j\omega t}\, dt \tag{13.48}$$

for which the inverse transform is

$$f(t) = \mathscr{F}^{-1}\{\bar{F}(j\omega)\} \doteq \frac{1}{2\pi} \int_{-\infty}^{\infty} \bar{F}(j\omega)e^{j\omega t}\, d\omega \tag{13.49}$$

It is important to note at this point that if the integral

$$\int_{-\infty}^{\infty} |f(t)|\, dt$$

exists, then the Fourier transform for $f(t)$ exists and the function may be described in terms of a complex function of ω, $\bar{F}(j\omega)$. At any given ω, $\bar{F}(j\omega)$ has a magnitude and phase angle analogous to the magnitude and phase angle of a harmonic term of the exponential Fourier series of a periodic function.

As with the Laplace transform, the inverse Fourier transform is unique. That is, there is a one-to-one relationship between a time function and its Fourier transform, so we can use Fourier transform pairs to find the inverse transform rather than using the integral of Equation 13.49.

Since the Fourier transform, like the Laplace transform, is an integral, it is linear. That is, $\mathcal{F}\{c_1 f_1(t) + c_2 f_2(t)\} = c_1 \mathcal{F}\{f_1(t)\} + c_2 \mathcal{F}\{f_2(t)\}$. By application of the definition, we can obtain Fourier transforms of some simple time functions as follows:

1. $\mathcal{F}\{\delta(t)\} = \displaystyle\int_{-\infty}^{\infty} \delta(t) e^{-j\omega t}\, dt = 1$

2. $\mathcal{F}\{\delta(t - nT)\} = e^{-jn\omega T}$

3. $\mathcal{F}\{e^{-at}u(t)\} = \displaystyle\int_{0}^{\infty} e^{-at} e^{-j\omega t}\, dt = \dfrac{1}{j\omega + a} \qquad a > 0$

4. $\mathcal{F}\{e^{-a|t|}\} = \mathcal{F}\{e^{at}u(-t) + e^{-at}u(t)\} \qquad a > 0$

$$= \dfrac{1}{a - j\omega} + \dfrac{1}{a + j\omega} = \dfrac{2a}{a^2 + \omega^2}$$

Since the inverse transform is unique, we can immediately write the following set of Fourier transform pairs:

1. $K \leftrightarrow K\delta(t)$

2. $Ke^{-jn\omega T} \leftrightarrow K\delta(t - nT)$

3. $\dfrac{1}{a + j\omega} \leftrightarrow e^{-at}u(t)$

4. $\dfrac{1}{a - j\omega} \leftrightarrow e^{at}u(-t)$

5. $\dfrac{2a}{a^2 + \omega^2} \leftrightarrow e^{-a|t|}$

The double arrow ($\leftrightarrow$) is often used to associate transform pairs—both Fourier and Laplace.

You should note the difference between the time functions $e^{-at}u(t)$ and $e^{at}u(-t)$. One is zero for $t > 0$. The other is zero for $t < 0$. The definition of $u(t)$ is the key.

We now find the Fourier transform for a very important function in communication theory—the unit pulse.

Example 13.10 ──

We wish to find the Fourier transform of the function shown in Figure 13.10.

$$f(t) = \begin{cases} 1 & -\dfrac{\alpha}{2} \le t \le \dfrac{\alpha}{2} \\[2mm] 0 & \text{elsewhere} \end{cases}$$

$$F(j\omega) = \int_{-\infty}^{\infty} f(t)e^{-j\omega t}\,dt = \int_{-\alpha/2}^{\alpha/2} e^{-j\omega t}\,dt$$

$$= -\frac{1}{j\omega}\left[e^{-j\omega t}\right]_{-\alpha/2}^{\alpha/2} = \frac{1}{j\omega}(e^{j\omega(\alpha/2)} - e^{-j\omega(\alpha/2)})$$

$$= \frac{2}{\omega}\sin\frac{\alpha}{2}\omega = \alpha\frac{\sin(\alpha/2)\omega}{(\alpha/2)\omega} \doteq \alpha\,\sin c\left(\frac{\alpha}{2}\right)\omega \qquad (13.50)$$

Figure 13.10
A unit pulse of duration α.

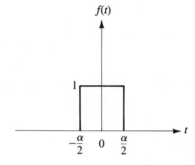

If we find the exponential Fourier series for the function of Figure 13.10 repeated every T seconds, as shown in Figure 13.11, we find that

Figure 13.11
Periodic function of repeated unit pulses of width α.

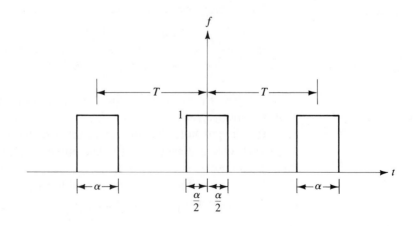

$$\bar{c}_n = \frac{1}{T}\int_{-\alpha/2}^{\alpha/2} e^{-jn\omega_0 t}\, dt = -\frac{1}{jn\omega_0 T}\left(e^{-jn\omega_0 t}\right)_{-\alpha/2}^{\alpha/2}$$

$$\bar{c}_n T = \frac{1}{jn\omega_0}(e^{jn\omega_0(\alpha/2)} - e^{-jn\omega_0(\alpha/2)})$$

$$= \alpha\frac{\sin n\omega_0(\alpha/2)}{n\omega_0(\alpha/2)} \doteq \alpha \sin c\left(\frac{\alpha}{2}\right)n\omega_0 \qquad (13.51)$$

For $\omega = n\omega_0$ the right sides of Equations 13.51 and 13.50 are identical. A sketch of the two equations is shown in Figure 13.12 for $\omega_0 = 2\pi/5\alpha$. The function $(\sin x)/x$ is zero for $x = K\pi$, where $K = \pm1, \pm2, \ldots$. For $\omega(\alpha/2) = \pm\pi$, $\omega = \pm(2\pi/\alpha)$.

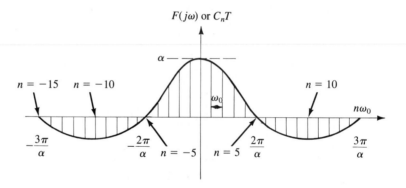

Figure 13.12
Sketch of $F(j\omega)$ for the unit pulse of Figure 13.10 and of $c_n T$ for the periodic function of Figure 13.11.

This example demonstrates that there is a close correspondence between the discrete-frequency spectrum of a function made up of repeated pulses as represented by its exponential Fourier series and the continuous-frequency spectrum of a single isolated pulse as represented by its Fourier transform. This relationship is exploited in a discrete-frequency version of the Fourier transform developed for numerical evaluation. The discrete Fourier transform (DFT) is not treated in this book, but it is usually discussed in texts on signals and systems. The DFT greatly expands the applications of the Fourier transform since both the transformation and the inverse can be calculated using a digital computer.

A compilation of a few useful transforms is seen in Table 13.4.

	$f(t)$	$\bar{F}(j\omega)$

Table 13.4
Fourier transforms
of some common
time functions

1.
$A\left[u\left(t + \dfrac{T}{2}\right) - u\left(t - \dfrac{T}{2}\right)\right]$
$AT\,\dfrac{\sin(\omega T/2)}{(\omega T/2)}$

2.
$Ae^{-at}u(t)$
$\dfrac{A}{j\omega + a}$

3.
$A\delta(t)$
A

4.
$A\left(1 - \dfrac{|t|}{2}\right)$
$|t| < \dfrac{T}{2}$
$\dfrac{AT}{2}\left[\dfrac{\sin(\omega T/4)}{(\omega T/4)}\right]^2$

5.
$Ae^{-a|t|}$
$\dfrac{2Aa}{a^2 + \omega^2}$

6.
$Ae^{-at}\sin(\omega_0 t)u(t)$
$\dfrac{A\omega_0}{(a + j\omega)^2 + \omega_0{}^2}$

7.
$Ae^{-at}\cos(\omega_0 t)u(t)$
$\dfrac{A(a + j\omega)}{(a + j\omega)^2 + \omega_0{}^2}$

8.
$\dfrac{A}{(b - a)}\,[e^{-at} - e^{-bt}]u(t)$
$\dfrac{A}{(j\omega + a)(j\omega + b)}$

13.9 BASIC PROPERTIES OF THE FOURIER TRANSFORM

Because of the symmetrical limits in the definition of the Fourier transform, some simplification results if the t-domain function is even or odd.

Theorem 13.8

Let $f(t)$ be even and let $\mathcal{F}\{f(t)\}$ exist; then $\bar{F}(j\omega)$ is real and even.

Theorem 13.9

Let $f(t)$ be odd and let $\mathcal{F}\{f(t)\}$ exist; then $\bar{F}(j\omega)$ is imaginary and odd.

Proof: To justify these theorems, we write $\bar{F}(j\omega)$ in the integral form.

$$\mathcal{F}\{f(t)\} = \int_{-\infty}^{\infty} f(t)e^{-j\omega t}\,dt$$

$$= \int_{-\infty}^{\infty} f(t)\cos \omega t\,dt - j\int_{-\infty}^{\infty} f(t)\sin \omega t\,dt \tag{13.52}$$

$$= A(\omega) - jB(\omega) \tag{13.53}$$

where $A(\omega)$ and $B(\omega)$ are real. From Equations 13.52 and 13.53, it is clear that a change of sign of ω changes the sign of $B(\omega)$. Thus $F(-j\omega) = F^*(j\omega)$.

It is clear that if $f(t)$ is even,

$$B(\omega) = 0$$

and

$$A(\omega) = 2\int_{0}^{\infty} f(t)\cos \omega t\,dt = A(-\omega) \tag{13.54}$$

If $f(t)$ is odd,

$$A(\omega) = 0$$

and

$$B(\omega) = 2\int_{0}^{\infty} f(t)\sin \omega t\,dt = -B(-\omega) \tag{13.55}$$

Since $A(\omega)$ is even and $B(\omega)$ is odd, for any $f(t)$ the definitions of the Fourier transform and inverse transform for even and odd time functions can be written as follows:

1.   Even time function $[B(\omega) = 0]$:

$$\mathcal{F}\{f(t)\} = A(\omega) = 2\int_{0}^{\infty} f(t)\cos \omega t\,dt \tag{13.56}$$

$$\mathcal{F}^{-1}\{F(\omega)\} = f(t) = \frac{1}{\pi}\int_{0}^{\infty} A(\omega)\cos \omega t\,d\omega \tag{13.57}$$

2.   Odd time function $[A(\omega) = 0]$:

$$\mathcal{F}\{f(t)\} = -j2\int_{0}^{\infty} f(t)\sin \omega t\,dt \tag{13.58}$$

$$\mathcal{F}^{-1}\{F(\omega)\} = f(t) = \frac{1}{\pi}\int_{0}^{\infty} B(\omega)\sin \omega t\,d\omega \tag{13.59}$$

We note the striking similarity of the transform and the inverse transform integrals in each case. In fact, this symmetry can be shown in a more general fashion. If we use the functional notation $\bar{F}(\omega)$ for the Fourier transform of $f(t)$—instead of $\bar{F}(j\omega)$—the symmetry becomes even more striking. Let us define

$$\mathscr{F}\{\bar{F}(\omega)\} = \int_{-\infty}^{\infty} \bar{F}(\omega)e^{-j\omega t}\, d\omega$$

Then, since

$$f(t) = \frac{1}{2\pi} \int_{-\infty}^{\infty} \bar{F}(\omega)e^{j\omega t}\, dt$$

$$\mathscr{F}\{\bar{F}(\omega)\} = 2\pi f(-t) \tag{13.60}$$

It is clear that interchanging the roles of ω and t will not affect the relationship. Thus

$$\mathscr{F}\{F(t)\} = 2\pi f(-\omega) \tag{13.61}$$

These relationships can be useful in finding transform pairs from those already known. For example, from

$$f(t) = \frac{e^{a|t|}}{2a} \quad\leftrightarrow\quad \frac{1}{a^2 + \omega^2} = F(\omega)$$

we can find the Fourier transform for

$$F(t) = \frac{1}{a^2 + t^2}$$

by the following reasoning:

$$\mathscr{F}\{F(t)\} = 2\pi f(-\omega)$$

$$= 2\pi\left(\frac{e^{a|-\omega|}}{2a}\right)$$

$$= \frac{\pi}{a}e^{a|\omega|}$$

Therefore,

$$\frac{1}{a^2 + t^2} \quad\leftrightarrow\quad \frac{\pi}{a}e^{a|\omega|}$$

With a more judicious choice of definitions for the Fourier transform, we could have avoided the 2π factor difference in transform and inverse transform and made the symmetry complete. This is done in some more advanced texts.

We learned in Chapter 12 that the Laplace transform could be used to transform t-domain differential equations to s-domain algebraic equations. As a result, we are able to model lumped systems in the s-domain and use matrix algebra to obtain solutions. We now show a similar property for the Fourier transform.

Theorem 13.10

Let the Fourier transform of $f(t)$ exist and let $f(t) \to 0$ as $|t| \to \infty$; then if $(d/dt)f(t)$ exists,

$$\mathscr{F}\left\{\frac{d}{dt}f(t)\right\} = j\omega\mathscr{F}\{f(t)\}$$

Proof: Let $(d/dt)f(t) \doteq f^{(1)}(t)$:

$$\mathscr{F}\{f^{(1)}(t)\} = \int_{-\infty}^{\infty} f^{(1)}(t)e^{-j\omega t}\, dt$$

Integrating by parts, we have

$$\mathscr{F}\{f^{(1)}(t)\} = \left[e^{-j\omega t}f(t)\right]_{-\infty}^{\infty} + j\omega \int_{-\infty}^{\infty} f(t)e^{-j\omega t}\, dt$$

The magnitude of $e^{-j\omega t}f(t)$ is no greater than $|f(t)|$, since $|e^{-j\omega t}|$ is never greater than 1. Thus $|e^{-j\omega t}f(t)| \to 0$ as $|t| \to \infty$, and the theorem is proved.

From this theorem we see that the Fourier transform takes inductor and capacitor t-domain models into ω-domain models as follows:

$$\mathscr{F}\left\{L\frac{di}{dt}\right\} = j\omega L\bar{I}(j\omega)$$

and

$$\mathscr{F}\left\{C\frac{dv}{dt}\right\} = j\omega C\bar{V}(j\omega)$$

Thus the same concepts of $\bar{Z}(j\omega)$ and $\bar{Y}(j\omega)$ that we learned in phasor modeling carry over to Fourier transform models. Also the $Z(s)$ and $Y(s)$ of Laplace-transformed network models may be converted for ω-domain analysis by the substitution of $j\omega$ for s.

If the function $f(t)$ has the property that the Fourier transform exists, then $f(t) \to 0$ at the infinite limits, and a system of first-order differential equations—such as the state equations—may be transformed into a set of algebraic equations in the ω-domain. Many functions that do not have Fourier transforms are Laplace-transformable because of the additional factor $e^{-\sigma t}$ in the integrand of the defining integral. When the Fourier transform of a function does exist, however, it is simpler in the sense that it is a function of a real variable ω instead of a complex variable s.

Theorem 13.10 may be extended to define the Fourier transform of the nth derivative of a function as follows:

Theorem 13.11

> Let $\mathcal{F}\{f(t)\}$ exist and let $f^{(1)}(t), f^{(2)}(t), \ldots, f^{(n)}(t)$ exist; then if $f^{(n-1)} \to 0$ as $|t| \to \infty$,
>
> $$\mathcal{F}\{f^{(n)}(t)\} = (j\omega)^n \mathcal{F}\{f(t)\}$$

As a result of Theorem 13.10, we see that the Fourier-transformed model of a network can be obtained simply by using the phasor model of each of the $R, L,$ and C components with ω left in as a variable. The Fourier transform (or Fourier series for periodic functions) of each source replaces the t-function in the ω-domain model. For example, consider a state model

$$\dot{\mathbf{x}} = \mathbf{A}\mathbf{x} + \mathbf{f}(t) \qquad (13.62)$$

The ω-domain equivalent is

$$[j\omega \mathbf{U} - \mathbf{A}]\mathcal{F}\{\mathbf{x}\} = \mathcal{F}\{\mathbf{f}(t)\} \qquad (13.63)$$

where the notation $\mathcal{F}\{\mathbf{x}\}$ means that we take the Fourier transform of each component of the vector $\mathbf{x}$. The ω-domain solution for $\mathbf{x}$ is then

$$\mathbf{x}(j\omega) = [j\omega \mathbf{U} - \mathbf{A}]^{-1} \mathbf{f}(j\omega) \qquad (13.64)$$

A listing of some useful Fourier transform operations is seen in Table 13.5.

Example 13.11

Consider the network of Figure 13.13.

Figure 13.13
(a) Time-domain series network model.
(b) Frequency-domain series network model for nonperiodic v-source.

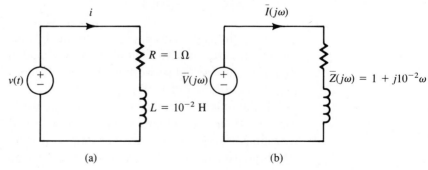

(a)   (b)

$$v(t) = \begin{cases} e^{-t} & t \geq 0 \\ 0 & t < 0 \end{cases}$$

$$V(j\omega) = \int_{-\infty}^{\infty} v(t)e^{-j\omega t}\, dt = \int_{0}^{\infty} e^{-t}e^{-j\omega t}\, dt$$

$$= \frac{1}{j\omega + 1}$$

$$I(j\omega) = \frac{V(j\omega)}{R + jL\omega} = \frac{100}{(j\omega + 1)(100 + j\omega)}$$

$$= \frac{100}{99}\left(\frac{1}{j\omega + 1} - \frac{1}{j\omega + 100}\right)$$

Taking the inverse transform term by term, we obtain

$$i(t) = \frac{100}{99}(e^{-t} - e^{-100t})\ \text{A} \tag{13.65}$$

This example demonstrates that the procedure of finding the inverse Fourier transform is similar to finding the inverse Laplace transform if the Fourier transform is a ratio of polynomials in $j\omega$. A plot of the $i(t)$ function of Equation 13.65 shown as Figure 13.14 indicates that it conforms rather closely to the shape of $v(t)$. An increase in the size of L will cause a greater deviation, while a decrease in L will result in a greater conformity.

Figure 13.14
Plot of the $v(t)$ and $i(t)$ functions for Example 13.11.

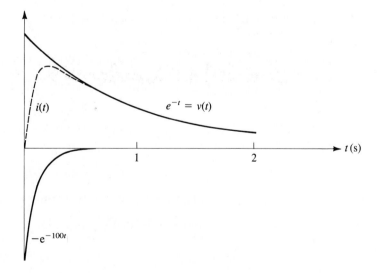

Table 13.5
Fourier transform
operations

Operation	$F(t)$	$\bar{F}(j\omega)$
Transformation	$f(t)$	$\displaystyle\int_{-\infty}^{\infty} f(t)e^{-j\omega t}\, dt$
Inverse transformation	$\displaystyle\frac{1}{2\pi}\int_{-\infty}^{\infty} \bar{F}(j\omega)e^{j\omega t}\, d\omega$	$\bar{F}(j\omega)$
Superposition	$af_1(t) + bf_2(t)$	$a\bar{F}_1(j\omega) + b\bar{F}_2(j\omega)$
Differentiation	$\dfrac{d^n}{dt^n}f(t)$	$(j\omega)^n\bar{F}(j\omega)$
Scaling	$f(at)$	$\dfrac{1}{|a|}\bar{F}\left(\dfrac{j\omega}{a}\right)$
Time shift	$f(t - t_0)$	$e^{-j\omega t_0}\bar{F}(j\omega)$
Frequency shift	$e^{j\omega_0 t}f(t)$	$\bar{F}[j(\omega - \omega_0)]$
Symmetry	$F(t)$	$2\pi f(-j\omega)$

Example 13.12

For our second example we investigate the response of a 2-port to a symmetrical voltage pulse. For the diagram of Figure 13.15,

$$\bar{V}_1(j\omega) = \frac{100}{(5 + j\omega)(5 - j\omega)}$$

and the 2-port voltage transfer function is

$$\bar{G}(j\omega) = \frac{10(j\omega + 1)}{(j\omega + 10)(j\omega + 20)}$$

Thus the Fourier transform of the output voltage is

$$\bar{V}_2(j\omega) = \frac{10^3(j\omega + 1)}{(j\omega + 10)(j\omega + 20)(5 + j\omega)(5 - j\omega)}$$

$$= \left[\frac{A}{(j\omega + 10)} + \frac{B}{(j\omega + 20)} + \frac{C}{(5 + j\omega)} + \frac{D}{(5 - j\omega)}\right]$$

Using the standard procedure for evaluating the constants, we get

$$A = \lim_{j\omega \to -10} (j\omega + 10)\bar{V}_2(j\omega) = 12$$

$$B = -5.1, \qquad C = -5.3, \qquad D = 1.6$$

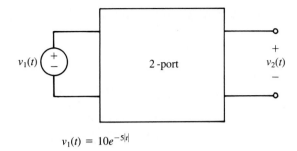

Figure 13.15
Network of Example
13.11.

Figure 13.15
Network of Example
13.12.

$$v_1(t) = 10e^{-5|t|}$$

Thus the ω-domain output voltage is

$$\bar{V}_2(j\omega) = \frac{12}{j\omega + 10} - \frac{5.1}{j\omega + 20} - \frac{5.3}{j\omega + 5} + \frac{1.6}{5 - j\omega}$$

The inverse transform is

$$v_2(t) = (12e^{-10t} - 5.1e^{-20t} - 5.3e^{-5t})u(t) + 1.6e^{5t}u(-t) \text{ V}$$

The first term of the solution applies for $t > 0$ and the second for $t < 0$. At $t = 0^-$ and $t = 0^+$ the solutions agree ($v_2(0) = 1.6$), which is a check on the accuracy of the calculations.

As a final comment on the Fourier transform, we extend the discussion of power considerations of Section 13.6 to include continuous-frequency spectra. Suppose we again talk about the power dissipated in a 1-Ω resistor. Then the energy dissipated over all time for a Fourier-transformable voltage $v(t)$ is

$$W = \int_{-\infty}^{\infty} v(t)^2 \, dt$$

(If we actually are interested in energy dissipated in a resistor R, of course, we merely write $v^2(t)/R$ or $i^2(t)R$ for the integrand.)

We now do a bit of trickery and write one of the $v(t)$ terms as an inverse Fourier transform,

$$v(t) = \frac{1}{2\pi} \int_{-\infty}^{\infty} \bar{V}(j\omega)e^{j\omega t} \, d\omega$$

and write

$$W = \frac{1}{2\pi} \int_{-\infty}^{\infty} v(t) \left[\int_{-\infty}^{\infty} \bar{V}(j\omega)e^{j\omega t} \, d\omega \right] dt$$

Now we interchange the order of integration to get

$$W = \frac{1}{2\pi} \int_{-\infty}^{\infty} \bar{V}(j\omega)\left(\int_{-\infty}^{\infty} v(t)e^{j\omega t} \, dt \right) d\omega$$

By the symmetry property discussed earlier (Equations 13.60 and 13.61),

$$\int_{-\infty}^{\infty} v(t)e^{j\omega t}\, dt = \bar{V}(-j\omega)$$

Therefore, the energy associated with $v(t)$ is

$$W = \int_{-\infty}^{\infty} v^2(t)\, dt = \frac{1}{2\pi} \int_{-\infty}^{\infty} \bar{V}(j\omega)\bar{V}(-j\omega)\, d\omega$$

$$= \frac{1}{2\pi} \int_{-\infty}^{\infty} |\bar{V}(j\omega)|^2\, d\omega \qquad (13.66)$$

since $\bar{V}(-j\omega) = \bar{V}*(j\omega)$. Equation 13.66 indicates that the energy associated with a voltage $v(t)$ may be calculated in the ω-domain as an integral over all ω, as well as in the time domain. Thus the energy associated with a given frequency band can be singled out for comparison with the energy associated with another band or the entire spectrum. This relationship is analogous to the result in Section 13.6 for the Fourier series and is also called Parseval's theorem. It is very useful in assessing the effect at a load on the energy available from a source through a filter.

Since a filter passes a given band of frequencies, the energy available at the output would be

$$W' = \frac{1}{2\pi} \int_{-\omega_0}^{\omega_0} |\bar{V}(j\omega)|^2\, d\omega$$

if the filter were ideal and the cutoff frequency were ω_0 rad/s.

The energy error ratio (EER) for a pulse-type voltage (or current) is defined in a fashion similar to the average power error ratio discussed earlier.

$$\text{EER} = \frac{W - W'}{W} = 1 - \frac{W'}{W}$$

Example 13.13

Let us consider the effect of an ideal filter on an exponential pulse voltage

$$v_1(t) = 10e^{-t}u(t) \text{ V}$$

The energy dissipated in a 1-Ω resistor by $v_1(t)$ is

$$W = \int_{-\infty}^{\infty} (10e^{-t})^2\, dt = 100 \int_{0}^{\infty} e^{-2t}\, dt = 50 \text{ J}$$

The energy at the output of the filter depends on the cutoff frequency ω_0.

$$W' = \frac{1}{2\pi} \int_{-\omega_0}^{\omega_0} \left(\frac{10}{j\omega + 1}\right)\left(\frac{10}{-j\omega + 1}\right) d\omega = \frac{50}{\pi} \int_{-\omega_0}^{\omega_0} \frac{d\omega}{\omega^2 + 1}$$

$$= \frac{100}{\pi} \int_0^{\omega_0} \frac{d\omega}{\omega^2 + 1} = \frac{100}{\pi} \tan^{-1} \omega_0 \text{ J}$$

Thus

$$\frac{W'}{W} = \frac{2}{\pi} \tan^{-1} \omega_0$$

if $\omega_0 \to \infty$, $W' \to 50$, and $\frac{W'}{W} = 1$.

Table 13.6 shows values of W'/W and the energy error ratio (EER) for several values of ω_0.

Table 13.6 EER values for Example 13.3

ω_0	$\dfrac{W'}{W}$	EER $\left(1 - \dfrac{W'}{W}\right)$
1	0.5	0.5
10	0.9365	0.0635
100	0.9936	0.0064
1000	0.9994	0.0006
∞	1.0000	0.0000

From these values a designer could decide how large the cutoff frequency $f_0 = \omega_0/2\pi$ must be to achieve the desired energy transfer.

13.10 SUMMARY

In this chapter we learned that many source functions of interest in electric network theory can be expressed in terms of functions of frequency. The Fourier series may be used to represent a periodic source function as a sum of sinusoidal time functions plus a constant. Since the frequencies of the sinusoidal functions are integral multiples of a fundamental frequency $2\pi/T$, we say that a periodic function has a *discrete-frequency spectrum*.

A Fourier series may be written in either the trigonometric or exponential form. Each term of the exponential series has the form of a time-varying phasor, and thus the phasor techniques of Chapter 9 may be used, without a transformation, to find a steady-state solution. Phasor techniques may, of course, also be used for the trigonometric series using the standard procedure.

The Fourier transform is an extension to continuous-frequency spectra of the Fourier series. It is applicable to nonperiodic pulse-type source functions and can be used to transform linear dynamic network models from the t-domain to algebraic ω-domain models—very much in the fashion of the Laplace transform. It is restricted, however, to a much smaller class of source functions than is the Laplace transform. In addition, the Fourier transform has no provisions for the inclusion of initial conditions, which are essential in the solving of simultaneous systems of linear differential equations. Thus the Laplace transform is much more useful *if a complete solution* is needed for a network model.

Part of the appeal of the Fourier series and Fourier transform of source functions lies in the ability of the analyst to determine average power and energy, respectively, associated with particular frequency spectra—discrete or continuous.

Another appealing feature is that the ω-domain network impedances ($\overline{Z}(j\omega)$) and admittances ($\overline{Y}(j\omega)$) for an exponential Fourier series analysis or a Fourier transform analysis are of the same form as those for a standard sinusoidal steady-state analysis.

Thus, if the response of a network is different at different frequencies (as is nearly always the case), some indication of the effect of that "filtering" can be obtained by an appropriate Fourier analysis. Often this analysis will involve the computation of an average power error or an energy error.

REFERENCES ———————————————————————————————O

1. McGillem, C. D., and G. R. Cooper, *Continuous and Discrete Signal and System Analysis*. New York: Holt, Rinehart and Winston, 1974, Chapter 5.

2. Scott, R. E., *Linear Circuits*, Part 2. Reading, Mass.: Addison-Wesley, 1960, Chapter 20.

3. Ziemer, R. E., W. H. Tranter, and D. R. Fannin, *Signals and Systems: Continuous and Discrete*. New York: Macmillan, 1983, Chapter 3.

PROBLEMS

13.1 Show that if $f_1(t) = \sin(nt + \alpha)$ and $f_2(t) = \sin(mt + \theta)$, where n and m are integers and $n \neq m$, then f_1 and f_2 are orthogonal over the interval $t = 2\pi$.

13.2 Show that $f_1(x) = e^{jnx}$ and $f_2(x) = e^{jmx}$ are orthogonal over the interval $x = 2\pi$ if $n \neq m$ and n and m are integers.

13.3 Define two functions made up of straight-line segments such that the functions are orthogonal over some specified interval.

13.4 Given that

$$f_1(t) = \begin{cases} 10 \sin 2\pi t & k \leq t \leq k + \tfrac{1}{2} \\ 0 & k + \tfrac{1}{2} < t < k + 1 \end{cases}$$
$$k = 0, \pm 1, \pm 2, \ldots$$

$$f_2(t) = \begin{cases} 5 \cos 2\pi t & k \leq t \leq k + \tfrac{1}{2} \\ 0 & k + \tfrac{1}{2} < t < k + 1 \end{cases}$$

(a) Sketch the functions over an interval $-1 < t < 1$.

(b) Test whether these functions are orthogonal over the interval $(k, k + 1)$.

13.5 Find the Fourier series for the square wave of Figure 13.16 by using the period $T = 2$ as shown and integrating with respect to x.

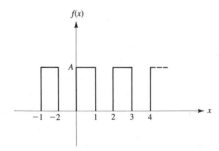

Figure 13.16

13.6 Convert the function of Problem 13.5 into one with a period of 2π and evaluate the coefficients for the Fourier series.

13.7 The function shown as Figure 13.17 is typical of the vertical sweep voltage used in television

receivers. Evaluate the Fourier series coefficients, working with the t variable.

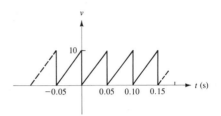

Figure 13.17

13.8 Convert the function of Figure 13.17 to one with a period of 2π and evaluate the Fourier series coefficients.

13.9 Shift the origin of Figure 13.16 to the right $\tfrac{1}{2}$ unit and evaluate the Fourier series coefficients.

13.10 Shift the origin of Figure 13.16 to the left $\tfrac{1}{2}$ unit and evaluate the Fourier series coefficients.

13.11 For the function of Figure 13.16, make an axis shift so that the resulting function $f_1(x)$ has half-wave symmetry and is an even function. Write the general expression for a_n for $f_1(x)$.

13.12 For the function of Figure 13.16, make an axis shift so that the resulting function $f_2(x)$ has half-wave symmetry and is an odd function. Write the general expression for b_n for $f_2(x)$.

13.13 Shift the axis of Figure 13.17 to create an odd function $v_1(t)$. Write the general expression for b_n for $v_1(t)$.

13.14 Shift the origin of Figure 13.17 to the right 0.025 s and evaluate the Fourier series coefficients.

For problems 13.15–13.21 you should use a numerical integration program such as NUMINT (Appendix C) to calculate the constant and the next four nonzero terms of the Fourier trigonometric series. The computer should also be used to calculate values of the sum of the truncated series. The truncated series should be plotted for one period (0 to T).

13.15 Find the Fourier series coefficients for the periodic function shown in Figure 13.18. Write the first five terms of the series.

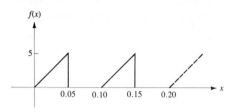

Figure 13.18

13.16 Find the Fourier series coefficients for the function shown in Figure 13.19. Write the first five terms of the series.

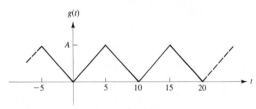

Figure 13.19

13.17 Find the Fourier series coefficients for the half-wave rectified sine function shown in Figure 13.20.

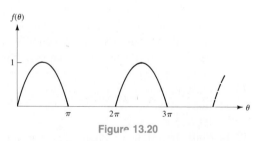

Figure 13.20

13.18 Find the Fourier series coefficients for the full-wave rectified sine function shown in Figure 13.21.

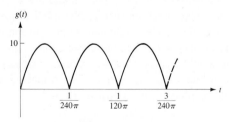

Figure 13.21

13.19 Shift the origin of Figure 13.20 to the right $\pi/2$ units and find the Fourier series coefficients. Write the first five terms of the series.

13.20 Shift the origin of Figure 13.21 $1/(480\pi)$ s to the right and find the Fourier series coefficients. Write the first five terms of the series.

13.21 Find the Fourier series coefficients for the function of Figure 13.22. Write the first five terms of the series. Is this an odd function?

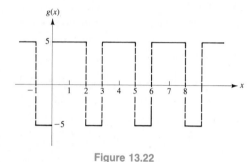

Figure 13.22

13.22 Find the Fourier series coefficients for the function of Figure 13.23.

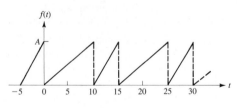

Figure 13.23

13.23 Find the Fourier series coefficients for the function of Figure 13.24 by use of the half-wave symmetry property. Does this function also have quarter-wave symmetry?

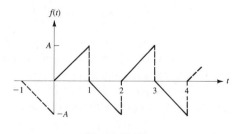

Figure 13.24

13.24 Use the symmetry properties of the function of Figure 13.25 to obtain the Fourier series coefficients.

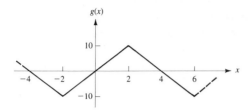

Figure 13.25

13.25 Can the x-origin of Figure 13.22 be shifted to make the Fourier series either a sine series or a cosine series plus a constant term? Demonstrate for each case, if possible, and explain your reasoning.

The program NUMINT may be used as the basis for the calculations specified in Problems 13.26–13.29.

13.26 Write a computer program to calculate the a_n coefficients for $f_1(x)$ of Problem 13.11, and find the first five nonzero coefficients.

13.27 Write a computer program to calculate the b_n coefficients for $f_2(x)$ of Problem 13.12, and find the first five nonzero coefficients.

13.28 Write a computer program to calculate the b_n coefficients for $v_1(t)$ of Problem 13.13, and find the first five nonzero coefficients.

13.29 Write a computer program to calculate the b_n coefficients for the function of Figure 13.25, and find the first five nonzero coefficients.

13.30 Obtain the Fourier series in the form

$$f(t) = a_0 + \sum_{k=1}^{\infty} c_k \cos(kt + \phi_k)$$

for the first three nonzero terms for Problems (a) 13.5, (b) 13.7, (c) 13.9, (d) 13.11, (e) 13.12, (f), 13.13, (g) 13.14, and (h) 13.15.

13.31 Assume that the function of Figure 13.17 is a voltage source applied to a series RL circuit of $R = 1\ \Omega$ and $L = 0.001$ H. Calculate the first four nonzero terms in the steady-state current that results. Plot the current and voltage versus time.

13.32 Suppose that the voltage source function for Figure 13.26 is

$$e(t) = \sum_{k=1}^{\infty} \frac{1}{k} \cos 1000kt \quad k = 1, 3, 5, \ldots$$

(a) Calculate the first three nonzero terms of the Fourier series for $i(t)$.

(b) Plot the functions of (a) and the sum of these three functions which approximates $i(t)$.

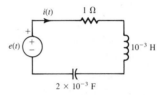

Figure 13.26

13.33 Find the exponential Fourier series coefficients $c_n = (a_n - jb_n)/2$ for the first three nonzero terms for Problems (a) 13.5, (b) 13.7, (c) 13.9, (d) 13.12, (e) 13.14, and (f) 13.15.

13.34 Find the APER for the Fourier series representation of Problem 13.26 (five nonzero terms).

13.35 Find the APER for the Fourier series representation of Problem 13.27.

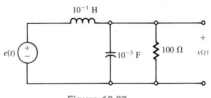

Figure 13.27
Low-pass filter network.

13.36 Find the APER for the Fourier series representation of Problem 13.28.

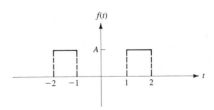

Figure 13.28

13.37 Find the APER for the Fourier series representation of Problem 13.29.

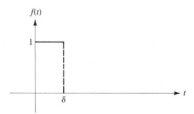

Figure 13.29

13.38 For the network of Figure 13.26, let
$C = 10^{-6}$ F, R and L be unchanged, and

$$e(t) = 10(\cos 2000\pi t + \tfrac{1}{3} \cos 6000\pi t$$
$$+ \tfrac{1}{5} \cos 10{,}000\pi t$$
$$+ \tfrac{1}{7} \cos 14{,}000\pi t) \text{ V}$$

Find the steady-state value of current as a
Fourier series. Calculate the average power
dissipated in the resistor for each term and
compare the results to the power available for
$e(t)$ (term by term) if applied to a 1-Ω resistor.

13.39 For the low-pass filter network of Figure 13.27,
the source voltage is

$$e(t) = 325|\cos 377t| \text{ V}$$

Find the first three nonzero terms of the
Fourier series for the output voltage $v(t)$. (Note
that the source is a full-rectified, 230-V (rms),
60-Hz voltage.)

13.40 Repeat Problem 13.39 for a periodic source
voltage such that

$$e(t) = \begin{cases} 325 \cos 377t \text{ V} & -\dfrac{\pi}{2} < 377t < \dfrac{\pi}{2} \\[2mm] 0 & \dfrac{\pi}{2} \le 377t < 3\dfrac{\pi}{2} \end{cases}$$

(This function is a half-rectified, 230-V (rms),
60-Hz voltage.)

13.41 Repeat Problem 13.39 for a periodic square-
wave voltage source

$$e(t) = \begin{cases} 500 \text{ V} & 0 < t < \pi \\ 0 & \pi < t < 2\pi \end{cases}$$

13.42 Find the Fourier transform of the function of
Figure 13.28.

13.43 Find the Fourier transform of the function of
Figure 13.29. Factor out $e^{j(\omega\delta/2)}$ and compare
the result to Equation 13.50.

13.44 Find the Fourier transform of the function of
Figure 13.30.

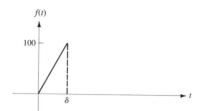

Figure 13.30

13.45 Find the Fourier transform of

$$f(t) = \begin{cases} e^{-t} & 0 < t < 1 \\ 0 & t > 1 \text{ and } t < 0 \end{cases}$$

13.46 Find the Fourier transform of the function of
Figure 13.31.

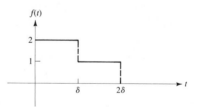

Figure 13.31

13.47 Find the Fourier transform of the function of
Figure 13.32. Compare this with the Fourier
transform of Problem 13.46.

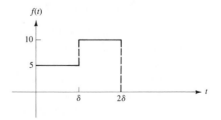

Figure 13.32

13.48 Find the Fourier transform of the function of Figure 13.33.

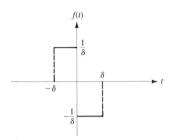

Figure 13.33

13.49 Starting with the general definition of the inverse Fourier transform, show that the inverse transform of an even function has the form of Equation 13.57.

13.50 Starting with the general definition of the inverse Fourier transform, show that the inverse transform of an odd function has the form of Equation 13.59.

13.51 Find the ω-domain form (Fourier transform) of i in the network shown as Figure 13.34 if

$$v(t) = \begin{cases} 10 \text{ V} & 0 < t < 1 \\ 0 & t < 0 \text{ and } t > 1 \end{cases}$$

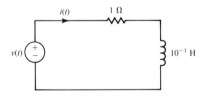

Figure 13.34

13.52 Find the Fourier transform of i for the network of Figure 13.35.

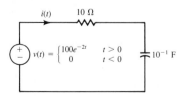

Figure 13.35

13.53 Find the Fourier transform of $v(t)$ for the network of Figure 13.36.

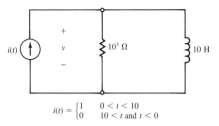

$$i(t) = \begin{cases} 1 & 0 < t < 10 \\ 0 & 10 < t \text{ and } t < 0 \end{cases}$$

Figure 13.36

13.54 Find the Fourier transform of $v(t)$ for the network of Figure 13.37.

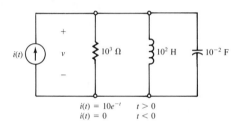

$i(t) = 10e^{-t}$ $t > 0$
$i(t) = 0$ $t < 0$

Figure 13.37

13.55 Suppose the square-wave voltage of Example 13.5 is applied to an ideal-filter 2-port with a bandpass of $11{,}000/(2\pi)$ Hz. Find the average power in a 1-Ω resistor at the output port of the filter.

13.56 Work Problem 13.55 for a 10-Ω resistor on the output port.

13.57 Explain why the average power error can never be negative.

13.58 Given that a transformation

$$\mathcal{G}^{-1}\{f(t)\} \doteq \int_{-\infty}^{\infty} f(t)e^{j\omega t}\, dt$$

Show that

$$\mathcal{G}^{-1}\{f(t)\} = F(-j\omega)$$

13.59 Assume that $F(j\omega) = \pi[\delta(\omega - w_0) + \delta(\omega + w_0)]$. Find the inverse transform. If we restrict the Fourier transform to integrable functions, what problem has developed?

13.60 Assume that $F(j\omega) = j\pi[\delta(\omega - w_0) - \delta(\omega + w_0)]$. Find the inverse transform. If we restrict the Fourier transform to integrable functions, what problem do we encounter? (Do not worry too much about this transform pair. Just recognize that it and similar ones are used regularly by respectable engineers and engineering professors.[1])

13.61 Use the numerical integration program, NUMINT (or other), to determine the energy error ratio for an ideal filter that passes frequencies up to $\omega = 2\pi \times 10^4$ rad/s applied to a voltage source $v(t) = [u(t + 10^{-4}) - u(t - 10^{-4})]$. Note the problem at $\omega = 0$.

13.62 Use the numerical integration program, NUMINT (or other), to determine the energy error ratio for the triangular pulse (Number 4) of Table 13.4 passed through an ideal filter, which passes all frequencies up to $\omega = 200$ rad/s. Let $A = 10$ and $T = 2\pi \times 10^{-2}$ s.

13.63 Repeat Problem 13.61 for an upper pass frequency of $\omega = 4\pi \times 10^4$ rad/s.

13.64 Repeat Problem 13.62 for an upper pass frequency of $\omega = 400$ rad/s.

13.65 Analytically determine the energy error ratio for the symmetrical exponential pulse voltage

$$v(t) = 100e^{-2|t|} \text{ V}$$

passed through a filter that passes all frequencies up to $\omega = 4$ rad/s.

13.66 Use the numerical integration routine, NUMINT (or other), to check the analytical results of Problem 13.65.

---

[1] As a matter of fact, some of the techniques used in evaluating discrete Fourier transforms require formal manipulations of this kind.

Giants of the profession
IEEE Centennial Hall of Fame

 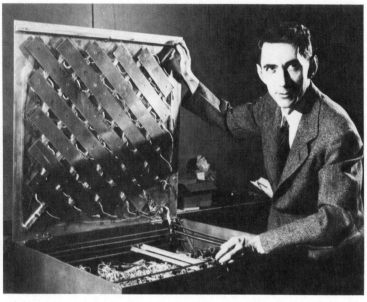

John R. Pierce (1910–   )
Specialist at Bell Laboratories in high-frequency electronic amplifiers; he was largely responsible for the Echo passive-communications satellite experiment; a noted science-fiction enthusiast and writer. Here he holds the traveling wave tube, 1946.

Claude E. Shannon (1916–   )
Engineer whose seminal paper, "A Mathematical Theory of Communication" (1948), launched the modern era in information theory. Shannon is showing the "mouse" maze, 1950.

Reprinted with permission from
"Centennial Hall of Fame,"
IEEE SPECTRUM, April 1984.

Laplace transform analysis of simple networks

14.1 INTRODUCTION

In Chapters 7 and 8 we formulated mathematical models in the t-domain for some simple networks with energy-storage elements. In the case of linear networks, these mathematical models were in the form of linear, constant-coefficient differential or integrodifferential equations. In Chapter 12 the Laplace transform was introduced as a very powerful technique for the analytical solution of these models. In this chapter our primary objective is to utilize the Laplace transform to obtain network solutions and to extend the elementary network theorems of resistive networks to cover s-domain models of RLC networks.

14.2 INITIAL CONDITIONS

We have seen, from our development of the Laplace transform, that the initial conditions needed for the solution of state models or integrodifferential equation loop or node models are inductor currents and capacitor voltages.

These are very desirable initial conditions because they are normally known at the beginning of the solution period (either directly or as an initially specified stored energy).

At times, however, as we have already seen, the network model may be formulated in terms of higher-order differential equations. In this case the application of the Laplace transform requires a knowledge of the initial values of some higher-order derivatives. These values are readily obtained from the network model by evaluating it at $t = 0$. This technique can best be presented by example.

Example 14.1

If we choose i_2 and i_4 as loop currents for the network shown in Figure 14.1, we have

$$2i_2 + 4 \int_0^t [i_2(\tau) - i_4(\tau)] \, d\tau + v_3(0) = e_1(t) \tag{14.1}$$

$$-4 \int_0^t [i_2(\tau) - i_4(\tau)] \, d\tau - v_3(0) + 3 \frac{di_4}{dt} = -e_5(t) \tag{14.2}$$

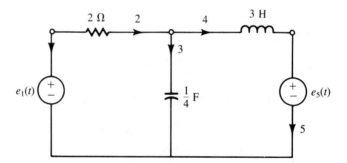

Figure 14.1
Network for Example 14.1.

If we use the Laplace transform to solve these equations, it is obvious that the necessary initial conditions are the capacitor voltage v_3 and the inductor current i_4 evaluated at time $t = 0^-$. The values of other variables and higher-order derivatives can be obtained from Equations 14.1 and 14.2 or from derivatives of these equations. For example, suppose we evaluate them at $t = 0^-$. Then we have

$$2i_2(0^-) + v_3(0^-) = e_1(0^-)$$

and

$$-v_3(0^-) + 3 \frac{di_4}{dt}(0^-) = -e_5(0^-)$$

Since $v_3(0^-)$ can be calculated from the initial energy storage and $e_1(t)$ and $e_5(t)$ are given functions of time, we have

$$i_2(0^-) = \frac{1}{2}[e_1(0^-) - v_3(0^-)] \tag{14.3}$$

and

$$\frac{di_4}{dt}(0^-) = \frac{1}{3}[v_3(0^-) - e_5(0^-)] \tag{14.4}$$

If the initial values of higher derivatives are desired, we first differentiate Equations 14.1 and 14.2 to obtain

$$\frac{2di_2}{dt} + 4i_2 - 4i_4 = \frac{de_1}{dt} \tag{14.5}$$

$$-4i_2 + 4i_4 + 3\frac{d^2i_4}{dt^2} = -\frac{de_5}{dt} \tag{14.6}$$

By evaluating this result at $t = 0^-$, we have

$$2\frac{di_2}{dt}(0^-) + 4i_2(0^-) - 4i_4(0^-) = \frac{de_1}{dt}(0^-)$$

and

$$-4i_2(0^-) + 4i_4(0^-) + 3\frac{d^2i_4}{dt^2}(0^-) = -\frac{de_5}{dt}(0^-)$$

Since $i_4(0^-)$ is given by initial energy storage, we have

$$\frac{di_2}{dt}(0^-) = \frac{1}{2}\left[\frac{de_1}{dt}(0^-) + 4i_4(0^-) - 4i_2(0^-)\right]$$

and

$$\frac{d^2i_4}{dt^2}(0^-) = \frac{1}{3}\left[-\frac{de_5}{dt}(0^-) + 4i_2(0^-) - 4i_4(0^-)\right]$$

which can both be assigned numerical values by substituting in the known value for $i_4(0^-)$, the value of $i_2(0^-)$ from Equation 14.3, and the values of the derivatives of the two sources, evaluated at $t = 0^-$.

If the initial values of the derivatives of other variables are desired, they can be obtained from the other equations of the network PRIMM. For example, since

$$v_3 = e_1(t) - 2i_2$$

we have

$$\frac{dv_3}{dt} = \frac{de_1}{dt} - 2\frac{di_2}{dt}$$

and

$$\frac{dv_3}{dt}(0^-) = \frac{de_1}{dt}(0^-) - 2\frac{di_2}{dt}(0^-)$$

At the risk of emphasizing the obvious, we note that the initial value of dv_3/dt can be nonzero even though the initial value of v_3 is constant. That is, $(dv_3/dt)(0^-)$ is the value of dv_3/dt evaluated at $t = 0^-$ and is not the derivative of $v_3(0^-)$. Similarly, $(di_2/dt)(0^-)$, for example, cannot be obtained by differentiation of Equation 14.3.

If the initial values of higher-order derivatives are desired, they can be obtained by continuing the process—that is, differentiate Equations 14.5 and 14.6, evaluate at $t = 0^-$, and substitute previous results.

The process illustrated in the above example is a very general process that can be applied to any network model to find the initial values of derivatives of any order for any of the network variables. We will, however, rarely have any need for any initial conditions other than the initial values of capacitor voltages and inductor currents.

If we elect to use state models for network analysis, the only initial conditions we ever need are inductor currents and capacitor voltages. This is one of the arguments for using the state-space approach to network modeling.

14.3   1-PORT MODELS IN THE s-DOMAIN— IMPEDANCE AND ADMITTANCE

Except for the phasor case, the majority of the mathematical models for the 1-port components that we have considered up to this point have been t-domain models. These t-domain models can be converted to s-domain models, for linear R, L, and C components and for v-sources, i-sources, and controlled sources by simply taking the Laplace transform of the t-domain component equations. In fact, this is the case for any 1-port with a component equation that is Laplace transformable. Thus we can readily write an s-domain component equation for a linear resistor, but the nonlinear resistor described by $v(t) = 10[i(t)]^3$ does not have a Laplace-transformed description. This is true in general for nonlinear components.

The s-domain component equations for linear components R, L, and C are summarized in Table 14.1. As previously noted, these s-domain component equations are obtained by Laplace-transforming the t-domain component equations.

All the component equations of Table 14.1 are either of the form

$$V(s) = Z(s)I(s) + E(s)$$

or of the form

$$I(s) = Y(s)V(s) + J(s)$$

where $E(s)$ and $J(s)$ are known functions and depend on the particular initial conditions. The functions $Z(s)$ and $Y(s)$ relate the transformed voltage to the transformed current (or vice versa) for zero initial conditions and consequently are quite logically referred to as the component's s-domain *impedance* and *admittance*, respectively. Thus we say that the s-domain impedances of the linear components R, L, and C are R, sL, and $1/sC$, respectively. Likewise, the admittances are G, $1/sL$, and sC.

Table 14.1 Component equations for linear passive elements

Component	t-domain component equation	s-domain component equation
R or	$v = Ri$ or $i = Gv$	$V(s) = RI(s)$ or $I(s) = GV(s)$
L or	$v = L\dfrac{di}{dt}$ or $i = \dfrac{1}{L}\displaystyle\int_0^t v(\tau)\,d\tau + i(0^-)$	$V(s) = sLI(s) - Li(0^-)$ or $I(s) = \dfrac{1}{sL}V(s) + \dfrac{i(0^-)}{s}$
C or	$v = \dfrac{1}{C}\displaystyle\int_0^t i(\tau)\,d\tau + v(0^-)$ or $i = C\dfrac{dv}{dt}$	$V(s) = \dfrac{1}{sC}I(s) + \dfrac{v(0^-)}{s}$ or $I(s) = sCV(s) - Cv(0^-)$

Finally, it should be noted that $Z(s) = 1/Y(s)$ for each of these three components.

The s-domain component equations for sources are not tabulated because of their varied forms. However, the s-domain component equation of any v-source, i-source, or controlled source is simply obtained by transforming the given t-domain component equation.

Finally, since KCL and KVL equations are algebraic summations, they can be converted to the s-domain by simply changing each variable to the s-domain. In other words, KCL and KVL equations can be written directly in the s-domain. This fact, coupled with the fact that the component equations can be written in the s-domain, means that we are now able to formulate network models directly in the s-domain. For example, loop equations may be written by summing voltages around the loops in terms of the transformed loop currents by using the s-domain component equations. This matter will be discussed later using examples. However, it should be noted that it is just a matter of whether we apply the Laplace transform before the formulation or after the equations are formulated.

14.4   SECOND-ORDER NETWORK FUNCTIONS

Second-order linear networks are characterized by an s-domain response function, which consists of a second-degree polynomial, or a quadratic function, in its denominator. Also, at times we may wish to isolate and concentrate upon a quadratic term in the analysis of higher-order networks. These second-order network functions have special characteristics that merit some extra attention.

Example 14.2

As an example of second-order network behavior, consider the network of Figure 14.2. If the initial conditions are zero, we can draw an s-domain equivalent network, as seen in Figure 14.3. In this network the s-domain characteristics of the passive components are given as admittances in anticipation of a nodal analysis. The node voltage equation is

$$GV(s) + \frac{1}{sL}V(s) + sCV(s) = \frac{10}{s} \tag{14.7}$$

which is the result that would be obtained if a t-domain nodal equation had been written for the network of Figure 14.2 and then transformed to the s-domain.

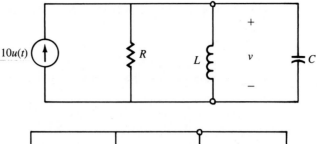

Figure 14.2
Network for Example 14.2.

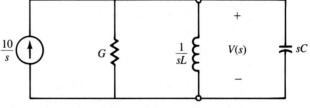

Figure 14.3
An s-domain equivalent
network for Figure 14.2.

Equation 14.7 can be solved for $V(s)$ to obtain

$$V(s) = \frac{10}{s\left(sC + G + \dfrac{1}{sL}\right)}$$

or

$$V(s) = \frac{\dfrac{10}{C}}{s^2 + \dfrac{G}{C}s + \dfrac{1}{LC}} \tag{14.8}$$

From this result and our experience with the Laplace transform in Chapter 12, we conclude that the form of the response $v(t)$ will depend upon the values for $G, L,$ and C. In order to examine this idea in more detail, suppose we calculate the roots of the denominator polynomial. By the quadratic formula, these roots are

$$s_1 = -\frac{G}{2C} + \sqrt{\left(\frac{G}{2C}\right)^2 - \frac{1}{LC}} \tag{14.9}$$

and

$$s_2 = -\frac{G}{2C} - \sqrt{\left(\frac{G}{2C}\right)^2 - \frac{1}{LC}} \tag{14.10}$$

In terms of these roots (poles), Equation 14.8 becomes

$$V(s) = \frac{\dfrac{10}{C}}{(s - s_1)(s - s_2)} \tag{14.11}$$

and, except for the case where $s_1 = s_2$, the corresponding t-domain function is

$$v(t) = (k_1 e^{s_1 t} + k_2 e^{s_2 t})u(t) \tag{14.12}$$

where k_1 and k_2 are the results of a partial-fraction expansion of Equation 14.11:

$$k_1 = \frac{10}{C(s_1 - s_2)} \qquad k_2 = \frac{10}{C(s_2 - s_1)}$$

Therefore, the voltage response becomes

$$v(t) = \frac{10}{C(s_1 - s_2)} (e^{s_1 t} - e^{s_2 t})u(t) \tag{14.13}$$

By examination of Equations 14.9 and 14.10, we see that the poles s_1 and s_2 can take three distinct forms.

Case 1.   *Real equal poles.* If $(G/2C)^2 = 1/LC$, then:

(a) $s_1 = s_2 = -\dfrac{G}{2C}$ (real and negative).

(b)   Rather than Equation 14.13, the solution is

$$v(t) = e^{-(G/2C)t} (A_1 + A_2 t)u(t)$$

where A_1 and A_2 are given by the procedure of Section 12.9.

Case 2.   *Real unique poles.* If $(G/2C)^2 > 1/LC$, then:

(a) $s_1 \neq s_2$, but both are real and negative. (We assume that G, L, and C are positive.)

(b)   The solution given by Equation 14.13 shows that the response is the algebraic sum of two negative exponentials. This response starts at zero for $t = 0$ and also decays toward zero as $t \to \infty$.

Case 3.   *Complex conjugate poles.* If $(G/2C)^2 < 1/LC$, then:

(a) s_1 and s_2 are complex and $s_1 = s_2^*$. That is,

$$s_1 = -\alpha + j\omega$$

$$s_2 = -\alpha - j\omega$$

where

$$\alpha = \frac{G}{2C}$$

and

$$\omega = \sqrt{\frac{1}{LC} - \left(\frac{G}{2C}\right)^2}$$

(b) The solution is given by Equation 14.13. However, because of the complex exponential, another form may be more desirable. This case will be developed in more detail shortly.

This example has been presented in the hope of accomplishing two goals. The first is an introduction to more general second-order network functions and their characteristics. The second goal is to show an example of nonnumerical, or symbolic, analysis of a network. Although most network analysis is done with numbers, it may be advantageous, on occasion, to do a symbolic analysis and then substitute numerical values near the end.

To this end consider the case where

$$L = 1.0 \text{ H}$$

and

$$C = 0.01 \text{ F}$$

Suppose we first calculate the value of G at which equal poles occur. When $s_1 = s_2$,

$$\left(\frac{G}{2(0.01)}\right)^2 = \frac{1}{1.0(.01)}$$

or

$$G = 0.2 \text{ S} \qquad (R = 5 \text{ }\Omega)$$

Therefore, when $R < 5 \text{ }\Omega$ ($G > 0.2$ S), Case 2 applies and when $R > 5 \text{ }\Omega$, Case 3 applies.

If $G = 0.4S$, Equations 14.9 and 14.10 give

$$s_1 = -2.68$$

and

$$s_2 = -37.32$$

from which

$$v(t) = 28.86(e^{-2.68t} - e^{-37.32t})u(t) \text{ V}$$

On the other hand, if $G = 0.1 \text{ } S$

$$s_1 = -5 + j8.66$$

and

$$s_2 = -5 - j8.66$$

In this case

$$v(t) = -j\frac{115.47}{2} [e^{(-5+j8.66)t} - e^{(-5-j8.66)t}]u(t)$$

This latter form is not particularly desirable because of the difficulty in interpreting it as a function of time (on an oscilloscope, for example). However, it can be rewritten as

$$v(t) = 115.47e^{-5t}\left[\frac{e^{j8.66t} - e^{-j8.66t}}{2j}\right]u(t)$$

or

$$v(t) = 115.47e^{-5t}(\sin 8.66t)u(t) \text{ V}$$

A generalized second-order function

When the roots of a quadratic term are real, a partial-fraction expansion that treats the resulting two poles as two separate terms is straightforward and gives meaningful results. However, when the roots of a quadratic yield complex conjugate poles (as often occurs in practice), an approach that treats the quadratic as a single term may be preferred. For this reason and because second-order functions occur often in many branches of linear system analysis, it is instructive to consider a generalized second-order s-domain function.

The s-domain function description of a linear network variable is often in the form of the ratio of two polynomials in the Laplace variable s. Symbolically, this can be expressed as

$$X(s) = \frac{N(s)}{D(s)} \tag{14.14}$$

where

$X(s)$ = Laplace transform of network variable

$N(s)$ = a polynomial in s

$D(s)$ = a polynomial in s

Suppose the denominator polynomial is factored to give

$$X(s) = \frac{N(s)}{(s^2 + 2\zeta\omega_n s + \omega_n^2)D_1(s)} \tag{14.15}$$

where ζ and ω_n are constants to be described in more detail shortly. This function can be expanded by partial fractions to obtain

$$X(s) = \frac{C_1 s + C_2}{s^2 + 2\zeta\omega_n s + \omega_n^2} + \text{terms due to } D_1(s)$$

where C_1 and C_2 are real constants that can be obtained by a straightforward extension of the partial-fraction methods of Chapter 12.

The solution in the time domain is given as

$$x(t) = \mathcal{L}^{-1}\left\{\frac{C_1 s + C_2}{s^2 + 2\zeta\omega_n s + \omega_n^2}\right\} + \mathcal{L}^{-1}\{\text{terms due to } D_1(s)\}$$

The terms due to $D_1(s)$ are handled by the techniques of Chapter 12 and we need only consider the quadratic term. Therefore, let us examine

$$Y(s) = \frac{C_1 s + C_2}{s^2 + 2\zeta\omega_n s + \omega_n^2} \tag{14.16}$$

Just as in the earlier example, the form of the response due to the quadratic term is dependent upon the nature of its roots.

The poles of the function given by Equation 14.16 are

$$s_1 = -\zeta\omega_n + \sqrt{(\zeta\omega_n)^2 - \omega_n^2}$$

$$s_2 = -\zeta\omega_n - \sqrt{(\zeta\omega_n)^2 - \omega_n^2}$$

which can be written compactly as

$$s_1, s_2 = \omega_n\left(-\zeta \pm \sqrt{\zeta^2 - 1}\right) \tag{14.17}$$

As a beginning toward understanding the meaning of these results, consider the case where $\zeta = 0$. Further suppose, for the sake of simplicity, that $C_1 = 0$. Then Equation 14.16 becomes

$$Y(s) = \frac{C_2}{s^2 + \omega_n^2} = \frac{C_2}{\omega_n}\frac{\omega_n}{s^2 + \omega_n^2}$$

and the corresponding time-domain function is

$$y(t) = \frac{C_2}{\omega_n}(\sin \omega_n t)u(t)$$

Therefore, the result when $\zeta = 0$ is a pure oscillation (a sine wave).

Next consider the case where $0 < \zeta < 1$. From Equation 14.17 we see that the poles are complex conjugate as given by

$$s_1, s_2 = -\zeta\omega_n \pm j\omega_n\sqrt{1 - \zeta^2} \tag{14.18}$$

Although the time-domain function could be found in terms of these two poles, it is advantageous to consider the quadratic function directly. In this case, Equation 14.16 is

$$Y(s) = \frac{C_2}{s^2 + 2\zeta\omega_n s + \omega_n^2}$$

which can be rewritten, by completing the square of the denominator, as

$$Y(s) = \frac{C_2}{(s + \zeta\omega_n)^2 + \omega_n^2(1 - \zeta^2)}$$

Suppose we define the following:

$$\alpha \doteq \zeta \omega_n$$

and

$$\omega^2 \doteq \omega_n^2 (1 - \zeta^2)$$

which leads to

$$\omega \doteq \omega_n \sqrt{1 - \zeta^2}$$

Then

$$Y(s) = \frac{C_2}{(s + \alpha)^2 + \omega^2} = \frac{C_2}{\omega} \frac{\omega}{(s + \alpha)^2 + \omega^2}$$

and from Table 12.1, we see that

$$y(t) = \frac{C_2}{\omega} e^{-\alpha t}(\sin \omega t)u(t)$$

As compared to the case where $\zeta = 0$, we see that the frequency of the sinusoidal term is now changed by the multiplicative factor $\sqrt{1 - \zeta^2}$. Further, we see that the sinusoidal oscillation is now damped by the $e^{-\alpha t}$ term. For these reasons, the constant ζ is generally referred to as the *damping ratio* (note that it is dimensionless) and ω_n is called the *undamped natural frequency*.

As a final note of interpretation of the significance of the constant ζ, we see from Equation 14.17 that when $\zeta = 1$, the poles are real and equal and when $\zeta > 1$, the poles are real and unequal. In this latter case the response has changed from an exponentially damped sinusoidal response to one that is the algebraic sum of two exponential functions.

Throughout this discussion we have tacitly assumed that the constant $\alpha = \zeta \omega_n$ is positive, and hence that $e^{-\alpha t}$ decays with time and does in fact cause a damping effect. In the most general sense, we would need to consider the possibility of an exponential term (either $e^{-\alpha t}$ or $e^{s_i t}$) of the form e^{kt} with k a positive constant. In this case the time-domain function will increase without bound as t becomes large. This possibility is quite remote in the networks that we have discussed. (Can you think of one possibility within the linear networks that we have considered?)

We are now ready to summarize the general results and establish some additional terminology. Just as in the example, we have three distinct cases. These are generally referred to as *critically damped*, *overdamped*, and *underdamped* because of their relationship to the damping ratio, ζ.

Case 1. *Critically damped.*

(a) $\zeta = 1$.

(b) Poles are real and equal:

$$s_1 = s_2 = -\omega_n$$

(c) Response is of the form

$$y(t) = e^{-\omega_n t}(A_1 + A_2 t)u(t)$$

Case 2. *Overdamped.*

(a) $\zeta > 1$.

(b) Poles s_1 and s_2 are real and not equal and are given by Equation 14.17.

(c) Response is of the form

$$y(t) = k_1 e^{s_1 t} + k_2 e^{s_1 t}$$

where k_1 and k_2 are found by the usual partial-function expansion.

Case 3. *Underdamped, or oscillatory.*

(a) $\zeta < 1$.

(b) Poles are a complex conjugate pair given by Equation 14.18 as

$$s_1, s_2 = -\zeta\omega_n \pm j\omega_n \sqrt{1 - \zeta^2}$$

or

$$s_1, s_2 = -\alpha \pm j\omega$$

(c) Response is of the form

$$y(t) = e^{-\alpha t}(K_1 \sin \omega t + K_2 \cos \omega t)u(t)$$

where K_1 and K_2 are constants that depend on the partial-fraction expansion of the quadratic term.

The background material that has been discussed in this section is utilized extensively in the ensuing sections. Any remaining questions you may have should be answered as we apply these concepts to examples of network solutions.

14.5 SOLUTIONS OF SIMPLE NETWORKS

In this section we exploit the fundamentals of the Laplace transform in the solution of network problems for networks with multiple energy-storage components. Although the emphasis is on second-order networks, the basic concepts can be extended to higher-order networks in a straightforward manner. For higher-order problems, nothing about the approach changes—only the complexity of the algebra involved is increased.

Example 14.3

If the network of Figure 14.4 has zero initial energy storage, it can be replaced by an s-domain equivalent as seen in Figure 14.5 (all components are shown as impedances). The loop equation is

$$\frac{50}{s} = \left(R + s + \frac{100}{s}\right)I(s)$$

and the solution for the current is

$$I(s) = \frac{50}{s(s + R + 100/s)} = \frac{50}{s^2 + Rs + 100}$$

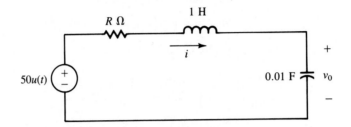

Figure 14.4
Network for Example 14.3.

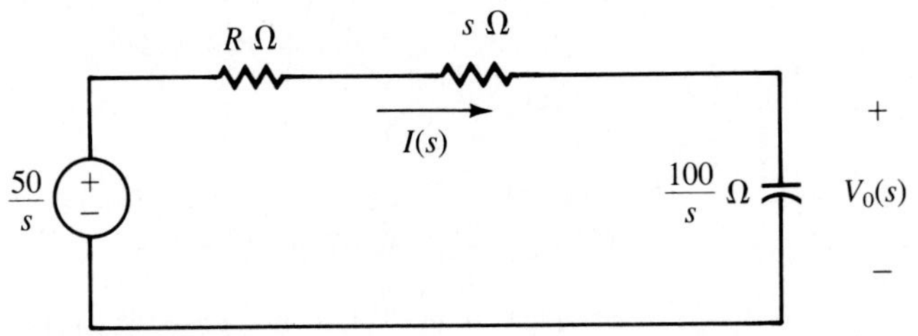

Figure 14.5
An s-domain equivalent
network for Figure 14.4.

Now from the s-domain form of the CE for the capacitor we can find

$$V_0(s) = \left(\frac{100}{s}\right)I(s)$$

or

$$V_0(s) = \frac{5000}{s(s^2 + Rs + 100)} = \frac{5000}{s(s^2 + 2\zeta\omega_n s + \omega_n^2)}$$

An examination of the quadratic term reveals that

$$\omega_n = \sqrt{100} = 10 \text{ rad/s}$$

$$2\zeta\omega_n = 20\zeta = R$$

or

$$\zeta = \frac{R}{20}$$

Thus the voltage $v_0(t)$ will be:

1. Critically damped for $R = 20$.
2. Overdamped for $R > 20$.
3. Underdamped for $R < 20$.

Suppose $R = 25 \ \Omega$. In this case

$$V_0(s) = \frac{5000}{s(s^2 + 25s + 100)} = \frac{5000}{s(s + 5)(s + 20)}$$

A partial-fraction expansion yields

$$V_0(s) = \frac{50}{s} - \frac{200/3}{s + 5} + \frac{50/3}{s + 20}$$

and the t-domain voltage is

$$v_0(t) = \left(50 - \frac{200}{3}e^{-5t} + \frac{50}{3}e^{-20t}\right)u(t) \text{ V}$$

which is the expected overdamped solution.

Suppose, however, that $R = 10 \ \Omega$. Then

$$V_0(s) = \frac{5000}{s(s^2 + 10s + 100)}$$

Since the response is underdamped, we choose to do a partial-fraction expansion that maintains the quadratic as a single term. Therefore,

$$V_0(s) = \frac{k_1}{s} + \frac{C_1 s + C_2}{s^2 + 10s + 100}$$

There are several approaches that can be used to obtain the constants k_1, C_1, and C_2. A straightforward approach is to consider the equation

$$\frac{5000}{s(s^2 + 10s + 100)} = \frac{k_1}{s} + \frac{C_1 s + C_2}{s^2 + 10s + 100}$$

We form a common denominator for the right-hand side of this equation and obtain

$$\frac{5000}{s(s^2 + 10s + 100)} = \frac{k_1(s^2 + 10s + 100) + s(C_1 s + C_2)}{s(s^2 + 10s + 100)}$$

This equation holds only if

$$k_1 + C_1 = 0 \qquad \text{(Coefficient of } s^2 \text{ terms)}$$

$$10k_1 + C_2 = 0 \qquad \text{(Coefficient of } s \text{ terms)}$$

$$100k_1 = 5000 \qquad \text{(From constant terms)}$$

Therefore, we have $k_1 = 50$, $C_1 = -50$, $C_2 = -500$, and

$$V_0(s) = \frac{50}{s} - 50\left(\frac{s + 10}{s^2 + 10s + 100}\right)$$

Suppose we rewrite this equation as

$$V_0(s) = \frac{50}{s} - 50\left[\frac{s + 5}{(s + 5)^2 + 75} + \frac{5}{(s + 5)^2 + 75)}\right]$$

Using Table 12.1 we obtain

$$v_0(t) = \left[50 - 50e^{-5t}\left(\cos \sqrt{75}t + \frac{5}{\sqrt{75}} \sin \sqrt{75}t\right)\right]u(t)$$

Example 14.4

The CE for the inductive 2-port of the network of Figure 14.6 is given by

$$\begin{bmatrix} 3 & 1 \\ 1 & 2 \end{bmatrix} \frac{d}{dt} \begin{bmatrix} i_3 \\ i_4 \end{bmatrix} = \begin{bmatrix} v_3 \\ v_4 \end{bmatrix} \tag{14.19}$$

or

$$\frac{d}{dt} \begin{bmatrix} i_3 \\ i_4 \end{bmatrix} = \frac{1}{5} \begin{bmatrix} 2 & -1 \\ -1 & 3 \end{bmatrix} \begin{bmatrix} v_3 \\ v_4 \end{bmatrix} \tag{14.20}$$

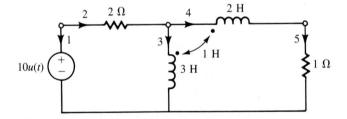

Figure 14.6
Network for Example 14.4.

If we decide to do a state-model formulation, these are the two equations that will become the state equations. In order to formulate these state equations, we need to solve for v_3 and v_4 in terms of i_3, i_4, and the v-source. The resistive network of Figure 14.7 is helpful. If a tree consisting of branches 1, 2, and 5 is chosen, both loop currents are specified by the i-sources (inductor currents).

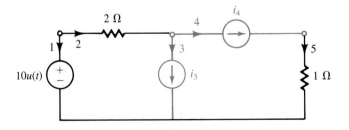

Figure 14.7
Network for formulation of state model for Example 14.4.

Thus we write, from inspection,

$$v_3 = v_1 - v_2 = 10u(t) - 2(i_3 + i_4)$$

and

$$v_4 = v_1 - v_2 - v_5 = 10u(t) - 2(i_3 + i_4) - i_4$$

In matrix form we have

$$\begin{bmatrix} v_3 \\ v_4 \end{bmatrix} = \begin{bmatrix} -2 & -2 \\ -2 & -3 \end{bmatrix} \begin{bmatrix} i_3 \\ i_4 \end{bmatrix} + \begin{bmatrix} 10u(t) \\ 10u(t) \end{bmatrix}$$

Substituting this result into Equation 14.20, we obtain

$$\frac{d}{dt}\begin{bmatrix} i_3 \\ i_4 \end{bmatrix} = \begin{bmatrix} -\dfrac{2}{5} & -\dfrac{1}{5} \\ -\dfrac{4}{5} & -\dfrac{7}{5} \end{bmatrix} \begin{bmatrix} i_3 \\ i_4 \end{bmatrix} + \begin{bmatrix} 2u(t) \\ 4u(t) \end{bmatrix}$$

If we take the Laplace transform for initial conditions given as $i_3(0^-) = 2$ A and $i_4(0^-) = 3$ A, we obtain

$$s\begin{bmatrix} I_3(s) \\ I_4(s) \end{bmatrix} - \begin{bmatrix} 2 \\ 3 \end{bmatrix} = \begin{bmatrix} -\dfrac{2}{5} & -\dfrac{1}{5} \\ -\dfrac{4}{5} & -\dfrac{7}{5} \end{bmatrix} \begin{bmatrix} I_3(s) \\ I_4(s) \end{bmatrix} + \begin{bmatrix} \dfrac{2}{s} \\ \dfrac{4}{s} \end{bmatrix}$$

Collecting terms and rewriting, we have

$$\begin{bmatrix} s + \dfrac{2}{5} & \dfrac{1}{5} \\ \dfrac{4}{5} & s + \dfrac{7}{5} \end{bmatrix} \begin{bmatrix} I_3(s) \\ I_4(s) \end{bmatrix} = \begin{bmatrix} 2 + \dfrac{2}{s} \\ 3 + \dfrac{4}{s} \end{bmatrix}$$

Therefore, the solutions for the s-domain currents are

$$\begin{bmatrix} I_3(s) \\ I_4(s) \end{bmatrix} = \frac{1}{s^2 + \frac{9}{5}s + \frac{10}{25}} \begin{bmatrix} s + \dfrac{7}{5} & -\dfrac{1}{5} \\ -\dfrac{4}{5} & s + \dfrac{2}{5} \end{bmatrix} \begin{bmatrix} 2 + \dfrac{2}{s} \\ 3 + \dfrac{4}{s} \end{bmatrix}$$

$$= \begin{bmatrix} \dfrac{2s + \frac{21}{5} + \frac{2}{s}}{s^2 + \frac{9}{5}s + \frac{10}{25}} \\[4mm] \dfrac{3s + \frac{18}{5}}{s^2 + \frac{9}{5}s + \frac{10}{25}} \end{bmatrix}$$

In order to obtain the t-domain solutions, we must take the inverse Laplace transform. For example,

$$I_4(s) = \frac{3s + \frac{18}{5}}{s^2 + \frac{9}{5}s + \frac{10}{25}} = \frac{3(s + 1.2)}{s^2 + 1.8s + 0.4} = \frac{3(s + 1.2)}{(s + 0.26)(s + 1.54)}$$

Using a partial-fraction expansion, we get

$$I_4(s) = \frac{2.203}{s + 0.26} + \frac{0.797}{s + 1.54}$$

and

$$i_4(t) = (2.203e^{-0.26t} + 0.797e^{-1.54t})u(t) \text{ A}$$

Likewise,

$$I_3(s) = \frac{2s^2 + 4.2s + 2}{s(s + 0.26)(s + 1.54)}$$

and a partial-fraction expansion gives

$$I_3(s) = \frac{4.995}{s} - \frac{3.1346}{s + 0.26} + \frac{0.1396}{s + 1.54}$$

The inverse Laplace transform yields

$$i_3(t) = (4.995 - 3.1346e^{-0.26t} + 0.1396e^{-1.54t})u(t)$$

Note that this result checks the initial value of i_3 exactly. However, the value as $t \to \infty$ shows some slight effect of rounding in the calculations.

14.6 EQUIVALENT 1-PORTS—THÉVENIN'S AND NORTON'S THEOREMS

The subjects of equivalent 1-port resistive networks, along with Thévenin's and Norton's theorems, were extensively treated in Chapter 4. In Chapter 9, these basic concepts were extended to include phasor models for networks in sinusoidal steady state. In both cases, we found that network reduction via equivalent networks was a valuable aid in the calculation of a network solution.

These techniques are even more valuable in the s-domain analysis and ultimate calculation of the complete dynamic response of a general linear network. For this reason, we now expand the basic equivalent network concepts to include s-domain models of linear 1-ports. Because of their importance, most of the basic concepts will be presented again in their new s-domain setting. The treatment largely parallels that in Chapter 4.

Consider a general linear network consisting of resistors, inductors, capacitors, v-sources, i-sources, and controlled sources (Figure 14.8). Two terminals, a and b, are emphasized for measurement. As we did previously, we wish to develop a 1-port model relating the terminal voltage to the terminal current.

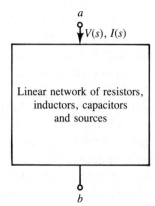

Figure 14.8
A linear 1-port network.

Theorem 14.1

A linear 1-port network consisting of some interconnection of resistors, inductors, capacitors, and sources[1] will have an s-domain component equation that is either of the form

$$V(s) = Z_T(s)I(s) + E_T(s) \tag{14.21}$$

or of the form

$$I(s) = Y_N(s)V(s) + I_N(s) \tag{14.22}$$

where $V(s)$ and $I(s)$ are the Laplace transforms of the terminal variables as illustrated by Figure 14.8.

Equation 14.21 is referred to as the *Thévenin equivalent component equation* and Equation 14.22 is called the *Norton equivalent component equation*. The terms in these equations are referred to as follows:

$Z_T(s)$: Thévenin equivalent impedance

$E_T(s)$: Thévenin equivalent voltage source

$Y_N(s)$: Norton equivalent admittance

$I_N(s)$: Norton equivalent current source

---

[1]Both branches of any controlled source must be included in the subnetwork being modeled by an equivalent component equation.

As before, we see that most networks will have both forms of equivalent component equations. Either form of the component equation can be solved for the alternate form unless either $Z_T(s)$ or $Y_N(s)$ is zero. This latter case, in fact, holds for v-sources and i-sources, respectively. That is, a v-source will only have a Thévenin-form CE and an i-source will only have a Norton-form CE.

The relationships, if they exist, between Z_T, Y_N, E_T, and I_N are readily obtained by simply solving for the alternate form. We will derive this equivalence when we discuss equivalent network realizations for equivalent component equations.

The symbolic-source method that we have used to find Thévenin- and Norton-form component equations has equal utility in finding an s-domain equation. We simply apply a symbolic source corresponding to the independent variable in the desired component equation and solve for the dependent variable. The result is the desired component equation.

Since initial conditions appear as knowns in the s-domain CE, the equivalent sources $E_T(s)$ and $I_N(s)$ result from initial conditions and independent sources in the network. That is, if all initial conditions were zero and the network contained no independent sources, then $E_T(s)$ and $I_N(s)$ would be zero. Further, the terms $Z_T(s)$ and $Y_N(s)$ will result from the passive components and the controlled sources. Armed with these ideas, let us examine the equivalent component equations in more detail.

Consider the Thévenin form of the component equation

$$V(s) = Z_T(s)I(s) + E_T(s) \tag{14.23}$$

Now if we set $I(s)$ equal to zero, we have

$$E_T(s) = V(s)\Big|_{I(s)=0} \tag{14.24}$$

which means that if we make no external connection to the terminals of the 1-port, then the Thévenin equivalent voltage source function can be found by calculating the voltage across the open-circuited terminals a and b. Note that this voltage will be zero if all initial conditions are zero and the network contains no independent sources.

Next, suppose we set all initial conditions and all independent sources equal to zero, thereby setting $E_T(s) = 0$. In this case we have

$$Z_T(s) = \frac{V(s)}{I(s)}\Big|_{\substack{\text{All initial conditions}=0 \\ \text{All independent sources}=0}} \tag{14.25}$$

The function of s that results from the calculation of Equation 14.25 is often called the *s-domain input impedance* or *driving-point impedance* at terminals a and b.

In keeping with past results, Equation 14.24 and Equation 14.25 are referred to as *Thévenin's theorem*. These results provide an alternative to the symbolic-source method for finding the Thévenin equivalent component equation. In order to find this equivalent component equation for a general network, we must find the two functions $Z_T(s)$ and $E_T(s)$. In the symbolic-source approach, the complete component equation—and consequently $Z_T(s)$ and $E_T(s)$—are found in one operation. If we apply the results of Thévenin's theorem, we use two separate operations or solutions in order to calculate $Z_T(s)$ and $E_T(s)$. Although two separate network analyses are required for this latter approach, this method is sometimes easier than the single analysis of the symbolic-source approach if the network does not contain controlled sources.

A few additional words are in order concerning the calculation of $Z_T(s)$ by Equation 14.25. First, how do we set all the independent sources in the network to zero? The answer, just as in the *t*-domain, lies in the reasoning that zero voltage exists across a short circuit and zero current flows through an open circuit. Therefore, just as before, we replace all *v*-sources with short circuits and all *i*-sources with open circuits. After all initial conditions and all independent sources are set to zero, Equation 14.25 indicates that we should apply a symbolic source $I(s)$ and calculate the voltage response, thereby obtaining

$$V(s) = Z_T(s)I(s)$$

Actually, we could just as well apply a symbolic voltage source $V(s)$ and calculate the current response as

$$I(s) = Y(s)V(s)$$

In this case, the input impedance is given by $Z_T(s) = 1/Y(s)$. In some cases, as we will see later, we will be able to evaluate $Z_T(s)$ in a more direct way, without applying a symbolic source. In any case, Equation 14.25 is the basic definition needed for the input impedance of a 1-port network.

Now let us turn our attention to the Norton form of the 1-port component equation.

$$I(s) = Y_N(s)V(s) + I_N(s) \tag{14.26}$$

We see immediately that

$$I_N(s) = I(s)\Big|_{V(s)=0} \tag{14.27}$$

and

$$Y_N(s) = \frac{I(s)}{V(s)}\Big|_{I_N(s)=0} \tag{14.28}$$

Since $V(s) = 0$ when terminals a and b are shorted together and since $I_N(s) = 0$ when all initial conditions and all independent sources are set to zero, we have the result

$$I_N(s) = I(s)\Big|_{V(s)=0 \quad \text{(terminals } a \text{ and } b \text{ shorted)}}$$

and

$$Y_N(s) = \frac{I(s)}{V(s)}\Big|_{\substack{\text{All initial conditions}=0 \\ \text{All independent sources}=0}}$$

This result is generally known as *Norton's theorem*.

The function $Y_N(s)$ is often called the *input* or *driving-point admittance* of the network. Comparison of the above results indicates that, not unexpectedly,

$$Z_T(s) = \frac{1}{Y_N(s)} \tag{14.29}$$

Equivalent networks

At times, during the analysis of a network, it is helpful to replace several components with a simpler equivalent network. This is an easy matter for either the Thévenin- or Norton-form component equation. For example, we see that the Thévenin-form component equation has a realization as shown in Figure 14.9. This is obvious since the terminal voltage $V(s)$ is the sum of two terms—that is,

$$V(s) = V_1(s) + V_2(s)$$

where

$$V_1(s) = Z_T(s)I(s)$$

and

$$V_2(s) = E_T(s)$$

and by a simple application of KVL, we have the desired result.

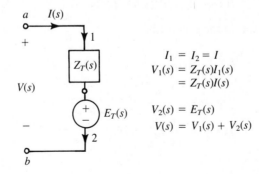

Figure 14.9
Thévenin equivalent network.

$$I_1 = I_2 = I$$
$$V_1(s) = Z_T(s)I_1(s)$$
$$= Z_T(s)I(s)$$
$$V_2(s) = E_T(s)$$
$$V(s) = V_1(s) + V_2(s)$$

Similarly, we see that the network of Figure 14.10 is a realization of the Norton-form component equation. Now the reason for the terminology *Thévenin's equivalent voltage source* and *Norton's equivalent current source* should be clear.

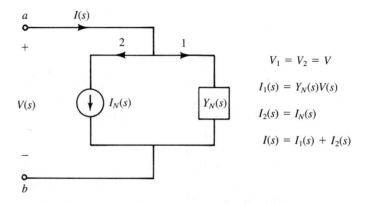

Figure 14.10
Norton equivalent network.

$$V_1 = V_2 = V$$

$$I_1(s) = Y_N(s)V(s)$$

$$I_2(s) = I_N(s)$$

$$I(s) = I_1(s) + I_2(s)$$

Series impedances and series *v*-sources

One of the simplest subnetwork configurations for which to derive a 1-port characteristic is a set of series components. We illustrate this concept by example.

Example 14.5 ——————————————————————————————————

Let us find the Thévenin-form component equation and equivalent network for the network and measurement diagram shown in Figure 14.11. If we apply a

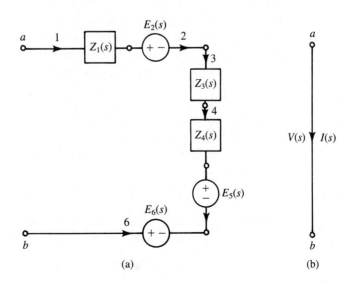

Figure 14.11
A 1-port network.

(a)

(b)

symbolic current source as shown in Figure 14.12, we can calculate $V(s)$ by a simple application of Kirchhoff's voltage law. Immediately we have

$$V(s) = V_1(s) + V_2(s) + V_3(s) + V_4(s) + V_5(s) - V_6(s)$$

$$= [Z_1(s) + Z_3(s) + Z_4(s)]I(s) + E_2(s) + E_5(s) - E_6(s)$$

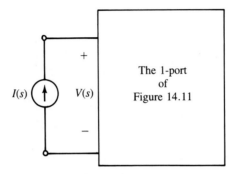

Figure 14.12
Symbolic source applied to the 1-port network.

Therefore,

$$Z_T(s) = Z_1(s) + Z_3(s) + Z_4(s)$$

and

$$E_T(s) = E_2(s) + E_5(s) - E_6(s)$$

Thus we see that the equivalent impedance of a series connection of impedances is the sum of the individual impedances and that the equivalent voltage source of a series of v-sources is the oriented sum of the individual v-source functions. This result is independent of the order of connection of the components. Furthermore, it is obvious that this result extends to any number of components. Note that in taking the oriented sum of the v-source functions, due account must be taken of the source polarity.

Finally, we note that for this example the same result can be obtained by a direct application of Thévenin's theorem.

Example 14.6

The results of Example 14.5 apply directly to a network described completely by impedances in series. This is illustrated by considering Figure 14.13, a network of n impedances in series. The input, or Thévenin equivalent impedance, is

$$Z_T(s) = Z_1(s) + Z_2(s) + \cdots + Z_n(s) \tag{14.30}$$

regardless of the form of the individual impedances. The component equation is

$$V(s) = [Z_1(s) + Z_2(s) + \cdots + Z_n(s)]I(s)$$

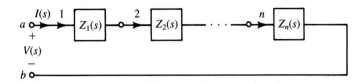

Figure 14.13
A series connection of n
impedances.

Therefore, the current response to an input voltage $V(s)$ is

$$I(s) = \frac{V(s)}{Z_1(s) + Z_2(s) + \cdots + Z_n(s)} = \frac{V(s)}{Z_T(s)}$$

and the individual voltages are

$$V_1(s) = Z_1(s)I(s) = \frac{Z_1(s)}{Z_T(s)}V(s)$$

$$V_2(s) = \frac{Z_2(s)}{Z_T(s)}V(s)$$

$$\vdots$$

$$V_n(s) = \frac{Z_n(s)}{Z_T(s)}V(s)$$

This latter result is another example of the voltage-divider rule.

If the individual impedances are all resistors, as shown in Figure 14.14(a), the equivalent network is a single equivalent resistor, as shown in Figure 14.14(b), with

$$R_T = R_1 + R_2 + \cdots + R_N$$

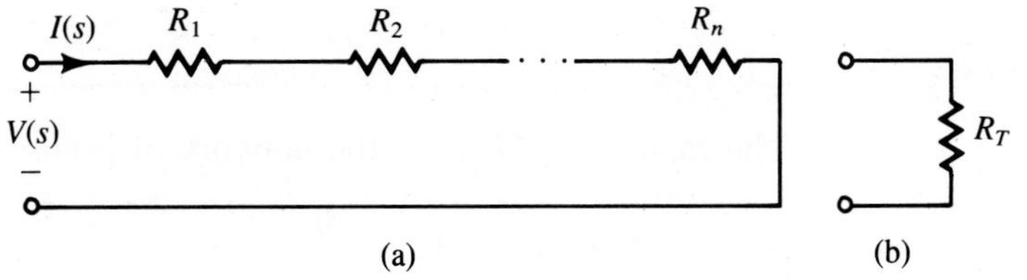

Figure 14.14
Series resistors.
(a) The original network.
(b) The equivalent
network.

(a)   (b)

Next, consider the network of series inductors of Figure 14.15(a). For all initial conditions equal to zero, each inductor is completely described by its impedance and

$$Z_T(s) = sL_1 + sL_2 + \cdots + sL_n$$

$$= s(L_1 + L_2 + \cdots + L_n)$$

Figure 14.15
Series inductors.
(a) The original network.
(b) The equivalent network.

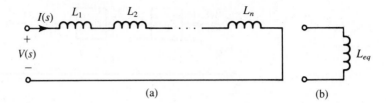

(a)   (b)

and we see that the network of Figure 14.15(b) is equivalent to the original network for

$$L_{eq} = L_1 + L_2 + \cdots + L_n$$

That is, the equivalent inductance of a set of inductances in series is the sum of the individual inductances. As in Chapter 8, in order to be equivalent under all conditions, the initial conditions of L_{eq} must be set to give the same $E_T(s)$ as does the original network.

Next, consider the network of Figure 14.16. The input impedance is

$$Z_T(s) = \frac{1}{sC_1} + \frac{1}{sC_2} + \cdots + \frac{1}{sC_n}$$

$$= \frac{1}{s}\left(\frac{1}{C_1} + \frac{1}{C_2} + \cdots + \frac{1}{C_n}\right)$$

Figure 14.16
Series capacitors.
(a) The original network.
(b) The equivalent network.

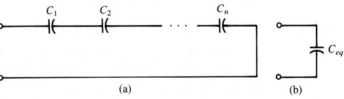

(a)   (b)

All these expressions verify earlier results.

Example 14.7 _____

The input impedance of the network of Figure 14.17 is

$$Z_T = 30 + 3s + \frac{10}{s}$$

Figure 14.17
A series RLC network.

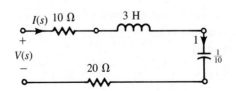

The capacitor voltage $V_1(s)$ is, by the voltage-divider rule,

$$V_1(s) = \frac{10/s}{30 + 3s + 10/s}V(s)$$

if $v(0) = 0$.

Example 14.8

The input impedance of the network of Figure 14.18 is

$$Z_T = 5 + \frac{5}{s}$$

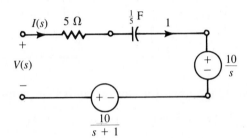

Figure 14.18
Network for Example 14.8.

The Thévenin equivalent network is shown in Figure 14.19. If the initial energy stored on the capacitor is zero, then

$$E_T(s) = \frac{10}{s} - \frac{10}{s + 1} = \frac{10}{s(s + 1)}$$

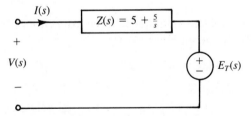

Figure 14.19
Thévenin equivalent network for Figure 14.18.

However, if the initial energy stored on the capacitor is not zero, then

$$E_T(s) = \frac{10}{s} - \frac{10}{s + 1} + \frac{v_1(0^-)}{s} = \frac{10 + v_1(0^-)(s + 1)}{s(s + 1)}$$

which can be obtained either by the symbolic-source method or by direct application of Thévenin's theorem. In either case, $Z_T(s)$ is unchanged.

Parallel admittances and parallel *i*-sources

By a simple analysis of Figure 14.20, we see that

$$I(s) = I_1(s) + I_2(s) + \cdots + I_n(s)$$

$$= [Y_1(s) + Y_2(s) + \cdots + Y_n(s)]V(s)$$

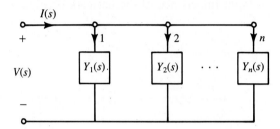

Figure 14.20
A network of parallel admittances.

Therefore, the input (or Norton-equivalent admittance) is

$$Y_N(s) = Y_1(s) + Y_2(s) + \cdots + Y_n(s)$$

For *n* resistors $R_1, R_2, \ldots, R_n$ connected in parallel, we have

$$G_{eq} = \frac{1}{R_{eq}} = G_1 + G_2 + \cdots + G_n$$

where

$$G_1 = \frac{1}{R_1}, G_2 = \frac{1}{R_2}, \ldots, G_n = \frac{1}{R_n}$$

The equivalent admittance of *n* capacitors $C_1, C_2, \ldots, C_n$ connected in parallel is given by

$$Y_C(s) = sC_1 + sC_2 + \cdots + sC_n$$

which leads to

$$C_{eq} = C_1 + C_2 + \cdots + C_n$$

Further, the equivalent admittance of *n* inductors $L_1, L_2, \ldots, L_n$ connected in parallel is

$$Y_L(s) = \frac{1}{sL_1} + \frac{1}{sL_2} + \cdots + \frac{1}{sL_n}$$

Therefore,

$$\frac{1}{L_{eq}} = \frac{1}{L_1} + \frac{1}{L_2} + \cdots + \frac{1}{L_n}$$

and

$$L_{eq} = \frac{1}{1/L_1 + 1/L_2 + \cdots + 1/L_n}$$

all of which verify earlier results.

Example 14.9

The input, or Norton equivalent admittance, of Figure 14.21 is

$$Y_N(s) = \frac{1}{20} + \frac{10}{s}$$

Figure 14.21
Network for Example 14.9.

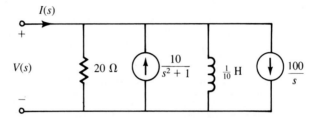

The Norton-form component equation for zero initial energy storage is

$$I(s) = \left(\frac{1}{20} + \frac{10}{s}\right)V(s) + \frac{100}{s} - \frac{10}{s^2 + 1}$$

We note that the parallel current sources add algebraically to obtain the equivalent current source, just as was the case in the *t*-domain models.

Some special results concerning two impedances in parallel are useful enough to justify some special attention. Consider the network of Figure 14.22. Immediately we see that

$$Y_N(s) = Y_1(s) + Y_2(s)$$

$$= \frac{1}{Z_1(s)} + \frac{1}{Z_2(s)}$$

Figure 14.22
Two impedances in parallel.

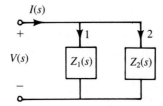

and that

$$Z_T(s) = \frac{1}{Y_n(s)} = \frac{1}{1/Z_1(s) + 1/Z_2(s)} = \frac{Z_1(s)Z_2(s)}{Z_1(s) + Z_2(s)} \tag{14.31}$$

Furthermore,

$$I_1(s) = \frac{V(s)}{Z_1(s)} = \frac{Z_T(s)I(s)}{Z_1(s)} = \frac{Z_2(s)}{Z_1(s) + Z_2(s)}I(s)$$

and

$$I_2(s) = \frac{V(s)}{Z_2(s)} = \frac{Z_1(s)}{Z_1(s) + Z_2(s)}I(s)$$

This latter result is another application of the *current-divider rule*.

Just as in resistive networks, rules for series and parallel connections of impedances can be used in conjunction to find the input impedance of many electric networks.

Example 14.10

Consider the network of Figure 14.23. The two parallel impedances can be replaced by a single impedance by use of Equation 14.31. This impedance is

$$Z_{bc}(s) = \frac{20(5/s)}{20 + 5/s} = \frac{100}{20s + 5} = \frac{20}{4s + 1}$$

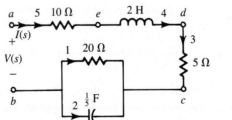

Figure 14.23
Network for Example 14.10.

The new equivalent network is shown in Figure 14.24(a). Since all impedances are in series, we have

$$Z_T(s) = 15 + 2s + \frac{20}{4s + 1} = \frac{8s^2 + 62s + 35}{4s + 1}$$

If the initial condition is zero and a voltage source, $v(t) = 10u(t)$, is applied to the terminals of this network, the resulting equivalent network is as illustrated by Figure 14.24(b). Since the 1-port is described by

$$V(s) = \frac{8s^2 + 62s + 35}{4s + 1}I(s)$$

Figure 14.24
Equivalent networks for
Example 14.10.

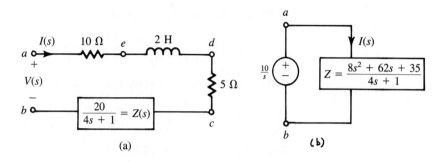

(a)   (b)

and $V(s)$ is given by the applied source as $V(s) = 10/s$, we have

$$I(s) = \frac{10/s}{(8s^2 + 62s + 35)/(4s + 1)} = \frac{10(4s + 1)}{s(8s^2 + 62s + 35)}$$

Here, $I_3(s) = I_4(s) = I_5(s) = I(s)$, and the voltages are

$$V_3(s) = 5I_3(s) = 5I(s)$$
$$V_4(s) = 2sI_4(s) = 2sI(s)$$
$$V_5(s) = 10I_5(s) = 10I(s)$$

and

$$V_{bc}(s) = V_1(s) = V_2(s) = \left(\frac{20}{4s + 1}\right)[-I(s)]$$

Finally, $I_1(s)$ and $I_2(s)$ can be found by the current-divider rule as

$$I_1(s) = \frac{5/s}{20 + 5/s}[-I(s)] = \frac{1}{4s + 1}[-I(s)]$$

and

$$I_2(s) = \frac{20}{20 + 5/s}[-I(s)] = \frac{4s}{4s + 1}[-I(s)]$$

Alternatively, these currents are

$$I_1(s) = \frac{V_{bc}(s)}{20}$$

and

$$I_2(s) = \frac{V_{bc}(s)}{5/s}$$

Time-domain answers can be obtained by finding the inverse transforms of the
s-domain expressions for the network variables.

For example, the expression for $I(s)$ can be rewritten as

$$I(s) = \frac{1.25(4s + 1)}{s(s + 0.613)(s + 7.137)}$$

and a partial-fraction expansion yields

$$I(s) = \frac{0.2857}{s} + \frac{0.4538}{s + 0.613} - \frac{0.7395}{s + 7.137}$$

The inverse transform yields

$$i(t) = (0.2857 + 0.4538e^{-0.613t} - 0.7395e^{-7.137t})u(t) \text{ A}$$

We note from this expression that

$$i(t)\Big|_{t=0} = 0.2857 + 0.4538 - 0.7395 = 0$$

and

$$\lim_{t \to \infty} i(t) = 0.2857 \text{ A}$$

These values verify known results. Since the current at $t = 0$ is specified by the initial current in the inductor, we have $i(0) = i_4(0) = 0$.

At steady state, the inductor becomes a short circuit and the capacitor an open circuit. Therefore, we see that

$$i_{ss} = \frac{10}{10 + 5 + 20} = 0.2857 \text{ A}$$

Other t-domain answers are left as exercises.

Source transformations

If the Thévenin-form CE of Equation 14.21 is solved for the current $I(s)$, we have

$$I(s) = \frac{1}{Z_T(s)}V(s) - \frac{1}{Z_T(s)}E_T(s)$$

By comparison to Equation 14.22, we see that

$$Y_N(s) = \frac{1}{Z_T(s)} \tag{14.32}$$

and

$$I_N(s) = -\frac{E_T(s)}{Z_T(s)} \tag{14.33}$$

Then, by rewriting Equation 14.33, we obtain

$$Z_T(s) = -\frac{E_T(s)}{I_N(s)}$$

That is, the input impedance of the network is the negative of the ratio of the open-circuit voltage to the short-circuit current (both in the s-domain).

Equations 14.32 and 14.33 can be used to transform a Thévenin equivalent network to a Norton equivalent network, or vice versa. This result is illustrated by Figure 14.25.

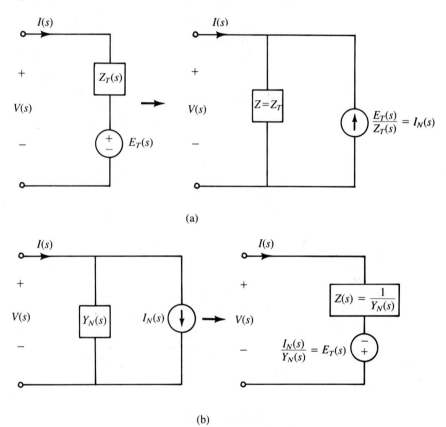

Figure 14.25
Source transformations.
(a) Transformation of Thévenin equivalent network to Norton equivalent network.
(b) Transformation of Norton equivalent network to Thévenin equivalent network.

We have now discussed three methods for finding the equivalent component equation or equivalent network for a given 1-port network:

1. The symbolic-source method—a basic, direct approach.

2. Application of Thévenin's and Norton's theorems.

3. Repeated use of source transformation and/or series-parallel impedance rules to reduce the network to the desired form.

In many cases, a combination of (2) and (3) is appropriate.

Methods 2 and 3 are often easier to apply than method 1 if the network has no controlled sources. In contrast, method 1 often yields the fastest results for networks with controlled sources.

Example 14.11

The s-domain Thévenin equivalent component equation is desired for the simple network of Figure 14.26(a) for a measurement diagram, as shown by Figure 14.26(b). Suppose we use the symbolic-source method and apply a source $I(s) = \mathcal{L}\{i(t)\}$, as shown in Figure 14.27. Any procedure to solve for $V(s)$ in terms of $I(s)$ will be adequate for our purposes.

Figure 14.26
Network for Example 14.11.

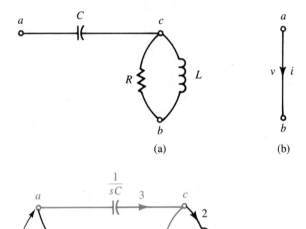

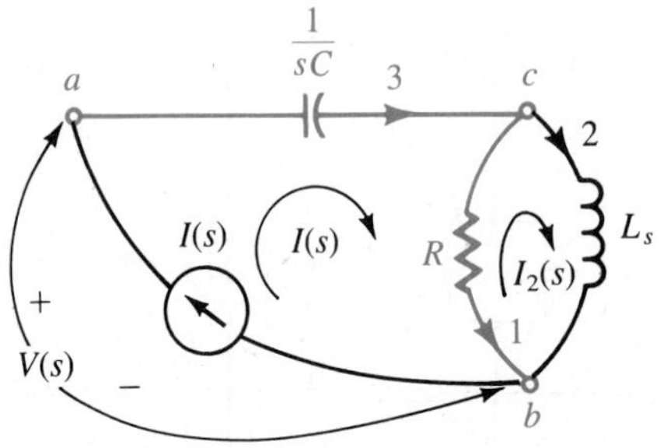

Figure 14.27
Network used to find Thévenin-form component equation.

Let us write the loop equations for the loop currents shown. Using our knowledge of the s-domain component equations, we write these equations directly in the s-domain by summing the s-domain voltages around the loops and expressing each voltage in terms of the loop currents. Thus we have

$$R[I_2(s) - I(s)] + sLI_2(s) - Li_2(0^-) = 0$$

and

$$V_{ab}(s) = V(s) = \frac{1}{sC}I(s) + \frac{v_3(0^-)}{s} + R[I(s) - I_2(s)]$$

By collecting terms and rearranging slightly, we have

$$(R + sL)I_2(s) - RI(s) = Li_2(0^-) \tag{14.34}$$

$$V(s) = \left[R + \frac{1}{sC}\right]I(s) - RI_2(s) + \frac{v_3(0^-)}{s} \tag{14.35}$$

Equation 14.35 is a dummy equation and will be used to solve for the voltage $V(s)$. From Equation 14.34,

$$I_2(s) = \frac{R}{R + sL}I(s) + \frac{L}{R + sL}i_2(0^-)$$

and when this result is substituted into Equation 14.35, we have

$$V(s) = \left[R + \frac{1}{sC} - \frac{R^2}{R + sL}\right]I(s) - \frac{RL}{R + sL}i_2(0^-) + \frac{v_3(0^-)}{s}$$

or

$$V(s) = \left[\frac{1}{sC} + \frac{RsL}{R + sL}\right]I(s) + \left[\frac{v_3(0^-)}{s} - \frac{RL}{R + sL}i_2(0^-)\right] \tag{14.36}$$

Therefore,

$$Z_T(s) = \frac{1}{sC} + \frac{RsL}{R + sL} \tag{14.37}$$

$$E_T(s) = \frac{v_3(0^-)}{s} - \frac{RL}{R + sL}i_2(0^-) \tag{14.38}$$

If we apply Thévenin's theorem directly to obtain the above results, we will obtain the same result for $Z_T(s)$, since the impedance of this network is the sum of the capacitor impedance and the equivalent impedance of the resistor and inductor in parallel. When we calculate the open-circuit voltage to find $E_T(s)$, the first term in Equation 14.38 is obvious for the network of Figure 14.26. However, the contribution of the initial inductor current is more subtle. You may find it helpful in this case to replace the inductor by an equivalent network, as shown in Figure 14.28. This equivalent is a direct result of the component equation for the inductor. Since the terminals are open,

$$E_T(s) = V_{ab} \text{ (open-circuit)} = \frac{v_3(0^-)}{s} - \frac{R}{sL + R}Li_2(0^-)$$

where the last term is calculated by the voltage-divider rule. Of course, we could also replace the capacitor by its Thévenin equivalent, but it is not really necessary to do so. In any case, you should be able to draw both the Thévenin

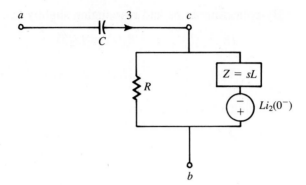

Figure 14.28
A network equivalent to
that of Figure 14.26.

and the Norton equivalent networks for the capacitor and the inductor. This is
done directly from the component equations, as shown in Table 14.1.

The component equations, in impedance and admittance form, are given in
Table 14.2 for several additional passive networks. In all cases, the measurement orientation is from top to bottom. These should be considered as practice
problems with answers.

Example 14.12 ──

The Norton-form component equation for the 1-port of Example 14.11 could
be obtained by solving Equation 14.36 for $I(s)$. However, since several points
are illustrated (including an s-domain nodal analysis), by ignoring the results of
Example 14.11 and reworking the problem with an applied symbolic v-source,
we proceed as if we had a new problem—to find the Norton-form component
equation for the network of Figure 14.26.

If we apply a symbolic v-source as shown in Figure 14.29 and write
s-domain nodal equations (node b as reference), we have

$$sC[V(s) - V_1(s)] - Cv_3(0^-) = \frac{V_1(s)}{R} + \frac{V_1(s)}{sL} + \frac{i_2(0^-)}{s}$$

and

$$I(s) = I_3(s) = sC[V(s) - V_1(s)] - Cv_3(0^-)$$

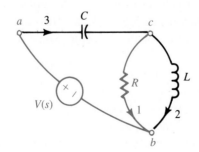

Figure 14.29
Network for Example
14.12.

By collecting terms and rearranging, we obtain

$$V_1(s)\left(\frac{1}{R} + \frac{1}{sL} + sC\right) = sCV(s) - Cv_3(0^-) - \frac{i_2(0^-)}{s} \qquad (14.39)$$

and

$$I(s) = sCV(s) - sCV_1(s) - Cv_3(0^-) \qquad (14.40)$$

where $V_1(s)$ is the unknown node voltage and Equation 14.40 is a dummy equation. Solving Equation 14.39 for $V_1(s)$, we have

$$V_1(s) = \frac{RLCs^2}{RLCs^2 + Ls + R}V(s)$$

$$- \frac{RLs}{RLCs^2 + Ls + R}\left[Cv_3(0^-) + \frac{i_2(0^-)}{s}\right]$$

Substituting this result into Equation 14.40, we have the Norton-form component equation

$$I(s) = \left[\frac{sC(R + sL)}{RLCs^2 + Ls + R}\right]V(s)$$

$$+ \frac{1}{RLCs^2 + Ls + R}[RLCs\, i_2(0^-) - C(R + sL)v_3(0^-)]$$

which is the same as that obtained by solving Equation 14.36 for $I(s)$.

Example 14.13

The Thévenin-form component equation of the 1-port of Figure 14.30 can be found for the case of zero initial conditions by applying Thévenin's theorem directly. For the measurement diagram shown, the equivalent source is given by

$$E_T(s) = V_{ba}(s)\Big|_{a-b \text{ open-circuited}}$$

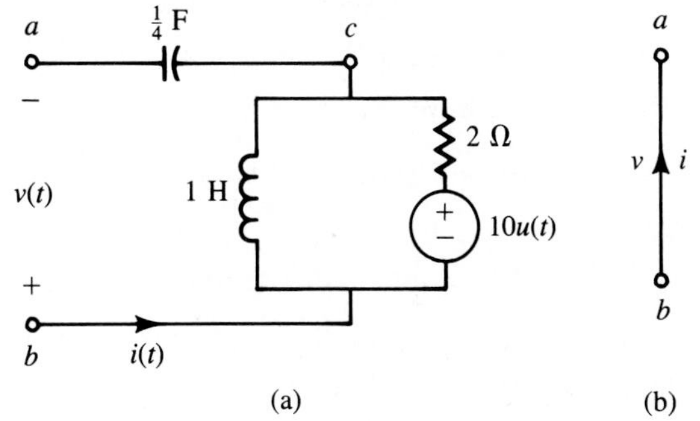

Figure 14.30
Network for Example
14.13.

(a)   (b)

or
$$E_T(s) = -\frac{s}{s+2}\frac{10}{s} = -\frac{10}{s+2} \qquad (14.41)$$

because no current flows through the capacitor, and $V_{ba} = V_{bc}$ can be calculated by the voltage-divider rule as the voltage across the 1-H inductor.

The input, or equivalent, impedance is (v-source replaced by a short circuit)

$$Z_T(s) = \frac{4}{s} + \frac{2s}{s+2} = \frac{2s^2 + 4s + 8}{s(s+2)} \qquad (14.42)$$

The equivalent network is shown in Figure 14.31.

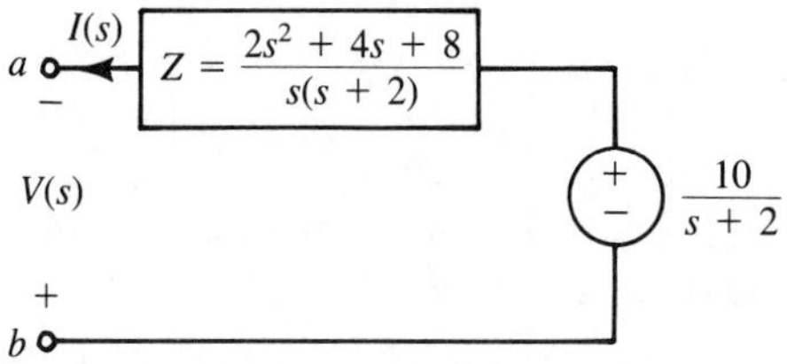

Figure 14.31
Thévenin equivalent
network for Example
14.13.

If a v-source $v_{ab} = 10u(t)$ is connected to the network of Figure 14.31, the current is

$$I(s) = \frac{10/(s+2) - 10/s}{(2s^2 + 4s + 8)/[s(s+2)]} = \frac{-10}{s^2 + 2s + 4} = \frac{-10}{(s+1)^2 + 3}$$

Therefore,

$$i(t) = \frac{-10}{\sqrt{3}}e^{-t}(\sin \sqrt{3}t)u(t)$$

On the other hand, suppose we connect a 2-Ω resistor between terminals a and b. Then the terminal voltage becomes

$$V(s) = \frac{-2}{2 + (2s^2 + 4s + 8)/[s(s+2)]}\frac{10}{(s+2)}$$

$$= \frac{-20s}{4s^2 + 8s + 8} = \frac{-5s}{s^2 + 2s + 2} = \frac{-5s}{(s+1)^2 + 1}$$

In this case we have

$$v(t) = 5e^{-t}(\sin t - \cos t)u(t) \text{ V}$$

and

$$i(t) = -2.5e^{-t}(\sin t - \cos t)u(t) \text{ A}$$

These results verify the initial and steady-state conditions obtained by examination of the original network.

Table 14.2   s-Domain component equations for some simple 1-port networks

Schematic	Thévenin CE	Norton CE
	$$V(s) = \frac{I(s)}{G + sC} + \frac{C}{G + sC}v(0^-)$$	$$I(s) = (G + sC)V(s) - Cv(0^-)$$
	$$V(s) = (R + sL)I(s) - Li(0^-)$$	$$I(s) = \frac{V(s)}{R + sL}V(s) + \frac{L}{R + sL}i(0^-)$$
	$$V(s) = \frac{I(s)}{sC + 1/(R + sL)}$$ $$+ \frac{Cv_c(0^-) - [L/(R + sL)]i_L(0^-)}{sC + 1/(R + sL)}$$	$$I(s) = \left(sC + \frac{1}{R + sL}\right)V(s)$$ $$+ \left[\frac{L}{R + sL}i_L(0^-) - Cv_c(0^-)\right]$$
	$$V(s) = \frac{I(s)}{G + sC + 1/sL}$$ $$+ \frac{Cv(0^-) - i_L(0^-)/s}{G + sC + 1/(sL)}$$	$$I(s) = \left(G + sC + \frac{1}{sL}\right)V(s)$$ $$- Cv(0^-) + \frac{i_L(0^-)}{s}$$
	$$V(s) = \left(R + sL + \frac{1}{sC}\right)I(s)$$ $$+ \frac{v_c(0^-)}{s} - Li(0^-)$$	$$I(s) = \frac{V(s)}{R + sL + 1/sC}$$ $$+ \frac{Li(0^-) - v_c(0^-)/s}{R + sL + 1/(sC)}$$

14.7   TRANSFER FUNCTIONS

The concept of a transfer function was introduced for the ω-domain model in Section 9.9. In the s-domain case, we have

$$T(s) = \frac{\text{output}(s)}{\text{input}(s)} = \frac{X(s)}{F(s)}$$

where the output $X(s)$ may be either the voltage or current variable associated with any network component and the input is either the s-domain description of a v-source or an i-source. Just as we discussed earlier, the network being described by the transfer function $T(s)$ cannot contain an independent source— the input is the only independent source. Also, in the calculation of $T(s)$, the initial conditions of the network are always set to zero.

Since the initial conditions are zero, each passive component is completely described by its impedance or its admittance, and the determination of $T(s)$ is a straightforward application of equivalent network concepts and some basic analysis techniques.

Example 14.14

An s-domain network is shown in Figure 14.32 with component values given as impedances. Suppose we find the transfer function

$$T(s) = \frac{V_0(s)}{V(s)}$$

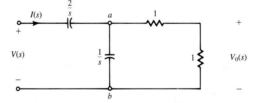

Figure 14.32
Network for Example 14.14.

We can find an equivalent network as seen in Figure 14.33 by calculating the equivalent impedance of the 1-F capacitor and the two resistors. From this network we see that

$$\frac{V_{ab}(s)}{V(s)} = \frac{2/(2s + 1)}{2/(2s + 1) + 2/s} = \frac{s}{3s + 1}$$

(Note that this expression is also a transfer function.) Since $V_0(s) = \frac{1}{2}V_{ab}(s)$,

$$T(s) = \frac{V_0(s)}{V(s)} = \frac{s}{2(3s + 1)}$$

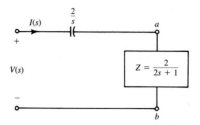

Figure 14.33
Equivalent network for
Figure 14.32.

If we want to find the output voltage, we have

$$V_0(s) = \left[\frac{s}{2(3s+1)}\right]V(s)$$

For any given input $v(t)$ and its s-domain expression $V(s)$, we can find $v_0(t)$ by the inverse transform. For example, suppose $v(t) = u(t)$. Then

$$V_0(s) = \left(\frac{s}{2(3s+1)}\right)\frac{1}{s} = \frac{1}{6(s+\frac{1}{3})}$$

and

$$v_0(t) = \left[\frac{1}{6}e^{-t/3}\right]u(t)\ V$$

Note that $v_0(0) = \frac{1}{6}$. Since the initial conditions are zero, how can this be correct?

Next suppose that $v(t) = 10\sin t$. Then

$$V_0(s) = \left[\frac{s}{6(s+\frac{1}{3})}\right]\left(\frac{10}{s^2+1}\right)$$

and the inverse transform can be used to find $v_0(t)$.

The basic ideas illustrated by this simple example can be used to work many network problems. Further details are left to the problems.

14.8 SUMMARY

In this chapter we utilized the power of the Laplace transform to calculate the complete response of some simple networks that contain energy-storage components. We also developed an s-domain extension of most of the fundamental concepts of earlier chapters. The ideas developed in this chapter are powerful tools in the analysis of linear networks.

In the next chapter, we pull all our tools together and bring our complete arsenal to bear in solving network problems.

PROBLEMS

14.1 The network of Figure 14.34 contains no energy storage at $t = 0^-$. Find dv_0/dt and d^2v_0/dt^2 at $t = 0^+$. Answers should be in terms of $i(t)$ and its derivatives.

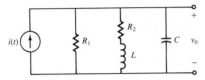

Figure 14.34

14.2 Find $v_4(t)$, $v_5(t)$, dv_4/dt, and dv_5/dt at $t = 0^+$ for the network of Figure 14.35 if it is unenergized at $t = 0^-$.

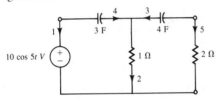

Figure 14.35

14.3 Find $v_0(t)$, dv_0/dt, and d^2v_0/dt^2 at $t = 0^+$ for the network of Figure 14.36 if it is unenergized at $t = 0^-$.

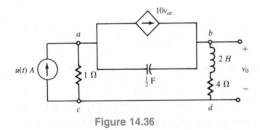

Figure 14.36

14.4 The network of Figure 14.37 has initial energy storage given by $v_2(0^-) = 0$. Calculate i_1, v_2, di_1/dt, and dv_2/dt at $t = 0^+$.

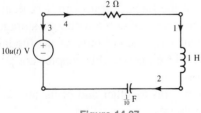

Figure 14.37

14.5 Find the impedance and admittance of each of the networks shown in Figure 14.38.

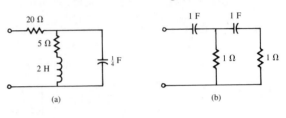

(a)   (b)

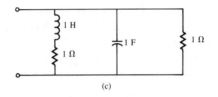

(c)

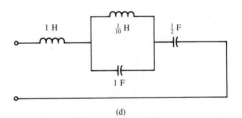

(d)

Figure 14.38

14.6 Find the impedance and admittance of each of the 1-point networks in Figure 14.39.

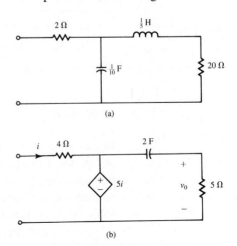

(a)

(b)

Figure 14.39

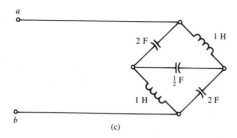

Figure 14.39 (continued)

14.7 Solve the network of Figure 14.37 for $i_1(t)$, $p_1(t)$, and $p_2(t)$, and the energy stored in the capacitor. Assume zero initial conditions.

14.8 Repeat Problem 14.7 for $R = 4\ \Omega$ and $C = \frac{1}{3}$ F.

14.9 Repeat Problem 14.7 for $R = 4\ \Omega$ and $C = \frac{1}{4}$ F.

14.10 Repeat Problem 14.7 for $R = 0\ \Omega$ and $C = \frac{1}{4}$ F.

14.11 Repeat Problem 14.7 for $v_2(0^-) = 20$ V.

14.12 Repeat Problem 14.7 for $i_1(0^-) = 10$ A.

14.13 For the network of Figure 14.40, formulate the state equations and solve for $v_3(t)$, $i_2(t)$, $v_4(t)$, and $i_5(t)$ for $e_5(t) = 10u(t)$ V and $v_3(0^-) = i_2(0^-) = 0$.

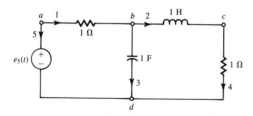

Figure 14.40

14.14 Repeat Problem 14.13 for $e_1(t) = 0$, $v_3(0^-) = 100$ V, and $i_2(0^-) = 5$ A.

14.15 Repeat Problem 14.13 for

$$e_1(t) = 10 \cos 10t\ u(t)\ \text{V}.$$

14.16 Formulate the integrodifferential mesh equations for the network of Figure 14.40. Use i_1 and i_2 as mesh currents and solve for $v_3(t)$, $i_2(t)$, $v_4(t)$, and $i_5(t)$ for the same source and initial conditions as in Problem 14.13.

14.17 Formulate the nodal equations for the network of Figure 14.40. Use node d as a reference and solve for $v_3(t)$, $i_2(t)$, $v_4(t)$, and $i_5(t)$ if $e_5(t) = 10u(t)$ V and $v_3(0^-) = i_2(0^-) = 0$.

14.18 Find the response $i_1(t)$ of the network of Figure 14.37 to an impulse source function $v_3(t) = 100\delta(t)$ V.

14.19 Find the response of the network of Figure 14.40 to a source function $e_5(t) = 100(t)$ V. Use the mesh current method.

14.20 Repeat Problem 14.19, but use node-voltage equations.

14.21 Find the s-domain Thévenin-form component equation for the network shown in Figure 14.41 for the measurement diagram shown.

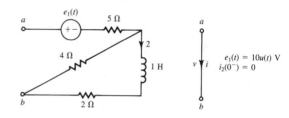

Figure 14.41

14.22 For the network of Problem 14.21, a 10-Ω resistor is connected between terminals a and b. Use the results of Problem 14.21 to calculate the voltage $V_{ab}(s)$ for this connection. Calculate $v_{ab}(t)$ and the instantaneous power for the 10-Ω resistor.

14.23 Repeat Problem 14.21 for $e_1(t) = 10 \sin t\, u(t)$ V and $i_2(0^-) = 0$.

14.24 Repeat Problem 14.21 for $e_1(t) = 0$ and $i_2(0^-) = 5$ A.

14.25 Find the s-domain Norton-form component equation for the network of Figure 14.41.

14.26 Find the s-domain Thévenin-form component equation for the network shown in Figure 14.42 for the measurement diagram shown.

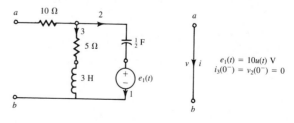

Figure 14.42

14.27 Repeat Problem 14.26 for
   $e_1(t) = 10 \cos 2t \, u(t)$ V.

14.28 Repeat Problem 14.26 for $e_1(t) = 0$, $v_2(0^-) = 100$ V, and $i_3(0^-) = 2$ A.

14.29 Find the s-domain Norton-form component equation for the network of Figure 14.42.

14.30 Find the transfer function $T(s) = V_4/V_5$ for the network of Figure 14.40.

14.31 Repeat Problem 14.30 for $T(s) = I_2/V_5$.

14.32 Find the transfer function $I(s) = V_5/V_1$ for the network of Figure 14.35.

14.33 Repeat Problem 14.32 for $T(s) = I_2/V_1$.

14.34 Repeat Problem 14.32 for $T(s) = I_2/I_1$.

14.35 Find the transfer function $T(s) = V_0/I$ for the network of Figure 14.36.

14.36 Find the transfer function $T(s) = V_0/I$ for the network of Figure 14.39(b).

Giants of the profession
IEEE Centennial Hall of Fame

John William Mauchly (1907–1980) Pioneer with J. P. Eckert in developing large electronic integrators and computers; coinventor of Eniac, Edvac, Univac, and Binac. Shown here with the ENIAC.

John Von Neumann (1903–1957) Mathematician who introduced the concept of a program written in a code that a computer would read, interpret, and execute; he was a consultant to Los Alamos National Laboratories. Shown here with the EDVAC.

Robert N. Noyce (1927–   ) Chairman of Intel Corp.; coinventor of the integrated circuit and developer of the planar process for manufacturing transistors; cofounder of Fairchild Semiconductor and Intel Corp. Shown here with his microprocessor chip.

Analysis of larger networks

15.1 INTRODUCTION

At last, we have accumulated the collection of formulation and solution techniques needed to tackle the analysis of large-scale networks. For this work we need a systematic procedure that takes advantage of explicit sets of equations in the PRIMM to eliminate the maximum number of equations from the set that must be solved simultaneously. The topological concepts of tree and cotree provide a systematic framework to define a convenient procedure, which applies equally well to large networks and to small.

Matrix algebra provides the symbolism to describe the procedures in a very general fashion. It is also quite useful in numerical calculations involving networks because of its precisely defined rules of manipulation. This is true both for hand and machine computation.

The Laplace transform rounds out the kit of tools needed for analytical solution. It also has precisely defined rules that aid in the systematic formulation and solution of network models.

In this chapter we bring all these tools to bear on the analysis of some larger networks. We would like to demonstrate these techniques on some truly large-scale networks, which include components of all types, but this is patently impossible. No one type of practical network includes all the various kinds of components we have discussed. More to the point, perhaps, is the fact that the model for any network we could dream up, with all the component types represented, would be too large to solve analytically in a reasonable amount of time.

We have all the tools needed to formulate models for large-scale networks, but to solve them we would need either large-order numerical-integration routines (for state models) or a computer program to determine zeros of large-degree polynomials for s-domain solutions. These types of programs are readily available (POLYROOT is one example), so, if you have mastered the formulation techniques, carrying through to solution should not pose a serious problem, given time and resources.

For the most part, therefore, we concentrate on utilizing the systematic formulation techniques on moderate-size networks with a diversity of component types and solving the resulting models by means of the Laplace transform.

As we progress through this chapter, you will undoubtedly be struck by the many opportunities for a slight error (often only a sign) that arise in the formulation and solution of models for even small networks. A great deal of patience and attention to detail is required to get through these procedures with absolute correctness—even if there is no question about what is to be done, and even if very systematic procedures are defined. A successful network analysis requires that every step in the procedure be done correctly. Therefore it behooves us all to work deliberately and check the results of each step before proceeding.

15.2   FORMULATION OF THE PRIMARY MATHEMATICAL MODEL

The model-formulation problem begins with the selection of a formulation tree. If selected properly, the tree provides the basis for KCL and KVL equations that will serve equally well for loop, supernode, or state equations (plus other models which we have not taken time to discuss).

There are no hard and fast rules that must be followed in choosing a formulation tree, and a tree that is suitable for supernode formulation may not be as well adapted for loop formulation. If you adhere to the following rules, however, you will find that the tree will serve equally well for all three formulations.

1. The tree should include all independent and dependent voltage sources.

2. The cotree should include all independent and dependent current sources.

3. All capacitors should be included in the tree, if possible.

4. All inductors should be included in the cotree, if possible.

If Rules 1 and 2 cannot be followed, the network does not have a unique solution and you may throw in the towel—if a complete solution is required. Rules 3 and 4 simply adapt the tree to state-model formulation. If all capacitors cannot be included in a tree and all inductors included in a cotree, no problems are caused in loop and supernode formulation. In state-model formulation, however, we encounter a case in which the number of state variables is less than the number of energy-storage branches. The formulation rules for this case are well known but are beyond the scope of this text.

Once the formulation tree is chosen, we write the KCL and KVL in matrix form:

$$\text{KCL:} \quad \mathbf{QI} = \mathbf{0} \tag{15.1}$$

$$\text{KVL:} \quad \mathbf{BV} = \mathbf{0} \tag{15.2}$$

The matrices $\mathbf{Q}$ and $\mathbf{B}$ are called the *supernode* and the *loop matrices*, respectively. If we put the tree variables first in $\mathbf{I}$ and $\mathbf{V}$, Equations 15.1 and 15.2 can be written

$$[\mathbf{U} \quad \mathbf{Q}_l]\begin{bmatrix} \mathbf{I}_t \\ \mathbf{I}_l \end{bmatrix} = \mathbf{0} \tag{15.3}$$

$$[\mathbf{B}_t \quad \mathbf{U}]\begin{bmatrix} \mathbf{V}_t \\ \mathbf{V}_l \end{bmatrix} = \mathbf{0} \tag{15.4}$$

where $\mathbf{U}$ is the unit matrix and subscripts t and l denote *tree* and *cotree* (links), respectively. Multiplying out Equations 15.3 and 15.4, we have

$$\mathbf{I}_t + \mathbf{Q}_l\mathbf{I}_l = \mathbf{0} \tag{15.5}$$

$$\mathbf{B}_t\mathbf{V}_t + \mathbf{V}_l = \mathbf{0} \tag{15.6}$$

Thus the tree currents can be written in terms of the link currents, and the link voltages can be written in terms of the tree voltages.

If we further subdivide the tree and cotree variables into sources and nonsources, we can identify the dummy KCL and KVL equations in matrix form. Suppose we let t_1 identify the voltage sources and l_2 the current sources. Then we could write Equations 15.3 and 15.4 as

$$\begin{bmatrix} \mathbf{U} & \mathbf{O} & \mathbf{Q}_{l_{11}} & \mathbf{Q}_{l_{12}} \\ \mathbf{O} & \mathbf{U} & \mathbf{Q}_{l_{21}} & \mathbf{Q}_{l_{22}} \end{bmatrix}\begin{bmatrix} \mathbf{I}_{t_1} \\ \mathbf{I}_{t_2} \\ \mathbf{I}_{l_1} \\ \mathbf{I}_{l_2} \end{bmatrix} = \mathbf{0} \tag{15.7}$$

from which

$$\mathbf{I}_{t_1} + \mathbf{Q}_{l_{11}}\mathbf{I}_{l_1} + \mathbf{Q}_{l_{12}}\mathbf{I}_{l_2} = \mathbf{0} \quad \text{(Dummy)} \tag{15.8}$$

$$\mathbf{I}_{t_2} + \mathbf{Q}_{l_{21}}\mathbf{I}_{l_1} + \mathbf{Q}_{l_{22}}\mathbf{I}_{l_2} = \mathbf{0} \tag{15.9}$$

Also,

$$\begin{bmatrix} \mathbf{B}_{t_{11}} & \mathbf{B}_{t_{12}} & \mathbf{U} & \mathbf{O} \\ \mathbf{B}_{t_{21}} & \mathbf{B}_{t_{22}} & \mathbf{O} & \mathbf{U} \end{bmatrix} \begin{bmatrix} \mathbf{V}_{t_1} \\ \mathbf{V}_{t_2} \\ \mathbf{V}_{l_1} \\ \mathbf{V}_{l_2} \end{bmatrix} = \mathbf{0} \tag{15.10}$$

from which

$$\mathbf{B}_{t_{11}}\mathbf{V}_{t_1} + \mathbf{B}_{t_{12}}\mathbf{V}_{t_2} + \mathbf{V}_{l_1} = \mathbf{0} \tag{15.11}$$

$$\mathbf{B}_{t_{21}}\mathbf{V}_{t_1} + \mathbf{B}_{t_{22}}\mathbf{V}_{t_2} + \mathbf{V}_{l_2} = \mathbf{0} \qquad \text{(Dummy)} \tag{15.12}$$

It should be clear that Equation 15.8 is a dummy matrix KCL equation since $\mathbf{I}_{t_1}$ is associated with the voltage sources. In like manner, Equation 15.12 is a dummy matrix KVL equation. It follows that Equations 15.9 and 15.11 are the KCL and KVL equations, respectively, which must be solved simultaneously with the component equations.

If you feel that we have taken unfair advantage in the dividing and subdividing of matrices and vectors in this exposition, we apologize. Frankly, we do not know how to make the equivalent presentation using scalar notation. We will, however, use scalar formulation in the examples to clarify the matrix formalism.

In formulating s-domain network models, one may either Laplace-transform the PRIMM and proceed, or do the loop-, supernode-, or state-model formulation in the time domain and then Laplace-transform the resulting equations.

Since the KCL and KVL equations are linear and algebraic, they have the same form in the s-domain as in the t-domain.

$$\mathbf{QI}(t) = \mathbf{0} \rightarrow \mathbf{QI}(s) = \mathbf{0} \tag{15.13}$$

$$\mathbf{BV}(t) = \mathbf{0} \rightarrow \mathbf{BV}(s) = \mathbf{0} \tag{15.14}$$

Thus these relationships between the currents and the voltages are unchanged by the transformation.

For the component equations, the linear algebraic relations also come through the transformation unchanged in form.

$$\mathbf{V}_R(t) = \mathbf{RI}_R(t) \rightarrow \mathbf{V}_R(s) = \mathbf{RI}_R(s) \tag{15.15}$$

The t-derivative CE transform as follows:

$$\mathbf{I}_C(t) = \mathbf{C}\frac{d}{dt}\mathbf{V}_C(t) \rightarrow \mathbf{I}_C(s) = s\mathbf{CV}_C(s) - \mathbf{CV}_C(0^-) \tag{15.16}$$

$$\mathbf{V}_L(t) = \mathbf{L}\frac{d}{dt}\mathbf{I}_L(t) \rightarrow \mathbf{V}_L(s) = s\mathbf{LI}_L(s) - \mathbf{LI}_L(0^-) \tag{15.17}$$

Since Equations 15.15–15.17 are linear, they may be solved for the alternate vector variable to yield the set:

$$\mathbf{I}_R(s) = \mathbf{R}^{-1}\mathbf{V}_R(s) \tag{15.18}$$

$$\mathbf{V}_C(s) = \frac{1}{s}\mathbf{C}^{-1}\mathbf{I}_C(s) + \frac{1}{s}\mathbf{V}_C(0^-) \tag{15.19}$$

$$\mathbf{I}_L(s) = \frac{1}{s}\mathbf{L}^{-1}\mathbf{V}_L(s) + \frac{1}{s}\mathbf{I}_L(0^-) \tag{15.20}$$

Then the proper set of equations can be chosen for the particular formulation desired. In these equations we have not included the transformed dependent sources, but—since they have linear algebraic CE—the transformation leaves each form unchanged.

We are now ready to formulate network models in each of the standard forms. Before going to that discussion, however, we present an inverse transformation technique that will prove useful.

Invariably in the solution of simultaneous differential equations by Laplace-transform techniques, every term in the s-domain solution has the same denominator polynomial. Rather than go through the partial-fraction expansion for each term, use of the following theorem often saves much effort.

Theorem 15.1

Let $F(s)$ be a ratio of polynomials in s with real constant coefficients,

$$F(s) = \frac{N(s)}{D(s)} = \frac{a_0 + a_1 s + a_2 s^2 + \cdots + a_n s^n}{D(s)}$$

where the degree of $D(s)$ is greater than that of $N(s)$. Then if

$$G(s) \doteq \frac{1}{D(s)} \quad \text{and} \quad g(t) = \mathcal{L}^{-1}\{G(s)\}$$

we have

$$f(t) = a_0 g(t) + a_1 g'(t) + a_2 g''(t) + \cdots + a_n \frac{d^n}{dt^n} g(t)$$

For this theorem to hold, it is crucial that the degree of $N(s)$ be less than the degree of $D(s)$. When this condition is true, $a_k s^k \rightarrow a_k (d^k/dt^k)g(t)$ for $k = 1, 2, \ldots, n$, since the associated initial conditions are zero.

Example 15.1

Given

$$F(s) = \frac{s + 1}{s(s + 2)(s + 3)}$$

$$G(s) = \frac{1}{s(s + 2)(s + 3)} = \frac{\frac{1}{6}}{s} + \frac{-\frac{1}{2}}{s + 2} + \frac{\frac{1}{3}}{s + 3}$$

$$g(t) = \left(\frac{1}{6} - \frac{1}{2}e^{-2t} + \frac{1}{3}e^{-3t}\right)u(t)$$

$$g'(t) = (e^{-2t} - e^{-3t})u(t)$$

Therefore,

$$f(t) = g'(t) + g(t)$$

$$= \left(\frac{1}{6} + \frac{1}{2}e^{-2t} - \frac{2}{3}e^{-3t}\right)u(t)$$

We now use the network of Figure 15.1 to illustrate the writing of the time-domain PRIMM in scalar and matrix form. Although not a large-scale network, this example has enough component diversity to provide some insight into systematic model formulation for a rather general network. Any resemblance of this network to an actual practical network is purely coincidental. It was devised to include a respectable number of common but diverse components and to be amenable to solution by Laplace-transform techniques.

Figure 15.1
Network for Example 15.2.

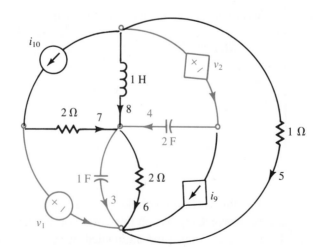

Example 15.2 ——

For the network of Figure 15.1, a formulation tree is chosen to include branches 1, 2, 3, and 4. This choice satisfies Rules 1 through 4.

In scalar form the KCL equations for the supernodes defined by the tree are

$$\left.\begin{array}{c} i_1 + i_7 - i_{10} = 0 \\ i_2 + i_5 + i_8 + i_{10} = 0 \end{array}\right\} \quad \text{(Dummy equations)}$$

$$i_3 + i_5 + i_6 - i_7 + i_9 + i_{10} = 0$$

$$i_4 + i_5 + i_8 + i_9 + i_{10} = 0$$

In matrix form these equations become $\mathbf{I}_t + \mathbf{Q}_l \mathbf{I}_l = 0$:

$$\left.\begin{array}{c}\text{(Dummy}\\\text{equations)}\end{array}\right\}\begin{bmatrix} i_1 \\ i_2 \\ \hline i_3 \\ i_4 \end{bmatrix} + \begin{bmatrix} 0 & 0 & 1 & 0 & 0 & -1 \\ 1 & 0 & 0 & 1 & 0 & 1 \\ \hline 1 & 1 & -1 & 0 & 1 & 1 \\ 1 & 0 & 0 & 1 & 1 & 1 \end{bmatrix} \begin{bmatrix} i_5 \\ i_6 \\ i_7 \\ i_8 \\ i_9 \\ i_{10} \end{bmatrix} = 0 \qquad (15.21)$$

The KVL equations in scalar form for the loops defined by the tree are

$$-v_2 - v_3 - v_4 + v_5 = 0$$

$$-v_3 + v_6 = 0$$

$$-v_1 + v_3 + v_7 = 0$$

$$-v_2 - v_4 + v_8 = 0$$

$$\left.\begin{array}{c} -v_3 - v_4 + v_9 = 0 \\ v_1 - v_2 - v_3 - v_4 + v_{10} = 0 \end{array}\right\} \quad \text{(Dummy equations)}$$

In matrix form these equations become $\mathbf{B}_t \mathbf{V}_t + \mathbf{V}_l = 0$:

$$\begin{bmatrix} 0 & -1 & -1 & -1 \\ 0 & 0 & -1 & 0 \\ -1 & 0 & 1 & 0 \\ 0 & -1 & 0 & -1 \\ \hline 0 & 0 & -1 & -1 \\ 1 & -1 & -1 & -1 \end{bmatrix} \begin{bmatrix} v_1 \\ v_2 \\ v_3 \\ v_4 \end{bmatrix} + \left.\begin{bmatrix} v_5 \\ v_6 \\ v_7 \\ v_8 \\ \hline v_9 \\ v_{10} \end{bmatrix}\right\} = 0 \qquad (15.22)$$

(Dummy equations) appears to the right of the lower partition.

The dotted lines in Equations 15.21 and 15.22 (which correspond to Equations 15.7 and 15.10) indicate the division between the dummy KCL and

KVL equations, respectively, and the equations that must be solved simultaneously with the CE.

We note that the $\mathbf{B}_t$ matrix of Equation 15.22 is equal to the negative transpose of $\mathbf{Q}_l$ of Equation 15.21. This is not a coincidence but is always true if the same tree is used for formulation and if the voltage and current vectors are arranged in the same order.

This relationship between $\mathbf{B}_t$ and $\mathbf{Q}_l$ leads to a convenient means for writing general loop and nodal equations in matrix form, as we will see. For now we note that since

$$\mathbf{B}_t = -\mathbf{Q}_l^T \left. \right)$$

and

$$\mathbf{Q}_l = -\mathbf{B}_t^T \left. \right)$$

(15.23)

we can write Equation 15.5,

$$\mathbf{I}_t = -\mathbf{Q}_l \mathbf{I}_l$$

as

$$\mathbf{I}_t = \mathbf{B}_t^T \mathbf{I}_l$$

(15.24)

Thus it follows that the complete current vector $\mathbf{I}$ can be written in terms of the cotree current vector $\mathbf{I}_l$ as follows:

$$\mathbf{I} = \begin{bmatrix} \mathbf{I}_t \\ \mathbf{I}_l \end{bmatrix} = \begin{bmatrix} \mathbf{B}_t^T \\ \mathbf{U} \end{bmatrix} \mathbf{I}_l = \mathbf{B}^T \mathbf{I}_l$$

(15.25)

In a similar fashion, we can start with Equation 15.6 and use Equation 15.23 to get

$$\mathbf{V}_l = -\mathbf{B}_t \mathbf{V}_t = \mathbf{Q}_l^T \mathbf{V}_t$$

(15.26)

Thus the complete voltage vector can be written in terms of the tree voltage vector as follows:

$$\mathbf{V} = \begin{bmatrix} \mathbf{V}_t \\ \mathbf{V}_l \end{bmatrix} = \begin{bmatrix} \mathbf{U} \\ \mathbf{Q}_l^T \end{bmatrix} \mathbf{V}_t = \mathbf{Q}^T \mathbf{V}_t$$

(15.27)

Equations 15.25 and 15.27 are always true, no matter what kind of network components are involved. They depend only on the topological (or interconnection) properties of the network and the formulation tree chosen. Thus we will see that it is not strictly necessary to write both KCL and KVL equations in order to formulate loop or nodal equations. It is good practice, however, to write both $\mathbf{B}$ and $\mathbf{Q}$ as a check on the correctness of each.

The CE for the network are

$$v_1(t) = 5\delta(t)$$

$$v_2(t) = 2v_7(t)$$

$$\frac{d}{dt}v_3(t) = i_3(t) \qquad v_3(0^-) = 10 \text{ V}$$

$$\frac{d}{dt}v_4(t) = \frac{1}{2}i_4(t) \qquad v_4(0^-) = 5 \text{ V}$$

$$v_5(t) = i_5(t)$$

$$v_6(t) = 2i_6(t)$$

$$v_7(t) = 2i_7(t)$$

$$v_8(t) = \frac{d}{dt}i_8(t) \qquad i_8(0^-) = 0$$

$$i_9(t) = 2i_6(t)$$

$$i_{10}(t) = 10\delta(t)$$

We will use this network PRIMM for examples of loop, supernode, and state-space modeling in later sections. Before moving on to those formulations, however, we note that one rather simple formulation scheme would be to eliminate tree currents and cotree voltages from the CE by substituting Equations 15.21 and 15.22 into them. This would yield eight equations in eight unknowns without additional manipulations.

The equations that result from this procedure are commonly called *hybrid equations* and relate tree-voltage and link-current unknowns. They are primarily useful when the CE are not amenable to loop, supernode, or state-model formulation. They can be used when the CE are nonlinear and nonexplicit or poorly conditioned in other ways for standard formulation procedures. The authors of most undergraduate textbooks do not discuss hybrid equations because they consider only well-behaved CE, such as we have. For the same reasons, with the exception of this brief mention, we follow suit.

15.3 LOOP FORMULATION

In formulating loop equations, the objective is to achieve a set of simultaneous algebraic equations relating the *s*-domain link currents. If the CE can be written in the form

$$\mathbf{V}(s) = \mathbf{Z}(s)\mathbf{I}(s) + \mathbf{E}(s) \tag{15.28}$$

then the substitution procedure of Chapter 4 can be followed exactly to yield the loop equations in matrix form.

First, the KCL are substituted into the CE to eliminate all tree currents. In matrix form this can be written

$$\mathbf{V}(s) = \mathbf{Z}(s)\mathbf{B}^T\mathbf{I}_l(s) + \mathbf{E}(s) \qquad (15.29)$$

using $\mathbf{I}(s) = \mathbf{B}^T\mathbf{I}_l(s)$ from Equation 15.25.

Next, the altered CE (Equation 15.29) are substituted in the KVL (Equation 15.14)

$$\mathbf{BV}(s) = \mathbf{0}$$

to yield

$$\mathbf{BZ}(s)\mathbf{B}^T\mathbf{I}_l(s) + \mathbf{BE}(s) = \mathbf{0} \qquad (15.30)$$

Equation 15.30 is a general algorithm for the formulation of loop equations and is restricted only to those networks in which the CE can be written in the voltage-explicit form, as shown in Equation 15.28.

The final set of equations corresponding to the PRIMM for the loop formulation is

$$\mathbf{I}(s) = \mathbf{B}^T\mathbf{I}_l(s) \qquad (15.25)$$

$$\mathbf{V}(s) = \mathbf{Z}(s)\mathbf{B}^T\mathbf{I}_l(s) + \mathbf{E}(s) \qquad (15.29)$$

$$\mathbf{BZ}(s)\mathbf{B}^T\mathbf{I}_l(s) = -\mathbf{BE}(s) \qquad (15.30)$$

Equation 15.30 is called the *matrix loop equation,* or *loop-current equation.* As is evident, once $\mathbf{I}_l$ is known from a solution of the loop equations, all variables of the network may be found using Equations 15.25 and 15.29.

Controlled-voltage sources fit into this formulation for all cases where the controlling variable is a current. For the controlled sources considered in this text, the controlling variable can always be written as either voltage or current.

Current sources—independent or controlled—do not fit into the matrix loop formulation symbolized as Equation 15.30. Thus we must do something special for this case.

The formulation with current sources of either type is complicated by two factors. First, $\mathbf{I}_l(s)$ now includes current sources and must be partitioned. Second, we do not use the dummy KVL equations of Equation 15.12; instead we carry out the final substitution only into Equation 15.11. This creates more complex matrix symbolism. If controlled-current sources are present, we have the additional complication of CE that do not fit the voltage-explicit pattern. If we make the controlling variable voltage and attempt to formulate with the controlling voltage explicit, we find that this voltage appears twice in the CE and thus Equation 15.30 does not hold.

All these complications combine to make an algorithmic formulation of the loop equations with current sources too complex for this text. We leave that formulation for more advanced courses. Instead, we will carry out the formulation of loop equations in scalar form, using the following KCL and KVL matrix equations to help us keep a perspective on what we are doing in the larger scheme of things.

$$\mathbf{I}_t(s) = -\mathbf{Q}_l\mathbf{I}_l(s) = \mathbf{B}_t^T\mathbf{I}_l(s) \tag{15.24}$$

$$[\mathbf{B}_t \quad \mathbf{U}]\begin{bmatrix} \mathbf{V}_t(s) \\ \mathbf{V}_l(s) \end{bmatrix} = \mathbf{0} \tag{15.4}$$

We formulate the loop equations in the following order:

1. Write all component equations (CE), including dependent sources, in terms of currents.

2. Use KCL to express all tree currents in terms of link currents.

3. Use results of (2) to write CE in terms of link currents.

4. Use CE of dependent current sources to eliminate dependent source currents from the other CE.

5. Substitute the resulting CE into the nondummy KVL equations to yield the loop-current equations. (These are also sometimes called *link-current equations*.)

If the controlled currents are paralleled by a passive network component, we can use a Thévenin transformation and Step 4 can be eliminated.

Example 15.3 ───

We now formulate loop equations for the network of Figure 15.2. As the first step we pick a formulation tree of branches 1, 2, and 4 in accordance with the rules of Section 15.2. Next we write the tree currents in terms of the link currents, using the fundamental KCL.

$$i_1 + i_3 + i_7 + i_6 = 0 \qquad \text{(Dummy)} \tag{15.31}$$

$$i_2 + i_3 + i_7 + i_6 = 0 \tag{15.32}$$

$$i_4 + i_5 - i_6 - i_7 = 0 \tag{15.33}$$

Next, the tree currents are eliminated from the CE by substitution:

$$V_2(s) = 3I_2(s) = -3[(I_3(s) + I_7(s) + I_6(s)] = -I_3(s) - I_7(s)$$

$$V_3(s) = \frac{1}{3}sI_3(s)$$

$$V_4(s) = \frac{9}{s}I_4(s) = \frac{9}{s}[I_6(s) + I_7(s) - I_5(s)]$$

$$= \frac{9}{s}\left[-\frac{2}{3}I_3(s) + \frac{1}{3}I_7(s) - I_5(s)\right]$$

$$V_7(s) = 2I_7(s)$$

$$I_6(s) = 2I_2(s) = -2[I_3(s) + I_7(s) + I_6(s)]$$

from which

$$I_6(s) = -\frac{2}{3}I_3(s) - \frac{2}{3}I_7(s)$$

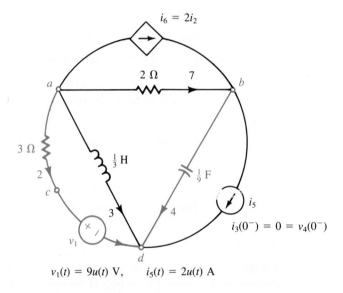

Figure 15.2
Network for Examples
15.3, 15.5, and 15.7.

$i_6 = 2i_2$

$2\,\Omega$ 7

a b

$3\,\Omega$

$\frac{1}{3}$ H

2

$\frac{1}{9}$ F

c

3 4 i_5

v_1

$i_3(0^-) = 0 = v_4(0^-)$

d

$v_1(t) = 9u(t)$ V, $i_5(t) = 2u(t)$ A

In matrix form, the CE are

$$
\begin{bmatrix} V_2(s) \\ V_4(s) \\ V_3(s) \\ V_7(s) \end{bmatrix}
=
\begin{bmatrix} -1 & -1 \\ -\dfrac{6}{s} & \dfrac{3}{s} \\ \dfrac{1}{3}s & 0 \\ 0 & 2 \end{bmatrix}
\begin{bmatrix} I_3(s) \\ I_7(s) \end{bmatrix}
+
\begin{bmatrix} 0 \\ -\dfrac{9}{s}I_5(s) \\ 0 \\ 0 \end{bmatrix}
\qquad (15.34)
$$

where the tree voltages are written first.

Next we substitute Equation 15.34 into the nondummy KVL (links 3 and 7):

$$\begin{bmatrix} -1 & 0 & 1 & 0 \\ -1 & 1 & 0 & 1 \end{bmatrix} \begin{bmatrix} V_2(s) \\ V_4(s) \\ V_3(s) \\ V_7(s) \end{bmatrix} = \begin{bmatrix} 1 \\ 1 \end{bmatrix} E_1(s) \tag{15.35}$$

The result is

$$\begin{bmatrix} \dfrac{s+3}{3} & 1 \\[2mm] \dfrac{s-6}{s} & \dfrac{3(s+1)}{s} \end{bmatrix} \begin{bmatrix} I_3(7) \\ I_7(s) \end{bmatrix} + \begin{bmatrix} 0 \\[2mm] -\dfrac{9}{s}I_5(s) \end{bmatrix} = \begin{bmatrix} 1 \\ 1 \end{bmatrix} E_1(s) \tag{15.36}$$

Equation 15.36 can be rewritten as

$$\begin{bmatrix} \dfrac{s+3}{3} & 1 \\[2mm] \dfrac{s-6}{s} & \dfrac{3(s+1)}{s} \end{bmatrix} \begin{bmatrix} I_3(s) \\ I_7(s) \end{bmatrix} = \begin{bmatrix} E_1(s) \\[2mm] \dfrac{9}{s}I_5(s) + E_1(s) \end{bmatrix} \tag{15.37}$$

The determinant of the coefficient matrix is

$$\Delta(s) = \frac{s^2 + 3s + 9}{s} \cong \frac{(s + 1.5 + j2.6)(s + 1.5 - j2.6)}{s}$$

$$= \frac{\phi(s)}{s} \tag{15.38}$$

and the solution to Equation 15.37 is

$$\begin{bmatrix} I_3(s) \\ I_7(s) \end{bmatrix} = \frac{s}{\phi(s)} \begin{bmatrix} \dfrac{3(s+1)}{s} & -1 \\[2mm] \dfrac{6-s}{s} & \dfrac{s+3}{3} \end{bmatrix} \begin{bmatrix} E_1(s) \\[2mm] \dfrac{9}{s}I_5(s) + E_1(s) \end{bmatrix} \tag{15.39}$$

We can simplify Equation 15.39 by factoring $1/s$ out of the coefficient matrix to produce

$$\begin{bmatrix} I_3(s) \\ I_7(s) \end{bmatrix} = \frac{1}{\phi(s)} \begin{bmatrix} 3(s+1) & -s \\[2mm] 6-s & \dfrac{s^2+3s}{3} \end{bmatrix} \begin{bmatrix} E_1(s) \\[2mm] \dfrac{9}{s}I_5(s) + E_1(s) \end{bmatrix} \tag{15.40}$$

$$= \frac{1}{\phi(s)} \begin{bmatrix} 3(s+1)\dfrac{9}{s} - \dfrac{18}{s} - \dfrac{9s}{s} \\[4mm] (6-s)\dfrac{9}{s} + 3(s+3)\dfrac{2}{s} + \dfrac{(s+3)3s}{s} \end{bmatrix} \tag{15.41}$$

$$\begin{bmatrix} I_3(s) \\ I_7(s) \end{bmatrix} = \frac{1}{s\phi(s)} \begin{bmatrix} 18s + 9 \\ 3s^2 + 6s + 72 \end{bmatrix} \tag{15.42}$$

We utilize Theorem 15.1 to find the solutions for $i_3(t)$ and $i_7(t)$. First, we find the inverse transform for

$$G(s) \doteq \frac{1}{s\phi(s)} \tag{15.43}$$

$$
\begin{aligned}
G(s) &= \frac{1}{s(s + 1.5 + j2.6)(s + 1.5 - j2.6)} \\
&= \frac{A}{s} + \frac{\bar{B}}{s + 1.5 + j2.6} + \frac{\bar{B}^*}{s + 1.5 - j2.6} \\
&= \frac{0.111}{s} + \frac{-0.0555 - j0.0320}{s + 1.5 + j2.6} \\
&\quad + \frac{-0.0555 + j0.0320}{s + 1.5 - j2.6}
\end{aligned}
\tag{15.44}
$$

Thus, for $t \geq 0$ we can write

$$
\begin{aligned}
g(t) &= 0.111 + e^{-1.5t}[(-0.0555 - j0.0320)e^{-j2.6t} \\
&\quad + (-0.0555 + j0.0320)e^{j2.6t}] \\
&= 0.111 + e^{-1.5t}(-0.111 \cos 2.6t - 0.064 \sin 2.6t) \quad (15.45)
\end{aligned}
$$

$$g'(t) = 0.3846e^{-1.5t} \sin 2.6t \tag{15.46}$$

$$g''(t) = e^{-1.5t}(\cos 2.6t - 0.5769 \sin 2.6t) \tag{15.47}$$

By Theorem 15.1 and Equation 15.42 we have, for $t \geq 0$,

$$
\begin{aligned}
i_3(t) &= 18g'(t) + 9g(t) \\
&= 0.999 + e^{-1.5t}(6.3468 \sin 2.6t - 1.000 \cos 2.6t) \quad (15.48)
\end{aligned}
$$

$$
\begin{aligned}
i_7(t) &= 3g''(t) + 6g'(t) + 72g(t) \\
&= 7.992 - e^{-1.5t}(4.0311 \sin 2.6t + 4.992 \cos 2.6t) \quad (15.49)
\end{aligned}
$$

From these solutions, all other currents can be found as linear combinations.

Example 15.4 _____

For the network of Figure 15.1, we formulate loop equations in the s-domain. As the first step we convert the voltage-controlled voltage source to a current-controlled voltage source.

$$V_2(s) = 2V_7(s) = 4I_7(s)$$

Since the controlling current in branch 6 (for the current-controlled current source, branch 9) is a link, no action is required to get $I_9(s)$ in terms of link currents.

$$I_9(s) = 2I_6(s)$$

Now we write the voltage-explicit equations and eliminate the tree currents and $I_9(s)$ by substitution. The result is, in matrix form,

$$
\begin{bmatrix} V_2(s) \\ V_3(s) \\ V_4(s) \\ V_5(s) \\ V_6(s) \\ V_7(s) \\ V_8(s) \end{bmatrix}
=
\begin{bmatrix}
0 & 0 & 4 & 0 \\
-\dfrac{1}{s} & -\dfrac{3}{s} & \dfrac{1}{s} & 0 \\
-\dfrac{1}{2s} & -\dfrac{1}{s} & 0 & -\dfrac{1}{2s} \\
1 & 0 & 0 & 0 \\
0 & 2 & 0 & 0 \\
0 & 0 & 2 & 0 \\
0 & 0 & 0 & s
\end{bmatrix}
\begin{bmatrix} I_5(s) \\ I_6(s) \\ I_7(s) \\ I_8(s) \end{bmatrix}
\qquad (15.50)
$$

We write the nondummy KVL equation for links 5, 6, 7, and 8 (Equation 15.22) as follows for convenience:

$$
\begin{bmatrix}
-1 & -1 & -1 & 1 & 0 & 0 & 0 \\
0 & -1 & 0 & 0 & 1 & 0 & 0 \\
0 & 1 & 0 & 0 & 0 & 1 & 0 \\
-1 & 0 & -1 & 0 & 0 & 0 & 1
\end{bmatrix}
\begin{bmatrix} V_2(s) \\ V_3(s) \\ V_4(s) \\ V_5(s) \\ V_6(s) \\ V_7(s) \\ V_8(s) \end{bmatrix}
+
\begin{bmatrix} 0 \\ 0 \\ -1 \\ 0 \end{bmatrix} V_1(s) = 0 \quad (15.51)
$$

When Equation 15.50 is substituted into Equation 15.51, the resulting loop equations are

$$
\begin{bmatrix}
\left(\dfrac{3}{2s}+1\right) & \dfrac{4}{s} & -\left(4+\dfrac{1}{s}\right) & \dfrac{1}{2s} \\
\dfrac{1}{s} & \dfrac{3}{s}+2 & -\dfrac{1}{s} & 0 \\
-\dfrac{1}{s} & -\dfrac{3}{s} & \dfrac{1}{s}+2 & 0 \\
\dfrac{1}{2s} & \dfrac{1}{s} & -4 & \dfrac{1}{2s}+s
\end{bmatrix}
\begin{bmatrix} I_5(s) \\ I_6(s) \\ I_7(s) \\ I_8(s) \end{bmatrix}
+
\begin{bmatrix} 0 \\ 0 \\ -5 \\ 0 \end{bmatrix} = 0 \quad (15.52)
$$

Since this formulation yields four equations in four unknowns, compared to three equations in three unknowns for state-model formulation, we leave the solution until Section 15.5. We will, however, put Equation 15.52 in slightly more docile form for solution by multiplying every scalar equation by s. The result is

$$
\begin{bmatrix}
\left(s + \dfrac{3}{2}\right) & 4 & -(4s + 1) & \dfrac{1}{2} \\[2mm]
1 & (2s + 3) & -1 & 0 \\[2mm]
-1 & -3 & (2s + 1) & 0 \\[2mm]
\dfrac{1}{2} & 1 & -4s & \left(s^2 + \dfrac{1}{2}\right)
\end{bmatrix}
\begin{bmatrix}
I_5(s) \\[2mm]
I_6(s) \\[2mm]
I_7(s) \\[2mm]
I_8(s)
\end{bmatrix}
=
\begin{bmatrix}
0 \\[2mm]
0 \\[2mm]
5s \\[2mm]
0
\end{bmatrix}
\tag{15.53}
$$

15.4   SUPERNODE FORMULATION

In formulating supernode equations, the objective is to achieve a set of simultaneous algebraic equations relating the s-domain tree voltages. These equations are named differently by different authors, but are variously known as *node-pair voltage equations*, *tree-voltage equations*, *cutset equations*, and *supernode equations*. We regard these equations as a generalization of the node equations and designate them by the term *supernode equations*, although supernode-voltage equations would be more descriptive.

If the CE can be written in the form

$$\mathbf{I}(s) = \mathbf{Y}(s)\mathbf{V}(s) + \mathbf{J}(s) \tag{15.54}$$

then the substitution procedure of Section 5.4 can be followed exactly to yield the supernode equations in matrix form.

First, the KVL are substituted into the CE to eliminate all link voltages. Using $\mathbf{V}(s) = \mathbf{Q}^T\mathbf{V}_t(s)$ from Equation 15.27 to substitute into Equation 15.54, we have

$$\mathbf{I}(s) = \mathbf{Y}(s)\mathbf{Q}^T\mathbf{V}_T(s) + \mathbf{J}(s) \tag{15.55}$$

Next, Equation 15.55 is substituted into the KCL

$$\mathbf{QI}(s) = \mathbf{0} \tag{15.13}$$

to yield

$$\mathbf{QY}(s)\mathbf{Q}^T\mathbf{V}_t(s) + \mathbf{QJ}(s) = \mathbf{0} \tag{15.56}$$

Equation 15.56 is a general algorithm for the formulation of supernode equations and is restricted only to those networks for which the CE can be written in the current-explicit form, as shown in Equation 15.54.

The final set of equations, corresponding to the PRIMM, for the supernode formulation is

$$\mathbf{V}(s) = \mathbf{Q}^T\mathbf{V}_t(s) \tag{15.27}$$

$$\mathbf{I}(s) = \mathbf{Y}(s)\mathbf{Q}^T\mathbf{V}_t(s) + \mathbf{J}(s) \tag{15.55}$$

$$\mathbf{Q}\mathbf{Y}(s)\mathbf{Q}^T\mathbf{V}_t(s) = -\mathbf{Q}\mathbf{J}(s) \tag{15.56}$$

Equation 15.56 is called the *matrix supernode equation*. As was pointed out in the last section for link currents, Equations 15.27 and 15.55 assure that a complete solution for the network is available once the supernode equations are solved for the tree-voltage vector $\mathbf{V}_t(s)$.

Controlled-current sources fit into this formulation for all cases where the controlling variable can be made a voltage. That, of course, includes all controlled-current sources considered in this book.

Voltage sources—independent or controlled—do not fit into the matrix supernode formulation symbolized as Equation 15.56. Thus we must take an alternate approach, which is completely analogous to the procedure discussed for loop formulation.

The formulation of supernode equations for a network with voltage sources is complicated by two factors. First, $\mathbf{V}_t(s)$ includes voltage sources and must be partitioned into two subvectors. Second, we do not use the dummy KCL of Equation 15.8; instead we carry out the substitution only into Equation 15.9. This creates more complex matrix symbolism. If controlled-voltage sources are present, we have the additional complication of CE that do not fit the current-explicit pattern. For reasons discussed in Section 15.3, we cannot make the controlling variable current and then write the CE current-explicit.

For all these reasons, it is not feasible to develop a matrix algorithmic approach to formulating supernode equations when voltage sources are present. Instead, we carry out the formulation of supernode equations in scalar form, using the matrix KVL and KCL equations as follows, to help us keep a perspective on what we are doing as we carry out the details.

$$\mathbf{V}_l = -\mathbf{B}_t\mathbf{V}_t(s) = \mathbf{Q}_l^T\mathbf{V}_t(s) \tag{15.26}$$

$$[\mathbf{U} \quad \mathbf{Q}_l]\begin{bmatrix}\mathbf{I}_t(s) \\ \mathbf{I}_l(s)\end{bmatrix} = \mathbf{0} \tag{15.3}$$

The order of the formulation procedure is as follows:

1. Write all component equations, including dependent sources, in terms of voltages.

2. Use KVL to express all link voltages in terms of tree voltages.

3. Use the results of (2) to write CE in terms of tree voltages.

4. Use CE of dependent voltage sources to eliminate dependent source voltages from the other CE.

5. Substitute the resulting CE into the nondummy KCL equations to yield the generalized node-voltage equations. (These are also sometimes called tree-voltage equations and supernode-voltage equations.)

Example 15.5 ━━

We now formulate s-domain supernode equations for the network of Figure 15.2 (Example 15.3). Our formulation tree consists of branches 1, 2, and 4, just as in Example 15.3. First, we write the link voltages in terms of the tree voltages using the fundamental KVL.

$$V_3(s) = V_2(s) + V_1(s) \tag{15.57}$$

$$V_7(s) = V_2(s) - V_4(s) + V_1(s) \tag{15.58}$$

Next we write the CE in current-explicit form (except for the voltage source) and substitute Equations 15.57 and 15.58 into them to eliminate the link voltages. In scalar form these are

$$I_2(s) = \frac{1}{3}V_2(s)$$

$$I_4(s) = \frac{s}{9}V_4(s)$$

$$I_3(s) = \frac{3}{s}V_3(s) = \frac{3}{s}[V_2(s) + V_1(s)]$$

$$I_6(s) = 2I_2(s) = \frac{2}{3}V_2(s)$$

$$I_7(s) = \frac{1}{2}V_7(s) = \frac{1}{2}[V_2(s) - V_4(s) + V_1(s)]$$

In matrix form and with $V_1(s) = 9/s$, the altered CE can be written

$$
\begin{bmatrix} I_2(s) \\ I_4(s) \\ I_3(s) \\ I_6(s) \\ I_7(s) \end{bmatrix}
=
\begin{bmatrix} \frac{1}{3} & 0 \\ 0 & \frac{s}{9} \\ \frac{3}{s} & 0 \\ \frac{2}{3} & 0 \\ \frac{1}{2} & -\frac{1}{2} \end{bmatrix}
\begin{bmatrix} V_2(s) \\ V_4(s) \end{bmatrix}
+
\begin{bmatrix} 0 \\ 0 \\ \frac{27}{s^2} \\ 0 \\ \frac{9}{2s} \end{bmatrix}
\tag{15.59}
$$

Next the nondummy KCL are written

$$\begin{bmatrix} 1 & 0 & 1 & 1 & 1 \\ 0 & 1 & 0 & -1 & -1 \end{bmatrix} \begin{bmatrix} I_2(s) \\ I_4(s) \\ I_3(s) \\ I_6(s) \\ I_7(s) \end{bmatrix} + \begin{bmatrix} 0 \\ 1 \end{bmatrix} I_5(s) = 0 \qquad (15.60)$$

When Equation 15.59 is substituted into Equation 15.60, and $I_5(s) = 2/s$ is inserted, we have the supernode equations.

$$\begin{bmatrix} \left(\dfrac{3}{s} + \dfrac{3}{2}\right) & -\dfrac{1}{2} \\ -\dfrac{7}{6} & \dfrac{2s + 9}{18} \end{bmatrix} \begin{bmatrix} V_2(s) \\ V_4(s) \end{bmatrix} + \begin{bmatrix} \dfrac{9}{2s^2}(s + 6) \\ \dfrac{2}{s} - \dfrac{9}{2s} \end{bmatrix} = 0 \qquad (15.61)$$

To simplify Equation 15.61 a bit for inversion, we multiply the first equation by $2s$ and the second by 18. The result is, after some combination,

$$\begin{bmatrix} 3(s + 2) & -s \\ -21 & 2s + 9 \end{bmatrix} \begin{bmatrix} V_2(s) \\ V_4(s) \end{bmatrix} + \begin{bmatrix} \dfrac{9}{s}(s + 6) \\ -\dfrac{45}{s} \end{bmatrix} = 0 \qquad (15.62)$$

The determinant of the coefficient equation is

$$\Delta(s) = 6(s^2 + 3s + 9) = 6\phi(s)$$

The s-domain solution for the unknown tree variables is

$$\begin{bmatrix} V_2(s) \\ V_4(s) \end{bmatrix} = -\frac{1}{6\phi(s)} \begin{bmatrix} 2s + 9 & s \\ 21 & 3s + 6 \end{bmatrix} \begin{bmatrix} \dfrac{9}{s}(s + 6) \\ -\dfrac{45}{s} \end{bmatrix}$$

$$= \frac{-9}{6s\phi(s)} \begin{bmatrix} 2s^2 + 16s + 54 \\ 6s + 96 \end{bmatrix} \qquad (15.63)$$

Since we carried the solution through for this network in Example 15.3, the t-domain solution is not found. We do have a check for $V_4(s)$, however, in the state-model solution in Example 15.7.

Example 15.6

For the network of Figure 15.1 we formulate supernode equations in the s-domain using the PRIMM of Example 15.2. As the first step, we write the s-domain CE with as many of them explicit in current as possible and eliminate link voltages by using Equation 15.6. We then use $V_2(s) = 10 - 2V_3(s)$ to eliminate $V_2(s)$ from the current-explicit CE.

$$V_1(s) = 5$$

$$V_2(s) = 2V_7(s) = 2[V_1(s) - V_3(s)] = 10 - 2V_3(s)$$

$$I_3(s) = sV_3(s) - 10$$

$$I_4(s) = 2sV_4(s) - 2v_4(0^-) = 2sV_4(s) - 10$$

$$I_5(s) = V_5(s) = [V_2(s) + V_3(s) + V_4(s)]$$

$$= 10 - V_3(s) + V_4(s)$$

$$I_6(s) = \frac{1}{2}V_6(s) = \frac{1}{2}V_3(s)$$

$$I_7(s) = \frac{1}{2}V_7(s) = \frac{1}{2}[5 - V_3(s)]$$

$$I_8(s) = \frac{1}{s}V_8(s) = \frac{1}{s}[V_2(s) + V_4(s)]$$

$$= \frac{1}{s}[10 - 2V_3(s) + V_4(s)]$$

$$I_9(s) = 2I_6(s) = V_3(s)$$

$$I_{10}(s) = 10$$

In matrix form the current-explicit altered CE can be written

$$
\begin{bmatrix}
I_3(s) \\
I_4(s) \\
I_5(s) \\
I_6(s) \\
I_7(s) \\
I_8(s) \\
I_9(s)
\end{bmatrix}
=
\begin{bmatrix}
s & 0 \\
0 & 2s \\
-1 & 1 \\
\frac{1}{2} & 0 \\
-\frac{1}{2} & 0 \\
-\frac{2}{s} & \frac{1}{s} \\
1 & 0
\end{bmatrix}
\begin{bmatrix}
V_3(s) \\
V_4(s)
\end{bmatrix}
+
\begin{bmatrix}
-10 \\
-10 \\
10 \\
0 \\
\frac{5}{2} \\
\frac{10}{s} \\
0
\end{bmatrix}
\qquad (15.64)
$$

Equation 15.64 is substituted into the nondummy KCL equations

$$\begin{bmatrix} 1 & 0 & 1 & 1 & -1 & 0 & 1 \\ 0 & 1 & 1 & 0 & 0 & 1 & 1 \end{bmatrix} \begin{bmatrix} I_3(s) \\ I_4(s) \\ I_5(s) \\ I_6(s) \\ I_7(s) \\ I_8(s) \\ I_9(s) \end{bmatrix} + \begin{bmatrix} 1 \\ 1 \end{bmatrix} 10 = 0 \qquad (15.65)$$

to produce the supernode equations

$$\begin{bmatrix} (s+1) & 1 \\ -\dfrac{2}{s} & 2s+1+\dfrac{1}{s} \end{bmatrix} \begin{bmatrix} V_3(s) \\ V_4(s) \end{bmatrix} + \begin{bmatrix} -\dfrac{5}{2}+10 \\ \dfrac{10}{s}+10 \end{bmatrix} = 0 \qquad (15.66)$$

Multiplying the second equation by s produces

$$\begin{bmatrix} s+1 & 1 \\ -2 & 2s^2+s+1 \end{bmatrix} \begin{bmatrix} V_3(s) \\ V_4(s) \end{bmatrix} = -\begin{bmatrix} \dfrac{15}{2} \\ 10(s+1) \end{bmatrix} \qquad (15.67)$$

The determinant of the coefficient matrix is

$$\begin{aligned} \Delta(s) &= 2s^3 + 3s^2 + 2s + 3 \\ &= 2(s^3 + 1.5s^2 + s + 1.5) \\ &= 2(s+1.5)(s+j)(s-j) \\ &= 2\beta(s) \end{aligned}$$

The solution for the unknown tree voltages in the s-domain then follows:

$$\begin{aligned} \begin{bmatrix} V_3(s) \\ V_4(s) \end{bmatrix} &= \frac{-1}{2\beta(s)} \begin{bmatrix} 2s^2+s+1 & -1 \\ 2 & s+1 \end{bmatrix} \begin{bmatrix} \dfrac{15}{2} \\ 10(s+1) \end{bmatrix} \\ &= \frac{1}{\beta(s)} \begin{bmatrix} -7.5s^2 + 1.25s + 1.25 \\ -5s^2 - 10s - 12.5 \end{bmatrix} \qquad (15.68) \end{aligned}$$

Since the state-model formulation includes both v_3 and v_4, we defer the t-domain solution until the next section.

15.5   STATE-MODEL FORMULATION ⎯⎯⎯⎯⎯⎯⎯⎯⎯⎯○

In the formulation of loop equations and supernode equations, we used s-domain KCL, KVL, and CE. In those cases we anticipated that the models would be solved by Laplace transform techniques and thus t-domain models would not be needed. When numerical methods are used to analyze the complete performance of a network—transient and steady-state—the state model is used almost invariably.

Therefore, in the discussion of state-model formulation, we work in the t-domain until the model is complete. Then the state model is Laplace-transformed for the purpose of obtaining a solution.

In our treatment of this subject we assume that a formulation tree can be selected in accordance with the rules of Section 15.2 with one further provision. The tree must include all capacitors and exclude all inductors. The case where this stipulation cannot be met is left to more advanced texts.

We begin the formulation of a state model by writing the CE for the dynamic (energy-storage) components in the first-order derivative-explicit form. In matrix notation they are written:

$$\frac{d}{dt}\mathbf{V}_c(t) = \mathbf{C}^{-1}\mathbf{I}_c(t) \tag{15.69}$$

$$\frac{d}{dt}\mathbf{I}_L(t) = \mathbf{L}^{-1}\mathbf{V}_L(t) \tag{15.70}$$

Next we construct an equivalent resistive network by replacing each capacitor with a symbolic voltage source and each inductor with a symbolic current source. Capacitor voltages and inductor currents are, of course, our state variables.

The variables $\mathbf{I}_C(t)$ and $\mathbf{V}_L(t)$ on the right-hand side of Equations 15.69 and 15.70 must be found from the equivalent resistive network. This procedure automatically assures that they are expressed as linear functions of the state variables and the independent sources. When they are substituted into Equations 15.69 and 15.70, the result is the network state equations.

Our chief problem in the formulation of a network state model, then, is the solution of the equivalent resistive network. For this solution we use the loop or supernode formulation methods of Chapter 5 (also Sections 15.3 and 15.4) and solve the resulting equations by matrix algebra or the equivalent.

Solution for the capacitor currents and inductor voltages from the equivalent resistive network always involves the use of dummy KCL and KVL equations, respectively. This follows because capacitors are represented in the network by symbolic voltage sources and inductors by symbolic current sources.

If we symbolize the solution for $\mathbf{I}_C(t)$ and $\mathbf{V}_L(t)$ in matrix form as

$$\mathbf{I}_C(t) = \mathbf{K}_{11}\mathbf{V}_C(t) + \mathbf{K}_{12}\mathbf{I}_L(t) + \mathbf{K}_{13}\mathbf{f}(t) \tag{15.71}$$

$$\mathbf{V}_L(t) = \mathbf{K}_{21}\mathbf{V}_C(t) + \mathbf{K}_{22}\mathbf{I}_L(t) + \mathbf{K}_{23}\mathbf{f}(t) \tag{15.72}$$

then the state equations are

$$\frac{d}{dt}\mathbf{V}_C(t) = \mathbf{C}^{-1}[\mathbf{K}_{11}\mathbf{V}_C(t) + \mathbf{K}_{12}\mathbf{I}_L(t) + \mathbf{K}_{13}\mathbf{f}(t)] \tag{15.73}$$

$$\frac{d}{dt}\mathbf{I}_L(t) = \mathbf{L}^{-1}[\mathbf{K}_{21}\mathbf{V}_C(t) + \mathbf{K}_{22}\mathbf{I}_L(t) + \mathbf{K}_{23}\mathbf{f}(t)] \tag{15.74}$$

Equations 15.73 and 15.74 can be rewritten in more compact matrix form as

$$\frac{d}{dt}\begin{bmatrix} \mathbf{V}_C(t) \\ \mathbf{I}_L(t) \end{bmatrix} = \begin{bmatrix} \mathbf{A}_{11} & \mathbf{A}_{12} \\ \mathbf{A}_{21} & \mathbf{A}_{22} \end{bmatrix}\begin{bmatrix} \mathbf{V}_C(t) \\ \mathbf{I}_L(t) \end{bmatrix} + \begin{bmatrix} \mathbf{B}_1 \\ \mathbf{B}_2 \end{bmatrix}\mathbf{f}(t) \tag{15.75}$$

or even more compactly as

$$\frac{d}{dt}\mathbf{x}(t) = \mathbf{A}\mathbf{x}(t) + \mathbf{B}\mathbf{f}(t) \tag{15.76}$$

where $\mathbf{x}$ is the state vector and $\mathbf{f}(t)$ is the vector of forcing functions resulting from the independent sources. The solution to Equation 15.75, together with the solution for the equivalent resistive network, provides a complete solution for the network.

Solution of Equation 15.76 by Laplace transform techniques is easily symbolized in matrix form. The Laplace transform of Equation 15.76 is

$$s\mathbf{X}(s) - \mathbf{X}(0^-) = \mathbf{A}\mathbf{X}(s) + \mathbf{B}\mathbf{F}(s) \tag{15.77}$$

This can be rewritten as

$$(s\mathbf{U} - \mathbf{A})\mathbf{X}(s) = \mathbf{X}(0^-) + \mathbf{B}\mathbf{F}(s) \tag{15.78}$$

From Equation 15.78 we have the s-domain solution for the state vector as

$$\mathbf{X}(s) = (s\mathbf{U} - \mathbf{A})^{-1}[\mathbf{X}(0^-) + \mathbf{B}\mathbf{F}(s)]$$

After working through the solutions for network models formulated by all three of the standard formulation procedures, you probably will have developed a preference for one over the others. We (the authors) prefer the state model in general for several reasons:

1. The formulation involves the solution of a resistive (linear algebraic) network and can be done numerically with a computer routine.

2. The Laplace-transformed state model involves only first-degree polynomials in s, and the initial conditions are entered in a very simple manner.

3. The determinant of $s\mathbf{U} - \mathbf{A}$ is a polynomial in s of degree equal to the order of the network.

4. The elements in $(s\mathbf{U} - \mathbf{A})^{-1}$ are rational functions in s (ratios of polynomials) with no simplifying manipulations required.

5. If computer solutions are desired, the state model is in the form needed for numerical integration.

Example 15.7

We now formulate state equations for the network of Figure 15.2. The equivalent resistive network is shown as Figure 15.3. We begin by writing the two differential equations in the state variables i_3 and v_4.

$$L_3 \frac{di_3}{dt} = v_3 \tag{15.79}$$

$$C_4 \frac{dv_4}{dt} = i_4 \tag{15.80}$$

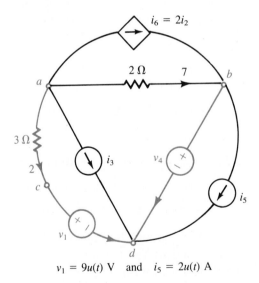

Figure 15.3
Equivalent resistive network for Example 15.7. The state variables are the inductor current i_3 and the capacitor voltage v_4.

$v_1 = 9u(t)$ V   and $i_5 = 2u(t)$ A

Thus we see that the task is to solve the equivalent resistive network for v_3 and i_4. Examination of the equivalent resistive network shows that it would be equally simple to solve by either the loop or supernode method. We elect to use the loop method and the same formulation tree used in Examples 15.3 and 15.5.

An inspection of Figure 15.3, the equivalent resistive network, indicates that only one loop equation in i_7 would be required. Therefore, we write the CE in terms of i_7 and the other link currents as follows: From the supernode equation for branch 2 of the tree, we get

$$i_2 + i_3 + i_7 + i_6 = 0$$

but

$$i_6 = 2i_2$$

and, therefore,

$$i_2 = -\frac{1}{3}i_7 - \frac{1}{3}i_3 \tag{15.81}$$

Thus the CE can be written in terms of the link currents as

$$\begin{bmatrix} v_2 \\ v_7 \end{bmatrix} = \begin{bmatrix} -1 \\ 2 \end{bmatrix} i_7 - \begin{bmatrix} 1 \\ 0 \end{bmatrix} i_3 \tag{15.82}$$

and

$$i_6 = 2i_2 = -\frac{2}{3}i_7 - \frac{2}{3}i_3 \tag{15.83}$$

When we put Equation 15.82 into the single nondummy KVL equation

$$v_7 + v_4 - v_1 - v_2 = 0$$

we get

$$(2i_7) + v_4 - v_1 - (-i_7 - i_3) = 0$$

or

$$3i_7 = -i_3 - v_4 + v_1$$

Therefore,

$$i_7 = -\frac{1}{3}i_3 - \frac{1}{3}v_4 + \frac{1}{3}v_1 \tag{15.84}$$

The state variables are i_3, v_4, and $v_1 = 9u(t)$ V. The equation

$$i_7 = -\frac{1}{3}i_3 - \frac{1}{3}v_4 + 3u(t) \tag{15.85}$$

can now be substituted into Equations 15.81–15.83 to yield

$$i_2 = \frac{1}{9}i_3 + \frac{1}{9}v_4 - u(t) - \frac{1}{3}i_3$$

$$= -\frac{2}{9}i_3 + \frac{1}{9}v_4 - u(t) \tag{15.86}$$

$$v_2 = -\frac{2}{3}i_3 + \frac{1}{3}v_4 - 3u(t) \tag{15.87}$$

$$v_7 = -\frac{2}{3}i_3 - \frac{2}{3}v_4 + 6u(t) \tag{15.88}$$

$$i_6 = -\frac{4}{9}i_3 + \frac{2}{9}v_4 - 2u(t) \tag{15.89}$$

We find i_4 and v_3 by utilizing these equations in the appropriate dummy KCL and KVL equations, respectively.

$$i_4 + i_5 = i_6 + i_7$$

$$= -\frac{7}{9}i_3 - \frac{1}{9}v_4 + u(t)$$

Therefore,

$$i_4 = -\frac{7}{9}i_3 - \frac{1}{9}v_4 - u(t) \tag{15.90}$$

$$v_3 = v_2 + v_1$$

$$= -\frac{2}{3}i_3 + \frac{1}{3}v_4 + 6u(t) \tag{15.91}$$

When Equations 15.84 and 15.85 are substituted into Equations 15.79 and 15.80, and $C = \frac{1}{9}$ F and $L = \frac{1}{3}$ H are inserted, we have the state equations

$$\frac{d}{dt}\begin{bmatrix} i_3 \\ v_4 \end{bmatrix} = \begin{bmatrix} -2 & 1 \\ -7 & -1 \end{bmatrix}\begin{bmatrix} i_3 \\ v_4 \end{bmatrix} + \begin{bmatrix} 18 \\ -9 \end{bmatrix}u(t) \tag{15.92}$$

To solve, we take the Laplace transform to get

$$\begin{bmatrix} s+2 & -1 \\ 7 & s+1 \end{bmatrix}\begin{bmatrix} I_3(s) \\ V_4(s) \end{bmatrix} = \frac{9}{s}\begin{bmatrix} 2 \\ -1 \end{bmatrix} \tag{15.93}$$

The determinant of the coefficient matrix is

$$\phi(s) = s^2 + 3s + 9 = (s + 1.5 + j2.6)(s + 1.5 - j2.6)$$

Therefore, the solution in the s-domain for the state variables can be written

$$\begin{bmatrix} I_3(s) \\ V_4(s) \end{bmatrix} = \frac{1}{\phi(s)}\begin{bmatrix} s+1 & 1 \\ -7 & s+2 \end{bmatrix}\begin{bmatrix} 2 \\ -1 \end{bmatrix}\frac{9}{s}$$

$$= \frac{9}{s\phi(s)}\begin{bmatrix} 2s+1 \\ -(s+16) \end{bmatrix} \tag{15.94}$$

Note that the solutions for $I_3(s)$ and $V_4(s)$ check those obtained in Examples 15.3 and 15.5, respectively. The t-domain solution for i_3 was found in Example 15.3. Since $\phi(s)$ of Example 15.3 is the same as $\phi(s)$ of this example, we may use the result

$$g(t) = \mathscr{L}^{-1}\left\{\frac{1}{s\phi(s)}\right\}$$

from that example to derive a t-domain solution for $v_4(t)$.
Thus

$$v_4(t) = -9[g'(t) + 16g(t)] \tag{15.95}$$

The functions $g(t)$ and $g'(t)$ are listed as Equations 15.45 and 15.46, respectively.

Example 15.8

Again we use the network of Figure 15.1 as an example for formulation. Figure 15.4 is the equivalent resistive network that we use to formulate the state model.

The state variables are v_3, v_4, and i_8. The starting point for the formulation is with the differential equations.

$$\frac{dv_3}{dt} = i_3 \tag{15.96}$$

$$\frac{dv_4}{dt} = \frac{1}{2}i_4 \tag{15.97}$$

$$\frac{di_8}{dt} = v_8 \tag{15.98}$$

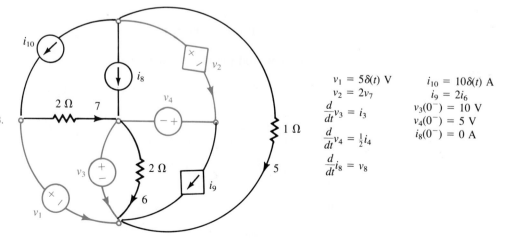

Figure 15.4
Equivalent resistive network for Example 15.8. The state variables are the capacitor voltages v_3 and v_4 and the inductor current i_8.

$v_1 = 5\delta(t)$ V $i_{10} = 10\delta(t)$ A
$v_2 = 2v_7$ $i_9 = 2i_6$
$\frac{d}{dt}v_3 = i_3$ $v_3(0^-) = 10$ V
$\frac{d}{dt}v_4 = \frac{1}{2}i_4$ $v_4(0^-) = 5$ V
$\frac{d}{dt}i_8 = v_8$ $i_8(0^-) = 0$ A

Now our task is to find i_3, i_4, and v_8 in terms of the state variables and the forcing functions. From the equivalent resistive network, we see that no solution of simultaneous equations is necessary since there is a complete tree of voltage sources and state variables. Thus all link voltages can be written in terms of those variables. Then the currents of all resistive links can be found. If this fortunate situation were not true, we would decide whether to use a loop or nodal formulation to solve the equivalent resistive network.

As is always the case, the variables on the right side of the differential equations must be determined using either the dummy KCL or KVL equations of the equivalent resistive network. In scalar form, these are

$$i_3 + i_5 + i_6 - i_7 + i_9 + i_{10} = 0 \tag{15.99}$$

$$i_4 + i_5 + i_8 + i_9 + i_{10} = 0 \tag{15.100}$$

$$v_8 - v_2 - v_4 = 0 \tag{15.101}$$

Thus we need to find i_5, i_6, i_7, i_9, and v_2. The other variables in the equations are either source variables or state variables.

We begin by writing the resistor link voltages in terms of the tree voltages.

$$v_5 = v_2 + v_3 + v_4$$

$$v_6 = v_3$$

$$v_7 = 5\delta(t) - v_3$$

Since

$$v_2 = 2v_7 = 10\delta(t) - 2v_3$$

then

$$v_5 = 10\delta(t) - v_3 + v_4$$

We can now find the resistor currents:

$$i_5 = 10\delta(t) - v_3 + v_4$$

$$i_6 = \frac{1}{2}v_3$$

$$i_7 = \frac{5}{2}\delta(t) - \frac{1}{2}v_3$$

and

$$i_9 = 2i_6 = v_3$$

Finally we have the necessary information to find i_3, i_4, and v_8 by substituting into Equations 15.99–15.101.

$$i_3 = -i_5 - i_6 + i_7 - i_9 - 10\delta(t)$$

$$= -[10\delta(t) - v_3 + v_4] - \frac{1}{2}v_3 + \left[\frac{5}{2}\delta(t) - \frac{1}{2}v_3\right] - v_3 - 10\delta(t)$$

$$\boxed{i_3 = -v_3 - v_4 - \frac{35}{2}\delta(t)}$$

$$i_4 = -i_5 - i_8 - i_9 - 10\delta(t)$$

$$= -[10\delta(t) - v_3 + v_4] - i_8 - v_3 - 10\delta(t)$$

$$\boxed{i_4 = -v_4 - i_8 - 20\delta(t)}$$

$$v_8 = v_2 + v_4 = 10\delta(t) - 2v_3 + v_4$$

$$\boxed{v_8 = -2v_3 + v_4 + 10\delta(t)}$$

Therefore, our state model is, in scalar form,

$$\frac{d}{dt}v_3 = -v_3 - v_4 - \frac{35}{2}\delta(t)$$

$$\frac{d}{dt}v_4 = -\frac{1}{2}v_4 - \frac{1}{2}i_8 - 10\delta(t)$$

$$\frac{d}{dt}i_8 = -2v_3 + v_4 + 10\delta(t)$$

In matrix form these are written

$$\frac{d}{dt}\begin{bmatrix} v_3 \\ v_4 \\ i_8 \end{bmatrix} = \begin{bmatrix} -1 & -1 & 0 \\ 0 & -\frac{1}{2} & -\frac{1}{2} \\ -2 & 1 & 0 \end{bmatrix}\begin{bmatrix} v_3 \\ v_4 \\ i_8 \end{bmatrix} + \begin{bmatrix} -\frac{35}{2} \\ -10 \\ 10 \end{bmatrix}\delta(t) \qquad (15.102)$$

After Laplace transformation, Equation 15.102 becomes

$$s\begin{bmatrix} V_3(s) \\ V_4(s) \\ I_8(s) \end{bmatrix} = \begin{bmatrix} -1 & -1 & 0 \\ 0 & -\frac{1}{2} & -\frac{1}{2} \\ -2 & 1 & 0 \end{bmatrix}\begin{bmatrix} V_3(s) \\ V_4(s) \\ I_8(s) \end{bmatrix} + \begin{bmatrix} -\frac{35}{2} + 10 \\ -10 + 5 \\ 10 \end{bmatrix}$$

or

$$\begin{bmatrix} s+1 & 1 & 0 \\ 0 & s+\dfrac{1}{2} & \dfrac{1}{2} \\ 2 & -1 & s \end{bmatrix} \begin{bmatrix} V_3(s) \\ V_4(s) \\ I_8(s) \end{bmatrix} = \begin{bmatrix} -\dfrac{15}{2} \\ -5 \\ 10 \end{bmatrix} \tag{15.103}$$

The determinant of the coefficient matrix is

$$\beta(s) = s^3 + 1.5s^2 + s + 1.5$$
$$= (s+1.5)(s-j)(s+j)$$

If we let

$$F(s) = \frac{1}{\beta(s)} = \frac{1}{(s+1.5)(s-j)(s+j)}$$

$$= \frac{0.3077}{(s+1.5)} - \frac{4}{13}\frac{s}{s^2+1} + \frac{6}{13}\frac{1}{s^2+1} \tag{15.104}$$

then

$$f(t) = 0.3077e^{-1.5t} - 0.3077\cos t + 0.4616\sin t \tag{15.105}$$

$$f'(t) = -0.4616e^{-1.5t} + 0.3077\sin t + 0.4616\cos t \tag{15.106}$$

$$f''(t) = 0.6924e^{-1.5t} + 0.3077\cos t - 0.4616\sin t \tag{15.107}$$

The s-domain solution of the state equation is

$$\begin{bmatrix} V_3(s) \\ V_4(s) \\ I_8(s) \end{bmatrix} = \frac{1}{\beta(s)} \begin{bmatrix} s^2+\dfrac{1}{2}s+\dfrac{1}{2} & -s & \dfrac{1}{2} \\ 1 & s^2+s & -\dfrac{s+1}{2} \\ -(2s+1) & s+3 & s^2+1.5s+0.5 \end{bmatrix} \begin{bmatrix} -\dfrac{15}{2} \\ -5 \\ 10 \end{bmatrix}$$

$$\begin{bmatrix} V_3(s) \\ V_4(s) \\ I_8(s) \end{bmatrix} = \frac{1}{\beta(s)} \begin{bmatrix} -7.5s^2+1.25s+1.25 \\ -5s^2-10s-12.5 \\ 10s^2+25s-17.5 \end{bmatrix} \tag{15.108}$$

The expressions for $V_3(s)$ and $V_4(s)$ check those obtained in Example 15.6.

By use of Theorem 15.1 and $f(t)$ (Equation 15.105) we can write the t-domain solutions:

$$v_3(t) = -7.5f''(t) + 1.25f'(t) + 1.25f(t) \tag{15.109}$$

$$v_4(t) = -5f''(t) - 10f'(t) - 12.5f(t) \tag{15.110}$$

$$i_8(t) = 10f''(t) + 25f'(t) - 17.5f(t) \tag{15.111}$$

As an example of how to organize the work to substitute the functions $f(t)$, $f'(t)$, and $f''(t)$ into Equations 15.109–15.111, we find $v_3(t)$. The others are left as exercises.

$$v_3(t) = e^{-1.5t}[(-7.5)(0.6924) + 1.25(-0.4616) + 1.25(0.3077)]$$
$$+ \cos t[(-7.5)(0.3077) + 1.25(0.4616) + 1.25(-0.3077)]$$
$$+ \sin t[(-7.5)(-0.4616) + 1.25(0.3077) + 1.25(0.4616)]$$
$$= -5.385e^{-1.5t} - 2.115 \cos t + 4.424 \sin t \text{ V}$$

15.6 SUMMARY

Now you have the whole story—for this textbook, at least. There are many choice tidbits, of course, left for more advanced courses in network analysis, network synthesis, computer-aided design, nonlinear network analysis, and so on, but you have the basic tools to tackle any one or all of them.

We presented network modeling as a science, but it is also very much an art. The art comes in choosing models for components, which are as simple as possible yet adequate for the analysis to be undertaken. We have not been concerned about the adequacy of the component models, since this is a judgment which can only be made with laboratory data available on each specific device. Rather, we have taken the standard linear types of component equations and concerned ourselves with formulating loop equations, nodal equations, and state equations for networks with rather idealized components.

We have learned how to transform a system of linear differential equations, determine the s-domain solution, and then find the inverse transform. But to keep things in perspective, all these elegant techniques are to no avail if the component models are not adequate to the task. As they say in the computer business, "Garbage in, garbage out!" So the analysis of a large-scale network must be preceded by some soul searching as to how simple—or complex—the component equations should be to simplify the solution problem but assure the accuracy desired.

All these problems and worries we leave to future courses or to professional practice. For now, congratulations! You can take well-earned pleasure in having climbed the first hill.

If you have found that homework in this section consumed an inordinate amount of time and was difficult to complete correctly the first time, take heart. If you are so fortunate as to work professionally in network or system modeling, you will probably work under more favorable time constraints. In an engineering job it is usually more important to get things done correctly than to get them done quickly. Unfortunately, that is not always true, of course, and we have some well-publicized engineering failures as evidence. In general, however, you can reasonably hope to have enough time allocated to an important analysis job that you can do it deliberately and carefully.

PROBLEMS

Please note: For all network model formulation problems, put variables in numerical order inside tree and cotree classifications when writing equations in matrix form. The rows in the KCL and KVL matrices should be in the same order as the corresponding links and tree branches, respectively. Every network in the problems should have each branch identified by number and orientation so that every voltage and current can be designated without ambiguity.

15.1 For the network of Figure 15.5, use a formulation tree of branches 1, 2, and 3 and write the fundamental loop matrix $\mathbf{B}$ and the fundamental supernode matrix $\mathbf{Q}$ in the form of those in Equations 15.3 and 15.4. The columns of each should be in numerical order. Check whether $\mathbf{Q}_l = -\mathbf{B}_t^T$. (If not, try again.)

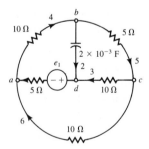

Figure 15.5

15.2 For the network of Figure 15.6, use a formulation tree of branches 5, 6, 7, and 8 and write the fundamental loop matrix $\mathbf{B}$ and the fundamental supernode matrix $\mathbf{Q}$ in the form of those in Equations 15.3 and 15.4. Use numerical order inside the tree and cotree classification. Check whether $\mathbf{B}_t = -\mathbf{Q}_l^T$. (If not, try again.)

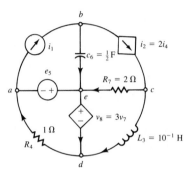

Figure 15.6

15.3 Work Problem 15.1 for a tree of branches 1, 3, and 5. Assume variables in numerical order inside tree and cotree classification. (Do not worry that the tree does not satisfy Rules 1–4. We are just working on writing fundamental KCL and KVL equations.)

15.4 Work Problem 15.2 for a tree of branches 2, 4, 5, and 6. (Do not worry that the tree does not satisfy Rules 1–4. We are not going to use these equations for formulation of a network model.)

15.5 For the network of Figure 15.7, formulate and

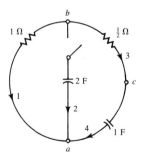

Figure 15.7

solve the s-domain loop equations for the initial conditions $v_2(0^-) = 10$ V and $v_4(0^-) = 0$. Write the CE in matrix form $\mathbf{V}(s) = \mathbf{Z}(s)\mathbf{B}^T\mathbf{I}_l(s)$ and substitute in KVL ($\mathbf{BV} = \mathbf{0}$). Use a formulation tree of branches 2 and 4.

15.6 Use a formulation tree of branches 1, 2, and 3 and write s-domain loop equations in matrix form for the network of Figure 15.5. Formulate by using the algorithm $\mathbf{BZ}(s)\mathbf{B}^T\mathbf{I}_l(s) + \mathbf{BE}(s) = \mathbf{0}$, and check by scalar formulation.

15.7 For general parameters and sources, formulate an s-domain loop model for the network of Figure 15.6. Use a tree of branches 5, 6, 7, and 8. Write the final result in matrix form.

15.8 Using a tree of branches 3, 5, and 6 in the network of Figure 15.8, formulate s-domain loop equations for a general $e_3(t)$. Write the final result in matrix form. Assume zero initial conditions on the capacitances.

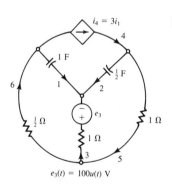

$e_3(t) = 100u(t)$ V

Figure 15.8

15.9 Use a tree of branches 5, 6, 7, and 8 to formulate s-domain loop equations for the network of Figure 15.6. Use general source functions. Write the final version in matrix form.

15.10 For the network of Figure 15.8, use a tree of branches 1, 2, and 3 to formulate s-domain loop equations. Set $e_3(t) = 100\delta(t)$ V, and use zero initial conditions for the capacitors. Find v_1 and v_2 for $t > 0$.

15.11 For the network of Figure 15.9, use a tree of branches 1, 4, 6 and 7 and formulate s-domain loop equations. The initial inductor currents are zero and $e_4(t) = 10u(t)$ V. Solve for the link currents.

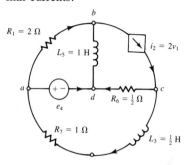

Figure 15.9

15.12 Given the network of Figure 15.10, use a T-equivalent network for the 2-port component and formulate s-domain loop equations for a tree of branches 1, 5, and 6.

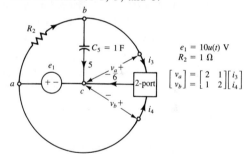

Figure 15.10

15.13 Given the network of Figure 15.11, use a tree of branches 3, 4, 6, and 8 to formulate s-domain loop equations. Assume $i_5(0^-) =$

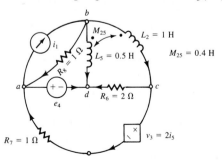

Figure 15.11

$i_2(0^-) = 0$, $i_1(t) = 20u(t)$ A, and $e_4(t) = 100u(t)$ V. Write the results in matrix form.

15.14 Formulate s-domain node equations in matrix form for the network of Figure 15.7. Use a formulation tree of branches 2 and 4, and set $v_2(0^-) = 10$ V and $v_4(0^-) = 0$. Write the CE in matrix form $I(s) = Y(s)Q^T V_t(s)$ and substitute into the KCL $(QI = 0)$.

15.15 Carry out the formulation of s-domain supernode equations for the network of Figure 15.5. Convert the source to a Norton equivalent and use the algorithm $QY(s)Q^T V_t(s) + QJ(s) = 0$. Check by scalar formulation. Use a tree of branches 2, 3, and 4.

15.16 For general parameters and sources, formulate an s-domain node model for the network of Figure 15.6. Use a formulation tree of branches 5, 6, 7, and 8. Write the final result in matrix form.

15.17 Convert the source of Figure 15.8 to a Norton equivalent, and use a formulation tree of branches 1, 2, and 3 to formulate s-domain node equations. Write in matrix form. Initial conditions are zero.

15.18 Given the network of Figure 15.10, use a T equivalent network for the 2-port component and formulate s-domain supernode equations. Use a tree of branches 1, 3, and 5, and assume $v_5(0^-) = 0$. Write the equations in matrix form and solve for the unknown tree voltages.

15.19 Repeat Problem 15.18, except use a π equivalent network for the 2-port component and include branches 1 and 5 in the formulation tree.

15.20 Given the network of Figure 15.12, use a for-

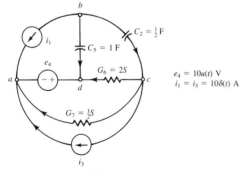

Figure 15.12

mulation tree of branches 2, 4, and 5 and formulate s-domain supernode equations. Write the equations in matrix form and solve. Use $v_2(0^-) = 10$ V and $v_5(0^-) = 5$ V.

15.21 Given the network of Figure 15.13, use a formulation tree of branches 3, 4, and 5 and formulate s-domain supernode equations. Write the equations in matrix form and solve. Use $v_3(0^-) = 15$ V and $v_5(0^-) = 5$ V.

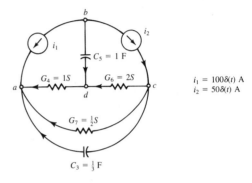

Figure 15.13

15.22 Formulate a state model for the network of Figure 15.7, and solve by use of the Laplace transform. Initial conditions are $v_2(0^-) = 10$ V and $v_4(0^-) = 0$.

15.23 For the network of Figure 15.5, formulate a state model and solve by use of the Laplace transform. Use a formulation tree of branches 1, 2, and 3 to solve the equivalent resistive network. Assume $e_1(t) = 100u(t)$ V and $v_2(0^-) = 0$.

15.24 Formulate a state model for the network of Figure 15.6 and write it in matrix form. Use general sources.

15.25 Formulate a state model for the network of Figure 15.8. Assume $v_1(0^-) = 10$ V and $v_2(0^-) = 20$ V, and solve for the state variables by use of the Laplace transform. Find $i_4(t)$.

15.26 Formulate a state model for the network of Figure 15.9. Use $e_4(t) = 50u(t)$ and zero initial inductor currents. Solve for the state variables and write $i_2(t)$.

15.27 Formulate a state model for the network of Figure 15.10. Solve for $v_5(0^-) = 0$.

15.28 For the network of Figure 15.11, assume that $i_5(0^-) = i_2(0^-) = 0$, $e_4(t) = 10\delta(t)$ V, and $i_1(t) = 5\delta(t)$ A. Formulate a state model. Laplace-transform the state equations and find the s-domain solution.

15.29 Formulate and solve the state equations for the network of Figure 15.12 for $v_2(0^-) = v_5(0^-) = 0$. Find $i_4(t)$.

15.30 Formulate and solve the state equations for the network of Figure 15.13 for $v_3(0^-) = v_5(0^-) = 0$. Find $v_1(t)$.

Note: Problems 15.31–15.37 require a numerical integration program such as TRAPZ1 or TRAPZ2 to solve network state models. Some judgment must be exercised concerning the time increment and the total time interval to be used. Each run should be long enough that the transient response has essentially died out. The time increment should be small enough that halving it does not result in a significant change in response—say 5%, for example, or some other arbitrary criterion. The state variables should be plotted versus time in each case.

15.31 Do Problem 15.22, but solve the state model numerically.

15.32 Do Problem 15.23, but solve the state model numerically.

15.33 Do Problem 15.25, but solve the state model numerically. Also print out and plot $i_4(t)$.

15.34 Do Problem 15.26, but solve the state model numerically. Also print out and plot $i_2(t)$.

15.35 Do Problem 15.27, but solve the state model numerically.

15.36 Do Problem 15.28, but solve the state model numerically for $e_4 = 10u(t)$ V and $i_1(t) = 5u(t)$ A.

15.37 For the network of Figure 15.9, solve the state model numerically if

$$e_4(t) = 20 \cos(100t)u(t) \text{ V},$$

$$\text{and } i_5(0^-) = i_3(0^-) = 0.$$

APPENDIX

Complex algebra

A.1 INTRODUCTION

The need for the concept of complex numbers arises when the solution of a quadratic equation of the form

$$z^2 + bz + c = 0 \tag{A.1}$$

is required and $b^2 < 4c$. The solution

$$z = \frac{-b}{2} \pm \sqrt{\left(\frac{b}{2}\right)^2 - c}$$

can be written

$$z = \frac{-b}{2} \pm \sqrt{\left|\left(\frac{b}{2}\right)^2 - c\right|(-1)}$$

$$= \frac{-b}{2} \pm \sqrt{-1} \sqrt{c - \left(\frac{b}{2}\right)^2} \tag{A.2}$$

Mathematicians usually use the symbol i to represent $\sqrt{-1}$, but because of the conflict with the traditional symbol for electric current, engineers often use j to symbolize $\sqrt{-1}$. Because of historical development, the square root of a negative number is called an *imaginary number*. Probably this came about because there is no real number which when squared will produce a negative number.

Use of the symbol j, which we will employ, allows us to write the solutions to Equation A.1 as

$$z = \frac{-b}{2} \pm j \sqrt{c - \left(\frac{b}{2}\right)^2}$$

(A.3)

A.2   DEFINITION OF A COMPLEX NUMBER

Any number that consists of a real part plus an imaginary part, either of which may be zero, is a *complex number*. The basic form of a complex number,

$$\bar{z} = a + jb$$

(A.4)

where a and b are real numbers, is called the *rectangular form*. The bar over the z denotes complex number to distinguish it from a real number. This may be conceived of as defining a unique point in a *complex plane* with the real axis corresponding to the axis of abscissas and imaginary axis corresponding to the axis of ordinates. Figure A.1 illustrates such a set of coordinate axes. The symbols Re $\bar{z}$ and Im $\bar{z}$ denote the real part of $\bar{z}$ and the imaginary part of $\bar{z}$, respectively.

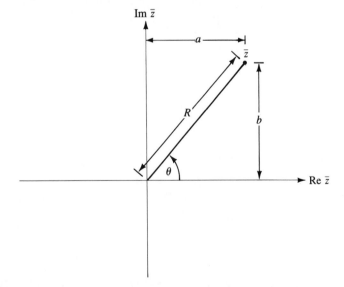

Figure A.1
Location of point $\bar{z} = a + jb$ in a complex plane.

In connection with Figure A.1, it should be noted that a and/or b may be either negative or positive. Positive a corresponds to the right half-plane, negative a to the left half-plane. Positive b indicates a point in the upper half-plane, negative b to a point in the lower half-plane.

The point $\bar{z}$ in the complex plane may also be specified by a distance from the origin (magnitude) and an angle measured in standard position. If R is the magnitude and θ the angle, then for any point $\bar{z}$ located on the complex plane of Figure A.1,

$$a = R \cos \theta$$

$$b = R \sin \theta$$

Thus the complex number $\bar{z}$ may be written

$$\bar{z} = R(\cos \theta + j \sin \theta) \tag{A.5}$$

This relation is sometimes called the *trigonometric form* of the complex number $\bar{z}$. Equation A.5 can be written more compactly by using Euler's relation,

$$e^{j\theta} = \cos \theta + j \sin \theta$$

as

$$\bar{z} = Re^{j\theta} \tag{A.6}$$

This relation is called the *exponential*, or *polar*, *form* of the complex number $\bar{z}$. This form turns up so much in engineering system analysis that to simplify its writing and printing it is common to symbolize the exponential by

$$\bar{z} = Re^{j\theta} \doteq R\underline{/\theta} \tag{A.7}$$

Two complex numbers

$$\bar{z}_1 = a_1 + jb_1$$

$$\bar{z}_2 = a_2 + jb_2$$

are said to be *equal* if and only if $a_1 = a_2$ and $b_1 = b_2$.

A.3 ADDITION AND SUBTRACTION ————————————————○

The definition of addition of complex numbers is best made with reference to the rectangular form. Let two complex numbers $\bar{z}_1$ and $\bar{z}_2$ be defined as

$$\bar{z}_1 = a_1 + jb_1$$

$$\bar{z}_2 = a_2 + jb_2$$

where a and b are real numbers. The sum $\bar{z}_3 = \bar{z}_1 + \bar{z}_2$ is defined to be

$$\bar{z}_3 = (a_1 + a_2) + j(b_1 + b_2) \tag{A.8}$$

The real part of the sum is the sum of the real parts and the imaginary part is the sum of the imaginary parts. Similarly, the difference $\bar{z}_4 = \bar{z}_1 - \bar{z}_2$ is

$$\bar{z}_4 = (a_1 - a_2) + j(b_1 - b_2) \tag{A.9}$$

In general, the only practical way to find a sum or difference of two complex numbers is to first put them in the rectangular form.

A.4   MULTIPLICATION

The operation of multiplication is probably best defined in terms of the exponential form. Let two complex numbers $\bar{z}_1$ and $\bar{z}_2$ be defined as

$$\bar{z}_1 = R_1 e^{j\theta_1} \doteq R_1\underline{/\theta_1}$$
$$\bar{z}_2 = R_2 e^{j\theta_2} \doteq R_2\underline{/\theta_2}$$

The product $\bar{z}_3 = \bar{z}_1\bar{z}_2$ is defined to be

$$\bar{z}_3 = R_1 R_2 e^{j(\theta_1+\theta_2)} \doteq R_1 R_2\underline{/\theta_1 + \theta_2} \tag{A.8}$$

The magnitude of the product is the product of the magnitudes and the angle of the product is the sum of the angles of the complex multiplicands.

It is often desirable to find a product directly in rectangular form. To derive the necessary relationship we write the complex numbers in trigonometric form as a step toward the rectangular form.

$$\bar{z}_1 = R_1 \cos\theta_1 + jR_1 \sin\theta_1 = a_1 + jb_1$$
$$\bar{z}_2 = R_2 \cos\theta_2 + jR_2 \sin\theta_2 = a_2 + jb_2$$

The product $\bar{z}_3$ (Equation A.8) written in trigonometric form is

$$\begin{aligned}
z_3 &= R_1 R_2[\cos(\theta_1 + \theta_2) + j\sin(\theta_1 + \theta_2)] \\
&= R_1 R_2(\cos\theta_1 \cos\theta_2 - \sin\theta_1 \sin\theta_2) \\
&\quad + jR_1 R_2(\sin\theta_1 \cos\theta_2 + \cos\theta_1 \sin\theta_2) \\
&= (a_1 a_2 - b_1 b_2) + j(a_1 b_2 + b_1 a_2) \\
&= a_3 + jb_3
\end{aligned} \tag{A.9}$$

The result is exactly what would be obtained in finding the conventional product of the two rectangular forms when $j^2 = -1$ is substituted into the result.

A.5   DIVISION

The operation of division is best defined in terms of the exponential form. If

$$\bar{z}_1 = R_1 e^{j\theta_1} \doteq R_1\underline{/\theta_1}$$
$$\bar{z}_2 = R_2 e^{j\theta_2} \doteq R_2\underline{/\theta_2}$$

then the quotient $\bar{z}_4 = \bar{z}_1/\bar{z}_2$ is defined to be

$$\bar{z}_4 = \frac{R_1}{R_2}\,e^{j(\theta_1 - \theta_2)} \doteq \frac{R_1}{R_2}\underline{/\theta_1 - \theta_2} \tag{A.10}$$

The magnitude of the quotient is the quotient of the magnitudes of the dividend over the divisor. The angle of the quotient is the angle of the dividend less the angle of the divisor. Division can be carried out directly in the rectangular form also, but we defer the discussion of that subject until the concept of complex conjugate has been discussed.

A.6 CONJUGATE OF A COMPLEX NUMBER ———————————O

The *conjugate of a complex number* $\bar{z}$ is symbolized by $\bar{z}*$ and is defined as follows: If $\bar{z} = a + jb$, then $\bar{z}* = a - jb$. The symbol $\bar{z}*$ is read "$\bar{z}$ conjugate." The definition in polar and exponential form becomes for $\bar{z} = Re^{j\theta}$,

$$\bar{z}* = Re^{-j\theta} = R\underline{/-\theta}$$

The concept of a complex conjugate is very useful in system analysis chiefly because of the following operations:

1. $\bar{z} + \bar{z}* = (a + jb) + (a - jb) = 2a$

$$= 2R\cos\theta \tag{A.11}$$

2. $\bar{z} - \bar{z}* = (a + jb) - (a - jb) = j2b$

$$= j2R\sin\theta \tag{A.12}$$

3. $\bar{z}\bar{z}* = a^2 + b^2 = R^2 = \bar{z}*\bar{z}$ $\tag{A.13}$

4. Let $\bar{z}_3 = \bar{z}_1 + \bar{z}_2$; then

$$\bar{z}_3^* = \bar{z}_1^* + \bar{z}_2^* \tag{A.14}$$

5. Let $\bar{z}_4 = \bar{z}_1\bar{z}_2$; then

$$\bar{z}_4^* = \bar{z}_1^*\bar{z}_2^* \tag{A.15}$$

Example A.1 ————————————————————————————

An application of Equations A.15 and A.11 is the following: Let

$$\bar{x} = \bar{z}e^{j\omega t} + \bar{z}*e^{-j\omega t}$$

Since $e^{j\omega t}$ is the conjugate of $e^{-j\omega t}$, we have $\bar{x}$ as a sum of conjugates. If $\bar{z} = Re^{j\theta}$,

$$x = Re^{j(\omega t + \theta)} + Re^{-j(\omega t + \theta)} = 2R\cos(\omega t + \theta)$$

A.7   DIVISION IN RECTANGULAR FORM ────────────────○

Very often a quotient of complex numbers must be computed from numbers originally in rectangular form. Further, the quotient itself may be needed in rectangular form for addition. This computation may be carried out directly by use of the complex conjugate. Let

$$\bar{z}_1 = a_1 + jb_1$$
$$\bar{z}_2 = a_2 + jb_2$$

and

$$\bar{z}_3 = \frac{\bar{z}_1}{\bar{z}_2} = a_3 + jb_3$$

In rectangular form

$$\bar{z}_3 = \frac{a_1 + jb_1}{a_2 + jb_2}$$

Now multiply numerator and denominator by the conjugate of the denominator, $\bar{z}_2^*$:

$$\bar{z}_3 = \frac{a_1 + jb_1}{a_2 + jb_2}\frac{a_2 - jb_2}{a_2 - jb_2} \equiv \frac{(a_1a_2 + b_1b_2) + j(a_2b_1 - a_1b_2)}{a_2^2 + b_2^2} \quad (A.16)$$

Since a and b are real numbers, a^2 and b^2 are positive and real and thus $\bar{z}_3$ of Equation A.16 is in rectangular form. The real and imaginary parts are

$$a_3 = \frac{a_1a_2 + b_1b_2}{a_2^2 + b_2^2}$$

$$b_3 = \frac{a_2b_1 - a_1b_2}{a_2^2 + b_2^2}$$

Example A.2 ────────────────

Given $\bar{z}_1 = 3 + j4$, $\bar{z}_2 = -2 - j1$, find $\bar{z}_3 = \frac{\bar{z}_2}{\bar{z}_1}$.

$$\bar{z}_3 = \frac{-2 - j}{3 + j4}\frac{3 - j4}{3 - j4}$$
$$= \frac{(-6 - 4) + j(8 - 3)}{3^2 + 4^2}$$
$$= \frac{1}{25}(-10 + j5)$$
$$= -\frac{2}{5} + \frac{j1}{5}$$

A.8   SUMMARY

A complex number can be expressed in several forms:

1. Rectangular: $\bar{z} = a + jb$
2. Trigonometric: $\bar{z} = R \cos \theta + jR \sin \theta$
3. Exponential: $\bar{z} = Re^{j\theta}$
4. Polar: $\bar{z} = R\underline{/\theta}$

where a, b, R, and θ are real numbers. The symbol for a complex number is conveniently distinguished from the symbol for a real number in various ways. In this book a bar over the symbol is used. In other texts this symbol may be defined differently, so care should be taken to avoid confusion.

To carry out each of the operations defined for complex numbers, the numbers involved in each operation should be put in the same form. This is not always necessary but confusion and errors are much more likely to occur if mixed forms are used.

PROBLEMS

A.1. Change the following complex numbers to rectangular form: (a) $10e^{j\pi}$, (b) $5e^{j\pi/3}$, (c) $10e^{-j0.6\pi}$, (d) $Ae^{j\alpha t}$.

A.2. Change the following complex numbers to exponential (polar) form: (a) $j6$, (b) $1 - j2$, (c) $-3 + j4$, (d) $3 + j4$.

A.3. Evaluate the following complex expressions and write both in rectangular and in exponential form (evaluate products and dividends in rectangular form).

(a) $(3 + j4)(3 - j4)$

(b) $\dfrac{1}{3 + j4}$

(c) $3 + \dfrac{10}{1 + j}$

(d) $\dfrac{2 + j3}{3 + j2}$

(e) $\dfrac{-3 - j2}{-2 + j3} + \dfrac{10}{1 + j}$

A.4. Evaluate the expressions of Problem A.3, but carry out evaluation of products and dividends in exponential form.

Matrix algebra

B.1 INTRODUCTION

The analysis of an electric network almost always involves the simultaneous solution of the system of equations that makes up the primary mathematical model of the system. For a linear network the primary mathematical model consists of a set of linear ordinary algebraic and differential equations with constant coefficients. With the aid of matrices, we can manipulate an entire system of linear equations with much the same facility and symbolism as we utilize in the solution of one scalar equation.

For our purpose matrix algebra is used to facilitate the formulation and the solution of mathematical models of systems that are too complex to be reduced easily to one equation in one unknown.

B.2 SOME DEFINITIONS OF MATRIX ALGEBRA

We shall need several definitions to establish the properties of matrices.

Definition B.1	**Matrix**
	A *matrix* is a rectangular array of elements each one of which may be a number, a function, or an operator, singly or in combination.

We shall confine our attention to matrices for which the elements obey the algebra of numbers.

As an example,

$$\mathbf{A} = \begin{bmatrix} a_{11} & a_{12} & a_{13} \\ a_{21} & a_{22} & a_{23} \\ a_{31} & a_{32} & a_{33} \end{bmatrix} \tag{B.1}$$

is a matrix with elements a_{11}, a_{12}, ... A boldface capital letter is used to symbolize a matrix, as contrasted with a scalar quantity. Brackets, [ ], are used to distinguish a matrix from a determinant, designated by $|\ |$.

Definition B.2

Row
Each complete horizontal set of elements of a matrix is called a *row*.

Example B.1

The first row of the matrix of Equation B.1 is the set of elements a_{11}, a_{12}, and a_{13}.

Definition B.3

Column
Each complete vertical set of elements of a matrix is called a column.

Example B.2

The third column of the matrix of Equation B.1 consists of the elements a_{13}, a_{23}, and a_{33}.

Definition B.4

Line
A *line* is either a row or a column of a matrix.

Definition B.5

Matrix Order
A matrix is said to be of *order* $m \times n$ if it consists of m rows and n columns.

In the specification of matrix order, the first number is always the number of rows and the second is the number of columns.

Definition B.6

Typical Element
A *typical element* of a matrix **A** is symbolized by a_{ij}, which represents the element in row i and column j.

As in the specification of matrix order, the order of the subscripts is important for the typical element.

B.3   MATRIX EQUALITY

One of the most important definitions pertaining to the algebra of matrices is the following.

Definition B.7

Matrix Equality
Two matrices **A** and **B** are *equal* if and only if $a_{ij} = b_{ij}$ for every i and j.

B.4 ADDITION AND SUBTRACTION OF MATRICES

Definition B.8

Matrix Sum
The *matrix sum* $\mathbf{C} = \mathbf{A} + \mathbf{B}$ is defined such that $c_{ij} = a_{ij} + b_{ij}$ for every i and j.

For the matrix sum to be defined, the matrices to be summed must be of the same order. When the order of two matrices is the same, the matrices are said to be *conformable for addition*.

Since the typical entries for a matrix obey the algebra of numbers, it follows that (1) matrix addition is commutative: $\mathbf{A} + \mathbf{B} = \mathbf{B} + \mathbf{A}$; and (2) matrix addition is associative: $(\mathbf{A} + \mathbf{B}) + \mathbf{C} = \mathbf{A} + (\mathbf{B} + \mathbf{C})$.

Matrix difference can be treated as a special case of the matrix sum; however, we shall give the operation a formal definition of its own.

Definition B.9

Matrix Difference
The *matrix difference* $\mathbf{C} = \mathbf{A} - \mathbf{B}$ is defined such that the typical element of $\mathbf{C}$ is $c_{ij} = a_{ij} + b_{ij}$ for every i and j.

It is clear that the conditions for conformability and the properties of commutativity and associativity for the matrix difference are identical with those of the matrix sum.

Example B.3

Let

$$\mathbf{A} = \begin{bmatrix} 1 & 2 & 0 \\ 3 & -1 & 2 \end{bmatrix} \quad \mathbf{B} = \begin{bmatrix} 2 & -1 & -2 \\ 1 & 0 & 3 \end{bmatrix}$$

Then

$$\mathbf{C} = \mathbf{A} + \mathbf{B} = \begin{bmatrix} 3 & 1 & -2 \\ 4 & -1 & 5 \end{bmatrix} \quad \mathbf{D} = \mathbf{A} - \mathbf{B} = \begin{bmatrix} -1 & 3 & 2 \\ 2 & -1 & -1 \end{bmatrix}$$

B.5   ZERO MATRIX ─────────────────────────────────○

The notion of a zero matrix is as useful as is the analogous term with scalar numbers.

Definition B.10

> ### Zero Matrix
>
> A matrix for which every element is zero is called a *zero matrix*.

Zero matrices of any order are commonly symbolized by **0**, just as is the scalar zero. The context in which the symbol is used will fix the proper meaning.

B.6   MATRIX MULTIPLICATION ─────────────────────────○

A very important operation in the development of an algebra of matrices is that of the product of matrices.

Definition B.11

> ### Matrix Product
>
> The *product* **C** of two matrices **A** and **B**; **C** = **AB**, is a matrix for which the typical element is
>
> $$c_{ij} = \sum_{k=1}^{n} a_{ik}b_{kj},$$
>
> where for every i and j, k ranges over the column order of **A** (and the row order of **B**).

Example B.4 ─────────────────────────────────

Let

$$\mathbf{A} = \begin{bmatrix} 1 & 1 & 0 & 2 \\ 2 & -1 & 0 & 1 \\ 0 & -2 & 1 & 0 \end{bmatrix} \qquad \mathbf{B} = \begin{bmatrix} 1 & 0 \\ 0 & 2 \\ 1 & 1 \\ 0 & 2 \end{bmatrix}$$

If $\mathbf{C} = \mathbf{AB}$,

$$c_{ij} = a_{i1}b_{1j} + a_{i2}b_{2j} + a_{i3}b_{3j} + a_{i4}b_{4j}$$
$$c_{11} = 1(1) + 1(0) + 0(1) + 2(0) = 1$$
$$c_{12} = 1(0) + 1(2) + 0(1) + 2(2) = 6$$

The detailed calculation of the remaining elements of $\mathbf{C}$ are left as an exercise. The matrix product is

$$\mathbf{C} = \begin{bmatrix} 1 & 6 \\ 2 & 0 \\ 1 & -3 \end{bmatrix}$$

The definition of matrix product implies that for $\mathbf{AB}$ to be defined, the column order of $\mathbf{A}$ must equal the row order of $\mathbf{B}$. If this is true, then $\mathbf{A}$ and $\mathbf{B}$ are said to be *conformable for multiplication*. In the matrix product $\mathbf{AB}$, $\mathbf{B}$ is said to be premultiplied by $\mathbf{A}$, and $\mathbf{A}$ is said to be postmultiplied by $\mathbf{B}$.

A somewhat easier concept of the multiplication process than that obtained directly from Definition B.11 can be described as follows. The *ij*th element of the matrix product $\mathbf{AB}$ is the sum of the products of the elements in row *i* of $\mathbf{A}$ by the corresponding elements in column *j* of $\mathbf{B}$. Thus the number of rows and the number of columns of the matrix product $\mathbf{AB}$ are equal to the number of rows of $\mathbf{A}$ and the number of columns of $\mathbf{B}$, respectively.

Theorem B.1

> Matrix multiplication is not commutative. That is, in general $\mathbf{AB} \neq \mathbf{BA}$.

This property can readily be recognized when it is noted that if two matrices $\mathbf{A}$ and $\mathbf{B}$ are conformable for multiplication in one order, such as $\mathbf{AB}$, there is no assurance that $\mathbf{BA}$ will even be defined, since the conformability requirement may not be met. Even if the matrices are of like order and square, and hence conformable for multiplication in either order, it is not difficult to find examples that illustrate the noncommutativity of the product of two matrices.

The two theorems that follow state important properties of matrix multiplication.

Theorem B.2

Matrix multiplication is associative. That is,

$$\mathbf{ABC} = (\mathbf{AB})\mathbf{C} = \mathbf{A}(\mathbf{BC})$$

Theorem B.3

Matrix multiplication is distributive over addition.

$$\mathbf{A}(\mathbf{B} + \mathbf{C}) = \mathbf{AB} + \mathbf{AC}$$

B.7 DIAGONAL MATRIX

There is one particular form of matrix that is of enough importance to warrant giving it a name and elaborating to some extent upon its properties. First we define a useful term.

Definition B.12

Main Diagonal

The *main diagonal* of a square matrix is the set of element locations for which the row and column subscripts are the same.

Example B.5

The elements on the main diagonal of a square matrix $\mathbf{C}$ of order n are c_{11}, c_{22}, . . . , c_{nn}.

Definition B.13

Diagonal Matrix

A square matrix in which the only nonzero elements are on the main diagonal is called a *diagonal matrix*.

From the definition, every element $d_{ij} = 0$ for $i \neq j$ for a diagonal matrix $\mathbf{D}$. Some, but not all, of the elements on the main diagonal may be zero. Because of the special characteristics of diagonal matrices, matrix products involving them have properties not typical of general matrix products. The following three theorems are concerned with such characteristics:

Theorem B.4

Let $\mathbf{D}_1$ and $\mathbf{D}_2$ be diagonal matrices of the same order. Then the matrix product

$$\mathbf{D}_3 = \mathbf{D}_1\mathbf{D}_2 = \mathbf{D}_2\mathbf{D}_1$$

is commutative and diagonal. The typical element of $\mathbf{D}_3$ is

$$(d_3)_{ij} = \begin{cases} 0 & i \neq j \\ (d_1)_{ii}(d_2)_{ii} & i = j \end{cases}$$

Theorem B.5

Let $\mathbf{A}$ be an $m \times n$ order matrix and $\mathbf{D}_1$ a diagonal matrix of order m. The matrix product $\mathbf{D}_1\mathbf{A}$ has a typical ijth element

$$(d_1)_{ii}a_{ij}$$

Thus in the matrix product $\mathbf{D}_1\mathbf{A}$, row i of $\mathbf{A}$ is multiplied by the iith element of $\mathbf{D}_1$.

Theorem B.6

Let $\mathbf{A}$ be an $m \times n$ order matrix and $\mathbf{D}_2$ a diagonal matrix of order n. The matrix product $\mathbf{A}\mathbf{D}_2$ has a typical ijth element

$$a_{ij}(d_2)_{jj}$$

As the typical element indicates, in the matrix product $\mathbf{A}\mathbf{D}_2$ column j of $\mathbf{A}$ is multiplied by the jjth element of $\mathbf{D}_2$.

Example B.6

Let

$$\mathbf{A} = \begin{bmatrix} a_{11} & a_{12} \\ a_{21} & a_{22} \\ a_{31} & a_{32} \end{bmatrix} \qquad \mathbf{D}_1 = \begin{bmatrix} (d_1)_{11} & 0 & 0 \\ 0 & (d_1)_{22} & 0 \\ 0 & 0 & (d_1)_{33} \end{bmatrix} \qquad \mathbf{D}_2 = \begin{bmatrix} (d_2)_{11} & 0 \\ 0 & (d_2)_{22} \end{bmatrix}$$

Then

$$\mathbf{D}_1\mathbf{A} = \begin{bmatrix} (d_1)_{11}a_{11} & (d_1)_{11}a_{12} \\ (d_1)_{22}a_{21} & (d_1)_{22}a_{22} \\ (d_1)_{33}a_{31} & (d_1)_{33}a_{32} \end{bmatrix} \qquad \mathbf{A}\mathbf{D}_2 = \begin{bmatrix} a_{11}(d_2)_{11} & a_{12}(d_2)_{22} \\ a_{21}(d_2)_{11} & a_{22}(d_2)_{22} \\ a_{31}(d_2)_{11} & a_{32}(d_2)_{22} \end{bmatrix}$$

B.8 UNIT MATRIX

The unit matrix in the algebra of matrices has properties analogous to those of unity in the algebra of scalar real numbers.

Definition B.14

Unit Matrix

A diagonal matrix with elements on the main diagonal equal to unity is called a *unit matrix*.

Theorem B.7

Let $\mathbf{A}$ be an $m \times n$ matrix and $\mathbf{U}_m$ and $\mathbf{U}_n$ be unit matrices of order m and n, respectively; then

$$\mathbf{U}_m\mathbf{A} = \mathbf{A}\mathbf{U}_n = \mathbf{A}$$

The proof of this theorem can be established by choosing the diagonal matrix to have unity on the main diagonal and using Theorems B.5 and B.6. The property stated in Theorem B.7 quite logically leads to the often-used term *identity matrix*.

B.9 SCALAR MULTIPLICATION

If every element on the main diagonal of a diagonal matrix $\mathbf{D}$ is the same and is symbolized by d, then for any matrix $\mathbf{A}$, and $\mathbf{D}$ of order so as to be conformable for multiplication,

$$\mathbf{DA} = \mathbf{AD}$$

In either case the typical element of the matrix product is $d(a_{ij})$. This operation is of enough importance to warrant defining it as a special case and calling it *scalar multiplication* of a matrix. This operation is usually symbolized as $d\mathbf{A}$, where multiplication of $\mathbf{A}$ by a scalar implies that if $\mathbf{B} = d\mathbf{A}$ the typical element of $\mathbf{B}$ is $b_{ij} = d(a_{ij})$. Scalar multiplication of a matrix is commutative; that is, $d\mathbf{A} = \mathbf{A}d$.

B.10   MATRIX TRANSPOSE ————————————————————○

One operation in matrix algebra that cannot have a scalar counterpart is defined as follows.

Definition B.15

Matrix Transpose
If $\mathbf{A}^T$ represents the *transpose* of $\mathbf{A}$, then the typical element a_{ij}^T of $\mathbf{A}^T$ is $$a_{ij}^T = a_{ji}$$

This definition suggests a commonly used scheme for forming a transpose by interchanging corresponding rows and columns.

Example B.7 ————————————————————

Find $\mathbf{A}^T$ if

$$\mathbf{A} = \begin{bmatrix} 1 & 2 & -1 & 3 \\ 0 & 1 & -1 & 1 \\ 2 & -3 & 2 & 1 \end{bmatrix}$$

$$\mathbf{A}^T = \begin{bmatrix} 1 & 0 & 2 \\ 2 & 1 & -3 \\ -1 & -1 & 2 \\ 3 & 1 & 1 \end{bmatrix}$$

Theorem B.8

For $\mathbf{A}$ and $\mathbf{B}$ conformable, $(\mathbf{AB})^T = \mathbf{B}^T\mathbf{A}^T$.

Proof: By the definition of matrix product, the typical element of $\mathbf{B}^T\mathbf{A}^T$ is

$$c_{ij} = \sum b_{ik}^T a_{kj}^T$$

Since a_{kj}^T and b_{ik}^T obey the algebra of numbers, the product is commutative and so

$$c_{ij} = \sum a_{kj}^T b_{ik}^T$$

By the definition of the typical element of a transposed matrix, $a_{kj}^T = a_{jk}$ and $b_{ik}^T = b_{ki}$. Therefore,

$$c_{ij} = \sum a_{jk} b_{ki}$$

which is the *ji*th element of $\mathbf{AB}$ or the *ij*th element of $(\mathbf{AB})^T$.

Definition B.16

Symmetric Matrix

A matrix $\mathbf{A}$ is *symmetric* if $\mathbf{A} = \mathbf{A}^T$.

Transposing a symmetric matrix, then, yields precisely the matrix transposed.

Theorem B.9

If a matrix is symmetric, it is square.

Theorem B.10

From the definition of the matrix transpose:

1. $(\mathbf{A} \pm \mathbf{B})^T = \mathbf{A}^T \pm \mathbf{B}^T$.
2. $(d\mathbf{A})^T = d\mathbf{A}^T$ (*d* is scalar).
3. $(\mathbf{A}^T)^T = \mathbf{A}$.

B.11   CRAMER'S RULE

One of the principal advantages of matrix algebra in network theory comes from its use in solving systems of linear algebraic equations. A solution algorithm suitable for computer implementation can be defined very simply and precisely in matrix terms. The process is commonly called *matrix inversion* and is the subject of the next section.

To prepare for that discussion, we review the basic rules of determinant theory and use them to justify the validity of a procedure for solving linear algebraic equations known as *Cramer's rule*. If you need more review on determinant theory, consult Chapter 2 or an elementary book on matrix algebra.

In the remainder of this section, we restrict our discussion to the determinant of a square matrix $\mathbf{A}$ and write it as det $\mathbf{A}$ or $|\mathbf{A}|$. There are three basic properties of a determinant that will be useful to us.

1. The value of a determinant is unchanged if a common factor of a row (column) is factored out.

2. The exchange of a pair of adjacent rows (or columns) of a determinant results in a change of sign.

3. The value of a determinant is unchanged if any row (or column) is multiplied by a factor and added to any other row (or column).

We now turn to Cramer's rule, which we justify on the basis of these rules. Consider the system of linear algebraic equations:

$$a_{11}x_1 + a_{12}x_2 + a_{13}x_3 = b_1$$
$$a_{21}x_1 + a_{22}x_2 + a_{23}x_3 = b_2 \tag{B.2}$$
$$a_{31}x_1 + a_{32}x_2 + a_{33}x_3 = b_3$$

Equations B.2 are compactly symbolized by the matrix equation $\mathbf{AX} = \mathbf{B}$:

$$\begin{bmatrix} a_{11} & a_{12} & a_{13} \\ a_{21} & a_{22} & a_{23} \\ a_{31} & a_{32} & a_{33} \end{bmatrix} \begin{bmatrix} x_1 \\ x_2 \\ x_3 \end{bmatrix} = \begin{bmatrix} b_1 \\ b_2 \\ b_3 \end{bmatrix} \tag{B.3}$$

Form the determinant of the coefficients of $\mathbf{A}$.

$$\det \mathbf{A} \equiv |\mathbf{A}| = \begin{bmatrix} a_{11} & a_{12} & a_{13} \\ a_{21} & a_{22} & a_{23} \\ a_{31} & a_{32} & a_{33} \end{bmatrix}$$

Then the solution to Equation B.2 by Cramer's rule can be written as

$$x_1 = \frac{\begin{vmatrix} b_1 & a_{12} & a_{13} \\ b_2 & a_{22} & a_{23} \\ b_3 & a_{32} & a_{33} \end{vmatrix}}{|\mathbf{A}|} \tag{B.4}$$

$$x_2 = \frac{\begin{vmatrix} a_{11} & b_1 & a_{13} \\ a_{21} & b_2 & a_{23} \\ a_{31} & b_3 & a_{33} \end{vmatrix}}{|\mathbf{A}|} \tag{B.5}$$

$$x_3 = \frac{\begin{vmatrix} a_{11} & a_{12} & b_1 \\ a_{21} & a_{22} & b_2 \\ a_{31} & a_{32} & b_3 \end{vmatrix}}{|\mathbf{A}|} \tag{B.6}$$

As a proof we examine the solution for x_1; we leave demonstration of the solutions for x_2 and x_3 to you.

First, form the following determinant (suggested by the left side of Equation B.2):

$$\begin{vmatrix} a_{11}x_1 & a_{12}x_2 & a_{13}x_3 \\ a_{21}x_1 & a_{22}x_2 & a_{23}x_3 \\ a_{31}x_1 & a_{32}x_2 & a_{33}x_3 \end{vmatrix} \tag{B.7}$$

By Property 3, the determinant of Equation B.7 is equal to Equation B.8:

$$\begin{vmatrix} (a_{11}x_1 + a_{12}x_2 + a_{13}x_3) & a_{12}x_2 & a_{13}x_3 \\ (a_{21}x_1 + a_{22}x_2 + a_{23}x_3) & a_{22}x_2 & a_{23}x_3 \\ (a_{31}x_1 + a_{32}x_2 + a_{33}x_3) & a_{32}x_2 & a_{33}x_3 \end{vmatrix} \tag{B.8}$$

This determinant is equal to

$$\begin{vmatrix} b_1 & a_{12}x_2 & a_{13}x_3 \\ b_2 & a_{22}x_2 & a_{23}x_3 \\ b_3 & a_{32}x_2 & a_{33}x_3 \end{vmatrix} \tag{B.9}$$

since Equation B.2 may be used to substitute for the first column. By Property 1, Equations B.9 and B.7 may be written as

$$x_2 x_3 \begin{vmatrix} b_1 & a_{12} & a_{13} \\ b_2 & a_{22} & a_{23} \\ b_3 & a_{32} & a_{33} \end{vmatrix} \tag{B.10}$$

and

$$x_1 x_2 x_3 \begin{vmatrix} a_{11} & a_{12} & a_{13} \\ a_{21} & a_{22} & a_{23} \\ a_{31} & a_{32} & a_{33} \end{vmatrix} \tag{B.11}$$

Since the determinants expressed by Equations B.10 and B.11 are equal for all values of x_1, x_2, and x_3, it follows that

$$x_1 \cdot |\mathbf{A}| = \begin{vmatrix} b_1 & a_{12} & a_{13} \\ b_2 & a_{22} & a_{23} \\ b_3 & a_{32} & a_{33} \end{vmatrix}$$

A similar development for x_1 and x_2 will confirm Equations B.5 and B.6, respectively, as solutions for these variables. It is clear that this kind of proof can be extended to fourth-order and higher-order determinants.

B.12   MATRIX INVERSE

We introduce the concept of matrix inverse by utilizing the Cramer's rule method of solving systems of linear algebraic equations. Consider the system of three equations in three unknowns from Section B.11.

$$a_{11}x_1 + a_{12}x_2 + a_{13}x_3 = b_1$$
$$a_{21}x_1 + a_{22}x_2 + a_{23}x_3 = b_2 \tag{B.2}$$
$$a_{31}x_1 + a_{32}x_2 + a_{33}x_3 = b_3$$

As we have seen, this system can be represented in matrix form as

$$\begin{bmatrix} a_{11} & a_{12} & a_{13} \\ a_{21} & a_{22} & a_{23} \\ a_{31} & a_{32} & a_{33} \end{bmatrix} \begin{bmatrix} x_1 \\ x_2 \\ x_3 \end{bmatrix} = \begin{bmatrix} b_1 \\ b_2 \\ b_3 \end{bmatrix} \tag{B.3}$$

or symbolically as

$$\mathbf{Ax} = \mathbf{b} \tag{B.12}$$

where $\mathbf{A}$ is called the *coefficient matrix* for the system of linear equations. The column matrices $\mathbf{x}$ and $\mathbf{b}$ in Equation B.12 are often called *column vectors* and the equation itself is called a *vector equation*. The symbol $\mathbf{x}$ can be called a *vector variable*, as contrasted to a scalar variable, and the symbol $\mathbf{b}$ a known vector. It should be evident that, although a vector can always be represented in matrix symbolism, a matrix is not necessarily a vector. In matrix symbolism the inner vector product $(\mathbf{x}, \mathbf{y})$ is defined as $\mathbf{x}^T\mathbf{y} = \mathbf{y}^T\mathbf{x}$. To make the solution by Cramer's rule applicable to matrix operations, we define the term *cofactor*.

Definition B.17

> ### Cofactor
>
> The *ij*th *cofactor* of a matrix $\mathbf{A}$ is $(-1)^{i+j}$ (minor of the *ij*th position).

To symbolize the *ij*th cofactor of a matrix $\mathbf{A}$, we use the symbol A_{ij} in contrast to a_{ij}, the symbol for the typical element of A. Using this symbolism for the cofactor, the solution for x_1 becomes

$$x_1 = \frac{1}{\det \mathbf{A}}(b_1 A_{11} + b_2 A_{21} + b_3 A_{31}) \tag{B.13}$$

where det $\mathbf{A}$ denotes the determinant of the matrix $\mathbf{A}$. Similarly,

$$x_2 = \frac{1}{\det \mathbf{A}}(b_1 A_{12} + b_2 A_{22} + b_3 A_{32}) \tag{B.14}$$

$$x_3 = \frac{1}{\det \mathbf{A}}(b_1 A_{13} + b_2 A_{23} + b_3 A_{33}) \tag{B.15}$$

In matrix notation, this solution can be written

$$\begin{bmatrix} x_1 \\ x_2 \\ x_3 \end{bmatrix} = \frac{1}{\det \mathbf{A}} \begin{bmatrix} A_{11} & A_{21} & A_{31} \\ A_{12} & A_{22} & A_{32} \\ A_{13} & A_{23} & A_{33} \end{bmatrix} \begin{bmatrix} b_1 \\ b_2 \\ b_3 \end{bmatrix} \tag{B.16}$$

The solution is said to exist for all $\mathbf{A}$ such that det $\mathbf{A} \neq 0$. When the determinant for a square matrix does not vanish, we say that the matrix is *nonsingular*. A system of linear algebraic equations with a nonsingular coefficient matrix always has a unique solution. Since det $\mathbf{A}$ is a scalar, Equation B.16 can also be written

$$\begin{bmatrix} x_1 \\ x_2 \\ x_3 \end{bmatrix} = \begin{bmatrix} \dfrac{A_{11}}{\det \mathbf{A}} & \dfrac{A_{21}}{\det \mathbf{A}} & \dfrac{A_{31}}{\det \mathbf{A}} \\[2mm] \dfrac{A_{12}}{\det \mathbf{A}} & \dfrac{A_{22}}{\det \mathbf{A}} & \dfrac{A_{32}}{\det \mathbf{A}} \\[2mm] \dfrac{A_{13}}{\det \mathbf{A}} & \dfrac{A_{23}}{\det \mathbf{A}} & \dfrac{A_{33}}{\det \mathbf{A}} \end{bmatrix} \begin{bmatrix} b_1 \\ b_2 \\ b_3 \end{bmatrix} \tag{B.17}$$

Symbolically,

$$\mathbf{x} = \mathbf{A}^{-1}\mathbf{b} \tag{B.18}$$

Equation B.18 is the solution to the vector equation $\mathbf{Ax} = \mathbf{b}$. Thus a vector equation such as Equation B.12 with a square matrix $\mathbf{A}$ can be solved by systematic procedures if det $\mathbf{A} \neq 0$.

The matrix symbolized by $\mathbf{A}^{-1}$ is called the *inverse* of $\mathbf{A}$. The solution of the system of equations given in Equation (B.2) can be found directly by matrix techniques if a matrix $\mathbf{C}$ can be found such that $\mathbf{CA} = \mathbf{U}$. If Equation B.12 is premultiplied by such a matrix on both sides of the equal sign, the result is

$$\mathbf{CAx} = \mathbf{Ux} = \mathbf{x} = \mathbf{CB}$$

By definition any matrix $\mathbf{P}$ which, when multiplied by a nonsingular matrix $\mathbf{A}$, produces a unit (identity) matrix is the inverse of $\mathbf{A}$. In mathematical symbols,

$$\text{if} \quad \mathbf{PA} = \mathbf{U} \quad \text{then} \quad \mathbf{P} \doteq \mathbf{A}^{-1}$$

At this point it may be helpful to note that there are three synonymous statements which can be made with regard to a square matrix $\mathbf{A}$: (1) det $\mathbf{A} \neq 0$, (2) $\mathbf{A}^{-1}$ exists, and (3) $\mathbf{A}$ is nonsingular.

If a matrix is not square, its determinant is not defined and such a matrix, therefore, cannot be nonsingular. We are now ready for a typical-element definition of the matrix inverse.

Definition B.18

> The inverse of a square matrix $\mathbf{A}$ is a matrix such that for all i and j the typical element is
>
> $$a_{ij}^{-1} = \frac{A_{ji}}{\det \mathbf{A}} = \frac{ji\text{th cofactor}}{\det \mathbf{A}}$$

The transpose relationship between the typical entry of $\mathbf{A}^{-1}$ and the corresponding cofactor of $\mathbf{A}$ is probably the major source of errors in the hand calculation of matrix inverses—particularly for students beginning matrix theory. The following concept may be helpful in avoiding this difficulty.

Definition B.19

Cofactor Matrix

The matrix $\mathbf{A}'$ for which the typical ijth element is the ijth cofactor of a square matrix $\mathbf{A}$ is called the *cofactor matrix* of $\mathbf{A}$.

In this notation, the inverse of $\mathbf{A}$ can be written

$$\mathbf{A}^{-1} = \frac{1}{\det \mathbf{A}} (\mathbf{A}')^T \doteq \frac{1}{\det \mathbf{A}} \mathbf{A}^*$$

where $A* = (\mathbf{A}')^T$ is called the *adjoint* of $\mathbf{A}$. It may be desirable, at least in the early stages of learning to calculate the matrix inverse, to find the cofactor matrix and transpose it, rather than calculate the adjoint matrix directly.

Example B.8

Consider the matrix

$$\mathbf{A} = \begin{bmatrix} 1 & -1 & 1 \\ 1 & 2 & 0 \\ 1 & 0 & -1 \end{bmatrix}$$

The cofactors of $\mathbf{A}$ are

$$A_{11} = (-1)^2(-2) = -2$$

$$A_{12} = (-1)^3(-1) = 1$$

$$A_{13} = (-1)^4(-2) = -2$$

$$A_{21} = (-1)^3(1) = -1$$

$$A_{22} = (-1)^4(-1 - 1) = -2$$

$$A_{23} = (-1)^5(1) = -1$$

$$A_{31} = (-1)^4(-2) = -2$$

$$A_{32} = (-1)^5(-1) = 1$$

$$A_{33} = (-1)^6(2 + 1) = 3$$

$$\mathbf{A}' = \begin{bmatrix} -2 & 1 & -2 \\ -1 & -2 & -1 \\ -2 & 1 & 3 \end{bmatrix} \qquad \text{(Cofactor matrix)}$$

$$\mathbf{A}* = (\mathbf{A}')^T = \begin{bmatrix} -2 & -1 & -2 \\ 1 & -2 & 1 \\ -2 & -1 & 3 \end{bmatrix} \qquad \text{(Adjoint matrix)}$$

$$\det \mathbf{A} = 1(-2) + 1(-1) + 1(-2)$$

$$= -5$$

$$\mathbf{A}^{-1} = \frac{1}{\det \mathbf{A}} \mathbf{A}* = -\frac{1}{5} \begin{bmatrix} -2 & -1 & -2 \\ 1 & -2 & 1 \\ -2 & -1 & 3 \end{bmatrix}$$

$$= \frac{1}{5} \begin{bmatrix} 2 & 1 & 2 \\ -1 & 2 & -1 \\ 2 & 1 & -3 \end{bmatrix}$$

There are methods other than using Cramer's rule for finding the inverse of a matrix. Often the calculations may be simpler when alternative methods are used. For the purpose of this text, however, the procedures discussed in this section and Section B.14 are sufficient. Consult one or more of the references for a more complete treatment of matrix theory.

The following theorems, stated without proof, summarize the most important properties of the matrix inverse.

Theorem B.11

> If $\mathbf{A}$ and $\mathbf{B}$ are square and $\mathbf{AB} = \mathbf{C}$, then $(\det \mathbf{A})(\det \mathbf{B}) = \det \mathbf{C}$.

From Theorem B.11, it follows that

Theorem B.12

> If $\mathbf{AB} = \mathbf{C}$ and $\mathbf{A}^{-1}$, $\mathbf{B}^{-1}$ exist, then $\mathbf{C}^{-1}$ exists.

Theorem B.13

> If any matrix in a product of square matrices is singular, then the product is singular.

Theorem B.14

> If $\mathbf{A}$ and $\mathbf{B}$ are square matrices and $\mathbf{AB} = \mathbf{U}$, then $\mathbf{B} = \mathbf{A}^{-1}$ and $\mathbf{A} = \mathbf{B}^{-1}$.

This theorem suggests perhaps the simplest method of checking to determine if a matrix inverse is correct. It also suggests that any method of finding a matrix $\mathbf{B}$ such that the product $\mathbf{BA} = \mathbf{U}$ is a valid means of finding $\mathbf{A}^{-1}$.

Theorem B.15

> The inverse of a scalar product $a\mathbf{B}$ is $(a\mathbf{B})^{-1} = (1/a)\mathbf{B}^{-1}$.

Theorem B.15 should be noted carefully. Confusion resulting from the difference in the procedure of factoring a scalar out of a matrix and out of a determinant is a major source of errors in the evaluation of matrix inverses.

Theorem B.16

If $\mathbf{D}$ is a diagonal matrix with all nonzero entries on the main diagonal, $\mathbf{D}^{-1}$ exists. The iith entry in $\mathbf{D}^{-1}$ is $1/d_{ii}$, where d_{ii} is the typical entry in $\mathbf{D}$.

Theorem B.17

If $\mathbf{A}^{-1}$ exists, then $\mathbf{A} = (\mathbf{A}^{-1})^{-1}$.

Theorem B.18

If $\mathbf{A}$ and $\mathbf{B}$ are the same order and nonsingular, then

$$(\mathbf{AB})^{-1} = \mathbf{B}^{-1}\mathbf{A}^{-1}$$

Theorem B.19

If $\mathbf{A}$ is symmetric and $\mathbf{A}^{-1}$ exists, then $\mathbf{A}^{-1}$ is also symmetric.

B.13 ELEMENTARY OPERATIONS ON SYSTEMS OF LINEAR ALGEBRAIC EQUATIONS

Let us consider a system of four linear algebraic equations with constant coefficients in four unknowns

$$a_{11}x_1 + a_{12}x_2 + a_{13}x_3 + a_{14}x_4 = b_1$$
$$a_{21}x_1 + a_{22}x_2 + a_{23}x_3 + a_{24}x_4 = b_2$$
$$a_{31}x_1 + a_{32}x_2 + a_{33}x_3 + a_{34}x_4 = b_3 \tag{B.19}$$
$$a_{41}x_1 + a_{42}x_2 + a_{43}x_3 + a_{44}x_4 = b_4$$

Application of Cramer's rule will demonstrate that the solution to this set of simultaneous equations is unchanged by any of the following operations:

1. Multiplication of any equation by a nonzero constant.

2. Replacement of any given equation in the system with an equation derived by adding to that equation any other equation in the set multiplied by a constant. (The constant may be positive or negative.)

3. Interchange of the order of any two equations in the system.

In the theory of linear algebra, these operations are called *elementary operations*. In matrix form, Equation B.19 is written as

$$
\begin{bmatrix}
a_{11} & a_{12} & a_{13} & a_{14} \\
a_{21} & a_{22} & a_{23} & a_{24} \\
a_{31} & a_{32} & a_{33} & a_{34} \\
a_{41} & a_{42} & a_{43} & a_{44}
\end{bmatrix}
\begin{bmatrix}
x_1 \\ x_2 \\ x_3 \\ x_4
\end{bmatrix}
=
\begin{bmatrix}
b_1 \\ b_2 \\ b_3 \\ b_4
\end{bmatrix}
\tag{B.20}
$$

It is clear that the three elementary operations on the system of equations in (B.19) are equivalent to the same operations on the rows of $\mathbf{A}$ and $\mathbf{b}$ in Equation B.20.

Two systems of n simultaneous linear algebraic equations in n variables are said to be *equivalent* if they have the same solution. Thus elementary operations on a system of linear algebraic equations produces an *equivalent system of equations*. This property may be used to convert a system of equations to a set that is more easily solved. To illustrate the general idea of equivalent systems of equations, we use two examples.

Example B.9

Consider the pair of equations

$$
x_1 + x_2 = 2 \tag{B.21}
$$

$$
x_1 - 2x_2 = -1 \tag{B.22}
$$

An equivalent system of equations can be obtained by multiplying either equation through by a nonzero constant and adding it (with either sign) to the other. The resulting equation and the one added form an equivalent system.

Thus

$$
x_1 + x_2 = 2
$$

$$
2x_1 - x_2 = 1
$$

which results from adding Equation B.21 to Equation B.22, is a system equivalent to the original one. It is not, however, any easier to solve than the original system.

If we had been a bit more judicious in our choice of multiplier for Equation B.21, we might have used -1. This gives

$$
x_1 + x_2 = 2 \; . \tag{B.21}
$$

$$
-3x_2 = -3 \tag{B.23}
$$

which is not only an equivalent system of equations but is also easier to solve than the original, since the second equation can be solved independently of the first. This is a property that we shall exploit to the fullest extent whenever possible.

This property can be described somewhat more generally. Equation B.21 contains a variable (x_1) that does not appear in the remainder of the set of equations (only one in this case). When a variable appears in only one equation of a set of simultaneous equations, it is not necessary to solve that equation simultaneously with the remaining equations. It may in effect be set aside and used to find the value of that one variable when the other variables have been determined.

We conclude the example by deriving another even simpler pair of equations by multiplying Equation B.23 by $\frac{1}{3}$ and adding this to Equation B.21 to obtain

$$x_1 = 1 \tag{B.24}$$

$$x_2 = 1 \tag{B.25}$$

Solving a system of simultaneous linear algebraic equations amounts to finding an equivalent set of equations (usually in easy stages) in which each variable appears in exactly one equation. A more complex example may be useful in further clarifying the points made in the previous example.

Example B.10

Given the set of equations

$$x_1 + x_2 + 2x_3 - x_4 = 3 \tag{B.26}$$

$$x_2 + x_3 + 5x_4 = 4 \tag{B.27}$$

$$x_3 - 2x_4 = 1 \tag{B.28}$$

$$2x_3 + x_4 = 2 \tag{B.29}$$

The first equation need not be solved simultaneously with the other three, since x_1 does not appear in those three. Equations B.27–B.29 may be solved, and x_1 can then be found using Equation B.26. Upon examination of Equations B.27–B.29, we see that x_2 appears only in the first equation; therefore, it may also be set aside until the remaining set is solved.

One way to solve Equations B.28 and B.29 would be to derive an equivalent system by multiplying Equation B.28 by -2 and adding it to Equation B.29, producing a complete equivalent system:

$$x_1 + x_2 + 2x_3 - x_4 = 3 \tag{B.26}$$

$$x_2 + x_3 + 5x_4 = 4 \tag{B.27}$$

$$x_3 - 2x_4 = 1 \tag{B.28}$$

$$5x_4 = 0 \tag{B.30}$$

In this system each equation from top to bottom contains a variable not contained in any of the equations below. Therefore, the solution to the set can be obtained by solving the last equation and substituting successively from the last equation toward the first. This gives

$$x_1 = -2$$

$$x_2 = 3$$

$$x_3 = 1$$

$$x_4 = 0$$

The steps demonstrated in Example B.10 are only one set of many possible that could be used to achieve the same result. They do exemplify, however, the basic procedure for solving systems of simultaneous equations by deriving successively simpler equivalent systems of equations.

If each equation of a set of linear algebraic equations contains one variable that does not appear in any of the remaining equations of the set, we say that the equations are *explicit* in those variables and call them *explicit equations*. A set of explicit equations contained in a larger system of equations is very convenient to use in deriving a simpler equivalent system. This results from the fact that explicit equations are useful in substituting to eliminate the explicit variables from the remaining equations.

The following example illustrates the use of explicit variables in carrying out the elementary operation called *substitution*.

Example B.11

The first two equations of the following set are explicit in the variables x_1 and x_2. They are explicit in the sense that x_1 does not appear in the second equation, nor does x_2 appear in the first.

$$x_1 \quad\quad + 2x_3 - \quad x_4 = 6 \tag{B.31}$$

$$x_2 + \quad x_3 + \quad x_4 = 1 \tag{B.32}$$

$$2x_1 + \quad x_2 + 6x_3 - \quad x_4 = 15 \tag{B.33}$$

$$x_1 + 2x_2 + 4x_3 + 2x_4 = 7 \tag{B.34}$$

Equations B.31 and B.32 can be used to eliminate x_1 and x_2, respectively, from the remaining equations by the procedure often called *substitution*, which was illustrated in Example B.10.

The elimination of x_1 results in

$$x_1 \qquad + 2x_3 - x_4 = 6 \tag{B.31}$$

$$x_2 + x_3 + x_4 = 1 \tag{B.32}$$

$$x_2 + 2x_3 + x_4 = 3 \tag{B.35}$$

$$2x_2 + 2x_3 + 3x_4 = 1 \tag{B.36}$$

For this system, only the last three equations need be solved simultaneously. The elimination of x_2 from Equations B.35 and B.36 yields

$$x_1 + 2x_3 - x_4 = 6 \tag{B.31}$$

$$x_2 + x_3 + x_4 = 1 \tag{B.32}$$

$$x_3 \qquad = 2 \tag{B.37}$$

$$x_4 = -1 \tag{B.38}$$

By coincidence, Eq. B.37 and B.38 are now solved for x_3 and x_4, respectively, and may be used to eliminate these variables from Equations B.31 and B.32. In the general case, of course, the result would be two equations in two variables, the solution for which might require one or two more simplifying steps.

B.14 GAUSS ELIMINATION

The method of *Gauss elimination* is often very useful for solving a vector equation or for finding a matrix inverse where actual numbers, rather than symbolic coefficients, are involved. To establish the basis for the method, consider the vector equation

$$\mathbf{Ax} = \mathbf{b} \tag{B.39}$$

where $\mathbf{A}$ is an $n \times n$ matrix, $\mathbf{x}$ is an n-vector unknown, and $\mathbf{b}$ is an n-vector that is known. A column matrix of n rows is often designated as an *n-vector*. As we shall use them, the terms column matrix and vector are synonymous.

Equation B.39 may be solved by the elementary operations described in Section B.13. In that section we discussed the operation of multiplying one equation by a constant and adding it to another equation to produce an equivalent set of equations. To carry out the equivalent procedure in matrix notation, we need to define two more elementary linear operations which result in an equivalent system of equations. The entire set of three is summarized below:

1. Multiply an equation by a nonzero constant.

2. Interchange equations.

3. Multiply one equation by a constant and add it to another equation.

If we apply these operations to Equation B.39, we see that they translate into row operations on **A** and **b** as follows:

1. Multiply the jth row of **A** and **b** by a nonzero constant.

2. Interchange the ith and jth rows of **A** and **b**.

3. Multiply the ith row of **A** and **b** by a constant and add the result to the jth row of **A** and **b**, respectively.

By successive applications of these operations, Equation B.39 can be reduced, if $\mathbf{A}^{-1}$ exists, to

$$\mathbf{Ux} = \mathbf{b}_1 \qquad\qquad (B.40)$$

where $\mathbf{x} = \mathbf{b}_1$ is the vector solution to Equation B.39. A systematic procedure to achieve the form of Equation B.40 is described next. The procedure is aimed at first reducing all terms below the main diagonal of **A** to zero and making the terms on the main diagonal unity, and next to reducing all terms above the main diagonal to zero. The procedure is described in terms of typical entries and then illustrated with an example:

1. Divide the first row of **A** and **b** by a_{11} to put 1 in the 1-1 position. If a_{11} is zero, interchange rows so as to bring a nonzero term into the 1-1 position. If this is impossible, then every entry in the first column is zero and $\mathbf{A}^{-1}$ does not exist.

2. Put a zero in each first column position by multiplying the first row by $-a_{i1}$ and adding it to the ith row of **A** and **b**. Call the resulting matrices $\mathbf{A}_1$ and $\mathbf{b}_1$ when the operations are completed.

3. Divide the second row by the term in the 2-2 position. If this term is zero, interchange rows of $\mathbf{A}_1$ and $\mathbf{b}_1$ so as to put a nonzero term in the 2-2 position. (Row 1 should be excluded from any interchange operation.)

4. Now with 1 in the 2-2 position, use row 2 to put zeros in column 2 below the main diagonal by multiplying row 2 of $\mathbf{A}_1$ and $\mathbf{b}_1$ by $-a_{i2}$ and adding the result to row i. When this set of operations is complete, call the resulting matrices $\mathbf{A}_2$ and $\mathbf{b}_2$.

5. Continue this process until all terms on the main diagonal are unity and all terms below the main diagonal are zero.

The solution for **x** may be obtained at this point by reading the value of x_n from the nth row and substituting it into the $(n - 1)$ row to obtain x_{n-1}. The next step would be to evaluate x_{n-2} by substituting x_n and x_{n-1} into the $(n-2)$ row. Thus successive substitution from bottom to top will yield the complete solution.

6. To obtain an explicit solution directly, however, we can continue the process already described to put zeros in all positions above the main diagonal. This time we work from the last column toward the first, however, and we begin by using the 1 in the nn position to eliminate all nonzero terms from the nth column. The procedure is analogous to that already described, but simpler, since the rows we operate with have only one nonzero element and that is always unity.

Example B.12

Consider the vector equation

$$\begin{bmatrix} 1 & -1 & 1 \\ 1 & 2 & 0 \\ 1 & 0 & -1 \end{bmatrix} \begin{bmatrix} x_1 \\ x_2 \\ x_3 \end{bmatrix} = \begin{bmatrix} 10 \\ 15 \\ -5 \end{bmatrix}$$

After using row 1 to eliminate nonzero terms in the 2-1 and 3-1 positions, we have

$$\begin{bmatrix} 1 & -1 & 1 \\ 0 & 3 & -1 \\ 0 & 1 & -2 \end{bmatrix} \begin{bmatrix} x_1 \\ x_2 \\ x_3 \end{bmatrix} = \begin{bmatrix} 10 \\ 5 \\ -15. \end{bmatrix} \qquad (B.41)$$

Next we divide row 2 by 3 to produce

$$\begin{bmatrix} 1 & -1 & 1 \\ 0 & 1 & -\frac{1}{3} \\ 0 & 1 & -2 \end{bmatrix} \begin{bmatrix} x_1 \\ x_2 \\ x_3 \end{bmatrix} = \begin{bmatrix} 10 \\ \frac{5}{3} \\ -15 \end{bmatrix}$$

Now we use row 2 to put a zero in the 3-2 position:

$$\begin{bmatrix} 1 & -1 & 1 \\ 0 & 1 & -\frac{1}{3} \\ 0 & 0 & -\frac{5}{3} \end{bmatrix} \begin{bmatrix} x_1 \\ x_3 \\ x_3 \end{bmatrix} \begin{bmatrix} 10 \\ \frac{5}{3} \\ -\frac{50}{3} \end{bmatrix}$$

After multiplication of the third row by $-\frac{3}{5}$, this becomes

$$\begin{bmatrix} 1 & -1 & 1 \\ 0 & 1 & -\frac{1}{3} \\ 0 & 0 & 1 \end{bmatrix} \begin{bmatrix} x_1 \\ x_2 \\ x_3 \end{bmatrix} = \begin{bmatrix} 10 \\ \frac{5}{3} \\ 10 \end{bmatrix}$$

At this point the solution for x_3 is available and the remaining variables may be determined by successive substitution.

We may continue to sweep out the off-diagonal terms, however, by using row 3 to put zeros in positions 1-3 and 2-3. The result is

$$\begin{bmatrix} 1 & -1 & 0 \\ 0 & 1 & 0 \\ 0 & 0 & 1 \end{bmatrix} \begin{bmatrix} x_1 \\ x_2 \\ x_3 \end{bmatrix} = \begin{bmatrix} 0 \\ 5 \\ 10 \end{bmatrix}$$

Finally, adding row 2 to row 1 yields the solution

$$\begin{bmatrix} 1 & 0 & 0 \\ 0 & 1 & 0 \\ 0 & 0 & 1 \end{bmatrix} \begin{bmatrix} x_1 \\ x_2 \\ x_3 \end{bmatrix} = \begin{bmatrix} 5 \\ 5 \\ 10 \end{bmatrix}$$

Example B.12 illustrates the direct solution of a matrix equation by the process of Gauss elimination. Many times the inverse of $\mathbf{A}$ rather than the solution of the equations may be of primary interest. In such cases the same general procedure may be used but with a little twist. Equation B.39 may be written

$$\mathbf{Ax} = \mathbf{Ub} \tag{B.42}$$

Now suppose that a set of elementary operations is applied to the system of scalar linear equations denoted by Equation B.42. It should be clear that these operations translate into row operations on $\mathbf{A}$ and on $\mathbf{U}$ (instead of on $\mathbf{b}$, as in the example). When a set of such operations is complete, the result can be denoted by

$$\mathbf{Ux} = \mathbf{Bb} \qquad \text{or} \qquad \mathbf{x} = \mathbf{Bb}$$

We have found the inverse, since

$$\mathbf{x} = \mathbf{A}^{-1}\mathbf{b}$$

and $\mathbf{A}^{-1}$ is unique. We now illustrate the beginning of the determination of an inverse by this procedure.

Example B.13

Consider the matrix equation

$$\begin{bmatrix} 1 & -1 & 1 \\ 1 & 2 & 0 \\ 1 & 0 & -1 \end{bmatrix} \begin{bmatrix} x_1 \\ x_2 \\ x_3 \end{bmatrix} = \begin{bmatrix} 1 & 0 & 0 \\ 0 & 1 & 0 \\ 0 & 0 & 1 \end{bmatrix} \begin{bmatrix} 10 \\ 15 \\ -5 \end{bmatrix}$$

We now carry along only the resulting square matrices. After reducing the first column to zeros, we have

$$\begin{bmatrix} 1 & -1 & 1 \\ 0 & 3 & -1 \\ 0 & 1 & -2 \end{bmatrix} \begin{bmatrix} 1 & 0 & 0 \\ -1 & 1 & 0 \\ -1 & 0 & 1 \end{bmatrix}$$

Next, divide row 2 by 3 to produce

$$\begin{bmatrix} 1 & -1 & 1 \\ 0 & 1 & -\frac{1}{3} \\ 0 & 1 & -2 \end{bmatrix} \begin{bmatrix} 1 & 0 & 0 \\ -\frac{1}{3} & \frac{1}{3} & 0 \\ -1 & 0 & 1 \end{bmatrix}$$

Now reduce the 3-2 entry to zero:

$$\begin{bmatrix} 1 & -1 & 1 \\ 0 & 1 & -\frac{1}{3} \\ 0 & 0 & -\frac{5}{3} \end{bmatrix} \begin{bmatrix} 1 & 0 & 0 \\ -\frac{1}{3} & \frac{1}{3} & 0 \\ -\frac{2}{3} & -\frac{1}{3} & 1 \end{bmatrix}$$

Next multiply the third row by $-\frac{3}{5}$ to yield

$$\begin{bmatrix} 1 & -1 & 1 \\ 0 & 1 & -\frac{1}{3} \\ 0 & 0 & 1 \end{bmatrix} \begin{bmatrix} 1 & 0 & 0 \\ -\frac{1}{3} & \frac{1}{3} & 0 \\ \frac{2}{5} & \frac{1}{5} & -\frac{3}{5} \end{bmatrix}$$

The remaining steps are left as an exercise. The matrix inverted here is that of Example B.12.

B.15 RANK

In describing the solution characteristics of a set of linear algebraic equations, the concept of *rank* is often useful. Suppose the equations are written in matrix form:

$$\mathbf{A}\mathbf{x} = \mathbf{b} \qquad (B.43)$$

where $\mathbf{A}$ is of order $m \times n$. Then the rank of the system of equations is defined to be the rank of the coefficient matrix $\mathbf{A}$. In order for Equation B.43 to have a unique solution, the matrix $\mathbf{A}$ should have rank n. As we will see, it follows that the number of equations (m) must be equal to or greater than the number of variables (n).

We now turn to the definition of the rank of a matrix.

Definition B.20

> ## Rank
>
> The *rank* of a matrix $\mathbf{A}$ of order $m \times n$, is the order of the largest nonzero determinant that can be formed (from) the rows (or columns) of $\mathbf{A}$.

The following properties follow from the definition:

1. The row rank is equal to the column rank.

2. The rank of a matrix is no larger than the minimum of (m, n).

3. Elementary operations on a matrix do not change the rank. Therefore, a matrix can be simplified, for purposes of checking rank, both by elementary row operations and elementary column operations. The *value* of the largest nonzero determinant is not needed—only the size. Therefore, it is not necessary to keep a record of the elementary operations carried out on the matrix being checked.

4. A matrix has rank zero if and only if every element is zero.

Example B.14

Given

$$\mathbf{A} = \begin{bmatrix} 1 & 0 & 2 & 1 & 3 \\ 1 & 1 & 2 & 1 & 2 \\ 2 & 1 & 4 & 2 & 5 \end{bmatrix}$$

for which $m = 3$ and $n = 5$.

First, we note that the rank of $\mathbf{A}$ is no greater than 3. By carrying out elementary row operations, we can get the following sequence of matrices—each of which has the same rank:

$$\begin{bmatrix} 1 & 0 & 2 & 1 & 3 \\ 1 & 1 & 2 & 1 & 2 \\ 2 & 1 & 4 & 2 & 5 \end{bmatrix} \rightarrow \begin{bmatrix} 1 & 0 & 2 & 1 & 3 \\ 0 & 1 & 0 & 0 & -1 \\ 2 & 1 & 4 & 2 & 5 \end{bmatrix}$$

$$\rightarrow \begin{bmatrix} 1 & 0 & 2 & 1 & 3 \\ 0 & 1 & 0 & 0 & -1 \\ 0 & 1 & 0 & 0 & -1 \end{bmatrix} \rightarrow \begin{bmatrix} 1 & 0 & 2 & 1 & 3 \\ 0 & 1 & 0 & 0 & -1 \\ 0 & 0 & 0 & 0 & 0 \end{bmatrix}$$

The three elementary operations used in this sequence are as follows:

1. Row 1 is subtracted from row 2 to produce new row 2.

2. Row 1 times 2 is subtracted from row 3 to produce new row 3.

3. Resulting row 2 is subtracted from resulting row 3.

It is now clear that the rank of **A** is no more than 2 and no less than 2. We can continue using elementary operations until at most one nonzero element remains in each row and column. Then the rank can be determined by counting the number of nonzero elements.

To illustrate this procedure, we continue the simplification of the last matrix found by elementary operations on rows. Now we elect to do elementary operations on columns. The first column can be used to sweep out the nonzero elements in the first row, as shown below.

$$\begin{bmatrix} 1 & 0 & 2 & 1 & 3 \\ 0 & 1 & 0 & 0 & -1 \\ 0 & 0 & 0 & 0 & 0 \end{bmatrix} \rightarrow \begin{bmatrix} 1 & 0 & 0 & 0 & 0 \\ 0 & 1 & 0 & 0 & -1 \\ 0 & 0 & 0 & 0 & 0 \end{bmatrix}$$

Next, the second column can be used to eliminate the only nonzero element in the fifth column.

$$\begin{bmatrix} 1 & 0 & 0 & 0 & 0 \\ 0 & 1 & 0 & 0 & 0 \\ 0 & 0 & 0 & 0 & 0 \end{bmatrix}$$

Note that we could have eliminated the nonzero element in column 2 by using column 5. There are obviously many variations on how to proceed, but the same outcome is assured—relative to rank.

BIBLIOGRAPHY

1. Browne, E. T., *The Theory of Determinants and Matrices*. (Chapel Hill, N.C.: The University of North Carolina Press, 1958).

2. Campbell, H. G., *Linear Algebra with Applications*, 2nd ed. (Englewood Cliffs, N.J.: Prentice-Hall, 1980).

3. Director, S. W., *Circuit Theory: A Computational Approach*. (New York: John Wiley & Sons, 1975), Chapter 9.

4. Hohn, F. E., *Elementary Matrix Algebra*. (New York: Macmillan, 1958).

5. Reed, M. B., *Alternating-Current Circuit Theory*, 2nd ed. (New York: Harper & Row, 1956), Chapter 9.

PROBLEMS

Given the following matrices:

$$A = \begin{bmatrix} 1 & 0 & 2 & 1 \\ 2 & -1 & 1 & 2 \\ 1 & 1 & 2 & 0 \end{bmatrix} \qquad B = \begin{bmatrix} 1 & 0 & 1 \\ 1 & 1 & 1 \\ 0 & 1 & 1 \end{bmatrix}$$

$$C = \begin{bmatrix} 2 & 1 & 1 \\ 1 & 0 & 1 \\ 1 & -2 & 1 \end{bmatrix} \qquad D_1 = \begin{bmatrix} 2 & 0 & 0 \\ 0 & -1 & 0 \\ 0 & 0 & 3 \end{bmatrix}$$

$$D_2 = \begin{bmatrix} -3 & 0 & 0 \\ 0 & 2 & 0 \\ 0 & 0 & -1 \end{bmatrix} \qquad E = \begin{bmatrix} 1 & 2 & 1 \\ 1 & 1 & 2 \\ 2 & -1 & 0 \\ 0 & 2 & 1 \end{bmatrix}$$

For Problems B.1 to B.10, find the matrices indicated.

B.1. $B + C$.

B.2. $C + D_1 - B$.

B.3. $2D_2 + C$.

B.4. $A + E^T$.

B.5. BA.

B.6. AE and EA.

B.7. $D_1 C$ and CD_1.

B.8. $D_2 B$ and BD_2.

B.9. $D_1 D_2$ and $D_2 D_1$.

B.10. $(AE + B)C$ and $AEC + BC$.

B.11. Demonstrate that $(AE)^T = E^T A^T$.

B.12. Calculate the cofactor matrix B'.

B.13. Calculate the cofactor matrix C'.

B.14. Using the cofactors found in Problem B.12, calculate det B and write B^{-1}.

B.15. Using the cofactors found in Problem B.13, calculate det C and write C^{-1}.

B.16. Find $(BC)^{-1}$ by the Gauss elimination process and demonstrate from the results of Problems B.14 and B.15 that

$$(BC)^{-1} = C^{-1}B^{-1}$$

B.17. Determine by Gauss elimination whether $(AE)^{-1}$ exists.

B.18. A *triangular matrix* is defined to be one for which the entries above or below the main diagonal are zero. If all entries on the main diagonal of a triangular matrix are nonzero, show that the matrix is nonsingular.

B.19. Find x from the matrix equation

$$Bx = b$$

where

$$x = \begin{bmatrix} x_1 \\ x_2 \\ x_3 \end{bmatrix} \qquad b = \begin{bmatrix} 1 \\ 2 \\ -3 \end{bmatrix}$$

(a) Use Gauss elimination to solve the matrix equation directly.

(b) Use the results of Problem B.14.

(c) Use Gauss elimination to find B^{-1}.

B.20. Complete the solution of Example B.13.

B.21. Find x from the matrix equation

$$Cx = b$$

where

$$x = \begin{bmatrix} x_1 \\ x_2 \\ x_3 \end{bmatrix} \qquad b = \begin{bmatrix} 10 \\ 5 \\ -15 \end{bmatrix}$$

(a) Solve directly by Gauss elimination.

(b) Use the results of Problem B.15.

(c) Calculate C^{-1} by Gauss elimination.

B.22. Solve the following matrix equations:

$$\begin{bmatrix} x_1 \\ x_2 \\ x_3 \end{bmatrix} = \begin{bmatrix} 1 & 1 & 0 \\ 1 & 0 & -1 \\ 1 & 1 & 0 \end{bmatrix} \begin{bmatrix} y_1 \\ y_2 \\ y_3 \end{bmatrix} \qquad (B.44)$$

$$\begin{bmatrix} 1 & -1 & 1 & 2 & 0 & -1 \\ 1 & 0 & 1 & 0 & 1 & 1 \\ 0 & 1 & 1 & -2 & 1 & 0 \end{bmatrix} \begin{bmatrix} x_1 \\ x_2 \\ x_3 \\ y_1 \\ y_2 \\ y_3 \end{bmatrix} = \begin{bmatrix} -5 \\ 15 \\ -10 \end{bmatrix}$$

$$(B.45)$$

(a) Write both matrix equations as one matrix equation and use Gauss elimination to solve.

(b) Write Equation B.45 in the form $\mathbf{Mx} + \mathbf{Ny} = \mathbf{k}$ and substitute for $\mathbf{x}$ from Equation B.44. If we symbolize Equation B.44 by $\mathbf{x} = \mathbf{Py}$, the result of this substitution will be

$$\mathbf{x} = \mathbf{Py} \tag{B.44}$$

$$[\mathbf{MP} + \mathbf{N}]\mathbf{y} = \mathbf{k} \tag{B.46}$$

The solution of Equation B.46 provides the solution for Equation B.44 and thus for the original system of equations. Solve by the cofactor method.

B.23. Develop the solution by Cramer's rule for x_2 (Equation B.5) corresponding to the development for x_1.

B.24. Develop the solution by Cramer's rule for x_3 (Equation B.6) corresponding to the development for x_1.

B.25. Solve the following set of equations using Cramer's rule:

$$\begin{bmatrix} 2 & -1 \\ 1 & 2 \end{bmatrix} \begin{bmatrix} x_1 \\ x_2 \end{bmatrix} = \begin{bmatrix} 1 \\ 3 \end{bmatrix}$$

(*Answer:* $x_1 = x_2 = 1$.)

B.26. Solve Problem B.19 using Cramer's rule. (*Answer:* $x_1 = 5, x_2 = 1, x_3 = -4$.)

B.27. Solve Problem B.21 using Cramer's rule. (*Answer:* $x_1 = -5, x_2 = 10, x_3 = 10$.)

B.28. Using basic determinant properties and Cramer's rule, show that the three elementary operations on sets of linear algebraic equations described in Section B.13 will leave the solution of the equations unchanged. (Deal with each elementary operation individually.)

B.29. Use a matrix-inverse computer program to solve Problem B.19.

B.30. Use a matrix-inverse computer program to solve Problem B.21.

The following problems refer to the matrices at the beginning of the problem section.

B.31. Check the rank of matrix $\mathbf{A}$.

B.32. Check the rank of matrix $\mathbf{E}$.

B.33. Check the rank of matrix $\mathbf{E}^T\mathbf{A}$.

B.34. Check the rank of matrix $\mathbf{BD}_1$.

Computer programs

The programs included in this appendix are intended for use in obtaining numerical solutions to problems which would take too much time to derive analytically, and to broaden the student's experience in finding solutions by any appropriate technique. No attempt was made to present the most elegant computer routines to accomplish a given task. Rather, our philosophy was to use simple algorithms in the hope that the student would benefit most by understanding the basis for the program and would thus be encouraged to modify it—and learn in the process.

The programs are written in BASIC and intended for implementation on a microcomputer. They have been tested on an IBM PC and thus should run on any personal computer using Microsoft BASIC. After some discussion we decided to have the data input from the keyboard and, except for two programs, the output directed to a printer. If the user does not have a printer available, it is a simple matter to direct the output to the screen and use the STOP command to keep the data from overflowing it.

Several programs use the LPRINT USING command in order to obtain the output in a convenient form. The user should be aware that there is always a possibility that this command may have to be altered to accommodate very small numbers or very large numbers. When printing out matrices the formatted printing is particularly desirable.

We originally intended to make this an appendix of subroutines rather than of complete programs. After a bit of reflection, however, we concluded that most instructors would much prefer that students at the sophomore-junior level spend most of the available time in studying network theory, rather than struggling with the problem of writing and debugging computer programs.

Particularly, we felt that the real and complex matrix inversion programs would take far too much time from a student's study of network theory. The other programs are shorter, and are of the nature of subroutines in that they must be modified to some extent for each individual special case.

In each of the programs, the noninteger real variables are declared as single precision to minimize the running time. The user must use some judgment as to when double precision is called for, and declare the appropriate variables accordingly.

These programs are available from the publisher on a floppy disk, which has a Users' Manual. The manual contains examples that illustrate uses of the programs. This material can be obtained through your course instructor.

Those interested in additional BASIC language programs, such as programs for finding the roots of functions, plotting subroutines, vector and matrix subroutines, etc., will find the following references helpful:

A. R. Miller, *BASIC Programs for Scientists and Engineers*, Sybex, Inc., Berkeley, CA, 1981.

F. R. Ruckdeschel, *BASIC Scientific Subroutines* (Volumes I and II), Byte Books, McGraw-Hill Publishing Co., New York, 1981.

P
R
O
G
R
A
M
S

C.1   COMPUTER PROGRAM 1 ─────────────────────────────○

Name: NUMINT

Purpose: The program uses trapezoidal integration to evaluate a definite integral with lower limit T_1 and upper limit T_2.

Algorithm: The definite integral is approximated by the trapezoidal technique as indicated below:

$$\int_{T_1}^{T_2} f(t) \, dt \cong (h/2) \sum_{n=1}^{N} \{ f[(n-1)h] + f(nh) \}$$

where $T_2 - T_1 = Nh$

Inputs: The program requires the lower limit T_1, the upper limit T_2, the maximum allowable error ratio E, the number of integration increments N, and the integrand function $FNF(T)$. If the integrand can be specified as a function, it should be defined in the function subroutine at line 500. If not, it can be defined as an n-dimensional array and read in as data.

Outputs: The program outputs are the number of runs, the value of the integral F_2, and the corresponding error ratio E_1.

Using the Program: The program prompts the user for all inputs. Error ratio is defined as the absolute value of the difference between the previous integral and the current integral divided by the current integral. If the specified error ratio is not satisfied, the integration increment is halved and the integral is reevaluated. Thus the integral is always calculated twice.

Comments: This program can be useful in evaluating coefficients for Fourier series and for finding average power and energy values for functions for which the Fourier transform is known.

P
R
O
G
R
A
M
S

Program listing for NUMINT

```
10 '   * PROGRAM INTEGRATES A FUNCTION FROM T1 TO T2, USING THE
20 '      TRAPEZOIDAL METHOD.  INPUTS NEEDED ARE T1, T2, NUMBER OF
30 '      INCREMENTS, AND ERROR RATIO CRITERION   (NUMINT) *
40 PRINT "      * NUMERICAL INTEGRATION PROGRAM *"
50 PRINT
60 PRINT " *  PLACE INTEGRAND FUNCTION AT LINE 1000   *"
70 PRINT
80 DEFSNG E,F,H
90 DEFINT I,K,N
100 '   * INPUT INITIAL AND FINAL TIMES  *
110 PRINT "INPUT T1 AND T2:"
120 INPUT "T1,T2";T1,T2
130 INPUT "NUMBER OF INCREMENTS";N
140 '   * ERROR CRITERION = CHANGE/(LAST INTEGRAL MAGNITUDE)   *
150 INPUT "ERROR RATIO";E
160 K=0
170 '   * INITIALIZE PREVIOUS VALUE OF INTEGRAL   *
180 F3=0
190 '   *   INITIALIZE PRESENT VALUE OF INTEGRAL   *
200 F2=0
210 LPRINT "RUN NO.","INTEGRAL",,"ERROR"
220 '   *  SET F3 EQUAL TO PRESENT VALUE OF INTEGRAL  *
230 F3=F2
240 '   *  SET INCREMENT OF INTEGRATION  *
250 H=(T2-T1)/N
260 GOSUB 1000
270 F2=0
280 FOR I=1 TO N
290 F1=0
300 F1=H*(FNF(T1+H*(I-1))+FNF(T1+H*I))/2
310 F2=F2+F1
320 NEXT I
330 K=K+1
340 '   *  CHECK ERROR RATIO  *
350 E1=(F2-F3)/F2
360 LPRINT
370 LPRINT K,F2,,E1
375 LPRINT
380 IF ABS(E1)<=E THEN 420
390 '   *  HALVE INCREMENT OF INTEGRATION  *
400 N=2*N
410 GOTO 230
420 END
980 '
990 ' *  FUNCTION SUBROUTINE  *
1000 DEF FNF(T)=T*T+T+1
1010 RETURN
```

C.2   COMPUTER PROGRAM 2 ————————————————————○

Name: NEWTON

Purpose: The program solves for the variables x_1 and x_2 which satisfy the nonlinear functions $F_1(x_1, x_2) = 0 = F_2(x_1, x_2)$.

Algorithm: The algorithm used is based on the technique commonly known as the Newton-Raphson method. The basis for the technique is presented in Section 4.8. Briefly, it utilizes the inverse of the second-order Jacobian matrix for F_1 and F_2 to solve for incremental changes in x_1 and x_2, which hopefully move an initial guess toward an acceptably accurate solution through a process of iteration.

Inputs: The program requires an initial estimate for the variables $X(1)$ and $X(2)$, a specification of the maximum allowable mismatch E, the functions $F(1)$ and $F(2)$, and the elements of the Jacobian matrix $J(I, K)$ for $F(1)$ and $F(2)$. The first three are input to the keyboard. The remainder are placed in the function subroutine.

Outputs: The outputs are the iteration number L, the maximum mismatch M, and the calculated values of $X(1)$ and $X(2)$ for that iteration.

Using the Program: After the appropriate functions have been placed in the function subroutine, the user is prompted for an initial estimate for the variables and a value of the maximum allowable mismatch. The maximum number of iterations is specified at line 210. If the program has not converged in that number of iterations, it is terminated, and a new estimate of the variables may be tried.

Comments: The mismatch in the solution is defined as the magnitude of the ratio of the increment for each variable to the calculated value of the variable. The maximum mismatch for the two variables is found for each iteration, and this is the basis for deciding whether to continue the process.

Note that the maximum mismatch may rise as one of the variables approaches zero, even though the process is converging. This occurs because the calculated value of the variable is in the denominator of the term. If at least one of the solutions occurs at zero, the magnitude of the variable increments could be used as a measure of mismatch.

P
R
O
G
R
A
M
S

The elements for the Jacobian matrix are the partial derivatives of the functions $f_1(x_1, x_2)$ and $f_2(x_1, x_2)$ with respect to the variables x_1 and x_2. That is, $J(I, K)$ is the partial derivative of f_i with respect to x_k.

Program listing for NEWTON

```
10  '   *   NEWTON-RAPHSON PROGRAM FOR 2 NONLINEAR ALGEBRAIC EQUATIONS   *
20  '   *   SOLVES FOR X1 AND X2 TO SATISFY F1(X1,X2) = F2(X1,X2) = 0    *
30  '
40  PRINT "* PLACE FUNCTIONS AND DERIVATIVES IN SUBROUTINE AT LINE 1000 *"
50  PRINT
60  DEFSNG D,M,X,F,E,J
70  DEFINT L,K,I
80  OPTION BASE 1
90  DIM J(2,2),F(2),X(2),D(2)
100 L=0
110 '   *   MAKE INITIAL ESTIMATE OF SOLUTION FOR X1 AND X2   *
120 INPUT "X1 ESTIMATE";X(1)
130 INPUT "X2 ESTIMATE";X(2)
140 '   *   SPECIFY MAXIMUM ALLOWABLE MISMATCH FOR X1 AND X2 SOLUTION   *
150 INPUT "MAXIMUM ALLOWABLE MISMATCH";E
160 LPRINT "ITERATION #     MAX MISMATCH        X(1)           X(2)"
170 LPRINT
180 M=999.999
190 '   *   PRINT INITIAL VALUES OF ESTIMATED VALUES AND MISMATCH   *
195 LPRINT L,
200 LPRINT USING "###.#######     ";M,X(1),X(2)
210 FOR K=1 TO 15
220 '   *   CALCULATE NEW ESTIMATED VALUES OF X1 AND X2   *
230 GOSUB 1000
240 D=J(1,1)*J(2,2)-J(1,2)*J(2,1)
250 D(1)=(-J(2,2)*F(1)+J(1,2)*F(2))/D
260 D(2)=(J(2,1)*F(1)-J(1,1)*F(2))/D
270 X(1)=X(1)+D(1)
280 X(2)=X(2)+D(2)
290 L=L+1
300 M=0
310 '   *   CHECK FOR MAXIMUM MISMATCH   *
320 FOR I=1 TO 2
330 IF ABS(D(I)/X(I))<M THEN 350
340 M=ABS (D(I)/X(I))
350 NEXT I
360 '   *   PRINT OUT RESULTS OF ITERATION   *
365 LPRINT L,
370 LPRINT USING "###.#######     ";M,X(1),X(2)
380 IF M<E THEN 400
390 NEXT K
400 END
960 '
970 '   *   FUNCTION SUBROUTINE   *
980 '
990 '   *   ELEMENTS IN THE JACOBIAN MATRIX   *
1000 J(1,1)=1+6*X(1)^2
1010 J(1,2)=1
1020 J(2,1)=1
1030 J(2,2)=1+12*EXP(-3*X(2))
1040 '   *   FUNCTIONS F1 AND F2   *
1050 F(1)=X(1)+2*X(1)^3+X(2)-2
1060 F(2)=X(1)+X(2)+4*(1-EXP(-3*X(2)))-4
1070 RETURN
```

C.3   COMPUTER PROGRAM 3 ————————————————————O

Name: RMATINV

Purpose: The program solves the set of real linear algebraic equations symbolized by the matrix equation $\mathbf{Ax} = \mathbf{b}$, by finding the inverse of $\mathbf{A}$.

Subroutines: The program uses a real matrix inverse subroutine (based on the Gauss elimination method), a matrix print subroutine, a matrix multiplication subroutine, and subroutines to save a matrix under a different name.

Inputs: The program requires the order of the square matrix $\mathbf{A}$, the real elements $A(I, J)$ of the matrix, and the real elements $B(I, J)$ of the vector $\mathbf{b}$.

Outputs: The outputs are the real elements of the matrix $\mathbf{A}$, the inverse of $\mathbf{A}$, and the product of $\mathbf{A}$ and $\mathbf{A}$-inverse. If the solution to $\mathbf{Ax} = \mathbf{b}$ is elected, the solution vector is also printed.

Using the Program: The user is prompted for all inputs. After the inverse is calculated the user is asked whether the solution to $\mathbf{Ax} = \mathbf{b}$ is desired. If not, the program is terminated.

The user must be on guard against the possibility of a singular matrix, since there is no warning flag. A check is provided for a valid matrix inverse, however, by multiplying the inverse times the original matrix. If a unit matrix is not produced, of course, the user is warned that a problem exists.

Comments: Since it is easy to make a mistake in inputting data from the keyboard for a large matrix, it is often desirable to replace the INPUT command by a READ/DATA command.

The matrix elements are declared as single precision variables in order to make the program run as fast as possible. The user may elect for more accuracy by declaring them double precision.

Subroutines from this program may be useful to the user in devising other matrix subroutines and programs.

Program listing for RMATINV

```
10 ' * PROGRAM TO SOLVE A SET OF REAL ALGEBRAIC EQUATIONS (RMATINV) *
20 PRINT "* THIS PROGRAM FINDS THE INVERSE OF A SQUARE MATRIX A, AND"
30 PRINT "  UTILIZES IT IN SOLVING THE MATRIX EQUATION, AX=B. *"
40 PRINT
45 DEFINT I,J,M,N
50 DEFSNG A,B,C
60 PRINT "ENTER MATRIX ORDER AND ELEMENTS OF A AS DIRECTED BY PROMPT."
70 PRINT
80 INPUT "MATRIX ORDER ";N
90 DIM A(N,N),B(N,2*N),C(N,N)
100 '    *ENTER MATRIX A *
110 FOR I=1 TO N
120 FOR J=1 TO N
130 PRINT "ENTER ";J;" ELEMENT OF ROW ";I;":";
140 INPUT A(I,J)
150 NEXT J
160 PRINT
170 NEXT I
180 M1=N
190 N1=N
200 '    * MOVE A TO C *
210 GOSUB 5000
220 M3=N
225 N3=N
230 '    * PRINT MATRIX A *
240 LPRINT
250 LPRINT "MATRIX A IS:"
260 LPRINT
270 GOSUB 2000
280 '    * FIND INVERSE OF A *
290 GOSUB 6000
300 M2=N
310 N2=N
320 '    * MOVE B = A-INVERSE  TO C FOR PRINTING *
330 GOSUB 4000
340 LPRINT "INVERSE OF A IS:"
350 M3=N
355 N3=N
360 GOSUB 2000
370 '    * CHECK RESULTS *
380 M1=N
390 N1=N
400 N2=N
410 GOSUB 3000
420 M3=N
425 N3=N
430 '    * PRINT RESULTS *
440 LPRINT "A TIMES A-INVERSE IS:"
450 GOSUB 2000
460 INPUT "SOLVE AX=B (Y,N)";Z$
470 IF Z$="N" THEN 760
490 '    * PUT A-INVERSE (B) INTO A *
500 FOR I=1 TO N
510 FOR J=1 TO N
520 A(I,J)=B(I,J)
530 NEXT J
540 NEXT I
550 '    * INPUT SOURCE VECTOR *
560 FOR I=1 TO N
570 PRINT "INPUT ";I;" ELEMENT OF B VECTOR."
580 INPUT B(I,1)
590 NEXT I
600 LPRINT
610 LPRINT "THE SOURCE VECTOR IS (IN ROW FORM):"
620 LPRINT
630 FOR I=1 TO N
```

RMATINV (*continued*)

```
640 LPRINT B(I,1),
650 NEXT I
660 LPRINT
670 '  * FIND SOLUTION VECTOR, C=A*B"
680 N2=1
690 GOSUB 3000
700 LPRINT
710 LPRINT "THE SOLUTION VECTOR IS:"
720 LPRINT
730 FOR I=1 TO N
740 LPRINT USING "###.###   ";C(I,1)
750 NEXT I
760 END
1960 '     * MATRIX PRINT SUBROUTINE (MATPRNT) *
1970 '       INPUT C(M3,N3)
1980 '       NO. COLUMNS LIMITED BY PRINTER
1990 '
2000 LPRINT
2010 FOR I=1 TO M3
2020 FOR J=1 TO N3
2030 LPRINT USING "###.###   ";C(I,J),
2040 NEXT J
2050 LPRINT
2060 NEXT I
2070 LPRINT
2080 RETURN
2980 '   *MATRIX MULTIPLICATION SUBROUTINE (MATMULT)
2990 '   C=A*B, A(M1,N1), B(N1,N2), C(M1,N2)
3000 FOR I=1 TO M1
3010 FOR J=1 TO N2
3020 C(I,J)=0
3030 FOR K=1 TO N1
3040 C(I,J)=C(I,J)+A(I,K)*B(K,J)
3050 NEXT K
3060 NEXT J
3070 NEXT I
3080 RETURN
3980 '   *MATRIX SAVE (B IN C) SUBROUTINE (MATSAVBC)*
3990 '    B(M2,N2)
4000 FOR I=1 TO M2
4010 FOR J=1 TO N2
4020 C(I,J)=B(I,J)
4030 NEXT J
4040 NEXT I
4050 RETURN
4980 '   *MATRIX SAVE (A IN C) ROUTINE (MATSAVAC)*
4990 '    A(M1.N1)
5000 FOR I=1 TO M1
5010 FOR J=1 TO N1
5020 C(I,J)=A(I,J)
5030 NEXT J
5040 NEXT I
5050 RETURN
5950 '   *MATRIX INVERSION SUBROUTINE (MATINV)*
5960 '     GAUSS-JORDAN ELIMINATION
5970 '     MATRIX A IS INPUT, MATRIX B IS OUTPUT
5980 '     DIM A(N,N),  TEMPORARY DIM B(N,2N)
5990 '     FIRST CREATE MATRIX WITH A ON LEFT AND I ON RIGHT
6000 FOR I=1 TO N
6010 FOR J=1 TO N
6020 B(I,N+J)=0
6030 B(I,J)=A(I,J)
6040 NEXT J
6050 B(I,N+I)=1
6060 NEXT I
```

P
R
O
G
R
A
M
S

RMATINV (*continued*)

```
6070 '   *PERFORM ROW OPERATIONS TO CONVERT THE LEFT-HAND SIDE OF B TO
6080 '    THE IDENTITY MATRIX.  THEN INVERSE OF A WILL THEN BE ON THE
6090 '    RIGHT SIDE OF B *
6100 FOR K=1 TO N
6110 IF K=N THEN 6240
6120 M=K
6130 '    *FIND MAXIMUM ELEMENT*
6140 FOR I=K+1 TO N
6150 IF ABS(B(I,K))>ABS(B(M,K)) THEN M=I
6160 NEXT I
6170 IF M=K THEN 6240
6180 FOR J=K TO 2*N
6190 B=B(K,J)
6200 B(K,J)=B(M,J)
6210 B(M,J)=B
6220 NEXT J
6230 '    *DIVIDE ROW K*
6240 FOR J=K+1 TO 2*N
6250 B(K,J)=B(K,J)/B(K,K)
6260 NEXT J
6270 IF K=1 THEN 6340
6280 FOR I=1 TO K-1
6290 FOR J=K+1 TO 2*N
6300 B(I,J)=B(I,J)-B(I,K)*B(K,J)
6310 NEXT J
6320 NEXT I
6330 IF K=N THEN 6410
6340 FOR I=K+1 TO N
6350 FOR J=K+1 TO 2*N
6360 B(I,J)=B(I,J)-B(I,K)*B(K,J)
6370 NEXT J
6380 NEXT I
6390 NEXT K
6400 '    * MOVE INVERSE TO REPLACE UNIT MATRIX *
6410 FOR I=1 TO N
6420 FOR J=1 TO N
6430 B(I,J)=B(I,N+J)
6440 NEXT J
6450 NEXT I
6460 RETURN
```

P
R
O
G
R
A
M
S

C.4   COMPUTER PROGRAM 4 ⎯⎯⎯⎯⎯⎯⎯⎯⎯⎯⎯⎯⎯⎯○

Name: CMATINV

Purpose: The program solves the set of complex linear algebraic equations symbolized by the matrix equation $\mathbf{Ax} = \mathbf{b}$ by finding the inverse of $\mathbf{A}$.

Subroutines: The program uses a real matrix inverse subroutine based on the Gauss elimination method. Also used are complex matrix input subroutines, complex matrix print subroutines, a real matrix multiplication subroutine, a subroutine to convert a complex number in rectangular form to the polar form, and subroutines to save a matrix under a different name.

The program is based on replacing a complex matrix of order n by an equivalent real matrix of order $2n$. Then the real matrix subroutines are used to find the inverse, and to find the solution to $\mathbf{Ax} = \mathbf{b}$. The complex matrix print routines then convert the real matrix back to an equivalent complex matrix, with the elements in rectangular form.

Inputs: The program requires the order of the square matrix $\mathbf{A}$, the complex elements $A(I, J)$ of the matrix in rectangular form, and the complex elements $B(I, J)$ of the vector $\mathbf{b}$.

Outputs: The outputs are the complex elements of the matrix $\mathbf{A}$, the inverse of $\mathbf{A}$, and the product of $\mathbf{A}$ and $\mathbf{A}$-inverse in rectangular form. If the solution to $\mathbf{Ax} = \mathbf{b}$ is elected, the solution vector is printed in both rectangular form and in polar form.

Using the Program: The user is prompted for all inputs. After the inverse is calculated the user is asked whether the solution to $\mathbf{Ax} = \mathbf{b}$ is desired. If not, the program is terminated.

The user must be on guard against the possibility of a singular matrix, since there is no warning flag. A check is provided for a valid matrix inverse, however, by multiplying the inverse times the original matrix. If a unit matrix is not produced, of course, the user is warned that a problem exists.

The complex matrix elements $A(I, J) = (a + jb)$ are represented by (a, b) in the input and the printouts.

Comments: This program is useful in finding solutions for the electric networks when phasor models are used.

Since it is easy to make a mistake in inputting data from the keyboard for a large complex matrix, it is often desirable to replace the INPUT command by a READ/DATA command.

The user may elect to use the compressed print option for matrices of order larger than three by putting the appropriate statement in the matrix print subroutines.

The matrix elements are declared as single-precision variables in order to make the program run as fast as possible. The user may elect for more accuracy by declaring them double precision.

Subroutines from this program may be useful to the user in devising other matrix subroutines and programs.

P
R
O
G
R
A
M
S

Program listing for CMATINV

```
10  ' * PROGRAM TO SOLVE A SET OF COMPLEX ALGEBRAIC EQUATIONS (CMATINV) *
20  PRINT "*THIS PROGRAM FINDS THE INVERSE OF A SQUARE MATRIX A, AND"
30  PRINT "UTILIZES IT IN SOLVING THE MATRIX EQUATION, AX=B."
40  PRINT
45  DEFINT I,J,M,N
50  DEFSNG A,B,C
60  PRINT "ENTER MATRIX ORDER AND ELEMENTS OF A AS DIRECTED BY PROMPT."
65  PRINT
70  PRINT
80  INPUT "MATRIX ORDER ";NN
90  '
100 '   * DIMENSION EQUIVALENT REAL MATRIX *
110 N=2*NN
120 DIM A(N,N),B(N,2*N),C(N,N)
130 '
140 '    *ENTER MATRIX A *
150 M1=N
160 N1=N
170 GOSUB 5000
180 '   * PRINT COMPLEX MATRIX A *
190 PRINT
200 LPRINT "THE COMPLEX MATRIX A IS:"
210 GOSUB 2000
220 '    * FIND INVERSE OF A *
230 GOSUB 9000
240 LPRINT
250 LPRINT "INVERSE OF COMPLEX MATRIX A IS:"
260 M2=N
270 N2=N
280 LPRINT
290 GOSUB 3000
300 '   * CHECK RESULTS *
310 M1=N
320 N1=N
330 N2=N
340 GOSUB 7000
350 M=N
360 '    * PRINT RESULTS *
365 LPRINT
370 LPRINT "A TIMES A-INVERSE IS:"
380 M3=N
390 N3=N
400 GOSUB 4000
410 INPUT "SOLVE AX=B (Y,N)";Z$
420 IF Z$="N" THEN 610
430 GOSUB 8000
440 '  * INPUT SOURCE VECTOR *
450 M2=N
460 N2=2
470 GOSUB 6000
480 '  * PRINT EXPANDED MATRIX B *
490 M2=N
500 N2=2
510 LPRINT "THE COMPLEX MATRIX B IS:
520 LPRINT
530 GOSUB 3000
540 '  * FIND SOLUTION VECTOR, C=A*B"
550 N2=2
560 GOSUB 7000
570 LPRINT "THE COMPLEX SOLUTION VECTOR IS:"
580 N3=2
590 GOSUB 4000
600 GOSUB 1000
610 END
960 '  * SUBROUTINE TO PUT COMPLEX VECTOR IN POLAR FORM (MATPOL) *
970 '
980 '  CONVERTS REAL EQUIVALENT M3 X 2 MATRIX TO POLAR-FORM VECTOR.
```

CMATINV (*continued*)

```
990 '
1000 LPRINT
1010 LPRINT "MAGNITUDE", "ANGLE (DEG)"
1020 LPRINT
1030 FOR I=1 TO M3 STEP 2
1040 CMAG=0
1050 CMAG=SQR(C(I,1)*C(I,1)+C(I,2)*C(I,2))
1060 BETA=0
1070 IF C(I,1)=0 AND C(I,2)>0 THEN BETA=90
1080 IF C(I,1)=0 AND C(I,2)<0 THEN BETA=-90
1090 IF ABS(C(I,1))>0 THEN BETA=ATN(C(I,2)/C(I,1))*57.296
1100 IF C(I,1)<0 AND C(I,2)>=0 THEN ANGLE=BETA+180
1110 IF C(I,1)<0 AND C(I,2)<0 THEN ANGLE=BETA-180
1120 IF C(I,1)>=0 THEN ANGLE=BETA
1130 LPRINT USING "####.###     ";CMAG,ANGLE
1140 NEXT I
1150 RETURN
1960 '    * COMPLEX MATRIX PRINT ROUTINE (CMATPTA) *
1970 '      INPUT A(M1,N1)
1980 '      NO. COLUNMS LIMITED BY PRINTER WIDTH
1990 '
2000 LPRINT
2010 FOR I=1 TO M1 STEP 2
2020 FOR J=1 TO N1 STEP 2
2025 LPRINT "(";
2030 LPRINT USING "####.###";A(I,J);
2035 LPRINT ", ";
2040 LPRINT USING "####.###";A(I,J+1);
2045 LPRINT ")  ";
2050 NEXT J
2060 LPRINT
2070 NEXT I
2075 LPRINT
2080 RETURN
2960 '    * COMPLEX MATRIX PRINT ROUTINE (CMATPTB) *
2970 '      INPUT B(M2,N2)
2980 '      NO. COLUMNS LIMITED BY PRINTER WIDTH
2990 '
3000 LPRINT
3010 FOR I=1 TO M2 STEP 2
3020 FOR J=1 TO N2 STEP 2
3025 LPRINT "(";
3030 LPRINT USING "####.###";B(I,J);
3035 LPRINT ", ";
3040 LPRINT USING "####.###";B(I,J+1);
3045 LPRINT ")  ";
3050 NEXT J
3060 LPRINT
3070 NEXT I
3075 LPRINT
3080 RETURN
3960 '    * COMPLEX MATRIX PRINT ROUTINE (CMATPTC) *
3970 '      INPUT C(M3,N3)
3980 '      NO. COLUMNS LIMITED BY PRINTER WIDTH
3990 '
4000 LPRINT
4010 FOR I=1 TO M3 STEP 2
4020 FOR J=1 TO N3 STEP 2
4025 LPRINT "(";
4030 LPRINT USING "####.###";C(I,J);
4035 LPRINT ", ";
4040 LPRINT USING "####.###";C(I,J+1);
4045 LPRINT ")  ";
4050 NEXT J
4060 LPRINT
4070 NEXT I
4075 LPRINT
```

CMATINV (*continued*)

```
4080 RETURN
4970 '    * COMPLEX MATRIX INPUT SUBROUTINE (CMATNPTA) *
4980 '      INPUT A(M1,N1)
4990 '
5000 PRINT "ENTER MATRIX A AS DIRECTED BY PROMPT:"
5010 PRINT
5020 FOR I=1 TO M1/2
5030 FOR J=1 TO N1/2
5040 PRINT "ENTER COMPLEX ELEMENT";J;"OF ROW";I;"IN FORM A1,A2:"
5050 INPUT D1,D2
5060 '    * CONSTRUCT EXPANDED EQUIVALENT REAL MATRIX *
5070 A(2*I-1,2*J-1)=D1
5080 A(2*I-1,2*J)=D2
5090 A(2*I,2*J-1)=-D2
5100 A(2*I,2*J)=D1
5110 NEXT J
5120 PRINT
5130 NEXT I
5140 RETURN
5970 '    * COMPLEX MATRIX INPUT SUBROUTINE (CMATNPTB) *
5980 '      INPUT B(M2,N2)
5990 '
6000 PRINT "ENTER MATRIX B AS DIRECTED BY PROMPT:"
6010 PRINT
6020 FOR I=1 TO M2/2
6030 FOR J=1 TO N2/2
6040 PRINT "ENTER COMPLEX ELEMENT";J;"OF ROW";I;"IN FORM B1,B2:"
6050 INPUT D1,D2
6060 '    * CONSTRUCT EXPANDED EQUIVALENT REAL MATRIX *
6070 B(2*I-1,2*J-1)=D1
6080 B(2*I-1,2*J)=D2
6090 B(2*I,2*J-1)=-D2
6100 B(2*I,2*J)=D1
6110 NEXT J
6120 PRINT
6130 NEXT I
6140 RETURN
6980 '   *MATRIX MULTIPLICATION SUBROUTINE (MATMULT)
6990 '  C=A*B, A(M1,N1), B(N1,N2), C(M1,N2)
7000 FOR I=1 TO M1
7010 FOR J=1 TO N2
7020 C(I,J)=0
7030 FOR K=1 TO N1
7040 C(I,J)=C(I,J)+A(I,K)*B(K,J)
7050 NEXT K
7060 NEXT J
7070 NEXT I
7080 RETURN
7980 '   *MATRIX SAVE (B IN A) SUBROUTINE (MATSAVBA)*
7990 '    B(M1,N1)
8000 FOR I=1 TO M1
8010 FOR J=1 TO N1
8020 A(I,J)=B(I,J)
8030 NEXT J
8040 NEXT I
8050 RETURN
8950 '   *MATRIX INVERSION SUBROUTINE (MATINV)*
8960 '    GAUSS-JORDAN.ELIMINATION
8970 '    MATRIX A IS INPUT, MATRIX B IS OUTPUT
8980 '    DIM A(N,N),  TEMPORARY DIM B(N,2N)
8990 '    FIRST CREATE MATRIX WITH A ON LEFT AND I ON RIGHT
9000 FOR I=1 TO N
9010 FOR J=1 TO N
9020 B(I,N+J)=0
9030 B(I,J)=A(I,J)
9040 NEXT J
```

CMATINV (*continued*)

```
9050 B(I,N+I)=1
9060 NEXT I
9070 '  *PERFORM ROW OPERATIONS TO CONVERT THE LEFT-HAND SIDE OF B TO
9080 '   THE IDENTITY MATRIX.  THEN INVERSE OF A WILL THEN BE ON THE
9090 '   RIGHT SIDE OF B. *
9100 FOR K=1 TO N
9110 IF K=N THEN 9240
9120 M=K
9130 '   *FIND MAXIMUM ELEMENT*
9140 FOR I=K+1 TO N
9150 IF ABS(B(I,K))>ABS(B(M,K)) THEN M=I
9160 NEXT I
9170 IF M=K THEN 9240
9180 FOR J=K TO 2*N
9190 B=B(K,J)
9200 B(K,J)=B(M,J)
9210 B(M,J)=B
9220 NEXT J
9230 '   *DIVIDE ROW K*
9240 FOR J=K+1 TO 2*N
9250 B(K,J)=B(K,J)/B(K,K)
9260 NEXT J
9270 IF K=1 THEN 9340
9280 FOR I=1 TO K-1
9290 FOR J=K+1 TO 2*N
9300 B(I,J)=B(I,J)-B(I,K)*B(K,J)
9310 NEXT J
9320 NEXT I
9330 IF K=N THEN 9410
9340 FOR I=K+1 TO N
9350 FOR J=K+1 TO 2*N
9360 B(I,J)=B(I,J)-B(I,K)*B(K,J)
9370 NEXT J
9380 NEXT I
9390 NEXT K
9400 '    * MOVE INVERSE TO REPLACE UNIT MATRIX *
9410 FOR I=1 TO N
9420 FOR J=1 TO N
9430 B(I,J)=B(I,N+J)
9440 NEXT J
9450 NEXT I
9460 RETURN
```

C.5   COMPUTER PROGRAM 5 ————————————————————————————○

Name: TRAPZ1

Purpose: The program uses trapezoidal integration to solve the first-order state equation $x' = ax + f(t)$, given the initial condition for x.

Algorithm:

$$x[(n + 1)T] = \frac{\{(1 + aT/2)x(nT) + (T/2)[f(nT) + f((n + 1)T)]\}}{(1 - aT/2)}$$

where T is the integration increment.

Inputs: The program requires the coefficient a (with proper sign), the initial condition $x(T_0)$, the length of the integration increment H, the number of integration increments per print interval NT, and the length of the solution time interval T. The forcing function is entered as FNF(T) at line 1000 by use of the function definition statement.

Outputs: The output is the state variable $X(1)$ tabulated versus time.

Using the Program: The user is prompted for all inputs. After each run the user has an opportunity to halve the integration increment and run again. Some judgment must be used as to when the increment is small enough to yield an acceptably accurate solution. An IF statement based on the maximum allowable fractional change in the state variable from the previous run can be set up at line 310 to decide whether to halve the integration increment and run again.

Comments: If $f(t)$ is discontinuous, this program may be used over each continuous interval successively, with the final value of one interval set equal to the initial value of the next.

The function $f(t)$ can be read in as an array if the time increment involved is the same as that chosen for the integration increment.

Program listing for TRAPZ1

```
10 PRINT "* TRAPEZOIDAL INTEGRATION PROGRAM FOR FIRST-ORDER NETWORKS *"
20 '        SOLVES (D/DT)X = A X + F.  REQUIRES A, X(0), F, TIME IN-
30 '        CREMENT, START TIME, AND RUN TIME.  (TRAPZ1)
35 PRINT
40 PRINT "*  PLACE FORCING FUNCTION AT LINE 1000  *"
45 PRINT
50 DEFINT I,J,N
60 DEFSNG A,F,K,T,X
70 GOSUB 1000
80 INPUT "INPUT THE COEFFICIENT A";A
90 INPUT "INITIAL X";X0
100 INPUT "INITIAL TIME, RUN TIME (SEC)";T0,T
110 LPRINT
120 LPRINT "TIME","SOLUTION"
130 LPRINT
140 INPUT "TIME INCREMENT";H
150 INPUT "PRINT INTERVAL IN NO. T-INCREMENTS";NT
160 T1=T0
170 K1=1+A*H/2
180 K2=1-A*H/2
185 '  *  GUARD AGAINST DIVIDE BY ZERO  *
190 IF K2=0 THEN PRINT "DIVIDE BY ZERO, CHANGE H" ELSE GOTO 210
200 GOTO 140
210 X1=X0
220 LPRINT T0,X0
230 WHILE T1<=T0+T+H*NT
240 FOR I=1 TO NT
250 X=(K1*X1+(FNF(T1)+FNF(T1+H))*H/2)/K2
260 T1=T1+H
270 X1=X
280 NEXT I
290 LPRINT T1,X
300 WEND
310 INPUT "TRY A SMALLER TIME INCREMENT (Y,N)";B$
320 IF B$="N" THEN 360
325 '  *  HALVE INTEGRATION INCREMENT; PRINT INTERVAL CONSTANT  *
330 H=H/2
340 NT=2*NT
350 GOTO 160
360 END
980 '
990 ' FUNCTION SUBROUTINE
1000 DEF FNF(T)=100*EXP(-10T)
1010 RETURN
```

C.6   COMPUTER PROGRAM 6 ⎯⎯⎯⎯⎯⎯⎯⎯⎯⎯⎯⎯⎯○

Name: TRAPZ2

Purpose: The program uses trapezoidal integration to solve the second-order matrix state equation $\mathbf{x}' = \mathbf{Ax} + \mathbf{f}(t)$, given the initial condition for $\mathbf{x}$.

Algorithm: $\mathbf{x}[(n + 1)T] =$

$$(\mathbf{U} - \mathbf{A}T/2)^{-1}\{(\mathbf{U} + \mathbf{A}T/2)\mathbf{x}(nT) + (T/2)[\mathbf{f}(nT) + \mathbf{f}((n + 1)T)]\}$$

where T is the integration increment.

Inputs: The program requires the two forcing functions FNF1 and FNF2 (in the function subroutine at lines 1000 and 1010), the initial conditions $X1(0)$ and $X2(0)$, the coefficients of the matrix A, the length of the integration increment H, the number of integration increments per print interval M, and the length of the solution time interval $T1$.

Outputs: The outputs are the state variables $X(1)$ and $X(2)$ tabulated versus time.

Using the Program: The user is prompted for all inputs. After each run the user has an opportunity to halve the integration increment and run again. Some judgment must be used as to when the increment is small enough to yield an acceptably accurate solution. An IF statement based on the maximum allowable fractional change in the state variable from the previous run can be set up at line 740 to decide whether to halve the integration increment and run again.

Comments: If the vector $\mathbf{f}(t)$ is discontinuous, this program may be used over each continuous interval successively, with the final values of one interval set equal to the initial values of the next.

The functions FNF1 and FNF2 can be read in as arrays if the time increment involved is the same as that chosen for the integration increment. This allows the program to be used in cases where the forcing functions cannot be expressed in analytic form.

Program listing for TRAPZ2

```
10 '  * TRAPEZOIDAL INTEGRATION PROGRAM FOR SECOND-ORDER STATE EQUATIONS. *
20 '    SOLVES (d/dt)X = A X + F(t).  INPUTS REQUIRED: ELEMENTS OF A,
30 '    INITIAL CONDITIONS, INTEGRATION INCREMENT, TIME INTERVAL.
40 PRINT "* SPECIFY FORCING FUNCTIONS AT LINES 1000 & 1010. *"
50 PRINT
60 DIM A(2,2),B(2,2),C(2,2),D(2,2)
70 DEFINT I,J,M,N
80 DEFSNG T
90 DEFSNG H,X,D,A,B,C,D,F
100 '  * INPUT MATRIX A  *
110 FOR I=1 TO 2
120 FOR J=1 TO 2
130 PRINT "ENTER ";J;" ELEMENT OF ROW ";I;" OF MATRIX A:";
140 INPUT A(I,J)
150 NEXT J
160 NEXT I
170 '  * INPUT INITIAL CONDITION  *
180 INPUT "X1(0),X2,(0)";X1(0),X2(0)
190 LPRINT
200 INPUT "INTEGRATION INCREMENT";H
210 INPUT "NUMBER OF INCREMENTS BETWEEN PRINT";M
220 INPUT "TOTAL TIME INTERVAL IN SECS";T1
230 GOSUB 1000
240 N=INT(1.5+T1/H)
250 FOR I=1 TO 2
260 FOR J=1 TO 2
270 B(I,J)=(H/2)*A(I,J)
280 NEXT J
290 NEXT I
300 '  * FIND C = (U - A*H/2)  *
310 C(1,1)=1-B(1,1)
320 C(1,2)=-B(1,2)
330 C(2,1)=-B(2,1)
340 C(2,2)=1-B(2,2)
350 '  * FIND D = (U + A*H/2)  *
360 D(1,1)=1+B(1,1)
370 D(1,2)=B(1,2)
380 D(2,1)=B(2,1)
390 D(2,2)=1+B(2,2)
400 '  * FIND DETERMINANT OF C  *
410 DTC=C(1,1)*C(2,2)-C(1,2)*C(2,1)
420 '  * GUARD AGAINST DIVIDE BY ZERO. *
430 IF DTC=0 THEN PRINT "DIVIDE BY ZERO, TRY NEW H" ELSE GOTO 450
440 GOTO 200
450 '  * FIND INVERSE OF (U - A*H/2)  *
460 B(1,1)=C(2,2)/DTC
470 B(1,2)=-C(1,2)/DTC
480 B(2,1)=-C(2,1)/DTC
490 B(2,2)=C(1,1)/DTC
500 '  * FIND (C-INVERSE)*D  *
510 C(1,1)=B(1,1)*D(1,1)+B(1,2)*D(2,1)
520 C(1,2)=B(1,1)*D(1,2)+B(1,2)*D(2,2)
530 C(2,1)=B(2,1)*D(1,1)+B(2,2)*D(2,1)
540 C(2,2)=B(2,1)*D(1,2)+B(2,2)*D(2,2)
550 X1=X1(0)
560 X2=X2(0)
570 H1=H/2
580 LPRINT
590 LPRINT "TIME","X1","X2"
600 LPRINT
610 '  * FIND X(K+1)  *
620 FOR K=0 TO N
630 X11=C(1,1)*X1+C(1,2)*X2
640 X12=B(1,1)*(FNF1(K*H)+FNF1((K+1)*H))*H1
650 X13=B(1,2)*(FNF2(K*H)+FNF2((K+1)*H))*H1
660 X21=C(2,1)*X1+C(2,2)*X2
```

TRAPZ2 *(continued)*

```
670 X22=B(2,1)*(FNF1(K*H)+FNF1((K+1)*H))*H1
680 X23=B(2,2)*(FNF2(K*H)+FNF2((K+1)*H))*H1
690 '  *  PRINT RESULTS  *
700 IF INT(K/M)=K/M THEN LPRINT USING "##.###        ";K*H; ELSE GOTO 710
705 LPRINT USING "###.#######    ";X1,X2
710 X1=X11+X12+X13
720 X2=X21+X22+X23
730 NEXT K
740 INPUT "HALVE INTEGRATION INCREMENT AND RUN AGAIN";R$
750 IF R$="N" THEN 810
760 '  *  HALVE INTEGRATION INCREMENT; PRINT INTERVAL HELD CONSTANT  *
770 PRINT
780 H=H/2
790 M=M*2
800 GOTO 220
810 END
990 '  *  FUNCTION SUBROUTINE  *
1000 DEF FNF1(T)=10*EXP(-.1*T)
1010 DEF FNF2(T)=0
1020 RETURN
```

C.7   COMPUTER PROGRAM 7

Name: FREQRES

Purpose: The program calculates the magnitude and phase angle of a real rational function in $j\omega$. It is used to find the response of a network transfer function to a sinusoidal input over a specified frequency range.

Algorithm: The program evaluates for each frequency chosen the complex value of the transfer function

$$T(s) = \frac{KN(s)}{D(s)}$$

when s is replaced by the imaginary number $j\omega$.

Inputs: The program requires the gain coefficient K, the degree N of the numerator polynomial $N(s)$, the degree D of the denominator polynomial $D(s)$, and the coefficients $A(I)$ and $B(I)$, respectively, of each. Each polynomial is assumed to be in the form

$$A(4)s^4 + A(3)s^3 + A(2)s^2 + A(1)s + A(0), \text{ etc.}$$

Also required are the low and high values (WL and WH) of the desired frequency range, and the number of frequency values $N1$ per decade (in powers of 2) for which the calculation is to be made.

Outputs: The outputs are the magnitude MAG and phase angle ANGLE of the transfer function tabulated versus frequency W.

Using the Program: The user is prompted for all inputs required. The program should be properly dimensioned at line 80 for polynomials of degree greater than 10.

Uniform spacing of frequencies on a logarithmic frequency scale is provided by the program. Some thought should be given to the frequency spacing required. This is dependent on the peaking characteristic of the transfer function.

P
R
O
G
R
A
M
S

Program listing for FREQRES

```
10 PRINT "*  FREQUENCY RESPONSE PROGRAM  *"
15 PRINT
20 '
30 'CALCULATES THE MAGNITUDE  AND PHASE ANGLE (IN DEG) OF A
40 'RATIONAL TRANSFER FUNCTION KG(S) AS A FUNCTION OF FREQUENCY.
50 'INPUTS NEEDED: GAIN CONSTANT K, LOWEST AND HIGHEST FREQUENCIES,
60 'NUMERATOR AND DENOMINATOR COEFFICIENTS (WITH SIGN).
70 '
80 DIM A(10),B(10),A1(10),A2(10),B1(10),B2(10)
90 DEFINT N,D,I
100 DEFSNG A,B,C,E,F,M,K,W
110 INPUT "GAIN CONSTANT";K
120 INPUT "DEGREE OF NUMERATOR, DEGREE OF DENOMINATOR";N,D
130 INPUT "LOWEST FREQUENCY, HIGHEST FREQUENCY";WL,WH
140 INPUT "HOW MANY POINTS PER DECADE (POWERS OF 2)";N1
150 I1=0
160 N2=N1
170 WHILE N2>=2
180 N2=N2/2
190 I1=I1+1
200 WEND
210 W1=10
220 FOR I=1 TO I1
230 W1=SQR(W1)
240 NEXT I
250 LPRINT
260 LPRINT "FREQUENCY","MAGNITUDE","ANGLE (DEG)"
270 LPRINT
280 FOR I=0 TO N
290 PRINT "INPUT NUMERATOR COEFFICIENT A(";I;"):"
300 INPUT A(I)
310 NEXT I
320 FOR I=0 TO D
330 PRINT "INPUT DENOMINATOR COEFFICIENT B(";I;"):"
340 INPUT B(I)
350 NEXT I
360 '   * SEPARATE TERMS BY SIGN, AND BY RE AND IM *
370 FOR I=0 TO N STEP 4
380 A1(I)=A(I)
390 NEXT I
400 FOR I=2 TO N STEP 4
410 A1(I)=-A(I)
420 NEXT I
430 FOR I=1 TO N STEP 4
440 A2(I)=A(I)
450 NEXT I
460 FOR I=3 TO N STEP 4
470 A2(I)=-A(I)
480 NEXT I
490 FOR I=0 TO D STEP 4
500 B1(I)=B(I)
510 NEXT I
520 FOR I=2 TO D STEP 4
530 B1(I)=-B(I)
540 NEXT I
550 FOR I=1 TO D STEP 4
560 B2(I)=B(I)
570 NEXT I
580 FOR I=3 TO D STEP 4
590 B2(I)=-B(I)
600 NEXT I
610 W=WL
620 WHILE W<=WH+W1
630 '   * FIND REAL PART OF NUMERATOR *
640 E1=0
650 FOR I=0 TO N STEP 2
```

FREQRES (*continued*)

```
660 C1=(A1(I))*W^I
670 E1=E1+C1
680 NEXT I
690 '    *find im part of numerator *
700 E2=0
710 FOR I=1 TO N STEP 2
720 C2=(A2(I))*W^I
730 E2=E2+C2
740 NEXT I
750 ' * Find re part of denominator *
760 F1=0
770 FOR I=0 TO D STEP 2
780 C3=(B1(I))*W^I
790 F1=F1+C3
800 NEXT I
810 ' * find im part of denominator *
820 F2=0
830 FOR I=1 TO D STEP 2
840 C4=(B2(I))*W^I
850 F2=F2+C4
860 NEXT I
870 F3=F1*F1+F2*F2
880 ' * find magnitudes of real and imag parts of g *
890 G1=(E1*F1+E2*F2)/F3
900 G2=(E2*F1-E1*F2)/F3
910 ' * find mag and angle of g *
920 MAG= K*SQR(G1*G1+G2*G2)
930 IF G1=0 AND G2>0 THEN ANGLE=90
940 IF G1=0 AND G2<0 THEN ANGLE=-90
950 IF ABS(G1)>0 THEN ETA=ATN(G2/G1)*57.296
960 IF G1<0 THEN ANGLE=ETA-180
970 IF G1>0 THEN ANGLE=ETA
980 LPRINT INT(1000*W+.5)/1000,INT(1000*MAG)/1000,ANGLE
990 ' * GO TO NEXT HIGHER FREQUENCY *
1000 W=W1*W
1010 WEND
1020 END
```

PROGRAMS

C.8   COMPUTER PROGRAM 8 ─────────────────────────────────────O
Name: POLYROOT

Purpose: The program uses the Newton-Raphson technique and the quadratic formula to find the roots of a real polynomial of degree two or higher, provided that the polynomial contains no more than one pair of complex roots.

Algorithms: After each real root is found a synthetic division subroutine is used to find a new polynomial with that factor removed. This process can be repeated as long as real roots remain. If the procedure finally yields a second-degree polynomial, the quadratic formula is applied to find the final two roots.

Inputs: The program requires the degree of the polynomial N, the coefficients $A(I)$, an initial guess $X0$, maximum number of iterations M, and convergence factor E.

Outputs: The program outputs are the value of each root X, the number of iterations required, and the coefficients $A(I)$ of the polynomial found by dividing the original polynomial by $(z - X)$.

Using the Program: The user is prompted for all inputs. The convergence factor E is a measure of the magnitude of the correcting increment. At the end of each set of iterations, the user may specify a smaller E and a new maximum number of additional iterations. When the root has been found to the satisfaction of the user, the synthetic-division routine is utilized to find a new polynomial with that factor removed. The process may be continued with a new initial guess until all real roots are found—or the process fails. If the process fails, and a real root is suspected to be present, a new initial guess may be successful.

Comments: The program works better for simple roots than for repeated roots. Even so, multiple roots can often be found.

The user may save time by getting approximate root locations from a program to plot the function over various ranges before using this program. A relaxed convergence factor may be used initially until the program converges on a root. Then additional accuracy may be obtained by specifying additional iterations and a smaller convergence factor. The user may wish to have the value of the polynomial printed out along with the root as a check on convergence.

Note: If the program has converged satisfactorily it should be terminated by the convergence factor, not the maximum number of iterations. To avoid excessive roundoff error in the synthetic division subroutine, the convergence factor should probably be set at 0.000001 or less.

P
R
O
G
R
A
M
S

Program listing for POLYROOT

```
10 '   * PROGRAM FOR FINDING THE SIMPLE ROOTS OF A POLYNOMIAL OF DEGREE
20 '      2 OR ABOVE AND WITH AT MOST ONE PAIR OF COMPLEX ROOTS *
30 '                  *  (POLYROOT)  *
40 '
50 PRINT "   *  THIS PROGRAM IS FOR A POLYNOMIAL A(0)+A(1)*X^1+A(2)*X^2...*"
60 PRINT "   *  THE COEFFICIENTS ARE INPUT IN RESPONSE TO PROMPT  *"
70 PRINT
80 DEFSNG D,F,Y,X,E
90 DEFINT I,N,M,K
100 INPUT "DEGREE OF POLYNOMIAL";N
110 PRINT
120 DIM A(N+1),C(N+1)
130 FOR I=0 TO N
140 PRINT "INPUT COEFFICIENT A(";I;"):";
150 INPUT A(I)
160 PRINT
170 NEXT I
180 IF N=2 THEN 720
190 PRINT
200 INPUT "WHAT IS THE CONVERGENCE FACTOR";E
210 PRINT
220 PRINT
230 K=0
240 PRINT "INPUT THE INITIAL GUESS:";
250 INPUT X0
260 PRINT
270 PRINT "MAXIMUM NUMBER OF ITERATIONS";
280 INPUT M
290 PRINT
300 PRINT
310 GOSUB 2000
320 PRINT "THE CALCULATED ROOT IS X = ";X
330 PRINT
340 PRINT "NUMBER OF ITERATIONS: ";K
350 PRINT
360 INPUT "TRY ANOTHER INITIAL GUESS (Y,N)";Z3$
370 IF Z3$="Y" THEN 220
380 PRINT
390 INPUT "MORE ITERATIONS (Y,N)";Z1$
400 IF Z1$="N" THEN 500
410 PRINT
420 INPUT "HOW MANY MORE ITERATIONS";M1
430 M=M+M1
440 PRINT
450 INPUT "NEW CONVERGENCE FACTOR (Y,N)";Z2$
460 PRINT
470 IF Z2$="N" THEN 310
480 INPUT "WHAT IS THE NEW CONVERGENCE FACTOR";E
485 PRINT
490 GOTO 310
500 FOR I=0 TO N
510 C(I)=A(I)
520 NEXT I
530 PRINT
540 B(0)=-X
550 B(1)=1
560 GOSUB 3000
570 PRINT
580 PRINT
590 PRINT "THE COEFFICIENTS OF THE RESULTING POLYNOMIAL ARE:"
600 PRINT
610 FOR I=0 TO N-1
620 PRINT "A(";I;") = ";A(I)
630 NEXT I
640 PRINT
650 PRINT
```

POLYROOT (*continued*)

```
660 INPUT "CONTINUE TO SEARCH FOR ROOTS (Y,N)";Z3$
670 IF Z3$="N" THEN 850
680 PRINT
690 N=N-1
700 K=0
710 IF N>2 THEN 240
720 IF N=2 THEN GOSUB 4000
730 PRINT
740 PRINT " QUADRATIC ROOTS ARE:"
750 PRINT
760 PRINT "      X1 = ";X1;
770 IF Y1>=0 THEN PRINT " +i";ABS(Y1)
780 IF Y1<0 THEN PRINT " -i";ABS(Y1)
790 PRINT
800 PRINT "      X2 = ";X2;
810 IF Y2>=0 THEN PRINT " +i";ABS(Y2)
820 IF Y2<0 THEN PRINT " -i";ABS(Y2)
830 PRINT
840 PRINT
850 END
980 '   ********************************************
990 '   *   POLYNOMIAL GENERATING SUBROUTINE *
1000 F=0
1010 '   *   GENERATE THE VALUE OF THE POLYNOMIAL   *
1020 FOR I=0 TO N
1030 DEF FNF(X)=A(I)*X^I+F
1040 F=FNF(X)
1050 NEXT I
1060 '   *   GENERATE THE VALUE OF THE DERIVATIVE   *
1070 D=0
1080 FOR I=1 TO N
1090 DEF FND(X)=I*A(I)*X^(I-1)+D
1100 D=FND(X)
1110 NEXT I
1120 RETURN
1920 '   ********************************************
1930 '   * NEWTON-RAPHSON SUBROUTINE (NEWTRAPH) *
1940 '   * THIS SUBROUTINE CALCULATES THE ZEROS OF A FUNCTION BY
1950 '       USING NEWTON'S METHOD. *
1960 '   * THE ROUTINE REQUIRES AN INITIAL GUESS, X0, A CONVERGENCE
1970 '       FACTOR E, AND A MAXIMUM NUMBER OF ITERATIONS M   *
1980 '
1990 '   * GET Y1 AND Y2 *
2000 X=X0
2010 GOSUB 1000
2020 '   * UPDATE ESTIMATE *
2030 Y1=F
2040 Y2=D
2050 '   *   PREVENT DIVISION BY ZERO   *
2060 IF D=0 THEN Y2=.0000001
2070 X0=X0-Y1/Y2
2080 K=K+1
2090 IF K>=M THEN RETURN
2100 IF ABS(Y1/Y2)>E THEN 2000
2110 RETURN
2910 '   ********************************************
2920 '   *    SYNTHETIC DIVISION SUBROUTINE   *
2930 '   * ASSUMES REAL POLYNOMIAL COEFFICIENTS *
2940 '   * FORM CALCULATED IS A(X) = C(X)/B(X). *
2950 '   * THE INPUT POLYNOMIAL COEFFICIENTS ARE C(I) AND B(I), AND
2960 '       THE RESULT IS A(I).   *
2970 '   * C(X) IS OF ORDER N, B(X) IS OF ORDER 1. *
2980 '   * RESULTANT A(X) IS OF MAXIMUM ORDER   *
2990 '
3000 FOR I=N TO 1 STEP -1
3010 A(I-1)=C(I)/B(1)
```

POLYROOT (*continued*)

```
3020 IF I=1 THEN 3060
3030 FOR J=0 TO 1
3040 C(I-J)=C(I-J)-A(I-1)*B(1-J)
3050 NEXT J
3060 NEXT I
3070 RETURN
3880 '    *****************************************
3890 '    *    QUADRATIC ROOT SUBROUTINE    *
3900 '    * CALCULATES THE ROOTS OF A SECOND-DEGREE POLYNOMIAL
3910 '       USING THE QUADRATIC EQUATION (QUADRAT)    *
3920 '
3930 '    * THE POLYNOMIAL IS ASSUMED TO BE OF THE FORM
3940 '            Y = A(2)*X^2 + A(1)*X + A(0)    *
3950 '    * THE TWO ROOTS ARE RETURNED IN THE FORM
3960 '            R1 = X1 + i Y
3970 '            R2 = X2 - I Y
3980 '
3990 '    * TEST FOR A(2) = 0
4000 IF A(2)<>0 THEN 4160
4010 PRINT "FUNCTION IS FIRST DEGREE."
4020 '    * TEST FOR A(1) = 0
4030 IF A(1)<>0 THEN 4100
4040 PRINT "FUNCTION IS NOT A POLYNOMIAL."
4050 X1=0
4060 X2=0
4070 Y1=0
4080 Y2=0
4090 RETURN
4100 X1=-A(0)/A1
4110 Y1=0
4120 X2=X1
4130 Y2=Y1
4140 RETURN
4150 '    *    APPLY QUADRATIC FORMULA    *
4160 A=-A(1)/(2*A(2))
4170 B1=A*A-A(0)/A(2)
4180 B=SQR(ABS(B1))
4190 '      * ESTABLISH SIGN *
4200 IF B1<0 THEN 4280
4210 '    *    CALCULATE REAL ROOTS    *
4220 X1=A+B
4230 X2=A-B
4240 Y1=0
4250 Y2=0
4260 RETURN
4270 '    *    CALCULATE COMPLEX ROOTS    *
4280 X1=A
4290 Y1=B
4300 X2=A
4310 Y2=-B
4320 RETURN
```

C.9   COMPUTER PROGRAM 9 ──────────────────────○

Name: PARFRACT

Purpose: This program evaluates a real rational function $A(z)/B(z)$ for a given complex value of z. (Note that z may be real.)

Algorithms: The program generates the real and imaginary parts of the numerator and denominator polynomials by standard complex number operations in rectangular form.

Inputs: The program requires the degrees $M1$ and $M2$, and the coefficients $A(I)$ and $B(I)$ of the numerator and denominator polynomials, respectively, and the value of z for which it is to be evaluated.

Outputs: The outputs are the real and imaginary parts of the rational function $C1$ and $C2$, and the magnitude CMAG and angle ANGLE.

Using the Program: The user is prompted for all inputs. If the program is to be used to evaluate a partial-fraction coefficient for a rational function with a simple complex root, the corresponding quadratic factor should be removed from the denominator polynomial to produce $B(z)$. A correction for this case to produce the correct coefficient has been incorporated in the program as an option. For repeated complex denominator roots the user must modify the application.

Comment: This program is primarily useful in the evaluation of partial-fraction coefficients for rational functions.

To get the rational function in the proper form to use this program, the previous program POLYROOT may be used successively to get the appropriate factors for the real roots removed. The synthetic division subroutine may also be modified to divide out the quadratic factors.

P
R
O
G
R
A
M
S

Program listing for PARFRACT

```
10 '  *  THIS PROGRAM EVALUATES A REAL RATIONAL FUNCTION, A(Z)/B(Z), FOR
20 '              A GIVEN COMPLEX Z. (PARFRACT)   *
30 '  *  TO EVALUATE A PARTIAL-FRACTION COEFFICIENT FOR A COMPLEX ROOT,
40 '     B(Z) SHOULD BE THE ORIGINAL DENOMINATOR POLYNOMIAL WITH THAT
50 '     QUADRATIC FACTOR REMOVED.  AN OPTION TO CORRECT FOR THIS CASE
60 '     HAS BEEN PROVIDED.  *
70 '
80 DEFSNG A,B,Z,C,D,N
90 DEFINT I,M
100 INPUT "DEGREE OF NUMERATOR POLYNOMIAL:";M1
110 PRINT
120 INPUT "DEGREE OF DENOMINATOR POLYNOMIAL:";M2
130 DIM A(M1+1),B(M2+1),A1(M1+1),B1(M2+1)
140 FOR I=0 TO M1
150 PRINT
160 PRINT "COEFFICIENT A(";I;")";:INPUT A(I)
170 NEXT I
180 PRINT
190 FOR I=0 TO M2
200 PRINT "COEFFICIENT B(";I;")";:INPUT B(I)
210 PRINT
220 NEXT I
230 PRINT
240 INPUT "VALUE OF COMPLEX Z (Z1,Z2)";Z1,Z2
250 PRINT
260 '  *  FIND REAL AND IMAGINARY NUMERATOR  *
270 A1(0)=1
280 A2(0)=0
290 NUM1=(A1(0))*A(0)
300 NUM2=(A2(0))*A(0)
310 FOR I=1 TO M1
320 A1(I)=Z1*A1(I-1)-Z2*A2(I-1)
330 A2(I)=Z1*A2(I-1)+Z2*A1(I-1)
340 NUM1=NUM1+(A1(I))*A(I)
350 NUM2=NUM2+(A2(I))*A(I)
360 NEXT I
370 '  *  FIND REAL AND IMAGINARY DENOMINATOR  *
380 B1(0)=1
390 B2(0)=0
400 DEN1=(B1(0))*B(0)
410 DEN2=(B2(0))*B(0)
420 FOR I=1 TO M2
430 B1(I)=Z1*B1(I-1)-Z2*B2(I-1)
440 B2(I)=Z1*B2(I-1)+Z2*B1(I-1)
450 DEN1=DEN1+(B1(I))*B(I)
460 DEN2=DEN2+(B2(I))*B(I)
470 NEXT I
480 '  *  CALCULATE QUOTIENT  *
490 D=DEN1*DEN1+DEN2*DEN2
500 C1=(NUM1*DEN1+NUM2*DEN2)/D
510 C2=(NUM2*DEN1-NUM1*DEN2)/D
520 INPUT "IS THIS A P-F EXPANSION FOR A COMPLEX ROOT Z (Y,N)";F$
530 IF F$="N" THEN 590
540 '  *  CORRECT FOR COMPLEX ROOT IN P-F EXPANSION  *
550 C11=C2/(2*Z2)
560 C2=-C1/(2*Z2)
570 C1=C11
580 '  *  CALCULATE MAGNITUDE AND ANGLE  *
590 CMAG=SQR(C1*C1+C2*C2)
600 IF C1=0 AND C2>0 THEN ANGLE=90
610 IF C1=0 AND C2<0 THEN ANGLE=-90
620 IF ABS(C1)>0 THEN ETA = ATN(C2/C1)*57.296
630 IF C1>0 THEN ANGLE=ETA
640 IF C1<0 AND C2>=0 THEN ANGLE=ETA+180
650 IF C1<0 AND C2<0 THEN ANGLE=ETA-180
660 PRINT
```

PARFRACT (*continued*)

```
670 PRINT " THE REAL AND IMAGINARY PARTS ARE:";C1;",";C2
680 PRINT
690 PRINT " THE MAGNITUDE IS:";CMAG
700 PRINT
710 PRINT " THE ANGLE IS:";ANGLE; "DEGREES"
720 PRINT
730 END
```

APPENDIX D

Answers to selected problems

Chapter 2

2.3 $+; -; v_1 \rightarrow +, v_2 \rightarrow -, v_3 \rightarrow +, v_4 \rightarrow -;$
$v_1 \rightarrow +, v_2 \rightarrow -, v_3 \rightarrow +$

2.5 (a) 10 A, 7.07 A, -10 A; (b) 0, 7.07 A, 0

2.7 (a) 5 V; (b) 20 V; (c) 0; (d) 5 V;
(e) -5 V; (f) 0

2.10 resistor, $R = 10 \ \Omega$

2.15 $t_1 = 5$ sec

2.16 $i(10) = 100$ A

2.21 (a) $i_1 = 5$ A for both cases; $v_{ab} = 25$ V for
$R = 5 \ \Omega$; $v_{ab} = 50$ V for $R = 10 \ \Omega$;
(b) $v_{ab} = 10$ V for both cases, if $R = 5 \ \Omega$,
$i_1 = 2$ A; if $R = 10 \ \Omega$, $i_1 = 1$ A

2.22 independent voltage source; $v = 50$ V; no

2.29 $R = 100|i|; v = -100$ V, $i = -1$ A

2.35 Node a: $i_1 + i_6 - i_4 = 0$
Node b: $i_1 - i_2 - i_5 = 0$
Node c: $i_6 + i_2 - i_3 = 0$
Node d: $i_3 - i_4 + i_5 = 0$
Loop $acba$: $v_6 - v_2 - v_1 = 0$
Loop $abda$: $v_6 + v_3 + v_4 = 0$
Loop $bcdb$: $v_2 + v_3 - v_5 = 0$
Loop $abcda$: $v_1 + v_2 + v_3 + v_4 = 0$
Loop $abda$: $v_1 + v_5 + v_4 = 0$

Chapter 3

3.5 (a) $p(t) = 50 \sin 10t$ W; absorbing energy
$0 \le t \le \pi/10$ s; delivering energy $\pi/10 < t$
$\le \pi/5$ s; (b) $w = 0$

3.8 $w = 10\pi$ J; no

3.10 (a) $p(t) = 50e^{-2t}$ W, $t \ge 0$; (b) $w =$
25 J; (c) $w = 25$ J

3.14 $w(1) = 2$ J

3.18 $w = 32,400$ J

Chapter 4

4.6 $i_1 = 5$ A; $v_2 = 15$ V; $v_4 = 25$ V; $v_5 =$
-30 V; $p_5 = -300$ W

4.7 $p_2 = -60$ W; $i_1 = 2$ A; $v_2 = -12$ V; $p_1 =$
20 W

4.12 $v_1 = 50$ V; $v_2 = 25$ V; $v_3 = -15$ V; $v_4 =$
25 V; $v_5 = 0$; $i_1 = -5$ A; $i_2 = 0$; $i_3 = -5$ A;
$i_4 = 5$ A; $i_5 = 0$

4.13 $i_3 = 7.63$ A; $v_{ab} = 1.69$ V

4.18 $p_1 = 1605.56$ W; $p_2 = 833.3$ W; $p_3 =$
-1700 W; $p_4 = -750$ W; $p_5 = 11.11$ W;
$v_2 = 50$ V; $v_1 = 170/3$ V

4.24 $i_4 = -2$ A; $i_1 = 2$ A; $i_3 = -3$ A

697

4.27 $v_1 = -5$ V; $i_1 = -5$ A; $v_2 = -15$ V; $i_2 = -5$ A; $v_3 = -11.43$ V; $i_3 = -5.72$ A; $v_4 = -21.43$ V; $i_4 = -4.29$ A; $v_5 = 10$ V; $i_5 = 0.72$ A

4.30 $i_3 = 2$ A; $v_1 = 55$ V

4.31 $v_1 = 91.4$ V; $i_3 = 2.14$ A; $i_2 = -6.72$ A

4.34 $v_2 = -1.672$ V; $i_3 = -0.39$ A

4.36 $i_1 = -3.65$ A; $p_1 = 266.5$ W; $i_3 = -3.26$ A; $p_3 = -890$ W

4.38 (a) $R = 5.95$ Ω;   (b) $i_y = 6.4$ A; $v_{cb} = 38.4$ V

4.42 $R = 13/9$ Ω

4.46 Thévenin-form component equation: $v(t) = 1.2i(t) - 60$

4.53 Thévenin-form component equation: $v(t) = 1.2i(t) + 2.66 \sin 5t + 2.66$

4.55 $i_2 = 16.67$ A

4.62 $i_2 = -1.2$ A

4.71 $R = 0.8$ Ω; $p = 45$ W

4.76 $R = 0.5$ Ω; $p = 728.5$ W

4.78 $i_2 \cong 2.4$ A

4.82 $i_2 = 2.431$ A

4.84 $i_2 = 3.1322$ A

Chapter 5

5.1   KVL: $v_4 - v_3 - v_7 = 0$
$v_5 + v_1 - v_2 = 0$
$v_6 + v_7 + v_3 - v_1 = 0$
$v_8 + v_2 - v_3 = 0$
KCL: $i_1 - i_5 + i_6 = 0$
$i_2 + i_5 - i_8 = 0$
$i_7 - i_6 + i_4 = 0$
$i_3 + i_4 - i_6 + i_8 = 0$

5.8 $i_7 = -5.27$ A; $i_8 = -5.09$ A; $v_5 = -36.45$ V; $v_6 = -128.25$ V

5.11 $i_4 = 40$ A; $i_1 = 55$ A; $i_2 = -45$ A; $i_3 = -50$ A; $v_1 = 110$ V; $v_4 = 160$ V; $v_6 = 10$ V; $v_5 = 40$ V

5.17 $v_1 = -9.2$ V; $v_2 = -11.6$ V; $v_3 = -1.8$ V; $v_4 = -0.6$ V; $v_5 = 9.2$ V; $v_6 = 11.6$ V; $i_3 = -0.6$ A; $i_4 = -0.6$ A; $i_5 = 2.1$ A; $i_6 = 1.4$ A

5.19 $v_3 = 1.74$ V; $v_4 = -12.04$ V; $i_1 = -0.407$ A; $i_2 = -3.026$ A

5.21 $v_4 = -2$ V; $v_5 = 18$ V; $v_6 = 10$ V; $i_4 = -1$ A; $i_5 = 4.5$ A; $i_6 = 2$ A; $i_1 = -6.5$ A; $i_2 = -5.5$ A; $i_3 = 1$ A

5.25 $i_4 = 4.67$ A; $i_3 = 6.67$ A; $i_5 = 13.34$ A; $i_2 = -11.34$ A; $i_1 = -6.67$ A; $v_2 = 23.35$ V; $v_3 = 13.34$ V; $v_4 = 23.35$ V; $v_5 = 10.01$ V; $v_6 = 0$

5.28 $v_4 = -20000$ V; $v_3 = 20000$ V; $v_5 = 19990$ V; $v_6 = 20000$ V; $v_7 = 19990$ V; $v_2 = -40000$ V; $i_3 = 4$ A; $i_4 = -2$ A; $i_5 = 0.9995$ A; $i_1 = -1.0005$ A; $i_2 = 5.0005$ A

5.35 $v_9 = -7.2$ V; $v_2 = 18.897$ V; $v_6 = -5.218$ V; $v_4 = 22.8$ V; $v_5 = 13.679$ V; $v_7 = -16.321$ V; $v_8 = 8.897$ V; $v_{10} = -1.697$ V; $i_2 = 1.575$ A; $i_4 = 7.6$ A; $i_5 = 2.28$ A; $i_6 = -0.652$ A; $i_7 = -1.632$ A; $i_8 = 1.78$ A; $i_9 = -3.6$ A; $i_1 = -2.22$ A; $i_3 = -9.232$ A

5.38 $i_4 = -10.757$ A; $i_6 = -6.112$ A; $i_7 = -5.559$ A; $i_8 = -7.212$ A; $v_9 = 80$ V; $i_1 = -49.095$ A; $i_2 = -43.536$ A; $i_3 = 3.545$ A; $i_5 = 18.883$ A; $v_3 = 17.725$ V; $v_4 = -32.271$ V; $v_5 = 18.883$ V; $v_6 = -61.12$ V; $v_7 = -11.118$ V; $v_8 = -28.848$ V

Chapter 6

6.5 $\begin{bmatrix} i_1 \\ i_2 \end{bmatrix} = \begin{bmatrix} 1/8 & -3/40 \\ -3/40 & 9/40 \end{bmatrix} \begin{bmatrix} v_1 \\ v_2 \end{bmatrix}$ short circuit parameters

$\begin{bmatrix} v_1 \\ v_2 \end{bmatrix} = \begin{bmatrix} 10 & 10/3 \\ 10/3 & 50/9 \end{bmatrix} \begin{bmatrix} i_1 \\ i_2 \end{bmatrix}$ open circuit parameters

6.7 $\begin{bmatrix} v_1 \\ v_2 \end{bmatrix} = \begin{bmatrix} 5.089 & 3.755 \\ 3.755 & 5.089 \end{bmatrix} \begin{bmatrix} i_1 \\ i_2 \end{bmatrix}$
$p(t) = 5.089i_1^2(t) + 7.51i_1(t)i_2(t) + 5.089i_2^2(t)$

6.10 $G_a = 0.318$ S; $G_b = 0.113$ S; $G_c = 0.113$ S
$R_1 = 1.335$ Ω; $R_2 = 1.335$ Ω; $R_3 = 3.757$ Ω

6.12 $R_1 = 0.667$ Ω; $R_2 = 0.667$ Ω; $R_3 = 0.078$ Ω

6.17 voltage gain: $\dfrac{v_2}{v_1} = -54.51$

power gain: $\dfrac{p_2}{p_1} = 1324.4$

6.22 $\dfrac{i_2}{i_1} = 39.8$; $\dfrac{v_2}{v_1} = -26.53$; % error = 0.503%

6.27 $\dfrac{v_2}{v_1} = -39.6$; $\dfrac{p_2}{p_1} = -39.6$

6.34 $v_0 = \dfrac{R_4(R_1 + R_2)}{R_2(R_3 + R_4)}v_2 - \dfrac{R_1}{R_2}v_1$;

$v_0 = \dfrac{R_1}{R_2}(v_2 - v_1)$

6.37 (a) $i_L = 7.33 \cos 100t$ mA;   (b) $i_L = 1.47$ cos $100t$ mA;   (c) $R_L = 1000\ \Omega$; $P_L = 0.242$ W

6.38 $i_L = 22 \cos 100t - 12.5$ mA

6.41 $\begin{bmatrix} v_1 \\ i_1 \end{bmatrix} = \begin{bmatrix} 1 & 0 \\ 0 & -R_2/R_1 \end{bmatrix}\begin{bmatrix} v_2 \\ i_2 \end{bmatrix}$

6.45 $v_1 = 34.19$ V; $v_2 = -14.19$ V

6.47 $i_1 = 4.86$ A; $v_2 = 65.38$ V

6.53 $i_1 = 99.775$ A; $v_2 = 14$ V

6.58 (a) $\dfrac{v_2}{v_i} = -52.1$; $\dfrac{p_2}{p_i} = 2581$

(b) $\dfrac{v_2}{v_i} = -50$; $\dfrac{p_2}{p_i} = 2500$

6.59 $\begin{bmatrix} v_1 \\ v_2 \end{bmatrix} = \begin{bmatrix} 4.235 & 0.767 \\ -0.661 & 2.666 \end{bmatrix}\begin{bmatrix} i_1 \\ i_2 \end{bmatrix}$ Thévenin-form CE

Chapter 7

7.1 (a) $i_1(t) = 50(1 - e^{-4t})$ A, $t \geq 0$
(b) $w(3/4) = 564.3$ J; $w(\infty) = 625$ J

7.4 $w(t) = 10^5(1 - 2e^{-0.01t} + e^{-0.02t})$ J, $t \geq 0$

7.10 $i_1(t) = -10 + 20e^{-0.5t}$ A, $t \geq 0$

7.12 $i(t) = 2 - 2e^{-2.5t}$ A, $t \geq 0$

7.14 $v_1(t) = 0$, $t \geq 0$, $v_2(t) = -5/3$ V, $t \geq 0$, $v_3(t) = 5/3$ V, $t \geq 0$

7.17 $v_1(t) = -3 + 3e^{-5t}$ V, $t \geq 0$

7.20 $v_3(t) = 50e^{-5t}ut$ V; $i_2(t) = 25e^{-5t}ut$ A

7.26

t	$v_1(t)$	$i_2(t)$	$p_6(t)$
0.1	−1.185185	−0.8487654	−19.36455
0.3	−2.335868	−0.9446557	−18.50189
0.4	−2.598241	−0.9665201	−18.30438
0.5	−2.756961	−0.9797467	−18.18459
0.7	−2.91106	−0.9925883	−18.06789

7.31

t	$v_1(t)$	$i_2(t)$	$p_6(t)$
5.00E-06	−6.910909	−0.3455455	−65.16705
2.00E-05	−20.99445	−1.049722	−38.76042
3.50E-05	−28.72372	−1.436186	−24.26804
5.00E-05	−32.96562	−1.648281	−16.31447
7.00E-05	−35.80696	−1.790348	−10.98695

7.35

t	$i_4(t)$
0.2	8.971044
0.4	14.72326
0.6	18.41155
0.8	20.77647
1.0	22.29285

Chapter 8

8.1 $C_{eq} = 0.571$ F

8.5 $C_{eq} = 17/7$ F

8.18

t	$v_1(t)$	$i_2(t)$
0.1	6.3873570	−28.7572900
0.2	16.1842300	−53.9779500
0.3	26.8863800	−75.8086400
0.4	37.2676800	−94.5524100
0.5	46.7808500	−110.5639000

8.19

t	$v_1(t)$	$i_4(t)$
2.0	−1.3935980	0.2058344
5.0	0.3282626	−0.2411345
8.0	−0.5587766	0.2374811
11.0	0.2384420	−0.2432153
14.0	−0.1369474	0.2382222

8.23

t	$v_1(t)$	$i_4(t)$
0.04	4.7111910	1.5752010
0.12	−3.0862560	1.3191530
0.20	−2.4006770	−0.2180595
0.28	0.4729703	−0.5115386
0.36	0.9498606	−0.0516040

8.25

t	$v_3(t)$	$i_4(t)$
0.005	7.7689440	1.8176930
0.020	9.9752100	4.4737620
0.035	9.9997130	5.8401410
0.050	9.9999690	6.5890070
0.065	9.9999690	6.9999780

Chapter 9

9.1 (b) $x = 25\ u(t)$;   (e) $\begin{bmatrix} x_1 \\ x_2 \end{bmatrix} = \begin{bmatrix} 30 \\ 25 \end{bmatrix} u(t)$

9.4 (b) $x(t) = \sqrt{10} \cos(t - 41.6°)$
(e) $x_1(t) = 2.28 \cos(2t - 58.4°)$; $x_2(t) = 4.59 \cos(2t - 62.4°)$

9.7 $i_1(t) = 4.17 \cos(40t - 49.6°)$ A; $i_2(t) = 4.06 \cos(40t - 54.7°)$ A; $i_3(t) = 4.17 \cos(40t + 130.4°)$ A; $i_4(t) = 2 \cos(40t + 90°)$ A; $i_5(t) = 2.69 \cos(40t - 29.2°)$ A; $i_6(t) = 0.383 \cos(40t + 20.7°)$ A

9.12 $i_1(t) = 2 \cos(10^4 t + 180°)$ A; $i_2(t) = \cos(10^4 t + 90°)$ A; $i_3(t) = \cos(10^4 t + 180°)$ A; $i_4(t) = 2 \cos(10^4 t + 180°)$ A; $i_5(t) = 2.236 \cos(10^4 t - 26.6°)$ A; $i_6(t) = 1.414 \cos(10^4 t + 45°)$ A; $i_7(t) = \cos 10^4 t$ A; $i_8(t) = 4 \cos(10^4 t + 180°)$ A

9.14 (i) $\bar{Z} = 0.883 + j3.27\ \Omega$; $\bar{Y} = 0.077 - j0.285$ S; $\bar{Z} = 50 - j5\ \Omega$; $\bar{Y} = 1.98 \times 10^{-2} + j1.976 \times 10^{-3}$ S; $\bar{Z} = 0.055 - j3.329\ \Omega$; $\bar{Y} = 0.005 + j0.2999$ S;   (j) $\bar{Z} = 5 - j2.5\ \Omega$; $\bar{Y} = 0.16 + j0.08$ S; $\bar{Z} = 2 + j1\ \Omega$; $\bar{Y} = 0.4 - j0.2$ S; $\bar{Z} = 0.588 + j7.642\ \Omega$; $\bar{Y} = 0.01 - j0.1306$ S

9.16 (b) $\bar{S} = 75 - j129.9$ VA;   (c) $\bar{S} = 2200 + j1650$ VA;   (f) $\bar{S} = 2000 + j1500$ VA

9.20 (b) E_1: load, supplying inductive vars, $\bar{S} = 997.5 - j2998.4$ VA; E_2: source, supplying inductive vars, $\bar{S} = -2998.4 - j997.5$ VA

9.22 (a) $\omega_0 = 2.236 \times 10^4$ rad/s; $\omega_1 = 2.186 \times 10^4$ rad/s; $\omega_2 = 2.286 \times 10^4$ rad/s;
(b) $\omega_0 = 2.236 \times 10^4$ rad/s; $\omega_1 = 2.211 \times 10^4$ rad/s; $\omega_2 = 2.261 \times 10^4$ rad/s;   (c) $\omega_0 \cong 3.16 \times 10^4$ rad/s; $\omega_1 \cong 31,094$ rad/s; $\omega_2 \cong 32,096$ rad/s

9.25 (b)
9.28
$$\begin{bmatrix} \bar{V}_1 \\ \bar{V}_2 \end{bmatrix} = \begin{bmatrix} R_1 + j\omega L & j\omega L \\ j\omega L & R_2 + j\omega L \end{bmatrix} \begin{bmatrix} \bar{I}_1 \\ \bar{I}_2 \end{bmatrix}$$

$$\begin{bmatrix} \bar{I}_1 \\ \bar{I}_2 \end{bmatrix} = \begin{bmatrix} 0.072 + j0.112 & -0.056 + j0.024 \\ -0.056 + j0.024 & 0.086 + j0.247 \end{bmatrix} \begin{bmatrix} \bar{V}_1 \\ \bar{V}_2 \end{bmatrix}$$

$$\begin{bmatrix} \bar{V}_1 \\ \bar{V}_2 \end{bmatrix} = \begin{bmatrix} 3.618 - j5.745 & -1.394 - j0.747 \\ -1.394 - j0.747 & 1.106 - j3.275 \end{bmatrix} \begin{bmatrix} \bar{I}_1 \\ \bar{I}_2 \end{bmatrix}$$

9.30 (c) $i(t) = 2.236 \cos(10t + 123.4°)$

9.31 (c) $f_3(t) = 15 \cos(377t - 60°)$

9.32 (1)(a) $R = 7.07\ \Omega$; $P = 1.035$ W;   (b) $R = 5.15\ \Omega$; $P = 8.12$ W   (c) $R = 13.46\ \Omega$; $P = 602.28$ W;   (d) $R = 6.32\ \Omega$; $P = 179.7$ W;   (e) $R = 7.07\ \Omega$; $P = 206.9$ W;
(2) $R = 11.48\ \Omega$; $P = 123.6$ W;   (3) $R = 0$; $P = \infty$;   (4) $R = 4.47\ \Omega$; $P = 295.06$ W

9.36 $v_0(t) = \dfrac{1000E}{\omega} \cos(\omega t + 90°)$ V

9.39 $v_0(t) = 4.975 \cos(10^3 t + 95.71°)$ V

9.42 $\bar{V}_2 = \dfrac{0.001}{0.002 + j(11/10^6)} \bar{E}$

9.45 $v_0(t) = 5 \cos(10^3 t + 90°)$ V

9.51 $\bar{T}(j\omega) = \dfrac{j\omega}{(j\omega)^2 + j\omega R + 1}$

9.56 $\bar{T}(j\omega) = \dfrac{j\omega R}{(j\omega)^2 R + j\omega + R}$

9.59 $\bar{T}(j\omega) = \dfrac{j\omega + 1}{(j\omega)^2 + j\omega 2 + 2}$

9.64 $\bar{T}(j\omega) =$
$$\dfrac{2(0.0004(j\omega)^4 + 0.05(j\omega)^2 + 1)}{0.0008(j\omega)^4 + 0.001(j\omega)^3 + 0.3(j\omega)^2 + 0.1(j\omega) + 2}$$

9.71 See problem 9.7

9.76 See problem 9.12

9.78 $\bar{V}_2 = 8.111 / -16.85°$ V;
$\bar{V}_3 = 3.919 / 148.965°$ V;
$\bar{V}_4 = 13.223 / 140.704°$ V;
$\bar{V}_1 = 22.08 / -4.29°$ V

Chapter 10

10.3 $\bar{V}_{ab} = 173.2 / 30°$ V; $\bar{V}_{bc} = 173.2 / -90°$ V; $\bar{V}_{ca} = 173.2 / 150°$ V

10.6 $\bar{I}_n = 0$; $\bar{I}_4 = 100 / -30°$ A; $\bar{I}_5 = 100 / -150°$ A; $\bar{I}_6 = 100 / -270°$ A

10.10 Same as problem 10.6

10.13 $\bar{I}_A = 7.98 / -148.6°$ A; $\bar{I}_B = 7.98 / -28.6°$ A; $\bar{I}_C = 7.98 / 91.4°$ A; $\bar{I}_1 = 13.83 / 121.4°$ A; $\bar{I}_2 = 13.82 / 61.4°$ A

10.16 $\bar{I}_1 = 350 / 149°$ A; $\bar{I}_2 = 350 / 29°$ A; $\bar{I}_3 = 350 / -91°$ A; $\bar{S}$ for the source: $-90,000 - j54,000$ VA

10.21 (a) $\bar{S}_2 = -j2.12$ kVA;   (b) $C = 9.68\ \mu$F

10.24 (a) $C = 84.9\ \mu$F

Chapter 11

11.3 $v_1(t) = \begin{cases} 0 & 0 \le t < T \\ -500 \text{ V} & T < t \le T + 2 \\ 0 & T + 2 < t \end{cases}$

$v_2(t) = \begin{cases} 0 & 0 \le t < T \\ 1000 \text{ V} & T < t \le T + 2 \\ 0 & T + 2 < t \end{cases}$

$v_3(t) = \begin{cases} 0 & 0 \le t < T \\ -250 \text{ V} & T < t \le T + 2 \\ 0 & T + 2 < t \end{cases}$

11.5 $v_1 = L_1 \dfrac{di_1}{dt} + M \dfrac{di_2}{dt}$

$v_2 = M \dfrac{di_1}{dt} + L_2 \dfrac{di_2}{dt}$

11.6 $v_1 = L_1 \dfrac{di_1}{dt} - M \dfrac{di_2}{dt}$

$v_2 = -M \dfrac{di_1}{dt} + L_2 \dfrac{di_2}{dt}$

11.11 A solution for polarity markings is: terminals a and f: dot; terminals a and c: triangle; terminals f and c: square.

11.14 $L = 11/3$ H; $L = 11/23$ H

11.17 $i_1(t) = 34.92 \cos(t - 65.2°)$ A; $i_2(t) = 15.62 \cos(t - 38.7°)$ A

11.20 $\dfrac{d}{dt} \begin{bmatrix} i_1 \\ i_2 \\ v_3 \end{bmatrix} = \begin{bmatrix} -1666 & -1666 & 8.33 \\ -4166 & -4166 & 33.33 \\ 0 & -800 & 0 \end{bmatrix} \begin{bmatrix} i_1 \\ i_2 \\ v_3 \end{bmatrix}$

$+ \begin{bmatrix} 8.33 \\ 33.3 \\ 0 \end{bmatrix} e(t)$

11.24 $i_1(t) = 1.93 \cos(2t - 71.66°)$ A; $i_2(t) = 0.93 \cos(2t - 128°)$ A

11.27 $\bar{I}_1 = 43.85\underline{/-15.26°}$ A; $\bar{I}_2 = 48\underline{/-168.7°}$ A

11.30 $\bar{I}_1 = 43.85\underline{/-15.26°}$ A

11.33 (a) $\bar{V}_{cd} = 48.5\underline{/204°}$ V; $\bar{V}_{ab} = 48.5\underline{/-76°}$ V

11.39 $N \cong 0.0328$; $\bar{I}_1 = 9.02\underline{/-34.4°}$ mA; $\bar{I}_2 = 0.275\underline{/-34.4°}$ A

11.41 $R_m = 19.2$ kΩ; $\omega L_{m_1} = 14.4$ kΩ
$R_1 = 0.32\ \Omega$; $\omega L_a = 0.24\ \Omega$
$R_2 = 0.0032\ \Omega$; $\omega L_b = 0.0024\ \Omega$

11.46 $|\bar{Z}_L| \le 0.001$

Chapter 12

12.6 $(s^3 + 5s^2 + 6s)X(s) = \dfrac{1}{S + 1}$

12.9 $\begin{bmatrix} V_1(s) \\ V_2(s) \end{bmatrix} = \dfrac{1}{s^2 + 4s + 3} \begin{bmatrix} s + 2 & 1 \\ 1 & s + 2 \end{bmatrix}$

$\begin{bmatrix} \dfrac{10s + 11}{s + 1} \\ \dfrac{-5s^2 + 2s - 125}{s^2 + 25} \end{bmatrix}$

12.13 $X_1(s) = \dfrac{10s(s + 7.5)}{(s + 0.5)(s + 11)(s^2 + 4)}$

$X_2(s) = \dfrac{70s}{(s + 0.5)(s + 11)(s^2 + 4)}$

12.15 (a) $a(t) = (-10/3 e^{-2t} + 40/3 e^{-5t})\, u(t)$
(c) $a(t) = (5/6 - 2/3 e^{-t} - 1/3 e^{-3t} + 1/6 e^{-4t})\, u(t)$

12.17 (a) $f(t) = (1.85 e^{-2t} - 10/9 t e^{-2t} - 1.85 e^{-5t} - 40/9 e^{-5t})\, u(t)$

12.22 $v_1(t) = (2.712 e^{-t} + 0.5t e^{-t} + 7.338 e^{-3t} - 0.05 \cos 5t + 0.046 \sin 5t)\, u(t)$
$v_2(t) = (2.212 e^{-t} + 0.5t e^{-t} - 7.338 e^{-3t} + 0.126 \cos 5t + 0.34 \sin 5t)\, u(t)$

12.24 (a) $x(t) = -3.536(e^{-0.293t} - e^{-1.707t})\, u(t)$
(b) $x(t) = (0.102 \cos(10t - 78°) + 0.0258 e^{-t}\cos(2t + 145.4°) + 2.5 e^{-t}\sin 2t)\, u(t)$

12.25 $x_1(t) = (-0.784 e^{-0.5t} - 0.293 e^{-11t} + 1.078 \cos 2t + 3.19 \sin 2t)\, u(t)$
$x_2(t) = (-0.784 e^{-0.5t} + 0.587 e^{-11t} + 0.198 \cos 2t + 3.03 \sin 2t)\, u(t)$

12.30 $v_2(t) = 166.67\, u(t)$ V

Chapter 13

13.6 $a_0 = A$; $a_n = 0$; $b_n = \begin{cases} \dfrac{2A}{\pi n} & \text{for } n \text{ odd} \\ 0 & \text{for } n \text{ even} \end{cases}$

13.10 $a_0 = A$; $a_n = \begin{cases} 0 & \text{for } n \text{ even} \\ \dfrac{2A}{\pi n} \sin \dfrac{n\pi}{2} & \text{for } n \text{ odd} \end{cases}$ $b_n = 0$

13.13 $b_n = \dfrac{20}{\pi^2 n^2} \sin \dfrac{n\pi}{2} - \dfrac{20}{\pi n}$

13.17 $f(\theta) = 0.318 + 0.5 \sin \theta - 0.212 \cos 2\theta - 0.425 \cos 4\theta - 0.018 \cos 6\theta$

13.19 $f(\theta) = 0.318 - 0.5 \cos \theta + 0.212 \cos 2\theta - 0.425 \cos 4\theta + 0.018 \cos 6\theta$

13.23 $a_n = \begin{cases} 0 & \text{for } n \text{ even} \\ \dfrac{-4A}{(\pi n)^2} & \text{for } n \text{ odd} \end{cases}$

$b_n = \begin{cases} 0 & \text{for } n \text{ even} \\ \dfrac{2A}{\pi n} & \text{for } n \text{ odd} \end{cases}$

13.26 $a_1 = 1.2732A$; $a_3 = -0.4241A$; $a_5 = 0.2546A$; $a_7 = -0.1819A$; $a_9 = 0.1414A$

13.30 $f(t) = 4.34 \cos(40\pi t + 90°) + 3.18 \cos(80\pi t + 90°) + 2.35 \cos(120\pi t + 90°) + \ldots$

13.34 APER = 0.0407

13.38 $i(t) = 0.0654 \cos(2000\pi t + 89.63°) + 0.0974 \cos(6000\pi t + 88.33°) + 1.847 \cos(10000\pi t + 22.54°) + 0.0672 \cos(14000\pi t - 87.3°)$

13.41 $v(t) = 250 + \dfrac{1000}{\pi} \cos(t - 89.94°) + 106.2 \cos(3t - 90.7°)$ V

13.46 $\bar{F}(j\omega) = \dfrac{2}{j\omega} - \dfrac{1}{j\omega}e^{-j\omega\delta} - \dfrac{1}{j\omega}e^{-j\omega2\delta}$

13.51 $\bar{I}(j\omega) = \dfrac{10(1 - e^{-j\omega})}{j\omega(1 + j0.1\omega)}$

13.55 0.5961 W

13.59 $f(t) = \cos \omega_0 t$

13.62 EER = 0.0029

Chapter 14

14.1 $\dfrac{dv_0}{dt}(0^-) = \dfrac{1}{C}i(0^-)$

$\dfrac{d^2v_0}{dt^2}(0^-) = \dfrac{1}{C}\dfrac{di(0^-)}{dt} - \dfrac{1}{R_1C^2}i(0^-)$

14.4 $i_1(0^+) = 0$; $v_2(0^+) = 0$; $\dfrac{di_1}{dt}(0^+) = 10$; $\dfrac{dv_2}{dt}(0^+) = 0$

14.5 **(a)** $Z_T(s) = \dfrac{40s^2 + 108s + 100}{2s^2 + 5s + 4}$

(b) $Z_T(s) = \dfrac{s^2 + 2s + 2}{s(s + 2)}$

(c) $Z_T(s) = \dfrac{s + 1}{s^2 + 2s + 2}$

(d) $Z_T(s) = \dfrac{s^4 + 13s^2 + 20}{s(s^2 + 10)}$

14.7 $i_1(t) = 10/3e^{-t}\sin 3t\, u(t)$ A
$p_1(t) = (50/3e^{-2t}\sin 6t - 100/9e^{-2t}\sin^2 3t)\, u(t)$ W
$w_2(t) = 5(1 + 1.054e^{-t}\cos(3t + 161.6°))^2\, u(t)$ J

14.11 See Problem 14.7.

14.13 $i_2(t) = 5 + 7.07e^{-t}\cos(t + 135°)\, u(t)$ A
$v_3(t) = 5 + 7.07e^{-t}\cos(t - 135°)\, u(t)$ V
$v_4(t) = 5 + 7.07e^{-t}\cos(t + 135°)\, u(t)$ V
$i_5(t) = -5 + 7.07e^{-t}\cos(t - 135°)\, u(t)$ A

14.17 See problem 14.13

14.19 $i_2(t) = 100e^{-t}\sin t\, u(t)$ A; $i_1(t) = 100\, \delta(t) - 100e^{-t}\cos t\, u(t)$ A; $i_3(t) = 100\delta(t) - 100e^{-t}(\cos t + \sin t)\, u(t)$ A; $v_2(t) = 100e^{-t}(\cos t - \sin t)\, u(t)$ V; $v_3(t) = 100e^{-t}\cos t\, u(t)$ V

14.21 $V(s) = \dfrac{9s + 38}{s + 6}I(s) + \dfrac{10}{s}$

14.25 $I(s) = \dfrac{s + 6}{9s + 38}V(s) - \dfrac{10(s + 6)}{s(9s + 38)}$

14.30 $T(s) = \dfrac{V_4(s)}{V_5(s)} = \dfrac{1}{s^2 + 2s + 2}$

14.32 $T(s) = \dfrac{V_5(s)}{V_1(s)} = \dfrac{24s^2}{24s^2 + 15s + 1}$

14.35 $T(s) = \dfrac{V_0(s)}{I(s)} = \dfrac{2s^2 + 44s + 80}{2s^2 + 5s + 22}$

Chapter 15

15.1

$$Q = \begin{matrix} & 1 & 2 & 3 & 4 & 5 & 6 \\ 1 & \begin{bmatrix} 1 & 0 & 0 & -1 & 0 & 1 \\ 0 & 1 & 0 & -1 & 1 & 0 \\ 0 & 0 & 1 & 0 & -1 & 0 \end{bmatrix} \\ 2 \\ 3 \end{matrix}$$

$$B = \begin{matrix} & 1 & 2 & 3 & 4 & 5 & 6 \\ 4 & \begin{bmatrix} 1 & 1 & 0 & 1 & 0 & 0 \\ 0 & -1 & 1 & 0 & 1 & 0 \\ -1 & 0 & -1 & 0 & 0 & 1 \end{bmatrix} \\ 5 \\ 6 \end{matrix}$$

15.5 $i_1(t) = (5.867e^{-0.314t} + 4.127e^{-3.186t})$
$u(t)$ A

$i_3(t) = (-2.185e^{-0.314t} + 22.175e^{-3.186t})$
$u(t)$ A

15.8
$$\begin{bmatrix} (3 + \int_0^t d\tau) & 1 & 0 \\ -2 & (2 \int_0^t d\tau + 2) & 0 \\ 5 & -1 & 1 \end{bmatrix}$$

$$\begin{bmatrix} i_1 \\ i_2 \\ v_4 \end{bmatrix} = \begin{bmatrix} 1 \\ 1 \\ 0 \end{bmatrix} e_3(t)$$

15.11 $i_3(t) = (60/11e^{-3t} - 60/11e^{2/3t}) u(t)$ A
$i_5(t) = (-15 + 15e^{2/3t}) u(t)$ A

15.14 $\begin{bmatrix} 2s + 3 & -2 \\ -2 & s + 2 \end{bmatrix} \begin{bmatrix} V_2(s) \\ V_4(s) \end{bmatrix} = \begin{bmatrix} 20 \\ 0 \end{bmatrix}$

15.18 $v_3(t) = (10 - 40/30e^{-t}) u(t)$ V; $v_5(t) = (40/3 - 40/3e^{-t}) u(t)$ V

15.20 $v_2(t) = (-5.33 + 35.33e^{-7.5t}) u(t)$ V
$v_5(t) = (-7.33 - 17.67e^{-7.5t}) u(t)$ V

15.25 $v_1(t) = (97.5 - 87.5e^{-0.5t} - 31.25te^{-0.5t})$
$u(t)$ V
$v_2(t) = (95 - 75e^{-0.5t} + 62.5te^{-0.5t}) u(t)$ V
$i_4(t) = (37.5e^{-0.5t} + 46.875te^{-0.5t}) u(t)$ A

15.28 $I_2(s) = \dfrac{-5.39s - 39.18}{(s - 3.663)(s + 1.605)}$

$I_5(s) = \dfrac{34.3s + 48.98}{(s - 3.663)(s + 1.605)}$

15.33

t	$v_1(t)$	$v_2(t)$
0.5	17.18613	60.92765
2.5	50.04767	118.27940
5.0	77.49243	114.49600
7.5	89.93132	104.26050
10.0	94.80606	98.70596

15.36

t	$i_2(t)$	$i_5(t)$
0.02	-6.423304	36.78196
0.04	-7.515441	39.45752
0.06	-8.671504	42.34023
0.08	-9.896958	45.44570
0.20	-19.066580	69.79318

Index

TRANSFORM PAIRS FOR SOME ELEMENTARY t-FUNCTIONS

	t-function	Laplace transform
1	$\delta(t)$	1
2	$u(t)$	$\dfrac{1}{s}$
3	t^n	$\dfrac{n!}{s^{n+1}}$
4	e^{-at}	$\dfrac{1}{s + a}$
5	$\cos \omega t$	$\dfrac{s}{s^2 + \omega^2}$
6	$\sin \omega t$	$\dfrac{\omega}{s^2 + \omega^2}$
7	$e^{-at}f(t)$	$F(s + a)$
8	$\dfrac{d}{dt} f(t)$	$sF(s) - f(0^-)$
9	$\displaystyle\int_0^t f(\tau)\, d\tau$	$\dfrac{F(s)}{s}$
10	$e^{-at} \cos \omega t$	$\dfrac{s + a}{(s + a)^2 + \omega^2}$
11	$e^{-at} \sin \omega t$	$\dfrac{\omega}{(s + a)^2 + \omega^2}$